THE BIG BOOK OF

includes the complete texts of

How to Say It® to Your Kids by Dr. Paul Coleman

&

How to Say It® to Teens by Richard Heyman, Ed.D.

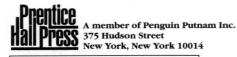

A member of Penguin Putnam Inc.
375 Hudson Street
New York, New York 10014

www.penguinputnam.com

Previously published as *How to Say It to Your Kids*®, copyright © 2000 by Dr. Paul Coleman and *How to Say It to Teens*®, copyright © 2001 by Richard Heyman, Ed.D.

Prentice Hall® is a registered trademark of Pearson Education, Inc.

Library of Congress Cataloging-in-Publication Data available upon request
Special Markets ISBN: 0-7352-418-7
Printed in the United States of America
10 9 8 7 6 5 4 3 2 1

Contents

How To Say It® to Your Kids

How To Say It® to Teens

How to Say It™

TO YOUR

THE RIGHT WORDS TO SOLVE
PROBLEMS, SOOTHE FEELINGS
& TEACH VALUES

Dr. Paul Coleman

Dedication

To my wife, Jody,
and our three children, Luke, Anna, and Julia.
I cherish you all.

And to the memory of my wonderful father, George Coleman.
I no longer hear your words,
but I do live by them.

Acknowledgments

First and foremost, I wish to thank my literary agents, Mike and Patricia Snell. They always have an idea, an encouraging word, and a cheery willingness to listen. A writer should be so lucky.

I wish to thank the following people who also made helpful contributions: Tom Power, senior editor at Prentice Hall, for his faith in my work; Sharon L. Gonzalez, production editor, and Rose Ann Ferrick, copy editor, who helped make the manuscript shine; John Coleman, my brother and assistant principal at J.F.K. Middle School in Enfield, Connecticut, for his insights into school safety and teaching issues; Kristen Fandl, C.S.W., my colleague. Although much of the time we just pass each other in the hall, I'm always glad to have you around; Gary Blum and Master Robert Blum at *Just for Kicks Martial Arts* for their assistance in rounding up stories for the book. And to Master Joseph Klee for his comments and insights on sportsmanship; Donna Berrios for her well-thought-out ideas; Robert and JoAnne Van Scoy, as well as Luanne and Tony Nappi, for their suggestions as we sat overlooking the lake; Paul Varricchio for his enthusiastic comments and sheer brilliance; Claire, Ann Marie, Jane, Debby, and John for always being there; My wife, Jody, and our children, Luke, Anna, and Julia, for their suggestions and tolerance while I was busy writing; And my parents, George and Frances Coleman. I love you and am forever grateful.

The difference between the right word and a word
is like the difference between lightning and a lightning bug.

—MARK TWAIN

Smart Talk:
The Six Ways We Speak
to Our Kids

Kathy glanced at the wall clock. Only fifteen minutes until the school bus arrived! Her two children were dawdling, trying to delay the inevitable moment when they must grab their belongings and head down the driveway for their first day back at school.

"Mark!" Kathy cried. "Why aren't your supplies in your book bag where they're supposed to be?"

Before he could respond, eight-year-old Jenny dropped a box of cereal on the floor, scattering its contents.

Kathy sighed loudly. "Jenny, aren't you finished with your breakfast? The bus will be here any minute!" She yelled to her ten-year-old son, "Mark, I need you to help your sister clean up. I'll get your book bag ready. Hurry!"

"But I didn't spill anything," he protested.

"I never said you did. Just help her, please. Now!"

Mark made a face and walked over to his younger sister. While she was bent over scooping up the cereal, he hit her just hard enough behind her knee to cause her to fall. "Mom," Jenny called. "Mark pushed me!"

"I did not!"

"Then why am I on the floor?"

Mark whispered back, "Because I hit you. But I didn't push you."

Kathy huffed back into the kitchen and stood over her arguing children. She felt like screaming. She just wanted her kids to be ready on time, and she wanted them to be in a reasonably good mood for school. The vision she'd had of giving them warm hugs before they left had vanished. The only wish that would come true now was that they would make it to the bus with seconds to spare. But she'd have to act like a drill sergeant to make it happen.

What could she possibly have said to improve the situation?

1

THE THREE OUTCOMES OF ALL COMMUNICATION

Talking to your kids isn't hard. But talking *smart* takes some forethought and a little practice. Communicating with children is an essential and important job of parents. Done well, it can bind a family together and prevent or heal many problems. Not done well, family life can be tense and confusing, and the child will venture into the world inadequately prepared to cope with all life has to offer.

Most parents overestimate the amount of meaningful conversation they have with their grade-school children. Recent findings at the University of Michigan showed that household conversation (just sitting and talking with children) had dropped nearly 100 percent in 1997 compared to 1981. One reason was that kids spent more time at before- and after-school activities, and family mealtime declined by an hour per week. Also, the time kids spent visiting with friends or talking on the phone tripled.

If you're like most busy parents, chatting with your children is brief and usually begins with one of the following:

"How did you sleep?" *("Fine . . .")*

"How was your day?" *("Fine . . .")*

"Where are you going?" *("Outside . . .")*

"When will you be back?" *("Later.")*

"What did you do at school today?" *("Nothing.")*

"Did you finish your homework?" *("I didn't have any.")*

"Stop that!" *("But she started it!")*

"How many times have I told you . . ." *("Oh, Mom!")*

For many parents these comments and others just like them make up the bulk of conversation on most days. Whether parents realize it or not, any communication attempt will have one of three consequences:

1. It will bring them closer to their children.
2. It will start an argument.
3. It will lead to avoidance or withdrawal.

Be honest. Do the majority of your conversations encourage closeness with your kids? Arguments are sometimes unavoidable, but they need not be poisonous to the relationship. As often as not they can end positively or at least without one or both sides feeling frustrated.

In too many families, conversations with children have a neutral effect at best. No harm was done, but neither was anything accomplished. The goal is to talk so that the parent-child relationship is enhanced, discipline is more effective, and your children will want to talk to you—not avoid you—when they have a problem. By knowing all six ways of communicating (instead of relying on just one or two) you can achieve those goals.

THE **TENDER** APPROACH TO COMMUNICATION

Kathy, the exasperated mom who was worried that her kids would miss the school bus, used—or, rather, misused—three of the six approaches to communication. Yes, she was able to get them to the bus on time, but at a high emotional price. She, Jenny, and Mark felt angry and put upon. What a way to start the school year. Had she used the approaches properly or in the right combination (a few seconds of forethought was all she needed), it still might have resulted in a mad dash for the school bus—but without the irritation and bad feelings that tainted everything.

The **TENDER** ways of speaking are **TEACHING** (criticism is a negative form of teaching), **EMPATHIZING, NEGOTIATING, DO'S & DON'TS** (commands, household rules), **ENCOURAGING** (including praise), and **REPORTING** (neutral comments, statement of facts, reporting your thoughts and feelings). When stressed, overtired, or preoccupied, parents are prone to responding to their children in limited ways. For example, four hours into a six-hour road trip, weary parents of bickering children might understandably yell, "Knock it off!" or, if trying to sound adultlike, they might say, "Must you fight like that!" (**DO'S & DON'TS** command). Will it work? Anyone who has been there will probably say, "Not for long." The main problem is that parents instinctively select a response without considering the alternatives, which are usually more effective. In fact, most stressed parents overuse some styles of talking (commands and criticism) and underuse others (especially **EMPATHIZING**). Even when not stressed, parents may be unsure of how to respond to a child's question or handle a predicament, and so they fall back on standby clichés and hope the child gets the point. One father, surprised when his son didn't win a trophy in a martial arts competition, didn't know how to console his son. "Life's not always fair," he finally said. Chances are that if the father knew more about the six ways of communicating, he would have come up with a more effective response.

When Kathy, the frazzled mom, said to Mark, "Why aren't your supplies in your book bag where they're supposed to be?" she was not really asking a question. She was criticizing Mark for his dawdling. The criticism was justified, but it complicated Kathy's situation in two ways. First, Mark thought she was being unfair, and he got angry. He'd intended to get his supplies together, but why did it have to be on his mother's timetable? Second, Kathy was not being clear about what she wanted. She really wasn't interested in *why* his book bag was still empty. She wanted it filled, but she didn't say that. Similarly, when she said to Jenny, "Aren't you finished with your breakfast?" she gave the appearance of asking a simple question (**REPORTING**) but in fact it was a veiled criticism. Imagine if instead she had said, "I'm sorry, Jenny, but we're running late. I know you are still hungry, but you can't have a second bowl of cereal. Grab an apple if you'd like." That would have been a clear statement of what Kathy wanted Jenny to do, and it would have been without the criticism.

When Kathy told Mark to help his sister clean up the spilled cereal, she was issuing a command (**DO'S & DON'TS**). Commands are fine and important, but in this case it only added to the tension that Kathy feared was already spoiling the morning. **EMPATHIZING** or praising ("You're a big help to me, Mark") might have taken the sting out of her command. Furthermore, and perhaps just as important, her choice of words might have lessened Kathy's irritation, too.

The more aggravated our speaking tone and the more harsh our words, the more upset we will become. The more we can speak calmly and pleasantly, the less upset we will become.

So if Kathy had used **REPORTING** to express her concern about being late for the school bus, without criticizing, and if she had balanced her commands (**DO'S & DON'TS**) by empathizing or encouraging, then the first-day-back-to-school blues might have been avoided.

INCREASING YOUR **TENDER** REPERTOIRE

At first glance you might believe that you regularly use all six communication styles. After all, what parent hasn't praised or empathized or taught or negotiated with their child, right? Guess again. When you run through the following list of common expressions that exemplify each of the six approaches, you may discover that you favor one or two approaches more than others. While it is easy to shift from one style to another when all is calm and the household is happy, people under stress tend to overuse certain styles. They might criticize more or bark out commands, or they might be overly sympathetic and lenient and not inclined to enforce rules. Interestingly, some couples balance each other out: One spouse emphasizes two or three styles while the other emphasizes the remaining styles. Together they are a complete set, but alone they lean to the left or right and then blame the other when matters get out of hand.

TEACHING

The "T" in **TENDER** stands for **TEACHING**. It is a rare day that parents don't teach their children. Teaching can be a warm, meaningful experience that bonds grown-ups with kids, such as when a parent patiently instructs her child how to ride a two-wheeler or tie a lure to a fishing line or scoop up ground balls. And children ask many questions that allow parents an opportunity to explain the ways of the world.

But teaching can degrade into lectures or nagging, and the message may get lost. Some parents feel comfortable teaching but uncomfortable showing much affection. Those same parents often get uneasy when their child is very emotional. They try to overcome their uneasiness by trying to get their child to understand the logic of the situation. They get impatient when logic doesn't help their child. ("Elizabeth, if you would just listen to what I am saying, then you would know how to do your math homework. Crying won't help!") Like each of the six styles, teaching has its benefits and its limitations. Is teaching a common style for you?

How to Say It

- "Let me explain . . ."
- "Watch how I do it, then you try."
- "Let's see if we can figure this out together."
- "Interesting choice. Why did you pick that answer?"
- "The answer is . . ."
- "I'm not sure what the answer is. Let's look it up."

- "Do it this way."
- "How would you feel if someone did that to you?"
- "When you told your sister she couldn't use your baseball glove, how do you think that made her feel?"
- "Making mistakes is one of the ways we learn things."
- "I want you to do this because . . ."
- "The reason you can't go is . . ."

Of course, tone of voice is key. Saying "Do it this way!" in a gruff, exasperated tone will be taken as a criticism. In fact, parents often slip into a critical teaching mode. It is not fatal, and used sparingly it may get the child's attention, but usually it adds to stress and lessens the likelihood your child will want you to help with problems.

How Not to Say It

- "I can't believe you did that!"
- "That's stupid!"
- "Never mind, I'll do it!"
- "If that's the way you're going to be, then you can take care of this by yourself."
- "That answer is wrong. I thought you said you studied for this test?"
- "You're acting like a baby!"
- "Why can't you be like your sister?"

Put-downs, name-calling, and comparisons are the worst kinds of statements you can make. Parents who use a critical teaching mode seldom use **EMPATHIZING**. Learning to speak more empathetically can actually help parents feel more patient.

The best time to use teaching is when:

anxiety or frustration (for either parent or child) is low;

children calmly ask questions;

children are not preoccupied with other things;

you are not likely to be critical.

EMPATHIZING

The first "E" in **TENDER** stands for **EMPATHIZING**. Empathy is important when your child is experiencing strong emotions. A child who calmly asks, "What is the capital of Kentucky?" will do fine with a straightforward answer. But if the child wads up his homework into a ball and yells, "I can never remember this stuff! Who cares what the capital of Kentucky is!" a little empathy may go a long way. "I don't blame you for being frustrated," a parent might say. "It's hard when you study your notes but still can't remember everything."

Parents trip up when it comes to showing genuine empathy. It's difficult to empathize when you're upset or angry or reeling from something your child has just said. Sometimes parents confuse empathy with encouragement and say things like, "Don't worry, I'm sure you'll do just fine." Sympathetic pep talks are encouraging, but they are not empathic. When you make an empathic response, you are not trying at that moment to solve problems or heal wounds. Instead, you are trying to understand your child's pain and talk about it in a way that helps the child realize you truly do understand.

When Annie came home crestfallen because a boy playmate preferred the company of another boy, her mother wanted Annie to feel better. She said, "Your sister will be home soon, and you can play with her." Mom was trying to be encouraging, but to show empathy she might have said, "That must make you feel sad and maybe a little angry, too." Annie would know that her feelings were being heard, not dismissed. That might have been sufficiently soothing, or it might have prompted Annie to talk even more about how she feels ("That happens to me at school sometimes, too"). Then Mom may have realized that her daughter's concerns were worth examining.

How to Say It

- "You're feeling sad [or mad or nervous or glad] about . . ."
- "It bothers you that your brother got to go on a class trip and you didn't."
- "I know you're feeling scared about . . ."
- "You wish Grandpa was here with you, don't you?"
- "You missed the goal, and you're worried you let your team down. Do I have that right?"

- "It feels good when you finally make friends at a new school."
- "The way you hung up the phone makes me think you're upset about something."
- "It's frustrating and sad when you look forward all week to the ball game but then get sick and have to stay home."
- "You're really excited about the class trip to the aquarium."

A true empathic response is like holding up a mirror to someone. What they hear you say is a reflection of how they feel. Empathic comments are without judgment. They do not contain solutions to a problem, but solutions fall more easily into place if you can empathize because you understand the problem better. When you are showing empathy, your child will likely talk more. It's easier for a child to reveal her concerns when someone can accurately describe her feelings. If your child looks troubled but refuses to talk, asking "Why won't you tell me?" is not empathic and probably won't help. Say instead, "You seem worried [or hurt or angry or sad, etc.] about something. I'd like to talk about it with you, but maybe you'd rather think about it by yourself for a while." That may gently coax your child to respond.

Clues that you are not being empathic (when you think you are):

You rush in with answers or solutions.

You find yourself debating with your child about how she should be feeling.

You are providing reassurances before you've clearly expressed your understanding of your child's concerns.

You want to get the conversation over with.

You are very angry.

How Not to Say It

- "I know how you must feel." (The feeling is not described.)
- "I understand." (Understand what?)
- "I still love you." (But is that your child's concern right now?)
- "You'll be fine." (Reassurance is not empathy.)
- "It's not as big a problem as you're making it." (You're telling your child he is wrong to feel the way he does.)

- "Life does that to you sometimes. The important thing is to think about something positive." (Your intent is to make her feel better, but this is not empathy.)

The best time to use empathy is:

> when your child is emotional and not likely to listen to reason (this is also the hardest time);
>
> when you're not sure what the real problem is (empathy can draw your child out);
>
> if your child is sensitive by nature;
>
> if you want your child to understand her emotions.

NEGOTIATING

The "N" in **TENDER** stands for **NEGOTIATING**. It should be used less often than parents realize. **NEGOTIATING** begins when your growing child requests more freedoms (choosing which clothes to buy, staying up later, etc.). You can then discuss with her the responsibilities that accompany those freedoms. Children are not your peers. They haven't the right—as do adults in contract disputes—to break off negotiations. Parents have the final say. Still, your children benefit when you hear them out, understand their reasons for wanting something, and sometimes negotiate an agreement with them.

When eleven-year-old Danny wanted to own an expensive pair of in-line skates, his father had two concerns. First, he wanted Danny to appreciate the value of money. Second, since his son tended to postpone getting his homework done by playing too much, the new skates would add to that problem. Dad expressed those concerns. Danny said he would do extra chores to earn the money. His father liked the idea, but the expensive skates would require a lot of chores. Dad really wanted the garage painted, but it wasn't a very big job because the first coat was nearly finished. Additional chores were required. Danny suggested they buy a cheaper pair of used skates so that extra chores would not be necessary. Dad agreed. Then Dad said that if Danny spent extra time playing and didn't finish his homework by nine o'clock, he would not be able to play the next day. Danny agreed. Obviously, Dad held all the cards in this negotiation. But because he believed his son would learn a valuable lesson, he took his son's ideas seriously.

The mistake parents make is when they negotiate out of desperation (that is also known as "bribery"). Maybe they are worried that their kids will misbehave during an important event, so they beg them to be good and promise them ice cream later. Or a mother screams, "Okay, you can have a new video game. Just stop yelling!" That situation is different from one where Mary must go grocery shopping and has to pull her two kids away from Nintendo to accompany her. She can start out by **EMPATHIZING** and saying, "I know it's no fun to go shopping when you'd rather play. But I promise I'll hurry, and if you two promise not to complain when we are in the store, we can have pizza for dinner tonight." Mary is not desperate. She wants to reward her kids for good behavior. If she also praises them once or twice in the supermarket for their pleasant behavior, she will increase the odds that her kids will cooperate even more in the future.

How to Say It

- "I know you've done a lot of work already, but we still have some more to do. I really appreciate your effort. Is there anything special you'd like to do later?"
- "I know you want to go to the lake today with your friend and her family. I think that would be nice but I have these concerns. . . . Any suggestions?"
- "Before I can consider what you want, I need these things to happen..."
- "Before we leave for the ball game, I want you to tidy up the house. Which rooms do you want to start with?"
- "I cannot agree to that. Is there something else you want instead?"

The parent who negotiates in the best way is a benevolent dictator. She is willing to make accommodations to her child's wishes because she believes it is deserved or that it is in her child's best interest. A benevolent dictator never loses sight of who is in charge.

How Not to Say It

- "Okay, you can sleep over your friend's house tonight, but remember you have a paper to write for school." (This is fine if your child is very responsible, but it is better to have an agreement ahead of time about your expectations. Kids are experts at putting fun ahead of responsibilities.)

- "Will you promise to be home on time if I let you play at the neighbor's?" (Of course your child will promise. If it is important that he not be late, discuss what the consequences will be if he is late.)
- "All right, all right. If you just be quiet for the next half hour, we'll go to McDonald's for dinner." (Using blackmail is a bad habit to get into.)

The best time to negotiate is when:

you are not desperate;

you want your child to take on more responsibilities;

you want to teach your child the art of negotiation and compromise and the consequences of keeping or breaking agreements.

DO'S & DON'TS

The "D" in **TENDER** stands for **DO'S & DON'TS**. Listen to Charlie and his mom:

"Charlie, put your coat on if you're going outside. You'll get cold."

"No, I won't get cold, Mom."

"Yes, you will. You'll freeze. Put your coat on."

"But Mom . . ."

"I don't like it when you don't wear a coat."

"But *I* like it!"

Mom is making two mistakes. First, she's confusing **DO'S & DON'TS** with **TEACHING**. If she absolutely wants Charlie to wear a coat, she should say that without explaining why. Rules and orders are not requests. When a parent gives a rationale for her command, the implication is that if the child can outwit her with logic, then the rule can be put aside. If you think that explaining your rule is important (**TEACHING**), feel free to do so. But if a debate begins, you must be ready to enforce the rule or open up negotiations. More explanations will not help.

Mom's second mistake was stating that she doesn't like it when Charlie goes outside without a coat. Again, that is *not* only not a command (she is **REPORTING** her opinion), but it gives Charlie an opportunity to whittle away Mom's resolve ("But *I* like it!").

Every parent has rules. While rules can be changed or even negotiated, they are meaningless if parents do not enforce them. When children are younger and the rules are being introduced, parents may use a teaching style to explain them ("No eating food on the couch because . . ."), but when kids are a little older, explaining the rule invites discussion ("But, Dad, I promise I'll be careful not to drip jelly on the new furniture") when discussion is not necessary. Children need the structure that rules provide. And the most important, nonnegotiable rules involve moral values and safety. When your eight-year-old refuses to wear a seatbelt, you do not negotiate. You may give an explanation, but chances are your child knows the reasons. It is better to say, "Until you wear your belt, we will not go to the mall."

Sometimes enforcing rules is best done when accompanied by an empathic statement. Telling your child sincerely that you know he is disappointed or angry can soften the blow a little. It is bad enough when a child feels he does not get what he wants, but it is worse when he also feels that his parent doesn't understand him—or care to understand.

How to Say It

- "Stop pushing each other right now."
- "Stop throwing a ball in the living room. That's not allowed."
- "I know that you don't agree, but the rule is . . ."
- "Hitting your sister is very wrong."
- "We made an agreement, and you have to stick by it. Thank you."
- "Bedtime is in five minutes. Brush your teeth now."
- "Turn off the television now. It's dinnertime."
- "You can ride your bike as far as the end of the block, but no farther."

The best rules are clear and concise. When stating a rule, ask yourself if it is really a teaching moment (giving reasons why) or if the rule is simply to be enforced. Also ask yourself if you are willing to negotiate. If not, stick to your guns.

How Not to Say It

- "What did we just talk about?"
- "How many times have I told you . . ."

- "What do you think you are doing?"
- "What's going on here?"
- "I don't like it when you talk back to me."
- "How much longer do I have to wait before you clean your room?"
- "Don't do that." "Stop it." "That's not allowed." (Don't do what? Stop what? Be specific.)

None of those comments is clear, and they invite irrelevant discussion. They will only aggravate you and your children. Be straightforward and clear when stating **DO'S AND DON'TS**. If you get angry or loud when enforcing a rule, you may be frustrated or upset by more things than just your child. The more confident you are about your parenting, the less you need to yell.

Rule of Thumb: Saying "please" not only models politeness, it actually can help aggravated parents to feel more in control of their emotions.

The best time to state **DO'S AND DON'TS** is when:

you have your child's full attention;

your child is causing or risking harm;

you are clear about what you want to happen;

you are capable of enforcing the rules.

ENCOURAGING

The second "E" in **TENDER** stands for **ENCOURAGING** (which also includes praising and reassuring). A common mistake parents make is that they infrequently praise good behavior and are quick to criticize bad behavior. Criticizing bad behavior is not helpful if parents don't show the child a desirable alternative. Also, many parents undermine their praise by following it with a criticism ("Yes, you stopped fighting, but only after I scolded you").

Praising effort, self-control, and thoughtful gestures will reap rewards for you and your child.

How to Say It

- "Remember how you practiced hard for the concert and performed so well? I bet you can practice just as hard this year, too." (Reminding of past efforts and successes.)

- "I'm happy and proud of the way you behaved today. I know it wasn't easy." (Praise followed by an empathic comment.)
- "Great job! I especially liked it when you . . ." (Being specific.)
- "You could have gotten mad at your sister and pushed her, but you didn't. That shows self-control, and you made me very happy." (Praising desirable behavior.)
- "I noticed you shared your pretzels with your friends. That was very thoughtful. Some children wouldn't have done that." (Praising desirable behavior.)

How Not to Say It

- "I'm sure you'll do fine." (Have you taken time to really understand your child's concerns? If not, your reassurances will not help.)
- "Nice job." (This is okay, but what specifically did you like? Elaborate. Don't miss an opportunity to praise your child's effort or self-control.)
- "Everybody loses once in a while." (She knows that. It's better to simply make empathic comments before offering a pep talk.)
- "You did okay, but you could have done better." (Be careful. Will such a comment actually discourage your child instead?)
- "That was incredible! Amazing! Unbelievable!" (Exaggerations are fine on occasion. Kids like to know you are enthused. But such overly exuberant commentary will have more impact when said infrequently. Besides, what will you say when they accomplish something that really is amazing?)
- "Yes, you did fine, but I expect you to act that way." (Faint praise is worse than no praise at all. Why miss an opportunity to help your child feel even better about his accomplishment?)

Growing children crave parental praise and encouragement. Done wisely, it will help shape desirable behaviors and improve esteem.

The best time to encourage, praise, or reassure is:

as soon as possible;

as often as possible;

when you see good effort, self-control, or thoughtful behavior.

REPORTING

The "R" in **TENDER** stands for **REPORTING**. This refers to:

statements of fact ("We're going to Grandma's today");

common questions ("How was school?");

personal opinion ("I like going to the lake . . .");

expressing feelings ("I'm annoyed that . . .");

making requests ("Please empty the dishwasher").

Typically, well-meaning parents use **REPORTING** as a poor substitute for some of the other approaches. Saying "I don't like it when you fight in the car" is reporting a feeling. But if the parent means "Stop fighting," she should say that. Parents caught up in New Age thinking assume they are showing respect to a youngster when they use sweet phrases like "We don't do that in this house, Kenny. Remember what I told you before?" The more words you use to get your point across to a child, the more likely you are being vague, confusing your child, and undermining your authority.

Sometimes a concerned parent talks about her own feelings and mistakes it for empathy ("I'm so sad that you hurt yourself"). Generally, normal everyday conversation includes a lot of **REPORTING** that fills in the gaps between opportunities to teach, praise, command, or empathize with your child. But don't confuse **REPORTING** with any of the other **TENDER** approaches. Otherwise, the message your child hears will not be the message you intend.

How to Say It

- "Tell me what you learned at your swimming lesson." (Make a statement instead of asking open-ended questions like "How was your swimming lesson?" You are more likely to get an informative response.)
- "We were late getting to the ball game and you missed seeing the home run. That's frustrating. I'm sorry." (Reporting a statement of fact as a preface to an empathic comment.)
- "Take off your headphones, please. I like it better when you are part of the family during dinner." (Reporting your preference after telling your child what to do.)

- "I love you."
- "I forgive you."
- "I'm sorry."

How Not to Say It

- Reporting that you like or dislike something when you really mean "Stop doing that!"

If your communication efforts have been less than satisfying, you've probably overused one or more of the **TENDER** approaches. Try your hand at a different approach or use some in combination. You will likely get better results.

Adoption

Michelle and Bill felt uneasy when their twelve-year-old adopted son, Brian, began asking if he would ever meet his birth parents.

"As far as I know the records are sealed, and he may never meet them," Michelle said. "I don't feel threatened, not really. But why am I so uncomfortable?"

Every week approximately thirteen hundred children are adopted in the United States. There are two common reasons why some adoptive parents are uncomfortable discussing adoption with their children. First, many parents decide to adopt because of infertility. Infertility can be a long, despairing process as the couple seeks treatment and tries for years to become pregnant to no avail. Thus, the decision to adopt is at least in the beginning a second-best choice. They then fear that their child will view his adoptive status as second-rate. Second, adoptive parents sometimes discover that their own parents are less enthusiastic about having a grandchild that is not of their bloodline. It is an attitude that certainly changes over time but nonetheless can create uncomfortable feelings.

By age five or six an adopted child should already know he is adopted. The task for parents is to answer the more detailed questions the child might have as he gets older. But another issue is what to say to the older brother or sister (who might not be adopted) when parents decide to adopt a child.

Things to Consider

➤ Adoption is not only legal, it has become a normal and quite beautiful way to bring a child into a loving family. If you talk about adoption with the attitude that it is normal and beautiful, there is nothing to be nervous about.

➤ Despite the previous point, it is not necessary to speak excessively about the fact that your child is adopted. He is your child, plain and simple. There isn't a need to draw a distinction between adopted children and children born to a family except to help your child initially understand. How a child gets to your family is not nearly as important as the fact that he is—and always will be—part of the family.

➤ Adopting an older child is a big adjustment to the children already in the family. Patience and understanding will be necessary.

How to Say It

- **REPORT** the basic facts. "You were born like any other child. A woman gave birth to you. But she was not able to take care of you, and she wanted you to live with people who could love you and take care of you. We were the lucky family you came to live with."
- "You are our real child. You belong to this family. We will always be your mother and father."
- "Sometimes adopted children have questions about their birth parents. If you ever have any questions, I'll answer them as best I can."
- If your child is furious one day and yells, "I wish you never adopted me!" say something like: "Well, I love you, and I'll always be happy you became my child."
- Reassure. "Once you are adopted, you are my child forever. I will never give you to another family."

How Not to Say It

- "Your birth mother was a drug addict . . ." Such a condemnation, even if true, is done to make yourself sound more loving and devoted than the birth parent. What insecurity do you have that warrants such a remark? It is far better to comment on the birth parents' circumstances (they were teenagers, they had no money, etc.) than to attack their character.
- "Your natural parents . . ." or "Your real parents . . ." You are the real and natural parent at this point—legally and emotionally. The term "birth mother," or "birth parents," is accurate and doesn't detract from your status.

If you already have an older child in the house and you decide to adopt, listen to questions and concerns your child might have, but do not give her the idea that her opinion will sway you one way or the other. The decision to adopt—like the decision to become pregnant—is the parents'.

What to Say to the Older Sibling

- "It sounds as if you're wishing you never had a younger brother. All children feel that way at times. Tell me what worries or saddens you."
- "I love your mom, but that doesn't mean I love you any less. I love both of you. And I am beginning to love your new brother, and that means I won't love you or Mom any less."
- "Your new brother may wonder if we love him as much as we love you. What do you think he is feeling? Any suggestions on how we might help him feel better?"
- "I liked the way you played with your new sister. You showed her what having an older brother can be like."

Smart Talk

A recent study involved 715 families with adopted children. The children had been adopted before their first birthday, and information was taken when the children were between twelve and sixteen years of age. Results showed a slight increase among some adoptees to engage in delinquent behavior compared with their nonadoptive siblings. There was also a slight increase among some adoptees to be more socially outgoing and helpful. The final conclusion was that adopted and nonadopted children are much more similar than they are different.

2

Angry Child

When kids get very angry, you might hear them yelling:

"I hate you, Mommy!"

"No, I won't stop, and you can't make me!"

"I don't have to listen to you! You're just my stepfather!"

"I won't love you anymore!"

"I don't want to talk about it!"

Younger children don't possess all the skills necessary to control their emotional outbursts (many adults don't, either). Parents and caretakers therefore need to uncover what is bothering the angry child, and they need to teach alternative ways to express anger. It can get confusing because if the child's anger is out of hand or obnoxious, parents don't always know what to focus on first—the underlying problem or the anger.

Rule of Thumb: Common sense says that if you address the problem that is causing your child's anger, the anger will diminish. However, the angrier or more out of control your child is, the less likely you will be able to discuss his underlying problem. In that case, calming the child down is necessary before any discussion can take place.

Things to Consider

➤ If you or your spouse has trouble controlling anger, your child will have a more difficult time controlling his. The old adage, "Physician, heal thyself," makes sense.

➤ When your child is very angry, speak in a conversational tone; otherwise, you run the risk of yelling.

➤ If your child is not breaking things or hurting anyone, be patient if she is unwilling to talk about what's bothering her just yet. Let her know you are very interested and available.

➤ According to psychiatrist David Viscott in his book *The Language of Feelings,* behind anger is hurt and sadness. Think about what is hurting your child instead of focusing on his anger, and you may hit pay dirt. People feel hurt when they lose their sense of being loved (or lose someone they love), when they suffer a loss of esteem or competence, or if life seems unfair or less in their control.

How to Say It

EMPATHIZING is usually your best bet for openers. Calmly REPORTING your observations or your reaction can also help.

- "When you're angry like that, I know you must be sad about something. Tell me what happened."
- "It hurt your feelings when your brother knocked your new bike over on purpose."
- "If you're angry, you must have a pretty good reason. Please tell me what it is."
- "When you're yelling, it is hard for me to concentrate. Please lower your voice."
- "You just slammed the door. That tells me you're hurt about something. I'd like you to tell me what's wrong."
- "I remember saying that to my father when I was a kid. I felt a lot better when we talked about it."
- "I can't force you to talk about it if you don't want to. I just hope you change your mind because talking usually helps. Besides, I hate to see you feeling so bad."

When your child is calmer, it is a good idea for each of you to sit while talking. Standing up increases the chances of another angry outburst or walking away prematurely. As the discussion nears the end, be ENCOURAGING. Praise your child for talking to you more calmly.

- "Even though you felt hurt and angry, I liked it much better when you talked more calmly. It made it easier for me to listen."
- "I noticed it when you started to speak more softly and with less anger. Good job. It isn't always easy to do that when you're upset."

Any **TEACHING** about how to handle angry emotions is best done in a friendly way when you are less annoyed. Role-playing is a good idea if you can make a game out of it.

- "Remember show-and-tell? When you are really angry or sad or upset about something, please tell me how you feel, but don't show it by yelling or calling people names or by stomping your feet or throwing things."
- "Let's pretend you are very mad at me about something. Can you say, 'Dad, I'm real mad right now,' instead of yelling at me?"
- "A friend of mine didn't know what to say when his son was very angry about something. What advice should I give him?" By referring to a third party, you make the topic less personal. That might make it easier for your child to offer his opinion.

How Not to Say It

- "Don't you talk to me in that tone of voice!" You may be right to feel angry (see the chapter on defiance and disrespect), but first consider what your goal is. Will a comment like that prompt your child to be more polite, or will it add fuel to the fire? It is very important to discuss the issue of disrespect, but that is best done a little later when the immediate problem is solved.
- "How dare you!" Same as above.
- "Don't you know how that makes me feel?" Trying to teach your child to empathize with your feelings is a good idea—but not as the first item. Your child is more concerned with her feelings, not anybody else's. Save that comeback for a little later in the conversation.
- "I refuse to talk to you as long as you're in that mood." Unless you are pretty sure that your child will change his tone, you run the risk that he will decide it is simply not worth talking to you. Then you've eliminated any way for either of you to approach the other without losing

face. It would be better to comment first that your child must be hurt about something and that you are available to talk. Or say something like "I want to hear about what's bothering you, I really do. But you'll have to change your tone a little bit. It's hard for me to pay attention when you're so mad."

- "You sound very angry." In their book *What Did I Just Say!*, Denis Donovan and Deborah McIntyre insightfully point out that validating a child's anger but not the hurt or sadness behind it can sometimes encourage more angry behavior. Telling a child he is angry may stir him up even more. Telling him he is sad is also accurate but more likely to lower aggressiveness.

3

Apologies

Karl and Pete were sitting on the back porch while their kids played. Pete's eight-year-old son, Joey, came out wearing his father's sport coat. It went down to his knees.

"I'm going to work now," Joey said.

"Don't spill anything on that jacket," Pete called out.

The boy went into the yard, and Karl chuckled. "I remember wearing my old man's stuff when I was a kid," he said. "Try walking down the stairs with a pair of size elevens!" He reached into a bowl of pretzels. "Of course, my father never liked me doing that. All I ever heard from him was complaints. And I never once heard him apologize. He never admitted to making mistakes. Not ever."

Kids yearn for their parents' love and approval. They like dressing up, pretending to be their mom or dad. They want their parents—especially their same-sex parent—to be proud of them. So when a parent makes mistakes and doesn't apologize, children feel deep down that they are unworthy. As they get older, they'll resent it. It's not enough for parents to teach their children to say they're sorry. Parents must admit when they are wrong and not feel ashamed to apologize to their kids when necessary.

Things to Consider

➤ Some parents show anger a lot. They are least likely to apologize and most likely to instill a sense of inadequacy in their children.

➤ While arguments and misunderstandings between a parent and child do happen, any negative effects are greatly diminished when there is positive closure. Not apologizing can leave the matter hanging and a child may believe his parent is still angry long after the incident has passed.

➤ You will not undermine your status or authority by apologizing. On the contrary, children are more likely to respect your authority and be less likely to rebel later.

How to Say It

REPORTING your apology and perhaps **EMPATHIZING** are called for.

- "I'm sorry. I shouldn't have yelled at you that way. Please forgive me."
- "I left for the store without asking if you wanted to come with me. Now you're upset. I'm sorry. Next time I'll remember to ask if you want to join me."
- "I probably should have apologized before now. I'm sure I hurt your feelings by waiting so long."
- "I was wrong to get so upset with you over such a small thing. I apologize."
- "I bet you're very hurt over what I said. I made a mistake. I was wrong, and I hope you'll forgive me."

How Not to Say It

- "I'm sorry, but I wouldn't have yelled at you in front of your friends if you'd done what I'd asked." That is more accusatory than remorseful.
- "Don't be so upset. You know I didn't mean it." If she's that upset, she did take it personally. Don't tell her she's wrong. Apologize.

When trying to get kids to apologize to you or someone else, don't insist they sound sincere. They probably won't sound sincere, at least not right away. The first thing they need to learn is that they were wrong to have done what they did. Later, when emotions are not so intense, help them to think about how they hurt someone else's feelings and what they might do to make amends.

How to Say It

- "This problem will not go away until you say you're sorry."
- "You broke your brother's toy on purpose. Tell me how you think he felt when you did that."

- "I know you were mad when you said those hurtful things, but that doesn't excuse what you did. It is important for you to apologize." (**EMPATHIZING** can soften his defensiveness.)
- "I heard you tell your sister you were sorry. That meant a lot to me. Good for you."
- "It's not like you to be this hurtful. Usually you are more kind. You need to apologize; otherwise, people's feelings will stay hurt." (It is always a good idea to balance complaints or criticisms with a positive remark.)
- "Don't apologize right this minute. I don't think you're ready. I'd like you to think about it for a while." This can be helpful if you sense your child will defy your request for an apology and you'd rather not butt heads. If your child wants to defy you, it allows her the chance to do so by not waiting to apologize but apologizing right away.

How Not to Say It

- "If you don't apologize, you can forget going swimming tomorrow." Applying an arbitrary punishment won't get you what you ultimately want—a child who is sincerely willing to apologize for being hurtful and who will try to avoid being hurtful in the future. It is better to say something like "I don't intend for us to be in the car together when you two haven't worked things out. I won't drive you anywhere when I know you'll just argue." That shows how not apologizing can have a natural consequence that might best be avoided by saying one is sorry.

A recent study in the journal *Child Development* showed that when parents tried to help their children empathize with the person who was hurt, as opposed to simply forcing their child to get along, the children did score higher on empathy and on the tendency to engage in positive social acts. The more often you ask your children to consider how they might have affected others, the more likely they will be better-acting kids.

4

Arguments
Between Two Adults

Katie often overheard her mother and grandmother arguing. She felt sad about it and tried to cope by occupying her mind with other things such as television or music. She was usually glad when the fighting stopped.

Bobbie overheard his parents arguing. Sometimes he would get in the middle and tell them to stop. Sometimes he'd start acting silly and giddy. Other times he'd get angry or aggressive.

Each child's style is different. Katie is concerned but uninvolved. If her caretakers argue frequently or if there are many unresolved fights (and certainly if there is violence), she is at risk for behavioral or emotional problems. Bobbie is already showing signs of disturbance. When a child intervenes in an adult argument, it is a sign that the arguing is of long standing and the child is overly involved. His occasional giddiness is not happiness but physical arousal that he cannot control. He is at high risk for acting out and developing more serious behavioral problems as he gets older.

Arguments between parents or caretakers happen, but their impact on a child depends on several factors, including how the adults respond to the child's concerns.

Things to Consider

➤ Prolonged conflicts or unresolved arguments between parents are damaging to a child's sense of security. It is not the arguing or yelling per se that is harmful, it is the child's belief that his security is threatened and that his environment is not trustworthy.

➤ Open hostility between parents is more likely to lead to behavioral problems in children than marital dissatisfaction without hostility.

➤ About one-half of all children are fearful when their parents argue.

➤ Children who witness spousal abuse engage in the same kinds of behavioral disturbances as do children who are victims of parental abuse.

➤ Children's anxiety is immediately lessened once they believe that their parents have resolved their argument. If parents who argue are observed smiling and holding hands later, the kids will breathe a sigh of relief and develop a sense of optimism that fighting won't lead to disaster.

How to Say It

- If you think your child overheard an argument you had with your mate, **EMPATHIZE** with her concerns. "I bet it made you worried or a little nervous."
- "Maybe you felt a little afraid."
- "I'm sorry you had to hear that. I'm sure it upset you."
- **REPORT.** Let your child know if matters have improved. He doesn't need to know the details but he needs to know if the situation has resolved. "I know you overheard that argument. You'll be happy to know that your mom and I have settled our differences, and we're not upset anymore."
- "Sometimes your mom and I get mad at each other, but we don't stay that way for very long. We still love each other very much."
- If your arguments remain unresolved, and especially if there is hostility, your child will feel insecure. Telling her that all is okay won't work. She'll know the truth by observing how you and your mate act toward each other. It is better to make any reassuring comment you can than say nothing. "Your dad and I are still upset with each other, but we're trying to work it out. I hope it will be soon. If this continues to trouble you, we'll talk about it."

How Not to Say It

- "That argument you overheard didn't bother you, did it?" Sometimes parents ask leading questions, using subtle tones and body language to make their children respond the way the parent wants to hear. If you really want to know how your child feels, make an **EMPATHIC** comment ("You must be upset over what you heard") instead of asking a question ("Did that argument bother you?")

- "I can't believe your mother!" Criticizing a mate to a child will not alleviate his anxiety; it will heighten it.
- "Don't look at me like that! I'm angry with you, too. When was the last time you cleaned your room!" Spillover effects can happen, but yelling at a child because you are upset with your mate only adds to the misery.

Rule of Thumb: Your children will eventually know how well you and your mate get along. You can't hide the truth. The issue is whether or not your children will feel worried and insecure about it.

Bed-wetting

Elliot is one of the 7 percent of eight-year-olds who wets his bed. He feels embarrassed and won't attend sleepovers or let his friends sleep at his house. While he has had many dry nights, the unpredictability of his bed-wetting haunts him and exasperates his parents. He has tried halting fluid intake after 7 P.M., but that has proved an inconvenience on hot summer nights. His pediatrician recommends a line of medication known as tricyclic antidepressants. His parents don't know what to do or how to console their son.

Things to Consider

➤ Bed-wetting is considered a problem if the child is at least five years of age and wets the bed twice a month or more.

➤ Eighty percent of bed-wetters have never achieved six months of continuous nighttime continence. That is called primary enuresis.

➤ Children who achieved continence for six months or more but then resumed wetting the bed (secondary enuresis) usually took longer to have dry nights and have more stress.

➤ About 3 percent of bed-wetters will continue this problem into early adulthood.

➤ By far the most successful treatment method is the urine alarm. The alarm goes off at the first sign of wetness and allows the child to interrupt the bed-wetting and use the toilet. Research is clear that this method far surpasses the use of medication. Tricyclic medications can have cardio-toxic effects if overdose occurs. Try the urine alarm before you try medications.

➤ Children over five who wet their pants during the day while awake are slower to improve.

How to Say It

- **TEACH** that the problem occurs in about one in fourteen children (age eight or under) and that it is treatable. **EMPATHY** is crucial. "I know you are very upset about this problem. You should know that you are not alone. There is probably one other child in your class with this problem. The good news is that you can stop having this problem with the urine alarm treatment."
- Reassure. "I'm glad we are tackling this problem. I know you'll feel so much better in time."
- After the bed is wet: "Okay, you pull off the sheets, and I'll get a fresh set. I'll help you make the bed." It is fine if your child prefers to make the bed alone. It is also fine if you tell the child he is to make it by himself (you are tired or busy). However, making the bed should not be viewed as a punishment. Your tone should not be scolding. Having to make a bed will not motivate your child to overcome the enuresis.

Rule of Thumb: Don't think your child will outgrow the problem. It is overcome by treatment and is likely to persist without treatment. Only 15 percent of eight-year-old bed-wetters stopped wetting within a year without treatment.

How Not to Say It

- "Can't you control yourself? You're nine years old already!" Scolding won't help, and it will definitely hurt. Your child feels bad enough as it is. If you find yourself scolding him, apologize soon. "I'm so sorry. I know it isn't your fault. I just wish you could feel better, and I think I took my frustrations out on you."
- "I'm not washing those smelly sheets. You do it." The critical tone is inappropriate. You are adding to your child's sense of shame.
- "Just try to sleep over at a friend's house. You might have a great time." Don't push it. Your child will feel humiliated if he wets the bed at a friend's house. Get the urine alarm and work on his training at home first.

6

Bossy or Domineering Child

Carol watched her daughter playing outside. The nine-year-old girl had her hands on her hips and was clearly bossing her friends. A few minutes later the girl came in the house.

"They didn't want to play with me anymore," the girl said.

Carol was not surprised.

To some extent bossiness can be part of a child's temperament. Shy, withdrawn children are less likely to try to dominate their peer group. Outgoing children can be bossy but often they are merely exuberant or filled with ideas and strategies. They are not so interested in taking charge but are willing to take the lead.

Bossy children are not leaders. They are rulers. They want things their way, and they think their way really is the best way. Bossy children may prefer playing with younger kids because it is easier to get their way. But domineering children run the risk of being rejected by their peers. To compensate, they may become even bossier.

Things to Consider

➤ Bossy, domineering behavior is probably being reinforced. The first place to look is the home. Is the bossy child one who has many responsibilities? A single-parent home or a home with an alcoholic or dysfunctional parent often relies on older children to abandon some of their childhood and join the ranks of the adults. Expecting these kids to do extra chores and look out for their younger siblings but not to be bossy with their peers may be expecting too much.

➤ Is the bossy child one who is frequently dominated at home? If so, he may be trying to balance the scales by dominating his playmates. If the way the siblings treat him is changed, the bossiness might take care of itself.

➤ Does the child show signs of perfectionism? If she is easily frustrated by her mistakes, afraid to take risks for fear of failing, or engages in compulsive rituals such as cleaning excessively or counting, she may have an anxiety disorder and should be examined by a professional.

How to Say It

A straightforward command that he stop being bossy and let his friends have their way probably won't work for long. Many reminders will be needed. Realize that this pattern of bossiness gives your child a sense of mastery or esteem and that alternative ways to achieve those ends are required. You may first want to help your child open up more.

- "I noticed you got upset when your friends didn't want to do things your way. Tell me more about that."
- "What is it like when somebody else wants things to go their way?"
- "When you told Jeremy that you wouldn't play with him unless he followed your rules, how do you think that made him feel?"
- "Would you want to play with someone who always had to get his way? No? Well, I'm worried that your friends won't want to play with you because you always want your way."

Plan ahead with your child. If you know he will be playing with friends, rehearse ways he can act more fairly and less bossy. Reward his efforts with praise and hugs.

- "I watched you agree to play soccer when you wanted to play dodge ball. That was terrific. I'm proud of you for letting other kids get their fair chance to have their way."
- "I saw you doing rocks, scissors, and paper. That was a very fair way to decide who goes first in the game. Good for you."
- "I think you like to be in charge with your friends because you also have a lot of responsibilities here at home. What could happen at home that would give you less work and more time for fun?" Be willing to negotiate. Children need responsibilities, and they also need to be children.

How Not to Say It

- "Nobody likes a bossy friend." First, that isn't always true. Some kids don't mind being led. Second, you don't want to suggest that being liked is the most important thing. Kids often make poor decisions just so they will be liked. It is better to say, "Kids who like you probably won't have fun playing with you unless they get to do what they want sometimes."

- "How was school? Did you try to cooperate more with your friends?" It is important to follow up when helping a child modify his behavior. But this question is vague (are you sure your child knows exactly what you mean by the word *cooperate*?), and it is a question that can be answered by yes or no and may therefore be uninformative. Be specific: "Tell me how you tried to be more fair and less bossy with your friends today." Ask how difficult or easy it was and exuberantly praise any improvements.

7

Bullies

Danny had been moody and lethargic for a few days. Ordinarily a happy eleven-year-old, something was the matter. It was only when he complained about going to school that his parents had their first clue. Finally, when Danny said he had lost his lunch money, his parents put two and two together. An older boy on the school bus had been bullying him. What began as mild teasing escalated to loud put-downs that got the attention of the other kids and finally resulted in forcefully taking Danny's lunch money. Danny was afraid and embarrassed. Like many children, especially preteens, he felt awkward about telling his parents.

Conservative estimates are that 75 percent of children will be bullied at some point in their school career. There is more violence in schools today than a generation ago. A study of fifty-three randomly selected middle schools in North Carolina showed that 3 percent of the students had carried a gun and over 14 percent had carried a knife or club. Consequently, the rules for dealing with bullies need to be modified.

Things to Consider

➤ Fighting back is risky given the prevalence of weapons. Think twice about teaching your child to use fists as a way to dissuade bullies. Also, many schools have a zero-tolerance policy for fighting, and children who are trying to defend themselves are still punished even though they did not start the fight.

➤ Phoning the bully's parents can help but do so only if you know the parents (even casually). The home life of the bully may not be ideal, and he or she may be a victim of abuse or living in a home where abuse is tolerated.

➤ Always get the school involved. Have a meeting with the principal, teachers, and any counselor. They need to know what is happening and are likely to have more clout.

➤ Some children are more vulnerable to being bullied. Children who are physically smaller than average, who cry easily, or who possess poor social skills (unable to effectively initiate conversation or less likely to offer help or kindness) are more frequently the prey. Teaching them assertiveness can help.

➤ Some bullying is physical (shoving, hitting, preventing movement), some is verbal, and some is nonverbal (obscene gestures, staring).

➤ Follow up by asking your child several weeks later if matters have improved. Don't presume the situation is fully resolved.

How to Say It

If you suspect a bully problem, **REPORTING** your observations and suspicions straightforwardly is best. Then you need to find out the details.

- "I think you are dealing with a bully. That happens to most kids, and it can be very upsetting. There are things that can be done to make it stop."
- "Tell me exactly what happened and when."

If your child tells you how he feels, an **EMPATHIC** response will help him feel understood and he will talk more.

- "So it's scary to play at recess now. A lot of kids know how that feels."
- "You feel embarrassed when you get teased in front of your classmates. I remember when I got teased like that."

An older child may be too humiliated to go into details. Empathizing by telling him he feels embarrassed to talk may actually make him more self-conscious. It is better to use general terms when trying to be empathic.

- "I bet it bothers you a lot. No one likes putting up with bullies."
- "It can really ruin a guy's day when a bully is around."

Finally, **TEACH** by role-playing with your child the various ways he might respond to being bullied. Rehearsing their response will improve their confidence in coping. There are no sure-fire formulas for dismissing a bully. However, experts agree that the most successful strategy involves two steps:

1. A brief, firm, and confident rebuff such as "I don't have to take this from you . . ." or "I don't have to put up with this!" (Rehearse this several times.)
2. Walking away with shoulders straight and head held high.

If your child has a capacity for entertainment and enjoys humor, he can respond by poking fun at himself after being taunted by a bully. "You're right! I am a freak! Aaagh!"

Bullies are more apt to stop their bullying if they are not getting a strong fear response from the other children. Ask your child to recall who witnessed the bullying and to report the bullying to a school official or you.

How Not to Say It

- "Just ignore him. He'll go away eventually." It is impossible to ignore a bully unless you spend your time in hiding. Fear is best overcome by teaching assertiveness.
- "But you're so tall and strong! You don't have to be pushed around by anyone." Size and strength are less a factor than your child's personality. Shyer or more sensitive children can be easily intimidated. It is better to coach him in effective responses and praise that performance.
- "You're getting older now. I can't solve all your problems for you. I'm sure you can figure this one out." The consequences of being bullied can be devastating. At best, kids are humiliated. At worst, they harbor deep resentments and may take matters into their own hands by finding a weapon. Your child needs your full support, the support of the school, and sensitivity to the feelings of humiliation or anger that can result.
- "He didn't hit you, he just called you names" or "He didn't tease you, he just stared at you." Don't underestimate how intimidating non-physical forms of bullying can be.

8

Cheating

Billy and Sam were stationed in front of the television playing their favorite video racing game. Every so often Billy would press the pause button and interrupt the game for a split second before restarting it. It had the effect of distracting Sam just enough to give Billy the edge he wanted.

"Stop doing that. It messes me up!" Sam said.

"Okay, okay," Billy said. But when it appeared that Sam would win the game, Billy pressed the pause button and managed to eke out a victory.

Most children will cheat at something. While parents understand that, it is a bothersome trait as the child gets older. Parents view it as a form of dishonesty similar to lying, and they don't want it encouraged. Plus, parents are aware that in order to get along with others, children must learn how to play fairly.

Things to Consider

➤ Sometimes children cheat merely to aggravate their opponent. It is a way of teasing a sibling; for example, a child may blatantly cheat and then watch the little sister get angry and hurt. If teasing is the motivation, address that instead.

➤ On average, cheating at games tends to diminish as the child gets older. The more pronounced it is for a child over ten, the more other areas of concern need to be probed. Are there upsetting things going on in the child's life?

How to Say It

- **REPORTING** your observation should come first, followed by a **DO & DON'T** reminder. "I just saw you switch cards. That's called cheating. Let's agree not to do that."

- "I saw you cheating again. I don't enjoy playing when you cheat. I'm going to stop playing now and we'll try again later."
- **ENCOURAGING** or praising noncheating behavior should be done periodically. "We've been playing this game for fifteen minutes, and you have played by the rules. That's great. I have much more fun when we play by the rules."
- "You just scored a point and you played by the rules. I bet that feels really good to know you accomplished something."
- Teach and encourage **EMPATHY**. "I wonder how your friend felt when you kept cheating at the game."
- "Sometimes you'll break the rules just to get that good feeling when you win. But that doesn't make it right."

How Not to Say It

- "You're a cheater. Nobody likes a cheater." Labels are unnecessary, much too critical, and not likely to help you achieve your goal. Besides, your child does not cheat all the time, so the label is wrong. Criticize the behavior, not the child's character.
- "We played a game, and you didn't cheat!" This is not a terrible thing to say and your intent is good—to praise your child for being honest—but whenever possible, praise what the child did that was positive (he was honest, he played by the rules) instead of praising the fact that he didn't do something (he didn't cheat). Teaching a child *not* to do something is not the same as teaching her an appropriate alternative.
- When you tell your child that she cheated, odds are that she will deny it. Don't say, "You're lying! Don't lie to me!" While her dishonesty may trouble you, stick to the issue at hand (see the chapter on lying for more advice). It is better to say, "I saw you move my piece on the game board. Maybe you don't think that is cheating, but I don't want to play with you when you move my pieces like that."
- Model appropriate self-talk during the game when you are excited or frustrated by your score in the game. In other words, teach tolerance and self-control. "I'm losing this game, and I want to win. I know I could try to cheat, but I don't want to win that way. If I lose, I'll try harder next time."

9

Chores

"How many times do I have to tell you to tidy up this room?" Dad said. He was feeling exasperated. The kids always have time for the computer, friends, and outside activities, but they never seem to have time to clean up after themselves.

"But I made my bed," six-year-old Anthony said.

"Yes, you did. Thank you," Dad said. "But that was last Friday."

It took them all of five minutes to tidy up.

"See how easy that was," Dad said. "Why do I have to tear my hair out to get you guys to help around here?"

Why, indeed.

Things to Consider

➤ Chores can be divided into two types. "Self tasks" involve activities that pertain to the person in question, such as making one's own bed, washing one's dishes, or cleaning up after oneself. "Family tasks" are those that benefit the family as a whole, such as mowing the lawn, doing laundry, feeding the dog, or shoveling the driveway. It's a good idea to have your children do both types, especially as they get older.

➤ Some parents have a managerial style. They assign chores and expect the child to take responsibility for getting it done. Other parents make requests and expect the child to help out when asked. Again, as they get older, children should bear responsibility for doing some chores without being asked.

➤ One study showed that adolescents who did family tasks were also more likely to be helpful to others in various contexts. Learning to clean up only after oneself may not teach about doing for others.

➤ Boys and girls do the same amount of self tasks, while girls do more family tasks.

➤ When chores don't get done, parents are usually inconsistent in enforcing the rules.

How to Say It

- **REPORT** accurately what you expect to be done, by whom, and when. "Before we leave at two o'clock I want you to pick up everything on the family room floor that doesn't belong there. Please throw away the things that are broken."

- "I want the leaves swept out of the garage. Tony, you do that. You can do it right after breakfast. It should take you ten minutes."

- You do not need to threaten punishments, but there can be natural consequences that would work to your advantage. "If you're not finished by two o'clock, we won't go to the party until it is finished. It's your choice."

- "If it's not done by nine tonight, you'll have to stop whatever you're doing then and get it done."

- "I've asked you to put away your papers and hang up your clothes, and you haven't done it. In five minutes the computer will be turned off, and it will stay off until those jobs get done."

- **NEGOTIATE.** Give kids age-appropriate choices. "Tommy, the dog needs to be exercised and given a bath. Also, the leaves need raking and the gutters need to be cleaned out. Which of those would you be willing to do today?"

- "I'd like you to do some regular chores. If you had your pick, which would you choose?"

- **EMPATHIZE** when your child seems disgruntled. "I know it isn't fun having to put your boots on to take the garbage out. But thanks for doing it."

- **ENCOURAGE** responsible behavior. "It helps out so much when you do your chores. I'm very grateful."

How Not to Say It

- Eliminate any vague commands such as "Clean up your room," "Tidy up the kitchen," and "Clean the countertop." According to whose standards? Your child's version of a clean room may be different from yours.

- "How many times have I asked you . . ." If you talk like that, it is a strong clue that you need to enforce the rules more consistently. You've probably allowed your child to get away with dawdling in the past. Give reasonable time limits and enforce them.

- "What am I, your servant?" What parent hasn't felt that way? Clarify with your child your expectations about what needs to be done and when. Then calmly but firmly enforce those expectations.

- "If you don't get your chores done, you can kiss the birthday party good-bye." If this works, it is only because your child has detected that you are losing your patience. The neat thing about clear expectations and clear consequences is that the consequences speak for you. You don't have to yell or get exasperated. Also, if you make threats you won't enforce, you are only whittling away your authority.

10

Initiating Conversation

Ed and his son, Ray, were driving home. It was raining and the streets were crowded with cars.

"Some weather, isn't it, Ray?" Ed said.

"Yeah."

"What did you say?"

"I said yeah."

"Oh." Ed continued to drive but was feeling self-conscious about the lack of real conversation. It wasn't for lack of trying. His son just tended to be closemouthed about a lot of things. Not always, but a lot of the time.

"Did you finish your homework, Ray?"

Ray stared out the window and said nothing.

"Ray, did you hear what I just said? Did you finish your homework?"

"Yeah."

"When?"

"This afternoon."

"What subject was it?"

"English."

Ed knew he'd have to pull teeth. He decided not to ask any more questions for the remainder of the ride home.

Some kids are not prone to conversation. Some tips might help.

Things to Consider

➤ Sometimes kids don't talk much to their parents because they already know what their parents will say. If your child was troubled or frustrated about something, would you have a standard comeback? Would you try to solve the problem? Would you say not to worry? Would you say something like "That's what happens when you don't follow rules"? If your responses are prepackaged, you are not truly listening to your child.

➤ Preteen and teen boys are prone to mulling things over before they discuss them. What looks like stonewalling is their effort to handle matters on their own. While that can be a strength, it is intensified for boys whose fathers are not as physically or psychologically available (due to overwork, divorce, etc.). These boys don't want to discuss some things with their mothers, so they have no one else to turn to for advice.

➤ When trying to draw out a quiet child, do something different. Talk about something new and exciting, change your verbal approach (use the **TENDER** guidelines), or change the environment (kids who do not open up in a car or the family room may do so at a restaurant or on a walk).

➤ Don't try to get your child to open up if you are busy doing something else or she is busy. Neither of you is sending a signal that you are ready to really listen to each other.

➤ If you talk to your child only when *you* feel like talking, don't be surprised if conversations are infrequent and less than satisfying.

How to Say It

- Ask questions that cannot be answered in one or two words. "What were some of the questions on your history test today?"

- If your usually not-too-verbal child asks or tells you anything, respond with comments that will invite more discussion, not shut it down. Usually, the best response is one where you show empathy or reflect back your child's feelings about something.

  "I can't wait until Saturday."

  "Oh, you're excited about going rafting."

  "Yeah."

  "If you had to convince someone to go rafting, what would be your three best reasons?"

- Ask your child to teach *you* something that you know she is interested in. "Tell me more about the exercise your teacher used in acting class. I always wanted to learn more about acting."

- If your child is brooding and feeling self-critical, don't automatically challenge her beliefs. She may just think you don't understand. **EMPATHIZE** first. "You put on makeup today, and none of your friends were impressed. Now you're telling me you feel ugly." That comment will probably invite more conversation. Telling her she is beautiful may make you feel better, but it may not be what she needs to hear just yet.

- Make the lull in conversation *your* problem and ask your child for help. "You know, I sometimes want to make conversation but don't always know how to keep it going. Could you help me by bringing up topics?"

- Praise any openness. "I like it when we can talk about these things. Everything that goes on in your life means a lot to me."

- Talk about something that excites you. Your enthusiasm might possibly be infectious, and your child will want to know more. "Wouldn't it be great if we could build an addition to the house? I've always wanted a large sunroom."

- If you try to respond effectively to a child's comment but her body language tells you that you missed the boat, let her know you really want to understand. "What you're telling me sounds really important, but I don't think I understand yet. Help me to understand. Has something I've said troubled you?"

- If you continue to feel frustrated that your child doesn't talk to you much, it's okay to ask if you are doing something wrong. Humility never hurts, and it might help. "Every time I try to talk to you it seems I say something wrong. Can you help me with this problem? What things do I say that turn you off?"

How Not to Say It

- "What am I? A head of lettuce? Why won't you talk to me?" This can work if your child enjoys your sense of humor, but if said with antagonism, you may get nowhere.

- "I hate it when I have to drag things out of you." This is a bit strong and has an accusatory tone. If children think they will be accused or criticized, they will definitely withhold conversation unless they have to. Talk using softer words. "It means a lot when we can have a conversation. I have a harder time when you give me short answers."
- "Why can't you be like your sister?" You've just increased the odds that he will talk even less.
- "Have you done something wrong? Is that why you don't talk much?" Don't make him feel paranoid or self-conscious.

11

Dawdling

"Lizzie, we should have left five minutes ago. Where are your shoes?"

"I can't find them."

"Then why were you watching television when you should have been searching for your shoes? You'll be late for your ballet class!"

A few minutes later the shoes were found, but Lizzie still wasn't ready to leave. First she had to brush her hair, then use the bathroom, then . . .

"Lizzie, you just have to be more organized from now on," her mom complained in the car. "I'm tired of running around at the last minute."

Tired, sure. But it will happen again and again. Lizzie's Mom is making two fundamental errors when she tries to get her daughter organized in the morning:

1. The words she uses are ineffective yet she keeps using them.
2. The only consequence to dawdling is that Lizzie must put up with a frustrated parent. Any kid can handle that.

Things to Consider

➤ Children who dawdle in the morning may be overtired. Children do not require eight hours of sleep per night; they require ten to twelve hours. Poor sleep habits will cause sluggishness in the morning.

➤ Teaching a child to be more organized and on time must usually be done for each and every situation. A child who no longer dawdles before school may dawdle before bedtime or as he prepares for an extracurricular activity such as dance or karate lessons.

➤ A child who awakens the first morning in Walt Disney World doesn't dawdle. He is motivated to be ready on time. Children are not always that motivated to hurry for school or shopping. Rewarding on-time behavior with check marks or stars that can be exchanged for something desirable (such as extra time at Nintendo) can help motivate a child. Praise is essential and ultimately more powerful than tangible rewards.

How to Say It

- Let the more rewarding morning activities (eating breakfast, watching TV) occur after your child has gotten himself better organized. "I'll be happy to serve you breakfast after you get your shoes on and put all your books in your bag."
- "This is your two-minute warning. In two minutes you have to stop everything you're doing and get ready to leave."
- Praise desirable behavior. "You got dressed before coming downstairs to breakfast. Good for you. That will give you more time to relax before school."
- "Right now I need you to do . . . [list the specific behaviors]. Any questions?"
- "You can take your time if you want, but if you miss the school bus you will have to pay me gas money from your allowance [or you'll have to clean the bathroom or do some other pre-agreed chore]." Under such circumstances you do not have to yell at your child to hurry up. Let the consequences be sufficient.

How Not to Say It

- Don't say "Put on your shoes!" when you mean to say "Stop everything and put your shoes on right now." When you ask a child to do something and then repeat it ten minutes later, your child often responds, "I was going to do it!" You were probably not specific about when you wanted the task completed.
- "Why are you never ready when it's time to go?" It simply wasn't that important to him. It would be better to ask yourself how you can speak more clearly to the kids and enforce your rules calmly but strictly.

- "Do I have to yell at you every day in order for you to be organized?" If you have to ask that question, the answer is yes. Your kids have learned the fine art of distinguishing between those moments when they can ignore your request and when they must obey. They've learned not to take you seriously until you get ballistic. Speak clearly, calmly, and firmly. Turn off all distractions. Reward efficiency and be willing to let your children deal with the natural consequences of being late.

- Teach them a lesson when you are disorganized. "See? I have to pay a late fee because I didn't pay this bill on time. It was hidden under all these other papers. If I was better organized, that would not have happened."

Smart Talk

In a study conducted at Rhodes College in Memphis, researchers concluded that children who procrastinate are more likely to have parents who do the same. These parents also procrastinated when they were youngsters. If your child is a slowpoke when it comes to organization and efficiency, first modify your own shortcomings. Are you sometimes late picking them up? Do you always sign their papers or report cards at the last minute? Do the kids overhear you complaining about bills that are overdue? Do you promise to do something only to say later, "I was too busy," "I didn't have time," or "I forgot . . ."?

The apple doesn't fall far from the tree when it comes to procrastination.

12

Death of an Adult Family Member

Maryanne and the kids had just turned into their street when the cell phone rang. She knew it was her mother. Her mom had called twice a day every day for the past week, ever since Maryanne's husband, Adam, had to be rehospitalized for cancer. She and the children had just visited him. He looked awful but his eyes shimmered in the presence of his wife and kids. They would return later in the day after their oldest son Scott's soccer game. A win would tie his team for the league lead. The boy loved soccer, and his parents wanted his daily life to be as familiar and routine as possible despite his father's setback.

"Hi, Mom," Maryanne said with a smile. "You could have left a message on the machine at home. You know I would have called you right back."

But it wasn't her mother; it was the hospital. Maryanne stopped the car just two houses away from her driveway, trying to grasp the full meaning of the message. Adam had died quite suddenly, not ten minutes after she had last seen him.

"Mom?" Scott said, looking wide-eyed at his mother.

Maryanne turned and looked at her son. The other two kids were now silent in the backseat, waiting. She knew she had to tell them, but how? Would things ever be the same again?

Things to Consider

➤ Some children between five and seven do not fully understand the finality of death. They may have to be retold that because a loved one has died, she will not be returning.

➤ Children will take their cue from their caretakers about how to mourn. If the adults cope with stoicism and unexpressed sadness, children will learn that showing feelings or asking questions is not allowed. They will then have to grieve alone somehow.

➤ Anticipate that the children will act out or withdraw emotionally if the deceased was very close and important to them. They may become argumentative, be less conscientious about schoolwork, or isolate themselves from pleasurable activities.

➤ If the death was unexpected or violent, children may suffer nightmares or other more intense forms of distress.

➤ Rituals can be crucial to the healing process. A memorial service, a wake, or a funeral helps to reinforce the reality that the loved one has indeed died. It also offers a clearer line of demarcation to help people move on.

➤ Reminisce. Look through photos or videos. While painful at first, a vital component of healing is allowing the happier memories to act as a warm blanket to the cold, sad reminders of loss. Children may always miss a loved one, but over time they can smile at the memory instead of cry.

➤ Experts agree that there is no "normal" length of time to grieve. Even when it appears that a child is faring well, there will be many moments of overwhelming sadness—especially during the first year. Holidays, birthdays, and anniversaries of special family times can trigger sadness.

How to Say It

- Be direct but sensitive. Let your nonverbal language convey that your child's response matters to you. "I have very sad news. Grandpa died this morning."

- If the children have questions, answer them honestly. Details that are frightening or grisly should be left out. "Remember that Grandpa had heart surgery? Well, he developed an infection called pneumonia. Pneumonia can usually be treated but Grandpa was so weak the medicines didn't work and he died."

- Children will worry about your safety and possibly their own. If a child asks whether he will die or whether you are going to die, it's okay to reassure her that you will live a long time and she will, too. "Everybody dies someday. But most people live to be very old. By the time I die you will be all grown up and living in your own house with your own children."

- Some children will be overprotective of you. They may worry when you are sick with a cold or when you are driving in bad weather. Make **EMPATHIC** comments and then *reassure* them that you are taking proper care of yourself. "You sound worried that I might die just as Daddy did. Those are scary thoughts. But you and your brothers are the most important things in my life, so you need to know that I take very good care of myself and always drive with my seatbelt on and very carefully."

- *Reassure* them by pointing out the other times they worried and everything turned out well. "Remember how last week you got worried when I had to take antibiotics for my bronchitis? But I got all better, didn't I?"

- Comment when you know your child is feeling sad but isn't saying anything to you. "Here we are having dinner, and Mommy isn't here. I miss her, too."

- Reinforce any religious beliefs. They can be a comfort. "I know Mommy is with God. And I truly believe she is watching us right now. She just can't talk to us. And every time you pray for her she will hear you. She died, but she didn't stop loving you."

- Most young children are capable of handling a wake and funeral. Take your cue from them. If they seem very frightened at the idea of viewing a dead body, let them know it is adults who mostly attend wakes and it is not necessary for them to go. Performing a ritual with them may be helpful—say a prayer together, send a balloon off "to heaven,"* or write a short letter to the deceased and then bury it.

- If your child is going to attend a wake, explain what he will see. "Daddy will be lying in a casket. His hands will be folded. He might not look exactly the way you remember because when we die our appearance changes a little. Everybody there will want to kneel down next to Daddy and say a prayer for him. If you want, you can do that,

---

*Where the Balloons Go by Paul Coleman is a story that helps children cope with loss. It is published by The Centering Corporation, a not-for-profit organization with an extensive and remarkably helpful list of books and brochures on the topic of loss. For a catalogue call 402-553-1200.

too. Or you can pray for him standing up." Explain how long you will spend at the funeral home.

- If your child sees you crying or upset even months later, don't pretend nothing was wrong. "I was thinking about Grandma and got very sad. Some days I miss her a lot."

How Not to Say It

- "I know how you feel, but Mommy would want you to be happy [or eat your supper . . .]." Any remark that tells a child he is wrong to feel the way he does can cause confusion, at the least. At the worst, he may feel guilty for not acting the way his dead relative would want him to act. It is better to say, "Mommy understands that you are sad now. She understands that you are not hungry. I understand, too. But I also believe that Mommy is looking forward to the day you can begin to feel less sad and more happy. But she knows it takes time."

- "Grandpa is taking a beautiful journey everyone takes one day." "Grandma is asleep forever." Children younger than eight or nine think in literal terms, not abstractions. Using words other than *dead* or *died* may confuse a child. He may never want to go on a *journey* or may be afraid to fall *asleep.*

- "Grandma died after she went to the hospital." "Grandma died because of an accident." Children go to hospitals sometimes, and all children have accidents. Don't imply that death commonly follows after such events. Instead, let your child know that the accident was severe and that accidents or routine hospitalizations don't usually cause death.

- "Grandma was sick . . ." Kids get sick, too. State that Grandma was extremely sick, and medicines that ordinarily work did not because she was so severely ill.

- "Don't worry, I will never die." But how do you explain that Daddy did? It is better to say that you don't expect to die until you are very old. If a child wonders what would happen to him if both you and your spouse died, you can explain the plans you made for providing a guardian. At the same time, reassure him that you don't expect it to happen.

- "It's been two years since Grandpa died. Everyone else feels better now, so why are you still upset?" The best way to forget is to remember. As contradictory as that seems, people are more able to move on from a loss when they have the freedom to remember the person who died and to feel sad. If your child surprises you by showing more sadness than you expected, use **EMPATHIC** comments to help you understand. Perhaps a friend's relative died, and it brought back sad memories. There could be many reasons. Say instead, "It's normal to have sad moments like this. What specifically were you thinking about that made you feel sad?"

Recovering emotionally from the death of a loved one can take time. Children who fare the best have caretakers who are supportive, who are able to provide for the children's ongoing needs, and who know how to offer comfort, reassurance, and a willingness to listen at all times.

13

Death of a Sibling

The death of a child is tragic to adults. For surviving brothers and sisters it can also be a disturbing reality because the child realizes she is not protected from death simply by being young. A deceased sibling was probably also a playmate, roommate, and everyday companion. Siblings share secrets and come to rely on one another in handling life's ups and downs. So when a sibling dies, a child can be truly lost, bewildered, and frightened. And that occurs at a time when the parents are themselves grieving a horrible, untimely loss. When talking to a child about a sibling's death, there are special considerations.

Things to Consider

➤ As with adults, children often go through stages of grief. The first is shock, then hurt and anger, and finally acceptance. These stages can overlap and take place over the course of many months or even longer. Yet, on a day-to-day basis, children seem to be able to grieve one minute and play ball the next.

➤ Parents tend to overprotect a surviving child. While understandable, it may inadvertently teach the child that life is fragile and death could happen to him at any moment.

➤ Some children cope with family tragedy or hardship by taking on adult responsibilities—even if it is just in their mind. They might feel they have to make a sad parent feel better, or they may want to be a "perfect" child so as not to make their parents any more upset. While learning compassion and responsibility is a good thing, children do best when they do not have to "grow up quickly."

➤ A surviving child may want to sleep with his parents for a while. That is fine.

How to Say It

- Encourage visits with the dying child. "Your brother loves it when you spend time with him. Even though he tires easily, it means so much."

- If a child is dying, you can let siblings know early enough so they have time to ask questions and make some preparations. "The doctors say that Jeremy may not live much longer. We will hope that he does live, but we are also sad thinking that he might die soon."

- According to psychologist and grief expert Dr. David Crenshaw, children often need to be told that one's body stops functioning after death. They may not understand that concept on their own. "Your sister's body completely stopped working. She feels no pain now. She does not feel hot or cold."

- A surviving child may feel guilty for past fights with the deceased. Don't automatically tell him he's wrong to feel that way. Be **EMPATHIZING** first; hear the details of the concern and then offer reassurance. "You're telling me you feel bad for all the times you fought with your brother. It's normal to feel that way. I felt bad for all the times I punished him. But you know what? I punished him because that's what parents do sometimes. And sometimes brothers fight. I don't feel bad for being a parent, and you don't have to feel bad for being a brother."

- "You feel bad about the times you and your sister didn't get along. But I remember that your sister still played with you afterward. You got over being mad, and she got over being mad because you loved each other."

- "You want to sleep with Mom and Dad tonight? It can be difficult sleeping on your own at a time like this. You won't feel the need to sleep with us every night, but for now it's okay." (A cot in the parents' room is also fine, as is any other arrangement that helps in the early days after a sibling's death.)

- "Looking at your brother's toys reminds you of him. Some days it can be easy to play with those toys, but some days you won't feel like it. Either way it's okay."

- Some children will feel guilty for having fun and feeling joyful when their parents are still grieving. "It brings joy to your mom and me that you can have fun. The sadness and grief of a child should not be the same as a parent's grief."
- "Today looks like a great day for sledding. How about getting your snowpants on and we'll go out." Grief expert David Crenshaw recommends that parents give children permission to have fun and take a break from grieving; otherwise, children can feel guilty for having fun.
- In the days or weeks after a child's death, quieter siblings might be encouraged to talk. "Let's take turns saying something about Tony. It can be whatever you like—some memory that makes you smile, something about your sadness, or any questions you might have."
- Use your religious beliefs to help provide consolation. "I don't understand why God let your sister die. But I believe she is very happy with God and will ask God to help us when we need help."
- "We will all be together in heaven one day, but we must live our lives as fully as we can in the way God would want us to."

How Not to Say It

Don't avoid discussing the deceased child on special days such as birthdays, family vacations, or holidays. In fact, have a special remembrance by saying a family prayer or bringing up pleasant memories of past holidays. Tell stories about the person. You need not dwell on the memory but the absent child should be acknowledged and everyone should be allowed to express feelings. Make specific plans ahead of time about how the child (or other deceased family member) will be remembered. Perhaps one sibling can recite a prayer, another place a memorial ornament on the Christmas tree, and so forth.

- "I can't imagine this family being happy ever again." Life will never be the same, but it can be beautiful and meaningful. There will be days you will all laugh. Reassure the surviving children that life will go on, that you will be involved in their school work and activities, that there will be vacations and fun times.
- "Your brother, God rest his soul, never gave me a hard time when I asked him to do chores. Why do you?" Don't make unfavorable comparisons—ever.

- "We'll discuss your brother's death later." Be willing to stop whatever you are doing to respond to your child's questions or comments.

Smart Talk

If your child is grieving, how should classmates welcome her back to school? According to experts David Crenshaw and Phyllis Rubin, in their videotape *Grief: How to Help Children Feel, Deal, and Heal,* you should take your cue from your child. Some children may feel too self-conscious if classmates make a big presentation. Other children might feel better knowing their grief is acknowledged and that they can talk about it to friends. Once you have an idea, discuss it with your child's teacher. Perhaps the class could make a card. Maybe students will be taught how to express their sadness to your child. Knowing that their classmates care can make a difference to many grieving children.

14

Death of a Pet

When Chance the golden retriever died, nine-year-old Mark was devastated. His sister was sad, too. But somehow Mark was particularly grieved. Mark's father recalled how at bedtime Mark's habit was to spend at least five minutes lying next to Chance and petting him. Chance seemed to look forward to it, too. (All Mom and Dad got was a good-night peck on the cheek from Mark if they were lucky.)

It was Mark who insisted that Chance be buried in their backyard. His parents agreed, but the request made them a little uneasy. They worried that a gravesite might be a constant reminder to Mark and would keep him feeling sad.

Often, a child's first experience with death happens when a pet dies. It can be a time when children learn about death and that life is precious, and discover that however sad such a loss can be, they can feel better over time. Talking to a child about death involves some of the same concepts and phrasings mentioned in the other chapters. But the death of a pet can have its own, unique aspects as well. In fact, since a pet was there every day, a child may have stronger emotional ties to the family dog than to a relative who visits less often.

Things to Consider

➤ A pet such as a dog or cat is as likely to die from an accident as it is from old age. A sudden, cruel death can be more upsetting than an expected death.

➤ Putting an animal to sleep, while humane, may not be understood by children. They may think you killed the animal or were willing to have it die because you no longer wanted to care for it.

➢ The death of a pet can be more difficult to cope with if it comes on the heels of some other death or loss.

➢ Don't replace the pet right away. Give your child several months to get used to the loss and to grieve.

➢ Don't presume that the death of a pet is either devastating or no big deal to your child. Find out, and take your time doing so. Overreacting or underreacting won't be as helpful to your child.

How to Say It

- When informing a child of a pet's unexpected death, use simple but clear words. Give the details if asked. "I came home from work today and found Pokey on the side of the road. A car had hit him, and he died." If the body is available, a child may wish to see the pet. Unless the body is badly mutilated, a child can handle seeing it. (Younger children might also handle it well but may not fully comprehend the meaning of death.) A blanket covering most of the body might be appropriate to hide some of the wounds.

- If the pet was brought to a veterinarian for disposal, a child may or may not be upset that he did not get a chance to see the body. If the child is upset, say, "I wanted to take Pokey to the veterinarian as soon as I could. Nothing could be done to save him." If it would be helpful for your child, ask the veterinarian to show your child where his pet was examined and how the animal was cared for.

- Putting an animal to sleep should be an adult decision, not a child's. The child may never want the animal to be put to sleep or may agree to the procedure only to feel guilty later on. Discuss as far ahead of time as possible that you intend to have the dog put to sleep. Explain your reasons. Empathize whenever possible. "The doctor said that Pokey cannot live much longer. While Pokey is alive, he is in a lot of pain, so the doctor will give Pokey a special medicine that only animals get. That medicine will make Pokey fall asleep, and then after a few minutes he will die. That way he does not have to suffer any more pain. I feel very sad that Pokey will die, but I'm glad we can help him so that he does not feel any pain."

- Use the death of a pet as a springboard for a discussion about death. "Tell me your understanding of what death means." "Do you have any questions about death?"

- You may want to remind your child what happens to a body at death. "Pokey's body has stopped working. He doesn't feel anything, not pain or heat or cold."

- Replacing a pet immediately might seem like a good idea, but it may not be necessary (the child may not be that upset by the loss or may not want a new pet). And sometimes it can backfire. The child might resent the pet, comparing it unfavorably with the dead one. Besides, it is best that children take time to grieve a loss without trying to cover those emotions with a new pet. "I like the idea of having another pet. It was fun playing with Pokey and taking care of him. But I want to wait awhile and remember Pokey. I also want to save up some extra money because it is important to have our new pet examined by a veterinarian and have shots."

How Not to Say It

- "It was just an animal." Maybe to you, but to your child the pet may have been a companion, a protector, a best friend.

- "If we get a new cat, I expect you to take more care of this one than you did with Mopsy." Now is not the time to suggest to your child that he was an inadequate caretaker.

- "If we go to the animal shelter to look for a new pet, will that make you happy?" A new pet will not necessarily make your child happy. It takes time to grieve for a beloved pet. Also, don't be too quick to get your child to feel better. Grief is natural and should be given its due. This is a sad but wonderful opportunity to connect to your child in a meaningful way over the loss.

- "If we get another pet, that one will die eventually, too. We shouldn't bother." If you absolutely do not want a new pet, you have that right. But don't suggest to a child that it is of no value loving something because it is not permanent. It is better to state your genuine reasons for not wanting a pet—particularly reasons your child is familiar with. "I decided not to get another pet. Remember how I worried about having enough money to pay the expenses?"

15

Comforting the Dying Child

Timmy's father walked into the boy's bedroom and opened the blinds. The leaves of the huge maple outside the window were a blazing orange, the same color as the pumpkins that dotted the front porches in the neighborhood in preparation for Halloween.

"How's my boy?" the father whispered, walking toward the twin bed.

Timmy smiled but was too weak to say anything. His father sat on the bed and began gently massaging his son's bony shoulders.

"It's a beautiful day, son. Would you like to sit on the porch with me later? Mom and your sister are going to pick apples before lunch. That means applesauce later on for you and me." The father smacked his lips comically, hoping to nudge a smile from his son.

"Yeah," Timmy said. Then he looked his father square in the eyes. "Dad, I'm going to die, aren't I?"

There may be nothing more heart wrenching than a child dying. Sadly, every year thousands of parents have to suffer what is arguably the most painful type of grief. For many of these parents there will be time to talk to their dying child about death and to say good-bye. To the very end, parents want to protect their children from any unnecessary suffering. Trying to decide how much a dying child should be told about his situation may seem confusing. Will it add to the child's fears? Will it make him more depressed? Will he lose the will to fight his illness? According to the research, families are usually better off when death can be discussed openly with the dying child. It is hard, but it can make an important difference in the final days of a child's life.

Things to Consider

➤ One purpose of the discussion is to alleviate fears, not enhance them. Your child will have many questions about death and the afterlife. This is an opportunity to put his mind at ease.

➤ The discussion will happen more than once. The first time will probably be the hardest.

How to Say It

- You may still be holding out hope for survival and don't want to upset your child unnecessarily. But if the odds of survival truly are diminishing, it is best to acknowledge the possibility of death. "Some children with your problem have died, but some haven't. The doctors still want to help you. They haven't quit."

- When it is clear that death is certain and you haven't spoken about that yet, do so honestly. You may want to emphasize what will happen to ensure his comfort. "At this point there is nothing more that can be done to help you get better. Yes, the doctors say you will die. But we will all be here with you and make you as comfortable as possible."

- *"Will dying hurt?"* "There are medicines that will make you feel comfortable. If you have pain, we can give you more medicine to take that pain away."

- *"I'm afraid. . . . I don't want to die."* "Nobody wants you to die. We all love you and will miss you. But when you die, you will not feel fear anymore. Your body will not feel pain anymore. [Here you can discuss religious beliefs.] You will be with God. While that is hard to understand, I believe with all my heart you will be happier than you've ever been. You will have no more pain and not be afraid at all."

- *"But you won't be with me."* "I will someday. I believe that in heaven a long time can feel like a very short time. You will be in heaven for what feels like a little while, and then I will join you and everybody you love will join you."

- *"What if there isn't a heaven?"* "There is. I know it, and I'm so glad that you will be in such a happy, wonderful place."

- *"Will I see Grandma?"* "Yes, Grandma is in heaven, and you will see her."

- *"Will I become a ghost?"* "Not the way you might think. We all have spirits that will leave our body after we die and go to see God. Your spirit is who you really are. Your body is like clothing. You won't be like ghosts you see on TV. You will be able to watch us from heaven, though."

How Not to Say It

- "You will be fine." When a child is seriously ill and death is probable, the odds are high she already has an inkling she is dying. If you tell her she will be fine, she may not believe other things you say about dying.
- "There is nothing to worry about, I'll take care of you." If your child has concerns, she needs those concerns addressed. Listen to her worries and answer them as honestly as you can.
- "You shouldn't be asking such questions. Save your energy to get better." Your child needs to ask those questions and have them answered. If you do not wish to let him talk, what other choice does he have? Don't suggest to him that he could be working harder to get better. He doesn't have that kind of power.

Dying at Home or in the Hospital

Researchers at the Medical College of Wisconsin studied families of children with a terminal illness. They wanted to know if it made a difference if parents chose to have their child die at home (in a home-care program) or in the hospital. Parents who cared for their dying child at home did suffer less depression and physical ailments after the child died. Spouses also got along better and tended to be less socially withdrawn. The siblings of the dying child also showed less fear and withdrawal after their brother or sister died.

If there is a choice, parents may want to consider having their dying child spend his last days at home. If that is not possible, anything the parents can do to make the hospital room more homelike might help. Regardless, it is always helpful and healing when family members have time to say their good-byes in an atmosphere of warmth and closeness.

16

Defiance and Disrespect

All children disobey. They sneak cookies, "forget" to clean a room, and play computer games when they promised Mom they would do homework. From a parent's viewpoint, disobedience is often similar to a minor driving infraction: It happens to the best of people, and it is hoped they learn something from it. But when children act defiantly, parents know that a line has been crossed. Defiant children are not simply disobeying but are challenging a parent's authority.

Defiance is disobedience with attitude.

Defiance, like beauty, is also in the eyes of the beholder. Imagine a boy who was teased on the bus by a classmate. Later that night the boy refuses to attend a birthday party, adamantly yelling, "No, I won't go, and you can't make me!" A perceptive parent might wonder if the boy is acting this way because he is afraid or anticipates further embarrassment. Was the boy acting defiantly? Technically, yes. But the parent who is aware of the boy's recent troubles might treat the situation with more concern and compassion.

Defiance becomes a problem for most parents when they attribute the defiant act to willful disrespect. When a twelve-year-old scoffs at a request to turn off the television at bedtime and responds contemptuously, "No. You can't tell me what to do!" a parent hears disrespect and sees red. In such a case, no alternative explanation for the defiance is obvious, so it is attributed to bold insolence. However, that does not mean alternate explanations don't exist.

Things to Consider

➤ Is this a new behavior or one that has been repeated often? If it is a recurrent problem, then any communication style you used before probably won't be effective this time, either. Try a different approach using the

TENDER guidelines. If this is a new problem, the suggestions in the How to Say It section are a good first step.

➤ Disrespect for authority is a serious issue. Don't be reluctant to have a follow-up discussion at a time when you are less angry and your child is likely to be more receptive. One father, stunned by his ten-year-old daughter's belligerent back talk, yelled at her immediately but was too tired to have a lengthy argument. The next day after school he invited her to play catch and then discussed his concerns during that time.

➤ Is it willful disrespect, or could your child be reacting to something else? Haven't you said things you didn't mean because you were frightened, ill, worried, or generally overstressed? Disrespect should not be excused, but it shouldn't prevent a parent from trying to understand.

➤ Keep in mind that many children today are dealing with divorce, something that can increase their anger at authority. Some children have to take on added responsibilities because they are living in a single-parent household or in a two-career family where parents are not always home when the children are. These children might view themselves as more grown up. There is also a misguided tendency among many adults to let their children's friends call them by their first name. Raising children to adult status like that gives them a mixed message when we also expect them to obey authority.

Smart Talk

Stressed parents may sometimes misinterpret bad behavior on the part of their child. In a 1994 research study, depressed parents were more likely to describe their children in negative, emotionally laden terms than were nondepressed parents. A parent's poor mood can interfere with the parent's ability to view his or her children more positively. Depressed parents in therapy were able to change the descriptions of their children to more positive ones.

How to Say It

If a disrespectful retort by your child is not part of your list of **DO'S & DON'TS**, it should be. Children will be dealing with authority figures throughout their school career and during their adult years. They need to learn how to *state* their upset feelings, not act them out.

Your first response most likely should be a **REPORTING** of your strong dislike for the way your child just spoke to you, and a firm reminder that such actions are unacceptable. (Exception: If your child is clearly distraught, then something deeper is bothering him. It is better to show some empathy and inquire what's wrong before sounding too strict. Say, "This isn't like you. Something is troubling you. Let's talk about it.")

Some opening responses you might try:

- "I am your mother [father, grandmother, etc.] and will not tolerate being spoken to that way."
- "What you just said makes me very angry."
- "You can be upset with me, you can disagree with me, you can be furious with me, but I won't put up with being spoken to like that. Now, can you think of a way to rephrase what you just said?"
- "We have two problems to discuss now: the fact that I won't let you go to your friend's house when you still have homework to complete and the fact that you just yelled at me and showed disrespect. Do you want to choose which topic to discuss first, or should I?"
- "What you just said has hurt me deeply. I expect you to think about your actions and come to me later with an apology. Then we'll discuss this further. Until then, don't expect me to feel as proud of you as I did before this."
- "Do you realize you just broke one of the Ten Commandments? When you talk back to me like you just did you are showing dishonor instead of honor."

Keep in mind that while you may be understandably furious and have good reason to raise your voice, this is also an opportunity to model for your child how to express anger and hurt in a clear, firm manner without treating him as he treated you. Otherwise, he may learn that showing disrespect is appropriate when one also possesses power and control.

What Else to Say

After first stating that you are angry and that the defiant behavior was not acceptable, exploring reasons why your child acted so defiantly may reveal some interesting concerns. **EMPATHY** helps here. Children are not as adept as adults at uncovering issues that are bothering them. Even if they are aware of what's bothering them, they may not be capable of reporting it adequately. A calmer tone of voice by the parent and a willingness to make some guesses might result in a new perspective on the child's motivations. After any discussion of problems with your child, you will believe one of two things: that your child is basically good but immature and bothered by some other stress or concern, or that your child is basically bad and must be kept in line. Be careful. Research has repeatedly shown that opinions adults have of children often become self-fulfilling. Here are some ideas of what else to say:

- "What you just did [defiant act] is not like you. My hunch is that something else is bothering you. Let's talk about that."
- "I've watched you be angry before without being so disrespectful. I know you can do better."
- "You're angry and you feel like lashing out. Everybody feels that way sometimes. Are you angry about something that happened today or earlier this week?"
- "I'm wondering if the fight you had with your sister has anything to do with why you just acted so disrespectfully and mean to me?"
- "Sometimes we say or do things that are wrong and hurtful. My guess is that you already realize you shouldn't have done what you did."
- "I get the sense that something else is bothering you but you don't want to discuss it now. I'll ask you again later. If you change your mind, I'm available."
- "I still don't like the way you treated me, but I'm beginning to understand you had a lot on your mind."
- "I know you've watched your father [or Grandma, Uncle Pete, etc.] speak to me [or someone else] that way. That must make it harder for you to realize it is always a wrong thing to do."

As you can see, the above comments are softer in tone, increasing the odds that some positive resolution of the problem will occur. They reflect a purposeful shift in goals. The original goal was to clarify that defiance and disrespect are unacceptable. The current goal is to change the atmosphere from hot to warm and allow for a meaningful dialogue. Don't wait until you feel less angry to say these things. The very act of trying to become more empathic can have a calming, warming effect on you.

Rule of Thumb: Research shows that when you are angry and speak in a tone louder than normal, you just get angrier. Having the presence of mind to speak in a tone *lower* than normal conversation can actually reduce your anger in a matter of seconds.

How Not to Say It

- Comments such as "Who do you think you are?" and "How dare you!" or "Never in my life have I heard such a thing!" may not do any harm if they are short and sweet. Tirades and long lectures are likely to be tuned out. Then you'll be angry about that ("You look at me when I'm talking to you. Do you hear me?"), and the all-important topic of defiance and disrespect may get buried. If you yell often, it won't get a child's attention, but speaking slowly and softly will. If you rarely yell, an initial outburst will get the child's attention, but don't belabor it.

- Don't administer impulsive and arbitrary punishments such as "You can forget about going to the sleepover this weekend." It is better to tell your child you will think about an appropriate punishment rather than lock yourself into something your child will argue is unfair and you cannot modify without losing face. (Punishments should fit the crime. Having a child write you a letter explaining why the behavior was wrong may have more impact. Or, temporarily add to the child's chores, thereby making your day easier.)

Be sure you notice and then **ENCOURAGE** your child every time he could have acted defiantly but did not.

- "I know you didn't like it when I told you no, but it meant a lot to me that you didn't speak to me disrespectfully."
- "Do you realize what you just did? You were angry, but you told me you were angry. You didn't show it by yelling at me. I'm impressed."
- "I've watched you all day [all week], and not once did you act defiantly even though you might have felt like it. That makes me feel wonderful."

Finally, when all is calm and everyone is in a better mood, many younger children enjoy a game of role-playing where they act out the right and wrong ways to talk to their parents. Children need more than being told what to do; they need an opportunity to practice it. (The last "R" in **TENDER** can also mean **REPEAT!**)

Divorce:
Telling the Children

"Well, when do you expect us to tell them, Jane? After I've left? Don't you think they should be given some warning?"

Jane cleared away the dinner dishes from the table and plopped them on the kitchen counter. "Of course they should be told sooner rather than later. But what do you intend to tell them? I doubt you'll speak the truth. Maybe they should know that their father is a middle-aged carouser."

Jack stood up from his seat. "The details are unimportant. The point is we fell out of love a long time ago."

"Let me get this straight. You want me to accompany you to the living room where we both will sit together and calmly explain to our children that we are getting a divorce. And you don't want me to tell them that I want to remain married or that the divorce is all your idea."

"I've been unhappy with you for years. Why didn't you do something about my concerns three years ago when I told you where things were heading?"

"The bottom line is that you decided to have an affair and leave your family. Now you want me to make it easy for you to tell them. Don't hold your breath."

Unfortunately, Jack and Jane's argument is common among couples planning a divorce. Often, one person does not want a divorce and wants to punish the spouse. Each holds the other more accountable. When bitter feelings emerge, it becomes easier to demonize a spouse—exaggerating his or her faults and character flaws. Not cooperating with the other in parenting then becomes easier to justify.

Nevertheless, when a separation or divorce happens, the children will be told something. What—and how—they are told can make a difference between adjustment and maladjustment later on.

Things to Consider

➤ Ideally, parents should inform the children together. That guards against their hearing two different versions of events. More important, according to experts, it helps preserve the children's sense of trust in the parental relationship at a time when the marital relationship is dissolving.

➤ Don't assassinate your partner's character. Unless your spouse has a history of harming your children, he or she will continue to have a relationship with the kids. They should not have to listen to derogatory comments about a person they still love.

➤ Children's immediate concerns will be how the divorce affects their life. Be prepared to tell them what their day-to-day life will be like.

➤ Divorce always affects children. They may feel depressed, blameworthy, or out of sorts at the disruption in their life. Some children fare better than others. The best predictors of positive adjustment are two factors: whether the children have adequate time with each parent (especially the father) and whether the parents get along as well as can be expected post-divorce (cooperate in parenting).

➤ When responding to kids' questions, anticipate having to repeat yourself over the course of weeks or even months. Children often have strong fantasies that parents will reunite.

How to Say It

- "For a long time Mom and Dad have not been getting along. We have tried in different ways to make our marriage happier, but we still are not happy. We have decided not to live together and to get a divorce."

- Children will likely protest and ask for more details. It is best to provide reasons that your children are already aware of rather than tell them things they know nothing about. "You've heard us fighting many nights." "You saw how unhappy we were during our last vacation." "You've noticed that Daddy has been spending less time at home and more at work."

- If your children are aware of specific personal problems that a parent might have, such as alcoholism or gambling, there is no use pretending they were not factors in the decision to divorce. However, demonizing a spouse can create more anxiety for your kids and may even backfire. Children often come to the defense of a parent they feel is being overcriticized. "Yes, your mother's drinking problem affected my decision to get a divorce. But it is more than that. We simply agreed we cannot live together any longer."

- If one parent wishes that the divorce would not happen but it clearly is going to happen, it is not worth blaming the divorce on the other spouse. The decision to divorce is not the cause of a divorce. People divorce for many complex reasons, and in most cases the decision is not impulsive but evolves over time. "It is true that your father does not believe we can work things out, and I would like to try a little longer. Still, the reason we are getting a divorce is that we cannot live together and be happy. And we have tried to make it work."

- If you are separating but may not divorce, try to give the children as much information as possible on the length of the separation. "We plan to live apart for the next six months. We will each see you practically every day, and nothing else in your life will change. At the end of six months we will decide if we want to stay separated or not."

- Children need to be reminded that they are not the cause of the breakup. "Your mom and I love you and will always love you. Our reasons for divorcing have nothing to do with you. We simply could not be happy together."

What Else to Say

- After the initial shock has worn off, be prepared for a full range of reactions from your children. They may be spiteful, uncooperative, depressed, withdrawn, or a combination of those. Their school performance may decline, but doing well in school may not be a sign that all is well. Some children cope by suppressing feelings and diverting attention to safe pursuits like schoolwork. However, they may be quietly suffering, unwilling to add to the family's pain by calling attention to themselves. Make **EMPATHIC** comments whenever possible. If your child makes hostile remarks ("You don't care about us!"), don't automatically defend yourself. "You sound real hurt and sad. You feel as if I've let you down."

- "It's been a few days since you've spoken about the divorce. I'm imagining you might be feeling sad and a little scared."

- "It's hard getting used to the idea that we all won't live together."

How Not to Say It

- "It's your father's fault." If your children will have a relationship with their father, it is harmful to make him the culprit and yourself a victim. Your children will cope much better if each parent supports—and doesn't sabotage—the other parent's relationship with them.

- "We don't know when we will actually separate." Until you do know, don't tell the children.

- "Mommy will need you to be the man of the house." A few extra responsibilities appropriate to a child's age will not be a problem, but do not rely on your children for more than that. You are the adult; they are the children.

- "Was I really that horrible to live with?" Never put your children in the middle. Never put them in a position where being loyal or helpful to you will make them feel disloyal to the other parent.

- "The divorce is for the best." Your child probably doesn't see it that way. Your task is to try to understand their feelings and *show* them (not simply tell them) that the divorce will work out fine. You do this by providing a loving home and by cooperating with your spouse in parenting.

Rule of Thumb: Rehearse telling the children about the divorce with your spouse. Anticipate their questions and how they will be answered. Otherwise, you run the risk of turning a difficult moment for all into an angry free-for-all.

It's okay to tell the kids you don't know all the answers to their questions but will tell them as soon as you can.

18

Divorce:
Introducing Your Child
to Your New Partner

Sabrina waltzed into her mother's house after spending the day with her father.

"Daddy's got a girlfriend," she announced.

Her mother quickly ended the phone conversation she was having and stared at her daughter. "What makes you say that?" she said, trying not to sound concerned.

"Because I met her today at the park. We had lunch together."

"Oh? What did she look like?"

"She was kind of pretty. She's a schoolteacher, and she knows lots of songs because she likes music."

"Oh."

An hour later Sabrina's mom and dad were arguing on the telephone. Why didn't he talk to her before about his girlfriend? Shouldn't they have discussed when it would be appropriate to introduce the new woman to their daughter?

In fact, Sabrina's dad did make mistakes in his approach. In this case it may have turned out all right, but he took some big and unnecessary risks.

Things to Consider

➢ Introduce your new partner only when you are sure you are in a committed relationship. Children should not have to grow attached to a new adult only to go through another loss if the relationship breaks up.

➢ You may be curious to know if your new friend will get along with your children. Don't let that curiosity force you into premature introductions. If you have any reservations about your new friend's qualifications to be a stepparent, then he or she may not be the best choice for a mate.

➤ Understand your motivations for introducing your children to your new friend. Some parents do so because it makes it easier to see both the friend and the children at the same time. Otherwise, one relationship may interfere with time for the other. It is better to sacrifice time with your new friend than risk introducing your children to someone who may not remain part of their lives.

➤ Do you want to irritate your ex-spouse by introducing your new friend to the kids? Don't.

➤ Don't surprise your children. A few weeks before the introduction you can inform your kids what you are planning. That gives you time to understand their concerns and feelings. If they sound positive about the meeting, don't presume they will always feel that way.

➤ If you have a child who is not yet a teenager but has begun puberty, you and she may be entering similar phases of life. Just as she is contemplating relationships with the opposite sex and may actually have started to talk on the phone with boys, you are now in the dating scene. Obviously, the dating rules for divorced adults are different for adolescents, but your child will be watching closely. Modeling virtue may never be more important than it is now.

How to Say It

- **REPORT** your wishes. "As you know, I have been seeing a woman from time to time since your mother and I divorced [separated]. This woman has become very special to me. Because she is special, I thought it was time for you to meet her. Tell me what you think about that."

- Either repeat back your child's words, or make an **EMPATHIC** comment if you detect underlying feelings that your child is not verbalizing. "You're saying that it is fine, but I'm wondering if it makes you feel kind of funny inside, maybe a little sad" or "You sound excited to meet her. What about it makes it seem exciting?"

- Give details about the upcoming meeting. "I thought she could visit us next Saturday, and then we would all go to the amusement park together. Do you like that idea?"

- "We'll talk about this again. Please come talk to me if you have any questions or concerns."

- If your child asks if you plan to marry this person, tell the truth. "We don't have definite plans just yet, but we both want to marry each other. As soon as we decide for sure, we'll let you know."

If your child does not want to meet the other person, try to understand why. Probably, she is still hurt and sad over the divorce and does not want to give up hope for a reconciliation. Also, your child may be concerned that she is being disloyal to her other parent.

- "You do not have to meet my friend just yet if it is going to be upsetting. But I want you to know that I will continue to spend time with her and that she is very special to me. I hope you'll change your mind soon about meeting her." It's okay to tell your child about times you spend with your friend. It can reaffirm the hard fact that the marriage is over and that you are moving on with your life.

Smart Talk

Do you plan to cohabit with your new friend? You may want to do it for companionship or convenience, but think twice if you think it will improve the odds of success in a remarriage. Researchers from the University of Nebraska discovered that cohabitation does not improve subsequent marriage quality or mate selection. In fact, cohabitors are more likely to eventually divorce their new mate compared with couples who did not cohabit before marriage. Researchers at the University of Wisconsin found that 40 percent of cohabitors end their relationship before marriage. Once married, couples who lived together prior to marriage have close to a 75-percent divorce rate. *More disturbing is that 64 percent of child abuse perpetrated by a nonparent is done by boyfriends. A child left alone with a boyfriend is statistically at risk for potential abuse.*

How Not to Say It

- "Don't you think she's wonderful?" "Isn't he nice?" "Aren't you happy I found him?" You can report how you feel ("I think he's nice . . ."), but don't suggest to your children that they should feel the same way. They probably don't, at least not yet. It is better to wait until the children spontaneously report their own positive feelings.

- "Don't tell Daddy that you met my friend." Never put your kids in the middle like that.

- "Look who's sitting over there, sweetheart—someone I've wanted you to meet. What a surprise!" Prepare your children ahead of time. It is a thoughtful thing to do for all parties involved.

- "I will be spending every weekend with her. If you want to see me, you will have to spend time with her, too." Your kids come first. Spend time alone with them. If you remarry, your children will have to adjust to that fact, although spending some time alone with your kids is still a good idea.

19

Divorce:
Saying Good-bye
After a Visit

"I simply hate it," Don said. He was the father of two boys. "I feel sad and miserable, and it sometimes takes me a day or two to get over it."

Saying good-bye to your kids after a weekend or a vacation together is something many separated or divorced parents never adjust to. They want to end the visit on an upbeat note, so they try to sound happy, but inside they feel like crying. Children, too, can get moody or downcast after returning from a visit with a parent. There is no way to take away the pain, but there are things to say that may help.

Things to Consider

➤ It can take a long time to adjust to visitation. Pace yourself.

➤ If at all possible, try to live close enough to your children that they can bike to your place. Knowing they can pop in at any time or that you can be with them on a few minutes' notice will definitely ease the separation pain.

➤ If you did not want the divorce, dropping your children off at your ex's will likely be more difficult than if you had wanted the divorce.

➤ If you and your ex argue a lot, drop-offs will also be more problematic. Your kids are best served when their parents are civil and reasonably cooperative with each other.

How to Say It

- Don't pretend you feel great when you feel awful. Your children sense how you really feel and they may get the message that unhappy feel-

ings are not allowed. It's best to **REPORT** any sad thoughts well before
the actual drop-off so that there is time for feelings to be discussed or
at least acknowledged. "We'll be getting ready to leave in a few hours.
I always feel sad around this time because I start to miss you. I wonder if you feel the same way."

- "The hardest part is right after I say good-bye. I feel better later,
  though, and I always look forward to your next visit."

- **TEACH** about mixed feelings. "Even though I'm sad I won't see you
  for a while, I get excited thinking about what we'll do when we're
  together next time. So I feel sad and excited at the same time."

- When the pain of separation is less raw, you can make a game out of
  everyone's feelings. "Here we are, the four dwarfs. Who wants to be
  Gloomy? Who wants to be Miserable? Is anybody Excited? No one try
  to be Sleepy or you'll miss dinner."

How Not to Say It

- "There's no need to cry. We'll be together on Wednesday night, and
  I'll call you tomorrow." Evidently there is a need to cry. It is better to
  acknowledge that their sadness is okay and understandable. Don't
  make them think it's wrong to feel the way they do. You can remind
  them of things to look forward to.

- "I'd better get you home on time. You know how your mother gets
  when I'm just five minutes late." Criticizing their mother will only add
  to the tense feelings.

- "Oh, next Saturday I won't be able to see you. I'll be away on business." Inform them of such things when you have time to discuss it.

- "You haven't been upset the last few times I've dropped you off. You
  guys are brave and strong." Don't praise them for not showing any
  emotional distress. They will learn that in order to please you they
  will have to pretend about their feelings. If they have begun handling
  the situation well, just let them know that you've noticed it's getting
  easier.

Picking up your children for a weekend or evening together can sometimes be awkward. Leaving one parent to be with the other is a reminder

of the realities of divorce. Some days they may wish they could have stayed at home and been with their friends. Then they might feel guilty. What could you say?

How to Say It

- Sounding upbeat when you first greet them is fine but pay attention to the emotional undertone. If the kids seem tired or a bit depressed or if there are awkward silences in the car, it's best to comment on those reactions by normalizing them. "I'm thinking you might feel weird some days when we get together. Even though you want to see me, I'm sure there are times when you're tired or busy with other things. On those days you might even wish Mom and Dad didn't get divorced."

- Older children (preteen and teen) may want to spend time with their friends on days or nights they are with you. "Since we have to schedule our visits, I bet there are times when you want to be somewhere else but you can't because the schedule says we have to be together. Sometimes we can work around that. Maybe we can figure a way to get together at a different time so you can then be with your friends. What do you think?"

- "I still want to be with you as often as I can. But I understand there will be times when you'll want to be with friends."

How Not to Say It

- "Your mom was in a bad mood as usual when I picked you up." Don't put the kids in the middle.

- "You can see your friends instead of me." Don't make it sound as if you are eager to get rid of them. If they want to see their friends, try to be flexible when possible, but don't push aside your relationship with them. Make arrangements with the custodial parent so that you can get extra time with the kids if an important function interferes with your visitation.

20

Divorce:
When One Parent
Abandons the Children

Charlie sat by the window, baseball glove in hand, waiting for his father to arrive.

"He said he'd be here," Charlie said quietly to his mother. "He promised."

"Your father has been busy," Mom said. What she wanted to say was that Charlie's father was unreliable and that he probably didn't even love his son. After all, he'd seen Charlie only once in the past six months. There was no excuse. Now she'd have to console Charlie one more time.

Charlie stood up and tossed his glove into the corner.

"Hey, I can play catch with you," Mom said. "I'm actually pretty good, you know."

Charlie didn't utter a word as he walked into his bedroom and closed the door.

After a divorce, many children expect that they will see each parent on a regular, predictable basis, only to realize that one parent (the noncustodial parent) has virtually abandoned them. While some of these parents walk out and never see their children again, typically the drifting apart occurs over time. These parents (usually the fathers since only 15 percent of divorced fathers live with their children) often stay involved the first year or so after a divorce and then slowly fade from their children's lives. Estimates are that less than half of divorced fathers see their children more than several times a year. One-third of fathers who remarry stop seeing their children altogether. The reasons are varied and often occur when the father and children live in different states. But sometimes the mothers—still bitter toward their ex-husbands—make the visitation a time to resume fighting, and the children suffer from the fallout.

Regardless, many children who were originally told that they were not to blame for the divorce begin wondering if they are truly worthwhile and lovable. What does a divorced mother say to a child whose father has consistently neglected him?

Things to Consider

➤ Look inward. Has unresolved anger toward your ex prompted you to hinder visitations or make them unnecessarily hostile? If so, your child is suffering. Make any changes you can.

➤ If you or your ex is considering a move that is more than two hours away from the other, please reconsider. Distance in miles is a natural barrier to parental involvement with children and sets the stage for what will inevitably be an emotional drifting. Within a few years the children will, at best, be the recipient of checks and gifts and phone calls but little else.

➤ Ridiculing your former spouse is never wise. However, if a parent truly has drifted from his children's lives, it is not your job to defend him. It is better to acknowledge the truth, but don't add fuel to the fire by taking potshots at your ex's character.

➤ It is vital to a child who has been virtually abandoned by a parent to have other adults who can serve as an appropriate and consistent role model. Your ex-spouse's parents may be wonderful grandparents and their relationship with your children need not be a casualty of the divorce.

➤ Younger children often put the absent parent on a pedestal. They fantasize about him as the good parent who simply cannot be there. Don't feel threatened. Your child will become disillusioned sooner or later.

How to Say It

Children need to hear three things: **EMPATHIZING** comments for their hurt feelings, a factual and fair **REPORTING** of your views about the abandonment, and **ENCOURAGING** words which reassure and indicate that they are loved, that you will not abandon them, and that their future can be happy.

- "It's your birthday, and you didn't get a card or phone call from Dad. Now you feel sad. I know it hurts when you don't hear from your father."

- "It looks as if your dad isn't going to show up again today. Even though you are trying not to show it, my guess is you feel pretty bad right now."
- "Now that your father has remarried and has a new family, he spends practically no time with you. That must feel awful."
- "I don't blame you for feeling angry."
- "Your father is wrong not to see you or talk to you much. You are my joy in life and your father is missing out by not being with you."
- "You are probably thinking that your dad doesn't love you. I don't know what is in his heart, but he certainly is not showing you love. There is no excuse for that."
- "You are lovable. Your mother does not know how to give love. I wish she did because you deserve much more of her time."
- "Some people don't know how to be a good parent. Your mother [father] is one of those people."
- "There is no way I would ever leave you. I will always be here for you. You are my wonderful child, and I'll love you forever."

How Not to Say It

- "What did you expect? Your father is a loser." Comments with a bitter edge can backfire. Children, especially as they enter adolescence, can resent such opinions.
- "Frankly, I'm glad you don't see her. She is not a good influence." You are missing the point. Chances are your child is hurting over the abandonment and doesn't really care about your opinion. Don't overlook the child's feelings.
- "I'm sure your father wanted to visit. He must be very busy." Don't pretend. If your ex-spouse wanted to visit, he would. Acknowledge the reality without attacking your mate and show understanding for your child's feelings.
- "Your father loves you." Don't say it unless you really believe it. Then be prepared to explain how it is he can love the child but not participate in the child's life. If you're unsure how your ex feels, say something like "The way he shows his love is not the way I show my love. He is making a mistake by not being involved in your life."

If you happen to be an absentee parent who cannot be as available as you would like, examine your reasons for being absent. Would you have to give up a better paying job in order to move closer to your children? Then give up the job. Why is the job more important? Is your new spouse objecting to your involvement with your children? You have an obligation to your children. Don't expect your children to understand your reasons for not seeing them. They may not openly complain about your reasons, but deep down those reasons will ring hollow. In such a circumstance, do all you can to be in very frequent—almost daily—contact with them. Mail short notes every day, use e-mail, or call on the phone. Do whatever you can to show your children they mean the world to you.

21

Divorce and Feelings About the New Stepparent

Carlos and Ana had a quiet moment alone with their father. They liked his new house and seemed to enjoy their weekend visits. Ana, the eight-year-old, particularly liked her stepmother, Maria. But her older brother was still standoffish.

"Want some more popcorn?" Dad asked.

"Carlos isn't eating his," Ana said. She pointed to an area behind the couch where much of Carlos's popcorn had somehow fallen.

"Carlos? What's that about?" Dad asked.

"Let Maria vacuum it up later," Carlos said. He tossed another piece on the floor.

"You pick those up right now," his father said. "You know better than that. Just because you have trouble getting along with Maria doesn't give you the right to make such a mess."

"Yeah, it does," Carlos said. He glared at his father, egging him on to make more of the issue.

His father just sighed and shook his head. "I wish you could see things the way your sister does."

Attitudes toward a parent's new companion are often a confusing jumble of emotions. On the plus side, children might like the stepparent and enjoy seeing Mom or Dad happy once again. But it is easy to resent the new grown-up in their life or be jealous of the parent's time with that person or to feel sad for the other parent who does not have a new companion. When feelings are mixed, a child can send confusing messages to the adults about those feelings. Imagine that Mom has remarried, but Dad is unhappy about it. What is likely to happen? If the child's mixed feelings are more positive than negative, she may learn not to praise the stepparent in front of Dad. If Dad doesn't hear good things, he may falsely conclude that the child does not like the stepparent. That same child might also learn not to reveal negative feelings about a stepparent when Mom is around. Mom, too, will get a distorted picture of what's really on the child's mind. In the case of Carlos and Ana, it *appeared* that Carlos disliked his stepmother, Maria, but that Ana liked her. The deeper truth might be that each child had mixed feelings, but Carlos displayed the negative side and Ana compensated by displaying the positive side. Ana may deny her own negative feelings because Carlos is negative enough for both of them. And Carlos may deny his positive feelings because Ana is acting positive enough for both of them.

Rule of Thumb: The more extreme and opposite your children's attitudes are from each other, the more likely neither child is displaying his truest feelings. It is best to assume that each child's feelings are more mixed than is apparent. Take time individually with each child and help them to sort through their positive and negative emotions. With patience and tolerance you may uncover your kid's genuine feelings. Then they can be addressed instead of overlooked.

Things to Consider

➤ The younger the child, the more likely she will adapt to the new stepparent.

➤ Whenever possible in a stepparent family, the birth parent should be the disciplinarian. Stepparents should have a say over rules but are better off taking a backseat when doling out punishments.

➤ Children often have mixed feelings toward their parents (loving and hating them at the same time). Stepparents are no exception.

➤ Your child is best served when he can learn to accept and get along with a stepparent. If you dislike your ex-spouse's new mate, don't automatically encourage your child's negative feelings. Your child may feel the way he does in large part because you feel the way you do.

➤ If you dislike your ex-spouse's mate and show it, your child has two choices: to resent the stepparent as a way to appease you or to feel guilty for liking the stepparent. Chronic resentment or guilt will harm your child.

➤ Look for clues to your children's feelings from the way they play or draw.

How to Say It

- Underneath anger is hurt or sadness. Getting at those deeper feelings will require an **EMPATHIC** response from you. However, if your child's behavior is truly disruptive—not just annoying—a clear statement about **DO'S & DON'TS** may first be required. "Pushing your step-mother like that will never be tolerated. I know it has been hard getting used to having a stepmother. You can feel angry but you cannot show it that way."

- "I'm glad we have this time alone together, I've missed that. Earlier today when I saw that you had thrown popcorn behind the couch, I knew it was still hard for you to accept that I've remarried. I'm wondering what the saddest part is for you."

- **TEACH** about mixed feelings. Many children might not know that it is okay to have opposite feelings existing at the same time. "Remember when you got mad at Shadow after he got his dirty paws on your school report? Remember how you also petted him a little while later? We all can feel different ways about something. We can change our minds every day. You can be mad at me for getting remarried and still love me."

- *"I hate my new stepfather!"* "Tell me about that . . ."

- *"She can't tell me what to do!"* "She is not your mother, but she is my wife. She can tell you what do. You don't always like it when I tell you to do things, and you may not like it when she tells you. But you still have to do it."

- "I know that the last time you were with your stepfather you didn't complain. You actually seemed to be enjoying yourself. You probably had some nice thoughts about him then. I wonder what they were."

- *"Daddy, I like my stepmother. But I feel bad for Mom."* "I'm sure you do. Maybe you feel guilty about liking my wife when you see Mom upset sometimes. That's normal. Mom and I talked, and we both want you to feel good about your stepmother. Mom understands your feelings."

How Not to Say It

- "You shouldn't feel that way. Ted [new boyfriend or spouse] is a wonderful guy." Don't dismiss your child's viewpoint. Be matter-of-fact and show a willingness to listen. "Oh? Tell me more about that."

- "I don't like your mother's new husband, either." Unless the new stepparent is harming your child, criticizing him in front of your child will only stir the pot. You could say instead, "I wish things hadn't turned out the way they did, but I hope we all make the best of the situation."

- "Why can't you learn to like her? After all, your brother likes her." Again, when siblings show opposite reactions, the truth about how each really feels may lie somewhere in the middle of the extremes. It is better to try to coax out a list of likes and dislikes from each child and thereby help them sort through their mixed emotions.

- "If you're going to act this way, you can stop coming over." Don't threaten rejection or abandonment.

- "If you don't like my new husband, then you and I will just spend our time alone together." You are giving your child too much power over the course of events. Besides, he has to learn to get along with (but not necessarily like) your new spouse. It is better to say, "I will try to have some time alone with you when you visit, but that won't always be possible. So we'll all have to do our best to get along as well as we can."

22

Drugs and Alcohol

Andy, age twelve, is a great kid. He is likable, smart, and has a variety of interests. He knows about the dangers of drug and alcohol use. He attended a D.A.R.E. (Drug Awareness and Resistance Education) program at school and has no obvious inclination to try drugs. Is he at risk?

Yes. Despite the fact that his parents are together and there is no drug use in the home, other factors place him at risk. One is simply his age. Now in middle school and preparing for high school, he will meet many new classmates, some of whom use drugs. (According to the American Medical Association, the average age that twelve- to seventeen-year-olds said they first tried alcohol was just under thirteen.) And as he approaches his teenage years, he increasingly needs to feel accepted by his peers. Unfortunately, he rarely sees many of his friends from grade-school, and he has to make new friends. Will they be the right ones? Also, while his parents have religious beliefs, they show little effort to go to church or discuss spiritual and religious issues—something that can reduce his vulnerability to later drug use.

Andy might survive adolescence without abusing drugs or alcohol. He certainly is at a lower risk than some other children. But a real risk is there. What can his parents do to help?

Things to Consider

➤ As children approach age thirteen, drugs, alcohol, and cigarettes become more readily available.

➤ Inhalants (glue, solvents, cleaning chemicals) are easily accessible. According to the American Academy of Pediatrics, about 25 percent of kids between the ages of ten and fourteen know someone who has used inhalants to get high. Children ages ten and eleven have no real knowledge about the dangers of inhalants (which can cause brain damage or even sudden death), yet they are exposed to them.

➤ Children who experiment with drugs before age fifteen are seven times more likely to use drugs regularly.

➤ Children who have been sexually abused, who do poorly in school, or who do not have enough parental influence are also at higher risk for substance abuse.

➤ Discussions about drugs and alcohol must be repeated and become more sophisticated as the children get older or attend different schools.

How to Say It

- Be the kind of parent that kids will feel free to talk to about any exposure they might have to drugs. Many children know that drugs are bad—so bad that they might be afraid to mention any exposure they have had to their parents. "I heard a story about a child who was afraid to tell his parents that some other kids tried to get him to use drugs. He was afraid his parents would get mad at him. Drugs are so harmful that I want you to know you can come to me anytime to talk about what you have seen at school or with your friends."

- "I want you to know a secret: When a parent gets mad because his child is caught with drugs, the parent is really very afraid. He is scared because he knows that his child is at great risk for harming or killing himself because of drugs."

- "Tell me what you have heard on the bus or at school or in the neighborhood about kids using drugs or alcohol."

- "If you wanted to get some marijuana or beer, do you know how you would get it?"

- TEACH appropriate ways that kids can say no to peer pressure. A child may believe that drug use is wrong but still be intimidated by peers. Rehearse assertive skills so your child has practice and more confidence in her ability to say no. "Here are some ways you can say no to kids who want you to use drugs:

    "'No way! You just want me to get in trouble!'

    "'You're crazy! I'm never going to use drugs!'

    "'Forget it!'

"'You're wasting your time. There is no way I'm going to try drugs or alcohol."

Remind your kids that they also need to walk away immediately. Getting into a discussion with a drug pusher may make it harder for them to resist.

- Praise your child for not trying drugs or alcohol or for resisting the temptation. "I'm sure that if you really wanted to, you could have tried some drugs or beer by now. I am so proud of you for doing the right thing. It isn't easy to say no when you see other kids trying it, but you showed that you can say no."

What to Say if Your Child Asks if You Ever Did Drugs

Most experts advise telling the truth. I generally agree, but exceptions are possible. The goal is to keep your children away from drugs or at least increase the time it takes before they start experimenting. If you used drugs when you were younger and you believe it was a mistake, will telling your child improve the odds he will resist drug use? The answer depends on how well you know your child. If you have a good relationship with your child and there is a good deal of parental supervision, your child may be able to handle the truth. You may feel ashamed and embarrassed, and you may not be the hero your kid thought you were but it can help. However, if your child tends to be impulsive or has been in trouble at school already, if there is little parental supervision between the hours of 4 and 6 P.M., if it is a single-parent family, or if your children's friends have been in trouble for using drugs or alcohol, think twice about telling the truth. You must also weigh the risk that your child will discover the truth from some other family member.

- "Yes, when I was in high school [or college], I did try marijuana, and I drank a lot of beer. I was stupid to have done that. I risked getting in a car accident and killing myself or someone else. I'm ashamed to tell you the truth, but I'm telling you so that I can convince you that using drugs or alcohol is dangerous and wrong."
- "I once told you I never used drugs, but you just overheard me talking to Uncle Pete about a time I did use drugs. I lied to you, and I probably shouldn't have. I did it because it scares me to think you might someday want to try drugs. I didn't want you to think that drug

use isn't risky because I managed to end up okay. Drug use is very risky. It can make you do poorly in school, it can get you arrested, and it can cause you to steal money or hurt yourself seriously."

Smart Talk

One consistent finding is that the more often the family eats dinner together during the week, the less likely the children will use drugs. Parents who insist on family mealtime tend to have more orderly lives, take an active interest in their children's well-being, and are more influential. Mealtime is often the only time parents and kids actually talk about their lives in a calm manner. How often does your family eat together? Think about the changes that would be necessary to increase the frequency of family mealtime. Chances are those changes need to be made anyway.

If your family is too busy to eat together, too many things are being given priority over family unity.

How Not to Say It

- "I know you may want to experiment someday, but be careful. Drug abuse begins by experimenting." Some parents believe that in order to get with the "real world" they must surrender to the idea that drug experimentation is inevitable and focus instead on how to resist continued drug use. Hogwash. Drug experimentation is not inevitable. The risk of experimentation does increase with age but is not a sure thing. Be firm that experimentation is wrong and risky.

- "You shouldn't be hanging around those other kids if you know they have used drugs or alcohol." If your child's friends use drugs or alcohol, then your child must not be able to see them. Period. But the above comment is phrased in a way that makes the parent sound weak instead of firm. The parent is using a **TEACHING** style but should be using a **DO'S & DON'TS** style. Saying "You shouldn't . . ." is not the same as saying "You can't . . ." or "I won't allow . . ." While you may not be able to enforce that rule when your child is at school, your child should never be in doubt about the firmness of your feelings.

- "If you ever drink beer, I want you to do it at home, not anywhere else. At least that way I know where you are." You are caving in. You are saying that beer drinking is acceptable. That is not a message a preteen or teen should hear.

Rule of Thumb: Children need rules and tools. **TEACHING** about drugs and alcohol and how to resist peer pressure without being clear about **DO'S & DON'TS** (tools but no rules) is evading your responsibility to make clear what is right and wrong. Stating **DO'S & DON'TS** without **TEACHING** about drugs and how to resist them (rules but no tools) is like sending your child into a danger zone unprepared.

23

Eat Your Vegetables!
Clean Your Room!

"Close your mouth while chewing! And wear a coat outside. It's freezing!"

Kids can trip up even the most adept parents over these issues. Parents can teach the intricacies of multiplication and assist with a science project where a volcano spouts lava; some parents even master the complexities of a video game. But many children still race outside without proper outerwear, and their bedrooms are filthy enough to grow the vegetables they will later refuse to eat.

I doubt there is a book or formula that will solve these issues once and for all even though they appear to be the simplest. Perhaps this is God's way of teaching parents humility. Still, if you are tired of yelling, there are things you can do to save your vocal cords from premature old age.

Things to Consider

➤ Assess just how important these issues are. Perhaps a child could tidy up his room every week or two instead of more frequently. You shouldn't have to be a short-order cook to please all members of your family, but giving kids a choice of vegetables from time to time may not be inconvenient. Besides, with most Americans on a diet and many allergic to certain foods, it is more common these days for family members to eat different foods at the same meal.

➤ Inconsistency is the main culprit. It is sometimes easier for busy parents to overlook a messy room or to make popcorn after dinner to compensate for lack of vegetables during dinner.

➤ Give kids an array of uncooked veggies as snacks. Topped with salad dressing, salsa, or peanut butter, these snacks can become favorites over time.

How to Say It

Sometimes parents shout demands not because they want vegetables finished or rooms cleaned, but because they feel underappreciated and overtired. It is better to focus on what needs to happen to feel more appreciated and talk about that—rather than barking out orders.

- "I'm beginning to feel overworked. Let's talk about ways I need you to help out more around here."

- Sometimes parents yell at kids because they are really angry at a spouse for a similar infraction. If you think your mate isn't helping enough with cleaning house, dinner preparation, or child care, don't holler at the kids just so he can overhear it. "I started to yell at the children to clean their rooms. But I guess what's bothering me is that I don't feel I get enough help from you, either. Can we talk about that?"

- If you want your children to eat their vegetables or clean their room, **REPORT** your expectation with firmness but without criticism. "From now on you must eat some vegetables. It is important to stay healthy. You can help me choose which ones, but even if you don't like them, you will have to eat them."

- "Your room does not have to be cleaned up every day, but when I start tripping over things, I know it's time for a cleaning. I'll tell you how I want you to do it, and I expect you to tidy up once a week. Which day is best for you?"

- **NEGOTIATE** if you have preferences. "Would you like to dust or use a vacuum? Do you want to clean up after breakfast or after lunch?"

- "Would you like me to make a cream sauce for these vegetables or do you want them plain?"

- **EMPATHIZE** when they give you a hard time, but don't back down. "I know you would prefer Jell-O instead of green beans, and I'm sure it annoys you. But I'm your father, and it's my job to make sure you have a healthy diet."

- "I know you'd rather play outside instead of clean your room. But we agreed you'd do it now, and it won't take long. Thanks."

How Not to Say It

- "For the last time, clean your room! . . . Eat your vegetables!" You are training your child to take you seriously only when you yell. You'll develop permanent laryngitis, and the veins in your neck may never retract. Ouch.

- "I'd really like it if you would eat your veggies tonight." You are polite but wimpy. Learn to be polite but firm.

- "How many times do I have to tell you . . ." If verbal persuasion doesn't work, there may need to be consequences. Not allowing a child to do something she wants until her room is cleaned makes sense. If she won't eat proper foods, don't allow her to eat junk food later because she is hungry.

- "You will sit at that table until you eat all your food." Be cautious. You may be in for a long night if your child has a stubborn streak. The better approach is to make sure he doesn't eat dessert, and then set up a time when the two of you can taste-test a whole bunch of vegetables in a manner he might consider fun. Vegetables don't taste horrible. Kids object because they want to get in a power struggle or because they've gotten away with it in the past. (Most children eat vegetables they might ordinarily push aside when dining at a friend's house.)

24

Embarrasses You in Public

Janet was divorced with two grade-school children. Engaged now to John, she was nervous about having him and his parents over for dinner. They had never met her before, and she was eager to make a good impression. The evening began with a bang, literally. Jason, age nine, was horsing around and bumped into an end table. He knocked over and broke his seven-year-old sister's handmade ceramic otter.

"Mommy!" little Kate cried as she ran into the kitchen where everyone was standing.

"It was an accident!" Jason said, running up behind her.

Kate shouted back. "You did it on purpose!"

"I did not!" Jason pushed his sister. "Besides, she farted in my face."

"Stop it, both of you. Can't you see we have guests?"

"But look what he did!" Kate showed her mother the broken ceramic pieces.

"It was a dumb thing anyway," Jason said. "It looked ugly."

Janet tried to keep her cool. "Jason, don't talk to your sister that way."

Right before the kids wrestled each other to the floor, Janet looked over her shoulder to see her fiancé and her in-laws-to-be staring slack-jawed at the scene. She pointed to the dinner table to distract their attention.

"Did I mention that those strawberries were freshly picked? Help yourselves while I take my kids into the other room."

The biggest mistake parents make when their children act up in public is being concerned about appearances. Fearing that others will view their kids as unruly or themselves as ineffective, some parents don't know how to act when their children need to be disciplined in public.

Things to Consider

➤ Children learn quickly that when guests are over, some rules may be easier to break. Some kids may purposely manipulate the situation, but they succeed only when the parents allow it.

➤ For particularly important public situations, plan ahead. Figure out how you will respond to some predictable fights, whininess, or rude remarks.

➤ Some public events such as group picnics or family reunions may get your kids wound up or make them bored and restless. Keep that in mind when disciplining them.

➤ You may have less patience for what might be considered "normal" but mildly annoying kid behavior (low frustration tolerance, crankiness, restlessness, etc.) when you are tense or the situation is important. Understand that when trying to get them to behave.

How to Say It

- An ounce of prevention . . . Whenever possible, discuss ahead of time how you want them to behave. Tell them what you will say or do if they act up. Once in a while you can **NEGOTIATE**. "The last time you went to a wedding, you started arguing in church. If you do that, I will remove one of you from your seat, and you will sit with Aunt Mary."

- "You may get bored tonight when we have a lot of guests and no kids to play with. If you guys act nice and don't fight, I'd like to do something special for you. Do you have any ideas?"

- **ENCOURAGE** (praise) good behavior frequently. "I'm very proud of you. It means a lot to me that you two are playing nice together while Mom and Dad entertain our guests."

- When disciplining the children in front of others, use a firm, stern voice that shows you are in charge but not intimidated. "You will stop fighting immediately." Don't hesitate to excuse yourself from your guests to discipline your kids in another room. There is no need for embarrassment; it is your job as a parent.

- "Come and sit down over here with me, and we'll talk about this for a minute." Sitting them down will actually improve the odds that they will calm down.

- When kids are being argumentative but not aggressive, acknowledge their feelings and then tell them what you expect. "You're angry at your sister. That happens sometimes. Right now I will talk to you about it, but I expect you to stop arguing."

- If you believe that your children are just trying to get attention, the best thing to do is give them attention—but on your terms, not theirs. "I wanted to stop talking to my guests and come in here to see how you were doing. Are you bored? What can I do that might make your night more interesting?"

How Not to Say It

Nonverbal signals to your kids (eye-rolling or raised eyebrows) done in place of verbal reprimands *may* work as a reminder to your kids, but often they signal that you are embarrassed and reluctant to discipline them. If your kids know you will not be afraid to correct them in public, they will be less likely to take advantage.

- "Remember what we talked about?" Your kids might take the hint, but if you have to say this more than once, it may be an insufficient response. The problem with a comment like this is that you are really trying to avoid a more public confrontation. If your kids know that you will not hesitate to correct them, they will more likely behave better.

- If you find yourself whispering harsh threats in your kids' ears ("Unless you stop fighting this instant, you can forget about your Halloween party next month"), take that as a cue that you are already at a disadvantage. Confident parenting does not require impulsive arbitrary threats. Once again, plan ahead of time how you will respond rather than have to think on your feet.

Rule of Thumb: The more anxious and nervous you are to appear calm and competent, the less likely you will be. Your kids should be nervous about misbehaving, not you.

Fostering Empathy and Emotional Intelligence

Davey and Steve stood in the cafeteria line on their first day at a new school. Steve was a year ahead of Davey. Each had a tray filled with food, and each stood on the side, looking around for a place to sit. Since empty seats were few in number, they had to choose which group of kids they would sit next to. Steve plunked down next to a group of boys he recognized from his class. Everyone said hello, but the boys tended to ignore him. Steve spoke up once or twice and tried to get in the conversation, but it didn't help. By meal's end he was feeling alone and rejected. In contrast, Davey selected a group of boys and seemed to have no problem connecting with them. By the end of lunch he was feeling great. What did Davey do that Steve did not?

Of course, there could be many reasons that Steve didn't fit in. Maybe the boys he sat next to were not interested in making a new friend. Still, some children are more adept at reading others. They sense when to speak up and when not to. They may have a better skill at empathizing, which might also help them make friends easier.

Emotional intelligence is a new term that is not clearly defined. Daniel Goleman, the originator of the concept, describes it as "the capacity for recognizing our own feelings and those of others, for motivating ourselves, and for managing emotions well in ourselves and in our relationships." In sum, just as children need to learn about their bodies and their world, they need to learn about their emotional life. It can help them immeasurably as they navigate through relationships and life's ups and downs.

Things to Consider

➤ Emotional intelligence does not refer to being nice. It does not mean wearing your feelings on your sleeve. It means understanding your own emotions enough that you can use them in decision making, manage them better during stress, and be able to understand and relate to others better.

➤ Children with a capacity for empathy have better relationships and even perform better in school.

➤ While a great number of emotions exist, the most basic emotions are mad, sad, glad, fear, surprise, and disgust. Parents will often pay attention to some emotions of their children and ignore others. Consequently, children may learn to suppress some emotions and overuse others.

How to Say It

- Use moments when your child expresses emotion to **TEACH** about that emotion.

    "You're feeling frustrated right now because we are late for the game."

    "It surprised you to learn that Grandma was coming for a visit."

    "You were joyous when your team won the playoffs."

    "Last time you got so angry, you took longer to finish your assignment. This time you decided it wasn't worth it to get angry, and you finished your assignment more quickly. I bet that makes you feel good about yourself."

- Use moments with other children or animals to **TEACH** about their emotions. That way your child can practice empathizing.

    "The puppy cries whenever we leave it. What do you think she is feeling?"

    "The dog is wagging its tail when it sees its owner. What do you think the dog is feeling?"

    "That child over there just struck out with the bases loaded. Now he has his head down. What do you think he feels?"

    "You just said it seems as if your stomach has butterflies. What feeling is that?"

    "After studying hard, you complained of a stomachache. Sometimes stomachaches are a sign that someone is nervous. Are you?"

    "What could someone say that would make you feel angry? Sad? Happy? Disgusted? Worried? What sensations would you feel in your body if you felt any of those emotions?"

- **ENCOURAGE** and praise accurate identification of emotions and praise empathy. "You let her play with your doll because you saw that she was sad. That was very kind of you."

Smart Talk

Siblings teach one another how to read emotions in others. Research at the Institute of Psychiatry in London showed that siblings who fought less often were also more adept at reading other people's emotions. Evidently, children who fought less were improving their skills at empathy and using those skills in other contexts. Some siblings have very different temperaments. These kids tended to fight more often unless the older child's temperament was easygoing.

One positive consequence of the high divorce rate and the fact that family size is smaller and relatives often live far away is that siblings must learn to pull together and rely on each other for support.

How Not to Say It

- "Never give in to your emotions." Be careful. You are right that a child who feels angry should not hit someone, and so forth, but there are times when emotions are important cues that should not be dismissed. What if your child's friends wanted to steal another child's bike, and he felt guilty and did not want the owner of the bike to feel bad? You would want him to pay attention to those feelings.
- "Feelings are a weakness. You have to be tough to make it in life." Without empathy your child will have a hard time establishing close friendships.

Estrangement from Extended Family

Emma overheard her father talking on the phone to his brother.

"Don't expect us to show up at the party if you invite them, too," her dad said.

Emma knew what her dad meant. She had often overheard him complain bitterly about his sister and her husband. Emma couldn't remember the last time she had even seen her aunt. All she knew was that her father was angry at his sister.

Hard feelings among adult members of an extended family are not uncommon. Old hurts, misunderstandings, betrayals, and favoritism can sometimes add up to estrangement and divided loyalties. Little children may be unaware of these feelings, but usually not grade-school kids. Once they understand that the grown-ups don't get along, parents have an uneasy question to answer. Should they tell their children the reasons for the estrangement and make an uncle or aunt or grandparent look bad in their children's eyes? Or should they be discreet?

Things to Consider

➤ The more estranged you are from your family or origin, the more inner conflict you may have with intimacy. You may want it but also be afraid of it, thus making your primary relationship inconsistent in terms of the degree of closeness.

➤ If a close family member has betrayed you, you will be more sensitive to that issue and may overreact in your marriage.

➤ Examine how your family has hurt you. Did they affect your self-esteem? Your sense of fairness? Your sense of being lovable? These will be sore spots and will undoubtedly show up in your marriage at some point.

➤ History has a tendency to repeat itself. The more intense the estrangement with your family, the greater the odds there will be future estrangement among your children when they grow up.

How to Say It

- If the children ask pointed questions or if you believe they know about the estrangement, briefly **REPORT** your view of the situation. If you hope for a reconciliation, emphasize that point. "Your uncle Ed and I had a big argument about some money that he owes me. Right now I am mad at him. But he is my brother and I want us to be good friends again. I hope we will work it out."

- "Your grandmother and I just don't get along. It seems that every time we see each other, we argue. We've tried to solve our problems, but so far we haven't. I'll keep trying, but right now I don't want to talk to her."

- "Your aunt Mary doesn't want to talk to me. We have had problems getting along for quite some time. I wish we could talk and be friends, but she does not want to yet. I hope it changes."

- "My brother has a very big problem with drugs and alcohol. He won't get help, but he wants me to help him whenever he gets in trouble or runs out of money. I've stopped giving him money until he gets help. He is angry with me about that. Say some prayers for him."

- If your child seems distressed or even mildly concerned, **EMPATHIZE**. "You seem a little sad that I don't speak with my family. It is sad, isn't it?"

- "You look worried. Do you feel bad that I don't get along with Grandpa?"

- "It must have been scary when you overheard me argue with your uncle."

- **TEACH** your values about family togetherness. "One reason it is sad that I don't talk with my sister is that families should always stick together. I would rather that she and I got along."

How Not to Say It

- Don't demonize the estranged family member. "Your cousin is an awful person. I wish he had never been part of this family." Even if that cousin has done terrible things (sexual abuse of minors, for example), you don't need to voice contempt. You could say, "Your cousin committed a bad crime, and I do not trust him. He has hurt some children, so I cannot have him around here anymore. I wish that were not the case, but it is."

- "I'm not going to talk to my sister. She has to make the first move." Your anger may well be legitimate, but if you want to be a model for your children, you may have to put reconciliation ahead of pride.

- "I will never forgive!" What happened to you may seem quite unforgivable, and you are entitled to withhold forgiveness. If your children are observing all this, however, you may be teaching them things you hadn't intended, such as how to hold on to anger and bitterness. It is better to say things like "I can't forgive right now. I hope someday I can."

27

Family Meetings

Jane and Everett decided they wanted to expand their house. They had to decide on a downstairs addition or building a second story to their ranch house. The logistics became even more complicated as they imagined how the sleeping arrangements would change. They had four children. Would the kids mind switching bedrooms? Would the girls still want to share a room? If they had a new bathroom, should it be large or small? Jane and Ev decided to call a family meeting. It wouldn't be the one and only meeting, but it made sense to hear from all parties at the same time instead of trying to hash things out more haphazardly.

Things to Consider

➤ Family meetings are perfect when trying to understand everyone's opinion.

➤ Family meetings can be frequent. They are ways to touch base with everyone, especially when school and work schedules and extracurricular activities get hectic and overlapping.

➤ One or two generations ago, families were often together at night, watching a few select television programs together. Now kids have their own TV sets, they are more involved in after-school activities than ever before, and family mealtime has gone the way of the dinosaur. Even a fifteen-minute, twice-a-month family meeting, perhaps on a Sunday night, can help clarify everyone's schedules for the week. Upcoming events or concerns can be discussed, allowing problems to be managed before a crisis occurs.

➤ You might assign roles to each child. One could be the organizer responsible for calling everyone to the meeting. Another might take notes and summarize them at the meeting's end.

How to Say It

- "Mom and I decided that every Sunday night around seven o'clock we are going to hold a family meeting because . . ."
- Older kids, especially preteens and teens, might be less interested in attending. You can certainly force the issue, but these meetings are best if the kids want to participate. First, inquire as to why they are not interested. "You often have good reasons for feeling a certain way. What reasons do you have for not wanting to attend a family meeting?"
- **NEGOTIATE.** "I'd like you to attend the first two meetings. After that, we can see how you feel and discuss ways you might attend sometimes and not attend other times."
- "On days you don't attend we might have to make decisions that affect you. Do your best to let us know how you feel about an issue before the meeting; otherwise, you may have to go along with something you don't like."
- "Please complete these sentences: 'During this week, I wish Mom and Dad would . . .' and 'Things that happen during every week that I usually dislike are . . .'"

During the meetings, use the time to find out new information. Every kid has a school project or report or assignment that is coming due. Now is an opportunity to check on the status. Or discuss plans for an upcoming vacation. You might discover that some of the family has a different set of expectations than you do.

How Not to Say It

- "Everybody keep quiet and let me finish . . ." Decorum helps, but try to make the meetings enjoyable and interesting, not tedious or stressful.
- "Who wants to have a meeting tonight?" It is best if the meetings are regular and predictable. If you have them only occasionally, state that you intend to hold a meeting—not that it's just a possibility—and the family will take it more seriously.
- "If you have nothing to say, then just be quiet and listen." Again, kids will not always be eager to hold a meeting. You can state your expec-

tation without a nasty tone. Otherwise, you run the risk that the meetings will turn into forums for contention. "I know you'd rather not sit through this meeting. It's clear you are annoyed. But I want you to listen so you won't be in the dark about our plans."

Rule of Thumb: An uninterested child often becomes interested if he overhears the others laughing and enjoying the meeting. Also, if he overhears his name being mentioned, it will make him curious.

28

Explaining Family Obligations

"Do we have to go?" Alyssa said. "It's no fun. Aunt Celia's house is boring!"

"We don't visit that often," Dad said. "Besides, you get along with your cousin, don't you?"

"Oh, sure. If you don't mind playing with dolls. That's all she wants to do."

"It's just for a couple of hours."

"To you, maybe," Alyssa said. "To me it's a lifetime."

Sometimes children don't understand family obligations. Family get-togethers can be fun, but not always for the kids, especially as they get older. Or maybe Grandma has to move in with you. What begins as fun or exciting could corrode if Grandma's presence imposes too many restrictions on family life. Or perhaps you have to spend weeks or months visiting a sick relative, caring for him and cleaning his house while you are too tired to do much for your own family. The right words can soothe in these situations.

Things to Consider

➤ Do you mutter to yourself about family obligations within earshot of the kids? You may be setting them up to complain aloud for you.

➤ Do you and your spouse disagree about these obligations? Getting the children to honor them may be more difficult.

How to Say It

- **REPORT** the facts and expectations. **EMPATHIZE** if you know your children will be disappointed. If it isn't necessary that the kids attend, give them a chance to opt out. "Next weekend is Uncle Ned's surprise party. You'll miss your class car wash, but it can't be helped. I'm sure it bothers you, and I wish the party was a different day."

- "Grandpa's been living with us for several months now. Even though you like having him here, I know it has been inconvenient for you, especially when you can't have friends over as you used to."

- **TEACH** what a shy or resistant child might say to relatives. "Your mother's brother has a real funny story about when he was in summer camp. Be sure to ask him about it."

- **NEGOTIATE.** "Is there an upcoming family get-together that you'd rather not attend? This one you must attend, but maybe some of the others you can skip. What do you think?"

- Be clear on the **DO'S & DON'TS.** "You keep trying to get me to change my mind. You can try if you want to, but the answer will always be no. The wedding is too important for you to miss. I'm sorry. I know it isn't your idea of excitement."

- **ENCOURAGE** and praise cooperative behavior. "Even though you really were upset about going, you've been very pleasant in the car. I appreciate that."

- "I want you to know I appreciate that you tried to have a good time today. These family get-togethers mean a lot to me, and you made the day more enjoyable."

- If your child is being a stick-in-the-mud at the event, try to be unaffected. "I can tell you're miserable. If you can think of something I can do for you while we're here, just let me know."

How Not to Say It

- "Did you ever think that I do a lot of things for you that I'd rather not do? Huh? Do you ever see me complaining? No. So stop your whining." A very understandable sentiment, but it may not help as much as you think. (The same goes for expressions such as "Tough!" or "I don't care what you think!") If you really want your child to understand that everyone in a family must make sacrifices, it's best to say that in a way that does not sound critical. Otherwise, you are telling your child to understand your feelings without showing that you can understand her feelings. It is better to say, "It sounds as if you don't want to give up your Saturday for a boring old visit to your uncle's. Makes sense. Some days I feel exactly the same, such as when I helped Aunt Jess move furniture when I had a report to write. But making sacrifices is part of being a family. Please try to understand."

- "Now that we're on our way, you'd better not have a lousy attitude when we arrive." Don't overdo the threats. If your child is accompanying you despite his earlier protest, suggest that he will be able to cooperate rather than suggest he will have a poor attitude. "I know you'd rather not be doing this. Thanks for doing your best to make it an okay day."

- When the event is finished, don't rub it in. "See, I told you it wouldn't be so bad." It would be better to simply discuss what the child liked about the day and empathize when he speaks about things he didn't like.

29

Fears at Nighttime

"I'm sleeping on the couch tonight," eight-year-old Emily said. "That way I'm closer to you if anything happens."

"What could possibly happen?" her dad asked.

"I've had some scary dreams, and when I wake up, I don't like being in my room all alone."

"I see. Tell me about those dreams."

"They're too scary to talk about."

"They're just dreams, you know. They aren't real."

"I know that and you know that but my stomach doesn't know that."

Nightmares and fears of ghosts and such are common childhood concerns. They are different from fears of animals or bugs or heights in that they are purely in the mind of the child, whereas a child with a fear of dogs may actually have been bitten. It's easy to prove to a child that a daddy longlegs is harmless (though perhaps quite yucky). It's harder to convince a child that ghosts aren't real or that bad dreams won't return.

Things to Consider

➢ Fears of the dark or of monsters under the bed are more typical of preschoolers. If your child outgrew those fears but is suddenly complaining about them, it is good to be curious. The reasons may be simple (she watched a scary movie), or there may be deeper concerns (maybe a relative died recently, and the child is worried about ghosts).

➢ Repetitive nightmares, especially if they continue over a few weeks, are a sign of some distress. Look for obvious stresses such as a new school, a serious illness of a member of the family, marital fighting, etc. Discussing those concerns may get rid of the nightmares.

➤ Children over age seven with separation anxiety suffer nightmares more than kids without separation anxiety. (See chapter 31 on dealing with that issue.)

➤ Accommodating to your child's wish to sleep elsewhere may be okay for one night. Many children are fine by the next night. Beyond that, you need to try alternative means to help your child get over her fears.

How to Say It

- **EMPATHIZE, TEACH,** and reassure. "Most kids feel this way once in a while. And most kids discover that if they try to think of more fun thoughts, they eventually go back to sleep."
- "Nightmares can be very scary. Even though they are not real, they feel real. Everybody gets nightmares, and everybody eventually learns to go to sleep after having one."
- "You've been feeling scared a lot lately. I wonder if some things are bothering you . . ."
- **NEGOTIATE.** "You're worried about going to bed tonight. Last night you slept with us. Tonight you can go back to your bed. If you want, I'll stay outside your door for a few minutes. What do you want me to do?"
- "You just had a nightmare. They are scary but won't hurt you. I'll sit with you for a while, and you'll begin to notice that you are feeling better."

How Not to Say It

Common mistakes are made by parents when they feel frustrated that their child is not overcoming the fear.

- "It's the middle of the night. How many times do I have to tell you there are no such things as ghosts?"
- "You have to be brave."

Most children are helped when their parents teach them to cope on their own, but in small doses. For example, if a child is afraid of going to bed without a parent, the parent might lie with the child the first night. On the second night the parent can sit on the floor near the bed or stand outside the door. The third night the parent may stand by the door for a minute, then leave for two minutes, return for a minute, etc. Using this pattern of small doses, a child soon learns she can handle her fears and anxieties.

Rule of Thumb: If the parents strongly disagree on how to help a child with his nighttime fears (one parent coddles the child, and the other advocates letting the child manage on his own), then a child's fears may persist. Parents need to agree on a plan that includes comforting, reassurance, and a willingness to let a child learn to manage some of his own fears.

30

Fears of Animals
and Insects

Lizzie and Anna were playing outside when a strange insect landed on Lizzie's arm.

"Oh, get it off me," Lizzie cried.

"I'm not touching that thing," Anna said.

"Do something," Lizzie said. She started getting more scared.

Anna's little sister, Julia, heard the excitement and came over to investigate. "Cool," she said, looking at the strange bug.

"Get it off me," Lizzie cried. Julia flicked a finger at the creature, and it flew about them. Anna and Lizzie screamed. Julia just laughed.

Some children are more skittish around unfamiliar animals or insects. Having anxiety does not mean they have a phobia. A phobia is a strong fear reaction that interferes in a person's life. A child afraid of animals may qualify as phobic if she lives in the country and refuses to go outside because many dogs roam the roads. Her lifestyle is adversely affected. But she may not be technically phobic if she lives in a large city where all dogs are leashed and she feels comfortable walking around.

Things to Consider

➤ Phobias do not necessarily begin by having a bad real-life experience. Many people are terrified of snakes although they rarely encounter them and may never have been threatened by one. You can develop intense fears by observing others being afraid or by observing threatening situations on television or in books.

➤ Many common childhood fears are mild and easily changed. Kids might believe that certain insects are gross or disgusting but are not terrified of them.

➤ Avoiding a feared object (such as all dogs) or escaping from a situation (the presence of a spider) actually strengthens the fear. The child gets relief by avoiding or escaping a scary situation and believes that such relief can only occur in that way.

➤ A child overcomes strong fears by learning that certain situations are not as threatening as once believed (for example, dogs can be friendly) and by discovering he can cope with his uncertainty by staying in the situation long enough for his doubts and fears to diminish.

➤ Make sure you teach children appropriate caution. Never approach a strange dog with big movements, don't touch a snake you don't recognize, and so forth.

➤ If a phobia interferes with a child's life in a meaningful way (refusing to go to school, for example), professional help is required.

How to Say It

- Ask what the child's worst fear is and offer comfort and reassurance. "You're afraid the dog will bite you or knock you down. He is very friendly, but he can get excited and jump sometimes. Just because you feel scared doesn't mean there is really something to be afraid about."
- "When I was your age, I used to be afraid that a bat flying in the night would come at me. It never happened, and I learned not to be afraid. In fact, the bats ate a lot of the mosquitoes, and that was a good thing."
- **TEACH** coping by modeling it. "I'm going to pet the dog and let it lick my hand. Watch."
- "I'm letting the spider crawl on my hand. It tickles."
- "You can watch the dog and me from the window. That way you will feel safe. After a while you can watch me from the porch. Then you can watch me close up."
- "You did that very well. It isn't easy to do something that makes you nervous, but you did."

How Not to Say It

- "C'mon. No one else is afraid." You run the risk that the child will feel even worse if he doesn't succeed.

- "You did it yesterday. Why won't you do it today?" Most intense fears are not overcome by one successful experience. A person needs many successful exposures. It is better to remind him of past successes, but don't push. Try for a smaller achievable goal. For example, playing with a puppy or a newborn dog is far less frightening than a grown dog.
- "You're being a baby." Put-downs won't help. And if he does succeed, he won't appreciate your help. He'll resent your attitude.
- "It's all right to avoid dogs if you don't like them." But it isn't practical and will inadvertently intensify the fear over time.

Fears of Harm
or Injury

Tina sat looking out the window as her father prepared to leave for work. It was a cold, snowy morning, and the driveway was almost invisible.

"Don't go," Tina said. "What if you get in an accident?"

"I'll be fine, sweetheart. The snow will stop soon, and I'm always very careful."

"But I'm worried that this time you might die."

"I'll be fine. You should get ready for school."

"I'm not going to school today. I don't feel good. My stomach hurts, and I feel as if I might throw up."

Dad was concerned about Tina. She was in the third grade and never seemed to be this worried. She always enjoyed school, but she'd been complaining recently that she hated being away from home. There were no obvious reasons for her distress. Everybody in the family was healthy. Everybody got along. School was great. What was troubling her?

Tina had separation anxiety. It is not the same as the kind of anxiety a toddler might experience. Tina had been fine until recently, but she worried excessively about bad things happening and convinced herself they were likely to happen.

Older children may develop fears for the welfare of family members or their own safety. The reasons are unclear. They may have inherited a sensitivity so that they get anxious more easily. Sometimes the concerns are minor and temporary. Sometimes they blossom into intense fears and may result in a refusal to go to school.

Things to Consider

➤ Sleep may be disturbed in children with separation anxiety. They may fear sleeping as it is a form of separation from parents.

➤ Refusing to go to school should not be allowed. Once a child has remained home from school because of unrealistic fear, it gets harder to go back. Eventually, he may get behind in his schoolwork or disconnected from friends.

➤ Is one of the parents depressed? Some children feel a need to protect or look after a parent they think is unhappy. They need to learn that their parent can be safe and reasonably happy without their having to stay home from school.

➤ Sudden, unexpected, and intense fears of being harmed should be investigated. The child might have been abused.

➤ As if parents don't have enough to worry about, the National Institute of Mental Health has discovered that some anxiety or tic disorders in children might be triggered by strep throat infections. PANDAS (pediatric autoimmune neuropsychiatric disorders associated with strep infection) are not common but do occur. Strep can worsen a preexisting condition. Consult a physician if you notice an eruption of behavior problems following a strep infection.

How to Say It

- Offer **ENCOURAGEMENT**, but don't give in to the fears. "I understand you are worried, but I'm not going to stay home. I know that you will feel better in a little while." Children with separation anxiety need to learn to cope with their feelings without their parents giving in to the fears.

- "Today is Saturday, and I don't have to work. I will leave for a while but will return in half an hour. I want you to say to yourself, 'I'll be okay,' and then do something to keep yourself busy. I'll come home for a while and then go back out again, this time for a little longer."

- "On days you are not so worried, what do you say to yourself that keeps you from being scared?" Identify coping skills your child already may possess.

- "You will go to school today, but you can call me once at work."

- "You've called me at work for the past three days. Today we will skip the phone call. I think you can handle it."

- "Do you know how our dog sometimes barks at sounds because he thinks they are threatening? Well, the part of your body that causes you to worry is like that. It is barking to protect you from things that really are not problems. You have to train your mind not to be so overprotective."
- "You were worried about my safety today, but then you told yourself I would be fine. Good for you!"

How Not to Say It

- "If you kids don't clean up your mess, I just may not come home tonight." Don't ever threaten abandonment as a way of coercing kids to behave. It can make the more sensitive, worried child even more upset.
- "You're being silly." Don't dismiss the fears like that. You can reassure your child that the fears are unfounded without criticizing.
- "Actually, I'm glad you stayed home today. Your company always cheers me up." Don't reward your child's fears.
- "If you don't snap out of it, I'm going to call the doctor." A professional should be consulted if the problem persists, but don't make it sound like a punishment.
- "You have a stomachache? Okay, you can stay home with me." Children who experience separation anxiety will have vague physical complaints that come and go. Do not allow them to be an excuse for staying home from school.

32

Teaching Forgiveness

It was the third time that Joe missed his son's baseball game; today it was by fifteen minutes. What made it more difficult was that he had promised more than once he would be there. When he drove to the park, he saw that the field was empty, the game over. Cars were leaving, and he assumed his son rode home with one of the other parents as he had done twice before. To his amazement, Joe saw his son standing by a car with one of the coaches. Joe honked his horn and got their attention.

Once inside the car, Joe was full of apologies. "I tried, I really did, son. But traffic was heavier than usual—" His son interrupted. "That's okay, Dad, I understand. That's why I waited before leaving. I knew you'd get here eventually."

Joe was stunned. His son's eyes were red, but the boy managed a smile. He was hurt, obviously, yet seemed willing and able to forgive.

Joe put his arm around his son for the rest of the drive home. He thought of his own faults: how he had a tendency to hold grudges, to give others a hard time if they let him down in any way. Yet, here was his son, who had reason to be angry, still able to be understanding and forgiving.

"And a little child shall lead them."

Without forgiveness, relationships are at best superficial. More often they are unworkable. Forgiveness is a profound concept, easy to talk about but difficult to do when the hurts against us are huge. While your children may be unable to fully understand forgiveness, it is important that they be taught empathy, compassion, and a willingness to give some people second and third chances. Without parental guidance, kids will be at the mercy of television, music, and peers.

Things to Consider

➤ Esteemed researcher Robert Enright at the University of Wisconsin* has said that children have a different view of forgiveness compared with adults. School-age children seek justice, offering forgiveness only if a penalty has been paid. Adolescents may be willing to forgive but often do so more out of peer pressure or a need to belong than a genuine compassion for the wrongdoer.

➤ You should not compel a child to forgive. In fact, you cannot. Forgiveness is a form of love and cannot be forced. You can compel a child not to act out his anger, however.

➤ If someone genuinely hurts your child and you are quick to preach forgiveness, you may be forcing your own needs (to be liked or to be seen as good) on your child. Genuine forgiveness often takes time.

➤ Forgiving someone is not the same thing as continuing to have a relationship with that person (reconciling). Your child may have been hurt by a friend and, while able to eventually forgive, may be unwilling to remain friends with the offender. That may show good judgment on your child's part.

How to Say It

• When a friend has hurt your child, empathize and understand before preaching forgiveness. "You overheard your best friend making fun of you behind your back. Now you never want to be her friend again. You must feel very sad."

• After your child's feelings have been expressed and understood, inquire as to what forgiveness means to your child. "It's been three days since you've spoken to Margie. What would have to happen for you to forgive her?" (The minimal likely answer: "She has to apologize. . . . She has to be punished.")

• "You can tell her how she hurt you and that you want an apology. What would make it easier for you to do that?"

---

*Dr. Enright is the founder of the International Forgiveness Institute, which has been a forum for groundbreaking research and workshops on the topic of forgiveness. Their quarterly publication *The World of Forgiveness* is available by writing to International Forgiveness Institute, 6313 Landfall Drive, Madison, Wisconsin 53705.

- Remind your child of times she has forgiven others. "You forgave your brother after he teased you on the bus. Sometimes when we forgive someone it feels unfair. But if you get even, that is not forgiveness. That's revenge."
- "Imagine you decided to get revenge. What else might happen after you do that?"
- "Imagine you forgave your friend. What might happen after you did that?"
- Foster **EMPATHY**. "Put yourself in your friend's shoes. Why do you think she said those bad things about you?"
- **TEACH** simple definitions and plant seeds. "Forgiveness is a willingness to give someone another chance when they do not deserve it. What do you think about that?"
- "When you forgive people, you are not approving of what they did. You are saying that what they did was wrong and hurtful but you are willing to forgive them anyway."
- If your child tells you that she and a friend made up, use that as a springboard for future discussions. "You and Margie have been friends again for over a week. Are you glad you forgave her? Why?"
- "It has been two weeks since you've spoken to your friend who hurt you. Tell me what you wish would happen."
- **ENCOURAGE** and praise efforts to forgive. "It must not have been easy to forgive her, but you did it. I'm proud of you."
- Give permission for some anger to emerge later. Children may forgive quickly to please a parent or may not be in touch with the degree of hurt they have experienced. If so, some residual anger may show up later on. Don't criticize that but try to help your child understand. "It's normal after you forgive somebody to still feel sad or mad at times. Do you need to talk to your friend again?"

How Not to Say It

- "He only broke a toy. We can replace the toy. You shouldn't hold a grudge." Young children are often hurt by events adults consider very minor. But to the child they are not minor. Fighting over toys is a perfect scenario to help your child deal with frustration and problem-solving. Be **EMPATHIC** first. "I don't blame you for feeling sad when he broke your toy on purpose. It really bothers you."

- "If you forgive your friend, he'll only hurt you again later on." Some friends will take advantage, but many won't. If your child is mistreated again, he may choose not to be friends with the other child. That may be appropriate and a good lesson. But if he offers forgiveness and the friendship flourishes, that, too, is a good outcome. If you teach your child that friendship means "one strike and you're out," he will never have friends.

- "He apologized. What more do you want?" True forgiveness can be hard, and a genuine apology may not take away the sting completely. But if your child wants more than an apology, find out what. It might be that he wants justice; perhaps he wants something replaced that the friend broke or lost. Or it might simply be that he is still hurt. It is better to acknowledge that and praise the effort to forgive. "Your friend apologized, but you still feel mad and hurt. I'm glad you want to become friends again, but sometimes it can take a while for the bad feelings to go away completely."

Rule of Thumb: Your own capacity to forgive others will help or hinder your effort to educate your child on forgiveness. You run the risk of trying to make your child be forgiving so as to alleviate your own guilt about being unforgiving. Or you run the risk of teaching nonforgiveness as a way of life. Do what you can to resolve your own hurts.

33

God:
Common Questions

Lily and her brother, Brian, watched the television news with concern. The scene was of devastation caused by an earthquake in another country. Families were crying as workers searched the rubble for dead or injured relatives. Lily seemed particularly troubled. Her mother reassured her that the earthquake was far away and that they were in no danger. Still, Lily was not satisfied.

It was the next day on their way to church that Lily finally spoke up. "You always said God was good."

"Yes," her mother said. "He is."

"Then why did he let the earthquake happen?"

Perhaps not even the most learned theologian could answer that question definitively. Parents do not have to know the right answers to questions their children ask about God. But if parents want their children to believe in God and to one day be devoted to God, they must be willing to clearly state what they believe.

Things to Consider

➤ Polls show that 96 percent of adult Americans believe in God. Your children will hear about these ideas regardless of your personal beliefs, but your influence will be most important.

➤ It is a mistake not to give your children any particular religious instruction on the grounds that they will make their own choice when they grow up. Belief in God requires faith, a willingness to believe despite clear evidence. Without faith that is nurtured at an early age and throughout childhood, your children will more likely wander aimlessly through their spiritual life and not venture far with any real conviction.

➤ According to research discussed in my book *The 30 Secrets of Happily Married Couples,* the odds of having a successful marriage increase if you and your mate share the same faith. In measures of happiness, same-faith couples are slightly happier than interfaith couples, who are happier than couples where one or both partners have no religious faith.

➤ Marriages where partners are not of the same faith can become stressed when it is decided that the children must be taught religion. Parents who agree ahead of time on the kind of religious instructions their children will have, and who show respect for any religious differences, fare the best.

➤ In their fine book *Where Does God Live?* Rabbi Marc Gellman and Monsignor Thomas Hartman state that answering questions is less important than living your religion. If you tell your child that God exists but do not connect any of your actions to God, you miss out on the most important way to teach.

How to Say It

Obviously, answers to questions about God reflect belief and opinion, not objective truth. While the content of your answers may differ from someone who possesses a different set of beliefs, the tone behind the words should show interest in the topic, reverence for God, and a sense that the mystical aspects of God cannot always be understood.

- *"What is God like?"* "I have never seen God, but I believe he is all loving and all powerful, and that he knows everything. He even knows that we are talking about him right now."

- *"What is heaven like?"* "Nobody knows for sure. We believe it is a place where we can be with God and with people we love and be very, very happy forever. I don't know if there are trees or flowers or lakes or mountains in heaven. What would you hope to see in heaven?"

- *"When our dog dies, will he go to heaven?"* "I'd like to think so. I think God wants us to be as happy as we can be, and he wants us to be with people and pets that we loved."

- *"What is a soul?"* "Our soul is the part of us we cannot see that is most like God. It is our spirit. It will never die. When our body dies, our soul continues to live forever."

- *"If God loves us so much, how come he lets bad things happen?"* "So many people get confused about that. One answer is that he gave people freedom to make good choices and bad choices, and some people make bad choices. When bad things like earthquakes or serious illnesses happen, God wants us to help people who are hurt or very sick. When we show love to other people, we are doing what God wants.

  "What God wants most of all is for all of his children to be with him in heaven. Sometimes when bad things happen, people talk to God and feel closer to him. Maybe some bad things happen so that people will turn to God."

- *"Does God punish me if I am bad?"* "He doesn't have to. If we do bad things, we usually pay for it at some point. If we treat other people in a mean way, they don't want to be around us. If we steal things, we might get caught or people will learn not to trust us. God wants us to be good and to try to love him."

- *"How can I love God if I've never met him?"* "There are at least two good ways. First, since God is part of people's soul, every time you do nice things for others you are doing good things for God. Second, he wants you to pray to him. You won't hear him answer the way I answer you, but talk to him all about your day and what is making you happy and sad. Pretty soon you will feel as though you know him."

- *"Are people who don't believe in God bad?"* "No. And some people who do believe in God do bad things. People who don't believe in God believe that once you die, that is it. There is no heaven and you won't see people you love. I don't believe that way. I know that even though I miss Grandma, she is with God and someday a long time from now I will be in heaven with her."

- *"Are angels real? Do I have a guardian angel?"* "If you believe in the Bible, then, yes, angels are real. Angels are good spirits whom God sends to help us. Angels want us to be good people and to love God. You can pray to your angel. You can even give him or her a name."

Rule of Thumb: Excessive devotion to the material things of this world will cause you to lose sight of the spiritual needs of your children.

How Not to Say It

- "Ask Grandma . . ." It is fine to say you do not know an answer and that your child can find out from someone else. Just don't give the impression that you are not interested.

- "You can believe whatever you want to believe." Technically, you are right. But it is better to teach them first what you believe and let them know that eventually they must choose to believe in God or not. Give guidance, state your beliefs, and try to live your beliefs. Tell your kids you are *choosing* to believe in God and love him. They will learn that they, too, have that choice.

- "If you don't obey me, God will punish you." The idea that God is a policeman or court judge is a very limiting idea. Besides, *you* should provide consequences to your children if they don't behave. That is why God made you the parent.

- "If you don't obey me, God won't love you." God should not be used as a threat. You want your child to approach God with warmth and respect, not fear.

- "Bad things happen to people who are bad." That simply isn't always true.

God: Prayer

Six-year-old Patty listened as her father said grace before their Sunday dinner. When he finished, Patty finally asked him the question that had perplexed her for some weeks.

"Dad," she said. "Why does God use paper towels?"

Now her father was perplexed. "Paper towels?"

"Yes. Why does he use them? Is it to wrap the food?"

Her father glanced at his wife, and they both looked at their daughter. "I have no idea what you are talking about, Patty," he said.

Patty tried to explain. "You said it in the prayer. You said, 'Bless us, Lord, and these gifts from your bounty.' Why does God use Bounty paper towels?"

For many children, saying prayers is the same as singing the national anthem or reciting the Pledge of Allegiance. Some of the words take on meanings the authors never intended. Ready-to-wear prayers are certainly not harmful and may give a child some comfort, especially if recited with a parent or just before sleep. But they can be limiting to a child who does not understand the words.

Since 90 percent of Americans admit to praying, it is logical to assume that parents would like their children to pray. But teaching prayer can get cumbersome. Many children do not comprehend its value or quickly lose interest. In an era of the internet and instant access, where kids can press control buttons and immediately affect the image on a video game screen, praying lacks both instant gratification and pizzazz. What's a parent to do?

Things to Consider

➤ The meaningfulness of prayer to a child will rise or fall depending on the meaningfulness of prayer to a parent.

➤ Don't be discouraged if your older children seem uninterested in prayer and require frequent reminders. They may not truly understand the value of prayer until they become parents themselves.

➤ Teaching children to pray for others—not just themselves—is important in the development of empathy and compassion.

➤ Discourage prayers where your child is only making requests for items, as if God were Santa Claus.

How to Say It

- **TEACH**. "Prayer is simply a conversation with God. Talk to him the same as you would talk to me. Tell him what's on your mind."
- "Prayers can be very short. Saying 'Good morning, God. Thanks for the day!' is a great prayer."
- "If you don't know what to pray about, think of things you are thankful for. God gave you to me, so I thank him that I have you."
- "You didn't realize it because I was silent, but I just said a quick prayer while we were walking. You can pray anytime, anywhere."

Your child may have other questions, such as:

- *"Does God answer my prayers?"* "God hears your prayers. But he knows what is best for you and sometimes says no and sometimes says yes, and sometimes he says, 'Not right now.'"
- *"If God knows everything, why do I have to pray to him when he knows what I want before I ask?"* "He wants you to talk to him. He wants you to think about him and realize how much he loves you. He doesn't want to be ignored."
- *"If I want something, should I ask God once, or should I keep bothering him about it?"* "You never bother God by talking to him. It is better to pray often because you may want to talk to God about many things other than what you want. He wants you to love him, and he knows you will learn to love him if you pray more often."
- *"What is the best prayer?"* "The best prayer is any prayer that is deeply felt by you, that you say from your heart. It shows that you believe God hears you and can answer your prayers if he thinks it is best."

- *"What if I don't get what I want?"* "When you pray for something, tell God that you will try to understand if he chooses not to give you what you ask for. That shows you trust God's judgment. You trust that he knows what is truly best for you in the long run."

- "Here is a fantastic secret that will help you for the rest of your life: Whenever you are really angry at somebody, say a prayer for that person. You will feel better, and God will smile."

- "Pray for people who don't pray."

How Not to Say It

- "After what you just did, you should tell God you are sorry for being so bad." Your intent is good and important. Showing remorse to God is healthy and builds character. But don't make it sound like a punishment. It is better to bring up the idea when feelings are calm and suggest to your child that he talk to God about what happened earlier in the day.

- "You don't need to pray. Just try to be a good person." If you believe in God, why would you discourage personal conversation with God? Besides, being a good person may be more easily accomplished if one already has an active prayer life.

- "Say your prayers before you go to sleep." This is fine as long as you are not teaching a child that the only time to pray is before bed. **ENCOURAGE** praying often during the day.

God:
"I Don't Want to Go to Church"

Phil and Donna wondered if it was really worth it. Most of the time their kids cooperated when it was time to get in the car and go to church. But some days—like today—were torture. The kids had been playing with their friends and didn't want to be interrupted. Their minor protests about going to church turned into more intense pleading and ended in a heated exchange. As the family car pulled into the church parking lot, the kids were angry and sulking. The tension was high.

"We're supposed to be going to church to worship God," Donna said to her sullen children. "Would you guys take those nasty looks off your faces and try to get in the right mood?"

"I'm staying in the car," one of the kids said.

"Me, too," said another.

"Get out of this car *now!*" Phil yelled into the vehicle.

The kids obeyed. But church services were not serene and meditative as Phil and Donna had anticipated just an hour earlier.

Church is a challenge when children act like chumps.

Things to Consider

➤ Ideally, the time before going to church or synagogue should not be rushed or chaotic. You increase the odds that churchgoing will be a chore.

➤ If you don't attend religious services regularly, your kids might challenge your decision to go on any given day. If it becomes part of the routine, they are more likely to cooperate.

➤ If only one parent attends regular services, the kids will question the fairness of being forced to attend.

➤ According to a groundbreaking Gallup survey, how often a couple prays together is a better prediction of happiness in marriage than how often they make love. Couples who pray together (compared with couples who don't) report having more respect for their spouse (83 percent versus 62 percent) and are more likely to agree on how to raise children (73 percent versus 59 percent).

How to Say It

For it to be meaningful, churchgoing should be a family ritual, not a once-in-a-while pastime. If your children give you a hard time about attending church, the first factor to examine is the frequency of churchgoing. If you decide you want the family to attend church more regularly, explain your reasons.

- "I understand that you might want to stay home. After all, that is what we have done most Sundays. But we have decided it was a poor idea to stay away from church, and we plan to go as often as possible."

- **EMPATHIZE** if your kids were in the middle of some game or project when it was time to leave for services. But be clear that worshiping God is a **DO**, not a **DON'T**. "I know it can be annoying to interrupt your game, but you know it is time for synagogue. You have five minutes to get ready. Thanks."

- Give them plenty of advance notice and one or two additional reminders before it is time to leave. You may head off major hassles if they register complaints early—before you are feeling rushed. "We're leaving for church in half an hour. You should be dressed and ready in fifteen minutes."

- "You don't have to like going to church, but you do have to go."

- "Just as you have to go to school on days you don't want to, you have to go to services. Mom and Dad believe it is important."

- "When you go to synagogue [or church], you have two choices. You can think about other things, or you can try to spend time talking to God and thanking him."

- **ENCOURAGE** and praise. "Thank you for being ready on time. I like it when we all go to church together and everyone is in a good mood and not rushed."

- **NEGOTIATE.** "If everyone is in a good mood this morning, we will all go out for breakfast after services. Or would you rather go out for lunch later on?"
- **REPORT** your feelings. "This is the part of the service I like the best . . ."
- **REPORT** during the week how important going to church or synagogue is to you. "I stopped off at church just to pray for a few minutes on my way home today. Sometimes I like doing that."

How Not to Say It

- "You should want to go." It is better to try to teach them the important and beautiful aspects of the service and pray that their desire to attend will increase.
- "I don't care what you think. You're going to church, and that's that." It is good that going to church becomes a routine and not a choice for the children. However, it is also a good idea to try to empathize with their complaints ("But, Mom, I get bored . . ." "I have homework to do . . ." "I want to go out and play . . ."), but don't give in to their pleading. Instead of saying you don't care what they think or feel, say, "I know how you feel. Some days I'd rather stay home, too. But it is important for us to go and give thanks to God and to pray for our family and people in the world."
- "I didn't see you praying at church. How do you expect to get anything out of the service if you don't put anything into it?" Many adults don't put much into it, either. Contemplating scripture requires a concentrated effort. It is better to discuss aspects of the readings later on and **TEACH** what was important to you.
- "If you act nice and don't cause trouble, we can skip church next week."
- "What will the priest [minister, rabbi] say if we don't show up for services this week?" What people think of you should not be a reason to go.

36

Gratitude

"What do you say, Natalie?" Mom said as Natalie grabbed the gift from her aunt.

"Thank you," Natalie said. She thrust her hand inside the package and pulled out a pair of decorative socks. It was not what she was hoping for.

"Aren't they pretty?" Mom said.

Natalie nodded. "They will look nice with my new dress," she said.

Natalie found a way to say thanks even though socks were not on her A-list.

She had learned how to be polite. Politeness is certainly a missing element for many children, but politeness is not gratitude. Gratitude goes deeper. It is a more heartfelt appreciation for what has been given you. It implies an awareness of what others must have sacrificed or went through in order to provide for you. Instilling a sense of gratitude in our children is critical for their well-being. Without it, they will possess a sense of entitlement whereby very little is appreciated and most things are taken for granted.

Things to Consider

➢ You must show gratitude if your children are to learn how to be grateful.

➢ Without appreciation for the small things, the big things will never truly satisfy.

➢ Gratitude at its fullest is other-focused. It rests upon empathy and joy. Without empathy, gratitude is superficial and even condescending. Without joy, gratitude is fleeting and hollow.

➢ If we spoil our children, we will take away their ability to feel truly grateful.

➤ What children will remember with fondness and gratitude is our time spent with them, not the time spent with toys. The more time you give your children, the fewer material things they will crave and the better able they will be to show gratitude.

➤ Saying grace before meals can instill a sense of gratitude for things most Americans take for granted.

How to Say It

- **TEACH** gratitude by explaining more in depth the time and thought that went into gifts. "Your grandma drove to the store thinking about what to get you. She went from shop to shop until she found something she hoped you would like. Then she paid for it with her money. All because she wanted you to smile and be happy."

- "When you make me things at school, I am very grateful because I know how much time you spent making it. That makes it special."

- "Imagine that you took the time to get me a special gift, and I wasn't grateful. How would that make you feel?"

- "Let's think of things we should be grateful for that we usually take for granted."

- "Everything on earth—the flowers, the water, the animals, the air, all the people, your family—are gifts from God. That is one reason we pray: to give thanks to God."

How Not to Say It

- "Tell Aunty Chris it was the best present you ever received and you'll love it as your favorite toy." Don't exaggerate. If the gift itself falls short, it's better to have your child appreciate all that went into making or purchasing it. Then she can express a more sincere form of gratitude that will mean more than inflated appreciation.

- "Saying thank-you is enough. You don't have to send a note." Going that extra step can help your children appreciate gifts they receive.

- Don't overlook day-to-day thoughtful gestures. "You found my sunglasses for me? I wondered where they were." Where is the gratitude? Use this as an opportunity to teach why the action (finding something you lost) meant a lot.

37

Hitting

"Bobby! Stop hitting your sister!"

"She hit me first!"

"No, I didn't," Karla cried. "He got mad at me because I won the card game."

"I did not!" Bobby screamed.

Mom was exasperated. "I don't care what the reason is. You know you're not supposed to hit your sister. Go to your room and come out when I tell you."

Every child will hit a sibling. Kids misbehave that way for a variety of reasons. The most common include getting even, to gain attention, to get one's way, being overtired, hungry, or ill. Parents must try to determine the reasons so they can respond appropriately.

Things to Consider

➤ If there is violence between the parents, a child is more likely to act violently.

➤ If parents disagree on how best to discipline a child who hits, the hitting behavior will probably not go away.

➤ No approach is perfect. When you try a new approach, stick with it for a while before you decide it is not effective.

➤ A helpful tool for reducing negative behaviors is to give a child a certain amount of "points" at the beginning of the week. Points are deducted for each wrong behavior. A child can trade in the points for certain pre-agreed items.

➢ Normal aggression must be distinguished from what is called conduct disorder. Conduct disorder is a persistent problem that does not seem to be affected by ordinary interventions. Children with conduct disorder are more defiant; often destroy property; are dishonest, impatient, and willing to take big risks; and often show a lack of empathy for others. Professional help is usually required, and teachers must often be involved in the process so that interventions are consistent.

➢ In recent years, violence in schools has been the focus of national attention. Children who commit more violent acts may give warning signs. These are the most common signs:

Feeling rejected and frequently picked on by peers

Decline in academic performance

Previous aggressive behavior

Drug or alcohol use

Easily angered over small things/loss of temper almost daily

Enjoying the hurting of animals

Writings or drawings that depict extreme violence

How to Say It

Proper discipline usually requires more than a verbal response from the parent. What a parent says is necessary but often insufficient if the goal is to help a child hit less often. However, saying the wrong words can aggravate the situation. Children ages ten to twelve especially may resent words they view as harsh or unfair. Then a parent has unwittingly added to the problem.

- **REPORT** your expectations as clearly as you can ahead of time. "When you two are playing together in the other room, I expect you to come to me if you have a problem or for the two of you to talk it out. Hitting is not allowed."
- **DO'S & DON'TS.** "Hitting when you get mad is wrong."

- **ENCOURAGE** and praise cooperative behavior whenever you can. If you are trying to reduce hitting behavior by a child, frequent praise will also serve as a positive reminder how to act. "You guys played so nicely together. Even when you argued about something, you didn't hit. That makes me very happy."

- After you correct a child for hitting, allow a minute of silence. Then listen to your child's reasons for his hitting behavior. Obviously, you don't agree that hitting was a solution, but you will fare better if you try to listen and, when possible, show **EMPATHY**. Don't try this until you have calmed down. If you are still angry at your child for hitting, you will dismiss his reasons too quickly. "Okay. Now I want to sit and listen for a minute. Please tell me why you chose to hit your sister. . . . Oh, I see. When she made a face at you after winning the game, you didn't like that. I'm sure it bothered you when she teased you like that."

- After you have shown some empathy, **TEACH**. Don't lecture. Instead, try to help your child figure out what he could have done differently. "When your sister teases you and you feel like hitting her, what other things could you do that would help the situation and not get you into trouble? . . . Good idea. Let's rehearse it now; it might be fun."

- Recurrent hitting should be punished. Ideally, explain ahead of time what the consequences will be. "If I see you hitting your little brother, you will have to stop playing for a half hour."

How Not to Say It

- *"Mom, she stuck her tongue out at me."* "Oh, just ignore her." If your child might ordinarily hit his sister but instead complains to you (which is what you asked), don't easily dismiss him. If he thinks you will not do anything, he will conclude that he must take matters into his own hands and probably end up hitting his sister again.

- "If you hit her once more, you will be punished." The first time he hits her should result in consequences. Telling him not to hit again does not teach him what he could do instead. Say instead, "I want you two to talk to each other about what's bothering you without hitting."

Smart Talk

A recent study at the University of Illinois examined three ways that parents might act when kids fight: ignore the conflict; teach children strategies such as negotiation, compromise, and problem solving; or punish the children. While both moms and dads believed that ignoring the problem was the least useful, parents used that approach three times as often as the other two approaches. When fathers used control strategies such as punishment, they did so because they lacked confidence in their skill at teaching children effective ways to negotiate or problem-solve, not because they felt it was the best approach overall. The upshot? Parents need confidence in helping their children learn to problem-solve. That takes a little time and practice, but the reward will be worth it.

38

HIV/AIDS

Phil mentioned to his family when he arrived home from work that he had donated blood earlier that day. Nine-year-old Sarah looked at him with fear. "Can't you get AIDS?"

Phil was surprised. How did Sarah hear about AIDS?

He shouldn't have been so shocked. Children hear about AIDS from television, older kids, discussions at school, and playmates. Some parents are understandably reluctant to discuss the subject with their grade-school children. It is yet another scary topic that seems to whittle away at a parent's fantasy that children can be spared from the harsher realities of life.

But a parent's wishes won't change the fact that children will hear about AIDS. It is better to inform them in a straightforward manner what AIDS is rather than allow them to be misinformed and unnecessarily afraid.

Things to Consider

➤ Know the facts. Many adults are misinformed and believe falsehoods that AIDS can be contracted from an infected person sneezing or by drinking from a shared cup—or that transfusions pose a high risk. According to the Centers for Disease Control, donated blood is tested not once but twice. While some risk always exists, the CDC said that at most, blood tainted with HIV may go unnoticed in one out of four hundred thousand pints, with the actual risk probably much lower than that.

➤ Unless your child is educated about human sexuality, there is no need to discuss the specific ways that AIDS is transmitted sexually. You know your child best and can determine what he is able to really understand at his age.

➤ Don't be stiff and formal or prepare a lecture. Simply have a brief conversation in which you give facts and answer your child's questions.

➤ Be prepared to discuss the topic again (and again) as your child matures and more advanced knowledge is necessary.

➤ The topic will come up unexpectedly—your child may overhear a commercial or news report, for example—so plan ahead.

➤ Research shows that parents who discuss AIDS with their kids overemphasize the medical end and ignore their children's emotional issues (fears of getting AIDS). Studies show that only one in five parents believes that kids worry about AIDS when in fact almost 60 percent of sixth to eighth graders are concerned.

How to Say It

Mostly you will be **TEACHING** facts and reassuring your child that he won't get AIDS from his normal activities.

- "I'm wondering if you have ever heard of AIDS and what questions you might have."

- "AIDS is caused by a virus called HIV. Some diseases such as a cold or flu are easy to get. AIDS is very, very difficult to get. You would have to mix your blood with the blood of someone who had the HIV virus."

- If your child asks if children get AIDS, say, "Yes, some children have been infected with HIV. Some were infected when they were born because their mother had the virus. Some children who needed extra blood when they were in the hospital got the virus from the blood. But all blood that is donated is tested for HIV, and blood that has the virus won't be used in hospitals."

- "You look worried as we talk about AIDS. Tell me what your concerns are."

- "Many people have died from AIDS but the medicines they use today help more than they used to. It is hoped there will be a cure someday."

- If your child worries that someone he plays with might have AIDS, more reassurance and facts are called for. "Since it is so hard to get AIDS, especially if you are a child, I believe that none of your friends has it. Did you know that if a person with AIDS has a bleeding cut, the virus is even more difficult to get because once it hits the air the virus gets very weak."

How Not to Say It

- "You get AIDS if you do drugs or try to have sex before you are married." Trying to scare your child to avoid drugs or sex won't work if you give them the wrong information. Once they learn the truth from books, teachers, or friends, you risk having them view you as ignorant or untrustworthy.

- "People who get AIDS have only themselves to blame." Many people have acquired AIDS through no fault of their own. Besides, talking about people who have AIDS is an opportunity to foster a sense of compassion in your child. Having HIV or dying of AIDS is a very sad thing that affects not only the AIDS patient but his or her family and friends. A better choice is suggesting that your child say a prayer for people with AIDS and their families.

- "AIDS is a disease that other people get. You don't have to worry about it." The tone is dismissive. What you are really communicating is "Let's drop the subject." Are you sure your child has no concerns? If your child is between five and eight, telling him AIDS is a disease is accurate and may be all that's required. But it is better to inquire if he has any questions and to leave him with the belief that you are available to talk about the subject at any time.

Smart Talk

When you speak to your child, keep in mind that you are communicating two things: verbal information and nonverbal information (body language). A child from age five to twelve becomes more adept at picking up on your body language. If she senses that you are uncomfortable with a topic, even though you are trying to act as if you are comfortable, she might choose to ignore that issue in the future. Either loosen up or let your child know that while the topic is not an easy one for you, it is important for you to discuss it. That way your child doesn't have to read between the lines and misread your intent.

39

Home Alone/Latchkey Kids

Gabriel said she didn't mind being home alone after school. During the two hours she waited for her father to arrive home from work, the twelve-year-old usually did her homework or watched television. She was good at monitoring the answering machine and not opening the door to just anybody who happened to knock. She liked the sense of being trustworthy and the feeling of independence that came with being home alone.

Her best friend, Cindy, didn't like being home alone after school. She understood the necessity of it, but she often felt afraid. On winter days when it was dark outside by 4 P.M., she grew more frightened.

With two out of three mothers of school-age kids in the workforce, latchkey kids are growing in numbers and total about seven million at last count. Helping them adapt depends on several factors.

Things to Consider

➢ While some kids may do fine being home alone, no study of "self-care" has shown it to have positive outcomes. The most optimistic reports conclude it has no negative outcomes.

➢ Children who are on their own for at least eleven hours a week are twice as likely to use alcohol, cigarettes, or drugs.

➢ Kids (fifth to seventh graders) home alone more than two days a week were four times as likely to report getting drunk in the past month.

➢ Self-care is more risky in urban environments than in suburban.

➢ Some kids stay with friends under adult supervision. Others use their free time after school to "hang out" with peers. The latter group is at higher risk for trouble than the former.

➤ Girls without supervision tend to be more at risk for problems than boys of the same age. That is probably due to the fact that girls develop physically at an earlier age and are more apt to hang out with older teens.

➤ A study that compared college students who were former latchkey kids with nonlatchkey kids showed no difference between the groups in personality or academics.

➤ A survey of 18 pediatricians, 96 police officers, and 209 parents asked at what ages kids can be left alone without supervision. For fifteen minutes or less, the average age given was nine. For an hour or more, the age was twelve. For babysitting, the age was fourteen.

➤ When more than one child is left alone, the children are likely to behave somewhat more disruptively or ignore each other than when a parent is present.

➤ Authoritarian parents (attentive, warm, but firm about discipline) are a buffer against a child conforming with antisocial peers (during and after school) compared with inattentive or more permissive parents. Tough but loving parents, take heart: You have the right idea.

How to Say It

Most kids are inadequately prepared to avoid injuries (burns, cuts, etc.), deal with emergencies, handle phone calls or visitors at the door, or cope with kidnapping or molestation possibilities. **TEACH** them what to say or do and rehearse with them.

- "Listen to the answering machine and don't pick up the phone unless it is someone you know well. Always say, 'Mom is busy at the moment,' and take a message."
- "Call 911 if you have any doubt about what to do. Here are the phone numbers for the neighbors who will be home."
- "The first-aid kit is always in the bathroom. Let's review how to use some of those items."
- Discuss ahead of time what your child plans to do when he arrives home. You should always know your child's home schedule. "Your plan is to make a sandwich, do your homework, and maybe play a video game. I'll call you and check in."

- "Don't go outside until I'm home." This is especially important in urban areas. Children in large cities are more likely to get into trouble when left to roam outside than are children in the suburbs.
- "You can't have any friends over until I get home."
- If your child expresses fear or dislike for the latchkey situation, take the concerns seriously. Find a way to provide supervision. "I feel bad for you. I can understand why you don't like being home by yourself. Let's figure out what can be done differently."
- "I know you'd like to have your friends over after school but there needs to be supervision. I'm sorry. I know it isn't fun."

How Not to Say It

- "Just keep the doors locked, don't answer the phone, and you'll be fine." Much more preparation is needed. Review as many scenarios as possible. Give them pop quizzes on occasion. "So what would you do if your brother cut himself badly?"
- "If you go out, be sure to leave me a note." Not advisable. With grade-school children you should know ahead of time where they plan to go, for how long, and how they plan to get there.
- "There really isn't anything to be afraid of. You'll get used to being home alone, and you'll probably like it." Your child may go along with it but may never learn to like it. Knowing that a parent is not in the next room can create much anxiety in some children even if they seem old enough. If your child remains anxious, you will have to do all you can to modify your schedule so you can be available to him. Perhaps in a year or two he'll be old enough.
- "You're such a big girl, being able to stay alone by yourself for an hour." If being home alone is infrequent, such praise is nice. But if a child must be home alone frequently, you may be making it harder for her to voice any objections. A better way to say it: "You certainly are taking on more responsibilities by being home alone. But it isn't always easy, and many kids don't like it. If you have any problem with it, let me know."

Rule of Thumb: Always phone your children when they are left alone. Get periodic updates on their attitude about staying home alone.

40

Homesickness

Tommy placed his backpack on the floor of his cousin's bedroom, the place that he'd call home for the next two weeks.

"It looks as if we got everything from the car," his dad said after their long drive. "We'll be going now, Tommy. Have lots of fun!"

Tommy's mother hugged him hard. "We'll miss you," she said. "But we want you to enjoy yourself. You always enjoy playing with your cousins."

Tommy's parents waved good-bye to their son and left. When they arrived home two hours later, the phone was ringing. "Mom!" Tommy said when she answered it. "I changed my mind. I don't want to stay. I want to come home."

Homesickness is not unusual, but parents can make the problem worse if they mishandle it.

Things to Consider

➤ While many children experience homesickness, most feel much better within a day or two. If you can handle their temporary discomfort, they will probably be able to handle it, too.

➤ Homesickness may be more pronounced if the family went through a recent loss or stressful period such as a death of a relative or marital separation.

➤ Homesickness, while uncomfortable, can make a child feel competent when he learns he can overcome it.

How to Say It

There are three phases: preparation, the actual leaving of the child, and postseparation. What you say at each phase can mean the difference between homesickness or away-from-home wellness.

- In the preparation phase, listen to your child's concerns and questions, and explain what he can expect while away. "Here is the brochure for camp. As you can see, every day you will take part in activities such as swimming and boating, plus you can pick certain things to do that are special such as archery."

- **TEACH** about homesickness if you think it is likely your child will feel lonesome. Don't belabor the point. "When you feel homesick, you may feel kind of sad in your stomach. It just means you miss us. But the feeling goes away after a day or so. It's just a feeling, and it won't hurt you."

- If your child asks what will happen if he misses you when away from home, **EMPATHIZE** and **TEACH** ways he can cope. "Most kids do feel a little lonesome. That's normal. When you feel that way, the best thing to do is some fun activity. Then later that night you can call me and tell me all about your day."

- If your child protests your leaving, try to find out if he has any legitimate concerns. Maybe he needs to be introduced to another child or the camp counselor to feel more at ease. "Tell me what your worst fear is right now. . . . What would have to happen for you to begin to feel better?"

- If your child calls you later on, be optimistic and upbeat. Reassure him that any concerns are normal and give suggestions where appropriate. Chances are your child will feel better soon. Hang in there. "I bet you did interesting things today. Tell me what you did."

- Find out what your child did that made him feel better and praise him. "So when you were feeling lonesome, you went swimming with the other kids. What a great idea."

- If your child is absolutely miserable and cannot be consoled, he simply may not be ready to be away from home for too long. "It's okay that you came home early. Maybe you have to be a little older to enjoy yourself away from your family."

How Not to Say It

- "No one else is feeling this way. You should be excited." That is not reassuring and can make him feel worse. It is better to let him know that it is normal to feel a little sad or scared.

- "Well, that was a waste of money. Next time you want to go away to camp, don't ask." You're not teaching him anything useful. He'll just feel bad about himself or bad about you. What good does that do?

- "We'll all miss you so much while you're gone. It won't be the same here without you." Don't make him feel guilty about leaving. Mastering separation from one's family is an important developmental task.

- "Remember, if you want to come home, just call us and we'll come right away. Call at any hour, day or night." Don't go overboard on the reassurance. You are actually planting the suggestion that he will have a hard time coping. Besides, since many children feel a little homesick, rushing in to rescue them never gives them the opportunity to see that the feeling can go away.

- "You're too old to get homesick." No, he's not, and he might be feeling that way for good reason. A seventh grader had to return home from a friend's house because he witnessed his friend's parents arguing and it scared him. Whatever the reason for homesickness, your child is experiencing it. Try to figure out the reasons.

Rule of Thumb: If you were very homesick as a child (or not at all homesick), you run the risk of overidentifying with your child. Your child may have feelings different from yours. Be open to that possibility.

41

Internet Concerns

Elliot typed in his favorite sport in the search engine of his internet site. He got more than he bargained for. Listed among the various sites he located were those that dealt with pornography.

Camille's friend showed her how to get into a chat room. Up until then the only communicating she'd done on the computer was to e-mail her friends. Now a whole new world was opened up. Fortunately, she told her friend she didn't like the chat room. Some other child, however, might have found it tantalizing talking to strangers.

The internet is like nothing the world has seen. Many parents are not computer literate, let alone internet savvy. Parents who would never let their children attend a PG-13 movie would be shocked at what is available to any knowledgeable user on the web.

And most kids are very knowledgeable when it comes to computers.

Things to Consider

➤ Place restrictive filters on the computer that don't allow access to certain websites. (This is a must if your child is used to spending time alone and unsupervised.) With powerful ads, lots of colors and games, and freebies to entice the audience, children are at risk for surfing areas they shouldn't.

➤ Place the computer in a family room or place where people gather. Kids who have computers in their room are likely to receive less supervision than is wise.

➤ Spend a few hours and get acquainted with the technology. The more you know about the internet, the better choices you can make for your children.

➤ Never allow your children to chat with strangers. Never allow your children to give their name or address (or your credit card number) to anybody on the internet.

How to Say It

- **DO'S & DON'TS**. Set very clear rules about using the internet. Enforce them and don't get lax in your supervision. "It's fine to use the internet to look up information for your school report, but I don't want you surfing around or downloading anything without my permission."
- "Sending e-mails to friends is fine if you limit the time to . . ."
- "Never use the internet unless I am here helping you."
- "Chat rooms are not allowed. They can be dangerous to young children like you. Some people chat who only want to take advantage of children."
- **TEACH** about risks and dangers. "Some people have been hurt by people they met in chat rooms."
- **ENCOURAGE** proper use. "You used the internet for your school report, and that was all. It is wonderful knowing I can trust you and that you are smart enough to avoid unnecessary risks."
- If your child gets annoyed with your cautiousness and insists that he can play it safe on the web, **TEACH** more about the dangers. "If somebody knocked on our door and wanted to teach you things about Satanism or wanted to show you dirty pictures, would I let him in? Of course not. People on the web care nothing about you personally. They only want to make money off you or lure you into trusting them."

How Not to Say It

- "I don't want you going online. It's dangerous." So many things are dangerous if misused. The internet can also be a marvelous source of important information. Besides, it will be necessary for your child to be computer and internet literate as he gets older. Teach the dangers and supervise when necessary, but let your child have access to the web.

- "Honey, come out of your room. You've been on that computer for hours." And it has been unsupervised. You may as well be allowing people who only want to take advantage of your child into her bedroom.

- "Isn't two hours long enough to be on the web?" You are too lax in supervision. Even if your child is not exploring inappropriate sites, computers can be addictive. Time spent doodling on a computer is time wasted.

42

Jealousy

"Why does she always get what she wants, and I never do?"

"How come they get to go to the beach, and we have to go to a dumb barbecue?"

"Why do I have to wait until I'm thirteen to get my ears pierced?"

"How come I have to wait for my birthday to get a new bike when all the other kids on the block have new bikes?"

"How come he always takes the bigger piece?"

"It's not fair!"

Kids get jealous. Just as an art expert might detect subtle shadings in a painting, grade-schoolers detect the subtlest variations in fairness. They keenly feel when they are getting the short end of things and demand justice. When it doesn't happen according to their sense of fair play, they get jealous.

Things to Consider

➤ Jealousy stems from a perception of loss. Jealous children may feel a loss of their lovableness, such as when they believe a parent or grandparent favors another child over them. It may stem from loss of esteem, as when a child is jealous of another child's skill. Or it may stem from loss of control (or the sense that matters are unfair) when something happens they can do nothing about such as a divorce (jealous of kids whose parents are together).

➤ Petty jealousies may come and go. If the jealousy persists, it is important to determine what the underlying loss might be.

➤ Parents who do not get along may unwittingly be more critical of a child who reminds them of their spouse. Unhealthy alliances may form (Mom and son on one side; Dad and daughter on the other) that can foster jealousy.

➤ Parents unhappy with their lot in life may reveal their jealousy of others and thereby encourage jealous thinking in their children.

➤ If a parent has a serious problem such as alcoholism or severe physical illness, one of the kids may have taken on adult responsibilities and become jealous of siblings who are more nurtured.

How to Say It

- **EMPATHIZE** and probe for the underlying loss. Don't rush in to make your child feel better; you may never understand what's really bothering him. "You seem hurt that Grandma gives a lot of attention to your little brother. Do you wonder if Grandma loves you as much as she loves him?"

- "Many of the kids in your class wanted to sign your friend's yearbook, but fewer wanted to sign yours. That hurts your feelings, and you feel a little jealous."

- "You're right. You've been doing so much extra housework because Mom and Dad have had to work longer hours, while your little sister hasn't had to do much at all. We haven't let you know just how grateful we are and what a good job you've been doing."

- **ENCOURAGE** your child by reminding her of past successes. "Yes, Kelley won the tournament and got her name in the paper. You won an award two years ago."

- **TEACH** your child to cope. "I understand that right now you're not feeling lovable [or competent or that life is fair]. But could you take a minute and think of the many ways you know that you are loved?"

- "Last week you felt jealous of your friend. You seem to be doing better today. What happened that helped you think differently?"

- "I know you're jealous of Tim. Have you ever wondered if he felt jealous of you?" (This can appeal to a child's sense of fairness. If jealousy goes both ways, it may not feel so bad.)

How Not to Say It

- "It's a sin to feel jealous." Yes, the Ten Commandments do prohibit envying thy neighbor. But stating such a rule won't help your child feel differently. He may simply learn that you cannot help him deal with difficult feelings. If you wish to use a biblical approach, say something like "God made all of us different. Nobody is the best at everything. Instead of being jealous, God wants you to focus on the things that you are thankful for. You can focus on what you don't have and be unhappy, or you can focus on what you do have and try to be thankful."

- "That's life. Who said it was supposed to be fair?" Trying to teach before showing empathy may close off communication and just frustrate your child more.

- "You're overreacting. You know Grandma loves you as much as she loves your brother." It is better to ask for specific examples of why your child feels jealous and challenge them. "Yes, you're right. Grandma did spend more time with him this weekend. But that was because she had to baby-sit, and your brother needed more of her attention. Whenever we are here to watch over your brother, Grandma spends more time with you."

- "Don't worry. I'll cut the cake so everybody gets exactly the same size piece." Don't worry about being so precise. It's okay for your kids to get used to the idea that life isn't always fair.

Rule of Thumb: Older children who receive less parental attention because they have a sibling who is very ill or disabled seem better able to accept the unequal treatment. Still, extra attention for those children can go a long way in helping them continue to cope well.

43

Little White Lies:
"Why Did You Lie About
Santa Claus?"

When seven-year-old Moiré learned the awful truth about Santa Claus from her highly-impressed-with-himself older brother, Sean, she had three immediate concerns.

1. Will Christmas ever be the same?
2. Why did her parents lie?
3. What else have they lied about?

Children vary in their reaction to learning the truth about Santa, the tooth fairy, and the Easter bunny. Some feel proud for having figured it out, but many find out the hard way: from friends or siblings who have no interest in letting them down easily. It need not be a traumatic event and is sometimes harder for the parents when they realize that more of their child's innocence has faded. Rarely do parents overreact to this issue, but often they underreact. Children, especially in the five- to eight-year-old range, may be confused or feel betrayed. They know how to think only in concrete, literal ways. They do not understand Santa Claus as an abstraction meant to signify love and sharing. They may therefore have specific concerns about what will happen differently next Christmas.

Things to Consider

➤ If your child seems particularly sad, moody, or withdrawn (or, conversely, is more disobedient), it is possible that the news about Santa is touching on some past loss. Has a grandmother died recently? Or a pet? Has the family relocated so the child moved away from old friends? Are you and your spouse arguing a lot? Have you separated or divorced? If so, you will have to take time to discuss those issues further.

➤ Some children still *want* to believe in Santa, and they are young enough (usually nine years or less) to be reconvinced Santa exists, at least for one more holiday. This is an option, especially if you want them to continue believing a while longer.

➤ The younger children may not fully grasp the concept of a *white lie*. Lying is lying is lying. Don't expect that any fancy reasoning on your part will help them fully understand. They simply must grow older.

➤ Once a child knows and believes the truth, don't automatically change your gift-buying strategies. Children may want to ease into their new understanding. They still may want to hear you mention Santa Claus and certainly be surprised on Christmas morning. A father of four children whose oldest son just found out the truth about Santa mistakenly saw it as an opportunity for his ten-year-old to help buy presents for his younger siblings. The child did help out, but with a distinct lack of enthusiasm. After many attempts to get the child to talk, the father finally realized that his son still wanted to *pretend* that Santa existed. Helping to purchase presents made it impossible for him to pretend.

Smart Talk

Sometimes parents can overidentify with their children, especially their same-sex children. How did you react when you learned the truth about Santa? Are you automatically assuming that your child will handle it the same way? Use your past for possible insights but consider that your child may react differently from the way you did.

How to Say It

The best way to begin is by using **EMPATHY**. Even if your child asks you a direct question such as "Is there really a Santa Claus?" or "Why did you lie to me?" you may be better off (and be able to delay the inevitable moment of truth) by saying such things as:

- "You sound really hurt [or worried]. Are you?"
- "This bothers you enough that you want to talk about it, right?"

- "You might be wondering what else isn't true that you once believed was true."
- "It made you upset when the older kids on the school bus told you about Santa."
- "Perhaps you are worried that Christmas won't be the same anymore."
- "I'm wondering if you feel I've let you down. You sure sound disappointed."

If your child is worried that next Christmas (or the next time she loses a tooth) it will all be different, reassure her:

- "No, next Christmas will be exactly like last Christmas. You'll still get toys, we'll still put up a Christmas tree, and you'll have a lot of fun with many surprises."
- "What would you like to see happen next Christmas that would still make it a special time, even if Santa is really Mommy and Daddy?"

If your child is troubled that you lied about Santa, using examples that he or she can understand might help:

- "Remember on Daddy's last birthday we told him we would be out shopping when he came home from work, but instead we surprised him at home with his present? It is true we lied to him, but we did it because we wanted him to be surprised. We wanted to make him happy."
- "Remember how excited you get when you get dressed up like a fire fighter? [or a cowboy or Superwoman or a ghost] on Halloween? You know you are only pretending, but you act as if it's true because it's fun to pretend and make believe. Mommy and Daddy have a lot of fun pretending about Santa Claus."
- "Remember how excited you were going back to the lake for vacation even though you hadn't been back there for a few years? At Christmas I remember how much fun it was for me when I was a kid, and I told you Santa was real so that you could have the same kind of fun I had."

If you think your child might want to be reconvinced that Santa exists, say:

- "Isn't it interesting that the weather reporters like to talk about Santa's whereabouts on Christmas Eve?"

- "Why do you think we have so many songs about Santa Claus?"
- "I just saw a shadow in the window. It looked an awful lot like an elf to me. Did you see it, too?"
- "I know some of the kids in school are saying Santa doesn't exist. I don't know about you, but I love to pretend that he does exist."

The above won't convince some children, but a child who still wants to believe may allow him- or herself to be convinced.

How Not to Say It

Anything that discounts your child's feelings or makes her wrong for feeling disappointed is a poor move, such as:

- "It's about time you learned the truth."
- "You're old enough to know. Many children find out when they are younger than you."
- "That's life. You'll learn many things are not what you think they are."
- "I've heard enough from you about this Santa Claus thing. Get over it."
- "You're making a big deal about nothing."

Finally, don't drag out the old newspaper clipping of "Yes, Virginia, There Is a Santa Claus." That sentimental favorite may touch the heart of adults, but children are unable to grasp Santa as a metaphor. Saying that Santa exists just as surely as love and joy and faith exist may only get you the following response: "That's nice, Dad, but is there *really* a Santa Claus?"

44

Lying

Julia, age nine, didn't mind making her tuna fish sandwich all by herself. She opened the can, dumped the tuna in a bowl, stirred in the mayonnaise, and slapped it all on bread. Her mom walked over to inspect the finished product.

"Looks delicious. Hey, how did this mayonnaise get smeared all over the counter?"

"I didn't do it," Julia said.

"Nobody else was in the kitchen except you, and you used the mayonnaise."

"But I didn't get any on the counter."

"Then who did?"

"I don't know but it wasn't me!"

Julia lied—or did she? She was genuinely surprised at the extent of the mess. She had no memory of doing it, so in her mind she was not guilty.

At other times kids lie and they know it. They do it to get out of trouble or to attract attention. Then it's a parent's job to do something.

Things to Consider

➤ Since every child will lie, a firm but low-key approach is best most of the time.

➤ Lying is much more serious when it is accompanied by violent behavior or stealing.

➤ Children who lie a lot probably have friends who do the same.

➤ While a child who lies may have honest parents, parents who lie or break rules are more likely to have children who do the same.

➤ Adults admit to lying about thirteen times a week (did they lie in the survey?). Many adults lie to make social interactions more acceptable (saying someone's new haircut looks great when thinking it looks awful).

How to Say It

- If the lie is over small matters ("I didn't mess up the counter, Mom"), don't debate it. "Well, however it happened, the counter needs cleaning. Grab a towel and start wiping, please."
- Don't debate when the evidence is clear that your child is lying. "You can say you didn't do it if you want, but I saw you throw the apple core behind the couch. Pick it up and throw it in the trash."
- Always correct a lie. "No, that's not the truth. The truth is . . ."
- Authors Jerry Wyckoff and Barbara Unell, in the book *How to Discipline Your Six- to Twelve-Year-Old*, recommend rehearsing telling the truth. "Millie, just please say, 'Dad, I was the one who accidentally erased the messages on the answering machine.'"
- If lying becomes more frequent or more serious, you will have to make lying an issue. "You're getting older, and I need to be able to trust you. If I think you are lying to me, then I will not be able to allow you to do things that require trust, such as spending a night at a friend's or carrying extra money."
- Recognize that children may lie to avoid disapproval, to make themselves appear better than others, or to deal with frustrations—in other words, as a way of coping with a flagging self-esteem. If you suspect any of the above, focus on the underlying concern the child might have. "I notice you tell stories about how strong you are. I wonder if some days you worry that other kids might not like you, and you want to impress them."
- "I think you lied to avoid getting into trouble. Actually, I'd be more proud of you for telling the truth even if I didn't like what you did."
- Praise truth telling, especially when your child could have lied. "Thank you for coming to me to say you broke the window. It means a lot when you tell the truth, especially when you think you might get into trouble for it."
- "Even though you lied today, I know you are someone who will try to tell the truth." Show that you have faith in him.

- **TEACH** by example. "When I came to pick you up at school today, I found a twenty-dollar bill in the parking lot. I turned it in to the office in case someone lost it."
- **TEACH** about white lies. Older children will understand that sometimes you might lie to protect someone's feelings. "Remember when Grandma gave me that sweater for my birthday and I told her I loved the color? Well, I didn't really love it, but I knew she had spent a long time looking for the right gift for me. I didn't want to hurt her feelings. What other examples of white lies can you think of?"

How Not to Say It

- "You're a liar." Don't label your child that way. Distinguish between the act and the person.
- If you already know the truth, don't ask, "Who broke the lamp? Did you?" That may set up your child to lie. Don't give him the opportunity to practice.
- "You did *what!*" Be careful not to punish truth telling. Yes, some wrong acts deserve punishment or corrective consequences, but make sure you praise telling the truth.
- "Are you sure you're telling me the truth? Kids lie, you know." You should convey to your child that you expect the truth, not that you expect lies.
- "You lie just like your father did." Deal with your children as they are, not as a projection of somebody else.

45

Manipulative Behavior ("But Mom Said I Could!")

"What are you doing, sweetheart?" Dad said to ten-year-old Vickie. She was thumbing through a jewelry catalog.

"I'm trying to decide which earrings to buy when I get my ears pierced," she said.

"You mean when you turn thirteen? That's a few years away."

"Thirteen? Mom said I could get them pierced this weekend!"

"She did?"

"Yes! Dad, all the girls in my class have their ears pierced. I'm the only one who doesn't."

"Well, I thought—"

"Dad, if Mom says I can get them pierced you have to let me. You just have to!"

Mom heard the ruckus and came in to investigate.

"Hon, did you tell Vickie she could get her ears pierced?"

Mom looked astonished. "Absolutely not. I told her that if you thought she was old enough, I *might* reconsider, but that's not the same as telling her it was okay."

Sometimes kids really do misinterpret what a parent says because they hear what they want to hear. Other times kids will try to divide and conquer.

Things to Consider

➤ This kind of behavior is normal and a sign of more sophisticated development. For some kids it can get out of hand, however.

➤ If parents disagree on child-rearing, kids will easily find a wedge and take advantage of it.

➤ If parents are overtired or overworked, they are vulnerable to the divide-and-conquer approach.

➤ While giving in to children's manipulations is bad strategy, so is being rigid and inflexible. In fact, the more rigid you are, the more likely your children will be manipulative to get what they want sometimes.

➤ Sometimes siblings pull together and gang up on a parent. Manipulative? Perhaps. But kids do not have much authority and may need to rely on such tactics. Hear them out; they may have a good point to make.

How to Say It

- **DO'S & DON'TS.** "This is the first I heard of this. Until I speak to your Mom [or Dad] I'll have to say no." This is especially important if your child frequently rushes you and insists you must make a decision immediately.
- "If you remember, the rule is that I don't agree to something I'm unsure about until your father and I have a chance to discuss it."
- "Let me talk to your mother now." This shows him he can't get away with manipulating, but neither are you rejecting his request out of hand.
- **REPORT** what troubles you. "Your friend called and invited you to sleep over. I said okay, and I assumed your friend's mom already said it was okay. Then I found out she had no idea what you kids were planning. That is not the way you go about asking for permission."
- "I need to think about it first" or "I need to speak to your friend's parents first."
- **ENCOURAGE** honest, straightforward requests with praise. "You asked me to think about your request and to talk it over with Dad. I really like that way of asking."

Smart Talk

In a study of 137 families with kids ranging in age from three to thirteen, parents were asked to judge whether or not children engaged in specific behaviors that were listed. Parents disagreed with each other twice as often as they agreed. Mothers tended to report more negative behaviors than did fathers. What does this signify? Don't presume you and your mate are on the same wavelength. Check out your presumptions early and often. Otherwise, your kids will have a field day trying to manipulate you.

How Not to Say It

- "You are being tricky and dishonest. I won't stand for it." This comes perilously close to calling your kid a petty criminal. Many good kids act in a manipulative way for one of three reasons: because in the past it was rewarded ("Daddy, *pleeeeease!*"), because parents don't agree on rules, or because a parent has been inflexible about rules that could be modified. If the behavior happens once in a while, it will likely diminish if it is not reinforced. If it happens frequently, the possibility is strong that other family or marital problems are lurking that need to be fixed.

- "It's fine with me if it's okay with your mom." Used sparingly and about noncontroversial issues, this statement is okay to make. It shows flexibility. It becomes problematic when parents say it out of laziness. Then the children learn that if they can soften up the parents one at a time, they will get what they want. Whenever possible, talk to your spouse directly about your child's request. Don't let the child be the go-between; messages can get misunderstood.

- "I wish you wouldn't ask me these things at the last minute." This is rather wimpy. If you don't want hurried, last-minute requests, don't reward them. Much of the time children can plan ahead and give you plenty of time to think about what you want to do.

46

Medical:
Shots, Blood Tests,
and Dental Procedures

Eight-year-old Debby clenched her jaw as the shot was being administered.

"Ugh, I'm glad that's over," she said. Then she watched the lab technician prepare a new syringe—a much bigger syringe.

"Another shot!" Debby cried.

"Oh, no, no," said her Mom. "This is a blood test. It's like a shot except they take blood from you. It feels the same as—"

"Noooo! You told me all I needed was a shot! You never said anything about blood!"

Debby had a point. Being surprised will only increase her apprehension the next time she visits the pediatrician. But her mom's reluctance to warn her about the blood test was understandable. She didn't want to hear the protests while driving to the doctor's office.

If you want to make doctor and dentist visits a little easier, try these suggestions:

Things to Consider

➤ Severely phobic children may need professional help. Fear and apprehension and saying "I hate shots" don't qualify as a phobia. A truly phobic child may feel and act terrified, may cry uncontrollably, or may physically resist the medical procedure.

➤ Almost all children are nervous about shots and dental work.

➤ Unlike other situations that might cause fear, the infrequency of shots and dental drilling make adapting to the situation harder.

➤ Most apprehensive school-age children will comply with getting shots, but they may try hard to get you to postpone it. Don't give in.

How to Say It

- Use words that are accurate but less painful sounding. "The shot of novocaine feels like a mosquito bite" or "It feels like a little bug bite, and then you'll feel some pressure."

- "It takes about three seconds for a shot [about one second to poke your finger *or* about thirty seconds to draw blood from your arm, which is about as long as singing Happy Birthday four times]."

- Tell the truth. If your child's experience is worse than you said it would be, he won't trust what else you say. "Shots can hurt like a little pinch hurts. Most kids don't like it much and are glad to get it over with."

- "The dentist drill sounds scary and you can feel it rumble on your tooth, but the most it should hurt is like a few mosquito bites."

- "Do you see how the third shot of novocaine didn't hurt at all? That's because the first two shots made your mouth numb so you won't feel pain."

- "When the nurse is taking blood from you, the only part that hurts a little is when they poke you with the needle. That takes a second. It doesn't hurt at all when the blood goes from your arm and into the tube."

- **TEACH** why the shot or the drilling or the blood test is necessary. "If your infection gets worse, it could become very painful. The shot will help you get rid of your infection."

- "The blood test will tell us what kind of treatment to give you. Without a blood test, the doctors might waste time giving you medicines you don't need."

- **TEACH** by rehearsing when possible. For example, to rehearse getting a shot, wipe an area of your child's arm with rubbing alcohol, gently pinch a fold of skin, and carefully squeeze a piece of skin between your fingernails. (Approximating the discomfort of a shot. Practice on yourself first.) "This is what will happen, and this is what it will feel like. I bet that feels like something you can handle. Doesn't it feel like a mosquito bite?"

- **EMPATHIZE.** "I know you feel scared and will be glad when it's done."

- "Your stomach may feel nervous. That's normal."

- Praise is also very important during the procedures. "You're doing great. It's almost over. The part that pinches is the hardest part, and that part is over." A reward after the procedure isn't a bad idea. Bribery (offering some reward ahead of time out of desperation) is not advisable, but since shots or blood tests are infrequent, a special treat afterward is fine.

How Not to Say It

- "This will sting" or "It feels like a little stabbing." Those words are too strong and scary. Even the words *hurt* and *pain* are vague. What will your child imagine when he hears those words?
- "You won't feel anything." Tell the truth.
- "You're older than your sister, and she didn't cry." It may not help, and it can make him feel worse. It is better to empathize with the anxiety and discomfort, and praise him for his achievement afterward.
- "Don't be a baby." You may get cooperation (or you may not), but you will definitely teach your child not to bother talking to you about upsetting feelings. You are adding insult to injury.
- "The doctor will get mad at you if you don't get the shot [if you don't get your teeth cleaned]." Your child may not care what the doctor thinks. Besides, teaching children to cooperate so they will be liked is potentially dangerous. Peers or adults who may want to take advantage of your child will often use that strategy.
- "Stop complaining. Look, if you promise to be really, really good, I'll buy you a toy later." This is dangerously close to emotional blackmail. The next time your child has a doctor's appointment, he may act up again, knowing he'll get a reward. Or your child may not care if he gets a present. If you want to reward your child, say this: "I thought it might be fun for us to get you a little present after your doctor's visit. That way we have something to look forward to." Try discussing that present during the medical procedure as a distraction.

Medical:
Hospitalization

When nine-year-old Christina ran through the family room and turned a corner, she tripped and hit her head on the television set. Her mom, Donna, knew that the cut was deep and immediately drove Christina to the emergency room. The girl was scared. It was her first time in a hospital, and she overheard the doctor say that stitches were required. Mom was nervous, too, but she also had an idea. Crouching next to her daughter's bed, she pulled the sheet over their heads, leaving only the head wound exposed, and together they sang Christina's favorite songs while the doctor stitched her up.

Some hospital stays are short. Some are longer. Some are unexpected. But parents can say things that can make a child's time in the hospital less scary.

Things to Consider

➤ School-age children are primarily concerned about suffering any pain from surgeries or medical tests. They may also worry about being separated from their parents.

➤ Most hospitals allow a parent to sleep in a child's room if necessary.

➤ A parent's attitude will have a large impact on the child's attitude.

➤ If a hospital stay is elective, let your child tour the facility ahead of time. Introduce her to a nurse or doctor whom she'll recognize later.

How to Say It

- **TEACH.** Inform your child what he can expect: the sign-in, any blood tests or X-rays, the surgery and postoperative experience. Be calm, matter-of-fact, and enthusiastic where appropriate. "Part of the fun is that you get to order the kind of food you want for supper, and you get to eat in bed. What's really neat is you are given a special medicine that makes you sleep, and you don't feel a thing during surgery. When you wake up, I'll be there waiting for you."

- Explain that it is okay to call a nurse (some children may be reluctant or may assume the adults will take care of everything). "If you need anything or have a question, all you have to do is press this button, and a nurse will come to you as soon as she is able."

- **NEGOTIATE.** It is not appropriate to plead with your child to cooperate with medical procedures and bribe her with goodies. However, since hospital stays are usually infrequent and stressful, you can discuss how you might celebrate when she returns home and is well again. "Would you like a little party with your friends? We could have it at a restaurant or at the house. Or would you prefer going to the amusement park?" The reward is not an enticement to cooperate but something to look forward to.

- **EMPATHIZE.** Resist the urge to reassure your child before you make empathic comments. Otherwise, you might cut off your child's concerns before she has fully expressed them. For example, if offering only reassurance, you might say, "No, it won't hurt." But an empathic comment might be: "You keep asking if the surgery will hurt. You're still worried that you will feel some pain during the surgery." That allows your child to express herself more fully and perhaps get to an underlying concern that has yet to be expressed. Other **EMPATHIC** comments include these:

  "You get worried when your friends tell you that going to a hospital is scary."

  "It can be a little exciting doing something you haven't done before."

  "You're upset that you might miss something fun at home while you are in the hospital."

- Reassure your child only after you believe you know his concerns. Be honest. "You won't feel a thing during surgery. You'll be asleep and won't even know you are having surgery. After you are awake, you might have a sore throat, but medications will help that, too."

Rule of Thumb: A hospitalization can cause some regression even in older children. Extra handholding is fine and helpful. Don't criticize your child if he acts younger than his age.

How Not to Say It

- "Most kids enjoy being in a hospital. It will be a lot of fun." Be honest. There can be enjoyable moments in a hospital, but most kids are glad to go home. The stay can be pleasant and interesting, however, so say that instead.

- "If you get upset, you'll have to stay longer [or they'll have to give you a shot]." Don't make the hospital a threatening place. Be sympathetic, not harsh.

- "You can go home if you want." If it isn't true, don't say it. Otherwise, your child will question the truthfulness of everything else you've said.

- "I'll feel so much better when you get back home." Tone down your own anxiety. It is better to say, "I'm glad the doctors are helping you, and I'm looking forward to Friday when you come home."

Smart Talk

If you are worried about your child's ability to cope with cancer, here's some good news. A 1997 study compared over three hundred cancer-surviving children with healthy children. The parents of these children were also evaluated for stress. Not only did children have fewer signs of stress than the parents did, but the cancer survivors were no different from their healthy counterparts in measures of stress. However, the parents of the sick children showed significant signs of post-traumatic stress disorder. Why? Those children were provided with tremendous social support, and they did not view the cancer as life threatening as had their parents. The bottom line: Parents of children with cancer need more support, and they need to remind themselves of the rise in the successful treatment of childhood cancers.

Medical:
When a Child Has
a Chronic Illness

Annie is one of five million children in the United States who suffers from asthma. According to the latest statistics, over 160,000 children will be hospitalized for asthma this year, and the number of new asthma cases has doubled in the last twenty years.

Arty is the unlucky one in a thousand children who suffer from juvenile arthritis. Sometimes for months at a time his knee swells up, and he has a hard time walking.

Severe food allergies, irritable bowel, migraine headaches, epilepsy, and diabetes are also among the chronic illnesses children face. Then there are the more debilitating diseases such as muscular dystrophy or diseases such as cancer that can sometimes be cured but that may require lengthy treatments. Kids who must deal with an acute medical problem know that they will soon feel better. But when a medical problem is chronic, children must learn to adapt to a more restrictive lifestyle.

Things to Consider

➤ You are not responsible for your child's chronic illness. Your responsibility is to see to it that your child receives appropriate care and treatment.

➤ Be on the alert for catastrophic thoughts ("She'll never have a normal childhood"). When treated properly, most chronic illnesses are not life threatening and are not usually too restrictive.

➤ Resist being overprotective. Research is clear that overprotective parents can unwittingly reinforce certain symptoms in children (such as pain and vague stomach or muscular aches). Similarly, don't grant your chronically ill child special privileges.

➤ Become an expert so you can teach your child how to manage his condition and how to detect warning signs.

How to Say It

- **TEACH** what the disease is in a matter-of-fact way. Don't be so serious or formal that your child worries unnecessarily. "You have asthma. That is an illness where once in a while you will have to work harder to breathe. It feels very uncomfortable, but the medicines we have will help a lot."

- "Many kids have allergies. Some children cannot drink milk or eat ice cream. Some kids can't eat corn or bread. Other kids can eat what they want, but they sneeze if they get near dogs or cats or certain flowers."

- "You are not an epileptic [an asthmatic, a diabetic, etc.]. You are a person with epilepsy."

- Offer **ENCOURAGEMENT**. "Many children have this problem. You are definitely not alone."

- As your child gets older, he needs to assume greater responsibility for taking proper medications, staying away from triggers that cause flare-ups, and recognizing the warning signs of a flare-up. "You remembered to use your ventilator before gym" [or "You remembered to tell Mrs. Jones you could not eat peanuts" or "You stayed away from the neighbor's new cat"]. Good for you!"

- "If you take your medicines properly and eat the right kinds of foods, you will feel good most of the time."

- Let your child down easily when restrictions are necessary. Suggest alternatives whenever possible. "No, you can't sleep over at Mary's because you are allergic to dog hair and it makes your asthma worse. I'm sorry. I wish you could go. Maybe I can talk to Mary's mom and see if you two could camp out in their backyard instead."

- **EMPATHIZE**. Chronic illnesses are by definition long-term. Your child will adapt but still be frustrated from time to time. "I know you felt disappointed when your class had a pizza party and you couldn't eat the pizza. What else did you feel?"

- "Some days taking your insulin shots makes you feel different from the other kids, and you wish you didn't have diabetes."

- "I know it can make you feel sad that you can't eat most of the Halloween candy. I'm glad you still got dressed in your costume and went out with your friends."

- If your child suffers a flare-up or goes through a difficult episode with her illness, speak as calmly and reassuringly as possible. "You are taking your medicine and know what to do. This flare-up is temporary. I know it feels a little scary and uncomfortable, but you've handled it before."

- Rehearse with your child some positive coping statements. "Next time you are upset that you walk with a limp and can't run as fast as the other kids, tell yourself 'I don't have to like this, but I can get used to it. I'm like every other kid: I'm better at some things and not as good in other things.'"

How Not to Say It

- "Your asthma is acting up? Let's get right home. We can go to the movies some other night." In their book *Natural Relief for Your Child's Asthma*, Drs. Steven and Ken Bock suggest you think twice about postponing enjoyable activities when the condition can be managed. Otherwise, children may not alert a parent when they are experiencing symptoms because they fear they will be forced to miss some activity.

- "You're feeling light-headed? Maybe it's your diabetes. Go lie down, and your brother can put away the dishes for you." When "illness behavior" is followed by some reward, the behavior can be reinforced. Don't let children out of their chores unless it is clearly necessary.

- "You've had diabetes for three years. You know you shouldn't be eating that!" You are right, of course, but you may be missing the point. A child who goes against medical advice (haven't you ever cheated on a diet?) is frustrated, not ignorant of the rules. It is better to empathize with her frustration than criticize her.

- "Be nicer to your sister. She has asthma." Your other children do need to be educated about their sibling's illness, but don't foster jealousy or resentment. If you ever overhear one of your other kids say "I wish *I* had diabetes," then you've overreacted.

- "Do you feel dizzy? Are you in any pain? Can you breathe okay? Are you sure you want to stay and play?" Overdone, your child may pay too much attention to his body and give in to the illness when he otherwise could get along fine despite having symptoms.

Smart Talk

In a study of seven- and eight-year-olds with migraines, treatment consisted of either biofeedback to reduce pain or biofeedback plus parental training in pain management. Both groups experienced less pain, but the second group did even better. What were parents trained to do? They encouraged normal activity for their children and encouraged the kids to try to manage the pain as much as possible by themselves. They did not ask children how much pain they were feeling and did not go overboard responding to their pain, and they asked the schoolteachers to follow the same guidelines.

In a different study of children with asthma, the father's role seemed influential in predicting school absences or asthma-related medical visits. Specifically, when fathers expressed a lot of criticism, the child was absent from school more often. The more time that fathers spent with their children on weekends, the fewer the medical visits for asthma needed by the child. This suggests either that fathers don't like spending time with asthmatic children or that asthma flare-ups can sometimes be triggered by emotions.

Medical:
Talking to Siblings of
Children with Chronic Illness

Ten-year-old Bruce did not hesitate to hold his younger brother's hand in the mall. His brother Tommy has Down's syndrome and looks up to Bruce.

"We're almost at the food court," Bruce said. "We can find a table while Mom buys our lunch."

Often, a heartwarming side effect of having a child with a disability or chronic illness is that siblings learn more about compassion and tolerance than they otherwise would. In fact, many of today's health care providers got their start by helping out at home with a family member who needed extra care or attention.

But there can be a downside. Siblings of kids with chronic conditions might receive less attention. They frequently take on added responsibilities or at least *feel* responsible for ensuring the safety of their brother or sister. In moderation that is not a problem. But if the illness is debilitating or if the parents are overwhelmed or overprotective, siblings may be saddled with too much stress.

Things to Consider

➤ Research evidence suggests that siblings understand and tolerate unequal treatment if there is a good explanation for it.

➤ Siblings can worry about their ill sister or brother, or may worry that they may become ill. They need to be educated and reassured.

➤ Were you a caretaker for a sibling (or even for a parent) when growing up? That background can make you either overly sensitive to your healthy children's needs or less sensitive. Try to adjust your reactions accordingly.

➤ Single parents or dual-career couples may expect more help from their children. Are your healthy kids involved too much in the care of the less healthy child because you are too busy?

How to Say It

- **TEACH** the basics of a sibling's illness and what effect it may have on their role in the family. "Your sister has severe asthma and sometimes has a hard time breathing. If you are playing with her and she has a flare-up, you might need to see that she uses her ventilator. Or you might have to get a teacher or grown-up to help her." Rehearse scenarios that are likely to occur.

- Offer reassurance if your child has unreasonable worries or concerns, perhaps asking "Will she die?" "No, she won't die. Many kids have this type of problem. But she can get real sick if we don't have her medications. Most of the time Mom and Dad will take care of her, but there may be times when you need to tell us what is happening."

- "No, her illness is not something you can catch."

- **EMPATHIZE** with their frustrations or worries. "You had to do most of the tidying up today because your brother was sick. I bet that can sometimes feel unfair."

- "You worry when your brother has to take his insulin shots."

- "Sometimes when you get mad at your sister, you feel guilty afterward because you know she is sick."

- "It's frustrating to have to turn around and go back home because we forgot the medicine. But we want to be prepared if we need the medicine."

- "It isn't easy some days having to look out for your little sister."

- **ENCOURAGE** and praise thoughtful behavior. Be willing to overlook some misbehavior when you know your child generally tries to be helpful and responsible. "You really are gentle with your brother when he needs your help" or "It's not always easy to be patient, but you were patient right now."

How Not to Say It

- "Don't fight like that with your sister! You know she's sick!" A recent study suggested that parents are willing to make excuses for their ill child's misbehavior but do not excuse the healthy child. Watch for that and make appropriate corrections. Sick children, just like adults, may be tempted to use their illness as a strategy to avoid responsibilities and excuse bad behavior.

- "It's your job to make sure your brother stays well." If medical emergencies are possible, do not expect a school-age child to take responsibility for the safety and welfare of the ill child. It should not be his "job." It is better to say, "You are not a doctor, so it is not your fault if there is a medical problem even when you help out and do your best."

- Don't say to a whining or demanding child, "You should be grateful you have your health [that you can walk, that you don't have cancer, that you don't have diabetes]." Don't try to make a child feel guilty for being healthier than a sibling. Kids will be kids, and that means they will take some things for granted (don't we all?) and whine when they don't get what they want. It is better to say something like "It's obvious you want that toy. I know you'd like it, but I'm sorry, the answer is no." Skip the lecture and don't make any references to the child with the medical problems.

- "Your brother is not like other children." Don't emphasize the differences. Your ill child is just like other children in every way.

Medical:
When a Parent Has a
Serious Physical Illness

Larry had been feeling weak and achy for months. Sometimes he had barely enough energy to fetch the morning mail before he wanted to go back to bed and sleep. After countless medical tests and reassurances from physicians that whatever he had would eventually go away, one specialist diagnosed fibromyalgia. Larry learned that fibromyalgia was similar to chronic fatigue syndrome and Epstein-Barr. The consequence would be periods of fatigue and pain that some days would be incapacitating. Larry's first thought was that he might not be able to keep his job. His second thought was that he might not be able to coach his daughter's basketball team.

Cancer, multiple sclerosis, degenerative nerve disorders, and severe respiratory or heart problems are just a few of the common illnesses that can affect a parent. When physical illnesses are severe or incapacitating, or if recovery takes a long time, the family has to reorganize in order to cope with the situation. Day-to-day life cannot go on exactly as it had before.

Things to Consider

➤ Children should not become mini-adults when a parent is sick. They may take on some added responsibilities but should retain their status as children. They should not feel responsible for the welfare of other family members.

➤ Parents whose responsibilities are limited due to physical illness sometimes pull back even further than they should (because of depression or insecurity), or they try to compensate by becoming overly involved in areas they can have a role in. Neither extreme is helpful. No matter how ill, children will look up to the parent as both boss and comforter. Don't underestimate your value just because of illness or disability.

➤ A recent study revealed that children are misinformed and undereducated about the causes of cancer. One in five believed it was caused by casual contact. Over half worried they would get cancer. If a parent has cancer, the children need to be educated about it.

➤ You have a tremendous opportunity to teach your children a valuable lesson: how to cope well during adversity.

How to Say It

- **TEACH**. Tell your children the basics of your condition and what they can expect in the near future. "The doctors told me I have breast cancer. They will do surgery to remove the cancer, and they will give me medications for many months to keep the cancer from returning. Some days I will feel sick from the medications, so I may not be able to go to work, clean up the house, play with you, or go shopping. I will be asking you to do a few more chores once in a while."

- "You don't get cancer from being with someone who has it. Just because I have cancer doesn't mean you will get it."

- Offer **ENCOURAGEMENT**. If your prognosis is uncertain, remain optimistic. You don't need to tell children the truth if the truth will leave them worried and without answers for the foreseeable future. If a child asks, "When will you be all better?" say, "I don't know exactly when, but the medications will do their job and I expect to feel much better as time goes on."

- If a child asks, "Will you die?" say, "No. I expect to live a long life." Even if there is a possibility you could die from the illness, it is best not to say that to children until you are closer to that stage.

- **EMPATHIZE**. "It's not easy coming home from school and having to tidy up the house when you'd rather play."

- "It worries you when you see me staying in bed most of the day."

- "I'm sure it's frustrating that we have to cancel our plans for today because Daddy is not feeling well."

- "You feel sad that Mommy couldn't watch your baseball game and see you get a hit."

- "You feel excited and happy that Dad feels well enough to go to the park with us."

- **REPORT** your opinions and feelings. "I'll be glad when the medications start to work and your mom feels better."
- Reassure children that they are not the cause of the illness or responsible for its worsening. "Daddy doesn't expect you to be well behaved every minute. He understands that you can have a bad day, too. He likes it when you guys get along and don't fight, but fighting won't make his illness worse."

Smart Talk

In a 1997 study of HIV-infected hemophiliac men, 45 percent informed their children of their illness. The parents were more likely to disclose the information the older their children were or the more advanced their illness. Researchers were interested in the impact of the disclosure on the children. Results showed that the most important factor was the overall quality of the parent-child relationship, not the disclosure (or lack of disclosure) per se. The better the relationship quality, the less depression or behavioral problems and the better the school performance after the disclosure of HIV illness.

How Not to Say It

- "Will you two stop fighting? Don't you want Daddy to get better?" Don't make them feel guilty for something they have no control over. Consider the possibility that they may be fighting out of worry for their father. Talking with your kids more about how they feel about a parent's illness may do more to reduce sibling arguments.
- "Since you are the oldest child, I expect you to make sure things run smoothly in the house while Mommy is in the hospital" or "You're the man of the house while Daddy is in the hospital." Children can have more chores, but they should not be given authority (in fact, siblings may not recognize that authority). Children need to believe that parents are still in charge. "Helping out" a parent is not the same as shouldering responsibility.

- "Mom could get worse, or she could get better. We just don't know." Don't let children worry unnecessarily. It is better to remain optimistic and remind the kids what is being done to make a parent feel better. "The treatment is continuing, and some days Mom feels a lot better. We don't know when Mom will be completely well."

- "I can't take this much longer . . ." You may have many days that can be overwhelming. You don't have to pretend you are coping well when you are struggling, but you don't have to suggest to your kids that you may fall apart completely. If you need professional help or an occasional visit with friends, do that. When feeling overwhelmed, tell your kids, "Some days it's harder for me to deal with Mommy's illness. I'll be fine in a while."

- "Can't you see I'm not feeling well and can't play that game with you?" Your kids may not be able to tell whether or not you are in the mood for games. Don't discourage them. It is better to say, "Gee, I'd love to play, but I'm not up to it now. But please ask me later."

51

Money and Allowance

Twelve-year-old Paulo greatly wanted an electric guitar and amplifier. His friend's older brother offered to sell him a used guitar and amp for $400. The agreement was that Paulo could take possession of the items, but he'd have to pay $40 a week for ten weeks. All the adults agreed. The problem was that Paulo needed to earn some of the money. His parents did not allow him to take it from his college savings. So Paulo knocked on neighbors' doors and tried to earn the money mowing lawns, raking leaves, and cleaning up garages.

The first three weeks he averaged only $30. He was underpaying his friend's brother and had to make it up the following weeks. By week seven Paulo decided the guitar wasn't worth the money after all. He was allowed to drop the deal and receive back one-half of the money he had paid. The rest was considered a rental fee for the time he had used the musical equipment. Paulo learned a valuable lesson.

Things to Consider

➢ Children need to learn the value of money and that many items must be earned.

➢ Allowances are fine as long as children are expected to do some chores for free since they have a responsibility to the family. Children should be expected to save a portion of money they earn.

➢ Talking to kids about the value of money is not the same as having them understand the meaning by paying for some things themselves.

➢ Many opportunities exist to teach kids about money such as looking for sale items, not buying something you would like because it is too expensive, or having kids earn lunch money they lost.

➤ When possible, don't agree to buy your child something on the condition he pays it back later. It is better for him to earn and pay his share ahead of time and then purchase the item.

➤ Are you over your budget? Do you pay bills on time? Do you and your spouse argue about spending? If so, you will have a more difficult time teaching your kids the proper way to deal with finances.

How to Say It

- **TEACH** about the high cost of items without criticizing your child for asking for things. "You want this new brand of sneakers because lots of kids have them? I'm sure it would make you feel good to have them, but we just bought you a new pair last month. Sneakers are too expensive. After you outgrow your current pair, we can discuss what kind to get you next."

- **DO'S & DON'TS**. "It costs too much. We can't go to Walt Disney World next year."

- "I know it's your money that you received for your birthday, but you still cannot spend it to get a tattoo." Don't hesitate to say no when your values are at stake. It is your duty as a parent.

- **NEGOTIATE**. This is a perfect issue on which to make a deal with your child. How much responsibility is he willing to take on? "You want me to help pay for your trick bike when you have a perfectly good twelve-speed in the garage. You will need to earn at least two hundred dollars. What ideas do you have to achieve that?"

- "If I buy you the item on credit and you don't do your chores or don't pay me money on time, what should I do?" Get your child's opinion on the consequences of failing to do his part in the deal. If reasonable, go along with his ideas.

- **EMPATHIZE** when the answer is no. "I'm sure you're disappointed. I know it would mean a lot to have that pair of designer jeans."

- **ENCOURAGE** and praise frugal or responsible handling of money. "You had to carry your lunch money, and you didn't lose it. Good job."

- "You are doing the extra work just as you promised you would. That shows me you can be counted on to do what you say you will do."

- "When I said we couldn't buy those skates for you, you didn't complain even though you were disappointed. That meant a lot to me."

- "Your father is late paying his support payments. As soon as he pays me, I can buy this for you." It is okay to tell your child that something is not affordable because of late support payments if that is the truth and you are not at fault. (Were payments late because you were being difficult and unfair on some other issue? Then don't paint your ex as the bad guy. It is better to say that you and your ex disagree about some things, and until you work it out, the support may be delayed.) Be cautious. If the father has been mostly reliable, don't plant the seeds of animosity in your child until you know the whole story.

How Not to Say It

- "Why do you think you can get whatever you want? Isn't it time you started thinking about others?" Trying to teach your child by criticizing him is not a good idea. He'll more likely remember your criticism than the underlying lesson.

- "When I was a kid, I had to earn everything I ever got. You kids today are spoiled." You are in charge. If you want your child to earn more of what she receives, then develop a strategy and implement it. Don't criticize your child for expecting to be given everything on a platter if that is what you have taught her over the years.

- "Okay, I'll buy you this. But I expect you to help out a lot more at home than you have been. And get those grades up, too." What does "help out" mean exactly? Be very specific on what you expect. Also, it's a better idea to have your child "help out" prior to your buying the item whenever possible. "I really think you need to do more work around the house before I spend the money on this CD. It is expensive, and I do need the help. If you will help me pick up your baby brother's toys before going to bed every night, and put all dishes in the dishwasher, we can come back in two weeks and buy this."

- "I know this is expensive, but I really want it. Don't tell your father." Don't put your child in a position where to feel loyal to you she must feel disloyal to her other parent.

52

Money:
Finances Are Tight/
Explaining Loss of Job

"I wasn't laid off," Bob said. "I was downsized. Somehow that word doesn't make it any easier."

That was the beginning of Bob's financial problems. Without a paycheck he had to pay extra for medical insurance since his company no longer provided that for him. Mortgage and car payments ate up his savings within six months. Job prospects he had counted on simply fizzled. But he wanted his children insulated from anxiety.

Things to Consider

➢ When parents can no longer afford certain extra things for their children such as dance lessons or the latest video game, they can be more upset than their children. Kids can handle such setbacks, and it can be beneficial for them to realize that the family can survive belt-tightening.

➢ Men in particular view their primary role as a provider. Out of work they can feel inadequate. Now is the time to enhance the quality and quantity of time spent with the kids. Once back at work you won't have the same opportunity.

➢ Make cutting back on expenses a fun and challenging family project instead of a frustrating experience. Kids can rise to the occasion and be willing to make sacrifices. Let them feel they are doing their part.

How to Say It

- **REPORT** the essential facts. "I was laid off at work. They no longer can afford to pay me, so until I find another job, we have to come up with ways to save money."

- **REPORT** some of your concerns but remain optimistic. "It doesn't come at a good time, and I worry about finding a job that will pay well. But I believe I eventually will find a job, and we'll get back to normal."

- **TEACH** being frugal. "It would help a lot if when we buy things we ask ourselves these questions: Can we get by without it for now? Can we find it at a cheaper price?"

- Explain what the implications are for the foreseeable future. "We will probably postpone our next vacation. Maybe instead we'll take more day trips. We'll have to cut back on gifts, too."

- **ENCOURAGE** creative ways to have family fun. "Yes, we'll have to forget about eating out for a while. Even fast food is expensive. What ways can we have more fun at mealtime?"

- Praise helpful attitudes and behavior. "I overheard you tell your brother that we should not go to the movies but wait until the movie comes out in video. That was a great idea on saving money. It must make you feel good knowing you can be patient."

- **EMPATHIZE** when children desire things they can't have because of finances. "I know it was hard when most of the other kids bought their food during the class trip while you had to pack a lunch."

- Reassure an overly concerned child. "I notice you yell at your brother when he wants to buy things we can't afford. You seem extra worried. Dad and I know what we can and cannot afford. Eventually we'll have more money, so you don't have to feel responsible for your brother."

- Reassure a child if you suspect she blames herself for the financial problems. "It is absolutely not your fault that we have less money to spend. In fact, I'd give up all the money in the world if I had to just to keep you. We don't have money because I lost my job. I hope to get another one soon."

How Not to Say It

- "We could lose the house. Is that what you want to happen?" Don't make the kids feel responsible if you have to sell a house or car. Children who cooperate with being frugal still *want* more things. That's to be expected. Praise them for their help and reassure them that the family will survive even if you have to move.

- "If Dad doesn't find the right job, we'll have to sell the house and move into an apartment." Children don't need to worry about that possibility. They can be told if it seems likely that such a thing will happen, but not before.

- "No, you can't have that cereal. It's a name brand, and it's too expensive. How many times do I have to tell you that!" Actually, if you're doing your job right, some younger children may forget that the family is in a financial squeeze. Gentle reminders and a little empathy will achieve your goal. "I wish we could buy that cereal. I know you like it. But see the price? It costs two dollars more than this brand. We have to save money."

53

Moving

"South Dakota?" asked eleven-year-old Scott. "Who do we know who lives in South Dakota?"

"We don't know anybody yet," his mother said. "But that's where my job offer came from and it's too good to pass up. You know I've tried for over a year to find a job nearby so we wouldn't have to move."

"I'm not going," Scott said.

"Scott—"

"I'm not going!"

Millions of children move every year to a new home, often to a new town or state. That means leaving behind friends, classmates, and the familiar neighborhood and venturing toward the unknown. For some kids it's an exciting adventure; for others it's an adventure laced with bittersweet feelings. A few kids are miserable, but they adjust.

Things to Consider

➤ The older the child, the more likely you will meet with resistance. Preteens are forming strong bonds with friends and may be unhappy about leaving them behind.

➤ Children who cope the best during difficult transitions tend to be more self-confident and have a close, supportive family. The adjustment will be longer if a family relocates because of a divorce, if a child is not close to a parent, or if a child feels insecure.

➤ Let the children be as involved in the house hunting as possible. Their excitement may increase when they see a large backyard or a driveway big enough to play hockey.

➤ What is your attitude toward the move? If you are reluctant or over-anxious, your children will have a harder time adjusting.

How to Say It

- Unless your children really do have a say in the decision to move, it's best to state that the move will happen instead of suggesting that it might happen. They will want to know why. "Mom and I decided we need a bigger house, and we'd like to live closer to my job. We're going to start looking soon. What kind of house would you like?"

- "My company is transferring me. We have to move to another state. Dad and I decided it is best for the family if I stay with my company."

- **EMPATHIZE** without trying to persuade your child to go along with the decision. If the kids have no choice but to go along with the decision, at least help them to know you understand their feelings. "You're telling me you don't like the idea of moving. Moving can be upsetting to some people. What don't you like about it?"

- "You're going to miss your friends. I can understand that. It's sad to leave friends behind. I'll miss my friends, too."

- "This is the only house you've known. I can see why you want to stay. I have many happy memories here."

- **NEGOTIATE**—not as a means of cajoling your children into liking the decision to move (they may not like it for a long while) but to give them some choices at a time when they are feeling powerless. "Do you want your own bedroom or bathroom? Does it matter if we have a swimming pool or not? Put your ideas together and Mom and I will see what we can do to make that happen. Of course, we may not be able to afford everything, but we'll do our best."

- **ENCOURAGE.** Remind them of past times when they adjusted to new things. "I remember when you graduated from fifth grade and went to a middle school. There were many new kids and teachers you didn't know, and you weren't very happy. But then you started to get used to it and now it feels comfortable."

- State what you are looking forward to. "The area we will be moving to is so pretty. I can't wait to see the mountains from our kitchen window."

- After you've empathized, it's okay to start making suggestions as to how the kids will adjust better. "We can look for a school that has a good drama club. I know that means a lot to you."
- Expect to repeat yourself if the kids are reluctant to move. They may ask "why" many times and try to talk you out of your decision. After you've given them an explanation two or three times, any more attempts to explain won't help. It is better to empathize and let them know that the decision is final. "You keep asking me why we have to move, so I know you really don't like the idea. It is a big change and will take some adjusting, but we will move. I know I can't say anything now to make you feel better."

How Not to Say It

- "I know you're upset but the new place will be wonderful!" You've made two mistakes. First, telling a child that you know he is upset and then rushing to change feelings is not empathy. Your child may not believe you really do understand how he feels. It is better to have your child talk more about why he is upset. Second, be careful about oversell. Is the place really wonderful? Emphasize the good points without overdoing it.
- "Look, I don't like this any more than you do, but we have no choice." If you can't find a way to be optimistic, don't expect your children to be. If you are unhappy, it is better to say, "I know exactly how you feel. I wish I didn't get transferred, either. But I know I will get used to it, and I know I will be happy there eventually."
- "We've been in the new house for a month and you're still moping around. I don't think you're even trying to like this place." Moping is just another way of complaining. Two things can help. First, putting him in touch with old friends by phone or e-mail (or even a visit to the old neighborhood, if feasible) can be a big mood lifter. Second, give him permission to mope. "I know you are still sad and frustrated that we had to move. It's okay if you want to walk around in a grumpy mood. I understand."

Making just one new friend and discovering that ties to old friends or classmates do not have to be completely severed will start to make moods improve.

54

Nagging

"I don't nag," Madge said. "I mean, I try not to. It usually starts out as a gentle reminder like 'Jason, sweetheart, don't forget your trombone. You have band practice today.' Then something happens. I repeat myself, and when Jason doesn't seem to be paying close attention, I speak louder and spread out my vowels like some opera singer. *Jaaaayyy-suuhn!'* Before I realize it, my eyes scrunch and my lower lip curls, and the next thing you know I'm a creature from a Steven King novel—all because of a trombone. Is there a cure?"

Nagging is an outgrowth of a parent's natural tendency to repeat him- or herself because of a child's natural tendency to ignore anything that doesn't have to do with eating, playing, or video games. It is also illusory. Nagging gives parents the impression that they are doing something important, but in reality they are accomplishing very little. (Sort of like being vice president of the country.)

Things to Consider

➤ Under stress, parents nag more. Nagging may be frustration toward another that is being displaced onto a child.

➤ If affection and quality time with a spouse is less than it should be, parents may nag more.

➤ Someone who frequently nags has underlying feelings of being less in control of their life than they should be.

➤ Is your spouse also guilty of what you nag your children about? (For example, do you nag your kids to pick up their clothes, and do so loud enough so your sloppy spouse overhears?) If so, you'd do better to work things out with your mate first.

How to Say It

- **DO'S & DON'TS.** Make your kids an offer they can't refuse. Tell them what you want done and when, and (most important) tell them what the consequences will be if they don't comply. Be calm and cool.

  "Your trombone is next to your book bag. Please remember to take it. But if you forget again, you'll have to do without it today. I won't bring it to school for you."

  "You can snack while watching television in the family room, but if I have to pick up the leftovers again when your show is over, you will eat only at the dining room table for the next two days. Thanks."

  "Wake up. This is your last warning. If you miss the bus, you'll have to pay me the cost of gas for the mileage. Now what can I get you for breakfast?"

  "I've been asking you to get your dirty clothes together so I can do laundry. At the commercial I'm turning off the TV, and I won't turn it back on until you get your clothes. Thanks. Any questions?"

  As you can see, the tone is not forceful or accusatory. When you are willing to apply consequences, then you don't have to nag. Let the consequences motivate your child, not your voice's decibel level.

- Praise compliance. "I asked you to set the table, and you did it right away. What a help you are."

How Not to Say It

- "How many times do I have to tell you . . ." That's nagging. It isn't necessary if you calmly apply consequences when the kids don't comply. However, you must be willing to let certain consequences happen. Will you allow your child to get a lower grade if he hands in homework late? (Or would you rather nag at him to get it in on time?)

- "If you had put your clothes in the hamper instead of on the floor, then your favorite shirt would be washed now and you could wear it. I tried to warn you." Let the natural consequences (in this case, no clean shirt to wear) do most of the speaking for you. There is no need to rub it in. It is better to say, "I wish you had a clean shirt to wear, too. If you want to try washing it now, you can."

- "After all I do for you kids, you can't even tidy up when I ask you." Your sentiment is understandable, but your words won't have anything but a short-term effect. Kids who delay following orders have learned that they can get away with it.

Smart Talk

In a study at Ohio State University of children in sixth, eighth, and tenth grades, parents and their kids were asked how frequently the children complied with helping tasks and how often they showed affection. The results showed that preteens and adolescents responded more positively when they felt more supported and connected to their parents. Girls were more helpful and affectionate than boys, and kids complied with moms more than dads. The better the connection to your kids, the less you will have to nag.

55

New Baby

Carol explained to the pediatrician how her six-year-old son, Tyler, seemed to whine for attention whenever she was feeding the new baby.

"I hope he gets over it," Carol said.

The pediatrician smiled. "Did Tyler ever try to get your attention when you were sitting and talking on the phone or with company?"

"Oh, sure," Carol said.

"So it isn't just the new baby. Tyler simply wants Mommy. It's pretty normal for children to feel that way, at least once in a while."

And so it is. Jealousy isn't fatal and it often is less of a problem for older children. Still, even when kids can't wait for the new baby brother or sister, there will be moments when they wished the stork plopped the bundle of joy somewhere else.

Things to Consider

➤ Older children may show their frustration at having less time with busy new parents by either withdrawing or acting passive-aggressively. They may get sloppier, more forgetful, or less reliable, thereby forcing parents to pay more attention to them.

➤ Having older children care for the baby (a nine-year-old can change diapers and assist with baths, for example) can help them bond—*if* the chore does not disgust them. Younger kids will want to help out but obviously require supervision.

➤ Children automatically seem older and more mature compared to an infant. But they are still kids, not mini-adults.

➤ In a blended family, a new baby can often unite the stepsiblings. They now have something in common—a little brother or sister who is genetically connected to them.

➤ In a blended family, a new baby might compel kids to give up their hopes of a parental reunion. A recent study showed that fathers who remarry pull away from their children from their first marriage if their new wife gives birth. Men seem to devote time to the "stable" family, but not the previous family. Don't let that happen.

➤ Some fathers worry more about finances after a baby arrives, and they spend more hours working. Now their older children see even less of their father, plus they have to share him with the newborn. Dads need to remember that their true worth is not their presents but their presence.

➤ Whenever appropriate, let the children be involved during the pregnancy; let them watch the sonogram, pick out supplies, etc.

How to Say It

- Older kids can be told as soon as a pregnancy becomes obvious. Enthusiasm and a willingness to let your children's feelings matter are the key attitudes. "Yes, we are having a new baby. I'm very excited. The baby should be born in March."

- TEACH how to handle frustrations by pretending the baby is already there. "Okay, Lynn, you pretend you are the baby, and Richie, you be yourself. Richie, make believe you are upset that I am spending all my time with Lynn. What can you say to me?"

- Praise your child for speaking up instead of acting out. "I like it when you tell me to spend more time with you. Then we can figure out a way to make it happen."

- Praise age-appropriate behavior. "You had to wait patiently before I could drive you to the game because the baby needed to be changed again. That's so helpful."

- ENCOURAGE speaking up by making sure it is rewarded with your time whenever possible. Otherwise, your child will learn that the surest way to get your attention is to act up. "I have about five minutes left to feed the baby. Then I'll put her down for a nap. What would you like to do together then?"

- **EMPATHIZE** when you cannot give your child the attention he wants. "I promised I'd be finished in five minutes, but the baby is cranky and won't sleep. That must be annoying to you."
- "Some older kids worry that their parents love the new baby more than they love them. Do you ever feel that way?"
- **NEGOTIATE.** "I've been so busy with the baby. What things could we do together that would make you feel better?"
- **DO'S & DON'TS.** Explain that babies require three basic things and that you must provide them. "Babies need ABC. A is for affection. Babies need to be held a lot. Otherwise, they can feel scared or get sick. B is for bottle. When a baby is hungry, he needs to be fed. He's not as capable as you are to wait for food. C is for change diapers. They need their diapers changed a lot because they can't use the toilet like you. Most of my time with the baby is spent doing those three things."
- Discuss the benefits of being an older child. "You're lucky. When you feel hungry, you can eat an apple or make a bowl of cereal. The baby has to wait for me to feed him."

How Not to Say It

- "You will love having a new baby brother. . . . I'm sure you'll be the best older sister around." That sounds nice, but it's better to let your child convey her own feelings instead of your presuming what they are.
- "You don't need all my attention; you just think you do." If he thinks he needs it, he needs it. Resist the temptation to view your older child as being more mature than he is.
- "You shouldn't say that about your baby sister!" If your child doesn't express his feelings, he will act them out. Do you have a preference? Criticizing a child for how he feels will make him feel even less important to you, and he will resent the baby even more. Empathize. "Calling your sister ugly makes me think you feel sad about something. Maybe you feel we love her more than we love you."
- "Act your age!" Actually, since regression is normal, your child is acting his age. He believes that if you act younger, you get more love and attention, and if you act your age, you get less. Once again, **EMPATHIZE** first, and then find ways to reward him for age-appropriate behavior. I know you're tired, but the best reward is your time.

Rule of Thumb: When a couple with stepchildren decides to have a baby, anxieties can be even higher. Parents may fear they will love the baby more than their stepchildren, and the stepchildren will fear the same thing. It is a good idea to announce the event privately to your biological child. That way, your child may feel more able to open up without feeling too self-conscious.

56

New Stepsibling

Put yourself in your child's shoes. First came the divorce. If your child was like most kids, he wasn't happy about it. Second was the parent's new girlfriend or boyfriend. That might be exciting or distressing, it all depends. Next came the announcement: "I'm getting remarried. Sally's two little boys will be living with me, so when you visit, you'll have two new friends."

When a divorce happens, kids lose control and consistency in their life. They had no control over the separation and no control over the new mate. But when it comes to the new stepsibling, it's a new ball game. It can be easier to fight against a stepsib than to fight the adults.

Things to Consider

➤ If you live with your stepchildren but see your biological children only on a scheduled basis, expect that your biological kids may feel jealous.

➤ Stepkids can easily displace bad feelings onto one another. They might also connect in a common bond.

How to Say It

- Discuss the upcoming first meeting ahead of time. Maybe show photos or have the kids write each other a letter of introduction. The more unknowns, the higher the anxiety. "His name is Matt. He's two years older than you and likes to play hockey. His father says he is a nice boy and easy to get along with. Here's his picture. Tell me your thoughts about meeting him."

- **EMPATHIZE** and accept the feelings. "You seem worried that you two might not get along" or "You worry that you are outnumbered and that they won't like you" or "You seem excited that Freddie trades baseball cards, too" or "You seem concerned that when you visit me, you'll be expected to spend more time with the kids than with me."

- **REPORT** your expectations. "I don't expect you and Megan to become best friends, though I hope you learn to really like each other. I do expect you guys to try to get along, just like you would with classmates."

- "Since Charlie is my new stepson, his mom and I agreed that if he misbehaves, she will be the disciplinarian. And I will discipline you. So if it looks as if I'm harder on you than on Charlie, I'm just doing what I agreed to do. What are your thoughts?"

- **ENCOURAGE** and praise cooperative behavior. "We all had a nice day together. It was especially nice watching you and your stepbrother get along so well. I give you a lot of credit."

How Not to Say It

- "How do you think it makes your stepmother feel when you fight with your stepsister?" Empathy training is a good idea but might best be saved for after you hear your child's concerns. Also, be sure your child really likes the stepparent; otherwise, he may not be interested in how she feels.

- "You guys have a lot in common. I'm sure you'll get along." Pointing out similarities is fine, but don't presume they will get along. Instead, leave room for the relationship to grow. It's better to say, "You guys have a lot in common. That might make your time together more enjoyable."

- "Your stepbrother obeyed us on the trip. Why couldn't you do that?" Don't make comparisons.

- "Of course you have to share your room. What else do you expect us to do?" Room sharing may be necessary. Don't add unnecessary resentment by failing to **EMPATHIZE** while you are being clear about the **DO'S & DON'TS**. "Yes, you will have to share a room. There is no other way. It's obvious you don't like that idea and I don't blame you. You can choose where you want the beds to go."

- "We're a bigger family now, and we'll do things together as a family." Carve out some time alone with your biological child.

57

Increasing Optimism

Jared and Kenny looked forward to receiving their new musical instruments for school band. They had each carefully considered which instrument they thought would be fun to play, and now they had arrived. Kenny chose the violin; Jared, the saxophone. Three weeks later Kenny was dutifully practicing his instrument, but Jared had all but given up.

"It's too hard," he complained.

"But you haven't tried for very long," his mother said. "It takes time."

"I did try, but when I blow into it, the sound that comes out isn't the right one. It doesn't even sound like a saxophone."

Mom was able to get Jared to practice that day, but his interest was not there. Maybe the saxophone wasn't the right instrument for him. Maybe she was expecting too much. Or maybe there was something else at the root of the problem. Come to think of it, Jared had a "why bother?" attitude about many things.

Things to Consider

➤ Optimism or a positive outlook in life requires a person to believe that resources are available to make things turn out okay. Resources may be within oneself (such as talent and motivation), or they may originate from outside (such as believing that parents or caretakers or God are looking out for you).

➤ Optimistic kids view themselves as capable and the world as reasonably safe. Thus, if they fail a test or if a friend betrays them, the setback is temporary. They believe they are still worthwhile and competent even if events turn out poorly.

➤ Optimists persevere. Pessimists quit at the early signs of difficulty because they haven't the faith in their effort. Quitting then results in failure that perpetuates the pessimistic outlook.

➤ Shy or highly active children may be more prone to pessimistic thinking because they cannot act in their world as successfully as kids more outgoing and patient.

➤ Pessimism and optimism can be learned by watching Mom and Dad.

How to Say It

- The essential ingredient to an optimistic outlook is faith that effort will more often than not result in progress or success and that all problems or setbacks are temporary. **TEACH** by giving examples a child will understand. "Do you remember when I wallpapered your room? I had to learn as I went along. It was frustrating and I made a lot of mistakes, but when I wallpaper your sister's room, I'll know better what to do."

- "When you helped train Fritz to sit and roll over, it took him a while to learn. But we all kept at it, and eventually he did learn."

- "Remember I kept throwing you ground balls so you could improve your ability? At first I threw the ball slowly, then I threw it harder and harder as you got more skilled. Hard work and effort paid off."

- **EMPATHIZE** to be sure you understand the extent of your child's concerns, then **TEACH** problem solving. "You don't want to audition for the school play because you don't think you'll get a part. But you seem sad about that, as though you wish you could get a part. You're right that auditioning is tough because there are more kids than there are parts in the play. Let's try to think of three reasons that auditioning is valuable even if a person doesn't get a role."

- "Ever since your mom and I separated, it seems to you that only bad things will happen in the future. I know that the separation was something that made you sad. That's normal. But what are some things you can trust will happen that you look forward to?"

- Give examples of how all problems are temporary. "When Grandma died, it was very hard for Grandpa to live all by himself. Even though there was no way Grandma could come back, there were many ways we could help Grandpa. That is why he spends a lot more time visiting your cousins and us. He still misses Grandma, but he's not as lonely as he was."

- "When I was out of work, we had a hard time paying our bills. While my new job doesn't pay me as much money as before, we have learned how to get by on less. We solved our problem."
- ENCOURAGE persistence and optimism. "You worked so hard on that school science project. Every week you would get more and more accomplished, and now it is finished. You should feel very proud."
- "When you first tried the pogo stick, you couldn't do it well. Now you can stay on it for ten minutes! Wow!"

Smart Talk

Researchers studied fourth, fifth, and sixth graders who had experienced at least four major stresses since birth (such as poverty or divorce). Some seemed resilient, able to bounce back and cope effectively with daily life, while others seemed to struggle. A key difference was outlook. Optimistic thinkers reported feeling less stress overall and less depression, and they felt more competent. When outside stress was high, those kids with positive expectations about the future did not think of themselves in a negative light even when they faltered.

How Not to Say It

- "Cheer up!" Telling a child he should feel better when he clearly feels depressed or cynical won't help. He'll just think you don't understand. Positive phrases should be saved for after you have empathized and given examples of past successes or reasons for optimism.
- "You can do it!" This is fine for a child who already believes in herself and just needs a pep talk. But if your child shows signs of pessimism, it's better to understand first her reasons for thinking that way and then gently remind her of past successes she is overlooking. Pessimists have distorted thinking. They ignore positive evidence and hone in on evidence that supports their negative outlook. They have to be shown over and over that they can do it, not just be told.

- "You have a bad attitude. You don't see other kids quitting this soon, do you?" Your negativity is showing. It doesn't sound as if you have as much faith in your child. It is better to let her know that her attitude makes some sense but is not helpful. Remind her of past efforts that succeeded and let her know you have confidence in her ability to try hard.
- "Why do you have to be so negative? Can't you look at the bright side?" These questions are not helpful to kids. They may be unable to figure out why. Or if they can come up with reasons, you have just prodded them to defend their style of thinking, not change it.

58

Parental Emotional Problems: Depression, Fears, Compulsions

Tammy's mom has obsessive-compulsive disorder. Her fear of germs is so strong that she washes her hands forty or more times a day. Sometimes she won't attend Tammy's ball games for fear of contamination.

Lyle's dad is severely depressed. He has just returned to work after a six-week leave and is feeling better. Still, he gets little enjoyment from things, never horses around with the kids, and seems tired and unmotivated.

Hilary's mom gets panic attacks. She is so frightened of them that she has stopped driving for fear she will get into an accident while panicking. Hilary can't understand why her mom won't go places with her anymore.

Right now 15 percent to 20 percent of the population suffer from depression or an anxiety disorder. The good news is they can be treated. But until a person has made significant improvements, their emotional problems can be a strain on them and their family.

Things to Consider

➤ In most cases, the problem can go away. In some, the problem may persist but be manageable.

➤ Once aware that something isn't right, children need to be educated as to the nature of the problem and the effects it will have on their life. They need to be reminded that it is not their fault and that in all likelihood the situation will improve.

➤ These problems are not cured by willpower. People suffering from depression or severe anxiety wish they were not feeling that way.

➤ Provide as much consistency in your child's life as possible. Regular mealtimes, favorite TV shows, bedtime stories, etc., offer comfort and reassurance that all is basically the same.

How to Say It

- **TEACH.** Explain the disorder in simple terms. "Just as some people are afraid of spiders and get really scared, your mom gets really afraid of germs, so she washes her hands too much. She realizes she shouldn't feel that way, but right now she can't help it. She is seeing a doctor to help her get over this problem, though."

- "Severe depression is more than feeling sad. The person gets no pleasure from anything and begins to feel as if nothing will help. It can take a few months sometimes to improve, but medications help a lot."

- Establish a plan of how the family will contend with the problem. "If your dad had a broken leg instead of depression, we wouldn't expect him to do all the things he usually does. Until he feels better, I'll need a little more help around the house. Is there some chore you'd be willing to do?"

- Reassure the child that matters will improve and she is not at fault. "Dad is not depressed because he's tired of being a father. His depression has nothing to do with you. There is a chemical in his body that he needs more of to feel better. The medicine is helping with that. He will definitely feel better. It just takes a little time."

- "You are not bothering Mommy with your problems. She wants to do things for you. She just can't right now. It's okay to ask her for things, but understand she may have to say no sometimes."

- Forewarn kids to upcoming changes in their routine. If they know what to expect, they have time to prepare. "Dad will be seeing a doctor called a therapist who will help Dad with his problem. In fact, we will all go together some times so we can all talk about what is happening and get our questions answered."

- **EMPATHIZE** with a child's feelings. Then offer **ENCOURAGEMENT.** "You worry that Mommy will never get better. A lot of kids might worry like that. But Mommy's problem is one that will get better."

- "You seem a little embarrassed when your friends come over and ask why your dad is not working. That's okay. It's no big deal to tell them he isn't feeling well but hopes to be better soon."

- "You're angry that we can't go on vacation this year because Mom isn't up to it. I'm disappointed, too. Can you help think of fun things we can do as a family when Mom feels better?"

Rule of Thumb: Talking matter-of-factly about the problem and how it might affect each person in the family will probably increase emotional closeness and overall family communication.

How Not to Say It

- "Nothing's wrong." If it is becoming obvious that something is wrong, tell the kids. Otherwise, they will be confused.

- "Stop doing that! Don't you understand your father's depressed?" If the kids are making a disturbance, a simple request to stop may suffice. If they persist, their behavior may be a sign of their own emotional insecurity about the parent's problem. If so, it is better to take them aside and inquire how they are feeling about the situation.

- "If you kids would stop fighting, maybe your mother wouldn't be under so much stress." Don't suggest that your children are in any way to blame for the problem.

- "Sometimes I just want to scream!" You're entitled to feel overwhelmed, but showing that to your kids will make them more anxious and perhaps afraid to speak up about their own concerns. If you say or do something you regret, let the kids know you made a mistake. "When I said 'I want to scream!' I guess I was feeling frustrated that things aren't better yet. But the truth is we have a lot to be thankful for despite the problem. Next time I'll try to simply say that I wish things were all better."

59

Parental Emotional Problems: Addictions and Bad Temper

Krysta couldn't think of a good enough excuse to prevent her neighbor and classmate Amy from coming to her house after school.

"I just want to stay fifteen minutes," Amy said. "My mom isn't home yet."

Krysta's heart started to pound. What if her father was drunk? His car was in the driveway. She imagined him sitting in front of the TV with a drink in his hand, swearing at the sports commentator. She arrived at the front door, took a deep breath, and opened it. . . .

While addictions and even severe problems with one's temper are listed as actual disorders, they tend to be problems that the person denies he has. Or else he admits to the problem but minimizes its negative impact and tends to blame others for making it necessary for him to do those things. Unlike disorders such as depression or phobias, an addict or a "rage-aholic" often will not seek treatment, so it is hard for family members to remain supportive and optimistic that the situation will improve. What do you say to a child whose parent has a serious disorder such as alcoholism, drug addiction, or gambling but who refuses to get the kind of help needed?

Things to Consider

➤ If you are the nonaddicted parent, the effectiveness of anything you say to your kids will depend on the extent you feel helpless or angry. The more you must submit to your spouse's ways, the more hopeless you feel; or the more resentful you are, the more your communications will have a neutral effect at best. More likely you will say the wrong thing and add tension and misery to an already difficult situation.

➤ If your partner is not getting help, you must. Seek out a therapist or try organizations such as Al-Anon. They can give you a sense of influence over your life. You need to feel empowered, not helpless.

➤ Divorce or separation is scary and a sad outcome for any marriage that once had promise. If your partner refuses help, you must weigh the impact on your family of divorce versus remaining together. Since you cannot change your partner's behavior, you must decide what you can and will tolerate.

How to Say It

- **TEACH** about the disease/disorder. "Your mother has alcoholism. She cannot control her drinking. She gets drunk and is unable to care for us the way we want."

  "Your dad has a very quick temper. He doesn't like it when he loses his temper but he has a hard time controlling it."

  "Your father is addicted to gambling. He has a strong urge to gamble our money and he cannot control it. That is what you have heard us fighting about."

  "Addictions make people have mood swings. Some days your mom will feel happy and other days she'll be angry and miserable. It's not your fault on those days. You aren't making her feel bad, her addiction is."

- Give practical advice. "If your dad is drinking . . . [If we are arguing . . . , If Dad's temper is getting out of hand . . .], leave the room and go to a neighbor's house. Call before you come home to see if it's a good time. You should not have to put up with this behavior."

- **EMPATHIZE.** This is essential not just for your child but for you. Empathy requires that you not deny a problem exists. Unfortunately, spouses of addicts often have their own level of denial. It can be easier to minimize a problem than face it. "It embarrasses you when you come from school with friends and your mother is asleep on the couch with beer bottles next to her. I don't blame you for feeling that way. It probably makes you feel sad, too."

  "It's scary listening to Mom and Dad fight all the time about gambling."

  "You worry that things will always stay this way."

  "Your father could get help, but he won't. Part of the disease is that he believes he doesn't have a problem. It's frustrating, isn't it?"

"Your father admitted he drinks too much, but he refuses to get help. That is his problem. I know you worry about him when he drives a car."

- Some children will try to be perfect and well behaved when they live in a dysfunctional family. They do this so as not to add more stress to an overstressed situation. However, don't mistake their good behavior (high grades in school, never in trouble, overly responsible) for healthy adjustment. They are hurting inside but won't let others know. "You are doing so well in school despite our problems. Sometimes I think you are sad inside but don't want to talk about it."

- Don't play into denial by making the problem a secret to outsiders. "You feel embarrassed that Mom gambles. It's okay to tell your friends about it. Your friends might find ways to help you feel better."

- Clarify expectations. "If your father won't get help by next week, I have plans for us to get a separation. I will not allow things to continue the way they have been."

- "Your dad's temper is too much for me. I'll be speaking to a therapist—a doctor who will help me decide what I can do to help you and me handle the situation better."

- ENCOURAGE normal, healthy activities. Praise when appropriate. Kids with addicted parents often suffer poor esteem. "I want you to take swimming lessons. I know you love swimming and are so good. I'm proud of what you've accomplished."

- ENCOURAGE talking to you about their worries. "Dad won't listen to your concerns. I'm sorry. I wish he would, but he can't. However, I can listen and will do my best to help you and me get through these hard times."

- As much as possible, smile, laugh, and have fun with your kids. They need the relief.

How Not to Say It

- "The person with the problem is your mother. Maybe if you talk to her, she will take her problems seriously." Children should not bear that responsibility. If the addicted parent or the one with the bad temper is not getting needed help, the other parent must take steps to protect the kids even if that means separating.

- "If we are all patient, things will improve someday." Don't kid your-self. Until the addict wants help, it won't occur. Your patience may show him that his intolerable behavior is tolerable. It is better to say the truth: "There is nothing we can do to solve Daddy's problem. We can be patient and loving and we can complain, but nothing we do will help. Only Daddy can get help when he decides."

- "Maybe I'll get a divorce." A divorce may be the natural consequence, but it is best to tell a child when you are pretty sure it will happen and happen soon. Don't leave your child hanging.

- "Don't complain about your father. How many times have I told you that I can't do anything about his problem?" You are angry with your child because her comments are revealing your own helplessness. A child who stops complaining isn't showing healthy adaptation. Your child may be going numb or learning that her feelings don't matter to either of her parents. Then you can expect acting out (mischief, petty crimes, poor school performance) or acting in (depression, self-criticism). At all times keep the lines of communication open even if you've heard the concerns before.

- "If she really loved you, she'd get the help she needs." It is only after they have been sober a while that addicts realize how hurtful their behaviors have been.

- "Your father loves you very, very much." If the addicted parent is not showing much love, don't try to persuade a child he is loved very much. It is too confusing. It is better to say that your child deserves to be shown love because he is a good and wonderful child.

- "How dare you tell the teacher!" Stop the secrecy. Outsiders need to know, especially a child's teachers. If they know what is happening at home, they can try to intervene so your child will have additional emotional support.

Rule of Thumb: Healthy adaptation to an addicted parent is not one of accommodation. Patience and understanding are necessary but not tolerating the status quo. Well-meaning spouses "enable" pathological behavior by tolerating it over time. By not tolerating the behavior, the person will get the help he or she needs, or the family may need to break up.

60

Peer Pressure

Craig attended seventh grade in a parochial school where uniforms were required. The children were allowed to wear shorts as part of their uniform until November. In late October, despite morning temperatures that were at freezing, Craig waited at the bus stop wearing shorts. Why? "Because most of the other kids are still wearing them," he said.

Ellen was in Craig's class. She is one of the 19 percent of seventh-grade students who admit to having engaged in sexual intercourse at least one time (according to a 1992 survey of students in Cedar Rapids, Iowa).

Anthony, age eleven, wants an earring, bleached blond hair, and a colorful underwear waistband that peeks out over his baggy pants—just like his new friend, Rich.

The influence of peers on growing children's attitudes and actions cannot be overlooked.

Things to Consider

➤ Preteens and adolescents improve their self-image by conforming to some peer group standards. With luck, those standards aren't so outrageous that parents will faint.

➤ At the same time, kids need to carve out a unique sense of themselves. Going along with new fads and trends is really a young adolescent's way of discovering who he is and new facets of his personality. It helps when parents don't overreact.

➤ Don't underestimate the impact of your values on your developing child. The majority of older kids and teens want to come to their parents to discuss problems and issues. Your opinions and values do count. (It just won't seem like it.)

➤ The goal is to help your child be confident enough to do what is right despite what his peers are doing.

➤ Do you cave into peer pressure because you want to be accepted by a group or don't want to displease others? Do you sometimes do things you shouldn't (speed, eat the wrong foods, swear in front of your kids while talking to friends, etc.) and comment that it's not a big deal because most people do it?

How to Say It

- **TEACH** about peer pressure but don't lecture. Examples from your life might be more interesting and useful. "A bunch of my friends had this pack of cigarettes and started smoking. They wanted me to try. I did take a puff, but I felt funny doing something I knew I shouldn't, so I stopped there. My friends teased me for a while, but then they stopped."

- "It's easy to go along with a crowd. The harder thing is to do what's right even when everyone else says it's okay to do what is wrong."

- **TEACH** ways to say no. "When your friends want you to do something you know is wrong, tell them 'I don't want to' or 'That has no interest to me,' and then walk away."

- **EMPATHIZE** with the need to feel like part of the crowd. "Everyone wants to feel accepted by a group of friends. It can feel awful when it seems as though you don't fit in."

- "Kids who say no to their friends and are able to resist pressure to do bad things feel a little unsure of themselves at first. But eventually they realize they are doing the right thing."

- **DO'S & DON'TS.** Now is the time to make clear to your children what you want or don't want them to do. The dilemma is how to state your view in a way that won't cause them to refuse to discuss the issue later on. You always want them to come to you with their concerns. "I'd be failing my job as a parent if I gave you the impression that drinking is okay. It is not. You are too young. But I'd also be failing my job as a parent if I made you feel afraid to talk to me when you feel pressured to follow the crowd."

- **ENCOURAGE** independent thinking. "In situations where friends are pressuring you, ask yourself: Is it illegal? Is it dishonest? Is it mean? Then decide for yourself whether you want to be someone who does those things."

How Not to Say It

- "I don't like the looks of your friend." Your growing child may not respect your making snap judgments on appearances only. Have the friend over and get to know her. You'll have more information to support or disprove your original view.

- "Why do you have to do things just because everyone else does?" You are coming dangerously close to repeating what parents of every generation have said: "If your friend jumped off a bridge, would you jump in after him?" What you want to do is get your child to realize he can be an independent thinker without alienating him. Questions like the above are accusatory and off-putting. Say something empathic like "It seems important to you to do exactly what others in your class are doing." You are planting a seed and opening the door for more communication later.

- "Don't you have a mind of your own?" Besides being harsh and critical, this comment is paradoxical. What you are really saying is "If you do what I want you to do, then you have a mind of your own. If you do what your friends want, you don't have a mind of your own."

- "Someone at your school got suspended for smoking pot? Good. Don't ever let me catch you smoking pot, or you'll never forget it." It is essential to be clear about your values, but you also want to be approachable.

61

Perfectionism

Sandy sat at the dining room table in tears. She'd been drawing a picture to give to her grandmother, and she made a small mistake. "It's no good," she cried. "I have to do it over again."

Sandy also had a nervous stomach. While she was a straight-A student, school made her uneasy because she always worried she might not get a high score on any of her tests. School projects often became a nightmare for her. She'd redo them until she felt they were perfect, but that meant she was still at work on them the night before they were due.

Things to Consider

➤ Perfectionistic kids (and adults) tend to be worriers. They worry about things that could go wrong, they worry about failure, and they worry about their parents. They look at negative possibilities and turn them into likely probabilities.

➤ Perfectionism is a misguided way to control anxiety and worry. A perfectionist tries to make his life perfect as a way to feel good.

➤ Perfectionists tend to be self-critical. Since they are imperfect and make mistakes, they judge themselves harshly. Helping a child to be less of a perfectionist takes time. (Parents, don't be too hard on yourselves if your efforts don't bring quick changes.)

➤ Certain parenting styles can contribute to perfectionism in kids. Parents who are overly strict and who believe that children must prove themselves worthy of love can prompt some kids to become perfectionists.

➤ In dysfunctional families such as those where at least one parent is alcoholic, one of the children (often the eldest) tends to "grow up early" and take on added responsibilities. These children often try to keep the household peaceful. They try to be overly good and helpful, and can develop perfectionistic tendencies. They won't change unless the parental problems improve.

How to Say It

- **TEACH** a child to deal with uncertainties by thinking rationally. Have your child say aloud during tasks such reassuring comments as "I'd like to get a perfect score, but it isn't terrible if I don't," "It's okay to make mistakes; everybody does," "I can do my best without having to be perfect," and "My parents love me no matter what."

- Use this analogy: "You've heard of guard dogs that protect their owners by barking at everybody, even friendly people. The guard dog worries too much. The part of you that worries is like a guard dog that barks. We want to train that worry part of you to worry (bark) less."

- Since perfectionists tend to do tasks at the last minute, help your child structure his time so that certain school projects are completed early. Resist the temptation to let your child check and recheck his work. "Your science report is due in three weeks. Let's figure out a schedule that will help you finish your report in two weeks."

- Offer **ENCOURAGEMENT** by pointing out the many worries that don't come true. "You worry that Daddy will get hurt, but he comes home from work every day and isn't hurt." "You worry that we will be mad at you if you don't get an A. Guess what? We're not mad at you, and we want you to enjoy doing your work."

- Identify tasks your child does where she is not a perfectionist (certain games, playing with dolls, doing certain chores, etc.). Point out that your child probably enjoys those tasks. "I noticed you weren't trying to play with your toys perfectly. You just had fun. If you don't try to be perfect at school, you might enjoy studying more."

- **REPORT** times when you make mistakes, and show that you can have a positive attitude. "I forgot to pay a bill on time, and now I have to pay a late fee. I'm usually good about paying bills on time, but on this occasion I forgot. No big deal." (You may want to purposely make mistakes—spill something, forget something, etc.—so you can demonstrate an "it's no big deal" attitude.

How Not to Say It

- "I see you spelled three words wrong on your test." Praise the overall grade and don't focus on critical details.
- "Hurry up!" "I'm very disappointed in you." "You know better than that." These phrases inflame perfectionistic tendencies. Watch your language for any signs of urgency, sharp criticism, or fault-finding. It is better to praise desirable behaviors.
- "Damn! I took a wrong turn!" Don't criticize yourself for making common mistakes. Your child will overhear and learn the wrong message.

62

Perseverance

Lee's parents could tell that their son was not enjoying piano lessons. Getting him to practice was an ordeal. They discussed the idea of letting him quit. Why should they force him to do something he hated? On the other hand, they had purchased a piano and had paid for months of lessons. Shouldn't he do his best for the time being?

It is a truism that the most successful people have experienced many failures. They succeed because they persevere. People who give up when the going gets tough have a tendency to develop depression and poor self-confidence, which makes it more likely they will not persist when future tasks become challenging.

If you want your child to persevere, you must be willing to let her fail. Then you must show her how to cope with failure—not by withdrawing from the task but by learning from mistakes and pressing forward. Overprotective parents may try to shield their kids from failure and miss teaching them a valuable lesson. But pushy, ambitious parents won't help their child persevere, either. Such parents are overly critical and value outcome more than effort. Children of these parents learn to fear making mistakes and consequently accept fewer challenges. They play it safe so as to not risk failure and rejection, and never learn how to dust themselves off and persevere.

Things to Consider

➤ Overprotective parents operate from fear. To ensure safety they keep their children from taking appropriate risks or give them permission to give up.

➤ Overly ambitious parents also operate from fear. They fear inadequacy and overcompensate by pushing their kids (and often themselves). They confuse "cracking the whip" with encouragement.

➤ Kids give up trying because they know someone else will do it for them or because they believe they do not have what it takes to succeed. While practicing a skill (such as long division) can enhance perceived competence, a more important skill is coping with frustration and anxiety when things don't go as planned.

➤ Perfectionistic kids won't persevere unless they feel assured they will succeed. They need help learning to see the value of failure and making mistakes.

How to Say It

True self-esteem does not develop from glowing accolades. It emerges from knowing one is truly loved and from succeeding at challenging tasks. Parents first need to examine why a child is not persistent. A good strategy is to identify tasks where the child did persist and find out what made that task different from one where the child gave up.

- "I noticed you kept practicing your flute even when you made mistakes. But you gave up playing basketball. What made it easier for you to practice the flute?"

- **EMPATHIZE.** This is a good way to help your child uncover his reasons for wanting to give up. "You seem frustrated with math. I'm wondering if you don't like it because you don't understand it."

- **DO'S & DON'TS.** If you invested money in an activity that your child really wanted to participate in but now he's showing no interest, you can insist he follow through. "We just bought you a uniform and paid the Little League fee. Now after three games you want to quit. I'm sorry, but you need to play for at least another month. If you need help, I'll be very happy to spend time practicing with you." The goal is not to punish your child, but teach him that his decisions do have consequences and that you won't always bail him out.

- **TEACH** how you persist at tasks despite setbacks. Give examples of famous people. "Even your favorite baseball player strikes out. He gets a hit only one out of three times at bat. What would you think of your favorite player if he quit because he didn't like striking out?"

- **ENCOURAGE**. This is most important. When you see your child correct a mistake or stay with a task that is frustrating, praise him. "You reread the chapter in your history book when you didn't know the answer to the question. When you still couldn't find the answer you looked it up in the encyclopedia. I'm very pleased and impressed. You showed you would not give up even when the task got difficult."
- Praise emotional control. The more agitated a child gets, the less likely she will complete a difficult task. Kids who can learn to control their emotions will persevere. "I saw you get frustrated with your homework. Then you took a break and threw the ball around with the dog before you went back to your work. Good for you. That was very smart to realize you needed a few minutes to enjoy yourself."

How Not to Say It

- "You promised you'd practice the piano if we bought you one. Well, we bought you one, and now you say you are bored. Tough." It may be a good idea to insist that your child follow through on his promise. However, a better approach would be to empathize with his feelings and try to learn underlying reasons why he has changed his mind.
- "Okay, we'll let you quit baseball, but don't expect us to pay for any other sport you want later on." This is unrealistic. Chances are you will oblige him later on. It is better to have consequences for his decision. Maybe he needs to earn back the money you spent on baseball equipment by doing extra chores.
- "Okay, we'll let you quit baseball even though we paid a registration fee. You can play soccer instead. But you'd better not quit that." What will happen if he does quit soccer? Kids will persevere more if they must pay a price for giving up. Perhaps the child could earn money to pay the registration fee.
- "You knew three months ago that your science fair project was due next week. Why are you just starting it now?" Kids procrastinate, at least in part, because the ability to be completely self-directed rarely develops before adolescence. Children need help learning to structure their time wisely. Parents need to be on top of their children's school assignments for that reason.

Smart Talk

Can Intelligence Be Improved?

Regardless of how smart or talented (or less capable) a child is, it is her *belief* of how smart or talented she is that will make a difference in perseverance. "Helpless" children believe that failure is due to lack of ability, so they do not persevere. "Mastery-oriented" children believe that if they keep trying, they can get smarter or succeed on a task. They persevere even when the task is challenging and mistakes are made. Easy success in school is not necessarily a good thing if your child never learns how to handle failure. Poor success is not necessarily a bad omen if the child attributes failure to lack of effort (not studying hard enough, etc.) rather than lack of ability.

Interestingly, a child with a helpless mind-set won't necessarily persevere after some successes. More important for that child is learning to use negative feedback as a message about effort and not a message about ability. If your child gives up easily, point out ways that her effort was low, not her ability, and help her use negative feedback (a poor test grade, etc.) as a clue to changes she can make that will make her smarter. (Students who don't think of themselves as smart but who believe they can become smarter perform much better than they did on previous tests.)

Praise effort lavishly. Praise outcome a little less.

63

Pets

The chant is universal and goes something like this: "If you kids want a dog, then you will have to take responsibility for it. I expect you to make sure it is fed and that you play with it. You'll have to clean up after it, too."

Of course, all kids agree to these conditions until the puppy has lived with them for, oh, two days, and then the kids slack off. What should parents say when the children want a puppy or a kitten or some other pet that requires care and feeding?

Things to Consider

➢ Don't get a pet unless you are prepared to do much, if not most, of the work involved. Yes, some children will eagerly take on the responsibility for pet care, but even they get bored.

➢ Kids can help with pet care and might even be reliable, but chances are they will need reminding.

➢ Research shows that pet ownership improves a child's sense of autonomy (taking care of himself) and self-confidence. This seemed especially true of children nearing adolescence.

➢ Cat owners will disagree, but when it comes to enhancing a child's self-esteem, dogs do the trick more than cats. The reason? Dogs are better able to give the impression that they like their owners.

How to Say It

- Skip the lecture about responsibility. Do make clear any expectations that you intend to truly enforce. "Okay, we can get a dog. But understand that twice a week I will send you into the yard with a pooper-scooper, and you will clean up after the dog—even if it's winter or you're in the middle of your homework."

- **EMPATHIZE** when kids don't want to take on responsibilities they had promised, but state **DO'S & DON'TS** clearly and calmly. "I know you want to ride bikes with your friend, but you promised you would give Pepper a bath before dinner. The hose is all set along with the shampoo. It will take ten minutes. I know you are annoyed, but I appreciate it when you keep your promises."

- Take advantage of opportunities to **TEACH** or **ENCOURAGE** values such as kindness, self-sacrifice, and compassion. "Scamp isn't feeling well after his operation. It's really nice of you to spend all that time petting him and making sure he is comfortable. That shows kindness and compassion."

- "You said it would be okay to stop buying those candy fruit snacks you like so that we could buy Fluffy a new pillow. That is very thoughtful."

How Not to Say It

- "We can get rid of this animal if you don't intend to take care of it." Since kids (and most adults) view pets as part of the family, you might as well be threatening to throw Grandma into the street. Praise appropriate pet care and expect that you might have to do a lot of the work, and you'll do fine.

- "Look at how the puppy chewed up the leg on the chair. Weren't you watching him?" That's what puppies do. Unless you place the puppy in a safer place, expect things to get chewed and don't blame the kids.

- "This isn't my cat, it's your cat." Children cannot take full responsibility for the welfare of a pet. They can help out, but you must be prepared to be the responsible one. Otherwise, it's better not to have the pet in the first place.

64

Concerns About Physical Appearance

Mark was noticeably overweight compared with his fourth-grade friends. While he occasionally was teased, most of the time his weight was not an issue.

Linda had braces. She hated them but understood the reasons they were necessary. She also endured some mild teasing, but her friends generally paid no attention to her braces.

Neil was short for his age. In fact, he was the shortest boy in his fifth-grade class. His parents noticed he was generally happy but that he got frustrated more easily. He hated being teased.

All of these children were noticed in some way for their appearance. Girls who are the first to develop breasts in their class may feel very self-conscious. Children who wear glasses sometimes feel the same way. We can't protect our kids from being teased about their appearance, but we can talk to them in a manner that might soothe the hurt feelings and provide them with a sturdier sense of esteem.

Things to Consider

➤ Concern about weight and body size tends to show up in girls more than boys and in white children more than African Americans.

➤ Children as young as preschool age believe that "fat is bad." Most preadolescent girls believe they are overweight, often because of fashion magazines and commercials that depict very thin models.

➤ Studies of children who are short in stature show mixed and contradictory results in terms of social, emotional, and academic functioning. That means short stature does not automatically mean a child will have difficulties. Height becomes more of an issue when children enter adolescence. Short children do better when their parents foster competence and self-reliance.

➤ Shorter children tend to avoid group activities such as basketball where they will feel self-conscious. They prefer more solitary sports such as swimming or hiking.

➤ One study showed that almost one-quarter of short-statured children repeated a grade, mostly because parents felt the child was immature. However, repeating a grade did not seem to change any academic or social skills.

How to Say It

Prevention is the best medicine. No matter what their appearance, skills, intelligence, or health status, children from loving homes with involved parents or caretakers who are firm but warm will be able to withstand most difficulties. Still, some ways to speak to them may be better than others.

- If your child's appearance bothers him, **EMPATHIC** statements may help him feel understood. Empathy does not mean you agree with your child's assessment, only that you understand why he might feel the way he does. "It bothers you that a kid in your class called you a name because you are not as tall [wear braces, are overweight, lack a certain skill, etc.]. I can't blame you. No one likes to be called names."

- "You think if you weigh more than the other kids, you might be laughed at."

- "You wish you were taller [more athletic, didn't have freckles, had a better singing voice, etc.]. Many kids wish they looked a little different from the way they do."

- **TEACH** coping with frustration or hurt feelings. Help them challenge their negative expectations. "Some kids aren't that smart, but still they have friends. Some kids aren't as good at basketball as other kids. Some kids are popular, some are not so popular. But they all have friends at school or in their neighborhood. Being well liked doesn't depend on how you look."

- "Haven't you ever seen kids who aren't that tall playing with their friends at school?"

- "We can start an exercise program for you, and we can make sure you don't eat any sugar. But some kids still can be very thin without trying and some gain weight easily. It isn't fair, but that's how it is sometimes."

- ENCOURAGE whatever skills your child possesses. Children with physical disabilities or limitations should be taught as much self-reliance as possible. "Let me see if you can do that by yourself. I bet you can."
- "See what you can accomplish just by trying hard and sticking to it?"

How Not to Say It

- Don't encourage obsessive preoccupation about appearance. "Don't eat that. Do you want to get fat?"
- "Make sure your clothes and hair look right. You want the boys to like you, don't you?"
- "Why do you keep wanting to lose weight? You look fine." Don't dismiss your child's concerns with platitudes, especially if she is very focused on being thin. Girls are at higher risk for eating disorders than boys. Instead, inquire further into your child's concerns. "You lost weight but still don't seem satisfied. You worry a lot about how you look, don't you?"
- "Don't let the other kids bother you. What do they know?" It isn't easy to ignore the scrutiny of peers. Your child may get the impression that you just don't understand.

(See chapters on bullying and teasing.)

Smart Talk

Dads, Listen Up!

In a study at Loyola University, about five hundred fifth- through ninth-grade students were "beeped" several times a day and asked to write down what they were thinking, feeling, and doing. One purpose was to determine how much the parents were involved in their children's experiences. The more a father was involved with his job, the less involvement he had in his daughter's life than his son's. In fact, the more satisfied a father was with his career, the less self-esteem his daughters had—presumably due in part to the father's reduced involvement. Girls very concerned about their appearance especially need a father's involvement in their lives.

65

Puppy Love

Eight-year-old Craig and his mom were buying school supplies. Craig grabbed an extra package of construction paper.

"We don't need any more paper," Mom said.

"It's not for me. It's for my teacher. She ran out of it."

"But the school will buy her the paper she needs," Mom answered.

Craig's face was downcast. "Okay," he said glumly.

Mom sensed what he was feeling. "Listen," she said. "Soon it will be Hanukkah and Christmas. I'm sure we can find your teacher an appropriate present."

Craig looked up and grinned.

Kids will develop crushes on their teachers, their schoolmates, or celebrities. It is the first stirring of romantic feelings that can confuse a youngster. A parent's job is to accept these feelings for what they are—normal emotions that should be neither trivialized nor a cause for concern. They are just additional signs that your child is growing older and that someone other than parents can be the object of his affections.

Things to Consider

➤ Infatuations are safe, distant ways to rehearse for the romantic moments that high school dating will probably bring.

➤ Initially, these feelings can confuse a child who may not understand why her heart beats rapidly when she sees a certain boy.

How to Say It

- Show interest and try to elicit more information about your child's feelings. **EMPATHIZE**. The goal is to let your child know that her feelings are normal, that you are interested, and that you can be someone to talk to whenever necessary. "It sounds as if Michelle is very special to you. What do you like about her?"
- "I remember liking my fourth-grade teacher a whole lot. I wonder if you feel the same way about your teacher."
- "It's kind of nice and exciting to imagine having Ricky Martin as your boyfriend."
- **TEACH** when appropriate. Since girls tend to mature more quickly than boys, some preteen boys are in the predicament of receiving phone calls from girls who like them. The problem is that the boys are not so interested. "Lisa called you. I think she kind of likes you. You can be polite to her but you don't have to feel obligated to stay on the phone for long if you feel uncomfortable. It's okay to say 'I gotta go.'"
- "I noticed you've written the name Jennifer on your notebook. Maybe she is someone you like. That's nice."
- **DO'S & DON'TS**. Guidelines about dating may be necessary if your child brings up the topic. If you mention it before she does, it might come across as a criticism. "No, you can't ask him for a date. You are too young. But you can invite him over to the house along with some other friends for a holiday party."
- **ENCOURAGE** appropriate expression of those early infatuation feelings. "I saw a poster of your favorite singer in the mall. Would you like one for your room?"

How Not to Say It

- "You're too young to have those feelings . . ." Don't trivialize your child's feelings. She will have them regardless of your opinion, and you may only succeed in preventing her from talking about them with you.
- "Don't be silly. You'll never meet Ricky Martin, let alone date him!"
- "It's called puppy love. They call it that because it's not the real thing." The feelings are real to your child, however innocent and immature they might be.

- "You can dream all you want, but you're too young to date so don't even think about that possibility." He might be too young to date, but it's better not to sound critical. He'll just think you don't understand.
- "Is he your boyfriend?" If said teasingly, this is definitely a put-down. If said sincerely, are you condoning having a boyfriend (or girlfriend) at that age? Many sixth to eighth graders who "date" are at risk for experimenting early with sex. Television, MTV, movies, and advertising are all very sexually suggestive (and explicit) and often give pre-teens the idea that having sex is acceptable. The older your child is when he/she begins dating, the more likely that sexual experimentation will be postponed.

66

Quarreling with Siblings

Imagine (it's not hard) that as you enter your house after a hectic day, you hear your beloved children screaming at each other. What would you do?

(a) Get back in the car and find someplace less stressful to be, such as a traffic jam.

(b) Hide in the bathroom until it blows over.

(c) Wait for your spouse to intervene (unless he is hiding in the bathroom, too).

(d) Yell at the kids for yelling at each other.

(e) Calmly and respectfully discuss with the children the effective ways to resolve arguments.

If you answered "e," you are either lying, a member of the clergy, or you just won $200 at the office pool and are too numb from excitement to really care what's going on.

Siblings will fight with each other. It's guaranteed. The best that parents can hope for is that the quarreling will be infrequent and not explode into *Wrestlemania: The Final Armageddon*.

Things to Consider

➤ Parents are rarely consistent when it comes to intervening in their children's arguments. Since most interventions will work once in a while, it can be confusing to know which intervention is best. Ideally, parents will try to teach their kids effective ways to discuss their differences and resolve disagreements. That requires some patience on the parents' part and a willingness to let the kids handle some situations by themselves.

➤ Do you tend to blame one child more than the other? Such blaming may be warranted but it could also be a clue to your bias. Do you tend to rescue the underdog? Does the more troublesome child remind you of someone you have issues with—such as your spouse? Do you expect the older child to act more maturely even though he is only seven years old?

➤ The more tense or unsatisfying the marital relationship, the more you can expect spillover into how you intervene with the kids. You may be harsher and less patient with them or too lenient.

➤ If you believe your spouse is too lenient, you may overcompensate and be stricter. Neither one of you may be handling the situation objectively.

➤ Hormones can make kids more irritable. At ages six to nine, the *adrenarche* phase of development begins. Levels of sex hormones increase and can cause moodiness, although no physical signs of puberty will be evident.

How to Say It

- The goals are to halt the potential for violence, calm down the kids just enough so you can help, and **TEACH** them to solve problems effectively. Don't immediately intervene (unless they might hurt each other). They may be able to resolve matters themselves. "Do you want me to help you solve this argument?" If they say yes, you have leverage as the invited guest. If they say no, give them a chance to figure things out on their own.

- Most arguments have to do with teasing and hurt feelings or unfairness. Step one is help them define the problem. "You are arguing over who sits on the loveseat while watching the movie. Why do you both think you have the right to sit there?"

- Step two is to brainstorm possible solutions. "Let's figure out three ways you might agree to solve this problem. John, you go first. What could happen that would make your sister think it was fair?"

- Step three is to agree on a plan. "Okay, John will sit on the loveseat for half an hour, then Jane will use it."

- Next argument, be a coach rather than a teacher. "Let's see if you guys can remember the steps to solving problems. You try to handle it yourselves, but I'll be available if you need assistance." Better still, when the kids are getting along and in a good mood, have them playact an argument followed by a try at calm problem solving. The rehearsal will help and may even be fun.

- Be cautious about taking sides. Siblings are experts at provoking each other in silent, subtle ways so that they appear to be innocent to the observer. "I don't know who started it, but I expect you two to find a way to solve it without arguing."

- Change the environment. "I want you two to sit at the kitchen table and don't leave until you have settled the problem." The change of scenery can help modify their feelings.

- **ENCOURAGE** any effort at problem solving. Praise desirable behavior. "Wow. I left you two alone, and you figured out a way to solve the problem. I'm impressed!"

- **EMPATHIZE** by digging deeper. Perhaps what's troubling one or more of the kids is not their sibling. Have they had a bad day at school? Did she lose the big game? Did his best friend move away recently? Are the parents not getting along? If you suspect an underlying issue, talk to that child privately. "I know your sister bugs you, but I was thinking that maybe you were still upset that Grandma is in the hospital. Tell me what you think about that."

- Say nothing. Grade-school children have had some experiences successfully resolving problems with friends. Grit your teeth, count to twenty, and see if your kids can manage without your help. If they can, everyone is better served.

How Not to Say It

- "Haven't I told you not to fight?" "Won't you kids ever learn to get along?" "What did I just tell you three minutes ago?" Every parent says these things at one time or another, but rarely do they help. It might stop the argument temporarily, but it doesn't show them how to solve the problem.

- "Who started it?" Never in the history of parenthood has a child answered this question accurately.

- "Wait until your father [mother] gets home." Handle the situation yourself.

- "If you don't stop arguing, I'm turning off the TV for the rest of the night." Try not to come up with arbitrary punishments. It's always better if the kids know ahead of time what the consequences will be. Or you might try saying, "It's too loud in here with you guys yelling and the TV blaring. If you can't discuss things more calmly, I will turn the TV off until you do. Thanks."

- "If you two don't fight, we will go out for ice cream later." Once in a great while this is okay, but some parents overuse it. Besides, what if they do fight and you tell them they'll get no ice cream? Now they have no incentive to get along. It is better to praise them frequently for cooperative behavior, teach problem solving, and apply quick and fair punishments when necessary. That will improve the odds that they will try to cooperate further.

67

Refusing Lessons

Marty wanted to take karate lessons real bad. His parents wisely signed him up on a temporary basis, just in case he later changed his mind. After three months, Marty still wanted to continue, so his parents paid for a year in advance (it was cheaper than paying month to month). But when Marty's friend John quit karate, Marty lost his interest as well. Should his parents force him to attend? How can they teach him accountability if they let him back out so easily? What should they say if he whines and complains that he hates karate?

Things to Consider

➤ Extremes are not advisable. Committing a child to a year of piano lessons when there are doubts she will persist or allowing the child to give up as soon as she loses interest can cause more problems.

➤ Make sure you are not trying to push your child into living out your dreams.

➤ Do you give up quickly on interests? Or do you stay in a miserable job out of a sense of duty? Either way, you may over- or underreact to your child's unwillingness to keep a commitment.

➤ Is your child's lack of interest playing into a power struggle between you and your mate (or ex-mate)? If you think your spouse is too lenient on the kids, you may insist your child stick with dance lessons. If you think your spouse is too strict, you may side with your child and say there is no point forcing him to do what he does not want to do. In either case, you are not necessarily seeing what is best for your child. You are simply opposing your mate.

How to Say It

- **REPORT** your expectations ahead of time. "I know you may decide that you don't like music lessons. That's okay before two months are up, but after two months you cannot change your mind."

- "We will buy you this inexpensive keyboard for practice. If you still want to take lessons after a year, we will buy a piano."

- **NEGOTIATE.** "If you really want an electric guitar and I buy one for you, you will have to pay half the cost of the guitar if you decide to stop taking lessons—unless you can think of some other way that is fair."

- Explore your child's reasons for wanting to quit. He might dislike a child in the group; maybe others laughed at him or maybe the teacher yelled at him, and he feels uncomfortable. Once you know the real reasons you may be able to resolve the problem without ending the lessons. "I know you promised you would stick with the lessons. Since you've changed your mind, I'm wondering if something happened that you haven't told me."

- **EMPATHIZE** when your child protests he has lost interest, but stick to the **DO'S & DON'TS** you agreed to. "You feel frustrated that you can't switch instruments. I can understand that. But you promised you would stick with the trombone, and we did buy you one."

- "Since we've paid for the trombone, I'm not willing to buy another instrument until we can sell yours. If you practice and keep up your lessons, I'll put an ad in the paper."

- **ENCOURAGE** those aspects of the lessons where your child does persist. "I know the warm-up exercises and stretching exercises are boring. That's one reason you want to quit dance lessons. But in three months you've learned how to tap very well, and I know you enjoy that part."

How Not to Say It

- "All right, all right. You can stop your lessons. But don't expect me to fork over the money the next time you want to learn something new." Don't give in to whining. If your child really is miserable taking lessons or is in over his head, you should probably cut your losses and chalk it up to immaturity. But it is better to end the lessons after he agrees to attend for one final month (or week).

- "But your grandmother was so excited when I told her you were taking horseback riding lessons." This addresses your reasons for wanting your child to hang in there but does not address her reasons for wanting to stop. It is best that a child take lessons in something that is not required by school and that she thinks she'll enjoy, not because it will please an adult.

- "How was your lesson today?" "Okay." "That's good." If you can't generate more enthusiasm for your child's efforts, don't be surprised if his enthusiasm wanes.

68

Refusing to Talk

"I can't get him to open up," Joy said to her husband. "You try."

"Maybe we should leave him alone," Al said. "He's old enough to sort through things by himself."

Joy sighed. "He's ten years old. The Dalai Lama he's not."

"All right, I'll give it a try. But I know what he'll say: 'Nothing's the matter.' Then what do I do?"

Getting kids to tell you what's on their mind can sometimes be a frustrating task. The first thing to think about is whether this is something new or a chronic pattern. If it's recent, you can probably make headway using empathy and intuition as you probe for what might be bothering your child. If it is a long-standing pattern, change your approach. Whatever you've done before hasn't worked.

Things to Consider

➤ Around age ten or so, boys tend to move away psychologically from their mothers and look more to their fathers for advice. But many men are not talkative. Some fathers are either psychologically or physically absent. When boys have no one to turn to, they learn to manage their feelings and problems on their own. That may teach self-sufficiency, but it also results in a boy who grows up to be a man uncomfortable with discussing feelings.

➤ If something is bothering your child, it likely has to do with self-esteem or issues of competence or incompetence. It may also concern issues of fairness or unfairness. Probe those areas first.

➤ Children do not possess great insight into why they feel the way they do. (Rising hormone levels present yet another complicating factor.) Asking "why" or "what" questions may not get you anywhere when you are probing for insightful answers. Questions with yes or no answers can help when a child is confused. (Note: One study showed that on average, dads asked more "wh—" questions while moms asked questions that yielded yes or no answers.)

➤ Hasty reassurances ("You shouldn't feel that way . . .") sound helpful but can actually make him feel dismissed or disqualified. Hold off on pep talks until you are sure you understand your child's concerns and have tried to empathize.

➤ Regular and meaningful "talk time" with your children—more than the simple exchanges that occur as you pass each other in the kitchen—will increase the odds that your child will want to discuss more upsetting or personal matters with you.

➤ Some children are sensitive to marital and family problems and do not want to add to a parent's burden by discussing their personal issues.

➤ Children who must take on added responsibilities of caring for younger siblings because of family strain may learn to keep their own problems to themselves.

How to Say It

- Probe but don't be pushy. Back off if your child is adamant about not talking. "I notice you've been very quiet ever since you got home from school, but when I ask what's wrong, you shake your head and say nothing. I'm thinking it might have something to do with the test you had to take." If your child just shakes her head no, she hasn't actually told you to back off. Keep up the probing, gently, until you get a clear message that she doesn't want to talk.

- Use **EMPATHY** by reflecting back your impressions. "I can see that talking about things isn't always something you like to do." (The use of the word *always* implies that he does open up once in a while. It is a good idea to use language that suggests your child might choose to open up later.)

- "Now doesn't seem to be the time you'd like to talk about it." (Implication: He will talk about it later.)

- "Maybe you want to think things over yourself. I have faith that if you need help with something, you'll talk about it when you are ready." Often, reluctant children do want to talk but are worried about doing so. Maybe they worry that you will be upset, or perhaps the topic is embarrassing. Saying you have faith in them helps. It gives them a gentle pat on the back, respects their privacy, and shows that you are approachable.
- "When you're ready, I'm here."
- "Is this something you'd rather talk about with your mother?" (Implication: Your child will want to discuss it with somebody.)
- "I can remember when I was your age, I didn't always know if I wanted to talk to my parents or not. But it always worked out better when I did."
- Have you been a good listener? If your tendency has been to criticize or trivialize your children's concerns, perhaps that is a reason for their reluctance now. "I know that in the past I haven't always been the easiest person to talk to about things. If that is your reason for not talking, I understand. I wouldn't want to talk to me, either. But I'm hoping you'll give me another chance." Such honesty and self-deprecating humor may shift the tone just enough to make it more likely he'll talk to you.

How Not to Say It

- "How do you expect me to help you if you don't tell me what's going on?" The idea is right, but the tone is wrong. A better approach: "I'd like to help. I'm at a loss to know what to do. Please tell me what's going on."
- "I'm not leaving until you tell me what's bothering you." State firmly that you are concerned but give your child room to take his time, mull things over, and perhaps come to you later.
- "You had your chance. If you need to talk, find someone else."
- "Do you really think you can solve all problems by yourself?" Actually, resilient children do solve some problems by themselves. Your role is important, but sometimes you can stand back and let your kids handle things themselves.
- "You're like your father. He doesn't talk, either." Making critical comparisons won't help.

- "I'm asking you a question! Don't sit there and say nothing. Talk to me!" Your frustration is understandable. It is better to **REPORT** it than to show it. "I'm frustrated. Something is on your mind that seems to be bothering you, and I'd like to see if I can help."

- "Finally you spoke up! Why couldn't you do that earlier? It would have saved me a lot of aggravation." It is better to praise him for confiding in you.

69

Running Away from Home

Amelia's parents received a phone call from the mother of Amelia's best friend. Apparently, Amelia showed up with a backpack full of clothes and wanted permission to stay for the weekend—"or maybe longer."

What was a twelve-year-old girl running away from home for?

One-quarter of a million kids under age thirteen will run away from home this year. The number is higher for teenagers. A 1998 study of teen runaways found that the majority left home because of perceived physical or emotional abuse. Those adolescents reported that running away was a last resort—not merely a bold attempt to annoy their parents—and many wanted an opportunity to reconcile with their families.

Things to Consider

➢ Err on the side of caution. Presume that running away is a sign your child has significant concerns.

➢ Most runaways end up at the home of friends or relatives.

➢ Younger children who run away simply because they are angry with a parent must be warned of the dangers of running away.

➢ Verbal and physical abuse are the reasons many children run away. Secondary reasons include inability to communicate with a parent, a chaotic household, or to accompany a friend who is running away from home.

How to Say It

- Use news reports of runaway children as an opportunity to **TEACH** ahead of time how serious and dangerous running away from home is. (Don't worry that you might give your child ideas he otherwise would not have.) "Most kids don't run away from home. When they do, it is often because there is a serious problem at home and the child does not believe he can talk things over with a parent. I want you to understand you can always talk to me. And I want you to understand that running away is very dangerous."

- If your child is threatening to run away, take time to consider what the underlying problem might be. "You rode your bike when I told you not to, so I punished you by not letting you ride your bike for a day. Now you are threatening to run away from home. I'm worried that something else might be bothering you. Let's talk about it."

- If your child threatens to run away, don't be intimidated. Use **DO'S & DON'TS**. "If I think you have run away, I will call the police. I will also speak to every one of your friends and their parents in order to find you."

- If your child threatens running away and is argumentative and trying to push your buttons, don't get sidetracked into more areas of conflict. Use words such as *nevertheless, but, still,* and *regardless* that will pull you back to the discussion at hand. "Regardless of your anger at me about not letting you go to the dance, I will call the police if you choose to run away," or "Still, despite your problems, I will call all your friends' parents to help find you if you choose to run away. We can solve your concerns in ways other than running from home."

- "Tell me what problem you will solve by running away from home." Running away is an attempt at resolving or escaping from some problem.

- If your child does bring up a concern, take it seriously. **EMPATHIZE** when appropriate. "You don't get along with your stepfather, so you want to leave home. I can imagine how hard it must be for you when you argue with him. Let's talk about ways that will help you two get along."

How Not to Say It

- "Run away if you want to. You'll be back." In the 1960s, *The Andy Griffith Show* was a popular television program. In one episode, the young son, Opie, decided to run away, and his father used "reverse psychology" and allowed his son to leave. Of course, the boy returned. There are too many dangers in today's society, however, to take that chance.

- "That's not a reason to run away . . ." You're missing the point. Your child evidently thought it was a good reason. It's better to listen to your child's concerns and take appropriate steps to solve those concerns.

- "You'll never amount to anything if you think you can just run away from your problems." Personal attacks on your child's character will add to her resentment. Criticize the behavior, not the whole being of the person. "I know when you think things through, you'll understand why running away is risky."

If your child ran away because of physical, sexual, or verbal abuse, steps must be taken immediately to halt the abuse; otherwise, the risk of running away in the future is high.

70

Saying "I Love You"

Linda told a story about one day when she was a little girl. Her father had come up behind her and put his arm around her. "You know," he had said, "every time I hear you humming in the morning I thank my lucky stars I have you."

It was a memory that always brought a tear to her eye. Her father had died not long after in a farming accident.

On average, adults who believe their parents loved them as children are not always able to admit that their parents showed them love. Many children have to read between the lines. They "know" a parent loves them but they do not always feel it. Telling children you love them is meaningless if your love is not demonstrated. However, showing love without saying "I love you" at least once in a while can cause some doubt or anxiety. Children need action *and* words.

Things to Consider

➤ Many marriages are less than satisfying because one spouse (often the husband) will rarely say "I love you" even though he may work hard and be devoted to his wife in other ways. Words without action are meaningless. Actions without words are meaningful but not intimate.

➤ You don't need to be a poet or sound like a greeting card. Think about the little things you love about your children and then tell them. If you repeat it once in a while, it might take on even more meaning to your child because it is unique and for him or her only.

How to Say It

- "My love for you is bigger than the sky. . . . No, bigger than the universe."
- "No matter what you do, no matter where you go, I will always love you."
- "I love you, son. Always remember that."
- "I'm not good at saying this, so listen up. I love you, and I always will. Now finish your breakfast."
- "You mean the world to me."
- "Do you know what cherish means? I cherish you."
- "It makes my day just being with you in the morning before you head off to school."
- "Just having you in my life makes life worth living."
- "If I could go back in time and do things differently, I'd still want you as my son.
- "Good night. I love you. God bless you."

How Not to Say It

- The only wrong way to say it is not to say it.

71

School:
Attending a New School

"I began my new job as a hospital nurse three weeks before my daughter started first grade," Marcie said. "It helped me understand what my daughter might be experiencing on her first day at school.

"First, I knew that my job was very important, so that made it all the more nerve-racking even though it was also exciting. Second, I barely knew anyone and didn't know my way around the hospital. That made me nervous. I watched other nurses do their work with ease, and I wondered if I really was up to the job. I had much more sympathy for my daughter, that's for sure."

Starting school or transferring to a new school can be an adjustment for most kids. It need not be traumatic, and once the children have adjusted, they can feel proud that they coped well. But until the transition has been successful, parents can make a difference in how well their kids adjust.

Things to Consider

➤ Ideally, avoid transferring your child to a new school in midyear. The curriculum is well under way by then and it might be harder for your child to catch up. Also, social groups may already have formed, and your child may have a difficult time establishing new friends.

➤ Adjusting to a new school will be harder when your child is adjusting to other changes such as parental separation or divorce or serious illness of a family member.

➤ Children will miss their friends from their former school. First-time students will be more anxious about the new environment.

➤ Anxiety is always higher when the number of unknowns is high. A visit to the new school is essential to reduce anxiety. If that is not possible, one parent might videotape the school or take snapshots. Or check to see if the school has a web page. A message from the principal or future class-mates will ease anxiety and bring a smile.

➢ If your child is having some difficulty adjusting, ask her teacher to pro-vide extra kind and encouraging words or introduce other kids to your child during lunch or recess.

➢ Find out from the teacher which student in your child's class was new to that school a year before. Seeing how that student has adjusted can encourage your child.

How to Say It

- Kids need practical information about their new school—what it looks like, what a typical day will be, the number of hours spent there every day, etc. The clearer the image, the better. Once those facts are pro-vided, the focus should be on your child's expectations. **EMPATHY** will help you probe. "I bet you'll be glad when you're all settled into the school and know where everything is."

- "What are you looking forward to the most, and what are you nervous about?"

- Encourage expression of thoughts and feelings. Performing some physical activity with your child while talking (play catch, ride bikes, go for a walk, jump rope, etc.) can make the dialogue feel less formal and serious. "How about throwing the ball around for fifteen minutes? You can tell me all about your day, and I'll tell you about mine."

- Children may wonder "What if I don't make any friends? What if they make fun of me? What if nobody asks me to play with them during recess?" Be ready to provide guidelines on coping with specific fears. But first try to discover why your child is fearing those things. "Many children worry about those things. What makes you worry about them?"

- "But the truth is you have always made friends. Once people get to know you, they do like you. If you want, we can have a party at our house soon, and you can invite your classmates."

- "Let's rehearse what you can say if you want to play with a group of other kids."

- **ENCOURAGE** by pinpointing successes in coping as your child pro-gresses through his first weeks of school. "Already you can tell me many of the teachers' names, and you have made two new friends. That must make you feel good."

- "It's only been a few weeks. It often takes longer to become comfortable with a new school. You're actually doing fine."

- "If you notice any new students who have just arrived, you can be the expert. You can tell them to come to you if they have questions, and you can show them around. How does that sound?"

- "We'll make sure we e-mail your friends at your old school, and you can tell them all about your new teachers."

Rule of Thumb: Most children are fairly well acclimated within three months. Remind yourself that your child will eventually get used to the new school.

How Not to Say It

- "This is no big deal. You'll be fine once you get used to it." You are closing off room for discussion. Encouraging your child should not be done at the expense of understanding and responding helpfully to his concerns. Encouragement is best when preceded by some empathy. "It's normal to feel nervous and a little excited. But I know as time goes on you'll feel more comfortable and less nervous. What could happen that would make you feel better?"

- "If you don't improve your attitude, no one will want to play with you." Scaring your child into a positive attitude is a contradiction.

- "You're making your little brother afraid to go to school. Try to be more positive." It's not your child's responsibility to prepare his younger sibling for school. Remember, your younger child is also watching you. Your role is more important.

- "I'm tired of hearing you complain." Often, children (and adults) whine or keep complaining because they never really felt listened to the first time. It is better to assume there is something you've missed about what's troubling your child. Also, encourage your child to list the things he likes about the new school in addition to listing his complaints.

- "Just introduce yourself to some kids" or "Just talk to the teacher if you have any questions." Kids who are nervous about the new school may need coaching on how to approach others. Don't just tell them, show them.

72

School:
"My Teacher Is Mean!"

Most kids will complain about a teacher sooner or later. Often the issue is one of perceived unfairness: The assignment was too hard or not enough time was given to study for a test. Children who report the most teacher unfairness also tend to be children with the most discipline problems. A child's view of his teacher is important. Dropout rates of high school students are highly correlated with belief that teachers are unfair or uninterested. According to an article in the *American Psychologist,* teachers view low-income students less positively and with lower achievement expectations, often basing their opinion not on scholastic abilities but on speech patterns and style of dress. These views can develop as early as kindergarten.

Parents shouldn't dismiss a child's concerns about a teacher, and shouldn't automatically regard their child's opinions as accurate. The goal is to uncover the true reasons for the child's views and take steps to improve the situation. Usually, greater involvement in your child's study habits and improving his ability to be well behaved will pay dividends.

Things to Consider

➤ Find out if having a "mean" teacher is adversely affecting your child's school performance. If not, having to cope with various adult personalities may be a fine lesson in life.

➤ Sometimes adults and children complain about someone when in fact it is someone else who is the real problem. (For example, a parent who complains that her children do not appreciate her might really be feeling unappreciated by her husband.) So a child who says a teacher dislikes him may also be feeling disliked by a friend. Probe for possibilities.

➤ A teacher's expectations can affect how well or poorly a child performs, though this effect is small. A recent study showed that the most powerful teacher expectation occurred when teachers *overestimated* the abilities of low-performing children. These kids rose to the occasion and did better than past test scores would have predicted.

➤ The best teacher will challenge your children to perform well and will not be content with mediocrity.

➤ Your expectations are more important than the teacher's. You set the standards of excellence. If a child is having trouble with schoolwork, look first on the home front. Have you taught good work habits? Do you check your child's schoolwork daily and monitor homework? Do you instill respect for authority? Do reading and writing come before TV and video games? If you've slipped up on these, don't be quick to judge your child's teacher as mean. She just may have higher standards than you do.

How to Say It

- The immediate goal is to get your child to explain as fully as possible why he thinks a teacher is mean. Elicit as much information as possible before you draw any conclusions about the accuracy of the claim. "What did your teacher say or do that made you think he was mean? . . . Anything else? . . . Has this happened before or was this the first time?"

- Find out if your child is troubled by the belief that the teacher is mean. "How much does it bother you? A little? A medium amount? A lot?"

- Explore alternative interpretations. "Sometimes teachers and parents do things kids don't like, but they do it because it is good for the children. Things like getting you to bed at a reasonable hour, not letting you eat too much candy, being sure you do your homework, and having you help around the house. Is it possible that your teacher thought he was being helpful?"

- Brainstorm solutions. Often, teaching your child to be more polite, inquisitive, and reliable with assignments can make the difference in a teacher's appraisals. "Are there times your teacher is not mean? Are there students your teacher is nice to? If so, what happens to make your teacher nice at those times?"

- If it seems to you that your child's teacher may simply be stricter than past teachers, **EMPATHIZE** with your child's feelings but **ENCOURAGE** obedience. "It isn't always easy having a strict teacher. Sometimes it feels unfair. But by being strict she is more likely to spend time on your lessons, and that is a good thing. Besides, she believes you have what it takes to follow her rules. She has faith in you."

- "I remember having a mean teacher when I was in sixth grade. Would you like to hear how I handled it?" Such stories can help your child cope and make him realize it is not necessarily a horrible thing to have a grumpy teacher.

- "You can always talk to me about your teacher. If necessary, I will talk to your teacher about the best way to handle matters. Do you have any thoughts about that?" Older children may prefer that you not say anything to their teacher. You must weigh that concern with their other concerns.

Smart Talk

How to Say It to Your Child's Teacher

If you have a concern about the teacher's methods, you may be interested in these three guidelines by author and former Secretary of Education William Bennett offered in his book *The Educated Child:*

1. *Gather the facts.* Your child may not be the best reporter of facts. Keep an open mind and don't automatically presume the teacher is at fault.

2. *See the teacher as an ally.* Assume the best about the teacher—that she wants your child to learn as much as possible. View her as on your team, not as an adversary. Treat her with respect.

3. *Follow the chain of command.* Don't automatically run to the principal. Try to work things out with the teacher. Once you do go above the teacher's head, you may never have a good relationship with that teacher. Choose your battles wisely.

To prevent difficulties with teachers, you may also want to do the following:

Be polite and gracious in all correspondence. Say words of genuine appreciation whenever you can. Teachers can use pats on the back.

Be involved in the school as much as possible so teachers know you. Volunteer at functions, chaperone a trip, help out with a holiday class party, give a talk to a class on a topic of interest, and so forth.

Follow up later on with a note of thanks after a problem has been resolved.

How Not to Say It

- "If your teacher was mean, she had a reason." Showing support for teachers is usually a good idea, but it's better to first probe for reasons why your child feels the way he does. "Oh? You think your teacher is mean? Tell me more."

- "You must have done something wrong." Again, don't jump to conclusions. This kind of comment closes off communication instead of enhancing it.

- "Your teacher sounds like an idiot. He had no right to say those things." There are two sides to every story. You are better off giving the teacher the benefit of the doubt. Your child will not respect her teacher if you show disrespect.

- "That's life. You have to learn how to deal with mean people." You are blocking off communication and missing an opportunity to probe for other problems.

73

School:
Homework Hassles

Joshua hovered over his math homework, writing furiously. He had five minutes to finish before his bus arrived.

"Mom!" he called. "Will you help me? I can't do this problem!"

"You told me you finished your math last night," Mom said.

"It was mostly finished. Will you do this problem for me? I'm going to miss my bus."

"No. You know how to do that—"

"Please!" Josh said. "I don't have the time!"

"You should have thought of that last night when—"

"Mom, you're not helping me!"

Helping your child to develop proper study skills will save you and him lots of needless aggravation.

Things to Consider

➢ There is no accepted standard for the amount of homework a child can reasonably expect to do on a daily basis. However, a common formula is to allow ten minutes a night for a first grader, and ten minutes per night added for each grade level. Thus, a fifth grader might average nearly an hour a day of homework while an eighth grader may average ninety minutes or more. (Note: Children watch between three and four hours of TV per day. Something is wrong.)

➢ Children often try to do other things while studying, such as watch television or talk on the phone. If so, they may spend double or triple the time it would take them if they simply sat at a desk and quietly did their homework.

➤ Unless you know what the homework assignments are and when they are due, you cannot help your child organize his time. One fourth-grade boy—with good intentions—began reading a book the night before his written book report was due. He completely underestimated the amount of time required to do the assignment.

➤ If your child rarely has homework or is able to complete it in school, she is not being challenged. You are doing your child a disservice to allow that to continue.

➤ Spelling words, historical facts, geography, etc., can be reviewed in the car when driving to a store. It's a great idea to use words or facts that the child has already been tested on to demonstrate how material can be forgotten unless it is reviewed. This technique is especially helpful for students who take comprehensive exams at the end of a quarter.

➤ Your children will eventually discipline themselves to do homework if you value such discipline. Do you do your work on time? Do the kids see you postponing necessary work and wasting time? Do they see you reading books and eager to learn new things?

➤ You will have made a huge, positive step when your children ask permission to watch television instead of your asking them to turn it off. TV should be an infrequent privilege, not a daily right.

How to Say It

- The most important thing to **TEACH** (repeatedly) is that you value education and you value homework as an essential tool for educating your child. Of course, most kids would rather play than do homework. You can **EMPATHIZE** without losing sight of your values. "I know that you'd rather not have any homework. I remember feeling that way, too. But I want you to learn as much as possible because I know you will have more choices when you get older if you do the best you can in school."

- Children need help persevering when assignments get difficult. For that to happen, they need to believe they have what it takes to succeed. At least they need to believe that solid effort will most often yield solid results. Praise specific study skills and praise effort. "You came right home from school and immediately went to your desk to do homework. That was smart. I noticed that you reviewed your chapter when you didn't know how to answer the homework problem. That was a smart idea, too."

- "I can see that you tried to figure this problem out yourself before you asked me for help. That shows good effort."

- "If you try hard, most of the time you will do pretty well. If you try but not very hard, sometimes you will do okay. If you don't try, you won't do well."

- When assisting a frustrated child with her homework, parents make one of three mistakes: They, too, get frustrated and therefore aggravate the situation; they do most of the work for the child (big mistake—it rewards whining and procrastination); or they pull away and offer less help. The better approach: "I can see that this is frustrating for you. I can do the first part of the problem for you and you can finish it, or you can do the first part and I will finish it. Which do you prefer?"

- "It seems as if no matter how I try to help, you are still frustrated. Maybe we both could use a five-minute break. How about a game of Go Fish?"

- Have your child speak aloud his thinking process as he works through a problem. That can help you detect where his confusion might lie. "Let me show you what I mean. I'll talk out loud while I do this addition problem. Six plus four is ten, so I put down the zero and carry the one . . ."

- Don't make overseeing homework a chore. If it's an aggravation for you, then your child will be less likely to enjoy it or less likely to ask for help when needed. "Oh, good. It's time to look over your homework. Let me finish drying my hands, and I'll be right over."

- "If you have a homework question, you can always come to me. If I am busy, I'll quickly stop what I'm doing and answer your questions." Show by your actions that homework issues are very important to you as a parent.

How Not to Say It

- "Did you do your homework? Good." Ask what the homework was and then check it over. Show an interest. It's an opportunity to catch mistakes or praise good effort.

- "You didn't have any homework today? Oh." Be more curious. Did your child have homework but finish it in school? Is not having homework typical? If so, the teacher is being negligent.

- "Okay, I'll do it for you this time. But next time you'd better have your assignment finished the day before it's due!" The problem here may be as much yours as the child's. If you are on top of his assignments, you'll be able to remind him ahead of time to get to work. Catching up on homework at the last minute is sometimes inevitable but should occur very infrequently.

- "Why didn't you tell me you had a science project due on Monday? Now we'll have to spend the entire weekend working on it!" Get your child into the habit of telling you what his assignments are daily. Some students must write their assignments in a book that you should have access to. If you don't inquire regularly, some assignments will slip through the cracks. Even bright children don't organize their time well and may underestimate how long a project takes to complete.

Smart Talk

Homework is even more of a hassle when parents disagree on how much help to give their child. Be careful about spousal power struggles. The husband who thinks his wife is too lenient may oversee homework in a strict, harsh way in order to compensate for his wife's leniency. But the wife may overindulge her child as a way of overcompensating for her husband's military style of teaching. In neither case is the child being truly helped. If this describes your marriage, begin with the premise that the best approach is what works for your particular child. Ideally, you want your child to be able to do as much of the work on her own but be able to ask for help when needed. Homework should be challenging but not too frustrating or overwhelming.

School:
"I'm Afraid to Ask Questions in Class!"

Mickey was a capable seventh-grade student. But when he was struggling with his homework, his parents discovered he had questions he could have asked the teacher but didn't.

"I feel funny asking questions," Mickey said.

His parents discovered no compelling reason for Mickey's reluctance. He was reasonably bright and never had an embarrassing incident in school that might make him shy. What could they do?

Things to Consider

➤ Children who are reluctant to ask questions in class are usually either shy or fear looking foolish. A parent-teacher conference can help. A teacher can praise children for asking questions and make sure such inquisitiveness is rewarded.

➤ Preteens get extremely self-conscious. A child who is worried about pimples on his face or how his hair looks may not want to call attention to himself by asking questions in class.

➤ If anxiety is at the foundation of a child's reluctance to ask questions, practice is essential. The only way to challenge their belief that something bad will happen if they ask questions is for them to ask questions and discover that the consequences are positive.

Smart Talk

Seeking help in a classroom is associated with better grades and improved confidence. Still, many students do not ask for help when needed. An extensive body of literature reveals the following findings:

Kids who feel competent are more likely to ask questions when needed. They are less concerned about looking foolish.

Younger kids, if taught that asking questions will help them learn, will ask more questions. Older children (seventh grade) will also weigh the costs of asking questions (appearing stupid, being criticized for not knowing something, etc.).

Children who need the most help (who are less capable) are least likely to ask questions. For them, asking questions only affirms their lack of competence.

Sometimes asking questions is a sign of *dependency* on the teacher. Asking for answers instead of asking for information that will help them understand material better is a clue to that dependency.

If asking questions is viewed as a reflection of inability or inadequacy, children are less likely to ask. If asking questions is viewed as a way to become more knowledgeable and competent, children are more likely to ask.

How to Say It

- **TEACH** that seeking help in a classroom will help the child learn and develop greater knowledge and skill. Discourage the belief that asking questions is a sign of lesser ability (it isn't). "It is a well-known fact that children who ask questions learn more and do better in school."
- "Asking a question is a way of showing that you want to learn more. Teachers like that attitude."
- The goal is to encourage your child without being pushy. A reluctant child will not feel more at ease if you get demanding, and a shy child needs gentle coaxing. "Let's make a list of three or four questions you

could ask your teacher. Then you tell me which of those you'd be willing to ask tomorrow."

- "A good time to practice asking questions is right when the class begins. The longer you wait, the more you might decide not to ask."
- "A simple question to ask your teacher might be: 'Could you repeat what you just said?'"
- "Let's rehearse speaking up. When we're at the restaurant, you can ask the waiter if they serve curly fries with the burgers."
- "Asking a question does not mean you are stupid. If you watch, you'll see that the smartest kids in the class ask questions. In fact, because they ask questions they do better in class."
- **ENCOURAGE.** "Your teacher told me you asked a question in class today. Good for you. Tell me what it was like."
- "Tell yourself, 'The more questions I ask, the smarter I am.'"

How Not to Say It

- "I expect you to ask at least one question in class tomorrow." If your child is fearful, making an order won't clear up the fear. **DO'S & DON'TS** are inappropriate in this case.
- "It's silly to be afraid to ask questions." If your child has some anxiety, you have just informed her that you really don't understand. You are not offering encouragement when you tell your child she is wrong to feel the way she does. It's better to understand, if possible, what her fears are and then offer some practical advice on how to overcome them.
- "If you don't start asking questions in class, I'll have to discuss this with your teacher." You make it sound like a threat. Your child should view you and her teacher as allies who only want to help. Say instead, "It is important to me that you feel comfortable asking questions. If you have difficulty, I'll chat with your teacher and together maybe we can help you."
- If a child asks you a question from his homework, don't respond by saying "I thought you knew that already. Why don't you know that answer? Did you forget?" Any comment by you that equates asking questions with poor ability or forgetfulness may prompt your child to stop asking questions.

School:
Poor Report Card

Jamie got a B in fourth-grade social studies. Across the county border in another school district, fourth-grader Laura earned a B for social studies. Is it reasonable to assume that these students learned pretty much the same thing and have about the same level of intelligence?

Absolutely not.

The truth is that the meaning of test scores, grades, and report cards varies from district to district. Teachers have varying standards, too. Some teachers grade on a curve, which means some students will get an A regardless of how well they understand the material. The self-esteem movement has prompted many schools to use more ambiguous measures of performance that toss out letter grades in favor of descriptions such as "Satisfactory" or "Improving." Some parents complain so much if their bright child receives a low grade that teachers relent and raise the grade to something more acceptable.

Ironically, a child with a "good" report card may be in more academic trouble these days. Parents unwittingly assume that an A or B student is doing well. In fact, the student's performance may be mediocre but the grades are inflated. That student will be in for a rude awakening if she attends a high school or college with more demanding standards.

Things to Consider

➤ If you do not know what specifically was taught and what the standards were for achieving the grades, the grades on the report card have little meaning. Talk to the teacher and find out exactly what an A means.

➤ Academic performance is not just a matter of ability. Research shows that involved and supportive parents who take a strong interest in their children's school performance will motivate their children to work harder.

➢ If a poor report card was a shock, you haven't been keeping tabs on your child's schoolwork during the quarter.

➢ Research also shows that the child's perception that his teacher "cares" can motivate him to work harder and perform better. What is a "caring" teacher? Someone who tries to understand a student's point of view, teaches him according to his individual abilities, and has expectations that the child will perform to the best of his abilities. (Good news! Kids want to be challenged to do their best! So why do some schools, teachers, or parents tolerate less?)

Smart Talk

Should You Pay Your Child for Good Grades?

Generally, no, you should not pay for good grades. While an occasional monetary reward may motivate a child to perform better, this practice has a number of pitfalls. First, it often reveals a lack of parental confidence that the child can get good grades any other way. It may also be a sign that the parents are not taking time to discover underlying reasons for poor school performance. Plus, it is based on the principle that the money is a motivator. What if it loses its appeal? Or what if the child requires a lot more of it to be motivated? Money should not replace parental involvement. If a parent insists that money is an appropriate reward, it should be accompanied by much praise ("You do well when you put your mind to it" or "You are doing a very good job on this report").

How to Say It

- When grades decline, don't first presume the child is lazy. A new school or a different teacher may have stricter standards. "Is the schoolwork getting harder for you?"
- "What has changed that makes getting better grades harder?"
- Try to figure out a plan of action. "What could you do differently that would make your grades improve? Any ideas?"

- Clarify that grades are important and that you will help your child become more organized and more prepared for tests. "It seems that your grade was based on homework plus test scores plus class participation. You did well on tests, but I know you sometimes were late with homework. That will be our first priority."

- Set a clear goal. Telling a child to "improve" his grades is vague. "What grade would you want to reach by your next report card? . . . To achieve that I'll review your homework every night and quiz you during the days before a test. What do you think?"

- Offer realistic **ENCOURAGEMENT**. "I've seen you get better grades. I know your work is harder this year, but I also know that when you take the time to learn something, you usually do well."

- "If you don't do well on a test, what do you think is the main reason?" Kids who attribute failure to lack of ability decide it isn't worth trying hard. Kids who attribute failure to reasons other than lack of ability (didn't study hard enough, etc.) usually perform well overall.

Rule of Thumb: A continuous decline (or sudden drop) in school performance signals a problem. Depression, anxiety, substance abuse, or family conflicts are common causes.

How Not to Say It

- "What am I going to do with you? Don't you want to be successful in life?" Frustration is understandable. It is better to search for underlying problems or at least convey that your child has the ability to make a solid effort.

- "You can forget video games until your grades improve." It might be necessary to curtail TV or video games. If so, it shouldn't be a form of punishment but rather a common-sense assessment of the obstacles to your child's best performance. A better way to say it: "I've noticed that you spend at least three hours a day on TV or video games. Much of that time needs to be spent studying. From now on you can play those games only after I've checked your homework and you've studied your lessons. The most important thing is for you to do the best you can in school."

- "Are you stupid or something?" A comment like this is not only inappropriate and unhelpful, it is a signal that home life may be tense. Inflammatory comments suggest that at least one of the parents is unhappy or angry and that there is spillover onto the children. An honest self-appraisal may prompt parents to improve their own life or seek counseling.

Smart Talk

Parents' influence on their children's school achievement is more profound than you might think. Recent research has demonstrated the following:

Parents' perceptions of their sixth-grade child's abilities in math and English were better predictors of that child's future performance than were the child's past grades.

Children who doubt their abilities do not persevere in difficult tasks. High-achieving children who nevertheless *underestimated* their academic abilities (had low confidence) were also viewed by their mothers as less competent. High-achieving kids who felt confident of their abilities had mothers who shared that view. In other words, what parents think of their children, the children will think of themselves.

Fathers are a very important influence for girls who later become successful in fields that are traditionally masculine. It seems that fathers are less likely than mothers to view their children's abilities in stereotyped ways. Mothers of daughters thought their girls had to exert more effort to be competent in math compared with mothers of sons. Mothers overestimate their daughters' abilities in English and underestimate their sons' abilities. Fathers showed no bias.

School:
Rejected by Classmates

In the wake of the tragic school shootings in such places as Littleton, Colorado and Jonesboro, Arkansas, there has been a keener concern about why some students become social outcasts. It has been known for years that children who are rejected by classmates are at higher risk for problems later on. Research shows that a snowball effect occurs whereby rejected kids are either more aggressive or withdrawn, which further leads to rejection. As someone involved in the care of children, you should know the following dozen facts:

➢ Rejected children show higher rates of criminal activity, substance abuse, and behavioral problems in school.

➢ Children rejected by peers in the third grade were three times more likely than nonrejected students to have poor adjustment in middle school.

➢ Peer rejection at age ten is associated with involvement in a deviant peer group at age twelve. Deviant peers are more likely to abuse drugs, engage in criminal activity, and drop out of school.

➢ Middle-school boys abused by peers (bullied, rejected) were depressed and had poor self-esteem ten years later.

➢ The single best predictor of peer rejection is aggressive or disruptive behavior.

➢ However, many rejected children are not aggressive at all. They are oversensitive, submissive, unassertive, and viewed as easily pushed around.

➤ Being viewed as shy by peers is not the same as being viewed as easily pushed around. Shy children were viewed as quiet, nondisruptive, and hesitant in social interaction but not viewed as oversensitive and easily bullied.

➤ Peers view well-liked students as being not too aggressive or disruptive, average in assertiveness, and especially kind, cooperative, and trustworthy.

➤ Well-liked students are viewed as capable of handling good-natured teasing. Aggressive children view teasing as an attack; submissive children view teasing as ridicule.

➤ Whether or not peers rejected an aggressive child or a withdrawn/submissive child seemed to be based on the child's ability to also show friendliness, cooperation with peers, and supportiveness toward others. The more positive behaviors children displayed, the more likely they would be accepted by peers even if they also acted aggressively or submissively.

➤ In a study of grades K–2, children relied heavily on teachers' comments about other children to form their opinions about their classmates. Thus, a disruptive child who was put down and not merely corrected by the teacher ("Billy, can't you ever sit still!") was more disliked by students. When teachers praised the good behavior of disruptive students ("Good, Billy. You're paying attention"), the other students had more favorable opinions of that child. Negative behavior that was corrected by a teacher (for example, "Billy, stop making paper airplanes and get back to work") had no effect on opinions.

➤ Boys who tend to be victimized often have overprotective mothers who treat them as younger than their age and who overcontrol the boys' spare-time activities. Victimized girls tend to have mothers who are hostile and critical of them, who threaten to leave, or who threaten to withdraw love if the girls misbehave. Fathers tend to be absent or uninvolved. Boys who are overprotected don't develop the kind of social skills respected by a peer group (rough play, autonomy, risk-taking, and acceptance of teasing). Girls who are rejected or criticized (with hostility) by mothers have a harder time developing the necessary social skills of empathy, cooperativeness, and sharing.

How to Say It

- Inquire as to the extent of the rejection. "Who is putting you down? Is it just one child, or do several kids do this?" The more children involved, the more likely the rejection will be harder to handle.

- "What do you say or do when these children do these things to you?" An overly submissive child is more likely to continue to be victimized. An aggressive child may be rejected but not bullied. Peers may later accept a child who can laugh it off and not withdraw.

- "How long has this been going on?" It is easier to change classmates' perceptions earlier than later. Asking a teacher to find ways to praise your child may also help, especially in the earlier grades.

- **EMPATHIZE.** "It really must hurt your feelings when that happens."

- "I imagine it makes you angry or sad."

- **TEACH** more socially desirable behaviors such as cooperativeness, use of humor, and kindness. These tend to counterbalance the negative views of others enough to end rejection. "I don't blame you for not wanting to be nice to the kids who mistreat you. But it has been shown that if your classmates view you as kind or cooperative, they will like you more. Want to try?" You must practice this daily until your child is adept.

- "How about twice a day for a week you say something kind to some of your classmates? You don't have to say it to the meanest ones just yet. Maybe you could tell someone he has a nice jacket or she asked a good question in class. What other things could you say?"

- If your child is aggressive, he is likely to interpret socially ambiguous acts (being bumped while standing in line, good-natured teasing) as having hostile intent. If he then acts with hostility, he is more likely to be rejected by peers. **TEACH** alternative ways of responding. "Let's pretend you're in the cafeteria line and someone bumps you. Instead of bumping back, what else could you do?"

- If your child is very sensitive to criticism, he may view good-natured teasing as ridicule. **TEACH** alternative ways of reacting. "For example, if someone laughs at the ink mark on your face, you could just smile and laugh."

- "I remember not being liked by some of the kids." Offering stories of hope can help. Give advice on how you coped while emphasizing how your child means the world to you.

How Not to Say It

- "Just join the crowd even if they don't like you. They'll learn to like you." Not necessarily. If your child lacks the social skills to handle criticism or to act his age or to initiate conversation appropriately, he will continue to be rejected. Teach him the necessary skills and remind him of his many good qualities.

- "You don't need them for friends. You have me. I love you and always will." This is well intended but not realistic (and it may be a clue that you are overprotective of your child which can be part of his problem). Kids still need to feel accepted by at least some of their peers. Minimizing that fact only informs your child that you really do not understand.

- "I'm going to talk to those other kids' parents!" Be careful, or you may do more harm than good. Older children may end up being even more disliked. You may get the other kids to stop teasing or bullying your child, but you won't make them like him. Teaching positive social skills is your best bet.

Finally, it can be helpful for rejected children to feel very accomplished in some area outside of school such as music, theater, gymnastics, or martial arts. Martial arts can improve a child's sense of physical competence (submissive children view themselves as weak) while the philosophy of martial arts also teaches physical restraint (so your child is less likely to use his skill aggressively). A class outside of the school setting can validate your child's worth and can help him cope with rejection from schoolmates.

School Safety Concerns

Olivia and her brother Pete couldn't help but watch the videotapes being replayed by the newscasters. The school shootings were a national story that had parents, teachers, and experts shaking their heads and wondering "Why?"

"Will that happen at our school?" Pete asked his mother.

"I'm afraid," Olivia said.

Fortunately, most schools are safe, especially in kindergarten through eighth grade. Still, many children get apprehensive when they hear news reports that undermine their sense of security.

Things to Consider

➢ The school shootings that made national headlines were newsworthy because the killers were themselves children or adolescents and because such killings are extremely rare. According to Richard Gelles, director of the Center for the Study and Prevention of Intimate Violence at the University of Rhode Island, fewer than one hundred homicides are committed annually by children under fourteen.

➢ Some elementary and middle schools do contain students in gangs or who use drugs.

➢ Unless steps are taken to make parents feel more confident about school safety, it will be hard for parents to reassure their children.

➢ There is always uncertainty. While experts can isolate the factors associated with an increased incidence of violence, it is very difficult to predict ahead of time who will commit a violent act. It is especially difficult when predicting homicide by children since the rates of occurrence are already so low.

➢ There can be no significant learning in an environment where safety is at risk and children are apprehensive.

➤ If you have any questions or concerns, talk to the school principal about the school's policy regarding student violence. Are violent acts immediately punished? In what way? What does a school do with repeat offenders?

➤ A nationally representative sample of eighth graders commented about the frequency of being victimized at school, about getting into trouble for bad behavior, and about concerns regarding school safety. The fascinating result: Those three conditions were significantly higher in schools that had only grades 6 to 8 or 7 to 9, compared with schools that had grades K to 8 or K to 12. If your child attends a middle school with no lower or higher grade levels, inquire more about school safety and policies regarding bully behavior.

➤ Does your school have school resource officers available? According to John Coleman and Bonnie Ryan-Spanswick, housemasters at John F. Kennedy Middle School in Enfield, Connecticut, an SRO can make a huge contribution to school safety. The SRO is a sworn police officer who is assigned to a specific school on a daily basis and spends most of the day interacting with students, teachers, and staff. The SRO is visible and available not merely to respond to a crisis but to discuss any concerns and, it is hoped, prevent a crisis. Parents also can feel free to discuss problems with the SRO and learn about such things as parents' rights and the legal consequences of certain troublesome behaviors by students.

How to Say It

- Don't be quick to reassure your child without finding out exactly what her worries are. Your child may be unconcerned about a possible shooting but still very concerned about being bullied, for example. "You seem more nervous about going to school. What do you think about that makes you nervous?"

- "When did you last feel comfortable and safe in school? How long ago? What has happened since then to change your mind?"

- "If you had the power to make your school completely safe, what would you be sure to do?"

- **EMPATHIZE** without quickly trying to reassure your child all is well. Hasty reassurances might halt further conversation and leave you in the dark about hidden worries. "I imagine when you watched the news report on TV, you wondered what you would do if that happened at your school."

- "It's very frightening and sad when something violent happens at school."
- **TEACH** what your child can do to help protect herself. "If you have any suspicion that a student wants to hurt somebody, it is okay and important to tell an adult."
- "If you think you are in danger, go quickly to a teacher."
- **REASSURE.** "I love you so much that I would never, never, *never* put you in a place where I believed you would be hurt."
- "School shootings are scary, but they also almost never happen. Your school is going to take some precautions to make sure nothing like that ever happens there."
- "If I thought you were at risk, I wouldn't let you go."
- "Let's say a prayer for the people who died and their families." Don't miss an opportunity to demonstrate your religious faith. Belief that God can and will offer comfort and that prayers can make a positive impact on the future course of events is a powerful tool.
- Don't hesitate to bring up the topic weeks later even if you think your child has forgotten the news story. You will not add to your child's fears, and you will have an opportunity for further discussion if your child still seems worried. "Remember a few weeks ago we talked about violence in schools and you were worried? You don't seem worried anymore. Is that true?"

How Not to Say It

- "Oh, that happened in another state. You don't have anything to worry about." Dismissing your child's worry may not alleviate it. He just may choose not to bring it up anymore. Furthermore, what if another school incident makes headlines? Your believability will be compromised.
- "You shouldn't watch that news report. Now, what would you like for dinner?" If your child knows about a frightening incident, it is best to discuss it, even briefly, to find out what your child thinks.
- "The world is a scary place." Your child will probably take your words to heart. Emphasize how bad things can happen but they are infrequent. Show him that you are not daunted.

78

Improving Self-confidence

Nine-year-old Meredith is seated at the dining room table working diligently on her math homework. Her mother peeks over Meredith's shoulder, studies her daughter's answers, and proceeds to tell her how amazingly intelligent she is. Mom often praises her daughter's intellect. A while later Meredith's father checks up on her. He watches how she erases a mistake and how intense her concentration seems. "You sure put in a lot of effort in your work, sweetheart," he says.

Whose comment, Mom's or Dad's, is more likely to increase Meredith's self-confidence? Would it surprise you to learn that one of the comments could increase Meredith's tendency to worry about failure?

Professional opinion about children's self-esteem has been a confusing mess of late. As the smoke has started to clear, the only consensus is that self-esteem may not be as vital a component of mental health as once thought. It is important but overrated. In the above example, Meredith might indeed feel self-confident about her intelligence if her mom praises her for being smart. But she is also likely to see intelligence as a fixed trait and may not persevere if a task seems difficult. Kids praised for being bright fear failing more than kids who are praised for their genuine hard effort to meet a challenge. And kids consistently praised for hard effort persevere when the going gets tough.

The self-esteem bandwagon resulted in many fundamental changes in schools over the past two decades. Failing students were often promoted to protect their esteem. Coaches refused to keep score in intramural games of basketball and baseball so as not to make the losing team feel bad. Many schools instituted a revised version of "Student of the Week" and made sure every student had a turn regardless of performance. In the science fair, everybody got a trophy. The upshot is that parents and teachers may feel better for trying, but children are less adept at handling failure.

Furthermore, numerous studies now suggest that many aggressive children have an overly positive view of themselves and their competence.

Smart Talk

Praising a child has always been a powerful tool in child-rearing and in helping kids feel good about themselves. But studies show that praise is effective because it is a part of a larger, more important factor called "Parental Responsiveness." A responsive parent does more than praise. He or she is actively involved and talks to a child about a wide variety of topics (and in a **TENDER** way). Praise is great, but it doesn't replace time together, affection, and other ways that parents show involvement and caring.

Things to Consider

➢ Think of self-confidence in specific, not just global, ways. A lower-than-average self-esteem may hide the fact that a child feels very proud in specific areas. Conversely, a child with high esteem can feel lousy about herself in areas not obvious to a parent.

➢ Since nobody is perfect, children (and adults) need to develop confidence in their ability to withstand disappointments and personal failures. *Resilience,* or the ability to bounce back from a letdown or be able to accept certain personal limitations (how tall a child is compared with peers, how athletic, how smart, etc.), does more to enhance esteem in the long run.

➢ One prominent researcher discovered after years of scientific study that teaching a child self-control is more important than broad attempts at self-esteem building. A child who masters self-control will not act or speak impulsively, will learn to persevere at a task despite feelings of anxiety or inadequacy, and will be more likely to resist peer pressure. The skill of self-control increases that child's chance of achieving meaningful goals—an outcome that will profoundly affect his or her self-confidence.

➢ Self-esteem, like love, may not be easily or precisely defined, but most people report greater self-confidence when they have reason to feel proud of themselves. That usually happens with a combination of knowing they are truly cherished despite their imperfections and by accomplishing difficult or challenging tasks. Love without accomplishment or accomplishment without love doesn't quite cut it. (Note: Youths in violent gangs feel appreciated by their group and often show mastery at violent or illegal behaviors. Their esteem can be quite high. Teaching the proper values cannot be overlooked.)

How to Say It

As your child grows, your level of overall responsiveness will act as an inoculation against many of the ups and downs that children experience. Just as a combination of good diet and exercise enhances our immune system's ability to fight disease, a supportive, loving family life enhances your child's psychological immune system. Global comments like "You are wonderful . . . the best kid in the entire world," etc., are terrific but must be balanced by more specific praise and encouragement such as:

- "You started tae kwon do eight months ago, and even on nights when you didn't feel like attending class, you showed up anyway. Now you've earned your orange belt. You should be proud of yourself for sticking to it."

- "Social studies has been a hard subject for you, yet you studied and let me ask you questions even though it was sometimes frustrating. That shows effort, and I'm impressed."

- "How about we go on a hike today? Just you and me." (Communicating that you simply want to spend time with them—and actually spending that time—conveys that they are truly special.)

- "Your friends wanted you to stay out longer than you should have, but you came home on time anyway. Going against your friends' wishes isn't always an easy thing to do. That took some courage."

- "What you just did [or said] showed patience. Good for you!" (Praise any of the virtues such as persistence, kindness, a sense of fairness, a willingness to share, or obedience.)

Rule of Thumb: Spend time with your child in meaningful activities. Self-worth can be enhanced whether or not the activity leads to an accomplishment.

If your child's self-confidence has been shaken recently, **EMPATHIZ-ING** is your best first move. Preface your remarks by briefly **REPORTING** what has prompted you to start the conversation.

- "You dropped the fly ball and your team lost. Now you can't seem to get that picture out of your head. Have I got that right?"

- "You look so unhappy. Tell me about it."

- "I've noticed you are keeping very quiet since your friends went bike riding without asking you to join them. It makes me think that your feelings were hurt."

- "I remember that you felt the same way two weeks ago when you didn't get chosen for a part in the play. That felt unfair, too." (Connecting the current hurt to a past hurt may help the child understand why her reaction is particularly intense. If the past hurt had healed, the child may begin to think that the current problem will be temporary.)

How Not to Say It

- Don't automatically ask, "Do you want to talk?" Your child may instinctively say no even though she might find the idea appealing.

- Asking "How do you feel?" can be a turnoff when your child is obviously upset. You may get a snippy response such as "How do you think I feel?" It is better to report your observations ("You're walking with your head down," "You just slammed the door," "Your eyes are red") and then state your interpretation ("so I think you're still very sad," "and that tells me you're very angry," or "It's hard to think about Grandpa and not cry").

- Don't ask what happened. Say, "Tell me what happened."

- Whenever possible, don't give any advice without getting clear acknowledgment that you have first understood what the problem is and how your child truly feels.

Often, children whose egos are bruised will use phrases that reveal global negative comments about themselves ("I'm stupid," "I can't do anything right," or "Nobody likes me") or global comments about others ("Everybody else is smart except me," "Nobody feels the way I do," or "All the boys know more than I do"). After you have demonstrated empathy, it is extremely important to **TEACH** your child how to think more rationally:

- "You're not stupid. You didn't study as hard this time."
- "I've watched everybody on your team make an error. You aren't the only one."
- "Remember how you played that video game and kept increasing your score? That shows me that you can improve over time if you work at it."
- "Yes, you made a mistake. That doesn't mean you'll never get it right. You've done well in the past, and you'll continue to do well most days."

It is very important that you not say the above examples before you've understood the real problem and expressed empathy. Otherwise, a sincere effort to get your child to appraise himself realistically ("You've made friends before, you'll make them again . . .") can sound as if you are dismissing his hurt feelings ("You shouldn't feel that way because . . ."). If he does not really believe you understand, he'll tune out your pep talk.

79

Self-critical Child

"I can't do it!" eight-year-old Audrey said. She threw the bat on the ground and walked away. "I'm just not good enough. I don't do anything right!"

Her older brother turned to the neighborhood kids who were standing nearby. "She gets that way a lot," he said.

"Come on back, Audrey," one of the other girls cried.

Audrey walked back into her house and shut the door.

Just about everybody can be self-critical at one time or another. "I can't believe I did that!" is a phrase many people mumble. But self-criticism can be extreme. When that happens, put-downs become all encompassing. Instead of saying "I'm not that good of a baseball player, but I still do okay," a strongly self-critical child will say, "I never do anything right!" Extreme self-criticism cuts to the core of the person. He or she is stupid, lazy, bad, weak, or ugly—qualities that define the whole person instead of commenting only on aspects of oneself.

Self-critical children are at risk for depression. Believing themselves incompetent, worthless, or bad, they never feel good about themselves even when they succeed. They tend to be perfectionists and pessimistic, striving for standards that are hard to maintain and feeling guilty or shameful when they can't live up to them.

Things to Consider

➤ Self-criticism tends to remain a stable quality of female adolescents through early adulthood. Self-critical teenage boys tend to feel more inner anger than depression when they reach adulthood.

➤ Younger children (especially preschool) tend to feel responsible for problems that are not their doing. They can feel blameworthy just by their existence. "It's my fault that Mom and Dad are unhappy."

➤ Guilt can be healthy if it leads to appropriate self-evaluation, reparation, and correction of one's behavior. The ability to empathize is strongly correlated with the ability to feel guilt. Children with chronically depressed parents often have a more complicated form of guilt where they assume an inappropriate level of responsibility for the events at home.

➤ In a study that began in 1951 and examined nearly four hundred children for decades (Caucasian, from two-parent families), it was found that five-year-old kids with very strict, demanding, unaffectionate parents were self-critical and depressed by age twelve.

➤ The behavior of the same-sex parent seems particularly important in the development of depression-prone children.

➤ Parents who often claim "It's my fault!" tend to have children with that same style of self-blame.

➤ Still, even in homes with chronically depressed parents or parents who are critical and cold, some children develop with a reasonably healthy ability to relate to others and avoid depression. There are no simple answers.

How to Say It

- First, be on the lookout for a child's self-criticism that seems harsh and overstated. Listen for words that are all-encompassing such as *never, nobody,* or *always,* as in "I'll never get it right," "Nobody likes me," or "I'll always be stupid." Then ask for more information. "I heard what you just said. Tell me what makes you say that."

- Challenge the overstated language your child uses. "It's not true that nobody likes you," "It's not true that you'll never learn how to play," or "It's not true that everybody thinks you are stupid. You are exaggerating."

- "When do you say those things to yourself? At school? With friends?"

- **TEACH** more appropriate self-evaluation by pointing out exceptions to your child's opinions. "You say you are stupid, but you get mostly A's on your report card. To me that means you are bright." Make these corrections as soon as possible after you hear your child's negative self-evaluations.

- "It isn't true that nobody likes you. I watch you on the playground, and I know the other boys play with you and enjoy being with you."

- "Just because you have to practice the piano a lot doesn't mean you are no good at it. In fact, the only way to be real good at it is to practice."
- "Yes, that girl preferred to play with someone other than you. Sometimes that happens, but it doesn't mean she hates you."
- Encourage your child to challenge his negative views. "What other examples can you give me that show you are much better than you think?"
- If you tend to be a more strict, demanding parent or uncomfortable with big shows of affection, it is important for you to loosen up. Start by allowing your child to get away with some messy activity. Be less concerned about neatness or being on time, act goofy, make mud pies or snow angels, or go haywire with modeling clay. "How about we rake the leaves into a big pile and then take turns jumping in them?"
- Again, the very strict or perfectionistic parent might want to ease up on expectations. "You don't have to clean up your room right now. It's okay to have it stay messy once in a while. This weekend would be a good time."

How Not to Say It

- Don't place any high-maturity demands on your child and watch out for all-encompassing language. "Your room must *always* be spotless," "You must *never* hurt anybody," "There is *no* reason you cannot get straight A's," "You should *never* undress where people can see you," or "*Nobody* will like you if you don't share."
- "You are a bad child." Don't label the child. Criticize specific actions, not the whole person.
- "If you feel guilty, then you must be guilty." This is not always true. Self-critical children assume guilt when it is not realistic.
- "If you continue to act this way, I just may leave for good" or "I won't love you anymore." These types of threats are very damaging. They undermine trust in others as well as any self-worth.

80

Sexuality and Reproduction

"Mom, what's sex?" seven-year-old Alex asked.

His mom turned away from the computer monitor, composed herself, and answered, "It's the difference between boys and girls," she said.

"Oh. What's for lunch?"

Mom's answer was sufficient for now. But soon her responses will necessarily be more detailed. She returned to her computer but couldn't concentrate very well.

Things to Consider

➤ It's a good idea to always be prepared to answer children's questions about sex. Questions occur unexpectedly and are best answered right then and there.

➤ "The talk" is a misleading concept. It suggests that the discussion, once completed, will be final. If you have a one-time only discussion about sex, it is not because you answered all questions satisfactorily, it is because your child would rather not raise the issue with you again.

➤ Take your cue from your child as to what constitutes a satisfactory answer. If your child is restless or inattentive, perhaps you have said enough for now.

➤ Take advantage of "teachable moments." Authors Charles Schaefer and Theresa Foy DiGeronimo point out that television shows make occasional sexual references that could be explained, or you and your children may happen to observe animals mating. These are perfect moments to teach a quick lesson and convey that the topic is one you can be comfortable with.

➤ Children will learn from their peers, usually before you think they are ready. But some of what they learn is incorrect. Don't take comfort knowing that your kids will learn about sex "from the streets."

How to Say It

- Use proper terminology. Words like penis, vagina, intercourse, semen, ejaculate, and sperm are accurate and leave no room for misunderstanding. The term "make love" may also be suitable, but be prepared to explain it. "How does a woman become pregnant? A man and woman get undressed. When they want to get pregnant, the man's penis gets larger and is put inside the woman's vagina—that is an opening between her legs. Sperm comes out of the penis and stays inside the woman. If the sperm reaches an egg, the egg grows and becomes a little baby."

- If you are uncomfortable talking about sex, say that up front. Otherwise, your child will detect your reluctance and may decide not to ask you more questions in the future. But admitting your discomfort shows that despite your feelings, you want to talk about sex. "My parents didn't talk about sex with me, so I'm a bit uncomfortable. Bear with me. Still, I'd much rather talk to you about it than say nothing."

- "What does having sex mean?" "Sometimes it means having intercourse which is how to make a baby. Sometimes it means touching each other in ways people ordinarily do not do unless they are married. A man will touch the woman's breasts and vagina and bottom. A woman will touch the man's penis and bottom."

- "How does a man's penis get big?" "The penis is made of spongy material. Blood flows into the penis and the spongy material swells up. That's called an erection."

- ENCOURAGE future questions. "I'm really glad you asked that question. It was a good question. Please come to me anytime you want to know more."

How Not to Say It

- "Where did you hear that word? Who told you those ideas? We don't talk about such things in this house." You are implying that anything which suggests sex is bad or dirty or a shameful topic. It is a natural act that children need to be properly educated about.

- "You are too young to know the answers to those questions." Sorry, you're wrong. Your answers can be short and sweet and age-appropriate. If your child is asking, it means he has heard things—usually in school or from siblings or friends—and deserves accurate and honest answers.
- "Well, in the woman are organs called ovaries, and they contain tiny eggs. Each month an egg is released into a long tunnel called the fallopian tube. The egg passes through this tunnel on its way to the uterus where it becomes fertilized. . . ." Accurate, yes. Necessary? Probably not. Does it sound like a classroom lecture? Definitely. It's best to keep answers short and sweet. If your child is keenly interested, you can add more details.

81

Sex Play with Other Children

Kevin was in third grade. "Guess what," he said to his father as he put his glove and ball in the garage. "Margo and I made out today!"

Dad's jaw fell.

"What's French kissing?" Kevin asked. "Margo said it's okay to kiss, but it's not okay to French kiss."

"Hey, shortstop," Dad said. "What else did you two do?" He was afraid to ask but felt he had little choice. His little shortstop was now in triple-A, on his way to the big leagues.

Most children will experiment with sex. It may be with siblings or friends or on themselves. Some children, like Kevin, are open about their endeavors because they haven't figured out that parents usually freak out (at least on the inside) over such things. Others know they are doing something their parents won't like and will be very reluctant to confess when confronted.

Things to Consider

➤ A recent study showed that nearly half of all parents reported that their child had engaged in some type of sex play with another child by the time their child was six. Follow-up revealed that such an activity had no bearing on functioning when the child was interviewed at age eighteen.

➤ While normal, such sex play should be gently discouraged.

How to Say It

- **TEACH** about personal privacy. "I don't want you to touch other children's private parts, and I don't want other children touching your private parts. Okay? That is why they are called private."

282

- "Many kids like to play those kissing games. It makes them feel more grown up. You are too young, and I don't want you playing them."
- If your child denies he did anything and you know he is lying, don't push him to confess. "I saw you behind the garage playing doctor, but I don't want you playing doctor. Your body is not to be used as a game."
- **EMPATHIZE.** "Many kids are curious about their bodies. It's normal to want to see other people's bodies, but I don't want you taking off your clothes as part of a game."
- "What you did is not something children should do. Okay? You aren't bad for doing it, but you shouldn't do it again."
- "If another child wants you to take off your clothes or to show your private parts, what will you say and do?" Rehearse strategies to say no.

How Not to Say It

- "Tell me what you did! You're not leaving here to play until you tell me!" If your child is not forthcoming about what happened, he already realizes it is not a subject you can handle well. It is better to state matter-of-factly what you know and teach your child proper behavior. Punishment is not necessary.
- "You did a horrible thing." Lighten up. It is not evil but a normal curiosity.
- "Stop touching yourself there! That's bad." Masturbation or rubbing oneself may occur in children. Gently **TEACH** your child that such behaviors are not appropriate in public and try to occupy his hands with some other toy.

82

Sex:
Child Reading
Adult Magazines

Steve came up to his wife in the kitchen holding a magazine.

"I found this under Jimmy's bed when I was looking for his socks," he said.

Christine looked at the cover of the *Playboy*. "It's six months old," she said. "Do you think he's had it all this time?"

Steve shrugged. "What should we do with it? Put it back and act as though we never found it?"

The couple decided it would be best to talk with Jimmy.

Things to Consider

➤ It is normal for preteens and teens to be interested in adult magazines, boys especially. As a parent you have the right to keep the magazines out of your house, but that won't keep your child from scanning them when they are available.

➤ Pornographic magazines can range in content from nudity to explicit sexual acts. Men's magazines often contain sexual acts between women. These topics should be discussed with your child if you discover he has been reading these magazines.

➤ You may want to discuss the difference between sexual curiosity, which is normal, and pornographic material, which views people (usually women) as purely sexual objects—an attitude that is harmful.

How to Say It

- It may be hard not to lecture, but do your best. Begin by **EMPATHIZING** to put your child at ease. If he thinks he's going to get into trouble, he won't listen to the important things you have to say. "A lot of boys like to read these magazines. It is normal to be curious about naked women and sex. But I noticed you were trying to hide the magazine. My guess is you figured out there may be something wrong about these magazines, too."

- If you have books on art that contain some nudity or if you and the children have visited a museum where there were statues or paintings of nudes, you can **TEACH** how nudity by itself is not bad or wrong. "Some of the greatest paintings have people with no clothes on. The human body is very beautiful to look at. It's understandable that you would be interested. But the pictures in these magazines are there for a different purpose. They make what can be a loving act between people into a purely sexual one, without the love that belongs there."

- "Slavery is wrong because slaves were viewed not as people but as objects to be owned and used for whatever purposes the slave owners wanted. Pornography is wrong because the people in the pictures are viewed by others as sex objects only. If someone cares about you only because of your body or your appearance, what happens when you get older and your body is less attractive?"

- "You have a mother and a sister. Would you want people not to care about them and only take advantage of them?"

- "Some of these pictures show homosexual acts. Have you heard the word *homosexual* before? Some people find it exciting to watch two people who are both men or both women have sex. But sex for the sake of sex cheapens human dignity."

- "I hope you'll decide to remember what I've told you the next time you see a magazine like this. For now, I'm going to throw this magazine away. I don't want it in our home."

How Not to Say It

- "Where did you get this trash? Did you buy it with your own money or did someone give it to you?" He now knows you object. But you probably lost the opportunity to teach him anything about why pornography is wrong.

- "I can't believe you would look at such things! Didn't I raise you better than this?" His behavior is really normal curiosity. Teach your values in a manner that will make it easier for him to listen.

- "If you're going to read that stuff, don't let me see it around the house." What values are you teaching? Giving permission shows that you recognize it is a normal curiosity to read such magazines, but you have a responsibility as a parent to teach your child your values.
- "That's disgusting!" What's disgusting? The sexual act portrayed or the fact that it is depicted in a manner devoid of love? Your child might want to know.

83

Sex:
Child Walks In on
You and Your Mate

Eleven-year-old Sam had been outside cleaning his bike and fixing the chain. But when he couldn't find his bicycle pump, he ran inside to ask his father.

"Dad?" he called out just as he opened the bedroom door.

The next thing he saw was his parents scrambling to find the blankets and hide themselves, but doing a pretty poor job of it.

Sam closed the door quickly behind him and paused for a moment. His eyes bugged out and his heart pounded. *Did I just see what I thought I saw?*

Things to Consider

➤ These moments are not traumatic but can be acutely embarrassing for everyone involved.

➤ You may be tempted to pretend it never happened, but don't. Your child may be scared, confused, or laughing hysterically. You're better off finding out his or her reaction and doing your best to clarify any misunderstandings.

➤ Young kids will be confused. Older kids will probably know what you were doing but still may be shaken or afraid they did something wrong.

➤ In the future: When in doubt, lock your door.

How to Say It

• Immediately get out of bed and put a robe on or get dressed. Don't wait until later to have the discussion. Don't ask, "Why didn't you knock?" By now your child is wishing he had knocked. "I'm sorry you came in when you did. Mom and Dad were making love. We should have made sure we had privacy, but we forgot."

- A child who hasn't had any formal sex education may be confused or scared. She may understand to some extent what she saw but will also be puzzled. Be calm, soft-spoken, and reassuring. "Moms and Dads make love like that as a way of showing their feelings toward each other. It is something that grown-ups do. You look a little nervous. I hope we didn't scare you."

- "Do you have any questions about what you saw?" A much older child probably understands what he saw, though he never actually witnessed it before. A little humor can ease the tension. "Well, this isn't the way I had planned to teach you about sex. I'm embarrassed, but I'll get over it. What questions do you have?"

How Not to Say It

- "Don't you know you're not supposed to barge into our room? Don't ever do that again." True, he should have knocked, but don't make that the issue. Believe me, from now on he'll give you plenty of warning. He doesn't ever want to see you two at it again.

- "What exactly did you see?" While you may be hoping she saw very little, don't ask this question. It can be embarrassing to have to give details. Presume she saw everything and do your best to correct any misunderstandings.

Single or divorced parents may be in bed with someone they are not married to. If your child catches you in the act with someone you have been dating, you have much more to explain than sex and anatomy. Children ages six and up will regard your relationship as serious. Older kids may feel you have betrayed their other parent. Read the chapters on introducing children to a new partner and how to handle matters when kids do not like the new person.

Rule of Thumb: Don't sleep with a new partner when your children are anywhere around unless that partner is living with you and you are in a committed relationship (married, or about to be). Anything less and you run the risk of your children getting confused, hurt, or angry.

84

Promoting
Sexual Abstinence

Karen, a divorced mother of a pubescent eighth-grade girl, spoke to her therapist about what had happened.

"I came home from work early because I wasn't feeling well. When I opened the door, I heard a rush of activity in my bedroom. Who did I find but my daughter and her boyfriend in my bed. Of course she is grounded. But I was proud of the way I handled the situation later on. I told my daughter all about condoms and safe sex. Can you believe she didn't have any condoms? We were calm and open. I really felt as if I was doing a good job as her mother."

Single parents have a tough job, but it is made tougher when society and the media claim that teenage sexual activity is inevitable, that abstinence is an old-fashioned, you-got-your-head-in-the-sand virtue, and that education about safety is paramount. Karen believed the propaganda that good parents teach good information about safe sex and that abstinence has gone the way of the typewriter.

Things to Consider

➤ Early sexual activity among children and teens is associated with early use of alcohol, drugs, criminal activity, and poorer social adjustment several years later.

➤ Once a teenager has had intercourse, frequency of church attendance declines. Grades fall significantly the year after the first sexual experience.

➤ Poor family relationships predict early sexual activity.

➤ Sexual experimentation does not cause experimentation with drugs or alcohol, but the three go together. A sexually active preteen or teen has probably experimented with these substances.

➤ Data from 1989 and 1992 show clearly that abortion rates are significantly lower for girls ages fifteen to seventeen in states with parental involvement legislation. This means that sexual activity is also lower in those states. Contact your legislator if you live in a state that overrules parental involvement.

➤ Statistics vary, but by twelfth grade more than half of all teens have engaged in sexual intercourse. In poor urban areas the statistics show that by age fourteen more than 80 percent of teens have had sex. A study in Iowa showed that 19 percent of seventh-grade students and 64 percent of twelfth-grade students had engaged in intercourse at least once.

➤ A sizable minority of students are able to postpone sexual intercourse beyond twelfth grade. Will your child be one?

How to Say It

- For preteens especially, make your values clear and explicit. Leave no room for doubt as to how you feel about teenage sexual experimentation. "Yes, sometimes children or teenagers have sex, but it is wrong to do that. It is a huge mistake. It increases the chance that the girl will get pregnant, but she will be too young to properly care for the baby. It's important to wait until you are grown up and able to provide a home and two parents for your baby before you have sex."

- **EMPATHIZE** but be clear about **DO'S & DON'TS**. "Many teenagers try to have sex. You will want to when you are a teenager, or someone else may want you to have sex. While it can be hard to say no, I want you to say no. The longer you wait to have sex, the better off you will be."

- "I will always want you to talk to me if you are tempted to have sex. I will not punish you for those feelings, but I will help you resist them because it is safer for you to resist them."

- "Another problem with having sex before you are grown up is that you have an increased chance of getting what is called a sexual disease. Many of these diseases can be treated with medications, but they can cause much pain and possibly some damage. Diseases like AIDS are not curable." (A report in the *New England Journal of Medicine* indicated that the strongest factor for cervical cancer was the human papillomavirus, one of the more prominent sexual diseases among younger women.)

Smart Talk

The Role of Nonverbal Communication

A study by Melody Graham at Mount Mercy College in Iowa showed that teens were less likely to engage in sex if:

They turned to their parents first for any problem.

Parents were available. Some parents communicate well but are too busy. They were less effective in helping their kids postpone sex.

They believed their parents would be very upset if they had sex. Interestingly, some parents were poor verbal communicators, but their teens got the clear message that sex was not allowed. Good communication was not effective in hindering sexual activity per se. A stronger factor was the teenagers' own values. Teens who thought having sex was okay and who had friends who engaged in sex were more likely to have sex themselves.

The message for parents: Your children are likely to postpone sexual activity if they believe you value abstinence, if they feel they can talk to you about anything, if family harmony is good, and if their friends are not sexually active.

How Not to Say It

- "You shouldn't have sex during high school, but if you do, please be sure you use a condom." While teaching that condom use reduces risks of pregnancy (but does not by any means eliminate that risk) is important, it is far more important to make a clear statement that premarital sexual activity is wrong and harmful. Saying "You shouldn't, but if you do . . ." is really saying that you accept the idea. It is a weak opinion. Kids need clear statements of your values. Teaching safe sex is important. Teaching abstinence is vastly more important.

- "Everybody has sex in high school eventually, so I expect that you probably will, too. Just be careful." You are really giving your permission. And you are telling your child that you have no faith in his or her ability to resist peer pressure or to make a mature decision regarding sex.

- "If I ever find out you had sex, I'll make your life a living hell." No question, your values are clear. But the best combination is clear values *plus* open lines of communication. This comment may teach your child never to approach you when peer pressure to have sex is high.

85

Sexual Abuse:
Alerting Your Child

Jim was listening to the local television news while preparing dinner. He wasn't paying close attention, but seven-year-old Alyson was. When he finally realized that the reporter was discussing the arrest of a man who had sexually abused children, he quickly shut off the television. Alyson looked up at him but didn't say anything. Later, he asked his wife if he should have spoken to his daughter about what she might have overheard.

"Probably," his wife said. "But I sure feel uncomfortable about the idea."

Most parents do. But according to best estimates, between 12 percent and 25 percent of children will experience some form of sexual abuse. The most vulnerable time is between the ages of eight and twelve. Girls are more vulnerable than boys. Abuse can be a single incident but typically occurs many times over the course of weeks, months, or years. Some sexual abuse may not involve touching; instead, the adult wishes to become sexually aroused by exposing himself or by showing erotic material to children. At a minimum, the child can be very uncomfortable. Psychological trauma is possible in more severe cases.

When Alyson heard the news report about a child molester, she didn't say anything to her father. While some children will ask parents, "What's sexual abuse?" or "What's a child molester?" many—perhaps a majority—will not. It is up to parents to inform their children because sexual abuse is common and is usually perpetrated by people children know—not strangers.

Things to Consider

➤ Much sexual abuse occurs before a parent has had an opportunity to explain the facts of life to their children. Parents are therefore compelled to warn their children about sex abuse using language and concepts they hadn't expected to say until a few years later. Before children can make sense of the concept of sexual abuse, they will need to understand some of the basics about human sexuality. That will include the names of a person's private parts (it really is best to use the actual terms: penis, vagina, anus, breasts).

➤ Next, it will be necessary to describe the idea of inappropriate touching, or any touching that can make a child feel uncomfortable, and distinguish it from acceptable touching (hugs, frolicking, visits to the doctor, etc.). Be matter-of-fact, and try not to sound frightened. You simply want to explain that certain kinds of touching are not allowed and that people do not have a right to touch children any way they wish.

➤ It is a good idea to give your child examples of ways they might be approached by a molester: the stranger in a car; someone who offers gifts or candy; someone who pays attention to her but then asks if she wants to play doctor; someone who asks for help searching for a lost animal. Remind your child that molesters are often friendly and try to entice children by giving them gifts or spending extra time with them. Role-playing effective ways to recognize and get away from a potential molester is also a very good idea.

➤ Girls are sexually assaulted at twice the rate of boys. The rate of assault for girls does not increase as the girl gets older—which means younger girls are at as great a risk as teenage girls.

How to Say It

- "The part of your body that your underwear covers we call your private parts. We call it that because nobody needs to see those parts of your body except sometimes your parents or a doctor. That is why you don't see people walking on the street without clothes on."

- "Some people want to touch your private parts. They might want to touch your bottom or your penis [vagina]. No one has a right to do that unless it is a doctor and I have given the doctor permission. Anytime you think someone wants to touch your private area, you can scream or say 'no' real loud and run away. You can tell me what happened."

- "No one has a right to even look at your private parts. That is why we call them private."

- "Sometimes the people who want to touch you in your private area first try to show you pictures of people with their clothes off. You might be curious about that but you should not trust that person."

All of the above is a form of **TEACHING**. Don't hesitate to make an **EMPATHIZING** remark if you think your child has a strong reaction.

- "You look worried, Molly. Are you wondering if something like that could happen to you?"
- **ENCOURAGE** your child to come to you with questions. "If you think this has happened to you before, or if someone touches you in a way I've just described, you must talk to me. You will never get in trouble for that. It is a good thing to talk to me."

What Else to Say

- If you are obviously ill at ease with the topic and think your child senses that, say, "It is a difficult topic because I don't like to think about someone hurting you or touching you in the wrong ways." If you give the impression that sex is an uncomfortable topic, your child may think twice about talking to you about it in the future.
- Follow up the initial conversation with your child, perhaps with your spouse also present. A husband might say to his wife, "I spoke to Molly today about that report on the radio about a child molester. I explained how some people might want to touch her in ways that could make her uncomfortable and how she should always come to one of us if she has any concerns about that."
- Offer reassurances. "I will always do my best to protect you. Most children are not abused but too many are." But remind her that such things happen when loving parents aren't looking, so she must be ready to say "no" and run away even if the person is someone she trusts.

How Not to Say It

There is no need to be dramatic or graphic. Descriptions of intercourse or masturbation are unnecessary unless your child understands sexual reproduction and feels comfortable with those terms.

- "Let me know if someone gets too friendly with you." That comment is too vague and underplays your concerns. Children think very literally. Be specific and clear.

- "Stay away from strangers." Most child abusers are people your children know. Besides, your kids watch you exchange pleasantries with many strangers (the meter reader, a checkout clerk, people sitting next to you in church or on a plane) and will get confused.

- Don't make it a one-time-only discussion. There will be other opportunities to remind your kids about the importance of saying no to uncomfortable touching. "Remember when I spoke to you about bad people who want to touch your private parts? That story you just heard was about a man who was arrested for doing that. What do think about that?"

With as many as one in four children being sexually abused at some point during childhood or adolescence, parents need to be alert to situations where abuse occurs. While the vast majority of adults who volunteer time to work with kids as coaches are decent, pedophiles often look for situations where their access to children is easy and fairly unrestricted. Remind your children about inappropriate touching and their need to tell an adult if abuse occurs or is suspected.

86

Sexual Abuse:
After It Happens

The trip back from the doctor's office was surreal. Marjorie had all she could do to concentrate on her driving and keep her eyes from filling with tears. She tried to sound reassuring to her eleven-year-old daughter, Samantha. The girl stayed quiet and pressed her face against the passenger window.

"It's over now, Sam," Marjorie said. She rubbed the back of her hand against Sam's cheek. "He'll never do that to you again."

What made the revelation of sexual abuse even more shocking to Marjorie was finding out who the perpetrator was—Alan, a neighbor just a few doors down. Alan was a father and respected member of the town. He was even at their house for a barbecue two weeks earlier. No one ever suspected a thing.

Since parents are often traumatized themselves when their child suffers severe abuse, they sometimes minimize or exaggerate the harm done. Neither extreme is helpful. Pretending that their child will eventually "get over it" or being panic stricken at the thought of the child ever going anywhere unaccompanied will complicate the recovery process.

Not all children who are sexually abused show any symptoms. The most reliable indicator of abuse is age-inappropriate sexual behavior or knowledge. Children who rub their genitals frequently, masturbate compulsively, or expose themselves to other children are often signaling for help. Or a child may have her dolls engage in sex play. Still, according to Cynthia Monahon, author of *Children and Trauma: A Guide for Parents and Professionals,* 20 percent to 60 percent of sexually abused children do not show any behavioral disturbances. Monahon also states that most children under eleven may not talk at length about shameful or painful feelings.

Healing after sexual abuse can be strengthened when parents say the right things. Patience is also important, since there are no quick solutions to overcoming trauma.

Things to Consider

➤ Don't be surprised if a child's school performance slips temporarily. Nightmares, phobias, and clinging behavior (wanting to sleep with parents) are also not unusual.

➤ In the immediate aftermath, protect your child from exposure to stimuli, such as violent or sexually provocative television shows, that might trigger bad memories.

➤ Don't assume that your child must talk out her feelings. Some children can only talk about the trauma for brief periods, while others talk every chance they can get. According to trauma expert Cynthia Monahon, a problem occurs when there is a mismatch between how much a parent needs to talk about what happened and how much a child needs to talk. Look to your child for clues and go at her pace.

➤ Be prepared to hear details that might horrify you. Do your best to convey to your child that you can handle it.

How to Say It

In the immediate aftermath, be **ENCOURAGING**. Your child needs reassurance that she will feel better over time, that she is deeply loved, and that she is not bad or in any way at fault.

- "We will always be here for you. You will not have to go through this alone."
- "All children who are abused are innocent. No matter what they did, they are not at fault for what the grown-up did."
- "The man who did this to you is bad. You are not bad."
- "You will start to feel better, not all at once but a little each day. Just like finding pretty shells on the beach—every day you add to your collection."

In the weeks or months that follow (depending on the severity and duration of the abuse and whether or not the abuser was a close relative), you might need to help your child cope with specific fears or vague anxieties. Girls tend to withdraw more; boys may act out more.

- "You'd rather sleep with your sister [or parents] tonight instead of alone in your room. That's fine for now, but soon you won't have to be doing that." (Your words should indicate that you expect she will feel better.)

- "You're feeling nervous inside right now. I can tell by the look on your face. Let's talk about ways that can help you feel better right now."

- Use encouragement by reminding her of past fears she overcame. "Remember two years ago when we had the car accident in the rain? You were scared to be a passenger for a little while, but then you got over it. You'll feel less afraid about this, too."

- Reassure her that anxiety and other symptoms of trauma are normal. "I do not expect you to act brave. It's normal to feel scared or have nightmares. But I know you won't always feel that way."

- During a nightmare or disturbing flashback, refocus the child's thoughts on the present. "I'm here with you, and we are safe in the house. You aren't with that man."

- "It's over. That was in the past."

How Not to Say It

- "You're fine. There's nothing to be afraid of." She is not fine, and her fears are real to her. It is better to say you understand she's feeling the way she is and reassure her that it is in the past and she will feel better eventually.

- "You're young. You probably won't even remember this when you get older." False. She will remember, and so will you.

- "Going to the mall with all those strange people is scary for you. Fine, we don't have to go." That comment subtly implies that avoidance is always reasonable and that the fears may last a long time. It would be better to empathize by saying that the mall *feels* scary (but it's just a feeling), and that the two of you can go some other time.

- "Why didn't you tell me right away!" This implies that your child was wrong or made a mistake. Molesters often use fear tactics to keep children from informing on them. Never blame your child.
- "You know you're not supposed to let anybody touch your private parts!" Again, you are telling the child he was in some way responsible. If you catch yourself saying these types of things, immediately correct yourself. "I'm sorry. You are in no way to blame. That man did those things to you and it must have been scary and confusing for you."

The more severe or prolonged the symptoms, or if the child refuses to attend school, it is wise to seek professional help.

87

Sharing

"Artie, share with your friend," his mom said. "You have plenty of time to play with that when your friend isn't visiting."

"But I'm playing with it now," the seven-year-old answered. "He can have it later."

"You have to learn to share," Mom said. "Now give him that toy."

Artie obeyed, but unwillingly. Was Mom right to make him share?

Things to Consider

➤ Sharing is important if children are to learn to get along favorably with peers. Preschoolers have a harder time sharing.

➤ The older the child (especially ten or older), the more he is capable of seeing the benefits to sharing instead of seeing only the costs.

➤ Some studies show that if a child's peer owns a toy, the parent is more likely to tell her child to let the owner have it back. But if her child owns the toy, the same parent is likely to tell her child to share. That bias can make it harder for kids to see the value in sharing.

➤ Studies show that children are more likely to share after observing a peer share than if they observed an adult share.

➤ Children ages nine to thirteen with mild retardation or cognitive deficits shared about one-quarter as often as same-age peers without such deficits.

➤ Some toys are very special and difficult to share. (Would you be willing to share your new car with your neighbor?) Before a play date, have your child select some toys he is willing to share and place the others out of the way.

How to Say It

- When possible, discuss the expectation of sharing before the event occurs. Preparation may help your child cooperate. "When your cousins come over, they will want to play some of your video games. Even though the games are yours, I want you to let them play games even if you don't want to play."
- "Are there some games you'd rather not let anybody play?"
- "What do you think about sharing your baseball glove when your cousins come over? Chances are some of them won't have their own glove. Would you be willing to play some innings without using your glove?"
- **EMPATHIZE** when necessary. "It isn't always fun to share. I know it can make you feel upset. But sometimes it makes you feel good."
- **TEACH** consequences by letting your child make up his own mind. "You don't have to share if you don't want to, but I'm concerned that your friends won't want to share with you next time."
- **ENCOURAGE** sharing by praising it. "I noticed you let your neighbor ride on your bike when his was broken. It was no fun for you because you had to stand around, but I'm proud of you for sharing. That was very kind."
- "I noticed that your friend shared his candy with you. That must have made you feel good. How would you have felt if he didn't want to share?"
- If your child refuses to share, consider that there may be underlying issues. "I wonder if not wanting to share your toys now has anything to do with the fact that our cat died a few days ago."
- "I notice that you especially don't like to share with Johnny. Is there something about him that bothers you?"

How Not to Say It

- "It's not nice to be selfish." You don't need to call names to make your point.
- "You have to share." Older children (budding attorneys) will tell you they do not have to; younger kids won't understand why, if they have ownership, they must give it up. Sometimes the fair thing is to let the

other child wait. (Be aware that sometimes parents urge sharing so as to avoid making an unfavorable impression on other adults. When that happens, you may be inconsistent in your guidelines.)

- "If you don't share, I'm going to punish you." Is it really important that your child share right then and there? You may get compliance, but you may worsen the problem. If your child feels he has nothing to call his own, he may become even more withholding in the future. Sometimes natural consequences work better. If your child doesn't share, perhaps later his sibling won't share with him; that will have more of an impact than a threat from you.

- "Actually, since I paid for the toys, they are mine, not yours. And I'm saying to share my toys." That won't fly—especially later when you want your child to clean up *his* toys.

88

Shyness

"What did you do in school today, Billy?" Uncle Ray asked.

Billy shrugged his shoulders.

"He's shy," Billy's father said. "Billy, tell Uncle Ray about your field trip. Tell him where you went."

"To the zoo," Billy said.

"Tell him what your favorite animal was."

"The giraffe."

"You had a great time, didn't you, Billy? Didn't you say you also liked the monorail because it took you all around the zoo? Tell Uncle Ray about the monorail . . ."

When a child is shy, conversations with unfamiliar people can be short and sweet. Parents often try to coax their shy children into becoming more involved. It is a good idea if done right.

Things to Consider

➤ About 10 percent to 15 percent of all children are shy or "slow to warm up." By adolescence at least a third of these children are no longer shy.

➤ Shyness can be painful when extreme, but it has its benefits, too. Shy children are less likely to take impulsive, fearless risks. Shy children are the least likely to act aggressively or criminally. Sensitive, they can develop empathy more easily.

➤ Peers do not necessarily dislike shy children. However, it may take shy children longer to make friends.

➤ The children who tend to overcome shyness have parents who do two things: Set clear rules and limits (the more vague the rules, the more likely a shy child can fade into the background) and help their child rehearse appropriate risk-taking.

➤ Don't force a shy child to perform.

➤ Don't answer questions for a shy child.

➤ Don't take over for a shy child when he could do it himself. Otherwise, shy children learn to become even more passive.

➤ Research shows that shy boys tend to marry later than non-shy boys. Not so for shy girls, who also tend to drop out of the workforce more in order to stay at home with their children.

How to Say It

- "Tell me what you did in math and science class today." These "Tell me" questions are better than "Did you . . ." or questions that can be answered briefly.

- **TEACH** assertiveness. "Let's practice talking loud on the phone." Shy children speak softly, which makes it more likely that others will stop speaking to them.

- "Let's practice what you can say when your aunt and uncle arrive. How about 'Hi, Aunt Mary. Did you eat at any fun restaurants on the drive down here?'"

- "Let's practice what you can say to a kid at school who is by himself."

- **ENCOURAGE** assertiveness by praising it. "You went right over to that group of kids and asked if you could play soccer with them. Good for you!"

How Not to Say It

- "Just go over there and introduce yourself. It's no big deal." Saying that is like telling someone who is claustrophobic to sit inside a closet. Practice ahead of time, then encourage.

- "No one will like you if you're shy." That won't help. In fact, it may make her more self-conscious. Besides, shy kids can be well liked once they make friends.

- "There's nothing to be afraid of." Not to you, maybe. It is better to say, "It isn't easy to speak up more, but it doesn't have to be hard all the time, either. Practice makes perfect."

- "C'mon. Please? Pretty please?" If you have to beg your child to be more assertive, you don't understand shyness. It is better to ask him what would make it easier for him to try.

89

Sportsmanship

The tae kwon do instructor watched as his team of eight- to ten-year-olds went down to defeat in the sparring competition. He congratulated the kids on their good effort and then gave them one more instruction.

"Go over and shake hands with the team that beat you. They taught you some things, and it's important to be a good sport."

Sportsmanship is a key ingredient to getting along well with other children. Plus, learning to lose gracefully and hope for the best the next time is a mark of a resilient, optimistic child.

Things to Consider

➤ Your influence is important, but so is the influence of the gym teacher and the athletic coach. Be sure to talk with them about their approach to teaching.

➤ Children with low self-esteem do very well with coaches who are supportive, who use positive words of encouragement, and who teach specific skills. High-self-esteem children can fare well with a coach who tends to be critical, but their low-esteem counterparts do not. If you place your child in a class such as martial arts to improve his esteem, make sure the instructor does not use criticism as a teaching technique.

How to Say It

- **TEACH** what you mean by sportsmanship. "Being a good sport means that even if you lose, you won't complain and you won't get angry at the player who beat you. It also means not making fun of any player you beat."

- "It isn't always easy, but good sportsmanship means trying harder the next time instead of giving up. That way you can inspire your team."
- **EMPATHIZE** after a loss or if your child feels he let the team down. Don't try to cheer him up without empathizing first. "It's normal to feel bad when your team loses."
- "All those who don't score a goal feel bad about it, especially if their team doesn't win."
- "It feels lousy when you are the only one who doesn't get a hit."
- **ENCOURAGE** sportsmanship by praising it. "I like the way you shook hands with the other player after the game and said, 'Good job.'"
- **TEACH** by asking questions about popular sports figures who misbehave. "That famous basketball player just got arrested" or "That baseball player was caught doing drugs. How do you think that affects his team?"
- "Someone is always watching you play. Maybe it's your family, maybe it's a big crowd, maybe it's just your opponent. But when the game is over, people will have an impression of you. Will it be positive or negative? . . . Why do you say that?"

How Not to Say It

- "Don't be a baby. Nobody can win every time." Name-calling won't help. It's better to empathize and show optimism. It simply will take a little time (usually a day) before your child feels better about a loss.
- "Hey, Coach, what's wrong with you? Why'd you take my kid out of the game so soon?" Questions for the coach are best asked privately. It can be disturbing for your child to see two people he (hopefully) respects—his parent and his coach—arguing.
- "If you played harder, you might have won that game." Your child knows that. If you really think your child was showing poor effort, you could inquire without making it sound like a criticism. "You seemed a little sluggish on the court today. Was that my imagination or was something on your mind?"

- "If you play your best, we can go for ice cream later." Do you really think that ice cream will be the main motivation? Not likely. Go out for ice cream whether she wins or loses and make it a fun time, regardless of the outcome of the game.

- "You really creamed your opponent," "You showed no mercy," "You were a killer on the court," or "Did you see his face when you beat him? Ha!" Tone it down. Be enthusiastic but don't encourage annihilation of the opposing team. **TEACH** having respect for the opponent.

Stealing

Joanne's parents told their daughter's teacher that some new felt-tip pens were missing from Joanne's desk, along with a brand-new notebook with a unique cover. The teacher investigated and found the pens and notebook in the possession of another little girl, who denied she had stolen them.

"I know that the girl stole them from your daughter," the teacher told Joanne's parents. "But her mother said she thinks she bought them. No one saw her take them, so we couldn't accuse her of stealing."

The teacher was in a dilemma. Circumstantial evidence showed the girl to be guilty, but there was no hard proof. What should parents and teachers do?

Things to Consider

➤ Most children will steal at least once. But a few will steal regularly and with increased sophistication. When first discovered, parents shouldn't overreact. Most children learn that stealing is wrong and will learn not to take other people's belongings.

➤ Frequent stealing among children ages ten to twelve is a predictor of court-recorded offenses later on. Frequent stealing is a sign of serious emotional problems.

➤ One study showed that a significant number of children who were referred for psychiatric assessment because they had been accused of stealing came from families where there was little parental warmth or personal attention.

➤ Stealing is hard to detect as kids get older. When stealing becomes a noticeable problem, you are better off taking the approach where your child has to prove his innocence rather than you prove his guilt. The little girl in the opening story who stole felt-tip pens got away with it because the teacher believed a child is innocent until proven guilty. Give children the benefit of the doubt at first. But if they are repeat offenders, you will make more headway if you make them prove their innocence.

How to Say It

- Younger children who are otherwise good kids are best taught that stealing is wrong (**DO'S & DON'TS**) without traumatizing them. "This toy doesn't belong to you. It is wrong to take things that are not yours."

- "It is called stealing when you take something that you did not pay for. Put it back."

- Use normal events to model honesty. "I just noticed that the woman at the checkout register overpaid me. Let's go and return the money to her."

- "This money on the table is for the waiter. The people who sat here before we did left it. Someone else might have taken this money and kept it. Let's make sure that the waiter gets his money."

- **EMPATHIZE** when your child really wanted something, but be sure to state that stealing is wrong. "You have the balloon in your pocket that we saw at the store. I know you really wanted it, but stealing is wrong. We'll go back to the store and return it."

- If infractions are more frequent and serious, consistent negative consequences are needed. If the child gets away with stealing even once in a while, it will become harder to break the habit. "This is the third time this week I've noticed money missing from my wallet. The first two times we found out that you stole it. Now I cannot trust you, and I have to believe that you stole the money again this time. Unless you can prove to me you were innocent, you will have to wash all the windows as a punishment."

- **ENCOURAGE** honesty by rewarding it with praise. "These cookies were on the counter all afternoon. I know you wanted some, but you didn't take any because you knew they were for the party. That shows honesty and trustworthiness."

Smart Talk

Signs That Your Child May Be Headed for Disaster

Prominent psychologist Jerome Kagan has outlined five categories to predict adolescents who are at risk for criminal behavior (such as stealing), teen pregnancy, or substance abuse. If your child fits even one of the categories, he or she is at risk.

Child has had chronic school failure.

There is a history of family abuse or neglect.

Child is easily vulnerable to peer pressure and peer values.

Child wants to prove he is fearless and is willing to take dangerous risks.

The child comes from a family that regards criminal behavior, teen pregnancy, and substance abuse as normal.

How Not to Say It

- "You're a thief!" Stealing is something all kids do at least once. Labeling them is an overreaction. Firmly tell them that what they did was wrong and why.
- "What am I going to do with you? Huh? Go to your room." If stealing is very infrequent and minor, you are overreacting. If the stealing has become more frequent and you are worried, try not to come up with arbitrary, spur-of-the-moment punishments. Instead, make the consequences clear and punitive, and apply them consistently.
- "If you keep that up, you'll get into real trouble someday." What you are saying is true but ineffective. Kids for whom stealing will become a problem do not think about long-term consequences.

Strangers

The mother leaned closer to the car window and began giving the driver directions. The driver had just pulled over, rolled down the window, and asked her if she knew where Prospect Street was. She held her child's hand while she spoke to the strange man.

When parents do these reasonable things, it can be confusing to kids who've been told not to talk to strangers. Evidently, parents can talk to them, but children shouldn't. When a parent casually says "hi" to a passerby, is that person still a stranger?

One man called a coworker at home. "Is your dad there?" he asked.

The little girl on the other end of the line spoke hesitantly. "Uh, no. He's . . . in the shower."

An hour later the man called back. "Is your dad there?" he asked again.

"Uh, no," the girl said. "He's in the shower."

"Can I speak to your mom then?"

"Uh, no. She's in the shower, too."

Parents try to teach their kids how to handle contact with strangers. It's just not that simple.

Things to Consider

➤ In 1988, 200 to 300 children were kidnapped by a stranger (taken more than fifty miles or ransomed, or murdered). Between 3,200 and 4,600 children were abducted by a stranger (taken, lured, or detained—usually to be sexually victimized). There were 115,000 reported unsuccessful abduction attempts. The rate of abduction by family members is much higher. A survey of children ages ten to sixteen in 1995 revealed that 3 percent reported having been abducted.

➤ Smaller children up to about age nine tend to think in black-and-white terms. Trying to teach them to distinguish between a safe and unsafe stranger can get confusing. It is better to talk about safe and unsafe *situations* and *behaviors* (inappropriate touching no matter who the person is, answering a door when you are home alone, etc.).

➤ Even familiar faces pose a potential danger. In most cases of sexual abuse the victim knows the perpetrator.

➤ Limit any unnecessary safety risks. Don't leave kids in a car unattended for any length of time. If no adult is home, let the answering machine pick up, not your child.

➤ Review, review, review. Kids can't remember all the rules. To pass the time, go over the rules while driving.

➤ Abductions by a parent during litigation are increasing. Studies show that such abductions are more likely to occur when a parent has a concern about an abusive or criminal environment for the child; when a parent has no respect for the law; when a parent is reluctant to seek help from the court; when the parent was not married to the other parent, was poorly educated, and had low income.

How to Say It

- **TEACH** about the danger posed by some people (not necessarily strangers). "There are people—grown-ups—who can act very friendly or as if they need your help. But really they are bad and might want to hurt other people. Most people are good, but it can be hard to tell the difference, so I don't want you speaking to people you don't know or standing close to them unless somebody you trust is there."

- Review a list of "nevers," such as:

     "Never get into a car with somebody you don't know even if it's raining or you are tired from walking."

     "Never tell anybody on the phone that you are home alone."

     "Never answer the door if you are home alone. If the other person says it's an emergency, call 911."

     "Never accept any food from somebody you don't know."

- Quiz your children on how they might handle certain situations. "What if a stranger asked you to go into the woods and help him find his dog? What would you do?" "What if somebody told you that I gave him permission to pick you up? What would you do?"
- "If you are not sure what to do, you can run away and you can scream. Then go to a place where you know somebody."
- "If you are at a mall or parking lot and feel threatened, yell out loud that the stranger is *not* your parent. Otherwise, some people will think you are just being a disobedient child."
- Offer reassurance if kids get too frightened. "As I said, most people are good and would not want to hurt you, but in order to be safe you must not trust many people. When you get older, you'll learn how to tell the difference better."

Smart Talk

How Best to Educate Your Child About Safety

Research shows that verbal instructions alone are inadequate. Four additional steps are essential.

Modeling. Demonstrate to your child what to say and do in a variety of unsafe situations.

Rehearsal. Have your child rehearse what to say and do, much like a child would rehearse a scene from a play.

Corrective feedback. Tell your child what he did well and what he did that was not helpful.

Practice. Review these methods frequently. Don't presume that as your child gets older (preteen or adolescent) he is prepared. *For reported cases of sexual assault, the majority of victims are teenagers.* (However, when asked retrospectively about prior victimization, 64 percent of adults claim they were sexually assaulted before the age of twelve.)

How Not to Say It

- "Be careful whom you speak to" or "Watch out for strange-looking people." Kids require very specific information, not vague, ambiguous rules. Saying "Be careful" is not the same as teaching a child to run away or scream.

- "Why didn't you answer the phone? It was an important message for me" or "Why didn't you accept the package when the mail carrier knocked on the door? Now I have to wait until tomorrow" or "Why didn't you act friendly to the adults at the party when they spoke to you?" Unless you give children specific *prior* instruction ("It's okay to answer the door if the mail carrier knocks. I'm expecting an important package"), don't criticize them for taking safety precautions.

- "Strangers sometimes kidnap little kids, take them away from their parents, hurt them, and kill them." Don't overly frighten your child. What if your child needs help and has only strangers to ask? All trustworthy people were strangers at one time.

Rule of Thumb: The best approach is to emphasize self-protective behaviors instead of emphasizing the negative consequences of failing to protect oneself.

Swearing

Mark and his sister, Melanie, were arguing about hogging the computer. Fourth-grader Mark ended the argument by calling his sister a bitch. Their mother was nearby and came running into the room.

"Mark! How dare you call your sister such a name!"

"Oh, it's not that bad, Mom. I only called her a female dog."

Mom was slightly taken aback, partly because she figured out that Mark must have looked up the word in a dictionary—perhaps the only time in his life he did that for something other than a homework assignment.

What should a parent do when his child swears?

Things to Consider

➤ Cursing and use of foul language have become a rite of initiation for many preteens and teens. You won't be able to prevent your child from swearing if his peers swear and he wants to fit in. But you can keep him from swearing at home.

➤ If you or your partner swears in front of the kids, even infrequently, your effort to prevent them from swearing will be seriously hindered.

➤ If you don't swear in front of your children, they will not swear in front of you.

➤ Frequent swearing by an adult (especially when aggravated) can actually increase anger. That can cause an increase in swearing. Teaching kids how to cope with frustrations without excessive anger or cursing is a wonderful thing to do.

How to Say It

- **TEACH** your values regarding swearing. "You don't hear me swear because even though it is common, it is like spitting on the sidewalk. It also offends many people, and we should show respect."
- If your child asks if you ever swear, **REPORT** the truth. "Yes, I do swear once in a while, but only if I'm alone or with somebody I know won't be offended. Frankly, swearing is a bad habit."
- Your preteen may object that curse words are just that—words. "But words have meaning, and they can offend people. If I called somebody stupid or made a racial remark, it is true that I'd be saying only words, but they would be hurtful words, offensive words. It would be wrong to say them."
- **EMPATHIZE** with a preteen's need to fit in. "Using bad words makes many kids your age feel cool. They want to fit in with their friends. That's understandable, but I'll be glad when you feel you can fit in without having to do things that are offensive."
- **DO'S & DON'TS**. "I still don't want to hear you swearing at home."
- **ENCOURAGE**. On occasion let your child know that you appreciate her use of proper language. "Some kids your age use curse words even at home. I'm proud of you for not doing that."

How Not to Say It

- "If you curse, I'll wash your mouth out with soap." You shouldn't have to take it that far. If you don't swear and your home life is reasonably happy, your children will respect your wishes. If they happen to swear in your presence, a firm reprimand will suffice.
- "Just because I swear doesn't mean you can." True. But don't expect compliance when you are modeling inappropriate behavior.
- "Jesus Christ!" Any swearing does not help you teach values such as patience, tolerance, or respect. Using a religious profanity also degrades God and your child's view of God. Since most Americans do have religious beliefs, you are undermining your efforts to teach religious values and love for God by using such language.

Tattling

"Mom!" cried eight-year-old Sabrina. "Ben is sneaking a cookie!"

"We don't like tattletales, Sabrina," Mom said.

Later on a neighbor knocked on the door and informed the mother that Ben was playing on the roof.

On the roof!

Mom ran upstairs to Ben's bedroom and found the window wide open. Sabrina was playing in the hallway. "Sabrina!" Mom said. "Why didn't you tell me that Ben was on the roof!"

"Because we don't like tattletales," she said.

Things to Consider

➤ Tattling is a quality most parents object to. However, parents still take action about the information the tattler gives. Consequently, parents give a mixed message.

➤ Tattling tends to be more frequent among kids up to age six.

➤ Children who tattle are rarely reprimanded, though tattling is discouraged.

➤ Parents seem to want the information a tattler reveals but dislike the (usually) self-serving motives of a tattler (to feel important, to get a sibling in trouble, etc.).

➤ Most kids outgrow tattling. Unnecessary tattling is sometimes punished by the one reported on—who gets even (often by finding something to tattle about). That natural consequence can curtail excessive tattling.

How to Say It

- You want to discourage your young children from being spies, police officers, and miniature parents, and learn to report on only serious or dangerous situations. Expect your child not to make the fine distinctions you would. "Anna, I know you like to tell me when your brother is doing something he shouldn't. Please tell me only if he is hurting someone or is in danger."
- "If you tattle just to get your sister in trouble, I won't appreciate it."
- "If you aren't sure whether to tell me, it's okay to tell me."
- "If you tell me something that I don't think was your business, I will say 'thank you,' but I probably won't do anything about it."
- Probe for underlying reasons for tattling. "Sometimes children like to tattle because it makes them feel good or they are mad about something. Tell me all your reasons."
- "You just tattled on your brother when he gave the dog his ham sandwich. What was your reason?"
- **ENCOURAGE** appropriate tattling. "Thank you for telling me that your brother went on the canoe without a life vest. It might have saved his life."

How Not to Say It

- "No one likes a tattletale." This really doesn't teach a child to properly discriminate between appropriate and inappropriate tattling.
- "Only little kids tattle. You should know better." Actually, an older child is more likely to learn the difference between safe and unsafe situations and when "telling" is appropriate.
- "I'm so glad you told me that your brother didn't brush his teeth." Encouraging tattling of minor infractions is not a good idea. You will create a monster.
- "You're a good helper for telling me the things your brother is doing wrong." Don't encourage her.

Being Teased

The neighborhood kids were tossing the football around. Occasionally, one of them would run for a pass or try to intercept a throw. At one point Jerry Scott grabbed the ball.

"Hey, don't let Scotty have it," a boy called out. "He doesn't know whether to dribble it or kick it!"

Everybody laughed. Jerry Scott took the ribbing good-naturedly. Later, he intercepted a throw and turned to the boy who just missed catching it. "Sorry, lady," he said. "Maybe next time."

Some teasing remarks are clearly mean-spirited and meant to ridicule. Some are obviously meant to be fun. However, much teasing can be hard to interpret unless one is keenly aware of the social context. A ribbing by a good friend is overlooked. The same comment by a new kid on the block might result in a war of words.

At some point everyone gets teased. Boys and men often define their friendships as one of good-natured but sometimes vicious put-downs. Insulting a buddy is a man's way of saying "I care about you."

Handling teasing among children is not always straightforward. Sometimes telling kids not to let teasing bother them is like telling a swimmer not to get wet.

Things to Consider

➤ Younger children regard teasing as hurtful most of the time.

➤ Eighth-grade boys rate teasing and being teased as a positive experience.

➤ According to reports, teasing is more a part of boys' lives than girls' lives.

➤ Teasing is a paradox. It can bring people closer together or create emotional distance.

➤ Children who were rejected by peers for being overly aggressive or submissive were often criticized for being unable to tolerate teasing. Coping with teasing and the ability to distinguish teasing from ridicule is a major task of children, especially as they get older. Rehearsing with them how not to overreact to teasing is crucial. They won't learn it by verbal instruction only.

How to Say It

- If your child is hurt by a teasing remark, your first response should be one of **EMPATHY**. "When your friend said that to you, it felt like he was making fun and that must have hurt."
- "It isn't fun when somebody teases you."
- "You felt sad when the kid on the bus laughed at your dress. It wasn't a very nice thing to do." (Often, an empathic remark makes the child feel understood and reassured that she is loved and cared about. That may be all that is required to help her get over the hurt.)
- If you believe that your child is taking it too hard or has misinterpreted a teasing remark, **TEACH** about alternative ways to interpret. "Remember how Uncle John and I tease each other a lot? We don't do that to be hurtful. It is our way of saying we love each other. I know that sounds strange, but it's true. I wonder if the boy who teased you really likes and admires you. Is that possible?"
- "Some kids make fun of other kids because they are jealous. Sometimes they are unhappy about things in their life, so they strike out at others with mean words. Is it possible that Jeffrey could be unhappy about things?"
- Get your child to imagine how other children successfully cope with teasing. "Have you ever seen a kid at school get teased and *not* feel bad about it later? Why do you think that was?"
- "I remember when Jason from next door teased you, but you didn't seem to be bothered. Why was that?"
- "There is a magic formula to handling being teased. If you smile and say nothing, the teaser will probably stop teasing. If he teased you

because he likes you, then he also liked it that you smiled. If he teased you because he wanted to be mean, he won't like it that you smiled and will probably stop teasing."

- **TEACH** by distinguishing good-natured teasing from ridicule. "Kids who want to be mean usually make mean faces when they tease you. Someone who likes you usually won't do that."

- "Someone who wants to hurt your feelings might show off in front of others by laughing at you and trying to get others to laugh at you. Someone who is just making a small joke may say it only to you and not try to get others to laugh at you."

- "If a good friend teases you, she probably doesn't mean to be hurtful. But if it bothers you, talk to her about it later. If she is really your friend, she'll stop teasing you that way."

- Tell stories about how you were teased when you were young. That often takes the sting out of it for your kids. "Oh, sure I remember being teased. When kids in my class thought it was cool to play the guitar, I took violin lessons. They teased me about that. But it didn't last long, and today I'm a pretty good violinist."

- A child who overreacts to teasing may well be troubled by other things. He may be feeling inadequate or unhappy or scared. Probe for possibilities. "How about we go for a ride and get an ice cream cone. I want to talk. I'm thinking that some things are bothering you and hoping you'll tell me what they are."

- A child who is very troubled by teasing may be someone who is being cruelly and repeatedly teased. This can be extremely harmful to your child and can result in severe behavioral disturbances. A loving, supportive family is crucial. You must also take steps to protect your child. "What those other kids are doing is very cruel. I will talk to the school principal and I will also speak to one of the parents whom I know. In the meantime, I want to rehearse with you how you can act when kids tease you. And remember, I love you with all my heart."

- "This may not help much, but I want you to know I think you are terrific. Every day for me is a happy one in large part because of you."

Rule of Thumb: If the home life is happy and secure, your child will most likely learn to handle being teased.

How Not to Say It

- "Hey, everybody gets teased. You'll get over it." This "don't worry, be happy" approach isn't necessary. Yes, your child probably will get over it (unless he is being mercilessly teased), but you can help by showing some **EMPATHY** first. "It sounds as if you had a rough time on the bus ride home."

- "Oh, quit your whining." You are coming perilously close to teasing your child because she is upset about being teased. You are validating her belief that there is something wrong or inadequate about her.

- "Stop teasing him. You're being mean." You may be right, but you may not be. Remember, the words themselves are less the problem than the context. If the kids still play together and enjoy each other's company, their teasing may be good-natured.

- "Oh, come on. I was just teasing you. Stop crying. Can't you take a joke?" Sometimes a parent teases a child hoping to get a laugh, but it backfires. When that happens, never add insult to injury ("Can't you take a joke?"). Apologize instead and offer comfort. When your child is less upset, you can try to explain what your intentions were.

- "How would you like it if someone teased you!?" This effort to instill empathy may not work if your child is eleven or older. Chances are he has begun to learn how to handle teasing. If he answered your question honestly, he'd probably say, "I wouldn't mind it if I got teased."

Trading Cards
and Mild Gambling

"I didn't think those pocket monster trading cards would be such a big deal to my kids," one mother said. "But they've taken over my children's lives. They're all they think about. When we're at the store they want me to buy them more cards. Then there is the issue of trading. It seems as though I'm watching young warriors at the stock market, the way they go at it. Should I be concerned?"

Kids have been trading cards ever since the first baseball card was printed a century ago. But today the characters being traded also have their likeness printed on hundreds of merchandising products and are the subject of movies and video games. It is hard to escape them. Like many things, it can get out of hand if parents are not observant.

Things to Consider

➢ For most children, trading cards will not become an obsession that interferes with their lives. But research suggests that children who tend to be more impulsive by nature do not foresee negative consequences and do not halt their actions quickly despite these consequences. They may be more likely to take some games to the limit.

➢ Trading has a gambling component. Kids are not always sure they made the best deal and may in fact lose out. Popular cards often have a limited printing that causes kids to keep purchasing more in hopes of finding the elusive ones.

➢ Many schools have banned trading cards because they pose too much of a disruption in schoolwork.

➤ High-frequency video game players gamble more than low-frequency video game players do. They also report that gambling makes them feel important.

➤ Gambling at age twelve predicts later substance abuse.

➤ Research has shown that parents overestimate the age at which their children first gambled and underestimate the probability that their child has already gambled.

➤ Trading cards can be fun and not dangerous. Parents can no longer presume it is completely innocent fun when in fact these items are marketed to entice kids to purchase more and more cards. Use common sense.

How to Say It

- Learn about your child's interests. It will help you decide whether any parental intervention is required. "Tell me all about these cards you have. What makes them interesting?"

- "How many cards do you get in a pack? How many different cards are there in all?"

- "Which friends have these cards? Do you trade with them?"

- TEACH about gambling. "When you buy a pack of cards, you may end up getting the same cards you already own, so you may waste your money. That's gambling. You are taking a chance with your money."

- DO'S & DON'TS. Parents must limit their children's involvement in activities that can get out of hand. "You can buy a new pack of trading cards every week [two weeks, etc.]."

- "No trading cards or talking about it with friends until your homework is done and corrected."

- "No looking on the web for more trading cards."

- EMPATHIZE. "It can be fun to collect as many cards as possible. Sometimes it gets frustrating when no matter how hard you try, you still can't collect them all."

How Not to Say It

- "I don't want you trading any cards." Trading is not a problem unless it becomes an intense preoccupation. Most kids outgrow the desire to collect the objects.

- "Buying trading cards is a complete waste. It's silly." You are probably right, but what are you achieving? If you don't want your child spending money on such things, say so. If you intend to let him purchase cards, then explain your concerns in a manner that doesn't sound insulting.

Trauma from an Accident or Natural Disaster

Kenny is a six-year-old admitted to a pediatric hospital in Boston. While his injuries after a bike accident were not life-threatening (350,000 children are injured each year from bicycle accidents), he had something more interesting to report: He had recently witnessed a stabbing. According to the *Journal of the American Medical Association,* 10 percent of hospitalized children (ages six and under) in Boston reported witnessing a shooting or stabbing. A study of sixth, eighth, and tenth graders in New Haven, Connecticut, revealed that 40 percent of these students had witnessed at least one violent crime in the past year. Almost all eighth graders knew someone who had been killed.

Three months after Hurricane Andrew devastated parts of Florida, one-third of children affected by the hurricane had significant symptoms of post-traumatic stress. After seven months many children improved except for those who had been more anxious and inattentive prior to the hurricane.

Too many children witness violence in the home or in their community. About 7 percent of children are regularly teased or bullied by peers. Odds are that by the time your child is ready to leave the nest, she will have witnessed or experienced some violent act, serious accident, or emotional trauma.

Things to Consider

➤ The impact of an extreme event can be reduced if the child lives in a loving, supportive home environment. But esteemed researcher and trauma expert Dr. Ronnie Janoff-Bulman at the University of Massachusetts in Amherst warns that the negative effects can be magnified if the child resides in an uncaring, abusive home.

➤ A caring family is not sufficient to help a child cope with disaster or trauma. Unless the parents or caretakers are willing to talk about the trauma on a regular basis, the barrier to communication will be a barrier to health. Parents should not conclude that discussing an upsetting event would retraumatize their child. Children need to talk about (or draw or playact) the painful events.

➤ Common symptoms after experiencing or witnessing a traumatic event include: bed-wetting, sleep difficulty, separation anxiety, intrusive thoughts about the event, physical complaints, and increased dependency. Girls tend to complain more about anxiety and depression than boys do, but boys may experience troublesome memories.

➤ Extreme symptoms are likely if the child experienced distress that was either life threatening, included scenes of grotesque destruction (mangled bodies, etc.), or involved serious injury to self or a family member.

➤ Greater effort to suppress upsetting thoughts or memories is associated with more severe symptoms.

➤ Children can exhibit intense symptoms when they have experienced mild trauma or mild symptoms when they have experienced extreme trauma. Don't judge the emotional impact on the basis of the seriousness of the accident alone. How parents react to the trauma has tremendous bearing on how the child reacts.

How to Say It

- Reassure your child that she is safe now and that the event has passed. "You are okay now. I am here with you, and all is safe. What happened was awful, but it's over. It's done. It's all gone." Be prepared to remind your child frequently that she is safe and that the event has passed.
- Speak calmly. Allow your child to say what he needs to. Encourage opening up. "When you are ready, you can tell me what happened."
- "I want to hear what happened . . ."
- "I want you to tell me what it was like for you . . ."
- "Even though it's over, I want you to be free to talk to me anytime about it."

- If your child shows symptoms that are upsetting to him (bed-wetting, fear of losing you, nightmares, etc.), reassure him that these are normal. "Children who go through what you went through usually wet their bed or have fears about doing certain things. The fears will go away soon."

- Guilt is a common aftereffect of surviving or witnessing trauma. Sometimes children believe they caused or could have prevented the event or injury. "These things happen. It was not your fault. The people who were injured were doing what they normally do, and yet they ended up getting hurt."

- "If you feel you'd like to do something for the people who were hurt, there are many things you can do. You can pray for them. If you'd like, we can stop in at church and say a special prayer. You can make a card. You can write a note. You can plant some flowers for them . . ."

- Observe your child at play and notice if she is trying to cope with the trauma by drawing or playing with dolls, etc. Use it as a springboard for a discussion later. "I noticed you were playing with the Barbie doll and you had her go to the hospital. Maybe you were thinking about the car accident . . ."

- ENCOURAGE dialogue. "I'm so glad you are talking about it with me. It's important to talk. Talking is like medicine. It will help you feel better."

Rule of Thumb: Initial signs that your child is okay can be misleading. Symptoms often occur many weeks or months later. Also, symptoms can reemerge on "anniversary" dates, especially if the event is shown on TV (a tornado, hurricane, flood, etc.).

How Not to Say It

- "Try to forget about it." Suppression of memory leads to more complications. If it is upsetting for you to talk about it, let your child talk to others or to a professional. (You should, too.)

- "I warned you not to go there," "I told you to wear a seatbelt," or "You knew better than to go with those other kids." If your child has experienced or witnessed some violent event, these comments will add to guilt and perhaps result in his not wanting to talk further about the event.

- "Oh, don't worry. You'll be fine. You'll get over it." You may be right, and your intent to be reassuring is good. However, be careful you don't give your child the impression that you do not want her to talk about it with you. Plus, really listen to her concerns before you start telling her to cheer up.

- "Oh, every time you talk about it, I shudder. I hate thinking about it." This is not a good idea because he may choose to keep quiet.

- "If you keep talking about it, you'll never get better." False. The opposite is true.

Violence and Sexual Material in Television and Movies

Wanda was careful about what she let her children watch on television. She was well aware that the sexual content of "family" programs had risen sharply. Still, she was surprised at how the objectionable material slipped into the television viewing. While watching an "allowed" show with her kids, a commercial came on advertising a show that was to air later that evening. In the preview two teenage girls were discussing their prom night. One lamented that she'd had a miserable time. "Why?" her friend asked. "Because my mom ended up sleeping with my boyfriend."

The line was supposed to get a laugh from the audience. Wanda was shocked, and she didn't know what to say to her eight- and ten-year-old children watching with her.

Television, movies, and video games play a huge role in the lives of most kids—even larger when the kids become teenagers. American kids watch between three and four hours of TV a day. Many movies try to attract preteens by using popular actors. Movies such as *Men in Black, Titanic, Ace Ventura,* and others boast a PG-13 rating, luring many kids younger than thirteen to more mature sexual or violent displays.

Things to Consider

➢ According to the research on the effects of television violence, there is overwhelming evidence of a link between TV violence and aggressiveness in children. The link is circular. Aggressiveness promotes the watching of violent programs, which fosters more aggressive tendencies. Obviously, media violence is just one of many links to aggressive behavior.

➢ Media violence puts some children at greater risk, particularly children with established emotional or behavioral disorders or children from homes where violence already exists.

➤ TV viewing adds to mindless daydreaming and detracts from a child's use of creative imagination.

➤ In a study of fourth and fifth graders, the students watched a low-grade violent film *(Karate Kid)* or a nonviolent sports program. They were later asked to monitor two children (shown on videotape) and ask for help if the two children needed assistance. Kids who watched the more violent film took longer to ask for help when the kids were fighting aggressively; in other words, they had a greater tolerance for watching real-life violence.

➤ Television news is downright frightening to children. It is best that they limit any viewing of news.

➤ One study in the journal *Pediatrics* showed that the onset of teen drinking was strongly related to the viewing of TV, music videos, and movie videos. The more they watched in ninth grade, the more likely they began drinking within the year. While it is not accurate to state that TV viewing caused drinking (perhaps teens who are inclined to drink like to watch more TV and videos), excessive viewing is a warning sign that drinking may follow.

➤ TV shows, music videos, and movies tend to show teen sexual behavior or partying as normal and risk free. Yet half of all teenage deaths due to injury are alcohol related, and 10 percent of teenage girls get pregnant each year.

Rule of Thumb: Parents must monitor and severely limit their children's TV viewing. It will improve the children's academic scores and reduce any effect TV violence or inappropriate sexual material may have.

How to Say It

- **DO'S & DON'TS.** "From now on you can watch TV only between the hours of . . ."
- "From now on you can watch only these programs . . ."
- "From now on the TV stays off during the week on school nights unless it is a special educational program or one I give you permission to watch." (You may want to unplug the TV after each use. It will help curtail impulsive TV viewing.)

- **TEACH** your values when objectionable material is shown. "That program showed two unmarried young people going to bed. I think that is a dangerous message for young people. Sex without love and commitment can increase the risk of unwanted pregnancy or disease."

- "That program makes fun of religion. Religion is very important to me and to many people. What are your thoughts?"

- "That racing-car video game shows women in two-piece swimsuits standing on the sidelines and cheering on the competitors. Why do you think that is?"

- **TEACH** younger children the difference between reality and fantasy. (One research study revealed that children with emotional or behavioral problems tended to prefer aggressive TV characters and more often believed fictional material to be true.) "Could somebody really jump out of a plane without a parachute and land on his feet?" or "Is it likely someone can drive that fast and dangerously and not get into an accident? Could that happen in real life?"

- **ENCOURAGE** alternatives to TV and video games. Even a half hour less of TV per night devoted to school or a family activity would pay huge dividends. **EMPATHIZE** with your child's initial frustration at having less TV time. "I know that not having the TV on as much can be boring. I know reading books is not something you look forward to. But I'm hoping you can spend some of the time playing games, learning new things, or with me."

How Not to Say It

Don't say anything that weakens your authority, sounds wishy-washy, or abandons your role as parent.

- "Why are you watching that junk?" Your sentiment is well taken, but what precisely do you mean? Do you want the TV off? Then say so. Did you want to explain why you don't like the show? Do that. Don't ask open-ended questions. Preteens and teens have answers for everything and are genetically programmed to be great defense attorneys.

- "I wish you wouldn't watch that show." Why be a wimp? You have the authority to enforce your views.

- "Are you sure that movie is okay for someone your age?" He's sure. But it still may be inappropriate and against your values. Don't ask his opinion. He thinks purple hair and body piercing are cool, too.

- "How long are you going to be playing that video game? Don't you have homework to do?" You sound so reasonable and fair, but it is okay to set a time limit for games. You don't have to let your child play as long as she wants. As a general rule, homework before pleasure makes sense. "When the show is over in ten minutes, please turn off the TV and start your homework. I know you have a test tomorrow."

Whiny and Demanding Child

"But why can't I see that movie? Everybody in my class saw it already!" Steve said.

"I doubt everybody saw it. It's rated PG-13, and you're only ten," Dad answered.

"They did see it! That's all they talk about."

"Well, just because other kids can do something doesn't mean it's right for you."

"It's not fair!" Steve plopped himself on the couch and sat like a statue, arms folded, face contorted with anger.

"It may not seem fair but—"

"How do you know I shouldn't watch it? Just because it's PG-13 doesn't mean I'm not old enough!"

The discussion continued a long while. Steve's form of whining was typical of older kids—complaining, debating, sulking, and facial expressions that could scare away a grizzly bear. Younger children like to stretch out their syllables ("Mommm! Pleeeease!) with a tone of voice as soothing as a dentist's drill.

Things to Consider

➢ All kids whine occasionally. Those who whine more have been rewarded for it.

➢ Many parents are guilt ridden because they have careers, are too busy, were previously divorced, or don't make enough money. Consequently, they overindulge their children just enough that the kids believe the world revolves around them.

➤ Spouses often don't deal with a whiny child in exactly the same way. One parent may be firm; the other may give in. That increases the likelihood of whining (not just by the child but by one of the frustrated parents, too).

➤ Sometimes kids whine because they have a legitimate complaint that the parent is ignoring. They may be overtired, very bored at an adult function, or frustrated by some other problem.

How to Say It

- Children can benefit from a four-step procedure. First, **TEACH** why whining bothers you:

    "It is as if you are hitting me with your voice."

    "Whining is not polite."

    "Whining is something younger children do, and you are older."

    "Whining after I say no to something is like disobeying me."

    "Whining gives me a headache."

- Next, demonstrate how to talk without whining. "If you want something and I say no, you could say, 'But I really want that. Can I talk to you about it again after lunch?'"

- "You could say, 'Mom, I'm tired and I want to go home please,' instead of whining, 'I want to go home right now!'"

- "You could say, 'I'm upset that other kids can see a movie and I can't. Please think about ways I could see it.'"

- Next, have your child rehearse speaking or complaining without whining. "Pretend you want something and I'm not agreeing to it. Talk to me in a way that is polite instead of whining."

- Finally, praise and **ENCOURAGE** appropriate behavior. "I like the way you asked me that. You weren't whining. You were being polite. I'm impressed."

- Anticipate whining situations and discuss it ahead of time with your child. "When we are in the supermarket, I know it will take us longer to shop than you would like. I'll do my best to hurry. Remember how you learned ways to talk to me without whining? Please practice them in the store." While shopping, periodically praise your child for not whining. Don't wait until the trip is over to praise. By the way, an occasional treat (ice cream cone, etc.) is fine as a reward, too.

- If your child is being polite and reasonable but you still must say no to a request, be careful. Your child may have no choice but to whine. It is better to **EMPATHIZE** and try to meet your child's legitimate needs at least partly. "You're right. It is hot and we have stayed here too long, but I can't leave yet. I don't blame you for being tired and upset. What could happen now that would make it easier for you to stay just a while longer?"
- Even if your child stops whining, he won't necessarily get his way. Be sure to **EMPATHIZE** then and thank him for cooperating. "I know it is upsetting that we can't drive to your cousin's house this weekend. You were looking forward to it. Let's figure out when we can go again. I appreciate it that you are being good about this."

How Not to Say It

- "Stop whining!" By itself this is not an effective technique. Perhaps you've noticed. If you've caved in to whining in the past, you helped create a monster. Stop rewarding unpleasant behavior and have your child rehearse better ways to try to manipulate you—er, I mean, better ways to converse with you.
- "If you don't stop your whining, I'll . . ." Threats may work for the moment, but you'll have a sulking, resentful child on your hands who will probably continue his whining later. It is better to approach this problem more systematically: Assess whether you've rewarded whining in the past and **TEACH** your child better ways to speak.
- "Grow up!" She will someday. She'll be dating boys with fast cars, an overabundance of testosterone, and God knows what kind of jewelry hanging from what parts of their bodies, and you'll wish she was seven again and whining like crazy. Parents are sure fickle.
- "You're driving me crazy!" That is what your child intended. Ignoring her is better than admitting she got to you.

Working Parent
(When You Used to Stay at Home)

Sylvia was a stay-at-home mom until her youngest child, Paula, entered first grade. The family could use the extra income, and Sylvia went back to work as a computer programmer—a job she gave up after the birth of her first child. But Sylvia had some concerns. Would she have enough energy at the end of the day to handle her home responsibilities? Would her husband help out more? Would the kids be at an emotional disadvantage because they had gotten used to having her around at all times? What happens when the kids get sick and have summer vacation? Could she handle the worry and stress that comes from trying to please a boss and a family at the same time?

Things to Consider

➤ More than half of all mothers are now in the workforce.

➤ There are spillover effects. A miserable job can add to family tension, though a happy family life can often make it easier to cope with a difficult job. Women who work at exciting or challenging jobs often report a greater ability to cope with the ups and downs of parenting than women with tedious jobs.

➤ Employment status is not the essential factor when assessing children's coping. The quality of home life overall is a more potent force.

➤ Extra income can add to a child's quality of life. However, research shows that if the frequency of shared parent-child activities is lessened due to employment, children may have poorer adjustments and show a decline in school performance.

➤ Working parents in a crunch for time spend more of it with younger kids. (Don't overlook the older kids.)

➤ Some evidence (though controversial) shows that infants in day care more than twenty hours per week for their first year of life have weaker attachments to parents and are more aggressive and noncompliant in school.

How to Say It

- Much depends on whether the parent is happy or unhappy about returning to work. **REPORT** by giving your child a clear idea of how your job will affect him. "I expect to leave for work after you get on the school bus and be home about an hour after you get home. That means you will be cared for by [Dad, yourself, your older sibling, Grandma, a neighbor, day care, etc.]."

- "I'll have less time to do housework, so I'll need you to do these extra chores to help out."

- "It is important to me that you and I still have time every day to share things like singing, reading books, homework, going for walks . . ."

- If you are looking forward to working, discuss why. If you are forced to work due to finances, try to sound optimistic. "The extra money will help pay for a new car that we really need. And we hope to save for a nice family vacation."

- **EMPATHIZE.** "I'm wondering if you feel worried about my working. Some kids do, some don't."

- "You seem excited. I'll have some interesting stories to tell about my day, won't I?"

- For a few months after you begin work, ask your child periodically how he is doing with the changes. Be careful not to ask leading questions. "I've been working for a week now. How was it for you?"

- If your child has relevant objections or concerns, do everything you can to fix things. The main objection will be that you have less time available. It is a reasonable objection with no easy answers for some people. "You're right. I do spend less time with you, and I hate that part. I have to work because I need the money. But I promise to try to plan my schedule a little differently. Do you have any ideas of how we could spend more time together?"

How Not to Say It

- "I'm taking a job, but I'm sure we'll all pitch in and do just fine." Don't be so reassuring just yet. Take time to spell out what the impact will be on your kids and listen to their responses. Otherwise, a child's uneasiness may be overlooked.

- "I can't help it if I have to work! You'll just have to get used to it. Other kids can handle it, so you should, too." It sounds as if you feel a little guilty for working and are lashing out at the kids. (Research shows that professional women don't feel they're doing enough for their kids even when they are doing more than their husbands.) Speak more tenderly to the kids (it's not their fault), look objectively at what you and your mate each do to help out at home, and get a grip.

- "You don't like it that I work, do you?" or "You like that I work, don't you?" Don't ask leading questions. Children may give you the answer you want to hear and not the answer they are really thinking about.

Rule of Thumb: You can't do it all. If both partners work, something will suffer. You will lose couple time, alone time, time for the kids, or time to do household chores. Research shows that couple time is usually sacrificed, which is a mistake. Ease up on housework, hire someone to mow the lawn, and spend the extra time with your mate.

Worried Child

Grandma's upcoming visit all the way from Michigan was on Hillary's mind. She was excited but worried, too.

"What if there's bad weather and the plane can't fly?" Hillary said. "Or what if the plane flies, but the pilot makes a mistake and the plane crashes?"

Mom tried to reassure her young daughter. "There's no need to worry," she said. "Grandma has visited many times, and she always has a safe trip."

"But what if . . ."

Hillary was off and running. She worried about everything: her grades, her health, the health of her family, and the future in general. About 3 percent of kids have anxiety severe enough to warrant a clinical diagnosis sometime during their childhood. But over 70 percent of kids ages eight to thirteen worry every few days to the point where it is hard for them to manage their concerns.

Things to Consider

➤ Highly anxious parents pose an obstacle to the successful treatment of highly anxious children unless the parents get treatment, too.

➤ Surveys indicate that school-age children worry frequently about school matters, dying, and social relationships. One study showed that global issues (pollution, starvation, and war) were high on the list of concerns for sixth graders.

➤ Parents underestimate the amount of worrying their children do.

How to Say It

- Probe for hidden concerns. "If I were to ask kids your age to list their top three worries, what do you think the answers would be?"

- Probe for coping skills. "If a child who was two years younger than you was worried about school grades [bullies, making friends, health, etc.], what advice would you give?"

- "A few weeks ago you were worried about the camp sleepover. What helped you to feel better? What did you do that made a difference?"

- **EMPATHIZE**. "You seem worried about your appearance. Some people worry about that. Do you think your friends are just as worried as you, or are they more worried?"

- "It must be hard for you to relax when you get so worried about things."

- **TEACH** alternative ways of viewing situations. "What is the evidence that people won't like you if you don't wear the right clothes? You've made many friends. Would they abandon you? Really?"

- "What is the evidence that you'll do poorly on that test?"

- "Once you think about the possibility that something bad could happen, you start to believe that the possibility is a strong likelihood. It's like seeing a small cloud and believing there will be a hurricane."

- "Make a list of everything you worry about for next week. Then we'll check off everything that comes true. I bet most of what you worry about never happens."

- "Next time you worry about something, tell yourself, 'My worry is like a balloon that I keep blowing into. It looks bigger and bigger, but it really is small when all the air is out of it.'"

- "Let's practice. I'll think of a few things to get nervous about and you try to show me why I'm exaggerating or worrying about something I can't control."

- "Tell yourself, 'I'm just having thoughts. Just because I think them doesn't mean they will happen.'"

- Find ways to praise and **ENCOURAGE** your child for reducing her worrisome thoughts. "You were worried about Grandma's safety, but then you told yourself she will be fine. Good for you."

How Not to Say It

- "It's silly to worry about those things." It isn't silly to your child. Help him to challenge his beliefs rather than dismiss his concerns as silly.
- "Don't worry about it." Nice try, but it probably won't work. Involving your child in some interesting activity may help.
- "You're just going through a phase." This is dismissive and doesn't help your child think more objectively about his concerns.

Smart Talk

At dinner or while driving in the car, practice being optimistic with your children. Ask, "What went right today? Let's think of as many things as we can." Later, have a discussion about things you can look forward to. Immediately challenge any pessimistic or fearful expectations with upbeat beliefs. The more positive expectations you possess, the easier it will be for your overly worried child to think positively. Tell your worried child to "turn your worry inside-out," and then give examples of how she can do that successfully. Praise her efforts.

When You Say It Right (but Things Still Go Wrong): Ten Winning Tips for Troubleshooters

Your world is probably filled with examples of "solutions" that used to work but don't anymore, or that work for other people but not you. Some solutions actually make the problem worse. For example:

A medication you take no longer is effective. You need something stronger.

Your dog follows the commands of a neighbor, but you can't get him to sit.

Your cold tablet stops your sniffles but makes you drowsy and unable to do your job.

You work longer hours to provide for your family, but now you rarely have time to see them.

You withdraw from an argument for fear of making it worse, only to grow increasingly resentful and distant from your spouse.

There are no perfect formulas to solve every child problem, but when common-sense solutions fail and creative solutions fail, chances are you have misidentified the problem. Giving your car a tune-up to make it run better won't help if the problem is bad gasoline. Wearing a sweater to keep warm is fine, but it doesn't fix the furnace.

Family life is complicated. People seek professional help because their efforts to resolve certain problems have failed and they don't know why. When reasonable efforts to parent your children backfire, something fundamental to the situation is being overlooked. This chapter will help you locate the culprits and fix them.

Reason #1: A Child Problem Is Really a Disguised Marital Problem

This takes many forms. One form occurs when a parent complains about a child's behavior (sloppy, inattentive, unappreciative, disrespectful, etc.) but the parent is hurt most by the belief that his spouse acts those ways, too. Thus, a man who is annoyed with his wife's inability to handle menial household chores by herself (such as a burned-out bulb or a tire with low air pressure) may yell at his daughter when she acts helpless. He is really angry with his wife. A wife who thinks her husband takes her for granted may find it difficult when the kids are whining while she's trying to eat lunch. She may mishandle that situation because her frustration with her husband is not being addressed.

When anger is misdirected at the children, yelling at them is often done within earshot of the spouse. "Will you kids please clean up your mess? How many times do I have to tell you!" may be a wife's way of yelling at her mate to help out more around the house.

Sometimes a child's behavior problem serves a hidden purpose. It gives a spouse an excuse to blame the mate for something. "See, I told you that you are too lenient [or harsh] with discipline. Now look at what he's done." When marital differences are annoying but unresolved, parents may have less flexibility when dealing with their children's problem behaviors, and those behaviors might then continue.

Finally, if a child's actions distract an unhappy couple from focusing on their relationship, the actions may persist despite reasonable efforts to resolve them. For example, a child who has many unrealistic fears and anxieties may keep parents from discussing (arguing about) an area of conflict. Instead, they may focus on the child. By bringing the parents together in a common cause, the child may subconsciously learn to develop symptoms.

If you want to assess your marriage, take the Argument Audit found in the Appendix. High scores may indicate that marital issues are interfering with your ability to effectively parent your child.

Reason #2: You Are Overly Involved or Underinvolved with Your Kids

Experts sometimes use the word *enmeshed* to describe an overly involved parent. Such parents mean well but actually tend to overprotect, smother, and stifle normal growth. They become uneasy with a child's growing independence because their own role is threatened. These parents use empathy a great deal and try to reason with their kids. This is not so bad, but usually they are trying to reason in ways that overprotect. Children in these cases tend to become more dependent and therefore require more involvement with their parents, so it is a self-perpetuating cycle. Some kids rebel and pull away from the smothering. Efforts to persuade them may fail—not because the words are ineffective but because the reason for the rebellion is being overlooked. Until Mom pulls back some (most enmeshed parents are mothers), nothing will change.

Underinvolved parents are referred to as "disengaged." They may care, but it takes a lot to get their attention. It will take a bloodcurdling shriek from a squabbling child before the parent (often a father) steps in and tells the kids to break it up. These parents admire autonomy and give their kids plenty of room. But, unfortunately, the kids receive less supervision and less affection as well. Such dads are good at giving orders but poor at affection or empathy.

You can see how these patterns can make it hard to communicate effectively. Imagine that the kids are fighting frequently (sound familiar?). An enmeshed mother jumps in to arbitrate, reason with the kids, and maybe tells them to be quiet. Ten minutes later the kids are at it again. A disengaged father may intervene if the fighting gets serious. But as soon as he goes back to the newspaper, the fight may resume, though at a slightly lower decibel level.

The mom is ineffective because instead of letting the kids work out their own squabbles, she teaches them that they can count on her to settle their differences for them. Dad is ineffective because if the only attention he gives the kids is negative attention, the kids will opt for that. Until Dad is more involved in the kids' lives overall (not just when they are fighting) and until Mom backs off a bit and lets the kids have a life without her, beautifully phrased communications will have no long-term effect.

Reason #3: You Are Depressed or Overwhelmed

When a parent's ability to take control is hampered by illness or depression, that parent's listening skills deteriorate. A depressed father will tune out the kids or limit his interactions with them. He may also interpret a child's misbehavior more harshly. The more overwhelmed a mother feels, the less capably she will handle any child situation.

Since dissatisfied couples are twenty-five times more likely to become depressed than are happy couples, it is important for a depressed person to look closely at the state of the marriage. Antidepressant medications can be very helpful. Support from other adults is also necessary when a person feels overwhelmed. Single parents have a very difficult task because they are on the job constantly.

Reason #4: Are You a Walking Contradiction?

When you teach "do as I say, not as I do," your credibility diminishes. You may want your children to obey rules, to put things back where they belong, to clean up their mess, and to show consideration, but you may act in the following ways:

> You change your mind about a supermarket item and place it back on the wrong aisle shelf for the sake of convenience.
>
> You find an expensive item on the ground and keep it instead of trying to locate the owner.
>
> You remark at a restaurant how the waiter forgot to charge you for something, and you say, "That's his problem, not mine."
>
> Your car is a mess.
>
> The top of your dresser is a mess.
>
> You routinely speed on the highway.
>
> You are frequently impatient with other drivers or when standing in a checkout line.
>
> You postpone work projects until the last minute.
>
> You are often late.

Children watch their parents carefully. As kids mature they are more likely to adopt a more casual set of values when their parents have done the same. Parenting will become more difficult.

Reason #5: You Overly Identify with Your Children

If your child is experiencing some difficulty that you once experienced, your background may help you understand—but it might also interfere. If you presume too much, you may stop listening to your child and miss some key elements of his concerns. For example, Fred was shy as a child, and he knew that his son, Danny, was shy, too. Not wanting Danny to feel bad about being shy (as Fred once did), Fred gave Danny encouraging pep talks but never really listened to any of his son's concerns. As a result, Danny was reluctant to talk to his father about the issue. Some parents are so convinced that their child is "just like me" that they overrule their spouse's opinions about the child, thereby setting the stage for spousal resentment.

In the book *Parenting by Heart,* psychologist Ron Taffel says that over-identification means you are reacting to your child but not truly connecting. Consequently, parenting may become more complicated because you think you know what is best when in fact you might not. You have to consider the possibility that you are not being objective. Ask for opinions from trusted friends or loved ones.

Reason #6: You Say, "I *Never* Want to Be Like My Parents!"

The more adamant you are about this, the more it usually backfires. For example, if your parents were frequently angry and you want to avoid feeling angry, you may become an ineffective disciplinarian. (Predictably, your spouse will be stricter, and you will yell at him for being harsh when in fact he is only balancing out the system.) If your parents were inattentive, you will want to give your children attention—but you may overdo it. Thus, your kids may become more dependent, or you may feel overwhelmed with time and work pressures but feel afraid to limit your time with the kids. (It's okay to do that sometimes. Kids need to learn patience and self-sufficiency.) Or you'll spend lots of time with the kids but have no time left over for yourself or your mate. It's funny but true: The parents who didn't raise you properly were trying to overcome factors present when their parents didn't raise them properly. If you take matters to extremes, you will lose perspective and effectiveness.

Reason #7: Your Expectations Are Self-fulfilling

A group of mothers who were convinced that their sons acted negatively when given sugar were divided into two groups. One group was told to play with their sons after the boys were given a sugary drink. The other mothers played with their sons when the boys were given an artificial sweetener. The boys had ankle and wrist "actometers" that measured their physical activity. In truth, none of the boys were given sugar, but the mothers who believed their sons had a sweet drink rated them as more active and difficult—despite the fact that their actometers revealed the boys to be less active than the other group.

Once you have labeled your child, that label will stick in your mind. A child who routinely delays doing his homework might prompt a parent to scold him when he is watching television instead of inquiring what the homework status is. That parental approach may cause more negative feelings on both sides and interfere with cooperation.

Reason #8: You Are Part of a New Stepfamily

Stepfamilies can run smoothly, but it usually takes time. Sometimes the adults are living together but unmarried, and that can be even more complicating because the nonparent has even less legitimate authority. Also, in some of these arrangements each party pays their individual bills, which further diminishes the sense that it is one big happy family. Generally, stepfamilies should follow these guidelines:

> The stepparent should help make rules but should not be the main enforcer.

> The stepparent should not try to replace the absent biological parent.

> The stepparent should find some quality one-on-one time with each of the kids. It is the best and fastest way to build rapport.

> Problems should be handled in family meetings until the stepparent is treated as a legitimate authority.

> Don't expect a stepparent to automatically love the stepchildren. Depending on the child's age, stepparents may never quite love their stepchildren the way they do their biological children, but treatment of all kids should be fair.

Reason #9: You Allow Stereotypes to Intrude in Your Family

Fathers who won't change diapers and mothers who won't play catch with their kids are not only missing out, they are messing up. It may seem small, but when you limit your activities with a child and let your mate take over, you limit your role in other ways, too. Eventually you will be a two-dimensional parent—very involved in your area of expertise but uninvolved in other areas. This can have far-reaching effects. One study showed that couples with one child, a girl, were 9 percent more likely to divorce than couples who had only a boy. Couples with two girls were 18 percent more likely to divorce than couples with two boys. Why? Evidently fathers spend more time in child-care activities with sons than with daughters. A dad's greater involvement usually improves marital satisfaction and reduces the risk of divorce. (Another study showed that if a girl had brothers, her father was more involved in her life than if she had no brothers.) While it is true that some parents are better skilled at some child-focused tasks than their mates, the less-skilled parent shouldn't abandon efforts to be useful in those areas.

Reason #10: You Don't Give New Approaches a Fair Shot

Ironically, frustrated parents have a tendency to overuse parenting approaches that haven't proved useful but give up on helpful approaches quickly. For example, parents who have found that taking away privileges from a child doesn't stop some unacceptable behavior will continue to take away privileges. They don't question the technique but just assume that their child is obstinate or extra difficult. But maybe they have misidentified the problem. Maybe the punishment is actually making matters worse. These same parents may try a new approach, but the first time they don't get the desired response, they abandon it and go back to the old standbys. If you have reason to believe that a different approach makes sense, try it for at least two weeks. If there is improvement but no resolution, then there is something about the approach that is working. Don't abandon it.

The happier and more stable your marriage, the more likely that parenting will be mostly a joy although certainly worrisome at times. A troubled marriage, however, can create problems with your children and in your ability to manage those problems effectively.

The Argument Audit below will give you clues about the status of your marriage. It will tell you if conflicts are minimal, if they are a bit troublesome but manageable, or if they have become seriously threatening to the marriage. The higher your score, the more you may want to consider marital counseling.

THE ARGUMENT AUDIT

Please mark your scores in the space provided at the end of each item. Use the following scale:

Rarely	0
Sometimes	1
Often.	2
Much of the time	3

When you complete the items, tally the individual scores. Compare your final score with the key presented at the bottom.

1. Do you feel you must assess your mate's mood before you feel free to speak to him/her? _____

2. Do the same arguments/conflicts occur repeatedly? _____

3. Do you feel out of sync with each other emotionally (for example, when he's ready for lovemaking, you're not, and vice versa)? _____

4. Are you accused of overreacting or underreacting to his or her behaviors or attitudes? _____

5. When the relationship seems to be going well, do you anticipate problems on the horizon? _____

6. Are you more invested in your spouse's changing some aspect of his/her behavior than he/she is? _____

7. When you believe that some problems are improving, do you view a setback as "back to square one"? _____

8. When you and your mate disagree, do you react more to his manner (tone of voice, attitude) than to the specifics of the disagreement? _____

9. Do you get defensive or offensive with your mate? _____

10. Do you anticipate (correctly or incorrectly) what your mate will say or do before it happens? _____

11. Do you act on those assumptions before checking them out with your mate? _____

12. Do you feel threatened that your mate has (or might be interested in having) some separate interest or hobbies? _____

13. Does one or both of you avoid discussing areas of conflict, or does at least one of you withdraw from that discussion prematurely? _____

14. Do you feel responsible for your mate's feelings/actions to the extent that if he/she is feeling blue, you wonder what you might have done to cause it? _____

15. Do you feel disowned by your parents or cut off from them emotionally? _____

Score

0–10 No problems. Any future problems will be avoided or caught early enough to resolve.

11–25 Some problems are developing but can be nipped in the bud.

26–35 Some problems have become difficult or unmanageable. Solutions do exist. Children may be affected.

36–45 Many unresolved problems. Marital satisfaction is low. A committed effort to resolve issues is absolutely essential.

A QUICK TEST FOR MARITAL HAPPINESS

If you are unsure whether your mate is happy in the marriage, there is a quick way to get a fairly accurate measurement. (Of course, talking with your mate about it is also a good idea.) This method is very reliable, assuming you and your mate are in good physical health.

1. Calculate the number of times you made love during a certain time frame (say, the past two weeks).

2. Calculate the number of arguments you've had during that same time period. (An argument is defined as any time you or your mate was "uncooperative.")

3. Subtract the number of arguments from the number of times that you made love.

4. If the difference is a positive number, you and your mate are probably happy. If the difference is a negative number, you and your mate are probably not happy.

Sources

Introduction: Smart Talk: The Six Ways We Speak to Our Kids

Hofferth, Sandra L. Changes in American children's time, 1981–1997. In *Brown University Child and Adolescent Behavior Letter* 15 (3), (March 1999).

Chapter 1: Adoption

Sharma, A., M. McGue, and P. Benson. The psychological adjustment of U.S. adopted adolescents and their non-adopted siblings. *Child Development* 69 (1998): 791–802.

Chapter 2: Angry Child

Donovan, Denis, and Deborah McIntyre. *What Did I Just Say?: How New Insights into Childhood Thinking Can Help You Communicate More Effectively with Your Child.* New York: Henry Holt, 1999.

Viscott, David. *The Language of Feelings.* New York: Pocket Books, 1976.

Chapter 3: Apologies

Krevaus, Julia, and John Gibbs. Parents' use of inductive discipline: Relationships to children's empathy and prosocial behavior. *Child Development* 67 (1996): 3263–77.

Chapter 4: Arguments Between Two Adults

Cummings, E. M., and P. Davies. *Children and Marital Conflict: The Impact of Family Dispute and Resolution.* New York: Guilford, 1994.

Davies, P., and E. M. Cummings. Marital conflict and child adjustment: An emotional security hypothesis. *Psychological Bulletin* 116 (1994): 387–411.

Chapter 5: Bed-wetting

Houts, A., J. Berman, and H. Abramson. Effectiveness of psychological and pharmacological treatments for nocturnal enuresis. *Journal of Consulting and Clinical Psychology* 62 (1994): 737–45.

Chapter 7: Bullies

DuRant, R., D. Krowchuk, and P. Kreiter. Weapon carrying on school property among middle school students. *Archives of Pediatric and Adolescent Medicine* 153 (1999): 21–26.

Chapter 15: Comforting the Dying Child

Mulhern, R. K., M. E. Lauer, and R. G. Hoffman. Death of a child at home or at the hospital: Subsequent psychological adjustment of the family. *Pediatrics* 71 (1983): 743–47.

Chapter 17: Divorce: Telling the Children

Ulrich, David N. Mobilizing family resources for constructive divorce. In Mark Karpel (ed.)., *Family Resources: The Hidden Partner in Family Therapy.* New York: Guilford, 1986, p. 401.

Chapter 18: Divorce: Introducing Your Child to Your New Partner

Neuman, M. Gary. *Helping Your Kids Cope with Divorce the Sandcastles Way*. New York: Random House, 1998.

Chapter 20: Divorce: When One Parent Abandons the Children

Booth, Alan, and David Johnson. Premarital cohabitation and marital success. *Journal of Family Issues* 9 (1988): 255–72.

Bumpass, Larry L., James A. Sweet, and Andrew Cherlin. The role of cohabitation in declining rates of marriage. *Journal of Marriage and the Family* 53 (1991): 913–27.

Margolin, Leslie. Child abuse and mother's boyfriends: Why the overrepresentation? *Child Abuse and Neglect* 16 (1992): 541–55.

Chapter 25: Fostering Empathy and Emotional Intelligence

Azar, Beth. Our siblings teach us how to read people's emotions. *APA Monitor* (September 1995): 29.

Goleman, Daniel. *Emotional Intelligence*. New York: Bantam Books, 1995.

Chapter 31: Fears of Harm or Injury

Swedo, Susan Anderson, and Henrietta L. Leonard. *Is It Just a Phase? How to Tell Common Childhood Phases from More Serious Problems*. New York: Golden Books, 1998.

Chapter 32: Teaching Forgiveness

Enright, Robert. Helping el nino to forgive. In *The World of Forgiveness*. Madison, WI: International Forgiveness Institute, 1998.

Chapter 33: God: Common Questions

Coleman, Paul. *The 30 Secrets of Happily Married Couples*. Holbrook, MA: Adams, 1992.

Gellman, Marc, and Thomas Hartman. *Where Does God Live? Questions and Answers for Parents and Children*. Liguori, MO: Triumph Books, 1991.

Glenn, Norval. Inter-religious marriages in the U.S.: Patterns and recent trends. *Journal of Marriage and the Family* 44 (3) (1982): 555–68.

Chapter 34: God: Prayer

Bel Geddes, Joan. *Children Praying: Why and How to Pray with Your Children*. Notre Dame, IN: Sorin Books, 1999.

Princeton Religion Research Center. *Religion in America: Will the Vitality of the Church Be the Surprise of the 21st Century? Princeton, NJ: Gallup Poll, 1996.

Chapter 35: God: "I Don't Want to Go to Church"

Greeley, Andrew. *Faithful Attraction: Discovering Intimacy, Love, and Fidelity in American Marriage*. New York: Tor Books, 1991, p. 190.

Chapter 37: Hitting

"Is your kid a killer?" *Psychology Today* (October 1999): 16.

Perozynski, L., and L. Kramer. Parental beliefs about managing sibling conflict. *Developmental Psychology* 35 (1999): 489–99.

Chapter 38: HIV/AIDS

Whalen, C., B. Henker, J. Hollingshead, and S. Burgess. Parent-adolescent dialogues about AIDS. *Journal of Family Psychology* 10 (1996): 343–57.

Chapter 39: Home Alone/Latchkey Kids

Galambor, N., and J. Maggs. Out-of-school care of young adolescents and self-reported behavior. *Developmental Psychology* 27 (1991): 644–55.

Kelly, P., M. Weir, A. Atkinson, and R. Lampe. Latchkey: Three voices with one message. *Clinical Pediatrics* 25 (1986): 462–65.

Messer, S., K. Wuensch, and J. Diamond. Former latchkey children: Personality and academic correlates. *Journal of Genetic Psychology* 150 (1989): 301–9.

Mulhall, P., D. Stone, and B. Stone. Home alone: Is it a risk factor for middle school youth and drug use? *Journal of Drug Education* 26 (1996): 39–48.

Chapter 44: Lying

Goleman, D. "Analyzed: Mental disorders or normal growth?" *New York Times,* May 17, 1988, p. 19.

Chapter 45: Manipulative Behavior ("But Mom Said I Could!")

Christensen, A., G. Margolin, and M. Sullaway. Interparental agreement on child behavior problems. *Psychological Assessment* 4 (1992): 419–25.

Shinnar, Shlomo. Epilepsy treatment in the 21st century. *Exceptional Parent* (October 1999): 64–74.

Chapter 47: Medical: Hospitalization

Barakat, L. P., A. Kazak, A. Meadows, R. Casey, K. Meeske, and M. Stuber. Families surviving childhood cancer: A comparison of post-traumatic stress symptoms with families of healthy children. *Journal of Pediatric Psychology* 22 (1997): 843–59.

Chapter 48: Medical: When a Child Has a Chronic Illness

Allen, K., and M. Shriver. The role of parent-mediated pain behavior management strategies in biofeedback treatment of childhood migraines. *Behavior Therapy* 29 (1998): 477–90.

Bock, Steven J., Kenneth Bock, and Nancy P. Bruning. *Natural Relief for Your Child's Asthma.* New York: HarperPerennial, 1999.

Gartland, H. J., and H. D. Day. Family predictors of the incidence of children's asthma symptoms: Expressed emotion, medications, parent control, and life events. *Journal of Clinical Psychology* 55 (1999): 573–84.

Johnson, Robert Wood, Sale Johnson, Casey Johnson, and Casey Kleinman. *Managing Your Child's Diabetes*. New York: Master Media, 1992.

Shinnar, Shlomo. Epilepsy treatment in the 21st century. *Exceptional Parent* (October 1999): 64–74.

Chapter 49: Medical: Talking to Siblings of Children with Chronic Illness

Walker, L., J. Garber, and D. Van Slyke. Do parents excuse the misbehavior of children with physical or emotional symptoms? An investigation of the pediatric sick role. *Journal of Pediatric Psychology* 20 (1995): 329–45.

Chapter 50: Medical: When a Parent Has a Serious Physical Illness

Armistead, L., K. Klein, R. Forehand, and M. Wierson. Disclosure of parental HIV infection to children in families of men with hemophilia: Description, outcomes, and the role of family process. *Journal of Family Psychology* 11 (1997): 49–61.

Chin, D., D. Schonfield, L. O'Hare, S. Maynes, P. Salovey, D. Showalter, and D. Cicchetti. Elementary school-age children's developmental understanding of the causes of cancer. *Journal of Developmental and Behavioral Pediatrics* 19 (1998): 397–403.

Chapter 54: Nagging

Brown University Child and Adolescent Behavior Letter 15 (7) (1999): 2.

Chapter 55: New Baby

Druckman, Amanda. Commitment crowded out. *Psychology Today* (November/December 1999): 21.

Chapter 57: Increasing Optimism

Evitt, Marie Faust. Comeback kids. *Child* (September 1999): 55–58.

Seligman, Martin E. P. *Learned Optimism*. New York: Pocket Books, 1990.

Chapter 58: Parental Emotional Problems: Depression, Fears, Compulsions

Beardslee, W. R., E. M. Versage, E. J. Wright, P. Solt, P. C. Rothberg, K. Drezner, and T. Gladstone. Examination of preventive interventions for families with depression: Evidence of change. *Developmental Psychopathology* 9 (1997): 109–30.

Chapter 62: Perseverance

Diener, C., and C. Dweck. An analysis of learned helplessness II: The processing of success. *Journal of Personality and Social Psychology* 29 (1980): 940–52.

Chapter 63: Pets

Van Houtle, B. A., and P. Jarvis. The role of pets in preadolescent psychosocial development. *Journal of Applied Developmental Psychology* 16 (1995): 463–79.

Chapter 64: Concerns About Physical Appearance

Drotar, D., R. Owens, and J. Gotthold. Personality adjustment of children and adolescents with hypopituitarism. *Child Psychiatry and Human Development* 11 (1980): 59–66.

Field, A., L. Cheung, and A. Wolf. Exposure to the mass media and weight concerns among girls. *Pediatrics* 103 (1999): 36–44.

Holmes, C., J. Karlsson, and R. Thompson. Social and school competencies in children with short stature: Longitudinal patterns. *Journal of Developmental and Behavioral Pediatrics* 6 (1985): 263–67.

Holmes, C., R. Thompson, and J. Hayford. Factors related to grade retention in children of short stature. *Child Care, Health, and Development* 10 (1984): 199–210.

Skuse, D. The psychological consequences of being small. *Journal of Child Psychology, Psychiatry, and Allied Disciplines* 28 (1987): 641–50.

Chapter 66: Quarreling with Siblings

Perozynski, L., and L. Kramer. Parental beliefs about managing sibling conflicts. *Developmental Psychology* 35 (1999): 489–99.

Chapter 68: Refusing to Talk

Leaper, C., K. Anderson, and P. Sanders. Moderators of gender effects on parents' talks with their children: A meta-analysis. *Developmental Psychology* 34 (1998): 3–27.

Chapter 69: Running Away from Home

Schaffner, Laurie. Searching for connections: A new look at teenage runaways. *Adolescence* 33 (1998): 619–27.

Chapter 72: School: "My Teacher Is Mean!"

Bennett, William, Chester E. Finn, and John T. Cribb. *The Educated Child: A Parent's Guide from Preschool Through Eighth Grade.* New York: The Free Press, 1999.

Madon, S., L. Jussim, and J. Eccles. In search of the powerful self-fulfilling prophecy. *Journal of Personality and Social Psychology* 72 (1997): 791–809.

McLoyd, Yonnie. Socioeconomic disadvantages and child development. *American Psychologist* 53 (1998): 185–204.

Murdock, Tamera. The social context of risk status and motivational predictors of alienation in middle school. *Journal of Educational Psychology* 91 (1999): 62–75.

Tal, Z., and E. Babad. The teacher's pet phenomenon: Rate of occurrence, correlates, and psychological cost. *Journal of Educational Psychology* 82 (1990): 637–45.

Chapter 74: School: "I'm Afraid to Ask a Question in Class"

Neuman, Richard. Children's help-seeking in the classroom: The role of motivational status and attitude. *Journal of Educational Psychology* 82 (1990): 71–80.

Chapter 75: School: Poor Report Card

Frome, P., and J. Eccles. Parents' influence on children's achievement-related perceptions. *Journal of Personality and Social Psychology* 74 (1998): 435–52.

Phillips, D., and M. Zimmerman. The developmental course of perceived competence and incompetence among competent children. In R. J. Sternberg and J. Kalligian, Jr. (eds.), *Competency Considered*. New Haven, CT: Yale University Press, 1990, pp. 41–66.

Wentzel, Kathryn. Student motivation in middle school: The role of perceived pedagogical caring. *Journal of Educational Psychology* 89 (1997): 411–19.

Chapter 76: School: Rejected by Classmates

Coie, J., J. Lochman, R. Terry, and C. Hyman. Predicting early adolescence disorders from childhood aggression and peer rejection. *Journal of Consulting and Clinical Psychology* 60 (1992): 783–92.

Finnegan, R., E. Hodges, and D. Perry. Victimization by peers: Association with children's reports of mother-child interactions. *Journal of Personality and Social Psychology* 75 (1998): 1076–86.

Hodges, E., and D. Perry. Personal and interpersonal antecedents and consequences of victimization by peers. *Journal of Personality and Social Psychology* 76 (1999): 677–85.

Ollendick, T., M. Weist, M. Borden, and R. Greene. Sociometric status and academic, behavioral, and psychological adaptation: A five-year longitudinal study. *Journal of Consulting and Clinical Psychology* 60 (1992): 80–87.

Parkhurst, J., and S. Asher. Peer rejection in middle school: Subgroup differences in behavior, loneliness, and interpersonal concerns. *Developmental Psychology* 28 (1992): 231–41.

White, K., and J. Kistner. The influence of teacher's feedback on young children's peer preferences and perceptions. *Developmental Psychology* 28 (1992): 933–40.

Chapter 77: School Safety Concerns

Anderman, E., and D. Kimweli. Victimization and safety in schools serving early adolescents. *Journal of Early Adolescence* 17 (1997): 408–38.

Gelles, Richard. Explaining the unthinkable: The Jonesboro tragedy. *Brown University Child and Adolescent Behavior Letter* (May 1998): 1, 5.

Ryan-Spanswick, B., and J. Coleman. Incorporating your school resource officer into the fabric of your middle school community. *Impact 1999*, 6 (1) (1999): 2–4.

Chapter 78: Improving Self-confidence

Baumeister, Roy F. Low self-esteem does not cause aggression. *APA Monitor* (January 1999): 7.

Chapter 79: Self-critical Child

Koestner, R., D. Zuroff, and T. Powers. Family origins of adolescent self-criticism and its continuity into adulthood. *Journal of Abnormal Psychology* 100 (1991): 191–97.

Zahn-Waxler, C., G. Kochanska, J. Krupnick, and D. McKnew. Patterns of guilt in children of depressed and well mothers. *Developmental Psychology* 26 (1990): 51–59.

Chapter 80: Sexuality and Reproduction

Schaefer, C., and T. DiGeronimo. *How to Talk to Your Kids About Really Important Things.* San Francisco: Jossey-Bass, 1994.

Chapter 84: Promoting Sexual Abstinence

Graham, Melody. *The Effects of Parent-Adolescent Communication on Adolescent Sexual Behavior.* Poster session presented at the Centennial Annual Convention of the American Psychological Association, Washington, D.C., August 1992.

Chapter 85: Sexual Abuse: Alerting Your Child

Finkelhor, D., and J. Dzuiba-Leatherman. Victimization of children. *American Psychologist* 49 (1994): 173–83.

Chapter 86: Sexual Abuse: After It Happens

Monahon, Cynthia. *Children and Trauma: A Guide for Parents and Professionals.* San Francisco: Jossey-Bass, 1997.

Chapter 87: Sharing

Owens, C., and F. Ascione. Effects of model's age, perceived similarity, and familiarity on children's donating. *Journal of Genetic Psychology* 152 (1992): 341–57.

Ross, Hildy. Negotiating principles of entitlement in sibling property disputes. *Developmental Psychology* 32 (1996): 90–101.

Siperstein, G., and J. Liffert. Managing limited resources: Do children with learning problems share? *Exceptional Children* 65 (1998): 187–99.

Chapter 88: Shyness

Kerr, M., W. Lambert, and D. Bem. Life course sequelae of childhood shyness in Sweden: Comparison with the U.S. *Developmental Psychology* 32 (1996): 1100–05.

Chapter 89: Sportsmanship

Smith, R., and F. Smoll. Self-esteem and children's reactions to youth sport coaching behaviors: A field study of self-enhancement processes. *Developmental Psychology* 26 (1990): 987–93.

Chapter 90: Stealing

Kagan, Jerome. Etiologies of adolescents at risk. *Journal of Adolescent Health* 12 (1992): 59–96.

Moore, D., P. Chamberlain, and L. Mukai. *Journal of Abnormal Child Psychology* 7 (1979): 345–55.

Seymour, F., and D. Epston. An approach to childhood stealing with an evaluation of 45 cases. *Australian and New Zealand Journal of Family Therapy* 10 (1989): 137–43.

Chapter 91: Strangers

Bovey-McCoy, S., and D. Finkelhor. Psychosocial sequelae of violent victimization in a national youth sample. *Journal of Consulting and Clinical Psychology* 63 (1995): 726–36.

Bromberg, D., and B. Johnson. Behavioral and traditional approaches to the prevention of child abductions. *School Psychology Review* 26 (1997): 622–33.

Finkelhor, D., and J. Dzuiba-Leatherman. Victimization of children. *American Psychologist* 49 (1994): 173–83.

Finkelhor, D., G. Hotoling, and A. Sedlah. The abduction of children by strangers and non-family members: Estimating the incidence using multiple methods. *Journal of Interpersonal Violence* 7 (1992): 226–43.

Johnston, J., L. Girdner, and I. Sagitun-Edwards. Developing profiles of risk for parental abduction of children from a comparison of families victimized by abduction with families litigating custody. *Behavioral Science and the Law* 17 (1999): 305–22.

Chapter 93: Tattling

Ross, H., and I. denBak-Lammers. Consistency and change in children's tattling on their siblings: Children's perspectives on the moral rules and procedures in family life. *Social Development* 7 (1998): 275–300.

Chapter 94: Being Teased

Keltner, D., R. Young, E. Heerey, C. Oemig, and N. Monarch. Teasing in hierarchical and intimate relationships. *Journal of Personality and Social Psychology* 75 (1998): 1231–47.

Chapter 96: Trauma from an Accident or Natural Disaster

Dollinger, S. Lightning-strike disasters among children. *British Journal of Medical Psychology* 18 (1985): 375–83.

Groves, B., B. Zuckerman, S. Marons, and D. Cohen. Silent victims: Children who witness violence. *Journal of the American Medical Association* 269 (1993): 262–64.

Janoff-Bulman, R. *Shattered Assumption: Towards a New Psychology of Trauma*. New York: The Free Press, 1992.

Kliewer, W., S. Lepore, D. Oskin, and P. Johnson. The role of social cognitive processes on children's adjustment to community violence. *Journal of Consulting and Clinical Psychology* 66 (1998): 199–209.

LaGreca, A., W. Silverman, and S. Wasserstein. Children's predisaster functioning as a predictor of post-traumatic stress following Hurricane Andrew. *Journal of Consulting and Clinical Psychology* 66 (1998): 883–92.

Marans, S., and D. Cohen. Children and inner-city violence: Strategies for intervention. In L. Leavitt and N. Fox (eds.), *The Psychological Effects of War and Violence on Children*. Hillsdale, NJ: Erlbaum, 1993, pp. 281–302.

Chapter 97: Violence and Sexual Material in Television and Movies

Comstock, G., and V. Strasburger. Deceptive appearances: Television violence and aggressive behavior. *Journal of Adolescent Health Law* 11 (1990): 31–44.

Godow, K., and J. Spratkin. Television violence and children with emotional and behavioral disorders. *Journal of Emotional and Behavioral Disorders* 1 (1993): 54–63.

Liebert, R., and R. Baron. Some immediate effects of television violence on children's behavior. *Developmental Psychology* 6 (1972): 469–75.

Molitor, F., and K. Hirsch. Children's tolerance of real-life aggression after exposure to media violence. *Child Study Journal* 24 (1995): 191–207.

Robinson, T., H. Chen, and J. Killen. Television and music video exposure and risk of adolescent alcohol use. *Pediatrics* 102 (1998): 54–66.

Valkenburg, P., and T. van der Voort. Influence of TV on daydreaming and creative imagination: A review of research. *Psychological Bulletin* 116 (1994): 316–39.

Chapter 98: Whiny and Demanding Child

Endo, G., H. Sloane, T. Hawkes, and W. Jenson. Reducing child whining through self-instructional parent training materials. *Child and Family Behavior Therapy* 13 (1991): 41–58.

Chapter 99: Working Parent (When You Used to Stay at Home)

Bryant, W., and C. Zick. An examination of parent-child shared time. *Journal of Marriage and the Family* 58 (1997): 227–37.

Moorehouse, Martha. Linking maternal employment patterns to mother-child activities and children's school competence. *Developmental Psychology* 27 (1991): 295–303.

Chapter 100: Worried Child

Cobham, V., M. Dadds, and S. Spence. The role of parental anxiety in the treatment of childhood anxiety. *Journal of Consulting and Clinical Psychology* 66 (1998): 893–905.

Gottlieb, D., and P. Bronstein. Parent's perceptions of children's worries in a changing world. *Journal of Genetic Psychology* 157 (1996): 104–18.

Muris, P., C. Meesters, H. Merckelbach, A. Sermon, and S. Zwakhalen. Worry in normal children. *Journal of the American Academy of Child and Adolescent Psychiatry* 37 (1998): 703–10.

When You Say It Right (but Things Still Go Wrong): Ten Winning Tips for Troubleshooters

Hover, D., and R. Milich. Effects of sugar ingestion: Expectations of mother–child interactions. *Journal of Abnormal Child Psychology* 22 (1994): 501–15.

Kerig, P., P. Cowan, and C. Cowan. Marital quality and gender differences in parent–child interactions. *Developmental Psychology* 29 (1993): 931–39.

Lindahl, K., M. Clements, and H. Markman. Predicting marital and parental functioning in dyads and triads: A longitudinal investigation of marital processes. *Journal of Family Psychology* 11 (1997): 139–51.

Taffel, Ron. *Parenting by Heart*. Reading, MA: Addison-Wesley, 1991.

Appendix

Coleman, Paul. *Getting to the Heart of the Matter*. Holbrook, MA: Adams Media, 1994.

Howard, J., and R. Dawes. Linear prediction of marital happiness. *Personality and Social Psychology Bulletin* 2 (1976): 478–80.

Index

Blaming
    children for sexual abuse, 300
    divorce and, 72
    HIV/AIDS and, 143
    marital problems and, 346
    parental emotional problems and, 207
    sibling quarrels and, 231
    trauma and, 330
Blood tests, 166-168
Bossy/domineering children, 32-34
Boys
    chores and, 41
    dealing with sexual abuse, 299
    discussing issues, 44
    effects of trauma on, 329
    interest in adult magazines, 284
    peer rejection and, 264
    self-criticism and, 276
    talking about feelings, 237
    teasing among, 321
    victimized by peers, 265
Bribery, overusing, 233
Bullies, 35-37
    trauma from, 328-331

C

Cancer
    children coping with, 171
    educating children about, 180
Cards, trading, 325-327
Catastrophic thoughts, 172
Caution, teaching, 116
Character assassination
    after divorce, 81-82
    during divorce, 70-71
    of estranged family members, 105
Cheating, 38-39. *See also* Lies; Stealing
Child problems, marital problems disguised
    as, 346
Children
    abandoned, 81-84
    sex play with other, 282-283
    worried, 342-344
Child/sexual abuse
    alerting children about, 293-296
    boyfriends and, 76
    dealing with, 297-300
    drugs and alcohol and, 90
    fear of harm or injury and, 119
    running away from home and, 241, 243
    strangers and, 313-316

Chores, 40-42
    church going as, 132
    overseeing homework as, 255
    room cleaning, 94-96
Chronic illness, 172-175
Church, attendance
    early sexual activity and, 289
    resisting, 132-134
Cigarettes, latchkey kids and, 144
Coaches
    styles of, 307
    talking to, 308
Cohabitation, divorce and, 76
Collecting, cards, 325-327
Communication. *See also* TENDER communi-
    cation
    three outcomes of, 2-3
    trauma and, 329
Compassion
    pets and, 223
    prayer and, 130
    teaching forgiveness and, 121
Complaining
    about family obligations, 109-111
    about moving, 191
    listening and, 248
Compulsions, parental, 205-207
Computers. *See* Internet
Conduct disorder, 138
Consequences
    appropriate, 69
    dawdling and, 48
    eating vegetables and, 96
    enforcing, instead of nagging, 193
    for hitting, 139
    immediate, 312
    for not sharing, 302
    room cleaning and, 96
    for stealing, 311
    unenforced, 42
Consistency
    enforcing rules, 42, 94
    of family meetings, 107
    intervening in children's arguments, 230
    parental emotional problems and, 205
    in talk time, 238
Conversation, initiating, 43-46
Criminal activity. *See also* Drugs
    adolescents at risk for, 312
    early sexual activity and, 289

How to Say It® to Teens

Talking About the Most Important Topics of Their Lives

Richard Heyman, Ed.D.

Prentice Hall Press

Acknowledgments

To Marilyn Samuels for her careful and professional critique of an early stage of this book.

To Don Braid for his endless encouragement and insightful comments, and for his friendship.

To Rielle Braid and Anna Hobbs for being articulate teenagers with good advice.

To Amanda Graves and David Heyman for taking time out of their very busy lives to give me invaluable help with style and content.

To Adam Heyman who gave me his experiences.

To Phoebe Heyman for her wise and enthusiastic editorial work, and her endless patience and forbearance with an obsessed writer.

To Tom Power, my editor, for his advice and encouragement, patience, and good humor.

To Pat and Mike Snell, my agents, for believing in me.

And to the endless numbers of students, parents, and colleagues who taught me so much.

Introduction

He was hard to communicate with even as an infant. He didn't seem to respond to us the way our other children did. Sometimes he'd wake up crying in the middle of the night. We'd ask him what was wrong. He wouldn't answer. He often seemed so sad, angry, and aloof—not like our other two kids—and it had been this way since we brought him home from the adoption agency.

He was our middle child. My wife, Phoebe, and I had been married for more than four years before we had our first child. We had held off having kids for three reasons. The first and most important one was that I wasn't ready for the responsibility. Phoebe was, but I wasn't. I couldn't imagine looking after a baby in addition to looking after my wife and myself.

Second, we wanted to enjoy each other's company alone for a while. We knew children would change our lives forever, and we weren't ready for that. We also wanted to be sure our marriage was a good one. It was, and is.

The final reason was probably the most important in terms of practical considerations. I had a medical problem and was advised not to have my own children. I had lost an eye to cancer as a two-year-old, and I was told that that form of cancer could be passed on to kids of my own. The doctor said I'd better adopt.

We spent two of our first four years of marriage living and teaching in East Africa, and adopting a child while we were there would have been difficult if not impossible. But during that time I decided I was ready for kids.

As soon as we returned to New York City, we applied to an adoption agency, which approved us. It couldn't very well have turned us down since it was the same agency from which my sister and I had been adopted. In the next thirty-six months we adopted two infant boys and accidentally had a biological child of our own, a girl. Fortunately, she never developed my problem, and all three of our wonderful children are now grown and successfully pursuing diverse careers.

But the journey through childhood and adolescence to adulthood for our middle child was a tough one. When he was quite young, we were so concerned by his lack of communication and some apparent motor skills problems that we had him tested to make sure he was within the normal range of development for his age. He was, and as an adult he turned out to be far above normal. But that didn't solve our problem with him when he was young.

The problem was that we couldn't communicate with him the way we could with our other two children. He never appeared to listen to anything we or any adults said. It was as though he knew more about everything than we did. This made it hard for us to have a normal parent-child relationship. We were never in control because he never listened to us, his grandparents, or his teachers in school, and he never talked to us freely about his life. By the time he was a teenager, we had really lost control.

The only communication we had with him seemed to be arguments or fights (not physical). We did our parenting talk, telling him our rules. But he had his own rules, so he generally ignored us and did what he wanted. We tried to be his friend. We tried to reason with him. A few times we seemed successful, but we generally didn't communicate.

This caused a number of problems for our family. It created great antagonism toward him by our other two kids. We wanted to be one big, happy family, but he made it hard because we always seemed to be fighting about something. He was never a good student. One day his high school principal called. Please come to school, she said. Your son has brought a bomb to school. It makes me smile now when I remember that I was comforted by the fact that it was, fortunately, only a small bomb.

Things went from bad to worse. As a teenager he harassed his girlfriend so much the courts put a restraining order on him, which he violated. He spent a night in jail as a result. When he came home, our communication with him was no better. We kept talking to him, but we didn't seem to connect. Our conversations were quite one-sided.

"What are you going to do about school?"

"I don't know."

"Don't you think you'd better start going to class?"

"Yeah, I guess."

"Well, are you going?"

"I don't know."

"You can't just lie around here all day."

"Just leave me alone, will you?"

"No, we can't leave you alone. You have responsibilities to yourself and to us."

"Give me a break."

We didn't know what to do or where to turn. Our only hope was that he knew how much we loved him and cared for him and that deep down he loved us, too. More important, we hoped that he would come to love and care for himself.

He turned eighteen, and he wasn't going to school and wasn't working. He would stay out until one or two in the morning and not get up until noon. After hours of talking about it, my wife and I agreed that he couldn't use our house as a hotel. If he wanted to live at home, he had to go to school or to work. If he was not willing to do either, then he had to leave.

"Can we talk for a minute?"

"Yeah."

"Your mom and I have talked about this, and we have to tell you that you can't simply use the house as a hotel. You're out all night, and you sleep half the day. If you go to school or get a job, you can live here as long as you like. But if you're not in school and not working, you have to find your own place to live. We'll give you a week to find a place."

"Okay."

We both had tears in our eyes as we said this, but we felt we had no other option. He left the next day and moved in with a friend.

Although we never lost touch with him, we're not sure how he survived over the next year and a half. On our visits to his small town house we noticed that he was losing a lot of weight. We were very concerned because we loved him very much, but we knew that he had to be responsible for himself since he had never acknowledged our authority when he lived with us.

In the course of my life I've noticed that people seem to enter our lives at just the right moment. This was true for our son. One day a friend of a friend offered him an apprenticeship mechanic position in his auto shop. From that point on his life changed. Cars, motorcycles, and engines were always his passion, and he had a genius for working on them. He was a good apprentice, did outstanding work in his classes at the local institute of technology, and finally went on to start his own business. He had found success and clearly began to like himself.

He is now one of the premier experts on rotary engines in North America. And most important, he is a wonderful man and never stops talking to us. He also has a son of his own, and I never tire of seeing him communicate so well with his child. Somehow, some way, our sad, lovely middle child turned into a successful, happy businessman and wonderful father.

Between those days and nights of fighting and crying, and now, my wife and I learned a few things about communicating with our kids. I've combined that experience with over thirty years of teaching and research to write this book and pass on what I hope are a few helpful hints. For example, I noticed that the people who had wonderful communication with children were those who were genuinely interested in listening to what kids had to say. This was true of parents, teachers, store clerks, and strangers. These special people all had a wonderful knack of being there completely for the kids in everything they said and did, and the kids picked up on that. Teenagers were especially good at it. They could also spot a phony a mile away.

Adults who had the most problems sounded as if they had only one overriding interest in the kids. They wanted to control them. There was no connection except an official one. Even when it was parents talking to their own kids, they sounded like police officers controlling traffic.

Some children are almost parent-proof. Like kids at school who learn well and succeed no matter how bad a teacher they may have, they will become well-adjusted, competent, and loving children no matter what their parents do.

But most kids are not parent-proof. They need the best you can give in order to flourish. I have seen families broken apart by parents who knew how to judge but not forgive, who valued money but not excellence, who loved humanity but not their children, who understood life but not themselves, who knew how to talk but not communicate.

It never surprises me when parents tell me they have trouble communicating with their teenagers. We all have trouble at some time or another, but some parents have a lot more problems than others.

There are no quick, easy solutions to them, but here are a few suggestions that you may find useful.

WHEN NOTHING SEEMS TO WORK

There are times when nothing we do with our kids seems to work. We try everything we know and still don't see tangible results. We're exhausted, mentally and physically. That's when we want to give up and write off the relationship. We tell ourselves we did our best but it wasn't good enough, so that's the end of it. No more trying to communicate. It's over.

That's precisely the time when it's crucial to keep on trying because if we keep trying, there is still some hope of success even if there are no guarantees. If we give up, we're guaranteed to fail. I unconsciously knew this then, and now I know it as the Communication Ethic. It teaches us to never stop trying to share our life and our love with our children no matter how tough things get. If we cut off or limit communication, even if it seems to have failed, we are cutting off our child's most important connection with us.

Peter Matthiessen, in *Nine-Headed Dragon River*, a wonderful book about one of his many spiritual adventures, describes meeting a crippled Tibetan holy man, the Lama of Shey, who lives in a hermitage on the Crystal Mountain. After weeks of trekking through the wild snow-clad mountains of a remote part of this mysterious country, he meets the lama one bright sunny morning at his hut on a mountain ledge. He has lived in isolation for eight years and, because he is crippled, may never leave, yet appears to be a very happy man with a wonderful smile and a great infectious laugh.

Through an interpreter Matthiessen asks how he feels about his circumstances. Is he happy to live in such isolation? His first response is a great burst of laughter. Then, "indicating his twisted legs without a trace of self-pity or bitterness . . . he casts his arms wide to the sky and the snow mountains, the high sun and dancing sheep, and cries, 'Of course I am happy here! It's wonderful! *Especially* when I have no choice!'"

We, as the parents of our children, have no more choice than the crippled holy man. When the only alternative to a relationship with our children, good or bad, is no relationship at all, we have no choice. Can we give up and cut off all communication? What kind of solution is that? And since we have no real choice, let's laugh out loud about it. Whatever life has given us, we have to make the best of it. What's the alternative?

For reasons I still don't fully understand, we never gave up on our son even after we asked him to move out. We visited him, talked on the phone, and he visited us. Gradually, in the next few years, we began to notice a change in our relationship. Things started to calm down. There was talk without arguments, without recriminations. All of a sudden we'd realize we were having a normal conversation with our son. And it's only gotten better and better.

COMMUNICATION IS THE CORE OF RELATIONSHIPS

The novelist Muriel Spark said, "Parents learn a lot from their children about coping with life." We certainly learned a lot from our son. He had no intention of letting us be "normal" parents, and there was precious little we could do about it. But we learned that good can come from bad. We learned how to keep the communication lines open in spite of everything because we had to. Our only other option was to give up on him and our relationship, and that we refused to do.

We learned that we can be responsible for our children only as far as they will let us. When they want to shut us out—and there can be a million reasons for this happening that have nothing to do with who we are as parents—we can't force them to change their minds.

We also learned that we can always talk to them whether they want us to or not. We never stopped talking to our son, no matter how often we had that talk thrown back in our faces. Although I don't think we understood it at the time, this talk was the most important thing we could have done, for his sake and for ours.

PART ONE

THE COMMUNICATION ETHIC

Five Universal Principles
of Communication

In doing the research for this book, I read many books and articles that emphasized the need for parents to be there for their kids. I've also found it in what teens say. "Kids need parents, not friends," said one teenager at a forum of parents and teenagers trying to find out what kids think about improving communication, how to keep kids safe from drugs and alcohol, and what a reasonable curfew is. The student continued: "You can't lose authority, and you can't have the kids running the show. I would imagine that kid who is [running the show] feels pretty lousy, actually."

Another student piped in: "As we move forward, the rules change. Kids gain responsibility, and they [parents] gain trust."

And another: "You can find out a lot about what your kid is doing by talking about things that have already happened instead of asking what they are doing now, who they are going with, stuff like that."

What do you want to say to your teenagers? Do you want to be able to tell them what the right thing is to say and do? Do you want to choose their friends? Do you want to ensure their success in school?

How much control do you want over your kids' lives? Needing control is like an addiction. As time goes on it takes more and more control to satisfy your need. You have to ask yourself what will happen when you can no longer control them. Will they have the necessary experience to control their own lives? We parents are often wrong, so why can't teenagers be wrong without our despairing that they are doomed? One author has written: "A child becomes an adult when he realizes that he has a right not only to be right but also to be wrong."

As our teenagers mature we want them to know what to do and why they should do it. This puts them in control of their own lives. They have the power in their knowledge of right and wrong. And they bear the responsibility for their behavior. We as parents can best use our talk to teach, not to command.

Teenagers are caught in between identities. They're children, yet they're no longer children. They're adults, yet they're not yet adults. As they search for identity, they look beyond parents and family to friends at school, to heroes in movies and magazines, and to pop music stars for answers to questions about what to like, what to say, what to wear, how to have their hair cut, what's cool, and what's not.

Many parents, I think, want their teens to be a clone of themselves. Someone said having children is the ultimate narcissistic act. Like Dr. Evil in the movie *Austin Powers: The Spy Who Shagged Me,* they want a "mini me" who thinks like them and will worship them for all their years as well as do whatever they say.

So when their teenager listens to "Limp Bizkit" rather than Lionel Ritchie, they feel betrayed. They actually dread the thought of their boys and girls becoming teenagers. They think of their sweet children turning into violent monsters hooked on drugs, sex, and rock and roll. The docile, well-behaved kids of family trips to the beach and playground, of Santa Claus, birthday parties, and the tooth fairy have turned overnight into rebels, scoffing at their parents, religion, and school, fueled by hormones run wild.

That's the stereotype. The reality is different, although not completely. Teenagers are searching for their identity and find it hard coping with all the changes and pressures that physical and mental adolescence brings with it. We all remember our teenage years as a time of searching for answers, finding them, and then discarding them for new ones. It was a time when friends were often more important than parents or teachers or clergy. We needed to belong, to be accepted, to be members of our group. Whether girl or boy, we needed to be like our friends, to do what they did, talk like they talked, like what they liked, hate what they hated.

We had more than our share of worries, dreams, hopes, and disappointments. There were concerns about school, sex, dating, clothes, summer jobs, getting into a good college. We wondered how we could afford that dress or piece of jewelry that would make our life complete. Or how we could ever save up enough money for a car. We had to be careful not to antagonize the kids who were gang members if we were not members ourselves. The last thing we wanted to do was fight although sometimes we had to. Should we join a club at school, try out for a team, or be part of student government? What our friends thought was the right thing to do was always a major consideration.

We're no longer teenagers, thank God! Now we're parents of teenagers. But that's even worse because we remember what we were like and the hell we put our parents through. Maybe we should send our kids away to military school until they're eighteen and then they're off to college. That might solve the problem of how to control our teens. Unfortunately, or maybe fortunately, most of us won't send our teenagers anywhere. They'll be with us at least until they leave for college or a job, and probably longer than that. So we'd better learn to cope. And even more than cope, we'd better learn how to communicate with these children-adults.

There is a way, and the purpose of this book is to show you that way. In this chapter I want to introduce you to the Communication Ethic, a set of five principles that will guide your talk with your kids. Everything you say can be improved by keeping these principles in mind as you decide what to say and how to say it.

An ethic is a standard of conduct, a morality, an expression of right behavior, a set of first principles. The Ten Commandments are an ethic, as is the Golden Rule. Like them, the Communication Ethic isn't tied to any particular family setting, any moment in time, any specific culture, or any particular society. It transcends all times and settings because it contains acknowledged truths about parent-child communication distilled from experience, common sense, and important research into the nature of talk. This book should help you translate these principles into important communication practices.

PRINCIPLE ONE: Be Involved

Communication with our kids is not an end in itself. Communication connects us to one another; it creates relationships. Good communication makes good relationships; poor communication inhibits relationships. But even poor communication is better than no communication at all because it means we are still involved in the lives of our teens. No communication means no relationship. If we're not communicating, we might as well live on different planets.

So the first principle of the communication ethic is *be involved.* That means being present in your teen's life in both body and mind. You should give your child the benefit of your whole being. That means complete focus and attention on what you're saying or doing together.

When you are totally involved in communicating with your teens, you're giving them the gift of yourself. In everything you say or do you are telling them that you value them. If you are talking, you should *just* talk. You should close your book, stop what you're doing in the kitchen or on the computer or in the workshop, and turn off the TV or radio. Your teens need and expect your full attention. If you give them only half of yourself, you are telling them that they are worth only half of you.

PRINCIPLE TWO: Make Love the Context

Everything you say to your teenagers makes sense to them in the context of the relationship you have built up between you over the years. So you have to ask yourself what kind of context you have created. When you *make love the context,* your teens will understand everything you say to them as an expression of that love. If you are praising them, they will hear it in the context of love. If you are disciplining them, they will hear it in the context of love. No matter what you say or do, you want your kids to think, "That's my mom (dad) showing that she (he) loves me and wants the best for me."

The context of love I am talking about is neither the romantic love of Hollywood nor the sentimental, self-centered love of TV sitcoms. This love is a selfless, egoless love. It's for your child's sake, not yours. You start building this context of love from the first moments you have with your children. It becomes a seen but unnoticed, taken-for-granted part of your relationship. It comes from what you say and do in moments of your talking, touching, kissing, comforting, and sharing. It comes from times of gentle conversation.

You can be responsible for your children only as far as they will let you. But you can always love them, whether they want you to or not. It's easy to love a child who's lovable. You must love your children whoever they are. Your unconditional love communicates the way you value them. You must not only love them but show that love in what you say and do.

Dr. Laura, a well-known "family values" radio talk show host, advocates that you turn your own kids in to the police if you catch them with drugs. Love is trust, and no child would ever trust a parent who did this. That's not to say your teen should go unpunished, but you should be a *guiding* light, not a *spot*light.

PRINCIPLE THREE: Listen More Than Talk

You have power over your teenagers—physical power (sometimes), legal power, moral power, and the power that comes from knowledge and experience. You may occasionally forget that having this power doesn't give you the right to dominate all communication with your teens. Good communication is two-way. It means you have to listen as much as talk. Because we seem to have a natural tendency to *talk at* our children much more than we *listen to* them, we must remember to *listen more than talk.*

Good communication means understanding. Understanding means being able to show it in what you say or do. If you don't listen to your kids, you will never know whether you understand one another or not. You must show your kids over and over again that you are there to listen. Listening means you don't interrupt, you don't jump to conclusions, you don't preach, you don't lecture. You just listen with full attention.

It's no more than common sense to say that if you want to understand your teenagers, you have to hear what they're saying. Their talk is the best window into their mind and soul. The last thing you want to do is discourage it. You want to prompt them to talk by asking open-ended questions— "Tell me what you think about . . ."—by nodding to show understanding while they're talking, by keeping silent when they have paused for a breath or to think about what to say next, by saying things like "Tell me more," by maintaining eye contact. If you do this on a regular basis, your kids will take your interest for granted, and you will give them the freedom to talk and yourself the freedom to listen. But don't forget sincerity. You can start a conversation mechanically, but if it hasn't taken flight on its own after a few seconds, wait a while and start again.

PRINCIPLE FOUR: Withhold Judgment

Your daughter is sixteen, and she just found out she might be pregnant. Would she tell you? If she did, how would you react? She would tell you if in the previous two thousand conversations you've had together, you've proven yourself a friend and worthy of her trust. These previous conversations, near meaningless at the time, pay off down the road.

Let me be clear. Withholding judgment doesn't mean you can't react to what your kids tell you. Second, it doesn't mean anything goes. Third, it doesn't mean there aren't consequences. But it does mean that any reaction to what your kids say must be held in abeyance, especially if you don't like what you hear initially. It does mean that you are open to your kids telling you everything and anything without telling them what *you* think about what they're saying. Consequences must flow naturally from their actions rather than from a knee-jerk reaction on your part before you have the whole story.

We all remember, to our everlasting regret, confiding in our parents, spouses, or friends, thinking they would understand, only to find that they didn't understand at all and reacted very badly. *Withholding judgment* is the way to create a relationship in which your teens will talk to you about anything because they know you will listen with an open mind. They know that the consequences of saying "the wrong thing" are small. They know this from experience and the trust that you have built up with them over the years, starting in early childhood.

I find that teenagers, after hearing themselves talk, pass their own judgment on their actions moments later, usually the same advice I would have given. Then it becomes a matter of mitigating the damage caused. "Here's what we do now . . ." A quick move from discussing the problem to acting on the solution works wonders, I find. A lot of times my suggested resolution is rejected, but teenagers seem to appreciate a list of options.

PRINCIPLE FIVE: Never Give Up

Relationships *are* communication. There are many times when communication with your kids breaks down. Your life is not like a TV sitcom in which problems between parents and kids appear and disappear in half an hour. You can have problems that last for weeks, months, years, or lifetimes when all communication seems futile. At times when everything you've tried with your teens has failed, you may be tempted to say, "I've had it! I've done my best, but it just isn't good enough. I give up."

That's something most of us have felt at one time or another. However, you have to realize that if you give up trying to communicate with your teens, you have lost. You have no real power over what your kids do if they don't give it to you. But you can control what *you* do. You can decide to give up trying, or you can decide never to give up. If you *never give up,* there is always the chance that someday you and your kids will connect again. You must always keep the lines of communication open. All the previous four principles depend on your still talking. Any communication, even one-sided, is better than no communication at all.

Taking Your Relationship to a New Level

These principles have made a great difference in my life and the lives of others. They are universals that aren't tied to any specific time or place or society. They find their home in no specific religion or faith. They are rooted in our human condition. They are not the product of fads, science, or cultural preferences but are what make us human in our relationships with others. If you apply these principles to your communication with your teenager, you will take your relationship to a new level.

A PARENT–TEENAGER COMMUNICATION SKILLS SELF-INVENTORY

Use the following questions to evaluate your communication skills. Find out how well you and your teen know and understand each other. Before you respond to each statement, reflect on how you presently talk to your teen. Decide whether each statement is mainly true or mainly false for you and your teen. If you're not sure what your teen would say, then ask. This is a personal inventory of what you know, what you feel, what you say, and how you tend to say it. It will give you a good starting point from which to improve your communication.

Remember, this is not a test, so be as honest as you can when you mark each statement either **T** for True or **F** for False.

I. How good are your communication skills?

1. I talk to my teenagers regularly. _____

2. I listen to my teenagers regularly. _____

3. I talk to my teenagers about important things. _____

4. I talk to my teenagers about unimportant things. _____

5. I can talk to my teenager about anything. _____

6. I don't preach at my teenagers. _____

7. I don't lecture my teenagers. _____

8. I always give my teenager an equal voice in the conversation. _____

9. I like talking to my teenager. _____

10. I like listening to my teenager. _____

11. I realize that my teenager may not understand me the way I intend. _____

12. I realize that I may not understand my teenager the way s/he intends. _____

13. I rarely lose my temper with my teenager. _____

14. I often compliment my teenager. _____

15. I often tell my teenager that I like her/him. _____

16. I often tell my teenager that I love her/him. _____

17. I often talk to my teenager just so I can hear the sound of her/his voice. _____

18. I often tease my teenager. _____

19. My teenager likes talking to me. _____

20. My teenager talks to me regularly. _____

21. My teenager listens to me regularly. _____

22. My teenager talks to me about important things. _____

23. My teenager talks to me about unimportant things. _____

24. My teenager can talk to me about anything. _____

25. My teenager rarely loses her/his temper with me. _____

Score 1 for each True response and 0 for False. Total for Section I (1–25): _____

II. How well do you and your teen know each other?

26. I like my teen. _____

27. I love my teen. _____

28. I know my teen's favorite music. _____

29. I know my teen's favorite movies. _____

30. I know my teen's favorite books. _____

31. I know my teen's favorite magazines. _____

32. I know my teen's favorite TV shows. _____

33. I know my teen's favorite Internet sites. _____

34. I know my teen's favorite sports. _____

35. I know my teen's friends. _____

36. I know what my teen likes to do best. _____

37. I like hugging my teen. _____

38. I value my teen's opinions. _____

39. I am flexible with my teen. _____

40. I usually say yes to my teen unless I have good reason to say no. _____

41. I value my teen's likes and dislikes. _____

42. I accept the fact that my teen knows more about some things than I do. _____

43. I can admit that I sometimes make mistakes. _____

44. I can admit to my teen when I am wrong. _____

45. I can admit that I don't always know best. _____

46. My teen likes me. _____

47. My teen loves me. _____

48. My teen knows my favorite music. _____

49. My teen knows my favorite movies. _____

50. My teen knows my favorite books. _____

51. My teen knows my favorite magazines. _____

52. My teen knows my favorite TV shows. _____

53. My teen knows my favorite Internet sites. _____

54. My teen knows my favorite sports. _____

55. My teen knows my friends. _____

56. My teen knows what I like to do best. _____

57. My teen likes hugging me. _____

58. My teen values my opinions. _____

59. My teen is flexible with me. _____

60. My teen usually says yes to me unless s/he has a good reason to say no. _____

61. My teen values my likes and dislikes. _____

62. My teen accepts the fact that I know more about some things than s/he does. _____

63. My teen can admit that s/he sometimes makes mistakes. _____

64. My teen can admit to me when s/he is wrong. _____

65. My teen can admit that s/he doesn't always know best. _____

Score 1 for each True response and 0 for False. Total for Section II (26–65): _____

III. Words I tend to use in conversation with my teen.

Positive words:

66. Believe	_____	79. Our	_____
67. Excellent	_____	80. Realize	_____
68. Family	_____	81. Safe	_____
69. Favorite	_____	82. Share	_____
70. Good	_____	83. Sympathize	_____
71. Help	_____	84. Together	_____
72. Honest	_____	85. Truth	_____
73. Kind	_____	86. Try	_____
74. Like	_____	87. Understand	_____
75. Listen	_____	88. Us	_____
76. Love	_____	89. We	_____
77. Nice	_____	90. Yes	_____
78. Okay	_____		

Score 1 for each True response and 0 for False. Total (66–90): _____

Negative words:

91.	Alone	_____	**104.** Never	_____
92.	Bad	_____	**105.** No	_____
93.	Busy	_____	**106.** Phony	_____
94.	Cheat	_____	**107.** Pigheaded	_____
95.	Dumb	_____	**108.** Shiftless	_____
96.	Failure	_____	**109.** Shut up	_____
97.	Good-for-nothing	_____	**110.** Slob	_____
98.	Hate	_____	**111.** Slut	_____
99.	Idiot	_____	**112.** Stop	_____
100.	Later	_____	**113.** Stupid	_____
101.	Lazy	_____	**114.** Worthless	_____
102.	Leave	_____	**115.** Wrong	_____
103.	Liar	_____		

Score 1 for each True response and 0 for False. Total (91–115): _____

Total for Section III (subtract the total of 91–115 from the total of 66–90): _____

Grand Total (add the totals for Sections I, II, and III): _____

WHAT YOUR SCORE MEANS

This is not a scientific assessment, but if done conscientiously, it can tell you much about your communication style, relationship, and attitudes. The higher your grand total, the better your communication with your teen should be.

60 to 90: Any score above 60 means that you probably have an excellent communication relationship with your teen.

40 to 59: This shows a good relationship. You are doing many things right, but there is still room for improvement.

20 to 39: You have work to do in order to get the communication lines open. You need to start improving your attitudes and skills.

10 to 19: Your communication is probably more destructive than constructive. You miscommunicate most of the time.

1 to 10: You and your teen rarely understand each other. You need serious help.

0 or less: A negative score means that you and your teen have no useful communication relationship.

If you scored over 75, you probably could have written this book yourself. If you scored more than 60, you probably will find most of what I suggest familiar and are already talking this way to your teen. If you scored below 60, you can really benefit from the communication practices I describe. They can help improve your relationship with your teen.

PART TWO

How to Talk About the Most Important Topics for You and Your Teens

E nough principles and stories! In Part One you learned some basic communication principles. Now for the other really important stuff: *how to use these principles in real conversations*—what to say and when, where, why, and how to say it. In this section you'll find all the tools you need to build your own conversational strategies and to begin conversations with your son or daughter.

Opening Scene: Each chapter begins with a specific parent-teen encounter that grounds the topic in a real-life situation. Even though your own situation may be different, you can see how the ideas and concerns surrounding the topic come to light. You will learn some words and phrases that you can use to talk to your teen in the context of your own family.

Things to Consider: This section helps you clarify your point of view, ideas, and values about each topic. You become aware of some choices you need to make. It teaches you to ask yourself, "What do I want to accomplish by talking to my teen about the topic?" You may find that you disagree with some of the values expressed in this section. That's all right. Thinking about how and why your values are different will help you talk to your teen more intelligently and sympathetically.

Three Things You Must Do: You should give these three things the highest priority. They often reflect the principles set out in Part One. You will probably think of others that are equally important to you. These will help you focus on immediate action in talking about this topic.

What to Say and Do: Here you will find examples of actual sentences and activities to use with your teen. You may not want to use them exactly as you find them; in fact, you may paraphrase them and change them to fit your teen and your circumstances. In any case, you are sure to find them a source of ideas on how to talk about each topic.

Words and Phrases to Use: This section gives you specific words and phrases that will help you talk about the topic with your teen in the most effective way. They express positive, compelling ideas and feelings that are designed to build and maintain the best possible relationship with your child.

What Not to Say: There are ways of talking about any of these topics that you must avoid because they will defeat your purpose. This section gives you examples of some of these sentences and briefly explains why you need to avoid them.

Words and Phrases to Avoid: Negative words and phrases will often alienate your teen and work against your relationship. You need to avoid them if you can. Most important, you need to think about these and others that don't work with your teen. The better your relationship with your teen, the smaller this list becomes.

A Note to Remember

Use Part Two as you would use a cookbook. When you need help on a specific topic, look it up, read what it has to say, and start talking. People who have read early drafts of this book said they enjoyed comparing their own ideas and practices with the ones presented even if they disagreed. So don't think that what you find here is the last word. Treat this book as a beginning rather than an end. Use it to open up the world of successful talk and relationships.

1 Anger

Anger is a short madness.

—Horace

Sheena came home late from school. She was furious about something, and her mother was worried because she hadn't come home at the normal time and didn't know where she was. Mom's first job was to calm her down, then try to find out what happened. Only then could she try to help solve the problem. Mom gave Sheena some tea and cookies and waited for her to start talking. It turned out that Sheena had been given detention by one of her teachers, and she was furious because she felt she had been treated unfairly.

Things to Consider

Teenagers get angry. Your teen may have a lot to get angry about. Older kids may bully her: "You have crappy hair." Schoolmates may say things behind her back or make her the butt of jokes: "Smelly Danielly." Teachers may tell her: "Stop doing that!" She may think you don't understand her: "I don't care what you promised your friend. No phone calls until you've finished your homework." She may not know exactly who she is or where she's going. She thinks she doesn't even control her own life. Anger is a natural reaction to all of this.

Anger can be destructive, but it can also be constructive. It's destructive when it hurts people or relationships. It's constructive when it is used for positive things, such as motivating one to work harder in school, deciding who one's real friends are, laughing at teasing and learning how to take and make jokes about oneself, and learning how to talk things through with parents or teachers who want to listen.

You are the key to having your teens talk about anger rather than acting it out. A relationship built on the Communication Ethic (Part 1) will make it more likely that your teenagers will feel comfortable coming to you with their feelings. But even if your relationship isn't everything it should be, and very few of us can boast that it is, there are still many important things you can do to help your teens cope with their anger.

Three Things You Must Do

1. *Understand* your teen's anger.

2. Help her *manage* it.

3. Help her *channel* it into productive emotions and actions.

What to Say and Do

Children like sympathy. If they feel they have got a sympathetic parent, they might offer information. If your teen is normally shy about talking to you but you suspect she is angry about something, show her you're there for her. Say such things as:

- ➤ You look angry. Is there anything wrong?
- ➤ I have a feeling that you're upset about something. Is it something I said?
- ➤ Whenever you talk that way, I know something is wrong. Would you like to talk about it?
- ➤ What do you mean you're not hungry? You're always hungry. Is something upsetting you?
- ➤ I think something is bothering you. Why don't we sit down and talk for a while.

If your teen is more open with you and says, "Gee, am I angry!" then say such things as:

- ➤ You *sound* angry. What happened to make you so mad?
- ➤ I know what you're feeling. I get angry, too. Tell me about it.
- ➤ Let's talk. You can tell me what's wrong.

Once you've begun talking, remember that you first want to *understand* the cause of the anger and how your teen is feeling about it. Try prompting her to open up. Say such things as:

- Talk to me.
- Look, I'm here for you. I'm not going to do anything but listen. So talk to me.
- I hate to see you so upset. What's wrong?
- Do you trust me enough to tell me what happened?
- I don't want to pry, but I want to hear about what happened. Will you tell me?

Then you want to help your teen *manage* her anger. Dwell on the positive. Try to relate her experience this time to other times she has been angry and how she successfully handled it, and to ways you cope with your own anger. Say such things as:

- I don't blame you for being so angry. I hated grade nine, too. But now you have to decide what to do about it that won't make things worse.
- The last time you were so angry, do you remember what you did to get over it? How did it work? How did it make you feel?
- Here's what I do when I'm angry.
- Let's take this anger apart, look at what caused it, and then figure out what you can do about it.
- It's good to talk when you're angry. Tell me what you'd like to do. Maybe I can help you.

Finally, once you and your teen understand the anger, you can help your teen channel it into something positive. Say such things as:

- What can you do to make sure it doesn't happen again?
- Which of these things would be best for you?
- If this happened to your sister/brother, how would you help her/him deal with it? What advice would you give?
- In situations like this one, what can you control and what can't you control?
- Have you ever made someone else angry? How did you do it? Why did you do it? How did it make him or her feel about you? Would you do it again?

The success of what you say may not be immediately obvious, but over time it will have positive results—if for no other reason than you and your teen are talking and creating a relationship of love, trust, and understanding.

WORDS AND PHRASES TO USE

⟫ help	⟫ I know	⟫ tell me	⟫ why
⟫ how do you feel	⟫ I understand	⟫ trust me	⟫ would you like to
⟫ I don't blame you	⟫ let's talk	⟫ what's good for you	⟫ you can tell me

What Not to Say and Do

Don't say such things as:

- I don't know why you're so angry.
- How can you be angry over nothing?
- Here's what I think you should do.
- You're such a baby.
- Why didn't you stand up for yourself?
- Can we talk later? I'm busy now.
- You'll just have to deal with it as best you can.
- I'd have punched his/her lights out.

We shouldn't use angry words and phrases. Don't say such things as:

- What do you want now?
- Can't you ever stay out of trouble?
- Don't bother me now. I'm busy.
- You'll just have to wait.
- Where the hell were you?
- Don't lose your temper with me, young lady/man!

WORDS AND PHRASES TO AVOID

⟫ be quiet	⟫ it's nothing	⟫ not again	⟫ wait until I tell your...
⟫ how can you	⟫ let me tell you	⟫ revenge	⟫ you're in trouble
⟫ I'm busy	⟫ never	⟫ stupid	⟫ you're silly

2 Anxiety

Life is what happens while you're busy making other plans.

—John Lennon

Something was wrong with Blake, their teenage son, but they didn't know what. Usually ravenous, he'd lost his appetite and was sitting on the couch silent, staring blankly at the TV. They tried chatting with him, but he just muttered something and went to his room.

The next morning they tried talking to him again, but he would say nothing. They asked if he was sick. He said he didn't feel very well and thought he'd better stay home from school. His parents asked him what exactly was the problem. He said he had a stomachache and felt a little dizzy. They suggested that they take him to see a doctor, but he said no, that he'd be all right the next day. So they said he could stay home, but if he wasn't better by tomorrow, he would have to see the doctor.

The next morning Blake said he felt a little better but still not well enough to go to school. He refused to go to the doctor. His parents insisted. The doctor examined him but found nothing physically wrong. She asked if there was anything else bothering him, something at school, for instance. He said no, school was fine. The doctor told his parents to keep an eye on him, that there were no signs of physical illness but perhaps he had experienced some kind of stress attack.

Saturday morning Blake seemed his old self once more. But Monday morning he seemed quiet, yet nervous. After continuous prodding he finally admitted that some boys at school were after him, and he was afraid they would beat him up. Now that his parents knew the problem, they were much relieved. They sat down with Blake to discuss the best course of action.

Things to Consider

Teens face anxiety daily. Their worries can be debilitating. They need to belong to their group; they need to succeed in school, make the team, wear the right clothes, have the right hairdo, say the right thing, have the right friends, ace the latest video game, and make their parents proud. The list is endless. Any one of these things can become so important that the thought of failing takes on gigantic proportions. Anxiety takes over unless you can help.

What should you do when you can see anxiety written on your teenager's face, in his movements, in what he says and does? When worry causes appetite and normal routine to disappear, replaced by unusual behavior or language, what should you say? How can you help him cope? It's hard for your teen to learn from *your* experience. Help him learn from his *own* experience.

Three Things You Must Do

1. *Show* that you care.

2. *Say* that you care.

3. *Be* available.

What to Say and Do

If your teen won't talk, you can still help. Say such things as:

- What's worrying you? Can you talk about it?
- Whatever is bothering you, you'll feel better if you talk about it.
- It's okay if you don't want to talk just now. Maybe later. I'll be here.
- You could write it down and let me read it.

If your teen wants to talk, let him. Hold your advice until he asks for it. Say such things as:

- Tell me all about it.
- I understand.
- Go on.

- Is there more?
- Why do you feel this way?
- Does anyone else feel this way?

Help to ease the anxiety. Say such things as:
- Have you felt this way before?
- What did you do then?
- How can we help you cope with this?
- What's the worst thing that can happen?
- That's not so bad, is it?
- Let's write the problem down. Putting things in writing helps make them more manageable.
- Let's write down some solutions. Then we can see which seems best.

To come to some kind of closure you can say such things as:
- Do you like feeling this way?
- Do you want to quit?
- What are your options? Can we come up with some?
- What do you want to do?
- I'll help you do it if you want me to.

WORDS AND PHRASES TO USE

after	help	other times	tell me	what
before	how long	solutions	think	will you
feel	I'll be here	talk to me	trust	write down

What Not to Say and Do

If your teen doesn't want to talk about it, avoid pressuring him. Don't say such things as:
- You've got to tell me what's bothering you.

> ✦ If you don't tell me what's wrong, I'm going to call the school [your friend, etcetera].
> ✦ If you don't stop this ridiculous behavior, you're grounded.

If your teen wants to talk, don't say such things as:

> ✦ How can you be worried about a little thing like that?
> ✦ Your sister/brother was never bothered by that.
> ✦ You should be grown up enough to cope with that.
> ✦ I'm going to speak with your school [coach, teacher, friend] about that.
> ✦ You'll just have to learn to cope with it by yourself.

Never say such things as:

> ✦ Don't bother me with your problems. I have enough of my own.
> ✦ I don't have any time to talk to you today. How about Saturday?
> ✦ Don't interrupt me. I know what's best.
> ✦ You're old enough to know better.
> ✦ What a silly thing to be upset about.

WORDS AND PHRASES TO AVOID

✦ baby	✦ immature	✦ later	✦ unimportant
✦ childish	✦ it's not the end of	✦ never	✦ you'll get over it
✦ don't	the world	✦ nonsense	✦ you're making a
✦ don't bother me	✦ it's your problem	✦ not now	mountain out of
✦ I'm busy	✦ just deal with it	✦ silly	a molehill

3 Appearance

Keep up appearances; there lies the test;
The world will give thee credit for the rest.

— CHARLES CHURCHILL

Sarah was about to turn eighteen and would graduate from high school in three weeks. She was starting college in September, which was going to put a heavy financial burden on her family. She realized she needed a job over the summer to help out with tuition. Her dad worked for a large oil company, and she had an interview there the following week for a job that would pay well and that would guarantee her employment each summer while in college. There was only one problem: Sarah had purple spiky hair, a ring in her nose, five earrings in each ear, and a stud through her tongue. She wore only black sweaters, black skirts, and black tights and shoes.

Things to Consider

It's a truism that teens need to fit in. Your teen has a distinct personality, likes and dislikes, talents, and interests that appeal to some groups of their peers more than others. Your teen may be a jock, a computer geek, a skater, or a student academic and social leader. Her music may sound like a broken dishwasher. Sometimes your teen's appearance tries your patience, but you have to cope. Teens want to sound alike and look alike. It's a badge of membership. We adults do the same thing. Go to a chamber of commerce meeting and try to find a man *not* in a dark business suit. In the corporate world, wearing suspenders is as brazen as a pink mohawk among teens. You must constantly ask yourself what is more important—your teen's need to be a member of a group or your desire to see him/her conform to your social norms of appearance?

You have a responsibility to teach your children that actions have consequences. They can appear any way they like, but people will judge them by that appearance. The consequences may be good or bad, but there will be consequences. Sometimes learning this lesson means hardship and disappointment. You have to decide where to draw the line between letting them appear as they choose and parenting them into appearing as you think they ought to.

Three Things You Must Do

1. *Understand* your teen's appearance as an expression of identity.

2. *Tolerate* your teen's appearance.

3. *Teach* your teen that appearances count.

What to Say and Do

Put your teen's appearance in the context of her peer group. Don't look at her in isolation because her reality is her group. Avoid commenting on your teen's appearance since it is almost always a losing battle. It's a very personal thing at any age beyond puberty, and you will hardly ever get any satisfaction from trying to convince your teen to dress the way you want her to even though you are paying the bills.

There are times, however, when you must tell your teen what you think of her appearance. Around the house or with friends she can wear what she wants, but when going out to dinner, dressing up is the rule because it shows respect for the place, the people, and the occasion.

If your teen is punk, you can begin jokingly. Say such things as:

+ Do all your friends look as good as you in black?

+ Green is my favorite color—even for hair.

+ How do you get your hair to stand up like that?

+ I used to look like you. My parents loved it.

- You're pierced in so many places, I'm worried you're going to spring a leak.
- If I told you to wear that leather jacket full of safety pins, you'd probably show up the next day in a polo sweater and Dockers.

Laugh about your differences. If your teen is just sloppy or dirty, say such things as:

- I always know when you're around even before I see you.
- Do you own anything that fits?
- You look as though you need spare change.

If your teen dresses the way you like, say such things as:

- Looking good, Billy Ray.
- You're such a good-looking girl/guy.
- Hey, two minutes in the penalty box for looking so good.
- Anytime you want to go clothes shopping, let me know.

For teens who are not aware of their appearance, say such things as:

- Would you let me take you shopping?
- I like that sweater, but I think you'd look even better in a different color.

For the teen who has to make a good impression, say such things as:

- What will you wear for the interview?
- Make your appearance fit the situation.
- What do you want your appearance to say about you?

WORDS AND PHRASES TO USE

▸ bizarre	▸ doesn't show you off to your best advantage	▸ is it hygienic	▸ safe
▸ colorful		▸ is this what your friends wear	▸ somewhat different
▸ dark			▸ unusual
▸ excellent	▸ flattering	▸ like	

What Not to Say and Do

Say nothing about your teen's appearance unless it's unlawful or so far out that you're afraid she or he is insane. There are a few things you should probably never say even jokingly because they immediately polarize the situation. Don't say such things as:

- You look positively awful.
- Go to your room and don't come out until you've taken all those things out of your body.
- You're not going to school looking like that.
- I don't care how your friends look. You're my child, and you'll do as I say.
- I would rather see you go out naked than looking like that.
- If you really think you look good like that, you need psychiatric help.

By the time your children are teenagers there is very little you can say or do short of financial and physical restraints that will change their appearance. It's something that has to come from them. To avoid confrontation over appearance unless absolutely necessary, say as little as possible.

WORDS AND PHRASES TO AVOID
(EXCEPT IN EXTREME CIRCUMSTANCES!)

- are you allergic to soap and water
- dreadful
- filthy
- hideous
- like a bum
- like a witch
- no child of mine is going to look like that
- sinful
- ugly
- you look awful
- you smell awful

4 Attitude

Life is not meant to be easy, my child; but take courage: it can be delightful.

—G. B. Shaw

Salvatore was depressed—not clinically depressed but intensely unhappy about the way his life was going. He was fifteen, had no girlfriend, and hadn't made the high school basketball team. Also, his grades could have been better than they were, so his parents weren't too pleased with him. Life had got him down, and he wasn't sure where to turn or what to do. He was so desperate that he finally decided to talk to his parents about the way he felt. They'd never been easy to talk to because they always started preaching. But maybe they could help him, and there was no one else to turn to.

Things to Consider

Your teen's attitude toward life can depend on many things over which you and he have little or no control: heredity, life experiences, health, family circumstances, talent and ability, opportunity, and luck. Attitude can also depend on things within his power, such as hard work, determination, ambition, resilience, faith, and self-esteem.

Your role as a parent is to help your teens with the things that are within your control and theirs. You can help your teens recognize and develop their talents, maintain their health, give them faith in themselves, achieve their ambitions, and work toward realistic goals. But the most valuable lesson you can teach them is this: The most important thing in life is not what happens to you but your attitude toward what happens to you.

You can teach this by telling your teens that this is the case, but you need to model this attitude for them as well. When your car dies in the middle of the busiest intersection in town or you don't get the promotion you wanted, show that you accept it as something fate has dished out to you. Show that acceptance doesn't mean defeat. Be a living example of how a positive attitude means that you will continue to do your best to achieve your goals. Then you will always come out a winner regardless of the result because you have given it your best shot.

What do you want when you're depressed? A lecture? No. You want a sounding board, a nonjudgmental, sympathetic ear.

Three Things You Must Do

1. *Listen* so you can understand your teen's attitude.

2. *Share* your own failures.

3. *Teach* him how to maintain a positive attitude toward himself and life in general.

What to Say and Do

Attitudes don't change overnight, so you should have a good sense of when your teen's attitude is upbeat or down. When it's up you should share in your teen's delight.

If you're not sure why he is so happy, say such things as:

- You seem awfully happy lately. Anything you want to share?

- It's great to see you so up. I hope it goes on forever.

- You keep smiling. What's the problem?

- Let's have a party and celebrate your happiness. What's the occasion?

If your teen seems unhappy, say things like:

- You seem awfully unhappy lately. Anything you want to share?

- What's wrong, honey?

- Why so down? Anything I can do to help?

- What's bothering you? You haven't been yourself lately.
- Let's sit down. I'd like you to tell me why you've been so unhappy.
- Are you having a problem in school? We can talk about it.

If your teen's attitude is generally optimistic, say such things as:

- You know, I really admire you. You seem to know how to make the best of everything.
- You have a terrific attitude. You seem able to rise above problems and work them out.
- You have such a positive attitude to things. Can you tell me your secret?

If your teen's attitude is generally pessimistic, try to get him to talk. Say such things as:

- You seem to be unhappy. Let's talk about it.
- What's the problem? You seem to be down all the time.
- I know things have been tough for you recently, but you seem so depressed, I think we need to talk about it.
- I want to help you be happy. Tell me what's wrong and let me see if I can help.
- Life isn't easy sometimes. We all have disappointments. I can help you if you'll let me.

Goal-setting games can help make life's troubles easier to handle. Ask your teen to write a list of all the bad things in his life. Then have him make a list of all the good things. Compare lists. See what is within his control and what is not. Plan strategies on how to fix the bad things that can be fixed.

WORDS AND PHRASES TO USE

• glad to see you happy	• realistic goals	• what can you control	• what makes you happy
• I like your attitude	• unrealistic goals	• what can't you control	• what makes you sad

What Not to Say and Do

Don't criticize or belittle your teen's attitude even if you don't like it. Seek to understand it. Being involved in a teen's life will give you an inside track on understanding his attitude. It is not always possible to be as involved as you would like to be, but you can be a good and sympathetic listener as well as a sensitive observer of your teen's moods, talk, and actions.

Don't be aggressive, sarcastic, or dismissive of your teen's attitude. Don't say such things as:

- You drive me crazy with your moods.
- You think you have it bad, wait until you hear about my problems.
- You're such a failure.
- I'm sorry you're my child.
- If you don't like your life here, then leave.
- You're lazy.
- You have a great talent for doing nothing.
- Shape up or ship out.
- You're better off than a million other kids.
- You just have a bad attitude.

WORDS AND PHRASES TO AVOID

- bad attitude	- lazy	- no talent	- spoiled
- dreamer	- never satisfied with anything	- quitter	- stupid
- dumb		- selfish	- useless
- failure	- no ambition	- sick	- warped

5 Authority

I don't like authority, at least I don't like other people's authority.

—A. C. BENSON

Theo's parents say he stopped acknowledging their authority over him when he was two. Now fourteen, he generally had refused to accept any adult authority whatsoever, which included parents, grandparents, uncles, aunts, teachers, principals, and neighbors. Fortunately, Theo never had any experience with the police. His parents used to despair when he was younger. In spite of their pleading, cajoling, and threatening, Theo continued to say that no one was "the boss of me." Now that he was a teen, Theo's parents told him, "If you won't listen to us, then you must take responsibility for your own actions. We will still be here for you, but since you refuse to accept our authority, we will stop telling you what to do and you'll have to live with the consequences of your own decisions." Although they were still legally responsible for him, they had decided to face the reality of the situation: They were his parents in name only.

Things to Consider

Believe me, there are children like Theo. I know because my wife and I had one. Kids like Theo refuse to be children; normal children, even the most recalcitrant, eventually give in to adult authority. But there are some, like Theo, who don't fit the mold. They always think they know best. What's the problem with these kids? They don't know best, so they constantly get into trouble. They make all kinds of mistakes that get them into trouble at home, school, and in the community.

If you have a teen like Theo or a teen who recognizes the authority of adults on a limited basis, you're not alone. Recognize the problem for what it

421

is. Don't blame yourselves since you are probably not directly responsible. It's just the way some teens are.

Nevertheless, even with kids like Theo, there are things you can say and do. Stay involved in their lives; know what they're doing and who they're doing it with. Tell them what you approve of and what you don't. Keep talking to them about their lives and yours. In what you say and do you must show them that you love them, no matter what. Above all, never give up on them. It's easy to love a child who wants your love. It's much harder to love a child who doesn't.

For the majority of teens, authority comes from our official position as parent, teacher, coach, or doctor. Or from the respect teens have for who we are as persons. The latter kind is the best. We want our authority to come from a teen's respect for who we are, not what we are. Whether or not it does depends on our relationship.

Three Things You Must Do

1. *Show* that the best authority is earned.

2. *Teach* that accepting authority is part of becoming an adult.

3. *Warn* your teenagers that flouting authority usually leads to trouble.

What to Say and Do

If you have a teenager who dislikes your authority but will normally give in, you can help him along. Say such things as:

▸ I'm not going to tell you that you have to do this for your own good because I don't think you'll believe me. But you should know that I wouldn't ask you to do it for any other reason.

▸ You like to think of yourself as getting close to being an adult. That means sometimes you have to do what others want you to do even if you don't want to.

- When I see you behaving in such a mature way, I know you're close to being a grown-up.
- There are some things we ask you to do, and we expect you to do them simply because we're your parents and we know best. But we are always happy to explain our reasoning to you.

With a teen who *strongly* resists your authority, talk things through. Say such things as:

- Why do we have to fight about everything we ask you to do? It doesn't make you happy, and it doesn't make us happy. Why don't we just talk these things through, and maybe you'll understand why you have to do them.
- You can resist what we say, but in the end it's you who will suffer the consequences.
- Some people have the authority to tell you what to do. You'll just have to accept that we have that authority over you.

To teenagers who resist teachers' authority and who occasionally get into trouble at school, say such things as:

- Your teacher seems unhappy with your behavior in class. What don't you like about her?
- We need to talk about school and find out why you are behaving the way you are.
- We think we need to have a conference with your teacher, and we want you to be there with us. It's about your unwillingness to do what she tells you to do in class.

With a teen who regularly gets into trouble at school, say such things as:

- Why don't you like school?
- If you were a teacher, what would you expect from your students?
- We want to have a conference with your school principal, and we want you to be there.
- The teachers and principal at your school think you have a serious problem with authority. We think so, too, but we need to get your side of the story. Do you think you have a problem? What do you think that is? Do you think it can be fixed?

WORDS AND PHRASES TO USE

- acceptance
- for everyone else's good
- legal authority
- making trouble for yourself
- maturity
- obedience
- people who want to help
- respect
- responsibility
- succeed
- things you could do
- understanding
- willingness

What Not to Say and Do

Don't taunt your teenager about fighting authority. Don't say such things as:

- You might as well give up fighting because you're going to lose.
- We're not going to discuss it. Just do what we say.
- If you fail in school, you're going to grow up to be a bum.
- How stupid can you get? Just do what you're told.
- There's no room for talk.

If your teenager absolutely rejects authority, don't say such things as:

- You're a disaster.
- You're going to end up in jail.
- I think you'd better leave home. We don't want you anymore.
- After all we did for you, how can you do this to us?
- I don't know what goes on in your head. You're the one who's going to suffer.

WORDS AND PHRASES TO AVOID

- a disaster
- bad
- delinquent
- dumb
- evil
- stupid
- useless
- why can't you act like a normal person
- wasted life
- you'll never grow up
- you'll end up in jail

6 Boys

Of all the animals, the boy is the most unmanageable.

—PLATO

Jessica was having boy trouble. She liked Sam, a boy in her high school, a lot, but she didn't know whether he really liked her. When it was just the two of them alone, he was attentive, affectionate, funny, and considerate. She liked being with him. But when any of Sam's friends came by, he seemed to forget that she existed and gave all his attention to them. As a result she felt neglected, hurt, and insecure. When they were alone, they talked about school, movies, books, and relationships. But when they were in a group, he only wanted to talk about computer games, the Internet, sports, and cars. Jessica didn't know what to do. She didn't understand Sam, and this was driving her crazy. Should she look elsewhere for a boyfriend, or were they all the same? Her girlfriends told her they were. She decided to talk to her mom about the problem, and maybe her dad. But her mom was easier to talk to about these things.

Things to Consider

Sex is the strongest motivating force in a teenager's life. Watching boys and girls interact in junior and senior high school is witnessing one of life's great rituals. Boys and girls flirt and tease; boys chase, and girls get chased. Same-sex groups huddle together to watch the other sex and speculate about existing and potential couples. Girls chat about relationships, and boys banter about chicks; both groups gather to establish the "ideology of cool." She's cool, he isn't. Belly button rings are, nose rings aren't. Kids either fit in or look for a new group with a different interpretation of cool.

You ignore these rituals at your peril. Your teen is almost certainly involved, and if she isn't, you should be more concerned than if she is. You can help your teenage daughter cope with boys as she tries to make her way through this ritual of the life force.

Your daughter needs to know a few basic things about boys if she's confused about them, and she probably is. If you think I'm commenting about the stereotypical boy, you're right. He may not really exist, but most boys share enough of these characteristics that talking about them will do no boy a serious injustice.

Boys find themselves attracted to girls and need to think themselves attractive to girls. They also need to belong to groups of boys. They need to compete for girls at the same time as they need to excel at sports, school, and games. Boys need to try hard to succeed in all these areas, while at the same time they must seem not to care. They must be "cool" about school, girls, sports, and all those things that really matter. Succeeding at these things gives them the security of membership and status in the male pack. Boys also need to show their independence from their families while they are still heavily dependent on them. Girls need to understand that teenage boys will seem caring, interested, and enthusiastic one moment, and insensitive, inconsiderate, and uncaring the next.

You can help explain these things to your daughter and give her the knowledge, confidence, and self-assurance to ride out a boy's stormy behavior if she thinks he's worth the trouble. As a former teenage boy myself, I can say from experience that boys are worth it even if they don't appear to be at the time.

Three Things You Must Do

1. *Recognize* the sexual forces at work in your daughter's life.

2. *Take an interest* in your daughter's relationships.

3. *Share* your knowledge and experience when asked.

What to Say and Do

When your daughter comes to you with any questions or stories about relationships with boys, welcome her with an open mind and listening ears.

Encourage her to talk. Say such things as:

- Tell me about it.
- I want to know as much as you're willing to tell me.
- Have I met him?
- What's he like?
- What do you like about him?
- How long have you liked him?
- What does he think about you?
- Do your friends like him?

All of these comments and questions present an interested but neutral face to your teen so that you are learning as much as you can without seeming to judge. You just want her to open up to you and share her thoughts and feelings so you can form some opinion of the relationship without having met the boy.

If your daughter has questions about the strange behavior of boys, say such things as:

- Boys are all different, but generally they're confused about who they are and who they want to be.
- Boys need girls to like them, but they also need to be one of the boys.
- Boys will do things sometimes for the benefit of girls and sometimes for the benefit of other boys. When that's the case, it doesn't mean they don't like you.
- You'll know if it is worth putting up with a boy. You know how you feel about him deep down, and you know how he treats you.
- You might not like my saying it, but you're better off not getting too serious about any one boy. Try to meet lots of them.

These are all ways of helping a conversation along. There is much more that can be said. Keep the conversation going so that your daughter can confide in you.

WORDS AND PHRASES TO USE

● boys are a puzzle	● gentle	● sense of humor	● what does he like
● boys often don't even understand themselves	● I know what you mean	● slowly	● what's he good at
	● interests	● tell me all about him	● where
● careful	● nice	● what does he look like	● who

What Not to Say and Do

Don't close down the conversation. Don't judge or patronize; your teen will stop confiding in you. Don't give advice until you're asked. Don't belittle your teen's feelings or underestimate her power. If you want to stay involved in her life, make it easy for her to talk to you about anything. Don't say such things as:

- ● You're too young to be involved with a boy.
- ● Boys can't be trusted. They're only after one thing. Once they have it, they'll drop you.
- ● You're so silly.
- ● You don't have time for boys. You need to concentrate on school.
- ● When I was your age, my dad would have killed me for getting involved with boys.
- ● Don't ever let me hear you talk about boys.
- ● Just because your girlfriends are being silly about boys doesn't mean that you have to be.
- ● I don't want to hear about your relationships with boys.
- ● You don't know what you're talking about.

WORDS AND PHRASES TO AVOID

● cheaters	● I don't want to know	● silly	● unacceptable
● don't trust them	● immature	● stupid	● waste of time
● I can't trust you anymore	● liars	● too young	● you can't

7 Bullying and Teasing

It is better to be a coward for a minute than dead for the rest of your life.

—IRISH PROVERB

"Jenna," her father said at dinner, "I read in today's paper that a fourteen-year-old boy in your high school killed himself by jumping off a bridge. He left a five-page letter to his fifteen-year-old brother that said how kids at school were bullying and teasing him a lot. He wrote, 'When people bully and tease me, I just smile a lot like it doesn't bug me but inside I cry.' Isn't that an awful thing? That bullying could make a kid commit suicide? Is there a lot of bullying at your school?"

"Dad, I don't know, but there's some. It can't be helped. Some kids just ask for it."

"I can't accept that. How do they ask for it?"

"They're strange or different or real wusses, or they're just small and weak, sort of gay. You know. They're just asking for somebody to beat up on them and make them normal."

"Are they the only kids who get bullied?"

"No. A lot of the younger kids get pushed around by the older ones."

"I don't believe what I'm hearing. There's that much bullying in your school, and no one does anything to stop it?"

"What can they do? It sometimes happens after school or on the way home."

"Does this happen to boys and girls, or just boys?"

"It's usually boys who do it to other boys, but sometimes they bully girls. And some girls do it to other girls."

"Have they ever tried to bully you?"

"Yes, once they did, but I got my friend Kelly, who's a senior on the football team, to protect me. He's big and really cool, and he told them he'd beat them up if they ever bothered me again. They haven't bugged me since."

"If anyone ever threatens you or touches you, I want you to tell me. Understood?"

Things to Consider

Bullying is a problem in most high schools even though it often goes unreported and unnoticed. Although it may be invisible to the administration, teachers may be aware of the more serious incidents and may be able to pick out most of the bullies in school if they had to.

You need to have the kind of relationship with your teens that encourages them to report any bullying or serious teasing. They need to trust your response. Teens won't tell parents who fly off the handle, rush down to the school threatening lawsuits, or take things into their own hands by threatening violence toward the bully. In most cases teens think that will just make things worse for them.

Be low-key. It's a very serious matter, but you need to talk about it calmly and reasonably, and, with your teen's help, work out a plan of action. You have options such as going to the school and talking to the principal, getting the name of the bully and calling his or her parents, or going to the police if the bullying warrants such a serious move. Some high schools have a police officer responsible for the school.

If you have a teen who wouldn't likely admit to being bullied, it's good to know these warning signs:

- ✦ missing valuable personal items such as a watch, Discman, or skateboard
- ✦ bruises that can't be accounted for by participation in sports or normal teen horsing around
- ✦ fear of school or skipping classes
- ✦ loss of appetite, stomachaches, or the appearance of anxiety or withdrawal
- ✦ a noticeable absence of friends, telephone calls, dates
- ✦ unexplained requests for money or money disappearing from your wallet

If you note any one or a combination of these signs, ask your teen about them. Don't be put off by initial denial. Be gentle but persistent. Explain that hiding the problem won't help it but may make it worse. Eventually you may be able to convince your teen that she needs your help. Tell your teen that bullies who get away with it often get bolder and more abusive. If you already have a good communication relationship, your teen will know that you are only interested in her safety and well-being.

Once you know there is a real problem, you can do a number of things:

- Collect any evidence of bullying. This can range from other kids willing to be witnesses to a written account detailing the abuse. Include the date, day, time, place, and details of the bullying, plus the names and phone numbers of witnesses. If the bullying includes extortion, list items or money taken.

- Go to the school. Get your teen to give you the names of those they trust and are willing for you to talk to.

- Get assurance that these discussions will be confidential until some action can be taken.

- If other kids have been bullied, join forces with them and approach the principal as a group.

- Find out what the school is planning to do and when.

- Go to the police if you think the bullying is serious and the school can't or won't deal with it.

- Bully-proof your child. Help her to have high self-esteem. Show how much you love and support her. Encourage her to join teams or clubs, which will give her a good support group. Coaches and teachers can also help and act as advisors and guardians.

Here is something else to consider. If your teen is the bully, you need to find out the cause and seriousness of the bullying. Ask your teen about it. Talk to your teen's friends. Talk to kids who have been bullied. Talk to the schoolteachers and/or principal. See if it's a one-time or habitual occurrence. If necessary, take your teen to counseling before it turns into something more serious.

Three Things You Must Do

1. *Realize* that bullying is a fact of life in many schools.

2. *Know* if your teen is a victim.

3. *Know* if your teen is a bully.

What to Say and Do

If you have a concern about bullying in your teen's school, don't hesitate to raise the issue with her. Get her used to talking about it. Your teen might be next. Say such things as:

- Is bullying a problem in your school?
- Who are the bullies in your school? Do your teachers know about them?
- What kinds of kids get bullied? What do bullies do to them?

Make sure your teen knows that she can always come to you if someone is "on her case." She will want you to help her, but not embarrass her or make things worse. Say such things as:

- You would always tell me if anybody tried to bully you, wouldn't you?
- If I can ever help you with this kind of situation, let me know.
- You know bullies won't go away until they are forced to.

If you notice any of the warning signs, talk to your teen to see if she is being victimized by a bully. Say such things as:

- Is everything all right? You don't seem to be your normal self.
- Did you lose your Discman? I haven't seen you using it in a while.

If your teen seems reluctant to talk about it, explain that not stopping the bullying now might make it worse. The violence or extortion will increase, not decrease. As long as the bully can get away with it, she will. Say such things as:

- If you're being bullied, we have to do something to stop it right now.
- Do they hit you? Do they ask you for money? Do they take things from you?
- It's only going to get worse unless we do something now.

Help bully-proof your child. You will want to raise her self-esteem and self-confidence. Go on outings together. Play sports. Encourage your teen to develop talents she has.

Your teen may be a bully. It may be serious or just a casual teasing done with others, with no hurtful intent. You have to find out and take appropriate action. Say such things as:

- I've heard rumors that you've been bullying younger kids. Is it true?
- What do you think about kids who bully or tease other kids and really hurt them?

WORDS AND PHRASES TO USE

❧ abuse	❧ extortion	❧ plan of action	❧ we have to do something
❧ advice	❧ hurt	❧ protection	❧ witnesses
❧ bruises	❧ information	❧ self-confidence	
❧ evidence	❧ it won't stop	❧ self-esteem	

What Not to Say and Do

Don't accept bullying in your teen's school. Don't say such things as:

- ❧ Bullying is no big deal.
- ❧ When I was in high school, I got bullied, and when I was big enough, I did some bullying.
- ❧ Kids today have no guts. They won't stand up for themselves.

If you find out that your teen is being bullied or teased, don't overreact. Don't rush down to the school threatening lawsuits or police action, or take things into your own hands by threatening violence toward the bully. In most cases teens think that will just make things worse for them.

Don't blame the victim. Don't blame your teen for being the object of a bullying. Don't say such things as:

- ❧ If someone's bullying you, it's your own fault.
- ❧ You've probably been asking for it.
- ❧ You have to fight back, stand up for yourself, or otherwise you deserve what you get.

Don't ignore the possibility that your son or daughter is a bully. Don't overlook evidence such as money, electronics, or bicycles that appear out of nowhere.

WORDS AND PHRASES TO AVOID

❧ break his bones	❧ it's a normal part of school life	❧ revenge	❧ you're a coward
❧ fight	❧ kill	❧ weakling	❧ you're overreacting
❧ I don't believe you	❧ loser	❧ you asked for it	❧ you're at fault

8 Careers

*There are very few jobs that actually require a penis or vagina. All other
jobs should be open to everybody.*

—FLORYNCE KENNEDY

*Katy was going into her senior year in high school. She did reasonably well in most of
her subjects, getting around a "B+" average. She got "A" in subjects she really liked, such
as English and social studies, but "B" in math, which she didn't like even though she
understood it quite well.*

*The big question now was what she wanted to do with her life. What kind of career
should she be thinking about? Most of her friends hadn't any better idea of what they
wanted to do than she did. The school guidance counselor wasn't much help since she
didn't really know Katy very well. Everything she said was based on Katy's grades and
scores on standardized tests.*

*Katy finally decided she'd better talk to her parents about things. They were easy to talk
to because they always listened and didn't just tell her what they thought she should do
unless she asked them to. And they would be paying for college if that was what she
decided to do.*

Things to Consider

Our teenagers can aspire to almost any career that suits them. There is still
racial, religious, and gender discrimination in many areas, but most people recognize that intelligence, skills, and a willingness to work are more important
than anything else.

You can help your teens discover their aptitudes and abilities and help
them choose the career path that suits them best. As a college professor I have

taught thousands of teens over the years. Three things seem to be most important in talking to them about their future. First, assess their talents. Do they have a special aptitude for academic subjects such as science and math? Are they talented in the arts? Do they have great people skills? Do they have mechanical skills?

Second, talk about their own desires. Know what excites them, what their daily life choices and interests are, their favorite subjects in school, the books and magazines they read, the websites they visit, the movies they watch, the groups they identify with, the interests of their friends.

Third, and in some respects most important of all, know your teen's personality. Whatever her talents and desires, personality plays a large part in determining success in her career. Ask yourself how you would describe your daughter or son to a stranger. Are they outgoing or quiet and reserved, cautious or risk-takers, careful about their appearance or sloppy, ambitious or laid-back, glamorous or plain, a leader or a follower, organized or disorganized, sensitive or callous, brave or timid?

If your advice is going to be helpful, consider how much you really know about your teens. The more you know, the better your guidance will be. The best way to get this knowledge is through good communication and consistent involvement in their lives.

Three Things You Must Do

1. *Involve* yourself in your teen's life so that you know her personality and interests.

2. *Assess* your teen's strengths and weaknesses.

3. *Listen* to your teen's own wishes.

What to Say and Do

When your kids were young, they might have said, "I want to be a doctor [pilot, teacher, or veterinarian]." Now that they're teenagers, they tell you they don't know what they want to be. Should you be concerned? Have a conversation about them. Say such things as:

- You're still young. You don't have to decide yet.
- You have so many options, it's no wonder you're confused about what you want to do.
- The most important thing is to make the right choice for you.
- Imagine yourself doing a job day after day and see what appeals to you.
- You may not find what you really like until you see what life offers.
- I think right now it's easier to rule out what you don't want to be.

Whether or not you're concerned about her indecision, there are things you can say and do to help guide her in the right direction. Say such things as:

- Let's list all the careers that you think might appeal to you and all the qualifications you think these careers require. I'll help you.
- Which of these qualifications do you have? Which ones do you think you'd enjoy getting?
- What kind of a person do you think you have to be to succeed in these careers you like?
- Are you that kind of person?
- If you could be anything in the world just by snapping your fingers, what would you choose?
- Let's do an inventory of things you like to do in your free time, to read about, to watch on TV, to see at the movies. What subjects do you like best at school? What are your best subjects?

WORDS AND PHRASES TO USE

ability	choice	intelligence	qualifications
advice	drive	likes and dislikes	realistic
ambition	hard work	our experience	talent
aptitude	help you	personality	together

What Not to Say and Do

Your opinion may differ from mine on this, but my belief is that you can help your teens best by listening very carefully to what they say and involving yourself in their lives in a quiet way, mainly as an observer. Get fully involved only when they or you think they need help. I tend not to be overly assertive or directive with teens. I don't patronize them. I don't say such things as:

- You'd better make up your mind about a career soon.
- We're not wasting money on college for you if you don't know what you want to do.
- When I was your age, I was already out working for a living.
- When I was your age, I already knew exactly what I wanted to do. That's why I'm successful.
- You're going to be a bum.
- You're wasting your life.
- When you're eighteen, you're on your own. *(If your child is a bum, this is okay to say.)*

WORDS AND PHRASES TO AVOID

✦ bum	✦ immature	✦ no talent	✦ ungrateful
✦ get a life	✦ lazy	✦ on your own	✦ wasting our money/ your life
✦ haven't a hope	✦ my advice to you	✦ stupid	✦ will never

9 Cars

Never lend your car to anyone to whom you have given birth.

—ERMA BOMBECK

Jason, a responsible seventeen-year-old, took driver education in summer school and passed his driver's test a week ago. Yesterday, Saturday, he uttered those words that strike fear in the hearts of all fathers: "Dad, may I borrow the car tonight?"

Dad was ready to say yes, but he wanted to make sure that he and Jason understood all the "rules of the road." He wanted to talk to Jason about the responsibilities that went along with the privilege of borrowing the car. He knew that he and Jason had to talk about things to make sure they understood each other.

Things to Consider

The summer I was sixteen I took a driver training course. I was a lifeguard during the day and took the course in the evenings at the local high school. I passed my driver's test the first time. When I asked my dad if I could borrow the car, I noticed a look of pain and horror quickly pass across his face. Nevertheless, he said yes. Off I went in the family Buick, solo. I was in heaven. What a feeling of power and freedom!

You need to put yourself in your teen's place when he asks to use the family car. In North America learning how to drive and "having your own wheels" are important parts of growing up. Don't automatically say no. Teach your teen how to use the car responsibly.

Life isn't perfect. You're not perfect. Don't expect your teen to be perfect. Putting a teen behind the wheel of a car means taking risks. Insurance statistics show that adolescent boys see the car as an extension of their identity and often use the car too aggressively. Adolescent girls are much better at driving responsibly. You have to decide what level of risk you can tolerate. If you will constantly worry about your car and your teen, then say no. Tell him that he'll have to wait until he can afford his own car and insurance, and is legally responsible for himself.

The best approach, however, is to give your teen the benefit of the doubt. Let him use the car until he proves himself unable to handle the responsibility. When you go out as a family, let your teen drive under your supervision. Set a good example with your own driving. Require your teen to help pay the cost of additional insurance coverage. Require successful completion of a driver education course that will improve driving skills and lower the cost of insurance.

Talk about your "rules of the road," such as no drinking and driving, and no friends driving. Have your teen contribute to gas and other car expenses in proportion to his use of the car. Help him save for his own car and help him find a good one.

I've had extensive and generally positive experience with teens and cars. We live in the country where, especially in winter, cars are the only way to get around. All my children took driver education as teens. My three children are only three years apart. At one point in their teenagehood we had six cars in the family. My wife and I, my daughter, and one of my sons each had one, and my other son had two. We also had a moped. Enough said. We had rules, but we also trusted our teens, and, that trust generally paid off.

Three Things You Must Do

1. *Teach* your teenager your rules.

2. *Trust* your teen.

3. *Be* a good example.

What to Say and Do

Establish the basic ground rules. Say such things as:

- If you want to drive, you have to learn to do it properly.
- You must take a driver education course. That will give me peace of mind and lower your insurance costs.
- If you pass the course and get your license, I will let you use our car.

When your teen has done this, you can talk about rules. Say such things as:

- Let's talk about the "rules of the road."
- Make sure you never drink and drive.
- If you've had a drink, you can call us anytime, anywhere, and we will come and get you.
- Your friends can't drive our car without our permission.

Talk about responsibilities. Say such things as:

- You are responsible for buying your own gas.
- You are responsible for a percentage of the extra insurance costs. *(Each family needs to decide what is appropriate for them.)*
- You'll need to keep your grades up in school, or you'll lose car privileges.
- You can use the family car as long as you use it responsibly and don't break the rules.

Share ideas. Say such things as:

- These are my rules. What do you think about them?
- Do you want to add any of your own?
- Let's write these rules down, and both you and I can sign them.

WORDS AND PHRASES TO USE

attention	insurance	no drinking and driving	save for your own car
care	mature	rules	using the car is a privilege
expenses	responsibility		

What Not to Say and Do

Don't let concerns about driving and cars come between you and your teen. Remember that your relationship is more important than anything else. Don't say such things as:

- I don't want you driving my car. It's too expensive.
- I don't care what you do, you won't drive until you're on your own.
- I don't trust you with anything of mine.
- Pass all the driver education courses and driver's tests you like. You still can't use the car.
- I don't want to hear any excuses from you. You broke the rules.
- I think you'll drink and drive.
- Give me one good reason why I should trust you.
- I don't care what your friends can do.
- I don't care why you need to use the car.

WORDS AND PHRASES TO AVOID

devious	liar	never	untrustworthy
careless	my car is more important to me than you	reckless	wild
immature		sneak	

10 Choices

I don't know the key to success, but the key to failure is trying to please everybody.

—BILL COSBY

Aaron had an important grade ten social studies exam the next morning. But his high school basketball team was playing its major rival that night and all his friends were planning to go to the game. He was a serious student and took pride in getting good grades in school, but he wanted to be one of the guys. If he didn't show up for the game because of the exam, his friends might start calling him names. He didn't know what to do.

His mother noticed that he looked somewhat distracted when he came home from school that afternoon, and she asked him if anything was the matter. After pretending that everything was fine, he finally admitted to her that he had a problem and didn't know what to do about it. He had to choose between his studies and his friends. It wasn't an easy choice to make.

Things to Consider

Life is filled with difficult choices. Teens are sometimes torn between pleasing themselves, their parents, their friends, their teachers, and, if they have a job, their bosses. You can help your children with these decisions through good communication. Your involvement in their lives, your willingness to listen and to be there for them, to hear what they have to say without judging them, and your unconditional love for them will make them come to you with their most perplexing choices as well as their less important ones.

Your perspective, based on your life experience, will be different from that of your teens. So try to put yourself into their shoes. Remember what it was like to be fifteen and still trying to find out who you really were. Don't assume that your choice of action will be right for your teens. Help them work through the options and the consequences of each option. From your experience you can add all kinds of contingencies to the situation that your teens may not think of. Sometimes choices have long-range consequences that they haven't considered.

Remember, too, that at the same time you are helping your teens make a choice, you are also teaching them how to make choices. If you have a good communication relationship, they will listen to what you say as you try to help them arrive at a decision. They will hear your reasons as emotional, logical, moral, ethical, or religious, although they may not use these labels. When they have to make choices on their own, they may remember how you worked through the options. Keep that in mind as you help them find their own way.

Three Things You Must Do

1. *Be involved* in your teen's life.

2. *Listen* to what he tells you.

3. *Teach* him to analyze the consequences of each choice.

What to Say and Do

Encourage your teen to talk about his difficult decisions. Say such things as:

- What can I do to help?
- Let's talk about your problem.
- Can you tell me what you think your choices are?
- Maybe there is a compromise choice.
- Let's examine all the consequences.
- Let me explain the process I use to make choices.
- Would you like me to tell you what I would do in your situation?

Work through the situation with your teen using this process. Say such things as:

- Let's talk through the situation so we both understand it the same way.
- Tell me what you think your choices are.
- Let's examine each choice.
- What's the best thing that could happen?
- What's the worst thing that could happen?
- What will happen if you do this or that?
- What would you like to happen?
- What do you think you'll do?
- How will that affect others?
- Is that a problem?

Give him practice by letting him help in making choices for the family. Say such things as:

- We're trying to choose between ____ and ____.
- What should we be thinking about?
- What do you think we should choose?
- We had to choose between those two things last year. Do you think we made the right choice?

WORDS AND PHRASES TO USE

• the best option/choice	• don't be afraid to make mistakes	• life isn't perfect	• responsibility
• dilemma	• effect on others/ on you	• most likely	• sensible
• difficult		• preferable	• short-/long-term effects
		• realistic	

What Not to Say and Do

Your job is to help your teen make choices, not to make them for him, unless it is quite beyond his competence or realm of responsibility and experience. Don't say such things as:

- There is only one possible choice.
- You're too young to decide.
- Don't be stupid. You can't do that.
- School must always come first.
- Family must always come first.
- Our wishes must always come first.
- It's not your decision to make.
- If you make the wrong choice, you'll be in big trouble.
- Your friends will understand.
- You don't understand the situation.

Don't say things that will damage your teen's self-esteem. Don't say such things as:

- You always make the wrong choices.
- You're so immature.
- I'm afraid to let you make any important decisions.
- Why didn't you come to me earlier?

Don't make your teen feel as though he is strictly on his own. Don't say such things as:

- I'm not interested in your problems.
- You'll just have to work it out for yourself.
- I'm tired of your getting yourself into these situations.
- I'm busy. Come back tomorrow, and we can talk then.

WORDS AND PHRASES TO AVOID

• a dumb choice	• I'll make all those decisions	• mindless	• that's no choice at all
• alone	• immature	• one problem after another	• you don't know what's best for you
• childish	• inconsiderate	• silly	• you're on your own
• I don't want to hear it	• irresponsible		

11 Chores

Work is much more fun than fun.

—Noel Coward

Charleen's job was to clean up each evening after supper. She also had to keep her own room clean and tidy. These had been her chores since she was eight, and now she was seventeen. She wasn't thrilled about having to do this. She loved going out in the evenings with her friends, to study or just to talk, and since she had a ten o'clock curfew on school nights, the earlier she got out, the more time she could have with them. At seventeen she shouldn't have to do childhood chores anymore. She decided it was time to get her parents to realize that girls her age had better things to do than clearing the dinner table, putting dishes in the dishwasher, and washing the pots and pans. That evening at dinner she was going to tell her parents that she thought it was time they treated her as an adult. Cleaning up after dinner was for kids.

Things to Consider

Sometimes you and your teen seem to live in two different worlds. Chores you think are reasonable for your teen to do as a member of the family are considered an imposition on her valuable time. When your teen complains, it leads to arguments.

Good communication strategies can help you resolve differences about doing chores. Start by asking your teens questions about why they are suddenly unhappy doing their normal work around the house, whatever it is. Teens often respond that they think it is more than their siblings do or that their friends don't have these obligations. Resist the impulse to yell that they shouldn't complain since you had to do three times as much when you were a teenager. Instead, ask them what they think their responsibilities should be. Ask them what they see as each family member's role. In other words, try to find out where they are coming from and where they are heading with their complaint. Do they want reduced chores? Do they want everyone else to do more? Do they want to do nothing at all?

Once you understand their positions, you can begin to point out mistakes in their thinking—if they are mistaken. Sometimes what is said is a shock, but if it is accurate, you will want to take action. But generally you want to make sure you understand each other. Then you can ask them to join with you in giving everyone in the family a fair share of the work around the house. You can even draw up contractual agreements to do specific chores for a particular reason, in a particular way, for a particular period of time. You can also use these discussions to teach them that the family is a unit in which everyone plays an important role. All teens should have responsibilities for helping out in the family. It's part of learning to be an adult.

Three Things You Must Do

1. *Understand* each other's view of chores.
2. *Review* the division of chores in the family.
3. *Negotiate* an agreement or impose one (a last resort).

What to Say and Do

Most teenagers don't like doing chores. Teach them from an early age that they have a responsibility to the family to do their share of the work around the home. Say such things as:

- ‣ Let's make sure you understand exactly what you're supposed to do.
- ‣ Let's sit down and make a list of everyone's jobs each week.
- ‣ Why don't you tell me what you're supposed to do, just so I know you understand.

If they are unhappy with their chores, listen to their complaints. Say such things as:

- ‣ Tell me why you don't like your job around the house.
- ‣ Do you think we're treating you unfairly?
- ‣ What do you think you should do?

Let them tell you what their friends do. Say such things as:

- Do you think we're being unfair to you, compared with your friends?
- What are their responsibilities?
- I think I will call your friend's mom and ask her what she has to do.

If it's appropriate for your family, you can offer to pay for chores instead of giving your teen a regular allowance. The obvious incentive is, no work, no pay. Say such things as:

- Since you don't have a regular job, why don't we pay you for your chores?
- Let's see what needs to be done, what we'd like you to do, what you'd like to do, and what it's worth.
- Let's draw up a schedule of jobs, days, and pay.

Divide chores into two categories: jobs that everyone in the family must do simply because they are members and jobs that the family will pay for. Your teen must do some of the first and can choose to do some of the second. Say such things as:

- You must keep your room clean.
- You must cut the grass each week.
- We'll pay you to wash the car.
- We'll pay you to take the paper, cans, and bottles to the recycling depot.

WORDS AND PHRASES TO USE

contribution	good attitude	may/must do	together
fairness	growing up	responsibility	volunteer
family	mandatory	sharing	willingness

What Not to Say and Do

Don't make it you against your teen or try to shame her. Don't say such things as:

- You're just a lazy slob.

- You're never willing to do your share.
- Why can't you grow up?

Don't make threats unless you are prepared to carry them out. Don't say such things as:

- Either you do your chores, or you have to get out of this house.
- If you won't pull your weight, you're no longer a member of this family.

Don't do comparisons. Don't say such things as:

- You're so lazy compared to your brother.
- I wish you were like your sister.
- Why can't you do what you're supposed to do like everyone else in the family does?

Don't play the martyr by threatening to do things for her. Don't say such things as:

- If you won't clean your room, then I'll have to.
- See what happens when you don't pick up your dirty laundry. I have to do it for you.

Doing chores is not the most important indicator of success in life. Don't say such things as:

- You're going to end up in jail if you don't shape up and do your chores.
- I can tell you're going to be lazy and selfish all your life.
- You're going in the wrong direction with your life.

Don't give up. Only the most difficult child will hold out against parents. Keep things low-key and positive. Be firm but don't fight.

WORDS AND PHRASES TO AVOID

- blind	- lazy	- uncaring	- worthless
- good for nothing	- selfish	- unloving	- you're a bum
- headed for disaster	- shiftless		

12 Clothes

You'd be surprised how much it costs to look this cheap.

—DOLLY PARTON

Antawn wanted a Tommy Hilfiger shirt more than anything. All his buddies at school had something with the Hilfiger logo on it. He didn't want to be left out. He just didn't have the money. He wanted to get a part-time job to pay for extras and special clothing, but his parents wouldn't let him because they didn't want anything to get in the way of his schoolwork. He needed a scholarship to go to college.

Antawn had to figure out how to get his folks to come up with the money for the shirt. His parents weren't poor, but they weren't rich, either, and the shirt cost much more than his ordinary school shirts. Maybe, he thought, if he explained to them how important it was for him to have what all his friends had, they'd let him buy it. He'd give it a try.

Things to Consider

Look around any high school, and you will see groups of almost identically dressed teenagers. You'll see clumps of preppies, jocks, goths, grunges, punks, and other styles that only teens would be able to name. Teens need to belong to one of these groups, and belonging means wearing the "uniform." Your job is to figure out how to pay for these clothes. As long as your teens are reasonable in their requests, don't waste your time and energy fighting. Teens need to dress in the style of their friends as much as you need to dress in a style acceptable to your peers, socially and at work. For example, you can't wear shorts and a T-shirt to work if the company uniform is a dress or shirt and tie unless you are willing to accept the consequences.

In any case, why would you want to fight them—other than the cost? To you teenage styles may seem ugly, extravagant, silly, stupid, or symptomatic of a bad attitude, but if you've been involved in your teens' lives, you'll know how important these clothes are. If you think they are a symbol of a bad attitude, then it's not the clothes that are the problem.

Unless the clothes are dangerous (such as platform wedgies), immoral, or illegal, I think you need to concentrate on the money problem and the reasonable limits problem. How do the clothes get paid for, and how many pairs of the "right" jeans or shoes or shirts do your teens really need? So don't get into arguments about style. Discuss the realities and jointly figure out what your teens can afford to pay for, either with your money or theirs, and how much is enough. Those are the real issues and the only ones on which you have a chance of reaching consensus.

Three Things You Must Do

1. *Accept* the fact that teens need to dress like their friends.
2. *Teach* them to be reasonable in their requests.
3. *Encourage* them to work for their fashionable clothes.

What to Say and Do

Separate clothing needs into two piles: needs and wants. Teens *need* such basics as socks, pantyhose, underwear, dresses, skirts, shirts, blouses, pants, slacks, jeans, sweaters, jackets, shoes, sneakers, and runners (or whatever you call sports shoes in your town). As long as the cost is within reason, any of these items can also be the "right" kind.

Your teen's *wants* may include more of their *needs* items, but definitely the "right" kind. Purchasing these with his own money should be his choice. It's a way of letting him learn to handle his own money wisely. But if he is going to use his money, you need to negotiate limits of reasonableness for your family circumstances and values.

You can begin by talking about needs and wants. Say such things as:

- Let's talk about your clothing needs.
- We'll tell you right up front that we're not going to argue with you about clothes.

- You can wear anything as long as it's not illegal, immoral, dangerous, or dirty.
- Let's talk about what you need and what you want.
- We'll pay for your *needs*.
- You can choose the style of your basic needs as long as it's not too expensive.
- Let's talk about your clothing *wants*.

Talk about the limitations and their responsibility. Say such things as:

- If you want more than the basics, then we have to figure out how you can afford them.
- You can spend money from your allowance and/or work for special clothing if you want to.
- We'll pay for special clothing for sports, parties, and concerts if we can, but you'll have to help.

You're entitled to tell your teen what you think of his clothes. Tell him as you would want someone to tell you, whether it's positive or negative. Say such things as:

- When you're going out with us, we expect you to dress appropriately.
- Remember that people will judge you by your appearance.
- Be sure people get the impression of you that you intend them to get.

WORDS AND PHRASES TO USE

- appropriate	- moral	- reasonable	- the impression you want to make
- clean	- needs	- safe	- wants
- legal	- personality	- style	- we'll share

What Not to Say and Do

Avoid fighting over clothes. You'll go a long way toward having a good relationship if you accept the fact that teen clothing styles come from their friends more than from you. Teens worry more about what their friends say about their clothing than what you have to say.

Don't create confrontations. Don't say such things as:

- You're going to wear what I say because I pay for your clothes.
- You'll wear what I want you to, or you'll go naked.
- No daughter/son of mine will be seen like that.

Don't focus on the negatives of clothes. Don't say such things as:

- You look like a tart/pimp/slut/slob/tramp/junkie/[or other such words].

Don't threaten. Don't say such things as:

- As long as you live in my house, you'll wear what I tell you to wear.

Don't ridicule their judgment. Don't say such things as:

- Why do you waste your money on a piece of clothing just for the label?
- These cheap sneakers are as good as those expensive ones. You just want the name.
- You buy such junk.

Don't blame them for wanting to be like others. Don't say such things as:

- You're such a conformist.
- You conform to the wrong things.

Don't make this a bigger issue than it needs to be. Don't say such things as:

- I don't want you hanging around with kids who dress like that.

Don't attack their bodies. Don't say such things as:

- You're too fat to wear that.
- You're too skinny to wear that.

WORDS AND PHRASES TO AVOID

• filthy	• I don't care what your friends wear/will think	• shock	• you'll dress the way I want you to
• I don't care what you like		• slob	
	• offend	• slut/tramp	• you're too young to know
• I won't allow it		• you can't	

13 College

Alicia's mother was a liberated career woman. Her father was a somewhat old-fashioned businessman. Alicia was eighteen and ready to start college in September. But, surprisingly, her parents suggested that she wait a year before continuing her formal education. Although they disagreed on a lot of things, they seemed to agree on this: that their beloved daughter was too young and immature to go to college now. She didn't have any idea what she wanted to do with her life.

Alicia was puzzled. All her friends were going off to college in the fall. What would she do? She'd be left all alone until she made new friends. Did they expect her to get a job? Or travel? What did they want from her? Maybe they didn't think she should go to college at all.

She needed her parents to explain their reasoning to her because as far as she was concerned, even though she didn't know what she wanted to study or what career path she wanted to follow, she didn't want to waste a year doing nothing.

Things to Consider

As a college professor I put a very high value on a college education because, when done right, it teaches important knowledge, skills, and understanding. These make most people better human beings than they would be without them. Everyone can benefit from college, not just "brains." But some teenagers are better off not going to college, and some are too young to start college right out of high school, no matter how well they may have done academically.

If you and your teen have discussed the many options and decided that college is the right option for her after high school, help her do well enough academically to get into the college of her choice. (Grades in school are a more accurate assessment of the options open to a student than they are a measure of what students know or understand. Good grades equal many options; poor grades equal few options.) Help her choose the right college and the right major. Decide on the right time. If your teen is mature and knows what she wants to study, then going to college at eighteen may be right for her. But many students get much more out of college in their twenties than if they had gone right from high school.

Know your teens so you can help guide their decisions. If you have been carefully observing them in high school, you know what directions their lives seemed to be taking. You know their academic ability, their personality, their level of maturity, their interests. Put that all into the mix as you talk to them about their future.

If your son or daughter will be going to college, the questions he or she need to answer are these: What do you want to study? What college? How much will it cost? What financial aid is available? What are the admission requirements?

Three Things You Must Do

1. *Advise* your teen on how to prepare for college academically.

2. *Help* your teen choose the right college and career path.

3. *Give* your teen the freedom to make her own choice about her future.

What to Say and Do

Deciding to go to college and choosing the right one are problems for some families and not for others. Every teen who has the ability should go to college because it opens up more career opportunities and because knowledge and understanding are valuable for their own sake. It is better to be well educated than not to be. If your teen is ambivalent about going, discuss the other options. Then talk about the intrinsic and economic value of a college education—the knowledge, skills, and understanding that make one's personal life fuller and richer.

If your teen is considering college, say such things as:

- Let's talk about college. Do you have any specific ones in mind?
- What do you think you'd like to study?
- We'd better make sure your grades are good enough to get in.
- Let's list your academic strengths and weaknesses.
- If you don't go to college, what would you do?
- What would you most like to do ten years from now? Let's see what you'd need to do that.
- We'd like you to go to college. What would you like?

If your teen is ambivalent or you think she is not ready, say such things as:

- As long as you have good grades, you can go to college anytime.
- What about taking a year off and working somewhere while you decide what you want to do?
- Why don't we explore all the options you have—college, work, apprenticeship, technical school, the military, travel—and see what appeals to you and what you're best qualified for?

If your teen is ready to go to college but doesn't know what to study, say such things as:

- Don't worry if you don't know what to major in. You can decide that once you've started.
- At your age it's more important to get a liberal education than specialize in one thing.
- Let's talk about the things you most like to do, read, watch, think about.

If finances are a problem, be up front about it. Say such things as:

- We want you to go to college. You have to help out financially by working summers.
- Do you think your grades are good enough to get a scholarship?

- We'll have to choose a low-cost college unless you can get some kind of scholarship.
- Let's go through the college guide and see which schools we can afford.

Find out what your teen wants, tell her what you want, and see if you fit together. Remember that it's her life. You must let her live it even if her wishes and yours don't coincide.

WORDS AND PHRASES TO USE

- career	- knowledge	- our finances	- will help
- choices	- not ready	- loans/scholarships	- your abilities/desires
- financial aid	- options	- skills	- your grades

What Not to Say and Do

Don't bully your teen and try to force her to go to college if she doesn't want to. Even though going to college is a good thing, your teen will not benefit from it if she doesn't want to be there.

Don't say that the world will end if she doesn't go. Don't say such things as:

- If you don't go to college, your life will be miserable.
- You have no choice. You must go to college.
- Only dummies don't go to college.
- You have the grades to go to college, so it's stupid not to go.
- You have no other talents, so you'd better go.

On the other hand, if she wants to go and you are not keen on it, you shouldn't stand in her way. Even if sending your child to college would be financially difficult, don't say such things as:

- We're not going to waste our money on you if you don't know what you want to study.
- Even though we know you want to go to college, we think you should go out and get a job.

- If you want to go to college, you'll have to pay for it yourself. We're not going to help.
- College isn't worth it. I learned more from working than you'll ever learn in college.

Help your child choose the right college for her, not for you. Don't say such things as:

- There's no choice. You'll go where I want you to go.
- If it was good enough for me, it's good enough for you.
- All colleges are the same, so let's choose the cheapest.
- Don't set your sights too high. You're not bright enough.

You have to ask yourself what is more important, your child or your opinions?

WORDS AND PHRASES TO AVOID

• choose a sensible major	• dummy	• trains you for a good career	• you'll do what we want you to
• college is a waste of time and money	• immature	• waste	• you'll go where we want you to
	• no brains	• you must go	
	• stupid		

14 Communication

I wish people who have trouble communicating would just shut up.

—Tom Lehrer

Carrie and her mother weren't communicating very well. They were both too busy, Carrie with schoolwork and Mom with her job. It was unusual for them not to spend part of each weekend together, catching up on the week's happenings in their lives, but lately Carrie had been spending her weekends at high school basketball games, on dates, at parties, or studying. Mom had year-end accounts to supervise, and that meant working nights and weekends. In the evening she was too tired to do anything but eat a late dinner and fall into bed.

Finally, Mom could stand it no longer. She suggested that the next weekend she and Carrie should spend all of Saturday and Sunday together. They could go shopping on Saturday, have dinner out, and see a movie. On Sunday they could go to church and then go for a hike in the country.

Carrie would love to, she said, but next weekend was all booked up already. Maybe they could do it the following weekend?

Things to Consider

After food, shelter, and safety, nothing is more important than good communication with your teen. Good communication is not simply a way to build a relationship, it *is* the relationship. Work at sharing your teen's life by keeping in constant touch with her thoughts, feelings, accomplishments, disappointments, and relationships. Good communication comes from constant and regular interaction. You and your teen will not understand each other if you don't have regular conversations. Understanding comes from knowing where the other person is coming from.

Teens are predisposed to reject you and your values. You wear dreary clothes. You have a stupid job. You listen to geeky "lite favorites" or opera on the radio. But good communication can change that impression. Chat about stuff they find cool and stuff you like. Leaf through their CD collection and play a few tracks. Help them build a model. Teach them how to make a dress. Invite them to sit at the table at one of your dinner parties.

Be in touch with your teens. Don't let other commitments prevent you from having a conversation with them at least once a day. Tell them they can call you at work. Talk about anything you like, but talk! Share experiences, ideas, feelings, worries, hopes. Talk about the weather, about work, about school, about boy- or girlfriends. Keep the lines of communication open. Take turns talking. Listen without judging. Tell stories. Express opinions. Talk about whatever is going on in your lives. Talk for the pleasure of hearing each other's voices. The most important part of what you say is just sharing your talk.

Three Things You Must Do

1. *Talk* to your teen every day.

2. *Listen* to your teen every day.

3. *Share* your teen's life every day.

What to Say and Do

Ask your teen questions about her life. Say such things as:

- ▶ What's happening in school?

- ▶ How's your relationship with _____ coming along?

- ▶ Any problems you want to talk about?

- ▶ Tell me more about what was bothering you the other day.

Tell your teen what you hope for in your relationship. Say such things as:

- ▶ I know I haven't given you enough of my time, but I'd like to change that starting right now.

- ▶ I want to be more involved in your life.

- I want to know more about what you're thinking, what's worrying you, what you want.
- From now on you can talk to me about anything you want, and I promise not to judge you. (You must be true to this promise, or your communication will never improve.)
- I know our relationship hasn't been everything it should have been, but with your help I'd like to change that starting right now.

Try sharing your thoughts and problems with your teen. Say such things as:

- May I ask your advice on a problem I'm having at work?
- I wanted to ask you what you thought about that movie we watched on TV last night.
- Let's go for a walk. There are things I've been thinking about that I'd like to share with you.

Whatever your teen says to you, don't shut her off. Say such things as:

- Why are you feeling that way?
- Those are harsh words. Do you really mean them?
- I don't care what you say as long as we keep talking.
- Call me at work if you want to talk.

Ask your teen for advice on improving your communication. Say such things as:

- What do you think you and I can do to make it easier for us to talk to each other?
- I want what I say to make sense to you, so tell me when you don't understand.
- What do you think makes for a good relationship between parents and kids?

WORDS AND PHRASES TO USE

- I love you	- I'm listening	- take turns	- what do you think
- I won't judge	- let's talk	- tell me about it	- what do you want
- I'll make time for you	- relationship	- together	- you can say anything you want

What Not to Say and Do

Nothing kills communication faster than one-way talk. Don't say such things as:

- Be quiet and listen to me.
- You're going to sit there and listen, and I'm going to talk.
- I'm not interested in what you have to say.

Don't preach at your teen. Don't say such things as:

- I'm your parent, and given my experience I know what's best.
- You're too young to know what's right.
- When you're older, you'll realize that I'm right.

Don't overreact to what your teen says. Don't say such things as:

- Don't you ever talk that way.
- Don't say any more.
- I don't want to hear it.

- How could you say/do/think such a thing?

Don't let good communication lead to bad consequences. Don't say such things as:

- How could you have done/said that? You're grounded.
- I'm ashamed of you.
- No daughter/son of mine would say/do a thing like that.
- I'm going to have to report this to the authorities.

Don't be too busy for your teen. Don't say such things as:

- Don't bother me now.
- Can't you see I'm busy?
- Can't it wait?
- Maybe we can talk tomorrow when I have some free time.

WORDS AND PHRASES TO AVOID

• be careful what you say	• how could you say such a thing	• I don't want to know	• shut up and sit down
• don't tell me	• I don't care what you have to say	• I'll do all the talking	• what a dumb thing to say
		• I'm not interested	

15 Competition

Excellence in life seems to me to be the way in which each human being makes the most of the adventure of living and becomes most truly and deeply oneself, fulfilling one's own nature in the context of a good life with other people.

—Eda J. LeShan

Adele was angry. She had worked very hard to prepare for last week's event. Long nights of work, weekends, every spare moment had been taken up with getting herself in shape. But she had lost. Not only had she lost, but she had been beaten by Joe. He had never beaten her before, and she was devastated that it had happened this time.

He had achieved a perfect score, while she had made one mistake. What had she lost? What was this contest that pitted boy against girl? It wasn't athletics or anything physical. It was a grade ten mathematics exam.

Adele thought she was the best. She had always been the best, always at the top of her class. Joe was never more than a close second. Now he had beaten her, and she was furious with herself and with Joe. She vowed she would never let it happen again.

When she talked about it to her mom and dad that evening, she could hardly contain her anger. Both parents knew that Adele was a very competitive girl who always tried to be the best at everything she did. They thought this was a good thing. However, this time they began to worry about the vehemence of her reaction. They decided to talk to her about how to channel her competitive drive and need to win into something constructive rather than destructive.

Things to Consider

Which would you worry about more—that your teen was fiercely competitive or that your teen was not competitive at all? Most of you, I'm sure, would think noncompetitiveness more troublesome. In our society we are taught that competition is good in all areas of life. As in most things, there is a happy medium. You need to encourage competitiveness in your teens because without it they might never achieve their potential, might never do their best. But you also need to discourage competitiveness when it starts to become an end in itself, when your teens seem to value winning above all else, when they view everything as a competition—for grades, for jobs, for love and affection, to be the first in line, or to be the first one away from a traffic light.

If you want the best for your children, then you must teach them that the best person to compete against is themselves. There will always be someone out there with more talent, more ability, better looks, better grades, more money, more "toys." It's up to you to teach them that their job is to make the most of what they have. Self-fulfillment comes from competing against oneself, from being all that one can be. Help your teens realize that trying to be better than the other person is ultimately self-defeating because there will always be someone else who is better than they are. Always competing against others will fill your teens' lives with disappointment.

On the other hand, when you teach your teens to compete against themselves, you are teaching them an essential and rewarding life skill. There is a realistic satisfaction in knowing they have done their very best at whatever they attempt. There is a Zen Buddhist saying that we are all perfect just the way we are. That doesn't mean we shouldn't strive to be better people; it just means that along the way we must accept ourselves for ourselves. When your teens learn to compete against themselves rather than others, then you have taught them to live their own lives and to measure their success by their own achievements rather than that of others.

Finally, a word of caution. Don't get carried away by your desire to see your child win. A competitive spirit is good, but don't become like many parents I've seen at their teen's sports event who constantly badger their child to do better and to win at all costs. You'll be giving your teen all the wrong messages. You might remember the most extreme example of this: a Texas mom who tried to kill a girl who was competing against her daughter for a cheerleading spot.

Three Things You Must Do

1. *Teach* them to love themselves for themselves.

2. *Show* them by example the importance of doing their best in whatever they do.

3. *Love* them for themselves.

What to Say and Do

Know how competitive your teen is and what effect it has on her. You can get a good idea of her reactions to winning and losing by playing games with her, or watching her play sports. Then you can explore her attitudes and feelings. Say such things as:

- How do you feel about winning/losing?
- Did you do your best?
- Why do you think you won/lost?
- What would you do differently next time?
- How do you think _____ feels about losing/winning?
- What's the most important thing you have learned by winning/losing?
- What have you learned about yourself?
- What have you learned about your competitors?

Competitive teens need to focus on doing their best for themselves. Say such things as:

- Don't worry about what anyone else is doing. Do this for yourself.
- It doesn't matter if you're not first as long as you have done your best.
- There will always be someone better than you. That's why you have to concentrate on living up to your own standards, not someone else's.

Make sure your teen knows how you feel about her. Say such things as:

- We love you for who you are, not what you win or lose.
- We don't love you any more or any less if you're first or last.
- We just want you to always do your best.

Relationships are more important than competitions. Say such things as:

- Winning doesn't make you a better person. Doing your best does.
- In any competition there are always winners and losers. The important thing is how you compete, not whether you win or lose.
- How does competing make you feel about the other people involved?
- What's more important to you, winning or your relationship with the other competitors?

With a noncompetitive teen you also need to talk about the importance of always doing her best for her own sake. Say such things as:

- We're not interested in your winning or losing but simply doing your best.
- Are you working up to your potential?
- We realize you don't like to compete. That's okay as long as it's not because you're just afraid of losing.
- Competition can be a good thing as long as you're competing against yourself.

Make what you say appropriate to your teen's personality and performance.

WORDS AND PHRASES TO USE

❥ be fair	❥ it's how you handle winning and losing that's most important	❥ put teamwork ahead of your own self-interests	❥ winning and losing are less important than competing in the right spirit
❥ be honest			
❥ fulfill your potential		❥ simply do your best and everything else will follow	
❥ love your opponent	❥ love yourself		❥ work to your own standards

---

What Not to Say and Do

Don't place your own need to win on your teen's shoulders. Don't say such things as:

- You know you can win. Now get out there and show me.
- If you win, you'll make me very proud.

> You can succeed where I didn't.

Don't belittle your teen if she loses. Don't say such things as:

> Nobody likes a loser.

> Winning isn't something, it's everything.

> I don't want any child of mine to be a loser.

Your love must not depend your teen's competing and winning. Don't say such things as:

> No child of mine would ever think about losing.

> If you don't win, don't look to me for comfort.

> If you lose, then the world knows you're a loser, and I won't stand for that.

Don't teach your teen unethical practices. Don't say such things as:

> You must win at all costs.

> Cheat if you have to. Everyone does it.

> There is no alternative to winning, so do whatever you have to to win.

WORDS AND PHRASES TO AVOID

> failure is unacceptable	> it's not how you play the game, it's whether you win or lose	> losers never make the headlines	> you're a failure
> I can't love a loser		> losing is unacceptable	> you're afraid to compete
> I'm ashamed of you	> life is only about winning	> no guts	> you're not good enough

16 Contraception

Contraceptives should be used on every conceivable occasion.

—The Goon Show

Jim and Mary were religious people. They believed that sex outside of wedlock was wrong and that teenage sex was both wrong and dangerous. They were the parents of two teenagers whom they loved very much. Their daughter, Allison, was seventeen, and their son, Tommy, sixteen. Although both children went to church with them every Sunday and didn't openly question its teachings, Jim and Mary knew there were pressures on both teens that could cause them to do things that neither the church nor their parents would approve of.

Jim and Mary decided to sit down with Allison and Tommy one Sunday after lunch to talk about sex in general and safe sex in particular. It wasn't going to be easy, but these were realistic parents who cherished their own values and principles and cherished the well-being of their children even more. They didn't stick their heads in the sand, thinking that the modern world and its values and pressures would disappear. Of course they had tried to instill their beliefs in their children, and they were confident that their teens would do the right thing. But they also believed in that old proverb, "An ounce of prevention is worth a pound of cure."

Things to Consider

You have tried to give your children the right values, but your teens have their own lives. You know that is what growing up means, and yet it's hard to accept. Your teenagers live in a world of pressures that sometimes make them do things they don't really want to do, although they may not realize it at the time. Help your teens cope with these pressures by always being there for them and by having a relationship in which they can come to you with any problem and you will listen without judging. Show them that there is no risk in talking to you about virtually anything, even things about which you disapprove.

Your job is to help your teens make decisions (when they ask for your help), to make sure they understand all the options, and to minimize the negative consequences of wrong decisions. It is okay for them to learn from their mistakes, but the consequences of some mistakes are too destructive.

Talking to your teens about sex and contraception isn't easy. Some of you think that just talking about it will encourage your children to do it. Some of you believe that the words "safe" and "sex" never go together for teenagers, that all teen sex is dangerous. Nevertheless, you may find that recognizing what might happen and helping your teen be prepared for it is preferable to believing that it could never happen and then wondering what to do when your teen gets pregnant or contracts a sexually transmitted disease such as syphilis, gonorrhea, HIV, or, worst of all, AIDS!

You can teach your teens that sex out of wedlock is a sin. You can teach them that birth control is a sin. You can teach them that the best contraceptive device is abstinence. But because you love them, you can also teach them about condoms, the pill, and other birth control methods so that they have the power that comes from knowledge and understanding. Having done all these things, you must trust them to do the right thing, and you must be there for them if they don't.

Three Things You Must Do

1. *Teach* them your values through word and deed.

2. *Teach* them the why and how of contraceptives.

3. *Trust* them to do the right thing.

What to Say and Do

Make clear to your teen what you believe is appropriate sexual behavior. If this means no sex before marriage and no contraception other than abstinence, you can say such things as:

- I realize what it's like to be a teen. I was one myself. I know the pressures and the urges. But you know what our values are, and I know you will respect them.

- Remember that contraception for us means no sex.

- I know you won't have sex because you know it's wrong. But I want to be sure that you know about safe sex. Do you know how to prevent disease and pregnancy?

If you think that your teen might have sexual intercourse, then you need to be up front about the need for protection. Say such things as:

- I don't think sex at your age is a good idea, but I want you to understand the consequences of unprotected sex and promise me that you will never have sex without using a condom.

- What have you learned about contraceptives in school? Do you know about the different kinds and how they are used?

- The pill will prevent pregnancy but not HIV or AIDS, syphilis, gonorrhea, chlamydia, genital warts, herpes, or hepatitis B and C.

- I will pay for your contraceptives.

- If your boyfriend/girlfriend wants sex without a condom, then he/she is putting you both in needless danger. Is this really love?

- Abstinence is the best contraceptive because there are some diseases that condoms won't stop.

You can approach your talk on contraception less confrontationally. Say such things as:

- Do you have any friends who have sex without using a condom? What do you think about that?

- Have you learned in sex ed how many sexually transmitted diseases there are?

- Do they teach you how to prevent them?

You need to talk to your teen about the consequences of not using a condom. Say such things as:

- Do you know what happens to you if you get AIDS?

- What would you do if you [or your girlfriend] got pregnant?

- Do you know any teen mothers or fathers?
- What do you do now that you couldn't do if you had a baby to care for?

WORDS AND PHRASES TO USE

- abstinence	- herpes	- parenting	- think of the consequences
- AIDS	- love	- pregnancy	
- condom	- maturity	- pressure	- trust
- contraception	- no sex is the safest sex	- responsibility	- values
			- venereal disease

What Not to Say and Do

Your teens are more important than most principles against sex and contraception I've ever heard. Talk to them in ways that build and maintain relationships of love and trust. Don't say such things as:

- Sex is sinful.
- The only reason for sex is to make babies.
- Abstinence is the only acceptable form of contraception.
- No child of mine would ever have sex before marriage.

- Don't do what I do. Do what I say.
- I could never love a child who had sex before marriage.
- If you ever get pregnant, don't bother coming home.
- You can't go on the pill.

Don't cut off conversations about sex. Don't say such things as:

- Don't talk to me about sex.
- I won't talk to you about sex. You're too young.
- I don't want to talk about contraception. Here's a book.

WORDS AND PHRASES TO AVOID

- bad boy/girl	- sinner	- slut	- whore
- evil	- sleaze	- stupid	- wicked

17 Cooperation

Jay was a junior on the high school football team. He was a wide receiver, and he thought he was pretty hot. There had been some college scouts at his team games, and they had told his coach they were going to be watching him closely this year and next. He seemed to have all the physical skills needed to be an outstanding college player; he was fast, fearless, and had good size and great hands. But they had a concern. They had watched him on some plays when another receiver needed downfield blocking, and what they'd seen disturbed them. Jay seemed unwilling to put his body on the line for his teammates.

Jay didn't seem to realize that football, like many activities in life, needed everyone to do his share, to cooperate for the good of the whole team. The scouts spoke to Jay's coach about this, and he in turn talked to Jay. Even though Jay's teammates had said things to him, their words, as the cliché goes, seemed to go in one ear and out the other. Jay seemed unaware that the team needed his cooperation to succeed. He didn't seem to understand his role as a team member. He seemed to think that he could succeed on his own even if his team lost, as long as he caught the passes thrown his way. He didn't understand cooperation—in this case, teamwork.

Jay's coach was frustrated by Jay's response to all this, so he decided to talk to Jay's parents. They would understand the importance of his cooperation if for no other reason than he might miss out on a college athletic scholarship because of it.

Things to Consider

Most teens don't have trouble cooperating with their peers. Their need to belong makes most of them quite sensitive to the needs of the group.

However, cooperating with you, other family members, teachers, and other adults doesn't seem to come quite as easily to teens because they are trying to develop an identity of their own. You find yourself getting into arguments about their unwillingness to cooperate with you on such matters as homework, curfews, chores, deadlines, and being kind to their siblings.

Show your teens the value of cooperation. Society couldn't exist without it. Cooperation creates governments, legal systems, buildings, companies, schools, cars, traffic controls, sports teams, and organizations. The list is endless. Challenge your teens to think of any good things in life that don't require cooperation.

Teach cooperation by modeling it. Show how you cooperate within the family, within the community, within your workplace. If your teens don't get the message, try suspending your cooperation with them, and point out the consequences. When they ask something of you, refuse to cooperate. They will learn the meaning of cooperation very quickly.

Teach them to cooperate for their own good. You know how you feel about people who don't want to cooperate. They're painful to be around. You start excluding them from your life because you know they're a hindrance, not a help. There must be people like that in your teens' lives. Point them out so your teens will be aware of them.

Some teens cooperate in all situations. Others compartmentalize their cooperative habits and use them with some people and not others. Help your teens broaden their cooperation compartments.

Three Things You Must Do

1. *Model* cooperation for your teen.

2. *Know* your teen's cooperative good and bad points.

3. *Encourage* your teen to be cooperative with everyone.

What to Say and Do

Give your teens lots of opportunities to show cooperation. Say such things as:

- I need help with housecleaning this weekend. Can I count on you?

➤ Your brother/sister needs some help with his/her homework. Would you mind?

➤ Will you go to the store for me? I'm busy with the laundry, and we need things for supper.

Stress that cooperation is in their own self-interest by pointing out how they feel about people who are uncooperative. Say such things as:

➤ You know how you feel when you want help from your friend and he is too busy.

➤ What do you think about someone who doesn't help your group get a job done?

➤ Nobody likes someone who only does things for himself and never helps the group.

➤ How do you feel about teammates who don't do their job or don't stay in shape?

Point out how much their friends need them to cooperate. Say such things as:

➤ If your best friend asked you to help him in school, would you say no?

➤ If you needed advice with a school project, would you expect your friends to help?

➤ You work in groups at school. Do you mind doing your share?

Talk about all the things in their everyday life that depend on cooperation. Say such things as:

➤ I just want to talk to you about the importance of cooperation. Let's look at some of the things we take for granted about life that depend on cooperation.

➤ If you were building a house, would you rather do it alone or with someone's help?

➤ Imagine building a bridge or an airplane without lots of people cooperating.

➤ School would be impossible if teachers and students didn't cooperate with each other.

➤ Team sports require cooperation.

- We all depend on one another.
- Cooperation is a two-way street.

If your teen is uncooperative with you or others, say such things as:

- I think you need to learn the value of cooperation. If you won't cooperate with me, then maybe I shouldn't cooperate with you. Do you think you can do everything for yourself?
- Imagine a world in which nobody cooperated with anyone else. What would it be like?
- What happens when you don't cooperate at school?
- Do you want to be known as someone who won't cooperate?

WORDS AND PHRASES TO USE

- cooperation makes life easier	- doing your share	- the Golden Rule— act toward others as you want others to act toward you	- the team
	- helping out		- we need you
- cooperation makes life possible	- no man is an island		- you need us

---

What Not to Say and Do

Don't set a bad example by saying such things as:

- I can't help you now. I have too much of my own work to do.
- See if you can get someone else to help you.
- Do it yourself. You don't need my help.

Don't make your teen think that he has to spend all his time helping others and have no time for himself. Don't say such things as:

- Your needs come last in this family.
- I don't care if you have homework to do. I need help painting the garage.

Don't make cooperation an end in itself. Don't say such things as:

- I don't care what your coach asked you to do, you should do it.

◆ You'd better cooperate with your teacher, or you'll have to answer to me.

◆ Whatever I ask you to do is more important than what you want to do.

WORDS AND PHRASES TO AVOID

◆ do it yourself	◆ I have no time for you	◆ later	◆ want
◆ I		◆ me	◆ you're lazy
◆ I don't care	◆ I wouldn't help you even if I could	◆ tomorrow	◆ you're selfish
◆ I'm too busy			

18 Criticism

Honest criticism is hard to take, particularly from a relative, a friend, an acquaintance, or a stranger.

— FRANKLIN P. JONES

Elaine was tired of being criticized by her mom and dad. In the eyes of this fifteen-year-old, her parents found fault with almost everything about her: clothes, hair, makeup, girlfriends, boyfriends, schoolwork, attitude, spending habits, and the way she spent her leisure time. It was really getting to her.

Whenever she confronted her parents, they said they were merely trying to help her. They clearly had no sense of the negative impact they were having on their daughter. Their constant criticism was affecting her self-esteem and her regard for her parents' opinions. She found herself thinking that just out of spite she would do things she knew her parents would criticize. Since they seemed to criticize everything anyway, what difference would it make?

Mom and Dad thought they were helping their daughter each time they voiced their opinion about some aspect of her life. They realized that their comments were negative, but there was so much yet to teach their daughter about life and so little time in which to do it.

They didn't understand that constant negative criticism does more harm than good. And they never realized that self-criticism is the best kind.

Things to Consider

Teens don't like being criticized any more than others do, even when it's for their own good. Being responsible for teaching your teens about life doesn't give you the right to openly criticize everything they do. Don't nag them If they haven't learned the first few times, nagging won't help. Try a new approach.

Two kinds of criticism work best. The first is criticism that is actively sought. When your teen asks for your opinion, give it, but always take your teen's feelings into account. Make your criticism constructive. First point out the good things, then the bad. Don't say things that you would not appreciate hearing yourself even if they are true.

The second is self-criticism. From an early age help your children think about their own behavior. Teach them to reflect on what they say and do, and how they interact with the rest of the world. Help them see that their actions have consequences.

Teach them appropriate behavior, but don't judge them by your standards alone. Your teens live in a world of other teens. Be sensitive to the standards of their peers. That doesn't mean accepting or approving those standards, but take them into account before you criticize your teens too harshly.

Keep your critical remarks to a minimum and make them constructive. Encourage self-criticism in your teens. Remember that the meaning of criticism is in the mind of the hearer. In other words, you may intend your criticism to be constructive, but your teens may hear it as destructive. Make sure you and your teens share the same framework for understanding each other.

Three Things You Must Do

1. *Encourage* your teen to be reflective and self-aware from an early age.

2. *Imagine* how your teen will hear your criticism.

3. *Realize* that your teen can't be perfect.

What to Say and Do

Before you criticize your teen for something, find out her side of the story. Say such things as:

- That was an interesting thing to do [say]. What's that all about?

- Can we talk about what you just did [said]? I want to know why you did [said] it.

- Your schoolwork seems to be suffering. Is there something I should know?

You can soften your criticism and make it more effective by framing it. Say such things as:

- I don't want to criticize you for something that isn't within your control, but I'm concerned about _____.
- Please understand what I'm going to say is my way of trying to help you.
- Tell me if I'm way out of line for saying this.

Encourage self-criticism. Say such things as:

- What do you think of what you did [said]?
- Have you thought this thing through?
- What were your options?
- If you had it to do over again, would you do the same thing?

Make your criticism constructive. Say such things as:

- I really like what you did there, but can I make a few suggestions?
- If you did this again, you might want to do a few things differently.
- Let's talk about how you might change your approach to this problem.
- Let's look at what you did, and you tell me if you think you did your best.

WORDS AND PHRASES TO USE

- am I out of line here	- how to make it better	- let's talk	- tell me what you think
- can you fill me in	- I've some suggestions	- may I help you	- together
- doing your best		- self-awareness	- what's your view
		- share	

What Not to Say and Do

Avoid creating a you-against-your-teen situation. Don't say such things as:

- I think that's terrible.
- I think that looks awful.
- Can't you do any better than that?

Don't criticize everything. Choose what is most important. Don't say such things as:

- I don't like your hair.
- I don't like your friends.
- I don't like your language.
- I don't like your clothes.
- I don't like your attitude.
- I don't like your music.

Don't overreact or use extreme words. Don't say such things as:

- That's the worst thing I've ever seen [heard].
- I hate your taste in _____.
- You look terrible.
- Your work is a disgrace.
- You have no sense of what's good or bad.

Don't make the consequences of refusing to accept your criticism too extreme. Don't say such things as:

- If you don't change, I'll cut off your allowance.
- If you don't improve your schoolwork, you might as well quit.

WORDS AND PHRASES TO AVOID

a terrible job	bad	listen to me	worthless
a waste of time and effort	do what I say	stupid	you have no sense
	horrible		

19 Curfews

Time is nature's way of keeping everything from happening at once.

—Anonymous

Peter, in his first year of high school, decided to ask his parents what his curfew was. All his friends had one, so he figured he'd better have one, too. They told him it was ten o'clock during the week and midnight on Friday and Saturday. Peter compared his curfew to his friends' curfew and discovered that his was later. Peter told his parents this (they had a good communication relationship, and he could tell them almost anything) and asked why they were so liberal. They replied that they knew they could trust him and that if they made his curfew later than everyone else's, he would rarely have cause to break it.

Peter's parents knew that the essential part of their relationship with him was trust. If they couldn't trust him to be sensible, then no curfew would be sufficient. If they could, then any curfew would do. In fact, they knew Peter didn't really need a curfew. He would usually come home at a reasonable time.

However, they did insist on three things whenever he went out. First, Peter had to tell them where he was going and let them know if his plans changed. Second, he had to call them when he was leaving for home. No matter where he was or what time it was, he had to call them so they knew he was on his way. Third, they would come and get him if he ever needed to be picked up. It didn't matter where or what time of the day or night it was, if he called them for a ride, they would come.

Things to Consider

Society is big on accountability. Politicians make noise about a rising rate of teenage crime and often blame parents for inadequate supervision of their teens. These people are wrong on two counts. Teen crime is falling, not rising. And inadequate parental supervision isn't the problem, although parental abuse of children often is. The problem is that teen tragedies make big headlines, and then everyone becomes an expert on what parents should have known about their kids.

In fact, you are probably doing your best with your teens, and in most cases your best is quite good. Your teens are basically good kids who can be trusted. That isn't to say you can't improve your parenting. You can spend more time listening and be more involved with their lives and less involved in yourself. You can talk with them so you know who they are.

Your teen may be one who needs an early curfew, but make the curfew reasonable in the context of your teen's friends. Don't make your teen come home at nine if his friends have a ten o'clock curfew. Think about some of the good reasons for giving teens a curfew:

- They are not getting enough sleep.
- They have an important event the next day and must be well rested for it.
- You know from experience that they can't be trusted.
- They are being punished.

Here are some of the bad reasons:

- Everyone knows that after a certain hour the only teens still out are up to no good.
- It makes your life easier.
- You had the same curfew when you were their age, and look what it did for you.

Three Things You Must Do

1. *Know* where your teen will be.
2. *Know* your teen's friends.
3. *Decide* on a reasonable curfew in consultation with your teen.

What to Say and Do

Talk to your teen about the reasons that curfews are important. Say such things as:

- I think you realize you need a curfew for school nights and for the weekend. You're a teenager, and you need nine hours of sleep each night even if you don't think you do.

- You have a later curfew because you have shown that we can trust you to be home at a reasonable hour. That's the important thing.

- I'm giving you a curfew so you know what the boundaries are. Sometimes you might forget that you have to give school and your health first priority.

- Your curfew will change as you develop a sense of responsibility for yourself.

Decide on a curfew with your teen so that it is in keeping with their friends' curfews. Unless your teen is a special problem, that will give you a good idea of what's reasonable for their group of friends. Say such things as:

- What's a good curfew for you? What do you think it should be?

- All your friends have curfews, and I think you should have one, too. I'm happy to make yours the same as theirs as long as theirs is reasonable.

Make it quite clear what the curfew is. Say such things as:

- You're a good kid, but you still have to be home at ___o'clock during the week and ___o'clock on Friday and Saturday nights.

- This is your curfew. If you have any questions about it, tell me.

- We expect you to follow your curfew, but if you think there'll be a problem some night, talk to us about it. We can make exceptions.

Talk to your teen about any rules that go with the curfew. Say such things as:

- We have three rules that we want you to follow regardless of your curfew time: First, we must always know where you are and who you're with. Second, we must know when you are leaving for home, especially if you're late. And third, you can call us any time of the night, and we will come and get you.

- Our first concern is you. That's why you have a curfew and rules.

- As long as you behave responsibly, we'll reward that behavior.

Above all, if your teen is reasonable and trustworthy, show that you will be reasonable, too.

WORDS AND PHRASES TO USE

▸ fair	▸ in keeping with your friends	▸ our concern for your health and safety	▸ reasonable
▸ good	▸ maturity	▸ responsibility	▸ sleep
			▸ trust

What Not to Say and Do

Don't impose an arbitrary curfew. Don't say such things as:

- ▸ Curfews are for your own good.
- ▸ I'm not going to discuss it.
- ▸ As long as you live in my house, I set the rules. I'm not interested in your opinion.

Don't set a curfew that is out of line with your teen's friends. Don't say such things as:

- ▸ I don't care what curfews your friends have.
- ▸ Your friends' curfews are their parents' business. Your curfew is mine.
- ▸ Your curfew is ____ o'clock. I don't care if it seems unreasonable to you.

Never refuse to discuss your teen's concerns. Don't say such things as:

- ▸ I don't want to talk to you about your curfew. It's not open to discussion.
- ▸ Go away.

Don't ignore your teen's good behavior. Don't say such things as:

- ▸ I don't care if you think you can be trusted.
- ▸ I was a teen once myself, so I know what you're like. I don't trust any teenagers.
- ▸ I don't care what you do or what you say, your curfew won't change.

As long as your teen is normal and has shown that he can be trusted, don't treat him as though he is a juvenile delinquent waiting for a chance to get into trouble.

WORDS AND PHRASES TO AVOID

▸ curfews are for my benefit, not yours	▸ I don't care about your friends	▸ juvenile delinquent	▸ you don't know what's best for you
▸ go away and leave me alone	▸ it's not about trust/ open to discussion	▸ keep you out of trouble	▸ you'll do as I say
		▸ this is it	

20 Dating

I have such poor vision, I can date anybody.

—Garry Shandling

Sherry was fourteen and just beginning to date. Her mom and dad told her they would like her to go out with lots of different boys, not just one. They believed she was much too young to go steady with just one boy. Sherry had a different idea. She had a mad crush on Tom, and if he were to ask her to go out with him, she would jump at the chance. If he asked her to go steady, she knew she'd say yes. To complicate things further, her girlfriends told her that if she was so keen on Tom, she should ask him out herself. Girls, they said, didn't have to wait around to be asked out on a date anymore. They could do the asking themselves.

Things to Consider

If you're concerned about your teen dating, you are not alone. Almost all parents of teenage girls and boys go through the same problems when their children start to date. All of a sudden your innocent child is a sexual being. What should you say or not say, allow or not allow? Here are a few things to consider.

First, remember that dating, like other sexual behavior, isn't a rational thing. Don't think that reasoning with your teen about dating is going to help. There are no guarantees.

Second, discuss appropriate dating behavior: how dates should treat each other. Talk about issues of respect, self-worth, kindness, independence, and responsibility.

Respect: Even in the most casual dating relationship, the other person deserves to be treated with respect.

Self-worth: No matter how long or short the relationship, teens must do nothing to hurt the self-worth of the other person.

Kindness: Dates deserve to be treated with kindness and not be the butt of jokes, insinuations, criticism, rumors, or psychological or sexual harassment.

Independence: Relationships among teens still need to allow for the independence of each teen. Dependency relationships can easily develop, especially if one teen partner has low self-esteem. These relationships are unhealthy and can be destructive.

Responsibility: Dates need to behave responsibly toward each other. They mustn't put the other person in situations that make them feel afraid, embarrassed, or uncomfortable.

Some experts report that one in three teen girls experiences some form of physical, psychological, or emotional violence in dating relationships. Even if it happens to one girl out of one hundred or one hundred thousand, it's unacceptable. Be alert to any signs of physical or emotional violence on your daughter's or son's body or changes in behavior. Don't wait for your teen to come to you. Have regular conversations about the ongoing relationship, and don't be afraid to ask direct questions about anything that concerns you. Don't be afraid to tell your boys the standards of behavior toward their girlfriends that you expect from them.

Remember that sexual relationships (broadly defined) at any age involve emotions and other irrational, illogical, and very powerful forces. If the situation seems to warrant firm action on your part, be authoritative. Let your teens know exactly where you stand. Be sure you have good evidence before you say or do anything drastic. Remember that with teens you're often dealing with first relationships that can set the tone for future, longer lasting ones. You want your teens to start off on the right foot.

Three Things You Must Do

1. *Accept* dating as a natural and exciting stage in becoming an adult.

2. *Talk* about proper dating behavior.

3. *Reject* all abusive relationships.

What to Say and Do

When your teen is beginning to date, talk to her about your own experiences of dating. Don't say anything that would discourage her from talking about her dates. You need to develop a habit of listening to her dating stories. Encourage her to talk. Say such things as:

- Did I ever tell you about my first date? I was nervous.
- Some of my dates were fun and some were the worst. It depended on who I was dating.
- I tried to date lots of different girls/boys, because my parents wanted me to. But it didn't always work out that way when I had a crush on someone in particular.

Encourage your teen to begin dating by going out with groups of teens rather than just one boy or girl. Express your opinion. Say such things as:

- I'd like it better if you went out with groups of kids, not just you and your date alone.
- I used to double-date, especially on the first date, just in case it didn't work out.

Dating is still very different for girls and boys. Boys are the pursuers and girls the pursued. Encourage your daughter to be more up front. If there is a boy she'd like to go out with, tell her to call him. Say such things as:

- Do your girlfriends ask boys out?
- How would you feel about asking a boy for a date?
- Do you like waiting for the phone to ring, or do you wish you could just call the boy you want to go out with?

Ask your son how he would feel about being asked out. Say such things as:

- Would it bother you if a girl asked you out?
- Do you think girls should be able to ask guys for a date?
- Do you think it's easier being a boy or being the girl?

Involve yourself in your teen's relationship. Don't be nosy, but don't be shy about asking questions, especially if you think the relationship isn't as good as it should be. Say such things as:

- How does _____ treat you when you're out together?
- Do you ever argue?

21 Death

Death is just a distant rumor to the young.

—ANDY ROONEY

Rod's best friend, Al, was killed in a traffic accident. A drunk driver ran a red light at midnight as Al was driving his girlfriend home after a high school post–football game party. Rod and Al had been best friends since elementary school. They played on the high school football and basketball teams together. They were planning to go to the same college next year. Now Al was dead.

In addition, Rod's grandfather had died during the summer. He and Rod had been very close. They hiked and fished together. They talked a lot about family, about life, about Rod's schoolwork and his plans for the future.

Rod's parents had spent many hours talking to him about death and dying when his grandfather died, and now they were going to have to do it again. But the death of a seventeen-year-old is much more difficult to make sense of than the death of an eighty-year-old. They realized, though, that talking things through is important for any kind of traumatic emotional upset, and they were ready and willing to do it again.

Things to Consider

When my daughter was fifteen, her boyfriend fell asleep at the wheel as he was driving his parents home from a hockey game in a distant town. He and his mom were seriously injured, and his father was killed. My daughter spent much of the rest of that relationship as an amateur therapist trying to help this boy cope with his feelings about the accident. He refused professional help. We all agreed that that was a big mistake. My daughter did as well as a fifteen-year-old could do under the circumstances, but the relationship did not last.

Death and dying are an inescapable part of life, but that doesn't make it easier to talk about them with your teenagers. Your beliefs about the purpose and meaning of life, whatever they are, will help put death into perspective. If your beliefs are part of an organized religion to which your teens belong, it may be easier to make sense of the death of a grandparent, parent, sibling, or friend. But it is never really easy since most of us don't really know what comes after life or why some people live to old age and others die before they reach their prime.

Here are some things to consider. One of the most important principles of coping with the death of a loved one or someone close to you is that grieving is a healthy and necessary thing. We must be allowed to grieve. We need to go through the stages of disbelief, anger, recognition, acceptance, and reconciliation. You will have to help your children through this. Above all, don't deny them their right to grieve.

Talk about the dead person, about your memories of him, about his plans, personality, and accomplishments. Talk about his strengths and weaknesses. Talk about how much you'll miss him. Talk about how difficult it will be to live without him. Share your favorite stories about him. It is one of the best ways to assist your teens through the grieving process. Don't be shy when it comes to talking about feelings. Don't do anything to prevent your teens from talking about their feelings or from showing them. Crying is okay for boys as well as girls.

Show your teens how to celebrate a person's life as well as mourn his death. Help your teens realize that whatever happens, life goes on. The old cliché is true: It doesn't matter what happens to us; what matters is how we deal with it.

Three Things You Must Do

1. *Encourage* grieving.

2. *Share* stories about the person.

3. *Celebrate* the person's life.

What to Say and Do

If a teen's friend is dying or dead, encourage your teen to express his anger, his frustration, his sorrow, and sometimes his guilt. Death disrupts the normal, taken-for-granted flow of everyday life. Help your teen put it into a normal context. Say such things as:

- Would you like to talk about _____?
- I've had friends die, and I know how hard it is.
- It's hard to understand why these things happen. But let's talk.

If the death seems to be affecting your teen seriously, encourage him to talk to a minister, mullah, priest, rabbi, or other clergy, or to a doctor who has extensive experience helping people cope with the death of someone close. Say such things as:

- Do you think you'd like to talk to [member of the clergy].
- I'm going to ask _____ if s/he would come over on Sunday so we can talk about this.
- You may not like this, but I'm going to make an appointment for you to see Dr._____. I think you need someone with more experience than I have to help you through this.

Encourage your daughter or son to get together with friends to talk, pray, tell stories, cry, hold each other, and share the grief. Say such things as:

- Are you and your friends planning anything to celebrate _____'s life?
- I think you need to share your feelings with your friends.
- You'll feel much better if you and your friends can grieve together.

If your teen has lost a parent, grandparent, sibling, or any other close relative, you need to let him see you grieve. Show him that it's all right to cry, to be sad, to be angry, to not understand. Above all, encourage him to express his feelings openly and not hold them in. Talk to him about the person, about the good things in her life. Help him understand that acceptance is easier after we have been grieving. But don't expect things to happen overnight. It can take months or years. Say such things as:

- I know you miss _____ terribly. So do I.

- It's okay to cry.
- Death is always hard, even when it's an old person.
- We'll miss her, but she'll always be there in our memories.
- Take your time getting through this. Don't try to shut out what happened. Don't try to make sense of it, either. It's just one of those things in life that happens whether we want it to or not. Even though you can't believe it right now, time will heal you.
- Think of _____. How would she want you to cope with this?

Encourage your teen to attend the funeral or memorial service. Whether it's for a friend, parent, or relative, it's very important for the teen to participate in this grieving ceremony. Talk to him about it if he has never been to one before. Help him see the importance of communal grieving and saying good-bye. Say such things as:

- Do you want to go to the service? It's a good way to say good-bye.
- Do you know what happens at a funeral or memorial service? Let me describe it to you.
- You don't have to be afraid you'll cry. We're supposed to cry at funerals.
- I think _____ would want you to be there.
- I know it's sad, but I think you'll feel better if you come.

Your involvement in your teen's life will pay off in this situation because you'll notice if the person's death has seriously affected him. You'll see changes in his behavior, interests, appetite, talk, schoolwork, and even personality. Allow for some changes, temporary or permanent, but be ready to get professional advice if the changes seem serious.

WORDS AND PHRASES TO USE

- a part of life	- dead	- life's mysteries	- sad
- affection	- death	- memorial	- time will heal
- caring	- don't be afraid to cry	- memories	- you'll miss her/him
- celebrate	- dying	- pray	

What Not to Say and Do

Don't say anything that will discourage your teen from expressing his feelings. Don't say such things as:

- Try to act like a grown-up.
- Only babies cry.
- We all die sooner or later, so get used to it.
- I don't want you slobbering all over the house.

Don't dismiss your teen's feelings for his friend. Don't say such things as:

- It can't be that bad. You hardly knew him.
- He probably brought it on himself.
- You kids ought to be more careful. You're always getting yourselves killed.
- Teens drink, do drugs, drive, have sex, and you're still just babies. No wonder some die.

Don't discount your teen's feelings at the death of an elderly family member. Don't say such things as:

- She was old, so it's not surprising she died.
- You don't have to feel sorry. She had a good, long life.
- You'll get over it soon enough.
- Don't waste your tears. She was very old.

Don't discourage your teen from grieving alone, with family or friends, or at formal ceremonies. Don't say such things as:

- Stop crying. It's enough already.
- She's dead and buried. Forget about it and get on with your life.
- I don't care if you go to the funeral or not. She won't know if you're not there.

WORDS AND PHRASES TO AVOID

• control yourself	• I don't want to talk about it	• keep your thoughts to yourself	• people die, didn't you know
• grow up	• it's not the end of the world	• life is just a way of passing time between birth and death	• stop crying
• s/he wasn't worth all these tears			• you'll get over it

22 Discipline

It is impossible to enjoy idling unless there is plenty of work to do.
—Jerome K. Jerome

Sam's parents were having a difficult time with him. He wasn't doing well in school, and he didn't seem to want to listen to their advice and guidance. They didn't know how to go about disciplining him. What should they say? What should they do? Other parents seemed to have boys and girls who listened to what they said. Why couldn't Sam be that way? It was a constant struggle to get him to do anything they wanted him to do. Where should they begin? How could they discipline him so that he would do the right thing and maybe even come to the point where he would discipline himself?

Things to Consider

As you know from the introduction to this book, I know about discipline problems from firsthand experience with one of our teenage sons. He was almost impossible to discipline. No matter how much we talked or what we did, he simply refused to acknowledge that we or any other adults "were the boss of him." What did we do? We told him that since he refused to allow us to "parent" him, he had to take responsibility for his own actions. But we never stopped loving him and giving him as much support as he would allow us to give. It all turned out well in the end. He's an excellent young man, husband, father, and businessman. How can our success help you discipline your teen? What should you do?

1. Make love the foundation of your relationship with your teen.
2. Minimize the harmful consequences of bad behavior.
3. Tell your teen what is acceptable and unacceptable behavior.

4. Let your teen experience the consequences of unacceptable behavior.

5. Look for patterns of behavior in what your teen does and says.

6. Know your teen's strengths and weaknesses.

7. Always look for the best solution for your teen's problems.

8. Decide how self-destructive the behavior is. If your teenager is likely to do things that will hurt him or others, you need to seek the help of a psychiatrist or psychologist.

9. Teenagers have reasons for what they do. Don't assume you can read your teen's mind. Encourage him to explain his behavior to you.

10. Make the punishment fit the crime.

11. Don't make threats you don't intend to keep or couldn't keep if you wanted to.

12. If all else fails, use a third party as a mediator in your disciplinary problems.

13. Your discipline must be fair and be perceived as fair. Talk it through so that you and your teen understand each other.

If you've involved yourself in your child's life so that you know what he is like, you will know how to discipline him appropriately. If you haven't taken the trouble to be involved, you're at a great disadvantage, but there is no time like the present to begin that involvement. It's never too late.

A final thing to consider: Whatever the problem, never give up trying to talk about it. Never cut off communication even if your teen won't talk to you or doesn't seem to listen.

Three Things You Must Do

1. *Teach* your teen the rules of acceptable behavior.

2. *Realize* that your teen needs to rebel against your rules and create his own set.

3. *Never* give up.

What to Say and Do

Give your teens boundaries. Set rules but tie them to specific occasions. Say such things as:

- Remember your curfew tonight is ten o'clock.
- Homework before pleasure.
- You can go out after you've done your chores.
- You can't use the car if you let your grades slip.

Make discipline your teen's responsibility. Say such things as:

- You need to be in charge of yourself. You're getting too old for me to tell you what you ought to be doing.
- You know the right thing to do.
- You know that nobody can help you if you don't help yourself.
- Self-discipline is the best kind.

Praise your teen for good behavior. Say such things as:

- I'm really proud of you.
- I wasn't sure you had the self-discipline to get that done, but you did. Good for you.
- You're a good person and a hard worker.
- It's wonderful to have a trustworthy daughter/son like you.

Talk things through when they go wrong. Say such things as:

- How did that happen? We'd better talk about it.
- I think you and I need to talk about your behavior since we seem to understand things differently.
- Let's compare versions of what happened.

Even when your teen seems out of control, you must control yourself. Say such things as:

- We don't seem to connect, but have to keep trying.
- I don't know what kind of trouble you're in now, but we're here for you.

> ✦ Whatever happens, we have to keep talking.
> ✦ You don't want to listen to what we say, so you have to be responsible for your own decisions and face the consequences.
> ✦ If you ever want to talk, we're here.

WORDS AND PHRASES TO USE

✦ accountable	✦ duty	✦ liability	✦ restraint
✦ careful	✦ for your own sake	✦ obligation	✦ role
✦ consequences	✦ good	✦ others	✦ self-control
✦ dependable	✦ in your own best interests	✦ reliability	✦ training
✦ direction		✦ responsibility	✦ trust

What Not to Say and Do

Remember the communication ethic. Don't judge your teen too harshly. What you say must depend on your teen's age and the severity of the discipline problem. Don't say such things as:

> ✦ Don't you have a brain in your head?
> ✦ You drive me crazy.
> ✦ Idiot!
> ✦ I'm doing this for your own good.

Don't give up on your teen. Threatening him with extreme consequences doesn't normally help. You'll often regret what you've said. Don't say such things as:

> ✦ Get out!
> ✦ You're grounded for a year.
> ✦ I'm calling the police (unless the situation truly warrants it).
> ✦ You're not my son/daughter anymore.
> ✦ I don't want to know you.

Don't polarize the situation, you against your teen. Don't say such things as:

- If you can't live with my rules, you're out of here.
- It's my way or the highway.
- I don't want to hear any more from you.
- I'm not interested in your excuses.

Stay involved in your teen's life. Don't close the door on him. Don't say such things as:

- I'm done with you.
- Get out of my life.
- You're nothing but trouble, and I disown you.
- Since I can't trust you, I don't care about you anymore.
- You can do what you like because you're not my son/daughter anymore.

WORDS AND PHRASES TO AVOID

bad	dumb	idiot	miserable
brainless	empty-headed	liar	slacker
careless	evil	loser	sneak
disown	fool	maniac	stupid

23 Divorce and Remarriage

I am a marvelous housekeeper. Every time I leave a man, I keep his house.
—Zsa Zsa Gabor

Sabrina's mom and dad got divorced two and a half years ago when she was thirteen. Now both her mom and dad are seeing new people. Sabrina lived with her mom but also spent alternate weekends with her dad because they lived in the same city. She was devastated by the divorce in the first place and now is having great difficulty accepting the fact that her mom and dad are dating other people. Her parents had both thought that divorce was the best way of ending a relationship poisoned by argument, verbal and psychological abuse, and general incompatibility. They would have divorced sooner but decided to wait until Sabrina was a teenager, thinking it would be easier for her to accept the separation at that age. They were wrong. Sabrina hadn't yet fully accepted the divorce, nor could she accept the fact that both parents needed new relationships. Her parents were at a loss as to what to say to her.

Things to Consider

You've been on an emotional roller coaster during the divorce. Whatever the circumstances, divorce is difficult. You are trying to put your personal life back together. Your teenager is angry and afraid of the divorce, afraid that she will also be divorced. For teens divorce destroys a known world and replaces it with an unknown one. For some teens a bad relationship between parents is preferable to no relationship. Teens, like all children, accept their family life as normal. It's a safe, stable, familiar world even if it's unsafe and unstable. It's their world.

You and your teen need to create a new world of love, safety, and stability. You also have to create a new world for yourself. Even casual dating can cause problems and may cause you and your teen to withdraw from each other, cutting off communication.

The first rule is the cliché: Time heals all wounds. Your teen needs time to work her way through the death of her family, like grieving a real death. This takes time. Allow for that. Your teen will not easily accept a new relationship in your life, especially if it happens too soon. Introduce any notion of a new relationship slowly and carefully.

Sex can be a problem if you have taught your teen that sex outside of marriage is wrong. Avoid one-night stands and other overt sexual behavior in any new relationship until your teen has had time to adjust to the divorce. Again, time is the most important factor. Introduce any new person slowly and gently.

Teens need the security of knowing that they still have the unconditional love of their parents. Make it obvious that they do. This will help them accept any new person in your life.

Understand that new partners cannot easily become new parents. The relationship between new partner and teen should be modeled on friendship, not parenting. The new partner will have to have a good sense of humor and high self-esteem to cope with the hostility he or she will likely face initially from teens, especially if the divorce was hostile.

Finally, the more you've been involved in your teen's life and the better your communication, the easier the transition from divorce to new relationship will be. Encourage your teen to talk freely about her feelings. Emphasize your love for your teen. Don't criticize your ex-spouse, no matter how you feel. Your teen won't understand or sympathize because you are talking about her parent, not ex-parent.

Three Things You Must Do

1. *Give* your teen time to grieve over the breakup.

2. *Encourage* your teen to talk about her feelings.

3. *Reassure* your teen that you love her as much as ever.

What to Say and Do

There is never a good time to tell your teen about divorce. Don't wait. Do it as early as possible to prepare her for the process. Give your teen the maximum time to grieve and adjust to the death of the world she has known. Say such things as:

> ✦ I need to talk to you about a problem your dad and I are having.

If possible, both of you should talk to your teen together. Say such things as:

> ✦ We need to talk to you about something very important.

Get to the point, but put it in the best possible context. Say such things as:

> ✦ We love you very much and don't want to hurt you, but your mom/dad and I have decided that we need some time apart. We want to talk to you about it so you'll understand what the problem is.

Teens may not understand. They probably want you to fix any problems and stay together. Don't expect them to agree or sympathize. Say such things as:

> ✦ We know you won't like this, but your mom/dad and I are going to separate and maybe get divorced. We don't expect you to understand the problem, and we don't expect you to agree that this is a good idea. But we want you to know that we both love you and will always love you even if you're living with only one of us at a time. That's why we wanted to talk to you about it.

Be realistic with your teens. Say such things as:

> ✦ Things will be different now that we're splitting up, but we both want only the best for you. We'll work hard to make sure that your life isn't too different.

> ✦ We don't want to move you away from your friends, so you're going to be staying here with me. But you'll get to visit your dad/mom at least two weekends each month.

> ✦ I know you're angry with us and probably a little bit afraid at what's happening. Let's talk about it. What are you thinking?

> ✦ What about any of your friends who've gone through a divorce with their parents? What do they tell you?

> I've never been through a divorce before, so I don't know much more about how things will work out than you do. But I can promise you one thing: We both love you and will do the best we can for you.

Slowly get your teen accustomed to a new relationship you may have. Say such things as:

> Your mom/dad and I have been apart for a year now. What would you think about my dating someone? I know it might seem strange, so I'd like to know your feelings.

> Now that we're settled in our new living arrangements, I have something to tell you. I've met someone I like, and we're going out to supper next week. Let me tell you something about him/her.

> I want you to understand that this is just a date and nothing more serious than that. I know you won't like it, but I need to have a social life.

> You know that I've been seeing _____. I'd like you to meet her/him, so would you come to lunch with us next Sunday at the pizza restaurant on Main Street.

> Even if I married _____, s/he wouldn't be taking the place of your mom/dad.

Listen, listen, listen. Talk, talk, talk. Say such things as:

> Let's go for a walk. I want to talk about how your life and mine are changing.

> I know this has been tough for you. How are you feeling about it?

> You know how much I value your opinion. Tell me what you think of

_____.

> Let's make sure we have time to talk each week. What can we do every Sunday morning together? You decide.

WORDS AND PHRASES TO USE

> a new beginning	> difficult changes	> sharing	> we're not abandoning you
> afraid/alone/angry	> love	> stability	
> confused	> new	> supportive	> your needs, my needs, and our needs
> dating	> sadness	> trust	

What Not to Say and Do

Be sympathetic to your teen's normal reaction of anger and fear. Your teen won't see separation or divorce as a solution. Don't say such things as:

- Your mom/dad and I are getting a divorce, and you'll just have to live with it.
- Don't worry. This will be better for everyone.
- I guess you'll be glad you don't have to hear us fighting anymore.

If you can avoid it, don't blame your spouse in front of your child no matter what you feel or what the circumstances of your separation or divorce and no matter who you think is at fault. Don't go into the gory details. Don't be openly hostile. Your teen loves both of you even if you no longer love each other. Don't use your teen to communicate with your ex. Don't say such things as:

- That bastard/bitch!
- I hope that when you marry you don't get stuck with someone like him/her.
- I hate that man/woman.
- Tell your father/mother from me that . . .

If you're going to start dating again, don't rush into it. Don't be too quick to introduce a new love into your teen's life. Don't be intimate in situations where your teen might accidentally discover you. Go slow. Don't say or do such things as:

- I know I've told you that sex outside marriage is wrong, but this is different.
- I'm asking my new girlfriend/ boyfriend to dinner on Saturday night. I want you to be here so you can meet her/him, and I want you to be nice to my new friend.
- You're going to have a new mom/dad someday, so you'd better get used to it.

Don't cut off lines of communication. Don't say such things as:

- I don't care what you think.
- If you don't like my new girlfriend/boyfriend, just keep it to yourself.
- Now that I'm on my own I won't have very much time for you.
- You have to choose. You either love me or your dad/mom.

WORDS AND PHRASES TO AVOID

bastard/bitch	deceiving	inconsiderate	miserable
cheat	I hate him/her	keep your thoughts to yourself	you'll have to choose

24 Drinking

Water, taken in moderation, cannot hurt anybody.

—MARK TWAIN

David was seventeen but got his driver's license when he was sixteen. He had his own car, bought with money earned at summer jobs. One night at a party a few miles from home, he drank too much beer. David called his parents. They had a long-standing policy with their children that they must call them anytime they needed help or simply to say that they were on their way home. The parents promised that there would be no recriminations, no moralizing, and no guilt trips, regardless of the circumstances. This policy paid off. David's parents drove to the party and found him looking very queasy and feeling worse. After some thank-you's to David's friends for looking after him, his mom drove him home, and his dad drove David's car home.

They had purposely introduced their teenagers to wine and beer on special occasions so that they would not be seen as mysterious forbidden fruit to be consumed when no one was looking. They themselves drank and believed that social drinking was not an evil as long as it was done responsibly and in moderation. They wanted their teenagers to understand this from both experience and example. And it appears they succeeded.

Things to Consider

You have your own beliefs, values, and rules about alcohol for yourself and your family. My advice on how to communicate your beliefs and rules to your teens is from my point of view and experience. The brief story above that introduces this topic tells of my experience with our son, David. I believe that drinking for most older teenagers is inevitable even if undesirable. Therefore, we have to teach our teens that the golden mean applies to drinking as it does to most things in life. Drinking is acceptable in moderation, but drinking and driving is forbidden.

505

If your habits, tastes, religion, or values tell you that drinking, even moderate drinking, is unacceptable, teach that to your teens. Decide whether you want to teach your teens never to drink or simply not to drink until they're of legal age. Begin to share your values with them when they are very young. Help them avoid situations where there might be alcohol. In other words, know your teen and your teen's friends.

Most teens have access to alcohol. Peer pressure can make them do things they might not ordinarily do. For them to resist alcohol when all their friends are drinking will take much self-discipline. Their values must be established early in life, and they must be strong in their convictions.

If your attitude toward alcohol is less stringent, if you yourself are a social drinker, communicate your views on appropriate drinking behavior to your children around age ten, because they will have access to alcohol at an early age. I grew up in New York City and had my first drink in a bar on Long Island when I was twelve. It was a Tom Collins. I remember it well. Your teenager may have the same opportunity. I have read that 90 percent of high school students have tried alcohol outside the home. Many report that they were able to buy their own.

Decide if you will do what my wife and I did. We gave our children a little wine at dinner, if they wanted it, on special occasions like Thanksgiving and Christmas. After the first time they often refused. Our purpose was to demystify alcohol. We wanted them to have their first experience with drinking under our supervision. When I was at a college in upstate New York, I saw many eighteen-year-olds who had no experience with alcohol stumble back to the dormitory on Friday night and be sick in the hall. They didn't know how to handle their drinking. We didn't want our teens to be like that.

Examine your own attitude toward drinking and make that attitude clear to your teens in conversation and by example. Decide if alcohol is absolutely forbidden or if it is not. Decide if you want your teens' first experiences with alcohol to be in your own home under your supervision, so you can teach them to have a healthy attitude toward drinking. Decide if this is preferable to having them learn about drinking secretly, alone or with friends, in a car or a vacant lot, or at a rowdy party.

Alcohol, like so many things in life, can be used or abused. It's your responsibility to involve yourself in your teenagers' lives to the extent that you can help them learn to abstain or to drink responsibly. Involve yourself through talk and by example. If you think that you or your teen has a problem with alcohol, get professional help.

Three Things You Must Do

1. *Teach* your attitudes and habits about drinking through talk and by example.

2. *Give* your teen rules about drinking and an escape route for him and his companions when faced with drinking and driving, such as a taxi credit card or calling home anytime.

3. *Trust* your teen unless you have good reason not to.

What to Say and Do

If you want your teen to abstain from alcohol for personal or religious reasons, teach him by word and example from an early age. Say such things as:

- I can't be around all the time to keep you from drinking, but I'm trusting you to do the right thing.

- You may think you know better than I do about what's good for you. But I think you'll find out as you grow older that drinking won't do you any good and can do a lot of harm.

If there is alcoholism in the family, you should warn your teen that a predisposition for it can pass down from one generation to the next. Say such things as:

- I think you need to know that _____ was an alcoholic, and I might have become one, too, if I hadn't decided to abstain. You need to be careful because alcoholism seems to have a genetic link and can be inherited.

If you approve of social drinking, tell your teen what your attitudes are. Say such things as:

- Studies have shown that a drink or two a day, especially red wine, can be good for you.

- I don't generally approve of teenage drinking, but I don't mind your having a little wine or beer with dinner on special occasions.

- Alcohol should be treated with respect. Drunkenness is never acceptable.

Explain your rules about drinking and driving. Say such things as:

- I know you'll be going to parties where there is beer and wine. Remember, *no* drinking and driving.
- You can call me any time of the night if you have been drinking, and I'll come and get you.
- You and your friends need to select a designated non-drinking driver when you go to parties.

WORDS AND PHRASES TO USE

- abstain
- alcoholism
- be responsible
- beer

- call me
- don't drink and drive
- drunkenness

- illegal
- moderation in all things
- social drinking

- spirits
- trust
- wine

What Not to Say and Do

Don't make drinking a bigger issue than it needs to be. Don't say such things as:

- You must never take a drink again, or I will disown you.
- You are a sinner.
- Alcohol is evil. If you drink, you are evil.

Don't judge your teen too harshly if he makes a mistake. Don't say such things as:

- If you get drunk, don't call me for help.
- I won't have any son or daughter of mine drinking.
- If I ever catch you drinking, you're grounded for a year.

Don't be unreasonable about drinking, especially if you are a drinker. Don't say such things as:

- I don't care if you're seventeen, you can't have a drink in this house until you're of legal age.

Don't encourage your teen to drink. Don't say such things as:

- Don't be a sissy. A little drink never hurt anybody.
- You need practice in holding your liquor. Let me see you drink this.
- When I was your age, I could drink my friends under the table.

WORDS AND PHRASES TO AVOID

baby	don't think you can depend on me	I don't want to hear about it	sneak
can't hold your liquor	drunkard	sinner	wuss
disown	evil		

25 Drugs

Reality is a crutch for people who can't cope with drugs.

—LILY TOMLIN

Like most parents of her generation Beverly had experimented with marijuana when she was in college. She remembered it made her feel relaxed and social. After college she smoked a few joints at occasional parties but never quite got used to the sweet, sickly smell of the burning weed. Remembering how prevalent drug use was at school—not just marijuana, but also LSD and cocaine—Bev and her husband were worried about their son and daughter, twelve and thirteen years old, getting involved. Their children went to a large high school, and the rumors were that drugs were available for those who could pay for them. They talked about how they would react and what they would say if they found out their kids were doing drugs of any sort. Both agreed that "an ounce of prevention was worth a pound of cure." They decided that talking to their kids about their concerns and their own experiences was a good way to start discussing the subject of drugs. Their talking relationship with their kids had been quite good through the early years of their childhood, and although they now seemed more interested in talking to their peers than to their parents, the lines of communication still seemed pretty open.

Things to Consider

You want to drug-proof your kids, to be confident that if they are ever asked, they will automatically say "No!" to marijuana, cocaine, LSD, sniffing glue or solvents, barbiturates, and tranquilizers. All these things are available, especially in larger towns and cities.

According to some estimates 15 to 20 percent of teens have tried marijuana, but those estimates are probably low. Kids are often introduced to drugs by their peers at age twelve or thirteen. They want to know what the experience is like. They want to please their friends and show that they are part of the crowd. Sometimes they keep using them to show that they can make their own decisions, because they have become addicted, or because they like the feeling it gives them. Shy kids may use drugs to show they belong; kids who worry a lot may use them to relieve stress; emotionally repressed kids may use them to let their feelings out; and abused kids may use them to escape.

Drugs are a part of our society. My daughter had a friend whose mom would supply her with "joints." Medically prescribed drugs make an important contribution to our quality of life, but so-called recreational and designer drugs to which people become addicted destroy life. And many of these drugs are cheap enough for teens to buy with their allowance or part-time job money. So you mustn't underestimate your teen's access to drugs.

You need to know what to say and do to help drug-proof your teens. Teach them from an early age how to make good decisions for themselves. Talk frequently and frankly about the dangers of giving in to drugs. Set an example of responsible drug use yourself. Know your teens' friends and their habits and home situation. Talk to your teens' teachers at school and to the school administrators about drug availability and use there. If you have concerns about your teens, know where to get help. If you didn't start doing all this when your kids were eight or nine, now is a good time to start.

Three Things You Must Do

1. *Recognize* that we live in a drug-using society.

2. *Teach* responsible medical drug use by example.

3. *Reject* recreational use of addictive or behavior-altering drugs.

What to Say and Do

People develop a dependency on drugs. Teach your teen that drugs may be a medical necessity and often a medical miracle, but that there is big difference between their medical use and their recreational use. Say such things as:

- We all use drugs, but even medical drugs should be used only when absolutely necessary.
- Drugs are wonderful things to help with illness and disease, even with headaches. But using drugs as an escape is dangerous when they are addictive.
- Drugs can never be a substitute for love, understanding, and feeling good about yourself.
- You know we can't prevent you from taking drugs, but let's talk about the consequences.

Try to find out your teen's experience with drugs. Say such things as:

- Do you know anyone who does drugs?
- What kinds of drugs—marijuana, hashish, cocaine, rock, ecstasy?
- Are there kids at your school who sell drugs?
- Have you experimented with drugs?

Don't be shy about asking your teen's high school principal or teachers about drugs in the school. Ask the police if you're really concerned.

Look for warning signs that your teen may be using drugs or thinking of using them because of stress, peer pressure, or other social or personal factors. Warning signs of drug use can include the following:

- a change in sleeping habits
- a change in eating habits
- disinterest in schoolwork
- moodiness and extreme mood swings
- a different set of friends
- slurred or strange speech
- secretiveness
- red eyes
- runny nose
- unusual scars
- needle marks

- increased sensitivity to simple remarks
- weight loss

Keep your communication lines open. Say such things as:

- How's your friend _____ doing? (Ask about a specific friend just to get the conversation started.)
- How's your math [physics, bio, or other subject] coming along? (Be specific. You should know schoolwork specifics if you've been involved.)
- What do you think about renting a movie and watching it together some night this week? You choose. Is there something you'd really like to see?
- Is everything going all right for you with _____? (Fill in the name of a boyfriend or girlfriend.)
- Are you feeling good about yourself these days?

Build a relationship so that your teen will talk to you about anything, including drugs. If you're too judgmental, your teen won't tell you things he thinks you won't want to hear. Build this kind of relationship over time by not overreacting.

WORDS AND PHRASES TO USE

- addiction
- are you okay
- coping
- drugs are only good for you when you're sick
- how are things going
- how do you feel
- medication
- overdose
- peer pressure
- side effects
- stress

What Not to Say and Do

Don't ignore your teen. Demands for attention can be a cry for help. Don't say such things as:

- I can't talk to you right now. Catch me later.
- You're old enough to cope with your own problems.
- I'm just too busy at work to worry about you right now.

Don't lose touch with your teen and your teen's friends. Don't say such things as:

- Just get out of here and leave me alone.
- I don't care who you're with, just stay out of trouble.
- Here's some money. Now go amuse yourself.

Don't encourage indiscriminate medication. Don't give your teen the idea that there is a pill for every problem. Don't say such things as:

- If you're not feeling well, we'll go to the doctor and get some pills to fix you up.
- These days there's a pill for everything.
- I don't know what I'd do if I didn't have my pills.

Don't ignore potential symptoms of drug use. Don't say such things as:

- You sleep too much, but then you're naturally lazy.
- Don't worry about that runny nose. There are a lot of colds going around these days.
- I'm glad you have a new group of friends. I never did like the other ones.

WORDS AND PHRASES TO AVOID

‣ don't bother me with it	‣ take a pill, and you'll feel fine	‣ you're fat	‣ you're on your own
‣ leave me alone	‣ you'll have to cope by yourself	‣ you're good for nothing	‣ you're stupid
			‣ you're worthless

26 Failure

The two hardest things to handle in life are failure and success.

—ANONYMOUS

Althea tried out for the high school cheerleading squad but wasn't chosen. She tried out for the girl's volleyball team but wasn't chosen. She auditioned for the school play but wasn't chosen. At age fifteen she felt like a failure. All her friends knew that she had failed while some of them had succeeded. One friend made the cheerleaders, the volleyball team, and the female lead in the play. That was the kind of girl everyone liked, valued, and admired, Althea thought, whereas she was a loser, and nobody admired a loser. Althea's parents were disappointed for her. They hurt almost as much as she did, perhaps even more. They wanted to help her through this difficult time and make something positive out of these failures. They knew that with the passage of time the hurt would ease, but they were afraid the scars would remain and prevent Althea from taking risks in the future. This is what they wanted to help avoid. They knew that a successful life depended on taking risks and trying new things, knowing that there was always the risk of failure but that without that risk there was no possibility of success. So they decided they and Althea needed to talk things through.

Things to Consider

You have experienced failure, and if you're like me, your failures have outnumbered your successes many times over. Failure is the risk of trying. When your teens fail to achieve a place on the team, a good grade, or the attention of the boy or girl they have fallen for, it hurts you as much or more than it hurts them. You want to protect your teen from failure, but you don't want to stop them from trying new things, scaling new heights, working toward new goals

515

Try to ease the pain when things don't go the way your teens had hoped. Talk about their options. Put things into perspective. Help them realize that sometimes it is better to have tried even if the attempt led to failure. But teach them that that is not always true.

Not all things are worth the risk. Your involvement with your teenagers will help you teach them that they need to consider their abilities, gifts, and aptitudes before trying out for a team just in case they have no chance of making it. Why should they subject themselves to almost certain failure? Self-examination might tell them that their talents lie elsewhere.

Failure can teach the importance of preparation and practice. Even if your teen is an excellent skier, she shouldn't go down a sixty-meter ski jump as a novice jumper. She should begin with the one-meter jump. She should perfect her technique on the small jumps and gradually work up to the big ones. Failure is a good opportunity to help teens reflect on and understand the importance of both talent and hard work to develop their talents to their full potential.

When your teens fail at something, use it as an opportunity for building their self-knowledge and self-esteem by teaching them how to make the best of a bad thing. If they learn how to handle disappointment at a young age, they will not be afraid to strive for what they want even though there is always the risk of failure.

Three Things You Must Do

1. *Teach* your teens that there is a risk of failure in everything we do.

2. *Help* your teens realize when to quit and when to carry on.

3. *Teach* them that good preparation can reduce the chance of failure.

What to Say and Do

Encourage your teen to get involved in activities. Say such things as:

- Let's talk about this and see what your options are. If you don't try, you won't know whether you would have been successful or not. If you do try, the best thing that can happen is that you'll succeed. The worst thing is that you won't. Now what do you think you should do?

- Give it a try. Otherwise you'll always be wondering if you could have done it.
- My attitude has always been that I'd rather regret having done something than not having done it. (Within the bounds of law, safety, and morality, of course.)

Talk through some of the considerations of success and failure. Say such things as:

- What you're trying takes some special talents and abilities. Do you think you have them? What do you think they are?
- If you decide to go for this and you don't make it, will that be okay?
- If you don't try, what else will you do?

Talk about personal reaction to failure and how to handle it. It can help your teen grow emotionally and assist her self-esteem. Say such things as:

- I've tried lots of things and failed, but those failures have taught me things about myself and about how to succeed next time. It could be the same for you.
- Do you think failing makes you any less a person?
- You need to learn how to handle failure because chances are you'll fail at more things than succeed. That's not a reflection on you, it's just the way life is.
- Maybe you haven't prepared yourself adequately. Maybe what you need to do is go back and work harder to get ready for this. Then try again and see if it works.
- Now you have a better idea of what it takes to succeed. You can try again and use this knowledge to prepare better.
- Nobody will think you're stupid or a loser if you don't make it, but they might if you don't even try.

WORDS AND PHRASES TO USE

- ability	- bold	- life is full of risks	- preparation
- accomplishments	- chance	- lose	- self-esteem
- achieve	- fail	- luck	- talent
- attempt	- hard work	- never give up	- try and try again

What Not to Say and Do

Don't discourage your teen from trying even at the risk of her failing. Don't say such things as:

- I don't see why you're even trying. You won't succeed.
- Give it up. You're only going to fail.
- You're just opening yourself up to failure.

Don't discourage your teen from facing life's challenges. Don't say such things as:

- Life is so full of disappointments, I don't think it's worth the effort.
- Don't even try since you'll probably fail anyway.
- It's not worth it. Better to just stay in your own little world.

Don't criticize your teen for trying. Don't say such things as:

- I don't think you're up to it.
- You don't have the guts to try.
- You fail at everything you try. Why don't you just give up?
- You're a failure, and you'll always be a failure.

WORDS AND PHRASES TO AVOID

• afraid	• failure	• no ability	• stupid
• brainless	• life will drag you down	• no talent	• you don't have the guts or the brains
• coward	• loser	• senseless	• you're not worth it

27 Family

. . . The family—that dear octopus from whose tentacles we never quite escape, nor, in our inmost hearts, ever quite wish to.

—Dodie Smith

Ben, Mae, and Rudy were siblings. Ben was sixteen, Mae was fourteen, and Rudy was thirteen. Their parents worked and yet they made sure that they always had time to spend with the kids in the evenings and on weekends. However, with everyone on different schedules and going off in different directions, it was hard to have good family time together. So the parents decided one evening that next Saturday morning they would have a family meeting and they would have such meetings twice a month. They decided that family relationships were the most important thing in life and that they needed to organize and structure something so there would be a regular time each month to talk to one another about good things and bad, about successes and failures, about smooth sailing and problems. They reasoned that these meetings would be a good time to teach the teens their responsibilities around the house, such as making beds, sorting laundry, washing up, and walking the dog. It was also a time to make up rules for using the computer, watching TV, and being on the telephone. Their family needed time for sharing, and family meetings turned out to be just the thing.

Things to Consider

Kids grow up thinking their family is normal even if they're being raised by drug-addled parents. If the family is violent (God forbid), violent is normal. My oldest son told me he was well into his teens before he realized that most kids did not have dads who were elbow-patch-wearing, pipe-smoking university professors. Whatever your family communication style, your children will grow up thinking that it's normal. But some styles are better than others.

No matter how large or small your family, no matter what its configuration, family communication is the core of your relationship with your children. Teenagers seem to value their peers more than their family, which makes it all the more important for you to have a regular time for family sharing. Sometimes this can be done at dinner, but with the kinds of schedules many families have these days, dinner is often eaten on the run and not with everyone sitting down together. You need to pick a time that's convenient for everyone. If it's just you and one child, it's easier. But as the family grows in size, regular sharing and good communication become more complex.

Teens need to share their feelings, thoughts, and stories. You need to share stories, concerns, plans, and responsibilities. You need good communication within the family, or your teens will not understand you—at least not the way you intend them to—nor will you understand them.

Sharing one-on-one is fine. Depending on your family size, you may want to do both individual sharing and family group sharing. If you find you need group sharing, then plan a regular meeting each month. You should also plan to rotate responsibilities for moderating the meeting; make rules about there being no personal attacks, yelling, or interrupting; create an agenda for each meeting; encourage nice talk such as praise, especially at the beginning, and then get onto the hard stuff; present solutions for the problems discussed; have someone write down the gist of what is agreed on and what actions will be taken. Keep the meetings short, end with stories or jokes, and follow up with a shared experience such as going out for pizza, a movie, or ice cream.

Finally, recognize that the essence of the family is trust and love. If you make promises, keep them. If your teen needs your love, don't ask why, just give it. Make it easy for your teen to talk to you by not judging, not overreacting, and not preaching or lecturing. Show your teen that family is and always will be her help and her strength in any situation.

Three Things You Must Do

1. *Talk* regularly, not just when there are problems.
2. *Share* thoughts and feelings.
3. *Show* love and trust through your talk and action.

What to Say and Do

The family must provide love and security. Take every opportunity to communicate to your teen that the family is her safe haven. You are there to listen, to understand, to protect, and to help when she needs it. Your teen will never admit she needs you to do this, of course, so sometimes you have to be subtle. Your teen might need help with something. Say such things as:

- I know you're almost an adult, but if there is anything I can do, just tell me.
- Let me know what I can do to help.
- I had a similar problem when I was your age. Would you like to know what I did?

Make opportunities for sharing by organizing outings, doing chores together, playing games or sports, taking trips. Say such things as:

- Let's go play some softball down at the park and then go for pizza and ice cream.
- Would you like to help me make dinner? I could really use the help.
- You choose a movie you'd like to see, and we'll all go. My treat!
- I think we need a family vacation because you guys are getting so old, you won't want to come with us anymore. It has to be some place we all want to go. Let's talk about where you want to go, and we'll see what we can afford.

If it suits your family, organize a time each week or month for a family meeting for sharing ideas, chores, responsibilities, and good and bad things that have happened. You can decide how formal it will be. It can be very informal, or it can include any or all of the following:

- Choose a chairperson who is responsible for calling the meeting and setting a day, time, and place. You can have a different chair each time.
- Have a written agenda for each family member.
- Choose someone to take notes and write up a summary of the meeting, including what you talked about, what you decided to do about each item on the agenda, who has the responsibility to carry out the decisions, what they must do, and when it must be done.
- Post the agenda items on the fridge to check off when they're done.

Keep your teen involved in family life. Don't let her become isolated or more dependent on friends than on the family for such things as love, attention, and understanding. Say such things as:

- You and I need to spend some time together since we're both so busy. How about having lunch with me on Saturday?
- May I see what you're doing in school these days?
- I'd like you to take a trip with me to visit my old college. I think you might like to go there someday.
- What has happened to _____? Are you still going out? Would you like to bring him/her home to dinner one weekend?
- I'm volunteering down at the food bank each Wednesday evening in November and December. Would you like to join me sometime? I'd love your company.

Trust, love, understanding, support, and safety. These are critical elements in the family that your teen should be able to take for granted, so don't be upset if she does take them for granted. She will quickly notice if they're not there even though she may not seem to notice when they are. In all that you say to your teen, recreate and reinforce these elements.

WORDS AND PHRASES TO USE

• affection	• share	• together	• we're all in this together
• family	• talk to me	• trust	
• member	• tell me how you feel	• we love you	• you're one of us

---

What Not to Say and Do

Never discourage honest, open conversation. Don't judge your teen without first making sure you know everything. Let some time pass before you do or say anything too harsh. Don't make her afraid of what the family will say. Don't say such things as:

- If you're in trouble again, I don't want to know.

- You're so stupid. How could you have done such a thing?
- We may be your family, but we can't always be there for you.
- We're your family, not your fairy godmother.

Never betray your teen's trust. What she confides in you should be as sacred as the confessional unless it is a matter of someone's safety. If you betray her trust without a reason that she understands and ultimately agrees with, your relationship will suffer. Don't say such things as:

- I know I promised not to say anything, but I had to.
- I'm calling the police (unless the situation truly warrants it).
- Don't tell me anything you wouldn't want me to repeat.
- I can't condone what you did, and I'm going to call your teacher/principal.

Never be violent in word or deed. Never say such things as:

- You rotten little creep!
- You stupid b—!
- Get out of my sight!
- Get out of this house!
- I never want to see or hear from you again!
- I'm going to beat your brains out!

Don't say or do anything that will make the family your teen's enemy. If your teen can't depend on the family for support, she will look elsewhere.

Teens need to be loved and valued. If they don't find that in their family, they will find it elsewhere. Boys may find it in gangs. Girls may find it in pimps.

WORDS AND PHRASES TO AVOID

- bastard/bitch	- don't talk to me	- I'm not interested	- we don't love you anymore
- criminal	- get out of here	- rotten	
- delinquent	- go away	- stupid	- you don't belong here anymore

28 Fear

> *The only thing we have to fear is fear itself.*
>
> —FRANKLIN D. ROOSEVELT

Sean was afraid to go to school. He had had a brief but ugly encounter with a boy named Rolf yesterday after school. Rolf was well known as a school bully, always picking on younger kids. He was a senior, and Sean was a freshman. He asked Sean for money, and Sean said no. Rolf grabbed him, went through his pockets, and took Sean's two dollars and some change. Then he told him that from now on he would beat him up unless Sean gave him a dollar a day.

Sean was only fourteen, and Rolf was a large seventeen-year-old. Sean was scared and didn't know what to do. He was afraid to tell his parents. He couldn't sleep that night, and the next morning he ate little breakfast. He still hadn't decided if he would go to school or not.

His mom noticed something was wrong and asked Sean what the problem was. After a few attempts at denial he broke down and said he would tell her what was wrong if she would promise not to call the school. She replied that she would make no promises until she heard the story. Sean was so afraid that he couldn't keep it in any longer and told her everything. She immediately called the high school and told the story to the principal. He had had other complaints of Rolf's bullying and extorting of money from younger students and asked her to come to his office with Sean to meet with the police. If they would sign a complaint against Rolf, he would now have sufficient grounds for expelling him from school. Bullying was a problem that he wanted to stop because it poisoned the culture of the school.

Things to Consider

Today's teenagers fear many things: physical violence such as shootings, stabbings, gang fights, and bullying, and psychological violence such as verbal

524

harassment, racism, and intolerance. They also fear failing tests, not getting into college, and not being part of the "in" group. Teenage girls fear not being pretty, not having the right body, and not having the right clothes. Teenage boys fear not being cool, not having the right clothes, not having the right body type, not making the team, and not having a cool car. Teens at "wealthy" schools and teens at "poor" schools share many of these fears.

Recent incidents of shootings in schools, as terrible as they may be, give people a false impression of violence in high schools. It is nothing new. American high schools have always been potentially violent places for students. Putting two hundred or more adolescent boys together in one building (my own high school in New York City had more than two thousand boys, ages fourteen to eighteen, with about an equal number of girls) is a recipe for all kinds of violence. The surprising thing is that most teenagers are not physically violent, and most high schools are relatively safe places in spite of the "raging hormones" of teenagers. Most teenagers don't fight, they cooperate.

All teenagers have some fears. Make sure that these are normal fears, such as fear of failing, fear of not being able to live up to one's heroes physically or mentally, fear of bullying or other physical violence, and fear of abuse or rejection from parents, friends, teachers, or peers.

Know your teens' fears. Have a relationship so your children will tell you almost everything. Show by your words and actions that they can talk to you about things that really worry them. Don't preach or yell or disparage their fears. Don't tell them they're being silly. Listen with sympathy, empathy, and without judging them. Encourage them to talk openly. Listen more than you talk. Give advice when they ask for it.

It's a wonderful thing when your teens trust you enough to come to you with their fears. With that trust you can help your teens cope and learn and go beyond. You can take appropriate action so that the cause of their fear gets removed. You can get in touch with the appropriate authorities; make phone calls; meet with school administrators, police, parents, and friends; and get counseling help when necessary. Or you can advise your teens on what action they can take.

There are many ways to deal with fear, short of physical violence. You need to know your children well enough so you can advise them about what to do to overcome their fears.

Three Things You Must Do

1. *Accept* your teen's fears as real.

2. *Understand* your teen's fears as reasonable for them.

3. *Support* your teen with whatever it takes to overcome his fears.

What to Say and Do

Your teen's fears are real regardless of how they seem to you. Treat them as real. Take them seriously. Say such things as:

- You seem worried. Are you afraid of something?
- I know something's bothering you. Want to talk about it?
- What's happened to make you feel like this?

Use words that show that you want to help. Say such things as:

- Is there anything I can do?
- I want to help you, but I can't if you won't tell me what's wrong.
- We're all behind you if you need us.

Accept your teen's fear as completely reasonable for him even if you think it is unreasonable. Offer your help in working things through. Say such things as:

- You have got to work this out, and I'm here to help.
- Tell me the problem, and let's see if we can come up with some solutions.
- I know you're scared, and you have every right to be. But here's another perspective on this.

Suggest a systematic approach to dealing with fear. Say such things as:

- How about writing down what's bothering you so we can look at it together?
- Let's write down the worst-case scenario and then the best one to get a better handle on things.
- What could happen that would get rid of your fear?

If your teen's fear seems to be a phobia or some kind of mental illness, don't hesitate to call for help. Find a psychiatrist or psychologist who can provide expert care.

WORDS AND PHRASES TO USE

- accept
- confident
- cope
- don't be afraid, we're here for you
- help
- I understand your fears
- let's talk things through carefully
- we all have our fears
- we'll protect you
- you're not alone

What Not to Say and Do

Never scoff at your teen's fears. Though they may seem irrational to you, they are very real to him. Scoffing will result in your teen's not confiding in you. Don't say such things as:

- Don't be silly. There's nothing to be afraid of.
- It's stupid to be afraid of that.
- Grow up.
- You're just a coward.

Never cut off discussion if your teen wants to talk. Don't say such things as:

- I don't want to hear about it.
- It's your problem, not mine, so keep it to yourself.
- Don't talk such nonsense.

- I don't have time now. Talk to me later.

Don't offer solutions and advice unless it's asked for. If you know your teen well, you can be the best judge of when he wants your help. Don't say such things as:

- I'm going to tell you what to do whether you want me to or not.
- Listen to me. I know what's best in a situation like this.
- Here's what you have to do.
- You either do this my way, or I don't want to hear any more about it.

Don't do an end run. Don't call people for help unless your teen agrees that it is the best way.

WORDS AND PHRASES TO AVOID

- baby/cry baby
- childish
- coward
- disaster
- don't tell me
- grow up
- how could you be afraid of that
- idiot
- I'm not interested
- immature
- unacceptable
- unbelievable
- unfounded
- you make me so angry

29 Feelings

In order to feel anything you need strength.

—ANNA MARIA OTESE

Saturday morning their dog died. Sarah was thirteen, and Josh was sixteen. Sarah cried. Josh didn't. He wouldn't let himself. His mom and dad, both quite weepy themselves, saw how upset he was and told him not to hold his feelings in. "Don't be afraid to cry. You'll feel much better." But Josh was adamant. "Men don't cry," he said. His mom and dad told him that was nonsense. Lots of men cry when they're sad. His dad said that he cried at long-distance telephone commercials. Josh was not amused. Sarah continued crying for her dead pet and felt much better for it. Josh wouldn't shed a tear in public, but in the privacy of his room he cried quietly to himself. Mom and dad wanted their son to be unashamed of his feelings and decided to talk to him about it.

Things to Consider

Your teens learn about gender stereotypes from a very young age. Girls are emotional and cry when they're hurt, sad, or happy. Boys are strong and cry when they're little but not when they're teenagers. Girls are nurturing and dependent. Boys are aggressive and independent. Girls show their feelings, and boys hide them.

You may have encouraged your boys to share their feelings openly, but did you succeed? It is not an easy thing for them because you have also taught them to be competitive and self-reliant in school, sports, jobs, and dating. Now you want them to express their feelings and to share them openly, but they resist. What do you say and do?

Consider the importance of your family context. Do you express your feelings easily? Do you hug and kiss one another? Do you cry openly when you're sad? Do you ever sing or dance with pleasure? In other words, what kind of models do your teens have for expressing feelings?

Feelings can be positive and negative. We don't want our boys and girls expressing their anger inappropriately. Anger and aggression need to be talked about but not acted out. Happiness and joy need to be expressed and shared.

Boys need dads as role models. Dads need to be involved in their sons' lives. Boys learn good things when this happens, such as how to be less overtly aggressive and competitive, and how to express feelings of sadness and fear. Boys need nurturing, and they need sensitive role models as much as girls do. They need to know how to express their own need for love, support, and dependence.

Three Things You Must Do

1. *Show* your own feelings.

2. *Encourage* your teen to express his feelings.

3. *Avoid* the tendency to gender-stereotype feelings.

What to Say and Do

Be a good role model for your teens. Be a parent who expresses his feelings. If you are sad, don't hide your tears. If you are happy, show it in what you say and do. If you are angry, show acceptable ways to express that anger (see Chapter 1). Create a family context in which it is good to share feelings, good or bad. Say such things as:

- In our house we're not ashamed of how we feel.
- I cry at the movies if they're sad.
- Men need to cry as much as women.
- I always enjoyed that TV program years ago where one of the young men always did his "dance of joy" when he was happy.

Encourage your teen to express his feelings. Listen to him. Make him comfortable doing it. Never scoff at or make fun of your son if he cries. Be open to his legitimate feelings and give him the love, attention, and sympathetic ear he needs. Say such things as:

- Tell me what's wrong.
- I'm here to listen and to help if I can.
- Tell me everything so I can understand your feelings.
- What are you feeling?
- You seem very happy. What's going on?

Know your child and treat him accordingly. Offer love and affection to both your girls and boys. Encourage your boys to express their feelings openly and truthfully. Don't discourage feelings of dependency or the need for love and affection. Help them manage feelings that can be destructive, such as anger, resentment, ambition, jealousy, and aggression. Show how they can be honestly felt, expressed, and controlled without doing anyone any damage. Say such things as:

- Don't hold back.
- It takes a strong person to show his feelings.
- It's healthy to express your feelings as long as you don't hurt anyone in doing so.
- I know you think men don't cry, but you're wrong. It's all right for men to cry.
- Feeling angry is okay as long as you don't do anything you'll regret. I usually do nothing when I'm angry until I've had a few days to think about it.

Create situations where you can see your teen honestly express his feelings. Involve yourself in his life so that you can share your feelings about your experiences together. Do such things as:

- Go out together to a movie, a ball game, the theater, lunch, or dinner.
- Go for hikes.
- Go skiing, skating, or swimming.
- Take your son to the ballet or your daughter to the car show.
- Play cards, chess, or other games.
- Go for a walk just to share yourselves and your feelings.

WORDS AND PHRASES TO USE

❥ are you happy	❥ both girls and boys need to share their feelings with someone	❥ I know how you feel	❥ share your feelings with me, and I'll share mine with you
❥ are you sad		❥ I understand	
❥ express your feelings		❥ I'm listening	❥ sympathy
	❥ go ahead and cry	❥ joy	❥ tell me about it

What Not to Say and Do

Never belittle your teen's feelings. If he has the courage to share them with you, accept them thankfully because most teens won't risk sharing their feelings with their parents. Don't say such things as:

- ❥ Grow up.
- ❥ What a silly way to feel.
- ❥ You have no right to feel that way.
- ❥ You're such a baby.
- ❥ I'm sick and tired of hearing how you feel about things.
- ❥ Welcome to the real world.
- ❥ You don't know what love is.

Never punish your teen for sharing his feelings with you. Listen without judging. Your teen simply wants a sympathetic ear. Provide one. Don't say such things as:

- ❥ I'm not interested in how you feel.
- ❥ You can't feel that way about him/her. I forbid you to see him/her again.
- ❥ If you can't stand up for yourself, you'll just have to take the consequences. Don't come running to me.
- ❥ You get what you deserve in this life.
- ❥ I'm glad you're feeling guilty. It's God's way of punishing you.

Don't treat your teens like gender stereotypes. Accept them for who they are and treat them accordingly. Don't say such things as:

- Boys don't cry.
- You're a sissy.
- You're overreacting.
- Don't give them sympathy. Get in there and beat the hell out of them.
- I don't care how you feel. If you're going to be man, get over it.
- That wouldn't scare a real boy.
- Girls don't feel that way. Be nice and gentle.

WORDS AND PHRASES TO AVOID

- be a man	- I'm not interested in how you feel	- sissy	- what a silly way to feel
- coward	- keep your feelings to yourself	- stop that silly crying	- you're just being immature
- don't bother me with such nonsense	- no daughter of mine would feel that way	- there's nothing to be afraid of	

30 Fitting In

I don't want to belong to any club that will accept me as a member.
— GROUCHO MARX

All teens face the problem of finding a place for themselves among their peers. A recent newspaper article explains how a seventeen-year-old boy solved this problem. A high school senior, he has a partially shaved head, speaks with a soft voice, carries a torn green school bag overflowing with crumpled school papers, two black drumsticks, an Orgy concert T-shirt, and videos of Marilyn Manson and Nine Inch Nails. He loves music and plays the snare drum in two school bands and the drums for a punk rock group.

Music, he says, makes it easier to balance his schoolwork, his part-time job at Wal-Mart, and coping with divorced parents. He quit the football team because he didn't like the way his teammates acted—too much pressure to be "cool." Instead he turned to drama where he didn't have to wear Tommy Hilfiger clothes and Nike shoes; he could have three ears and four eyes and people didn't care as long as he was a nice person. He disliked school cliques that encouraged inequality and some groups didn't like kids who didn't fit in. His solution was a small group of friends who didn't pick on people but accepted them for who they were. His opinion on loners who shoot their schoolmates: "If they went off and did something like that, they were already pretty messed up in the head."

Things to Consider

As always with teenagers, it's a case of who's in, who's out, what's in, and what's out—in sports, clothes, music, and academics. In junior and senior high schools teens begin to identify with other kids who share their interests and values. Teens need to be accepted by those kids.

You have no control over whether those kids accept your teens as a member of the group. It can break your heart to see your teens rejected by others. You must provide as much love and support as you can, knowing that it can't make up for their rejection. If they're accepted, you must make it your business to know as much as you can about that group. How do they dress? How do they spend their time? What music do they listen to? What do they do in school and after school? What are their collective values and ambitions? Talk to your teens regularly. Spend time with them. Show that you love and support them so that they don't have to depend on others for what they should be getting from their parents.

You have helped make your teens their own persons by being a role model. They have learned by watching how you behave toward members of your own group and outsiders. Children learn normal behavior from their parents—but only to a point. After that the peer group takes over and sets the standards of dress, talk, interests, and behavior.

Some groups have kids who are noisier, more noticed by others, and more imitated in tastes of dress, music, and activities. They are the pacesetters, the popular clique. But there are many other cliques in schools. It is hoped that your teens' group are nonviolent and non-drug-using or abusing. You can tolerate their strange clothes, language, and music. Gang membership is another matter. You might have to take drastic measures to protect your teens, such as professional counselling.

You can help your teens fit in by helping them be the same as their group. Don't make arbitrary rules about ways to dress, curfews, leisure time, and other matters that will make them different or prevent them from taking part in their group's everyday life. You should not sacrifice your moral or religious beliefs for the sake of your child's fitting in, but your parenting should take account of your teens' very real and important need to fit in.

Three Things You Must Do

1. *Recognize* that your teen needs to fit in with some group.

2. *Understand* that you have very little say as to which group accepts them.

3. *Know* as much as you can about your teen's group.

What to Say and Do

It is best for you to have always been involved in your teen's life and have a good talking relationship with him. You can talk to him easily about the importance of fitting in while emphasizing that the most important thing is who you are and how you treat others. Say such things as:

- What are the cliques like at school?
- Which are in and which are out?
- What are the "in" things just now?
- Do the jocks hassle people?
- Do you still hang out with the same people?

Fitting in always has its problems. See if you can get your teen to talk about any "fitting-in" fears he may have. Say such things as:

- Any problems at school?
- Are you getting along with your friends okay?
- What's new in your life? Any concerns?
- Do kids spread nasty rumors about other kids at your school?
- How do the cliques at your school get along?
- Are you happy with your group of friends?

You can discuss the pros and cons of cliques. Discuss values, self-esteem, discrimination, inclusion, and exclusion. Say such things as:

- I know you need to belong, to fit in at school, but it is important to consider other things, such as people's feelings and being nice to people.
- I know that your clique has some good values, particularly that you value everyone for who they are. But we both know that not all cliques are like that.
- You would never want to belong to a group that discriminated against other kids simply because they were different, would you?
- In your clique how do you decide who gets in and who doesn't?
- The most important thing is your self-esteem. If you value yourself, then you don't have to worry about fitting in or not.

If your teen belongs or wants to belong to a gang, you need to do whatever you can to stop him. Gangs are a symptom of an environment of fear, mistrust, and territoriality. Teen gangs attract members who are afraid, need security, and typically have low self-esteem and low self-confidence. If your child belongs to a gang, you need to reevaluate your relationship with him. Get expert help from psychologists, social workers, or police youth gang officers. Do whatever you can to get your teen out of that situation.

WORDS AND PHRASES TO USE

✦ be yourself	✦ exclusionary	✦ membership	✦ tolerance
✦ belonging	✦ fashion	✦ peers	✦ values
✦ clique	✦ gang	✦ self-confidence	✦ violence
✦ confidence	✦ kindness	✦ self-esteem	✦ who's in, who's out

What Not to Say and Do

Don't say anything that will hurt your teen's self-esteem. He may think that other kids don't value him for who he is. Don't make it worse by saying such things as:

- ✦ I'm not surprised you haven't impressed your schoolmates.
- ✦ I'm not surprised that nobody wants you in their clique.
- ✦ You're a loser.
- ✦ Get a life, will you?

Don't neglect your teen. Don't avoid being involved in your teen's life. Don't say such things as:

- ✦ I don't have time for you now.
- ✦ I'd like to, but I'm too busy.
- ✦ Don't bring your teenage world home to me.
- ✦ I don't want to meet your friends.
- ✦ You call that music? Turn that garbage off.

Don't encourage your teen to join exclusionary cliques. Don't say such things as:

- ▶ I'm all in favor of discrimination. Some kinds of people are just bad.
- ▶ You don't want to be friends with just anybody.

Don't set a bad example for your teen.

Don't belong to clubs that discriminate against people.

Don't make jokes that demean other groups in society.

Don't encourage any kind of violent behavior against others.

WORDS AND PHRASES TO AVOID

▶ hate	▶ kill	▶ stupid	▶ you'll never fit in
▶ I don't like whites, blacks, Asians, or Latinos	▶ no wonder you don't have any friends	▶ they're ruining our country	▶ you're stupid
▶ keep them out	▶ nobody would want you in his clique	▶ you can't trust anyone but yourself	

31 Food

Never eat more than you can lift.

—Miss Piggy

"Lauren! Coke, chips, and cheese doodles do not make a balanced diet."

"It's okay, Mom. I eat lots of other things, too."

"I know you do, and, no, it's not okay. You fill up with a lot of empty calories, and then you add real ones on top of that. You seem to be eating all the time. I'm going to make you a balanced lunch to take to school, and you'd better eat it and not that other stuff."

Teenagers don't have a great sense of nutrition. Lauren didn't. She thought any calories were better than no calories. She was close to being a compulsive eater. And her sister, Carrie, thought that anything with no calories was better than anything with calories. Their parents watched Lauren getting fat from eating too much, while Carrie looked anorexic from not eating enough. Lauren constantly ate junk food when she was out and everything in sight when she was home. Carrie was too thin and getting thinner even though she thought she was fat. Both children had eating problems and needed professional help.

Things to Consider

Teenage girls have problems with food. Some of them tend to extremes and have eating disorders. Some become compulsive eaters, take comfort in food, eat too much, and get fat. Some have a distorted sense of their own bodies and have anorexia nervosa (self-induced starvation) or bulimia nervosa (binge eating and purging). In either case, food is a problem for them—either too much or too little. But it is more than food. In fact, these diseases often have little to do with food. These are serious psychological and physiological problems.

Teenage boys have it easier. Only 5 to 10 percent of teens with eating disorders are boys. They don't worry too much about body image, although more boys now compare their bodies to TV images such as the guys on *Baywatch*. For most boys the problem is getting the right kind of food in sufficient quantities. If allowed, they will eat everything in sight.

Ensure good nutrition for your teens and make sure that they have a healthy diet and a healthy image of themselves to go along with it. Your teens are no longer at home as much as they used to be, and you don't have the same control over what they eat. They're concerned about fitting in and often have an extreme sensitivity about their weight. Girls complain about fat thighs and stomachs. Boys don't want to be the skinny or fat kid in the bathing suit. Help them be aware of the truth about their bodies and their habits. If your teens exhibit any signs of an eating disorder, seek professional help right away. Don't think you can treat it yourself.

However, there are some things you can do. Carefully monitor your daughter's weight and eating habits. Some estimates say that 2 percent of girls between the ages of fourteen and twenty-five are anorexic. Acquire information on anorexia and bulimia, and look for any of the warning signs. The signs of anorexia:

- an obsession about food
- unusual eating habits such as cutting food into tiny pieces
- constantly feeling cold
- noticeable weight loss
- excessive exercising

The signs of bulimia:

- eating large amounts of foods but with little weight gain
- excessive sensitivity, secrecy, and irritability about food
- going to the bathroom after meals to vomit in secret
- chronic sore throat and hoarseness
- evidence of vomiting or using a laxative

If your teens exhibit these symptoms, tell your physician immediately.

Know your teens. Know their sensitivities and plan a healthy diet around them. Help them with their self-esteem and to cope with their body type, whatever it is. Encourage good eating habits and good exercise habits. Talk about the latest research that suggests we are more or less stuck with our body type. Show your teens that you eat right, exercise often, and have a good self-image. Have only a small supply of junk food and drink in the house for special occasions. Discuss the male and female body stereotypes we get from movies, TV, and magazines. Advise your teens on clothing styles that are right for their body type.

You can do all these things and more to make sure your teens eat well and think well of themselves.

Three Things You Must Do

1. *Know* your teen's eating habits.
2. *Help* your teen accept her body.
3. *Be alert* to signs of eating disorders.

What to Say and Do

Listen to your teen talk about herself and her friends. Pay attention to how she talks about food, eating, her body and anyone else's. Say such things as:

- Do you guys eat a lot of junk food at school? I like a little junk food sometimes as a treat.
- Do you think s/he has a good body? How do you suppose s/he gets a body like that?
- I think teenage guys and girls don't eat very well. What do you think?

Talk about dieting and body type. Talk about whether your teen really needs to be thinner and what to do if she does. Say such things as:

- Our doctor can tell you how to lose weight sensibly and how to keep it off.
- Did you know that we all have our own weight set point that our bodies try to maintain? That's why some of us are heavier or lighter than others even though we eat the same amount of food. We can lower the set point through good eating and good exercise.
- If you could look different, how would you like to look? Why?

Help your teen's self-esteem. Say things that will encourage her to accept her body type and make the most of it. Say such things as:

- No matter how good you look, you'll always be able to find someone with a prettier face, a better body, or a smaller waist, or someone who's more handsome, more muscular, taller, or stronger. You need to make the most of what you have.
- Don't be ashamed because you like to eat. Eat sensibly and don't eat more than you need.
- We love you because of who you are. We think you look great just as you are.

Talk about eating disorders. Talk about the symptoms. If you think your teen suffers from one of these disorders, ask her about it. But don't assume she will tell you the truth or that you can treat a disorder without professional help. If your teen comes to you and says she has such a disorder, treat her as you would if she had pneumonia or hepatitis and take her to the doctor.

Talk to your teen about the elements of a good diet. Tell her how important it is for her looks and complexion. Write it out for her and put it on the fridge door.

WORDS AND PHRASES TO USE

a balanced diet	compulsive eating	five food groups	overweight
anorexia nervosa	dieting	good health	underweight
body image	eating disorders	junk food	vitamins
bulimia nervosa	exercise	nutrition	

What Not to Say and Do

Don't make a big thing about your teen's weight as long as it is in the normal range. Don't say such things as:

- You're a big fat tub, aren't you?
- You can never be too rich or too thin.
- One moment on the lips, a lifetime on the hips.

Don't encourage your child to eat junk food. Don't have it around the house. Don't eat lots of it yourself. Keep the sour cream, onion chips, Cheez Doodles, and Oreo cookies for special occasions.

Don't encourage indiscriminate dieting. Don't say such things as:

- You need to get on a serious diet.
- You'll never lose weight unless you diet.
- I have got a great diet to show you.

Don't think you can treat an eating disorder without professional help. And don't trust your teen to cure herself or be honest with you about her eating habits.

Don't trust food chains to provide a balanced diet for your teen or yourself. Their staples are meat, salt, and fat, which are fine in moderation but not without dairy products, vegetables, fruits, and whole grains.

Don't trust your teen to feed herself. Don't say such things as:

- I'm depending on you to make your own meals. I'm just too busy at work.
- You can do the shopping and cooking for yourself. You're a big boy/girl now.

Don't use mealtimes as an opportunity to lecture your kids. Don't say such things as:

- Let me give you some advice.
- Now listen to me. I wanted to talk to you about that terrible thing you did the other day.

WORDS AND PHRASES TO AVOID

• exercise is no good for you	• I'll give you money to eat lunch and dinner each day at that hamburger place	• you could look like a movie star if you wanted to
• I don't care what you eat as long as you stop complaining that you're hungry all the time	• start a diet	• you have to finish everything on your plate
	• when are you going to lose some weight	• you're a little fatty, aren't you

32 Friends

Friends may come and go, but enemies accumulate.

—Thomas Jones

Jack's parents were worried about two of his friends. They didn't know much about them, but what they knew they didn't like. Jack was a sophomore in high school, but these friends were either seniors or not in school anymore. He still palled around with his old friends from elementary school who were also sophomores, but he seemed to value these new friends more.

When asked about them, he said they were cool guys who knew their way around. Knew their way around what? He never actually came out and said what. Jack's parents worried that that meant drugs and other illicit things, although they never suspected Jack of taking drugs or doing anything illegal. Nevertheless, they were not happy about these friends and decided to try to find out more about them, not just for Jack's sake but for their own.

Things to Consider

Know as much as you can about your teens' friends. They are a window into the lives of your teens. You can often see your teens' interests, talents, and weaknesses reflected in their friends. The better you know your teens' friends, the better you will know your teens.

Sometimes your teens' friends won't be all that you think they should be. This should have nothing to do with their appearance, race, religion, ethnicity, or any stereotypical label. Legitimate concerns are that these friends are a bad influence on your children, causing them to neglect schoolwork, do drugs, steal, or generally get them into trouble.

Keep track of your teens' friends by being involved in your teens' lives. Have regular conversations about what they do when they're not home. Have them invite their friends over for lunch or dinner. Make your home a place where your teens' friends are always welcome. Let your teens have a party at your house. Make friends with your teens' friends.

My wife and I made our house a place where our teens and their friends would feel comfortable, and this has paid off. We had kids around talking, playing, watching TV, listening to music, and sleeping over. We knew some of our teens' friends almost as well as we knew our teens.

We didn't preach, judge, or yell at them or their friends. We trusted these kids to do the right thing, and most of the time they did—not always, but there were no serious transgressions. And we had conversations because we were interested in them, in their schoolwork, sports, families, pets, tastes in movies, books, and music. We treated their friends as we would treat our own friends.

One word of caution: You can't pick your teens' friends. You can make your feelings known, but don't expect your teens to accept or reject a friend on your say-so. With some teens, your objection will make them more devoted to that friend. Know your teens, and know their friends before you try to interfere because it may backfire.

Three Things You Must Do

1. *Be involved* in your teen's life.
2. *Know* as much about their friends as you can.
3. *Make* your home a welcoming and friendly place.

What to Say and Do

Talk about your teen's friends. Ask questions about them. Say such things as:

- How's _____ doing? You two still hang out together a lot, don't you?
- Made any new friends at school? Tell me about them.
- I like your friend _____. How's s/he doing?

My niece went through a serious "punk" period. Her mother sat down one day and told her that looking punk could have consequences. She said such things as:

- You can wear your hair pink and in spikes. I don't mind. But some of your friends' parents may not like their kids having a punk teenager as a friend. If you're okay with this so am I.

- We have an appointment with your school counselor to talk about your schoolwork in the coming term and I'm going to ask her to tell you how some kids might treat you because of the way you look. I'm sure she'll tell you the same thing I have—that your punk look will make some kids reject you. Again, if you're okay with this so am I.

Make friends with your teen's friends. Invite them to stay for lunch or dinner. Talk to them about their lives. Show that you're interested in them. Say such things as:

- Would you like a soda?

- Are you and _____ in the same classes at school?

- Any brothers or sisters?

- Are you on any teams or clubs at school?

- Would you like to stay for lunch/dinner?

Friends are the people who love you for what you are. But teens can be fickle friends. You can talk to your teen about problems he will inevitably have. Say such things as:

- Even friends can be mean sometimes and tease you. Try to laugh it off. Make a joke of it if you can.

- If your friends make a joke about your size, your looks, your hair, or your boobs, try to laugh also. DON'T TAKE IT SERIOUSLY. If you laugh too, they will stop doing it.

- Real friends will never put you in danger or ask you to break the law.

- Real friends love you and want the best for you.

WORDS AND PHRASES TO USE

- affectionate	- good friends don't judge because they know who you are	- real friends	- trustworthy
- faithful/honest		- safe	- with good friends you can think out loud
- fun	- love	- sense of humor	
		- teasing	

What Not to Say and Do

Don't think your teen will accept your choice of friends for him. If your teen's friends are really dangerous for him, you might have to take drastic action. But if you don't like him because of the way he looks or talks, what you think may not matter. Don't say such things as:

- S/he isn't a suitable friend for you. I don't care what you think, I don't want you associating with him/her.
- You are never to see him/her again, and I certainly don't want him/her in my house.

Don't put your desire for a clean, orderly house above your teen's need to have friends over. Don't say such things as:

- You can't have your friends over. They always make a mess.
- You can't have a party. You'll wreck the house.
- If you want to be with your friends, go to their house.

If your teen seems isolated, without friends, don't blame her. You may need to get professional help for your teen. Don't make a bad situation worse by saying such things as:

- The way you look I'm not surprised you have no friends.
- Who'd want to be your friend? I wouldn't.
- You'd make a terrible friend.

Don't ignore your teen's friends. Don't say such things as:

- I'm not interested in who your friends are.
- I don't want to meet your friends. One teenager in this house is more than enough.
- Your friends are your business.
- Keep your friends away from me.
- Your friends are probably a bunch of crack-head dope pushers.

WORDS AND PHRASES TO AVOID

- crack-head	- losers	- slackers	- villain
- criminal	- miserable	- stupid	- your friends are terrible
- dope pusher	- rowdy	- thieves	

33 Girls

Girls are always running through my mind. They don't dare walk.

—Andy Gibb

Bobby had a crush on Jeanne. They were both fifteen and sophomores in high school. Bobby had first noticed her last year. This year she was in his math class. She was smart and beautiful. He was smitten, but he was shy. He had never taken a girl out alone before. He wanted to ask her to a movie but didn't have the courage. He was afraid she'd say no. He talked to his friends about her. They suggested he ask her girlfriends if she was going out with anyone. A friend of his asked a friend of hers and learned that she wasn't going out with anyone else. He called her on a Tuesday evening. With his hands shaking slightly and his voice thin and nervous he asked if she had seen the latest hit movie. She hadn't. Would she like to go with him this Saturday night? After what seemed to Bobby like an eternity of waiting, she said she would. After he hung up, he began to wonder about how he could impress her. His mom might have some advice for him, he thought. After all, she was a girl once, he thought. He would ask her.

Things to Consider

Girls are just like boys, only different. Does that make sense? Probably no more sense than girls make to most boys. What can you tell your teenage son about teenage girls that would help both him and the girl of his affections? Getting him to talk about the girl and the way he feels would be a good beginning, and one that would allow you to talk about girls in general and this girl in particular.

The most important thing to say to your son about girls is that he must treat them with respect. He must be kind, thoughtful, and considerate of their feelings and needs. He mustn't think of them as objects or stereotypes. He must never be abusive or put them in any danger.

Having said that, you need to impress upon him that girls are not help-less, fragile creatures that need to be protected. They aren't the stereotypical girls of many Hollywood movies who scream with fright or faint at the sight of blood, who stand terrified while a boyfriend is dismembered by a maniac returned from the grave. Real girls are strong, courageous people who can be ambitious and aggressive as well as sensitive and supportive. They need to be valued for the independent, competent people they are.

You can tell your son what experts have said: that girls and boys grow up in different worlds even within the same family. Girls learn cooperation and equal-ity while boys learn power and control. But you can also tell him what I have pointed out in an earlier book on communication: Generalized gender differences don't tell us how to best relate to the woman or man in front of us because each has a distinct history, personality, talents, abilities, dreams, and goals.

Tell your son that he can best impress and be successful with the girl of his affections by getting to know her as a real person and then treating her as she likes to be treated. But also warn him that a thing we call "chemistry" is what finally determines how she feels about him. If the chemistry isn't there, she won't really go for him even if he is the nicest boy in the world.

Three Things You Must Do

1. *Tell* your son that girls are individual persons, not stereotypes.

2. *Teach* your son to treat girls with respect and consideration.

3. *Show* your son that girls can be as strong and courageous in their own way as boys.

What to Say and Do

Tell your son that the most important thing to remember about girls is that they want to be treated with respect, kindness, and understanding. In that respect they are no different from boys. Say such things as:

- If you want to impress your date, be nice to her. Listen to what she says, admire the way she looks, and treat her the way you would like her to treat you.

- Girls like boys who consider their feelings and their likes and dislikes.
- Girls like boys who don't put them in uncomfortable, embarrassing, or dangerous situations.

Point out that each girl must be understood as an individual. Tell him that although we tend to generalize about girls and boys, in reality those are often hollow comments. Say such things as:

- Do you think all boys are the same? Then don't assume that all girls are the same.
- Forget about Hollywood images of females. They're fiction.
- Generalizations about girls don't tell you how to interact with them.

Girls, like boys, can be strong, courageous, caring, and supportive, depending on what the situation calls for. Say such things as:

- Boys may be physically stronger than girls, but that doesn't mean girls are weak.
- Girls have goals, ambitions, and desires and will work hard to achieve them.
- Don't believe those films where the girl screams and watches while the bad guy fights with her boyfriend. A real girl would assist in fending off the bad guy.

Chemistry is the thing that makes the difference. It's sometimes heartbreaking but true. Unless the girl feels that certain something, which is indefinable and often inexplicable, your son doesn't stand a chance, no matter how nice, understanding, and handsome he may be. But tell your son there is also a plus side to this. It means that almost any boy has a chance with almost any girl because girls, once the initial rush is over, do not look at boys the same way boys look at girls. A boy may not be handsome or even good looking, yet there is some girl out there who will find him as attractive as Leonardo Di Caprio.

Finally, and this really should be done first, let your son tell you how he feels about girls in general and about any special girl in particular. Say such things as:

- I've done most of the talking. It's your turn to tell me what you think about girls.

> ◆ Tell me about the girls you know. Is there anyone really special? What makes her so special?
> ◆ What kind of girl do you find most attractive?

WORDS AND PHRASES TO USE

◆ ambitious	◆ brave	◆ nice	◆ smart
◆ athletic	◆ clever	◆ sensitive	◆ strong
◆ attractive	◆ courageous	◆ sexy	◆ supportive
◆ beautiful	◆ intelligent	◆ sincere	

What Not to Say and Do

Don't reinforce the stereotypes by talking about girls as though they were all helpless, flighty, boy-crazy teenagers who read romance novels and *Seventeen* magazine. Don't say such things as:

> ◆ Girls only need to go to college to find a good husband.
> ◆ A girl doesn't need a career because she's only going to get married and have kids anyway.
> ◆ Girls shouldn't play most sports. It's very unladylike.
> ◆ Girls are only interested in boys and clothes.

If you are antifeminist, don't get carried away by it. Try to give a balanced picture to your son. Don't such say things as:

> ◆ I think a girl's first responsibility is to grow up to be a good wife and mother.
> ◆ I'm against women who want as much power as men. Men have to be in charge.
> ◆ A woman only goes into business because she can't find a good man.

Don't try to keep your son from dating girls. Most teens start dating in high school, some as young as junior high. A good age is fourteen for group gatherings, sixteen for solo dates. Don't say such things as:

- I don't care what your friends do, you can't date until you're eighteen.
- I wouldn't let you go out with a girl whose parents let her go out before she's eighteen.

Don't encourage or reinforce your son in any misogynistic attitudes or behaviors. Don't say such things as:

- I don't know what you see in that slut.
- That tramp is only interested in one thing.
- Girls are worthless. I ought to know since I am one.
- I've never met a girl who was the equal of any boy her own age.
- You should never take girls seriously.
- Only ugly girls are feminists.
- No girl is good enough for my son.

WORDS AND PHRASES TO AVOID

- brainless	- it's just PMS	- slut	- tramp
- cowardly	- just a pretty face	- they're only interested in boys and clothes	- vain
- empty-headed	- scatterbrained		- weak
- flighty	- shallow		

34 Goals

The future is much like the present, only longer.

—Don Quisenberry

Louise's mom and dad had concerns over her apparent lack of goals. She did fairly well in school but seemed to have no need to excel. She liked sports and belonged to the soccer and volleyball teams but didn't seem to care whether she won or lost. Her parents talked to her about college, hoping to find that Louise had some career goals or at least some general goals in life. They were disappointed to find that she had no plans for what she was going to do after high school, to say nothing of what she wanted to do with her life. Louise's main goal seemed to be to get by in school, with her friends, and with her parents. Other than that she loved clothes and music, and was planning to get a part-time job after school and on weekends so that she could better afford to buy the things she liked. Her mom and dad decided to talk to Louise about the importance of having specific goals to strive for that would help give meaning and direction to her life.

Things to Consider

Know your teenagers' attitudes toward goals in life in order to know whether goals are their thing. For most teens having goals is a positive thing, and you can help them on the road to achieving them. First, help your teenagers evaluate their talents, abilities, likes, and dislikes in relation to possible goals in life as a way of choosing appropriate goals. If your teenagers are shy and don't like meeting new people, their goal should not be to become president of the United States. If they can't do long division and don't understand compound interest, becoming an accountant should not be a career goal.

Second, help your teens work out a plan for achieving their ambitions. If going to a fine college is a goal, you can send for a copy of that college's catalogue or look up its admission requirements on the Internet. Work backward from this goal to plan your teens' high school program. If they want to be a musician or singer, you can help them with lessons, a good instrument, and a place to practice.

But what should you say to teens who have no obvious goals in life other than to enjoy being teens? Involve yourself in your teens' lives so that you know how they spend their time, what they like to do, and how well they do it. Know how well your children are doing in high school and the subjects they excel in. Talk to their teachers about their work and their interests in school. If they're on a team, watch them play, watch them interact with other kids, and talk to their coach about their attitude and work ethic.

Don't despair if your children have no goals unless they are also real problem children. If your children do well in school and have obvious talents for other things, have no trouble making and keeping friends, and are nice people, accept their lack of goals as their way of living. It's a personality thing more than a lack of ambition or intelligence. You have children who are more willing to go with life's flow. Their goal is to see what life brings them rather than to actively seek it out. Accept this as a legitimate approach to living.

Three Things You Must Do

1. *Know* your teen's attitude to goal setting.

2. *Help* your teen set realistic goals and good plans for reaching them.

3. *Accept* your teen who is not goal-oriented or a plan maker.

What to Say and Do

Know what your teenager thinks about goal setting and talk accordingly. Say such things as:

- Do you have any plans for college?
- Are you hoping to get an "A" in math this year?
- Tell me what your goals are, and I'll tell you mine.

You and your teen should talk about her talents, abilities, likes, and dislikes in relation to her goals. You can help her to be ambitious but realistic. Say such things as:

- You're really good at _____. Do you like doing it?
- What do you think you're best at in school?
- If you could be anything you wanted to be, what would you choose? What do you need to be that?

Help your teen work out a plan for reaching her goals. Say such things as:

- You want to achieve this. Let's look at how you can best do it.
- If you want to go to Harvard, you need more than top grades because everyone who applies to Harvard has top grades. You need those grades plus all kinds of outside activities in sports, the community, volunteer work, and summer jobs. Let's see what you have and what you need.
- If you want to make the soccer team next year, you need to start training right now to improve your skills. Let's get some instructional videos and see what you can work on.

If your teen has no obvious goals in life other than to enjoy being a teen, talk to her about what she wants out of life. Don't criticize her approach. Say such things as:

- What courses are you taking in school? How are you doing?
- What are you going to do this summer?
- Have you given any thought to college?

If your child does well in school and has obvious talent for other things, has no trouble making and keeping friends, and is a nice person, accept her lack of goals as her way of living. Say such things as:

- You don't like making plans, do you?
- I know you don't like setting goals for yourself, but there are times when you need to plan ahead if you want to do something later. Like going to college means you have to meet the admission requirements.
- I know the kind of person you are, and I love you for it. I just want you to be prepared for what life gives you since you are not the kind of person who goes after what you want.

WORDS AND PHRASES TO USE

✦ abilities	✦ goals	✦ I love you for who you are	✦ realistic
✦ action	✦ happiness	✦ plan ahead to reach your goals	✦ take what comes
✦ ambitions	✦ how to get what you want		✦ talents
✦ drive			

What Not to Say and Do

Accept your teen for who she is. Don't criticize her for not having specific goals. Don't say such things as:

- ✦ If you don't set your goals now and go after them, you're a loser.
- ✦ I don't how you can waste your life by not knowing where you're going.
- ✦ I want you to sit down now and write out your goals, and I'll tell you if they're right for you.
- ✦ If you don't have goals and plans on how to reach them, you'll be a failure in life.
- ✦ I think you're a lazy bum. You have no ambition.

Don't encourage your teen to set unrealistic goals. You may simply be trying to live your fantasy life through your teen, and it isn't fair to her. Don't say such things as:

- ✦ I don't care what you say. If you wanted to be the quarterback on the football team, you could if you were willing to work hard enough.
- ✦ You could go to M.I.T. if you wanted to. You can get "A" in math if you try harder.
- ✦ I don't care if you don't want to be a lawyer. It's a good job for a woman. Someday you could be the first woman President of the United States.

Don't discourage your teen from discussing her hopes and dreams with you. Don't belittle her or be always too busy to listen. Don't say such things as:

- ✦ I'm not interested in dreams, just results.
- ✦ Don't be silly. You don't have the brains to go to college.

- We can talk later. I'm too busy to talk now.
- I want you to go into a profession. I'm not interested in hearing anything else from you.
- You can do what you want. Just don't expect me to be here for you if you don't do what I want you to do.
- That's a dumb goal. You'll never do it.

WORDS AND PHRASES TO AVOID

- bum	- lazy	- you can't just drift through life	- you have to have a plan
- dumb	- stupid	- you have no ambition	- you have to have goals
- failure	- unfocused		
- I'm too busy			

35 Gratitude

The best way to get praise is to die.

—Italian Proverb

Sophie's mom worked for weeks on Sophie's dress for the senior prom. They had gone together to the fabric store and picked out a pattern and some material. After that Mom spread out the cloth on the dining room table, pinned the pattern to it, and cut on the dotted line. She spent the next two weeks working in the evenings and on weekends sewing it together, fitting it on Sophie, and making adjustments for her shape which wasn't a perfect size six but close enough for there to be only a few minor changes. The dress was finally finished the evening of the prom. Sophie modeled it for her parents. They thought she looked beautiful. Sophie said a quick thank-you to her mom and went off to get ready for her date. On Monday afternoon a bouquet of beautiful flowers was delivered to Sophie's mom with a card that said, "Thanks, Mom. I love you. Sophie" Sophie's dad had suggested it as a way for her to show her appreciation for all the work her mom had done on her dress. Sophie loved the idea and wondered why she hadn't thought of it herself. She went to the local florist at lunchtime and paid for the flowers out of her allowance.

Things to Consider

When was the last time you were really grateful for someone's help but forgot to thank him appropriately? Did you think, I'm sure he knows how much I appreciate what he has done for me. I don't really have to call him or send a card or flowers or some other kind of gift. He would be embarrassed.

It happens to the best of us. Teens are not noted for their outward expression of gratitude. It isn't cool. Besides, teens are usually too busy thinking about themselves. We all do that, only teens do it a lot. Your teen has an infinite capacity for self-absorption. Life is a novel, and your teens are the main characters. Often, when reminded that someone deserves a really big thank-you, teens will say the person must know how grateful they are already. Your teens will shout, scream, and jump up and down for music or sports, but saying a sincere thank-you can be an effort.

Teens sometimes need to be taught how to say thank-you. It's not a character flaw. If they have grown up surrounded by a loving family that is eager to help them in any and every way, they take it for granted that this is the way families are. You are just doing your job. You don't need to be thanked. Teens need reminding that everyone needs to be appreciated for what they do.

No one likes to be taken for granted. It means we disappear. If we hold the door for people, make a phone call on their behalf, coach them in a sport, help them with schoolwork, write a job reference for them, give them a gift, or make them a dress, we need to be thanked. It shows the person noticed that we did something we didn't have to do. On the deepest level gratitude shows love. Taking kindness for granted is a form of aggression, the opposite of love. Teens need reminding on how to show gratitude since adolescents, especially boys, often seem to prefer aggression to love.

Don't hesitate to remind your teens to thank Grandma and Grandpa for their lovely Christmas present or to thank their coach, teacher, friends, and family for all the things they've done for them. Teach them that being too grateful, though gauche, is forgivable, especially in teens. But not being grateful enough is unforgivable. Point out that gratitude needs explicit expression. Teens mustn't count on people reading their minds. Say it, show it, be it. Teach your teens how to show gratitude by setting a good example in your own life.

Three Things You Must Do

1. *Teach* your teen the importance of saying thank-you.

2. *Teach* her by your own example.

3. *Teach* your teen that gratitude is an expression of love.

What to Say and Do

Remind your teen that everyone needs to be appreciated for what she does. Point out situations in which people didn't have to do what they did. Ask your teen what she thinks about the situation. Say such things as:

- ✦ Wasn't that nice of _____ to do what she did for you?
- ✦ Did you notice what _____ did?
- ✦ Isn't it wonderful how kind some people can be? Did you notice what he did?

Never assume that your teen will remember to thank someone. She may take much for granted, and other people's kindness may go unremarked by her. Say such things as:

- ✦ Please remember to call _____ and thank him/her.
- ✦ Have you called _____ to say thank-you?
- ✦ Don't forget to send _____ a thank-you note.
- ✦ I think what she did deserves some flowers, don't you?

Point out that what someone did was out of the ordinary. Make it clear that this was above and beyond the call of duty. Say such things as:

- ✦ You realize that _____ didn't have to do what he did, don't you?
- ✦ How are you going to thank her for that special kindness?
- ✦ He must think very highly of you to have done that for you.

Help your teen realize that expressing gratitude is a way of showing love. When she shows this nonromantic form of love, she helps make it possible for us to live in peace with one another. When she takes kindness for granted, she shows a form of aggression that pushes people away. Say such things as:

- ✦ People don't like being taken for granted. It makes it seem as though they don't exist.
- ✦ Gratitude is a great thing. It says you appreciate the kindness done to you, and you are returning it by showing you're grateful.
- ✦ If you don't thank people, you offend them.

Your teen mustn't count on people reading her mind. Help her understand that she has to say it, show it, be it. Say such things as:

- I know you're grateful to _____, but I think you need to show her how grateful you are.
- Don't assume that _____ can read your mind. Tell her how grateful you are for what she did.
- Why don't you give _____ a small present, such as a book, flowers, or chocolates, to show them just how much you appreciate what they've done for you?

Set a good example for your teen by showing your gratitude toward others for every kindness they show you. It is best if this comes naturally and isn't phony or forced.

WORDS AND PHRASES TO USE

appreciation	expression of thanks	present	thanks
beyond the call of duty	gratitude	reminder	thank-you note
don't expect someone to know what you're thinking	kindness	show how much it means to you	token of appreciation
	love	taken for granted	

What Not to Say and Do

The rule here is not to let your teen take someone for granted. Don't say such things as:

- You don't have to thank them. They were only doing their job.
- Forget about thanking them. They owed me one.
- You said thanks. That's enough.

Don't set a bad example by being ungrateful. Don't say such things as:

- I got what I deserved.

- It was the least they could have done.
- Saying thank-you is a form of weakness.

Don't discourage your teen from showing gratitude. Don't say such things as:

- You don't have to write a note. They know how grateful you are.
- Save your money. They won't notice it anyway.
- Don't give them flowers. What they did wasn't that great.
- If you give them a gift, they'll think you're a phony.

WORDS AND PHRASES TO AVOID

- anyone else would have done as much	- it was nothing out of the ordinary	- save your money - she doesn't deserve to be thanked	- they know you're grateful
- don't bother to thank him	- nothing special		- you deserved it

36 Guns

There is nothing more exhilarating than to be shot at without result.
—Winston Churchill

Nigel and his parents were sitting at the dinner table the day after the shootings at Columbine High School in Littleton, Colorado. He couldn't understand how kids could do a terrible thing like that. Now seventeen, he had owned a gun since he was eight when his father bought him a .22-caliber rifle so he could go hunting squirrels and rabbits with him. The first thing his father taught him was to always make sure it was unloaded when he wasn't out hunting. In the house his gun was kept locked up in the cabinet with his father's other guns. His father had the key. He knew that the ammunition was locked in a drawer in a cabinet in another room. His father had that key, too.

"What's wrong with those kids?" his mom wondered.

"It happens too much in our country," said his father. "Parents don't bring their kids up right," he continued.

"I don't think it's just that," said his mom. "I don't think kids should have guns."

"That's nonsense," said his father. "Guns don't kill people, people kill people. I blame these killings on a lack of discipline at home and in school."

Things to Consider

Nigel's dad is right. People kill. But he is also wrong. Guns kill. That's what guns do. They kill people and animals. That is why most countries in the civilized world have restrictive laws concerning gun ownership. Very few mass shootings of schoolchildren take place outside the United States, partly because guns are not easily available. And it's almost impossible to kill a roomful of people with a knife or a stick.

A recent survey found that 42 percent of households in the United States have guns. Fortunately, most of these guns don't get used to kill people. But enough do to make it important that you decide what your family gun policy is.

We may never be sure why some kids shoot others. We can say that it's caused by a lack of parental discipline or by violence in movies, television, and pop music videos. But we'll never know for sure. That's all the more reason to make guns hard to get, especially for teens.

Talk about the need for guns in your house. Talk about the kinds of guns you have and why you have them. Are they for protection, for hunting, for target shooting, for collecting? Talk about guns and killing, and help your teens understand your views. Let them tell you theirs. If you hunt, talk about the reasons for killing animals for sport.

Talk about the precautions you take with your guns. They should be locked away and the ammunition stored separately. They should have childproof locks. They should never be kept loaded.

Make sure your teen has proper training in the use and care of firearms. If you hunt, send him to a hunter safety course. If you target shoot, have him take a club safety course. Teach him how to hunt safely. Let him see what happens when you aim at a deer and pull the trigger.

Many adults speculate that kids don't understand the consequences of pulling a trigger because they see death on TV and it's not real. Don't believe this for a second. Teens know the difference between fiction and reality as well as adults. They know that real guns kill real people. Teenage boys can be quite aggressive, and sometimes these aggressive feelings overpower reason and concern for consequences. Teens haven't had enough life experience to know how to handle these emotions, and they sometimes lead to terrible things. Talk with your teen about how to manage these feelings.

The major cause of gun deaths among teens is not from their shooting their classmates. It is accidental shootings and suicide. If teens have ready access to guns, then guns will be played with or used to kill themselves. The best reason for not having guns around the house is to protect teens from themselves. Know your teen well enough to know the likelihood of his causing an accident or something worse.

Three Things You Must Do

1. *Evaluate* your need to have guns in the house.

2. *Keep* all guns locked up.

3. *Teach* your child the safe use of guns.

What to Say and Do

Talk to your teen about the need for guns in your house. Say such things as:

- ❧ We have guns for hunting. We are responsible gun owners.

- ❧ We have guns for target shooting. It's safe and it's fun. It's an Olympic sport.

- ❧ We have guns for protection. There have been too many break-ins and assaults.

You have to decide what your household rules will be. If you have guns, make it clear who has access to them, when, why, and how. Talk it through with your teens. Say such things as:

- ❧ I don't want you around your friends when they have their guns out.

- ❧ We have guns for hunting/target shooting/protection. They're locked away when they're not being used. I have the only key. No one touches a gun without my being there.

- ❧ Once you have passed the safety course and you are sixteen, you can use the .22 for hunting/target shooting at the club on your own.

Talk about guns and killing, and help them understand your views. Say such things as:

- ❧ Guns kill. We all know that. But they are also things we use for sport and pleasure. As long as we use them responsibly, they're okay.

- ❧ I see no reason that ordinary people should own guns.

- ❧ I have no objection to target shooting and hunting. I think that guns for those purposes should be limited to certain types, and people should need a license to own one.

Talk about the precautions you take. Make the reasons clear to your teen. Say such things as:

- All our guns and ammunition are locked safely away. I don't want them easy to get at.
- Guns should never be used by the wrong person, at the wrong time, or for the wrong reason.
- The greatest danger with guns is accidental shooting. You are never to play with one.

Make sure your teen has proper training in the use and care of firearms. Tell him that he will not be allowed to use a gun until he has passed the appropriate training safety course.

Be a good role model and teach your teen that he must never point a gun at anything he doesn't want to kill.

WORDS AND PHRASES TO USE

+ accidental shootings	+ keep them under lock and key	+ responsible	+ target shooting
+ care		+ safety	+ training
+ hunting	+ killing	+ supervision	+ you must never play with guns
	+ protection		

What Not to Say and Do

Never allow your teen easy access to guns. Don't say such things as:

- I know you're responsible, so I'm not going to lock up the guns.
- I always keep the guns loaded because you never know when you might need to use one in a hurry.

Don't teach your teen to use a gun in anger or fear. Don't say such things as:

- If you hear someone in the house at night, don't hesitate to shoot him.
- You know where the guns are. I expect you to protect our property.

> ♦ If that guy bothers you again, take the shotgun and tell him if he doesn't leave you alone, you'll shoot him.

Don't encourage indiscriminate hunting and don't use words that make killing seem like something else. Don't say such things as:

> ♦ See if you can kill that little bird in the tree over there.
> ♦ Shooting deer is just like harvesting a crop.
> ♦ I'm just culling the herd.

Don't allow your teens to shoot or hunt without proper training. Don't say such things as:

> ♦ Anyone who knows how to shoot a gun straight can hunt.
> ♦ I never took a course, and I'm a safe hunter.
> ♦ Those courses are for sissies.

Don't dismiss arguments in favor of some gun control. Don't say such things as:

> ♦ Guns don't kill people. People kill people.
> ♦ It's our constitutional right to have guns, and nobody is going to take that away.
> ♦ Gun control won't keep the bad guys from getting guns.

WORDS AND PHRASES TO AVOID

♦ culling	♦ harvesting	♦ I have the right to own any kind of gun I want	♦ people who want gun control are sissies
♦ don't worry about safety	♦ I don't need to keep my guns locked up	♦ I'll never give up my guns	♦ training courses are for people who have no common sense
♦ guns are our birthright			

37 Harassment

Either I'm missing something, or nothing has been going on.

—K. E. GORDON

Eric and his friends never thought the teasing they did was anything more than innocent fun. They thought all the girls knew that. It sometimes got out of hand, but they didn't mean any harm. But that morning everything changed. Their homeroom teacher told Eric, Charlie, and Clay to report to the principal's office right away. When they got there, they found Deirdre sitting there with her parents and the principal, Mrs. Ziegler. Mrs. Ziegler told them that they were being accused of harassing Deirdre, sexually and psychologically. Specifically, Deirdre said that they had touched her inappropriately and were always making rude remarks about the way she looked and the kind of girl she was. The boys denied doing anything wrong. They said they didn't do anything to her that was different from what they did to the other girls. What did they do to the other girls? They would walk up behind them and grab their knapsacks or pieces of clothing or maybe even pat their butts. The girls would get angry, and maybe they would wrestle with them a bit. But that's all. And sure they would tease them about their clothes or their hair or their attitude, but that was normal. All the boys did it to all the girls. The girls never really complained. They liked it, the boys said. Mrs. Ziegler said they were wrong and that they were to apologize to Deirdre and her parents, and they were never to bother her or any of the other girls again. Did they understand? The boys said they understood. They would stop. But they didn't really understand.

Things to Consider

Harassment has become a major issue in society. An extreme example that comes to mind is the teasing of a few students at Columbine High School that may have contributed to the shootings. Normally it refers to unwanted or intimidating remarks, attention, or actions that offend or threaten a person physically or psychologically. In other words, it's not just what you do but the context in which you do it.

Teenage boys are sexually aggressive, and teenage girls are the targets of that aggression. This plays itself out over and over again in school and out, in ways that are often unacceptable in modern society. What used to be considered harmless teasing now has a new name: harassment.

Boys are typically the culprits and girls the victims in harassment cases, and what I advise can be applied to any harassment concerns. Teach your teenage son to treat girls with sensitivity and consideration for how they feel about what he says and does. Boys will say that you can't read a girl's mind, that she may say stop but not really mean it.

That may be true, but it doesn't matter. What matters is that the girl says "No!" Teach your son that if she says no, it means no. More than that, tell him to be considerate of the girl's feelings. Ask him how he would feel about someone treating him that way, especially someone physically bigger and stronger than he was.

Girls can protect themselves against unwanted remarks and attention. Tell your girls to speak up. Tell them not to expect boys to read their minds. If a boy's behavior bothers them, they must say so clearly and directly.

Although it may seem like an obvious point, teach your boys the Golden Rule and how they can apply it to girls at school. If they always try to consider their feelings as they would want someone to consider theirs, many unfortunate situations will be avoided.

Most teen harassment happens innocently enough even though the consequences may be serious. Your best weapon in preventing harassment is talking to your teen about its meaning, the way it typically happens, its consequences, and the ways it can be avoided.

Be a good role model. Teens learn from your attitudes and actions.

Three Things You Must Do

1. *Teach* your teen the meaning of harassment and give him examples.

2. *Teach* your teen that no means no.

3. *Teach* your teen the Golden Rule.

What to Say and Do

Teach your teen what harassment is. Make sure he understands that it includes what is said and done and the context in which it happens. Say such things as:

- ✦ Do you know what harassment is? Let's talk about it.

- ✦ Did you know there are at least three kinds of harassment: physical, sexual, and psychological?

- ✦ Harassment has more to do with the way someone thinks about what you say or do to them than what your intentions are. You can harass someone without knowing you're doing it.

The best way to prevent harassment is to teach your teen to be sensitive to the feelings of others and to pick up on cues from others that the attention is unwanted. Say such things as:

- ✦ You don't pick on other kids, do you?

- ✦ If you're going to tease people, you need to be really careful about how they feel about it.

- ✦ You know what it means when a girl says no, don't you? It means stop whatever you're doing.

Teach your teen the Golden Rule: "Do unto others as you would have others do unto you." Make sure he knows it and what it means. Say such things as:

- ✦ Do you know the Golden Rule? It's a wonderful principle to keep in mind in all your relationships with others. It tells you to treat others as you would like others to treat you.

- ✦ I know you think teasing is innocent fun, but it isn't if it hurts someone.

- ✦ Imagine yourself being teased by someone like you. Would you always like it?

Encourage your teen to take a harassment workshop at school. Say such things as:

- ✦ Sometimes you may be harassing someone and not even realize you're doing it. You need to be aware of what others are feeling. Does your school have a class or workshop on that?

Your attitudes and actions should present a good model for your teen. Make sure you are sensitive to the harassment issue at home and at work. Talk to your teen about any instances you've observed where someone has been charged with harassment. Use these examples as a teaching tool. If you happen to see harassment on television or read about it in the newspaper or a magazine, use it as a teaching tool.

WORDS AND PHRASES TO USE

- anticipate
- be sensitive
- don't carry teasing too far
- empathize
- innocent fun can turn ugly
- no means no
- perceptions are more important than intentions
- respect others' feelings

What Not to Say and Do

Don't dismiss harassment as a feminist plot against the white male. Don't say such things as:

- It's just a woman's way to get back at us.
- If women are equal, why do they claim harassment so much? Can't they stand up for themselves?
- They're so sensitive. They can't take a joke.
- This political correctness stuff has gone too far.

Don't encourage your teen to be insensitive to others' feelings. Don't say such things as:

- You're a good kid. I don't see why you have to stop doing what you've always done.
- Everyone is hypersensitive these days. What a crock.
- If they're so touchy about these things, there's something wrong with them.

Don't blame the victim. Don't say such things as:

- If she's going to dress like that, what can she expect?

- Girls say no but really mean yes.
- They're all nice and sexy, but when you react like a normal guy, they scream "harassment."

Don't set a bad example. Don't make sexist remarks. Don't dismiss the notion of sexual harassment.

WORDS AND PHRASES TO AVOID

- can't take a joke	- just good, healthy fun	- nonsense	- she was teasing you
- feminist plot		- ridiculous	- sissy
- hypersensitive	- no really means yes		

38 Hate

Few people can be happy unless they hate some other person, nation, or creed.

—BERTRAND RUSSELL

Tony was not a great student. He wasn't a great athlete, either. He was quite insecure, his self-esteem was low, and he built himself up by tearing other people down. Most of the time he just hung out with a few friends and kept a pretty low profile. There were skinheads in his neighborhood, and just now he was thinking of joining them. Belonging to a gang was important, he thought, because if you didn't have people to protect you, you could get hurt. Since Tony wasn't African American or Hispanic or Asian, he figured he'd better be a skinhead. They hated everyone who wasn't white and Christian, and that suited him fine. He didn't like the idea of all these foreigners getting handouts and scholarships, and special treatment while he got nothing unless he worked for it. He hated them for it.

Things to Consider

Hate is a hateful emotion. It is often all-consuming. It is always wasteful. And it is inevitably worse for the "hater" than the "hatee" in the sense that if you hate me, I've got you hooked. You're thinking about me, but I don't have to give you a second thought. Your life is bound to mine, but not mine to yours.

I have always found it difficult to understand people who hate groups. I can understand hating an individual, although I think that, too, is unfortunate, but hating a group is senseless since it is really hating a nonentity, a stereotype, something that doesn't exist.

Teens who hate others may have psychological problems that require professional help. They may just need to fit in with their peer group in a school that is divided along racial, religious, or ethnic lines. Or they may have been taught to hate by their parents.

You can do a number of things to keep your teen from hating those who are nominally different from them. First, be a good role model. Do a self-assessment of your own views about others. Do your thoughts, words, or deeds teach your teen that hating African Americans, gays, Asians, Hispanics, Native Americans (First Nations in Canada), East Indians, Pakistanis, Jews, or any other identifiable group is okay? You may not be explicit, but the little things you say or do may communicate that message. Make sure that you don't.

Second, actively combat hatred. If you see or hear evidence of it, make a point of commenting on it. Don't be part of the conspiracy of silence. Don't belong to or support any group or organization that implicitly or explicitly condones hatred.

Third, talk to your teen about issues of hatred and prejudice. Ask him how he feels about instances of hate. Visit the Internet hate websites if you have the courage and have a conversation about what you see there. Make your opposition clear and reasonable. Find out how your teen thinks about these things.

Finally, stay closely involved in your teen's life so that you know who his friends are; what groups, clubs, or gangs he belongs to; what music he listens to, films he sees, games he plays, Internet sites he visits. Do this casually and without interfering with your teen's privacy and independence. You can learn these things through having regular conversations with your kids, not like some police interrogation.

If you find your child seriously involved in a hate group or hate activities, seek professional counseling. There are psychologists who can help your teen get to the root of his problem. It is a very serious matter and needs to be addressed quickly and expertly.

Three Things You Must Do

1. *Teach* your teen love, not hatred.

2. *Know* your teen's views and his friends' views.

3. *Make* your opposition to hate clear in what you say and do.

What to Say and Do

If you find your teen involved in activities that promote hatred of any kind, you must decide whether he has psychological problems that require professional help or is just trying to fit in with his peer group. You need to have a close involvement with your teen in order to know this.

Ask yourself if you could be the cause of any symptoms of hate in your teen.

- Have you been a good role model? Do you hate any identifiable groups? The little things you say or do may communicate that message.

To actively combat hatred, point out to your teen that you don't belong to or support any group or organization that implicitly or explicitly condones hatred. Say such things as:

- Those people have nothing better to do with their lives than hate others.
- What a waste of one's life to spend it in hatred.
- People who hate others hate themselves even more.

Talk to your teen about issues of hatred and prejudice. Say such things as:

- Did you see that story about someone burning down those churches? Isn't that terrible?
- Have you ever visited an Internet hate website? I don't have the courage, but if you want to, I'll do it with you.
- Have you ever seen any of the literature these people distribute? It's really filled with hate.
- Do you think free speech should protect these hate mongers? It's a difficult question to answer. What do you think?

Know what is going on in your teen's life and with his friends. Say such things as:

- Do you have any race trouble at school?
- I've heard about some racist rock groups that have a lot of hate lyrics. Have you heard them?
- Ever visit an Internet hate website?

WORDS AND PHRASES TO USE

* acceptance
* affection
* brotherhood
* differences
* equality
* fairness
* justice
* love
* mentally ill
* peace
* protection
* respect/tolerance
* sisterhood
* understanding
* we must live in harmony

What Not to Say and Do

Don't underestimate the problem of hate among teens. It exists in individuals, gangs, and groups, and causes violent incidents in schools, at rock concerts, at raves (all night teen dance parties), and in the community. Don't say such things as:

* So you hate some kids at your school. That's not a problem. I hate some people myself.
* Those damned _____ deserve everything they get!
* You either love 'em or you hate 'em.

Don't perpetuate the myths and stereotypes that feed the hate. Don't say such things as:

* They're planning to take over the world.
* They're polluting our race.
* They're not really human beings. They're more like animals.

Don't be a bad role model. Don't teach your teen to hate through your example. Don't say such things as:

* I hate those friggin' _____.
* They get all the breaks. I really hate them for that.
* All you have to do to succeed these days is be a minority. They get everything, and the majority get nothing.
* Everybody knows they're scoundrels. They'll even cheat their own kind just to make a buck.

Don't ignore the symptoms of a serious psychological problem if your teen shows irrational hatred for some person or group. This can lead to mass killing at school or in the workplace. Don't be understanding and think it's just youthful energy misdirected.

WORDS AND PHRASES TO AVOID

▶ all the hateful slang names for ethnic, racial, and religious minorities	▶ destroy	▶ murder	▶ shoot
	▶ detest/hate	▶ pollute	▶ they don't deserve to live
	▶ fight	▶ rebellion	
▶ cheat	▶ kill	▶ secret plot	▶ wipe out

39 Health

Health nuts are going to feel stupid someday, lying in a hospital dying of nothing.

—REDD FOXX

Janie was like many of her teen friends. She smoked, but not in front of her parents, and drank at parties. She spent evenings after homework talking on the phone half the night, then had trouble getting up in the mornings for school. She was thin but thought she could be still thinner. Even when it was bitter cold with snow and ice, she wore a short skirt with panty hose, a sweater that exposed her navel, platforms, and a flimsy jacket. Fashion was far more important to her than warmth, comfort, or safety. She wasn't into sports and rarely got proper exercise. Her mother scheduled annual checkups with their family physician, but these were sometimes missed. Janie regularly got colds, the flu, and whatever else was going around. Her parents worried about her but were afraid to say too much because in the past Janie had gotten very angry and told them that it was her life, not theirs. They didn't know what to say or do after that.

Things to Consider

Teens think they will live forever. They don't think much about nutrition, proper clothing, adequate sleep, or exercise. Teens smoke and drink if they have a chance, and some take drugs. They can be quite reckless in what they do, judged by adult standards. They are driven by a desperate need to belong, to fit in with their crowd.

Talking to your teen about proper health care may force you to take the risk of alienating your teen to some extent. If she is like Janie, above, she'll resent your interference in her life. Nevertheless, be assertive if your teen doesn't seem to take proper care of herself.

If your teen is reasonable about your role in maintaining her good health, as most teens are, your job is less demanding. Ensure that your teen eats well, gets sufficient sleep and proper exercise, and wears appropriate clothing, which, by the way, can also be fashionable. Monitor your teen's eating habits, weight, complexion, energy level, and temperament. If she appears ill, make an appointment with your doctor (make sure you have a family doctor).

Encourage your teen to be active in sports, not necessarily team sports or varsity sports, but in some kind of physical game. It can be jogging, swimming, tennis, pick-up-basketball, stickball, or golf. Not every teen has the ability, motivation, or opportunity to play a sport for her school. Teens need the exercise, fun, and change of pace that sports provide. If it's a sport that they can do with you as well as with friends, so much the better.

Make sure your teen knows the dangers of smoking. These days girls seem more at risk to become smokers than boys. Talk to your teen about what she can do to be a member of her group without smoking. You might even want to bribe her not to smoke.

Teens often don't allow enough time in their schedule for adequate sleep and therefore experience chronic sleep deprivation. According to the latest medical research, they need a minimum of nine hours a night and may need as much as eleven. Help them schedule their lives so that sufficient sleep time is available. A well-rested teen is healthier and nicer to be around.

Teen health shouldn't be left to chance. Know about your teen's health needs, schedule regular checkups, and ensure that appropriate inoculations are administered. Monitor your teen's growth, habits, and appearance, and talk about personal health issues. Look after yourself the way you want your teens to look after themselves.

Three Things You Must Do

1. *Monitor* your teen's health personally and professionally.

2. *Teach* your teen how to look after herself properly.

3. *Model* good personal health care for your teen.

What to Say and Do

Talk to your teen about the importance of good health, especially during these years of rapid growth and physical and psychological change. Say such things as:

- It doesn't matter how much money, success, talent, or intelligence you have if you don't have good health to go with it.

- Being healthy and staying fit will make you a nicer person and make your life much easier.

If your teenager is concerned about her looks and her body, talk to her about how good health makes a person look better. Say such things as:

- To look as good as some of those women in those magazines, you have be really healthy.

- Did you know that smoking causes wrinkles?

- You will look your best and feel good about yourself if you're fit and healthy.

- If you promise to go to bed each night by ten, I'll lend you the car on the weekends.

- Let's write up a schedule of your responsibilities so that you can get enough sleep each night.

If your teen is already involved in a fitness regime, talk about it, praise her for it, and tell her how good she looks. Say such things as:

- Your fitness work is really paying off. You look great.

- Tell me exactly what you do to stay fit.

- Whatever you're doing, it's working. You look so fit.

Encourage your teen to do some kind of sports or exercise. Say such things as:

- How about playing tennis with me this weekend?

- I'd like to get you to play golf. Are you interested?

- How about going for a run with me?

If your teen rejects your concerns about her health, try bribing her. Say such things as:

- I know you don't think your health is a problem, but I do. I want you to get a checkup, and I'll buy you that dress/shirt/shoes that you want so much if you go with me to the doctor.

- Your friends smoke and you think it's cool, so I'll make you a deal. For every day you go without a cigarette, I'll give you $____ [whatever you think would be an incentive]. If you give up smoking, I'll buy you a car. If you start smoking again, I'll take back the car. How about it?

With a difficult older teen, there comes a time when you have to pass the responsibility for her health on to her. Say such things as:

- You won't listen to my advice about your health, so now you're responsible for yourself.

- I'm not going to tell you what to do about keeping fit.

- I'll always be here for you, but now you're on your own. You have to look after yourself.

WORDS AND PHRASES TO USE

♦ appearance	♦ eating habits	♦ good health is very important	♦ responsibility
♦ checkup	♦ exercise		♦ sleep
♦ doctor	♦ fitness	♦ nutrition	♦ sports

What Not to Say and Do

Don't threaten or fight with your teen. Be firm, consistent, and authoritative, but don't use name-calling or any other form of abuse. Don't say such things as:

- You stupid kid. You're going to the doctor or else.

- Monkey see, monkey do. Your friends are stupid enough to smoke, so you do the same thing.

> ♦ How did I end up with an idiot like you? Don't you know how to take care of yourself?

Don't discourage your teen from engaging in exercise, whatever it is. Any exercise is better than none. Don't say such things as:

> ♦ If you had worked harder at getting into shape, you'd have made the team. Now you're going to play that sissy game.
>
> ♦ I don't see why you bother running. It doesn't get you anywhere. You'd be better off spending that time on school.
>
> ♦ Golf isn't good exercise. Look at how many fat women and men are golf pros.

Don't try to control your older teen's bedtime with rules. Negotiate with her and arrange trade-offs to make sure she gets enough sleep. Don't say such things as:

> ♦ I don't care if you are seventeen, be in bed by 10 P.M. or I'm going to cut off your allowance.
>
> ♦ What your friends are allowed to do makes no difference to me. You'll do what I say as long as you live in this house.

Don't be a bad role model. Show your teen what a healthy lifestyle is. Don't say such things as:

> ♦ People go to the doctor too much these days. I only go when I'm really sick.
>
> ♦ Every time I feel the urge to get some exercise, I lie down until it passes.
>
> ♦ Sure I smoke and drink. Life's too short to worry about doing the right thing.

WORDS AND PHRASES TO AVOID

♦ crazy	♦ go and buy me some cigarettes	♦ idiot	♦ you sleep too much
♦ dumb		♦ I like smoking	♦ you'll follow our rules
♦ exercise is just a fad	♦ how long you live is just a matter of chance	♦ sissy sports	
		♦ stupid	♦ your stupid friends

40 Homosexuality

If there were a pill for becoming heterosexual, I would take it immediately, because life would be so much easier and it would be nice to have children.

—Daniel Pinard

"Hey, Mom," Richie said at breakfast. "Guess what? You know my friend Sam? Yesterday he told me that he was gay. I've known him for three years, ever since we were freshmen, and I had no idea. I don't think it makes any difference. He's still the same guy I've always known, but now I'm not sure what to think. I don't want to treat him any differently and I don't think I will, but it's not something I can just forget about. I guess we'll never be competing for the same girl, and that's a good thing. He's never come on to me and I know he never will, so that's not a problem. There are a few openly gay kids in the school, boys and girls. They mainly hang out together. Some of the kids tease them and play practical jokes, especially the jocks. But generally everyone just lets them alone. Sam doesn't hang out with them. He's always been one of our crowd. Nothing's really different now. But I'm not sure. Maybe it is. What do you think?"

Things to Consider

There is good evidence that homosexuality is caused by certain structures in the brain; however, many people firmly believe that it is a lifestyle choice which is immoral, socially undesirable, and generally against God's law. But who, you might ask, would choose a lifestyle that would cause themselves so much pain and trouble? Ask yourself if your own sexual orientation is a choice. If you are honest, you must answer no. You do not choose to love men or women. You just do.

Much of what your teens think about homosexuality will come from your expressed feelings. If you hate gays, want to convert them to good family values, or find no problem with violence against them, your teen will likely share your views. If you accept homosexuality as simply a different sexual orientation from your own, your teen will be more open to this view.

In *The Birdcage,* a film in which two of the lead characters are homosexual, this gay couple exemplifies good family values while the "straight" family is totally dysfunctional. This proves nothing but the fact that neither homosexuality nor heterosexuality tells you anything about people's values.

Your moral or religious beliefs may be different from mine, but I recommend to you the idea that the best attitude to teach your teen about gays or anyone else who is "different" is love and understanding. Good communication about homosexuality will be reasoned, open, and without judging. Teach your teen that whatever you may feel about homosexuality as a lifestyle, you believe that everyone deserves a chance at a safe, happy life free from fear of discrimination and violence.

You want your teen to see in your words and deeds a set of values that emphasizes bringing people together rather than separating them. The fundamental message of the founder of every major religion is the same. In the words of the Bible, "Thou shalt love thy neighbor as thyself" (Leviticus 19:18, Matthew 19:19). Should we not follow that example and teach that there is no better way to treat others whatever their race, religion, ethnic background, or sexual orientation?

Three Things You Must Do

1. *Assess* your own feelings about homosexuality.

2. *Remember* that your teen will learn your values.

3. *Teach* your teen tolerance.

What to Say and Do

If you or your teen has concerns about homosexuality, take the time to research the scientific explanation. Say such things as:

- I don't know what to think about homosexuality, but scientists seem to believe it's caused by a certain structuring in the brain.

- Let's see what the Bible says about homosexuality. I know there are references to it there.
- What are your views about homosexuality?

Even if you think homosexuality is a sin, try to approach it with love and compassion. Say such things as:

- Even though I think homosexuality is wrong, I still pray for these people.
- Homosexuality is against God's law; we must deplore the sin but love the sinner.
- Whatever you or I believe about homosexuality, these people deserve the same rights, freedoms, and responsibilities as the rest of us.

If your teen is gay or *thinks* he is gay, you must be supportive. You know your teen and the kind of person he is. Don't be blinded to that by stereotypes and dogma. Say such things as:

- You are my child, and I love you for who you are no matter what that may be.
- You are a good person. I will love you and support you whatever your sexual orientation.
- The only important thing is what kind of person you are.

If your teen has a gay friend, encourage him to be as open to that friendship as to any other as long as that person is a good friend. Say such things as:

- Having a gay friend doesn't mean having a sexual relationship any more than having a heterosexual friend does.
- If your friend is a good person, that's all that matters.
- Gays are no less and no more deserving of our friendship than anyone else. It depends on who they are as people.

Encourage your teen to treat all people with love and respect, including gays. Say such things as:

- Our world thrives on differences.
- Differences in people and all other living things of the world enrich our lives.
- You have to love the person next door as well as society, the environment, animals, and the world in general. That means gays as well as straights.

WORDS AND PHRASES TO USE

❧ accepting	❧ kindness	❧ openness	❧ sexual orientation
❧ choice or no choice	❧ lifestyle	❧ reality	❧ supportive
❧ differences enrich us	❧ loving	❧ scientific evidence	❧ tolerance

What Not to Say and Do

Don't encourage blind prejudice against gays. Don't say such things as:

- ❧ Gays live a life of sin.
- ❧ I hate gays. I find them revolting.
- ❧ It's only bleeding heart liberals who are soft on gays.
- ❧ I'm against extending our rights and freedoms to include gays specifically.
- ❧ I don't have a problem with discrimination against gays.

If your teen is gay, don't disown him. You may not be able to accept his homosexuality easily, but your feelings will not change it. Don't say such things as:

- ❧ I'll have no child of mine like that.
- ❧ You can be gay if you want to, but don't expect me to accept it.
- ❧ All gays are an abomination.
- ❧ You've made the wrong choice.
- ❧ I think you're disgusting.

Approximately one in ten people is gay. It is not a disease or any kind of mental affliction. If your teen thinks he is gay and can't discuss it with you because of your strong feelings against homosexuality, the resulting feelings of loneliness and isolation can lead your teen to suicide. Don't say such things as:

- ❧ People who are gay are sick people.
- ❧ If you're gay, you must be crazy.
- ❧ Hanging around gays will make you gay, too.
- ❧ If you ever said you were gay, I'd have a heart attack, but first I'd throw you out of the house.
- ❧ I don't want you to ever talk to me about homosexuality. I'm not interested in those perverts.
- ❧ Don't ever bring any of your gay friends around here. They're not welcome.

WORDS AND PHRASES TO AVOID

❧ abomination	❧ discriminate	❧ perverted	❧ sinful
❧ awful	❧ diseased mind	❧ queer	❧ unacceptable
❧ crazy	❧ disgusting	❧ revolting	❧ unnatural
❧ degenerate	❧ hateful	❧ sick	❧ unwelcome

41 Honesty

Though I am not naturally honest, I am so sometimes by chance.

—SHAKESPEARE

"What did you do last night?" Howie's mother asked him at breakfast.

"Nothing much," he answered. "Just hung out with the guys."

In fact, Howie, who is sixteen, and his friends got an older brother of one of them to buy them a couple of six packs, and they spent the evening drinking in the kitchen of his friend whose parents were away. Howie knew that if he told the truth, his mom would get very angry. She didn't like his drinking at his age. But it doesn't do him any harm, he thought, and if he didn't drink with the guys, they'd call him a wuss and he'd be left out.

Telling his mom the truth wasn't an option. It wasn't as though he was drinking and driving. He didn't have his own car but could borrow the family car when he needed transport, and none of the other guys could drive. Drinking and driving was something he wouldn't do.

What was the harm in a few beers, he wondered, and what was the harm in not being totally honest with his mom? He didn't actually lie anyway, he realized. He did hang out with the guys last night. Leaving out exactly what he did wasn't lying. Last night he had coughed a few times and blown his nose, laughed a lot, and sat on a chair. But he didn't tell his mom that, and nobody would call him a liar for leaving that out. Only if his mom asked him if he drank any beer last night and he answered no would he really be lying.

Honesty was fine, he thought, but sometimes a guy couldn't tell his mom everything. As long as he didn't get into trouble or get hurt, she should trust him.

Things to Consider

How much do you really want to know about your teens' lives? You need to be involved in their lives. You need to know your teens' friends, what your teens do with them, and any clubs, teams, or gangs your teens belong to. Being involved in your teens' lives is crucial to good communication because it gives you a better context for understanding what they say.

Expecting teens to tell you all the things they do when they're not home is not the same as being involved in their lives. If you quiz them in detail about their lives, asking specific questions about what they've done, they'll think you're getting too nosy. If you're very strict and the consequences of their doing anything wrong are too severe, they probably won't tell you the truth anyway. Then if the truth should come out, they'll really be in trouble. They're caught in a catch-22 position. If they're honest with you, they're in big trouble, and if they're dishonest with you, they're in equally big trouble.

What's the answer? Trust your teens to be honest when it's important to be honest. At other times, don't ask questions to which you won't like the answers. I suggest a pragmatic approach. If you think your teens are involved in dangerous, unlawful, or immoral activities, you must try to find out the truth for their sake and the sake of others. But if what they're doing won't cause anybody any real harm, even if it's not exactly what you'd like them to be doing, leave it alone. Don't ask them to be honest with you.

It is desirable that you have been a parent who trusts his children know the difference between right and wrong. You've never been arbitrarily hard on your teens and given harsh punishments for minor transgressions. Your reactions to things your teens have told you have not been needlessly moralistic or judgmental. If you've been this way, you know that your teens will be honest with you about most things and sometimes tell you things you really don't want to know. You've built a relationship in which honesty is rewarded, not punished.

We are all dishonest to some degree. A friend says, "Hi, how are you?" You're not feeling well, but you don't have time to chat, so you answer, "I'm fine. How are you?" If you had told the truth, your friend would have had to ask what's wrong, and then you'd have to talk about it. But you're in a hurry, so you lie. We all sacrifice honesty for the sake of friendship or politeness. If you don't like a friend's dress, makeup, or new car, you don't tell her. You say nothing, or you lie. And that's okay.

Know whether you can trust your teens to be honest when it's right to be honest, and judiciously quiet when honesty would create more problems than it would solve. Give your teens the benefit of the doubt. Honesty isn't always the best policy for any of us.

Three Things You Must Do

1. *Trust* your teen to be honest when honesty is called for.

2. *Don't* be too nosy.

3. *Build* a relationship in which the penalties for breaking your rules do not encourage lying.

What to Say and Do

Create a good relationship with your teen by trusting him to generally do the right thing. Say such things as:

- You can tell me the truth. You know I won't make a big thing out of a little thing.
- I only want to know about trouble. You're old enough to know the right thing to do.
- You can be honest with me about most things, but I don't expect you to tell me about every little thing you do.

With the right relationship between you and your teen you can expect honest answers to certain kinds of questions. Say such things as:

- You know I only ask you specific questions about things you do that might be a real problem. And I expect you to tell me the truth.
- I trust you to do the right thing, so you have to trust me when I ask you a specific question about something you've done. When I do, I need an honest answer.

> ✦ I don't want to put you on the spot, so I'm not going to ask you for the details of what you do with your friends. I know you'll tell me if there is ever any problem.

Talk to your teen about the uses and abuses of honesty. Give him examples of when it is okay not to be totally honest for the sake of friendship and others' feelings. Say such things as:

> ✦ You know there are times when being completely honest isn't the right thing to do.

> ✦ A white lie is saying something that isn't true because you don't want to hurt someone's feelings.

> ✦ If a boy you don't like asks for a date, you can say you're busy even if you're not. You shouldn't say you won't go out with him because you think he's gross or ugly or a bore because that will hurt him for no good reason.

WORDS AND PHRASES TO USE

✦ be considerate	✦ feelings	✦ sin of omission	✦ truth is a relative term
✦ be understanding	✦ flexibility	✦ there's no absolute truth	
✦ compassion	✦ judiciously silent		✦ white lie
✦ don't be rigid	✦ nonjudgmental	✦ trust	

What Not to Say and Do

Don't insist on honesty at any price. In most situations your relationship with your teen is more important. Don't say things that will wreck that relationship, such as:

> ✦ You have to be honest with me in every circumstance.

> ✦ I'm not interested in excuses. There is no excuse for lying.

> ✦ If you ever lie to me, you're no longer my son/daughter.

Don't preach honesty as though you never twisted the truth when you were a kid. Don't say such things as:

- If my dad ever caught me lying, he'd beat me.
- When I was your age, I never lied to my folks.

Don't condone lying about important matters. Don't say such things as:

- I don't care if you cheat on a test as long as you don't get caught.
- Everybody lies. Honesty is a joke in this world.
- You lie better than a politician. I like that in a kid.

Don't dismiss or underestimate the importance of trust in your relationship with your teen. Don't say such things as:

- I never believe a word you say.
- Why should I trust you? I don't think you're ever really honest with me.
- I don't trust you, and you don't trust me.

WORDS AND PHRASES TO AVOID

- anger	- distrust	- if I ever catch you lying, I will never trust you again	- lying to me is the worst thing you could ever do
- dishonesty is the best policy	- I don't believe you	- lie when you have to	- truth at any cost

42 Hopes

Hope is the feeling you have that the feeling you have isn't permanent.

—JEAN KERR

Rose had hopes and dreams. As a seventeen-year-old in her senior year of high school, her first thoughts were about next year. She hoped to go to college to study psychology. She had already sent applications to five colleges across the United States and to her state college near her home. She hoped to get into her first choice but would be happy to be accepted anywhere. A combination of talent and hard work made it likely that she would get her wish. She had taken her College Boards but hadn't yet got her results. She hoped her scores were high enough to send her on her way toward her goal—to eventually get her Ph.D. and become a child psychologist.

Her brother, Dan, was fourteen, in his freshman year in high school, and his hopes were much less career oriented or forward looking. His main hopes were to become a regular on the football team and to get at least a "B" in English. Being a starting member of the team was always an important part of Dan's dreams. He always hoped to belong and to become recognized as a good athlete. Girls liked that, and Dan liked girls, one in particular. He hoped that she liked him as much as he liked her.

Rose and Dan were both good kids. They had hopes for the present and the future that were realistic and positive. They talked a lot with their parents about their hopes and received good and useful feedback. Mom and Dad were supportive and encouraged their kids to work hard for what they wanted and showed them how to do it, by example in their own lives and by offering advice. Most important, they taught them how to cope with disappointment, how to persevere, and how to keep their hopes and dreams in perspective by living in the present while working toward the future.

Things to Consider

Your teenagers have hopes. They will happily share some of them with you, and some they'll keep private. In this respect they are no different from adults. In another respect however, teens are very different. Their future is still a big question mark. What they will become as adults will be shaped by so many factors, including many that you and your teens have no control over.

On the one hand, teenagers' hopes need to be tied realistically to talent, ability, ambition, drive, and family circumstances. On the other hand, as a parent you hope for all possible success in every aspect of your teens' present and future lives. When their hopes are dashed by not making an "A" in class, not being chosen for the team, or loving and not being loved in return, you ache for them.

Like all of us, teens need to learn how to rebound when hopes are not fulfilled. You have to be there for support and advice, and to provide a good example of how to cope with disappointment. Three important things you can teach your teens are (1) don't confuse reasonable hopes with fantastic dreams that are beyond the realm of possibility, (2) hope without action rarely succeeds, and (3) regardless of hopes realized or unrealized, you need to accept the present while working for the future.

Your teen can dream about becoming a famous pop star, but to pin his hopes on doing so would be silly. Your teen needs to see the link between hope and action. The most realistic hopes are those he has some control over and can realize through his own actions. Hopes may or may not be fulfilled. Your teen needs to recognize that as long as he has done his best, no more can be asked or expected. He needs to accept success or disappointment as a natural part of life while continuing to pursue his fondest hopes.

Your teen will learn from how you cope with success and failure. Be a model of realistic optimism, perseverance, and acceptance. Share your hopes with your teen. Let him understand your ways of working to fulfill them while adjusting to the reality of life as it unfolds. Involve yourself in your teen's hopes and wishes, and share in his joys and sorrows.

Three Things You Must Do

1. *Be* close enough to know your teen's fondest hopes.

2. *Teach* your teen how to realize those hopes.

3. *Help* your teen through the failures and disappointments.

What to Say and Do

Know your teen's hopes. Talk about them in casual conversation. If you're involved in your teen's life, you'll already know what they are. Take the opportunity to share some of your own hopes with your teen. Say such things as:

- That's a good ambition, a nice thing to hope for.
- Do you have any special hopes or wishes that we haven't talked about?
- Did I ever tell you my fondest hope when I was in high school?

Help your teen be realistic. Talk to him about how hopes can sometimes be tied to things within his control and sometimes to things beyond his control, such as talent, ability, ambition, drive, and family circumstances. Say such things as:

- What do you think you need to achieve that?
- I think you have the talent to do that. The question is whether you have the drive.
- I know you'd like to go to _____ college, but unless you get a scholarship, I don't think we can afford it. So in a way it's up to you. Are you willing to work to get your wish?

Teach your teen how to rebound when hopes are not fulfilled. Tell him how you cope with disappointment. Ask him how he copes. Say such things as:

- Many of the things I've hoped for have happened, but many have not. I've never found it easy to accept it when something I've really wanted doesn't happen. I tend to be fatalistic and think that everything happens for a good reason even if I don't agree with it at the time.

- I've watched how you handle disappointment, and I think you're pretty good. What's your secret?
- You know, the more you hope for, the more likely you'll be disappointed. Are you ready for that?

I've found three things to remember about hopes: (1) I don't confuse reasonable hope with dreams that are beyond the realm of possibility, (2) hope without action rarely succeeds, and (3) I try to accept whatever happens but don't stop working for the future.

The most realistic hopes are those that your teen has some control over. Talk about this in the context of his life. Say such things as:

- If you hope to go to a good college, you can help your chances by working hard and getting the best grades you can.
- Hoping is not enough. If there's something you can do to attain your goal, you should do it because it will help you get what you want.
- Most of us don't have fairy godmothers to grant our fondest wishes. Realistically, if you want something, you have to go after it.

WORDS AND PHRASES TO USE

⋗ ambitions	⋗ do your best	⋗ fantasy	⋗ perseverance
⋗ coping	⋗ don't expect to get everything you want	⋗ fond hopes	⋗ rebound
⋗ desires		⋗ hard work	⋗ under your control
⋗ disappointments	⋗ expectations	⋗ hoping is not enough	
	⋗ failures		

What Not to Say and Do

Don't pry into hopes and dreams your teen would rather not talk about. Don't say such things as:

- What do you want out of life? I need to know.
- You never tell me your thoughts. I can't read your mind, you know.
- I'm sure you tell your friends a lot more than you tell me.

Don't criticize your teen for his hopes even if they are different from what you think they should be. Don't say such things as:

- You have to set your sights higher than that.
- Is that all you hope to do with your life?
- You have a miserable set of goals for your life.

Don't encourage your teen to be unrealistic. Don't say such things as:

- Whatever you hope for can be yours.
- You don't need talent to be successful.

Don't set a poor example for your teen. Don't be cynical or pessimistic in the face of disappointed hopes and desires. Don't say such things as:

- Life is such a series of disappointments.
- Sometimes I think it is not worth the trouble.
- You work and work and hope that something good will come of it, but it doesn't.

WORDS AND PHRASES TO AVOID

- dismal
- don't waste your time hoping things will go well
- face the facts, you're not going to get what you hoped for
- life is a crapshoot
- nothing good ever happens
- stop dreaming
- the only thing worth hoping for is money
- wasted hopes
- what really makes the difference is luck

43 Hypocrisy

A good deed never goes unpunished.

—Gore Vidal

"Dad, I don't know how you can be so hypocritical. You say you want to protect the environment, but now you're going to vote for a politician who's in the pocket of the developers."

These were Marcy's words to her father one morning at breakfast. They had been talking about the upcoming election and the issues involved. Marcy was particularly interested in getting her mom's and dad's views because her class had been discussing it in social studies all week, and she was going to be giving a detailed rundown today of each candidate and party in the district, including positions and track records on each of the important campaign issues.

Marcy was angry with her dad but not surprised. Now sixteen, she had learned long ago that grown-ups were generally hypocrites. They professed ideals, went to church or synagogue, and preached good values to their kids, but when things came to a head, they thought about little but their own selfish interests. At election time they voted for the politician who promised the best deal, regardless of the social, moral, or ecological issues involved. Development, growth, and profits were more important than people or the environment.

Whenever Marcy raised this issue with her mom and dad, they said they were sympathetic but had to be realistic. It was nice to be idealistic, but ideals didn't create jobs, pave the roads, build hospitals and schools, or pay the mortgage. One day, they said, when Marcy was older and had responsibilities for a family, she would understand. That would come with maturity.

If being an adult meant that she would have to be less idealistic and less caring, Marcy hoped she would never grow up.

Things to Consider

Teenagers ought to be idealistic. If they are too realistic or pragmatic at that young age, chances are good they'll be confirmed cynics by the time they're thirty. Teenage idealism and anger at what appears to be the hypocrisy of adults is healthy and needs to be encouraged.

When I was a teen, I thought I had the answers to all the world's problems. My parents, especially my dad, never seemed to get upset the way I did at the problems of poverty, homelessness, racial and religious discrimination, and the blatant hypocrisy of religious leaders. We had wonderful discussions—dare I say arguments—at the dinner table. No one ever won them, but they confirmed my belief that grown-ups were unable to see the logic and justice of my proposed redistribution of wealth and power in the United States. My dad was a corporate executive and disliked unions. I was a student in high school and thought the working person was exploited.

Although we argued, my parents never really criticized me for my views even when I called them hypocrites. I thought they were saying one thing and doing another, but they thought they were being flexible and pragmatic. In a sense, I was the real hypocrite. I wanted to save the world as long as I didn't have to sacrifice any of my own wealth, creature comforts, or social position to do it.

Give your teenager's idealism tender treatment. That doesn't mean giving in to your teen or not arguing your position. It means giving your teen credit for thinking about more than herself. For the most part, the ideals of teens are wonderful, imagining a world in which goodness and virtue are rewarded, and greed, insensitivity, and injustice are punished. Encourage and nurture them before adulthood and the realities of the world make such ideals untenable for all but the most ardent believer. Accept the fact that teens think most adults are hypocrites, but talk about why real life makes hypocrites of us all to some degree.

Three Things You Must Do

1. *Encourage* your teen's idealism.

2. *Accept* the inevitability of your own hypocrisy.

3. *Explain* the inevitability of some hypocrisy in us all.

What to Say and Do

Be more concerned if your teen isn't an idealist than if she is. Talk about your teen's ideals. Don't be afraid to question them. Make your teen think hard and defend her position. Say such things as:

- Do you really think you can save the world?
- Why should the world fit your ideal?
- What if people reject your version of the world?

If your teen doesn't want to save the world, try to find out why. Say such things as:

- Do you think the world is fine the way it is?
- Why aren't you upset about poverty, disease, global warming, and all the other things that kids your age are upset about?

If your teen calls you a hypocrite, discuss the issues in detail and don't let her get away with name-calling. Explain your position and get her to explain hers. Say such things as:

- It's no good your calling me names. Let's discuss this rationally.
- Have you ever said one thing and done the opposite?
- I want to hear your ideas on this, and then I want you to listen to mine.

You can use this kind of occasion to talk about the problems you face in making your ideals fit reality. Don't preach or whine. Explain how you cope with having to compromise your ideals in the face of the demands of everyday life. Invite your teen's reactions and suggestions. Give concrete examples. Tell stories about your experiences. Say such things as:

- I have ideals that I live by, but so do other people. Sometimes our ideals collide, and we all have to compromise.
- Everyone doesn't think the same way I do or you do. If I were God or king, I could say "my way or the highway." But since I'm just an ordinary person, I have got to meet people halfway even if I don't like what they say or do.
- I've learned that the world doesn't usually fit my picture of the way it should be. That's not the world's problem, it's mine.
- Here's an example of the kind of thing I face almost every day in my business. Tell me what you think I ought to do.

WORDS AND PHRASES TO USE

✦ compromise	✦ ego	✦ open to the needs of the moment	✦ rigidity
✦ contradictions	✦ flexibility		✦ truth
✦ demands of everyday life	✦ honesty	✦ pragmatism	✦ we're all hypocrites to some degree
	✦ ideals	✦ problem solving	

What Not to Say and Do

Don't criticize your teen's ideals. Don't say such things as:

- ✦ You have got your head in the clouds.
- ✦ You need to live in the real world. Then you'd know who the hypocrites are.
- ✦ The world will never be the way you want it to be.

Don't get angry if you're called a hypocrite. Don't say such things as:

- ✦ Don't you call me names.
- ✦ You have no right to call me a hypocrite.
- ✦ You're just a dumb teenager.
- ✦ You don't know what you're talking about.

Don't cut off discussion of differences between talk and action. Don't say such things as:

- ✦ I don't care what you say. This discussion is over.
- ✦ I can say what I like and do what I like, and you can't tell me not to.
- ✦ Don't talk to me about your high ideals. I'm not interested. I do what I have to do.
- ✦ You'll never understand what it means to be an adult until you have responsibilities like mine, so there's no point in talking about it anymore.

WORDS AND PHRASES TO AVOID

✦ blind	✦ ignorant	✦ pigheaded	✦ unrealistic
✦ don't you ever call me that	✦ immature	✦ shut up	✦ you don't know anything
	✦ innocent idealist	✦ stupid	
✦ dumb	✦ mindless	✦ uncompromising	✦ you think you know everything

44 Identity

Start every day off with a smile and get it over with.

—W. C. FIELDS

Liz's parents worried about her. She was in her second year of high school and seemed to have no sense of who she was or who she wanted to become. She had no consistent serious pursuits. At home she spent her time in her room listening to music, "talking" in a computer chat room, surfing the Internet, or phoning friends about boys, clothes, and school. Her parents thought she needed to have a more focused life, building on her strengths and compensating for her weaknesses in school and in her leisure activities. They wondered if they shouldn't talk to Liz about her career goals, her schoolwork, why she wasn't on any teams, why she didn't belong to any clubs, why she had given up dance classes, why she just seemed happy to do a little bit of this, and a little bit of that but nothing with great seriousness of purpose. She seemed to have no driving force. They asked her why she wasn't like her brother who seemed to know exactly who he was, his strengths and weaknesses, and what he did and didn't like.

Liz's parents confused her. Sometimes they treated her like a little girl but then expected her to behave like a grown-up. They got angry with the way she dressed, her makeup, and the rings in her ears. Then they expected her to be responsible for her schoolwork, for getting a part-time job, and for not smoking or drinking. She thought she was basically a good girl, but her mom and dad made it difficult because they overreacted. All she wanted was for her mom and dad to help her when she asked for it and trust her to get through things in her own time and in her own way. She wanted them to see her for who she was, not who they wanted her to be, even though she wasn't quite sure who she really was.

Things to Consider

Teenagers often struggle to discover who they are. With increasing life choices for women in our society, some people believe that identity struggle for teenage girls is more difficult than for boys. Yet the problem for girls and boys is basically the same.

A teenage identity crisis may also be a crisis for you. How do you help your teen find out who she really is? What do you say or do to give her direction and a sense of self-worth? What's your role in this journey of self-discovery?

You should know your teens and recognize that their pushing against the limits you have set up doesn't mean they aren't good kids. Teens are still kids. They don't have your experience of life and have to gain it for themselves, just as you did. By challenging your rules and values they discover their own. The hard part for you is allowing them to make mistakes. Don't allow your need to protect to smother them or, worse, alienate them.

Some of your rules and concerns are appropriate, such as those on smoking, drinking, sex, drugs, and crime. Your teen may challenge them without really wanting them to change. See these challenges as part of that self-discovery process. Don't give in to them but don't expect blind obedience. Use them as an opportunity for talk and involvement.

Other rules—on curfews, clothing, and dating—may be inappropriate. Use these challenges as a chance for negotiation, talking about your teens' rights and responsibilities as well as your own as a parent. Help your teens gain that knowledge and experience for themselves. Don't overreact to minor problems. Decide on the level of risk you can tolerate for your teens. It will ensure safety for your teens but not prevent them from being part of their group.

Taking risks, testing limits, changing self-images, and challenging rules and conventions are all part of teenagers' search for identity. You have the difficult job of helping them while being nurturer, protector, teacher, coach, and critic. Don't expect teens to understand your roles or to thank you for them. They'll come to appreciate you later on.

Three Things You Must Do

1. *Understand* your teen's need to find her identity.
2. *Recognize* that this involves finding her own values by pushing against yours.
3. *Maintain* your authority *and* your flexibility for your teen's sake, not yours.

What to Say and Do

Help your teen become someone instead of just being your child. Encourage her to try things, to challenge herself, to test her abilities and discover her likes and dislikes. Say such things as:

- ‣ If you want to do that, go ahead. I'll give you my support.

- ‣ Don't say you don't like it without at least learning more about it.

- ‣ I don't like the thought of your doing that, but as long as it's not dangerous, immoral, or illegal, I guess it's okay.

Your teenager's identity crisis may create problems for you. How can you give her direction and a sense of self-worth? Say such things as:

- ‣ You're at an age where you're always going to find out new things about yourself. Don't worry about it. It's normal.

- ‣ The important thing is not to do anything that will hurt your options later on.

- ‣ Now is the time to explore things. You're always going to be discovering new things that you like or don't like.

Your teen will test the limits you've set up. It doesn't mean your teen has gone bad. Accept this as part of adolescent searching for identity. Say things that open up the conversation:

- ‣ Why did you do that?

- ‣ Do you think you should be allowed to make your own rules?

- ‣ I don't like what you did, but I think I understand why you did it. Do you want to tell me why?

Use challenges as an opportunity for talk and involvement. Say such things as:

- ‣ I'm willing to be flexible on some things, but not on things that can mean serious trouble.

- ‣ There are better ways of finding out who you are than experimenting with smoking and drugs. I think we need to talk about this. I'd like to know why you might want to try them, and you should know why I don't want you to.

Rules on curfews, clothing, dating, and other safe issues can be an opportunity to talk about your teen's rights and responsibilities as well as your own as a parent. Say such things as:

- You can't have rights without responsibilities. I make rules because I am responsible for you.
- How much responsibility are you willing to take for yourself? What can you do that I won't have to do anymore?
- As you take more responsibility for yourself, you get to make more of your own rules.

As a parent you nurture, protect, teach, coach, and criticize your teen. You have to maintain your authority in the face of mild and fierce hostility for your child's sake. You also have to be flexible when the issues are not dangerous or morally compelling.

WORDS AND PHRASES TO USE

▸ adolescent	▸ believe	▸ identity	▸ responsibilities
▸ adult	▸ challenge	▸ issues	▸ rights
▸ authority	▸ choices/options	▸ likes and dislikes	▸ rules
▸ bad taste	▸ common sense	▸ protect	▸ test

What Not to Say and Do

Don't smother your teens or, worse, alienate them. Don't say such things as:

- You'll do what I say until you're living on your own and supporting yourself.
- I know what's best for you, and if you were more mature, you'd realize that.
- You're still just a kid. You have to do what I say.

Don't give in to teens, but don't expect blind obedience. Don't say such things as:

- Who gave you the right to make that decision?
- Don't ask questions, just do it.
- Don't you dare question my authority.

Don't overreact to minor problems. Don't say such things as:

- Go upstairs and take off that makeup right now.
- You're not going to school wearing that.
- You call that clean? There will be no computer or telephone privileges for you for a week.

Don't despair. Don't say such things as:

- I'm finished trying to be your parent. Do what you like.
- You're just a stupid kid.
- You're not my child anymore.

Don't be patronizing by suggesting that you have all the answers, or that their problems aren't significant. Don't say such things as:

- I know you're just going through that rebellious stage. It will pass.
- You're just going through a typical teenage stage, it's really nothing.
- Come to me with your little identity problems, and I'll show you how to get over them.

WORDS AND PHRASES TO AVOID

▶ adolescent nonsense	▶ delinquent	▶ immature	▶ stupid values
▶ authority	▶ disregard	▶ irresponsible	▶ you're on your own from now on
▶ childish	▶ dumb	▶ malicious	
	▶ I can't cope	▶ rebel	

45 Injustice

Injustice is relatively easy to bear; what stings is justice.

—H. L. Mencken

Carolyn had been talking about feminism with her friends at school, one of whom had a mom who was quite prominent in the women's movement. Men's oppression of women had been high on the list of injustices in the world. It made Carolyn wonder why every woman wasn't a feminist. She and her friends, both boys and girls, agreed that they would do everything they could to gain equal rights for women in every area of life in every country in the world.

Carolyn and her friends also had a long list of society's mistreatment of people who didn't have enough to eat or to care for their families, of animals who were hunted or used in medical experiments, and of the destruction of the environment through the greedy exploitation of nonrenewable resources by government, industry, and individuals. There were so many injustices in the world that they really didn't know where to start.

It was the kind of thing they talked about among themselves and also with their teachers, who were generally sympathetic but didn't seem particularly ready to get involved in any action themselves. Carolyn and her friends were thinking of starting a student club at school that would campaign and raise awareness among students of these great injustices. They knew of a high school in which a teacher and students had formed a very successful association to combat racism. Its purpose was to fight racism in school and society through education and public awareness. Carolyn thought that their club could use that association as a model.

Things to Consider

Your teenagers may be very idealistic about things like justice. They may have a strong sense of what is fair and what is not. Thousands of issues offer themselves as injustices that need putting right by those with ideals.

Don't let your experience or cynicism dampen your children's desire to see a better world. Offer support and understanding in ways which will tell them that you care, that you wish the world were a better place, and that you do what you can within the realm of possibility and responsibility to help. Make it clear that you're not a saint (which they'll know already) or a hypocrite (which they may doubt). Also, there's a limit to what you or any average person can do other than be nice to others, respect people's differences that are respectful, abhor racism or any form of arbitrary discrimination, and share some of your resources with people who need help.

You can encourage your teens to be active in organizations that aim to help others. You can seize opportunities to talk about concern for injustice. It is certainly worthwhile to explore issues in some detail.

Talk about the fact that most adults realize it is fruitless and sometimes self-defeating to dwell on all the bad things in the world while forgetting about the good. Teens need to understand, probably through their own experience but also from conversations with you, that even people like Mother Teresa, who devoted her life to helping the poor, couldn't be all things to all people. And very few of us can come close to being like her.

You might want to suggest that in the final analysis the best thing your teens can do to fight injustice is do their best to act justly toward everyone and everything they encounter in the world in everyday life. If everyone did that, the problems would start solving themselves.

Three Things You Must Do

1. *Accept* teen idealism.

2. *Support* your teen's concern about injustice.

3. *Talk* about the need for ideals, reason, and practical action.

What to Say and Do

Your teenager may have a strong sense of injustices that need to be put right. These can include things in the family, the community, the nation, or the world. It's good to talk about these things at the dinner table. Teens can benefit from your insights and experience. Say such things as:

- I think you're right. That's a horrible injustice. What do you think can be done?
- It's always easy to think of injustices. It's hard to think of good solutions. It's even harder to think of practical solutions.
- The first thing you need to do when you talk about these things is make sure you have your facts straight. It's hard to know the truth, but it's worth trying to find it.

It is good to offer your support and understanding. Tell your teen that you care, that you wish the world were a better place, and that you do what you can within the realm of possibility and responsibility to help. Explain what you do if she doesn't already know, which she may not.

- I hear what you are saying. It is important to help in any way you can.
- I'm on the board of the children's hospital.
- I volunteer at the food bank.
- You could do volunteer work, too, if you wanted to.

Explain that while you are not a saint, you still have a social conscience. Talk about your own way of making the world a better place. Say such things as:

- I'm not perfect, but I try to be nice to others.
- I try to respect people's differences as long as they are respectful of others.
- I am not racist and reject racism in any form.
- I believe I have an obligation to help people in our world who can't help themselves.
- I think I need to share some of my assets with people who are poor.

Encourage your teen to live her ideals. Say such things as:

- I think you should join some organization that aims to help others.
- Are there any clubs at school that concentrate on good works?
- Our church [synagogue, mosque] has plenty of things you could do to help others.

Seize opportunities to talk about your teen's concern for injustice. Help her be aware of the possibility that idealism can also lead to injustice. Say such things as:

- Sometimes fighting injustice leads to other injustice. People get so caught up in their ideals that they forget about real people.
- Your concerns are important. Just don't forget to look at all the possible effects your actions might have on people who get caught in the middle.
- Sometimes it is a case of choosing between the lesser of two injustices.

Tell your teen not to dwell on all the bad things in the world and forget about the good. Say such things as:

- I know you see a lot of the evil in the world. Don't forget that there is a lot of good, too.
- Let's see if we can name one good thing for every injustice you can name.

Suggest that your teen fight injustice by acting justly toward everyone and everything in the world in everyday life. Say such things as:

- It is always good to have some control over what you want to achieve. You can help the cause of justice by being just in everything you do. But don't expect everyone to agree with you.
- If everyone tried to be just themselves, it might help the problem a lot.

Warn your teen that she mustn't look outside herself for rewards or satisfaction for her work against injustice. Say such things as:

- There is an old saying, "Virtue is its own reward." It means that you should do things for their own sake, not because you think others will think you're great or wonderful for doing them.

WORDS AND PHRASES TO USE

active	equity	help others	prejudice
altruistic	fair	idealistic	racism
committed	favoritism	justice	virtuous
discrimination	feminism	meaningful	volunteer

What Not to Say and Do

Don't let your experience or cynicism dampen your teen's idealism. Don't say such things as:

- Grow up. The world is a tough place, and it will never change.
- You're just another do-gooder.
- We don't need any more bleeding heart liberals in this world.

Don't stand in the way of your teen getting involved. Don't say such things as:

- Don't waste your time. It won't do any good.
- You'd be better off spending your spare time doing homework or getting a job.
- You're just going to make enemies out of the people who you're going to be working for someday.

Don't make snide remarks about your teen's ambitions. Don't say such things as:

- Who do you think you are, Mother Teresa?
- You want to be a saint?
- Get real. You have to accept the world as it is.

WORDS AND PHRASES TO AVOID

• be realistic	• goody two-shoes	• might is right	• you're wasting your time and energy
• blind idealist	• life isn't fair and never will be	• you have your head in the clouds	
• do-gooder			

46 Independence

Life does not begin at the moment of conception or the moment of birth. It begins when the kids leave home and the dog dies.

—ANONYMOUS

Jake was fourteen, a freshman in high school. His parents had just given him his own room in the basement so he didn't have to share with his younger brother. He had made the football team and just got his first part-time job working in McDonald's. The pay was low, but his parents promised he could use it as he pleased. They suggested he save up for something big rather than spend it all every week, and they said that was all the advice they'd give him unless he asked for more.

Jake's sister, Margaret, was sixteen and seemed to be fully independent. She'd always had a room of her own, went out on dates, wore makeup, and was saving for a car. Mom and Dad said they'd match any money she saved up. She was working hard in school so that she would get into a good college. She wanted to be a doctor.

Jake and Margaret's parents wanted their kids to become good adults, so they gradually gave them as much independence as they could reasonably handle. They thought the best way to help their kids become responsible grown-ups was to let them gradually make many of their own decisions. If parents always made the decisions, how would children learn to make their own?

Their teens' independence combined rights and responsibilities for things such as getting schoolwork done and done well, the right to private spaces, responsibility for house and yard cleaning, control over their disposable income, the right to choose their own clothes, the right to save up for a car and the responsibility for maintaining it, the right to having a dating relationship with another teen, and the responsibility for getting enough sleep.

Things to Consider

Your job is to provide your teens with food, shelter, clothes, security, education, and love, but also to point them toward freedom and to put them on the road to becoming responsible and independent adults. Your dilemma is how to do both at the same time.

Your teens can't become independent young adults if you control everything they do. If you tell them how to spend their money, what movies are good for them, what music not to listen to, and what Internet sites are off limits, your approach is too controlling, too protecting, and too untrusting.

For the last twelve or thirteen years you've kept your children from harm and taught them to know right from wrong. Now you need to see how good a job you've done. Start giving up some control. Your children need to become independent in their own way over the next five or six years. Independence means having the right to make mistakes. You have to let them make their mistakes.

Don't dump everything on them at once. Ask what they want to control. Discuss the options. Give them responsibility for making choices about how they spend their time and their money. Sometimes you will need to say no for their own protection. Or say, "Let's think this through." You can talk about their options and consequences.

If you can, give them their own private space. Private physical space is important for teens. Private social and psychological space is even more important. Keep out unless you're invited. Start cutting the ties that bind. The most important part of your relationship will always be there if you have the courage to recognize and encourage your teens' growing independence from you.

Three Things You Must Do

1. *Recognize* your teen's need for independence from you.

2. *Give* your teen increasing control over her own decisions.

3. *Talk* to your teen regularly about her independence and intervene if things are threatening her welfare.

What to Say and Do

Begin by gradually giving up control over her life. Let her make decisions. Say such things as:

- I'm not going to tell you how to spend your money. You decide what you want to do with it.

- You're the best judge of your own taste in movies, music, and reading material. If you want my opinion, you can ask for it. Otherwise, it's your choice.

- You and I both know there is a lot of terrible stuff on the Internet, but I've decided that I'm not going to try to censor what you do online. I'm trusting you to do the right thing.

You've tried to keep your child safe and to know right from wrong. Say such things as:

- You and I have both worked at helping you think for yourself and learn how to make good decisions. Now we'll see how well we've done.

- I know you for who you are. I want to trust you to make your own choices about lots more things in your life—not everything but more things each year until you're on your own.

Start giving up control gradually. Say such things as:

- I want you to be more independent in making decisions that affect your life.

- You'll still need help with some things. If you want me to help, just ask.

Don't dump everything on your teen. Talk about what she wants to control. Say such things as:

- I want you to have more independence. What do you think you need to have control over?

- Let's talk about my role in your life. Where do you still need my help, and where do you want to take care of things yourself?

- Let's talk about sharing power and responsibility. I want to give you more power, but I also need you to take more responsibility. What do you think?

You have responsibility for your teenager until she is eighteen. Say such things as:

➤ No! I just can't let you do that, or I'd be shirking my responsibility as a parent.

➤ Let's think this through. I want to talk to you about the consequences of what you want to do. I think there may be other options that you haven't thought about.

Privacy is important for teens. Always knock before entering. Don't enter until you are invited unless it's an emergency.

WORDS AND PHRASES TO USE

➤ advice	➤ decision-making	➤ privacy	➤ sensible
➤ choices/options	➤ growing up	➤ responsibility	➤ the right to make mistakes
➤ consequences	➤ maturity	➤ rights	
➤ cooperation	➤ power	➤ self-confidence	➤ trust

What Not to Say and Do

Unless your teen is very immature or not trustworthy, don't say such things as:

➤ You'll do what I say.

➤ As long as you live under my roof, I control you.

➤ You're not old enough to make your own decisions.

Don't belittle your teen's transition into adulthood. Don't say such things as:

➤ You're such a baby.

➤ Aren't you ever going to grow up?

➤ You're so immature.

➤ How can I trust you to make your own decisions when you're still so young?

Don't idealize your own teenage years. The danger sign is when you begin your sentence with "When I was your age . . ." Don't say such things as:

➤ When I was your age, I was already out earning my own living.

➤ When I was your age, I didn't make such stupid mistakes.

➤ When I was your age, my parents knew they could trust me to do the right thing.

When your teen wants to do something that is reasonable, don't interfere. Don't be one of those parents who say no unless they have a good reason to say yes. Say yes unless you have a good reason to say no. Don't automatically say such things as:

➤ No!

➤ You can't do that.

➤ You don't have my permission.

➤ You're better off staying home.

➤ I don't like your doing that.

➤ That's not good for you.

WORDS AND PHRASES TO AVOID

➤ absolutely not	➤ immature	➤ not until you're responsible for yourself	➤ you'll only make some stupid mistake
➤ bad	➤ maybe next year		➤ you're too young
➤ forget it	➤ never	➤ you don't have enough experience	
➤ get out of here	➤ no		
➤ I don't trust you	➤ no way	➤ you don't know what's good for you	
➤ ignorant kid	➤ not a chance		

47 Internet

The computer is down. I hope it's something serious.

—Stanton Delaplane

Adam was a fifteen-year-old computer junkie. He visited chat rooms, typing his comments on everything from school and sex to football and new software. He once spent six straight hours playing a computer game.

His thirteen-year-old sister, Rhonda, spent much of her spare, and not so spare, time on the computer as well. She was into creating websites, visiting her favorite teen chat rooms, and playing computer games that she had downloaded from the Internet.

Their parents had bought them a computer for schoolwork. Their parents did some e-shopping, played games, and visited websites. Their dad, a writer, did a chat room interview on his last book.

Although they encouraged their teens to use their computers wisely and responsibly, they were concerned about the availability of certain websites, specifically hate sites and porno sites. They were out there, and they knew their kids might visit them. Their dilemma was that facing most parents of teens: Should they censor their kids' computer use or trust their teens to use their good judgment and reject porn and hate sites?

Things to Consider

A recent (1999) *Time* magazine survey of thirteen to seventeen-year-olds reported that 82 percent said they used the Internet for e-mail, chat rooms, and websites; 44 percent said they had seen sex websites; 25 percent had seen hate sites; 14 percent, sites that teach how to build bombs; and 12 percent, sites that show where or how to buy a gun. When asked about their parents' rules for Internet use, 31 percent said they had rules and always followed them,

26 percent that they had rules but didn't always follow them, and 43 percent said they had no rules.

The teens were then asked if they had ever encountered people online whom they suspected were not who they said they were. Seventy-two percent of girls and 57 percent of boys said yes; 66 percent of girls and 54 percent of boys said these people said offensive things; and 58 percent of girls and 39 percent of boys said they asked for personal information such as address or phone number.

When asked if they trusted the information they got from the Internet, 13 percent said a great deal, 62 percent said somewhat, and 24 percent said no. Seventy-eight percent thought it was a good idea for teens to have access to the Internet, 13 percent said it was a bad idea, and 8 percent said it made no difference.

Conclusion: The Internet is a wonderful resource when used responsibly, but it can put kids at risk since it doesn't discriminate when it comes to communication and the exchange of information between honest, reliable people and organizations, and those who seek to exploit the young, innocent, and gullible. The Internet allows people who would otherwise never talk to each other, to communicate; it offers all of us a variety of knowledge, information, and opportunities to search, find, and sell goods and services. But its strength is also its weakness. Anyone can have a website, anyone can say anything he wants, anyone can offer things for sale, anyone can pretend to be someone or something he is not.

Talk to your teens about the pros and cons of the Internet. Watch them use the computer to see how they handle the dangers and possibilities of using chat rooms, e-mail, or visiting websites where people can disguise their identities and intentions. Teach your teens to censor, to evaluate, and to critique what they see and hear.

You can monitor your teens' Internet activity by scanning e-mail addresses, watching incoming e-mail, or observing things that come snailmail from objectionable organizations. Make sure that your teens do not have a credit card, which is necessary to access most porn sites. Check your monthly bills carefully to make sure your teens' charges don't include such things. Teach your teens never to give out personal information. Place your computer in a high-traffic area of your house, such as a kitchen or hallway. Although I consider this the least desirable option, you can buy software that will block sites you don't want your teens visiting. But the best safeguard against Internet misuse is having teenagers you can trust to be their own censor.

Three Things You Must Do

1. *Know* what your teen knows about the Internet.

2. *Teach* your teen to be his own critic and censor.

3. *Know* the best and least obtrusive ways to monitor your teen's Internet activity.

What to Say and Do

Talk to your teens about how they use the Internet. Say such things as:

- Do you mind if I see what you're doing?
- How about showing me your sites?

If necessary, ask your teen to teach you about the Internet. Say such things as:

- You're the computer whiz in the family. How about teaching me what you know?
- I want to learn more about the Internet. Will you teach me?
- (Teasingly) Time for payback. I'd like you to teach me how to use the Internet.

Talk about the rules for sensible Internet use. Tell your teen to please observe the following:

- Never give out your personal information to chat rooms, bulletin boards, or e-mail strangers.
- Never agree to a real-life meeting without my permission.
- Don't answer threatening or uncomfortable messages and don't hesitate to tell me about them.
- Remember that people you meet on the Internet may not be who or what they tell you.

- There are people out there who are sexual predators, crooks, and hate-mongers.
- Although I am your parent and responsible for you, you must also take responsibility for being an intelligent user, critic, and censor.

Ask your teen about his experiences on the net. Say such things as:

- Have you ever met people online who you thought were not who they said they were?
- Have you ever met people who said offensive things?
- Have you ever met people who asked for personal information such as address or phone number?

Know the level of your teen's Internet sophistication. Say such things as:

- I like it because you can get a lot of useful information, and you can search for things you might want to buy. What kinds of things have you found there?
- You know, anyone can say anything he wants, anyone can offer things for sale, anyone can pretend to be someone or something he isn't. I think that's a real problem, don't you?

Here are some sources where you can get help if you want to protect your teen from the dangers of the net:

- http://www.cyberangels.org/. An online Internet safety program.
- http://www.safekids.com/. Ways to make kids' online experience fun and more productive.
- http://www.soc-um.org/. Tracks pedophiles and child pornography websites.
- http://www.netnanny.com/netnanny/. Provides software that will monitor and filter net use. Other software filters include: Cybersitter, CyberPatrol, Cyber Snoop, Surfwatch, and Rated P-G.

WORDS AND PHRASES TO USE

a great tool	communication	don't trust everyone you meet	hate/porn sites
be sensible	computer literacy		Internet literacy
caution	critically	e-mail	pros and cons

What Not to Say and Do

Don't talk about the Internet if you don't know anything about it. Don't say such things as:

- I don't want you surfing the Internet. It's filled with things you shouldn't see.
- The Internet does more harm than good with its pornography and hate.

Don't assume you can really control what sites your teen visits. Don't say such things as:

- You're not to look at any sex on the Internet.
- If I catch you looking at dirty sites, your computer privileges will be revoked.
- You are not permitted to go on the net without my being present.

Don't abdicate your responsibility for monitoring (not censoring) your teen's Internet use. Don't say such things as:

- I don't care what you look at.

- You're such a bad kid. I give up on you.

Don't reject computers and the net because you're worried about illicit use by your teen. Less than 3.5 percent of the net has "inappropriate content," according to one expert. Don't say such things as:

- We're not having a computer in this house.
- We can have a computer, but we're not going online.
- I don't want you using the Internet.

Don't overreact if your teen has been looking at "forbidden" sites. Remember how you were as a teenager. Sometimes overreacting is worse than the misdeed. Don't say such things as:

- You dirty little bugger.
- I can't trust you for a moment.
- How could you look at such filth?

WORDS AND PHRASES TO AVOID

- computers are dangerous things
- I can't trust you
- I won't have it in the house
- I'm going to censor your Internet use
- it's disgusting
- they do more harm than good
- you can do what you please
- you don't have my permission to use the net
- you'll just abuse it
- you're untrustworthy

48 Jealousy

Jealousy consists of revealing how little we think of ourselves and how much we think of the other person.

—Anonymous

Gary was jealous of Jonah. Everything seemed to come easy to him. Not only did Jonah get straight "A" grades in school without much apparent effort, but he was great-looking, so all the girls wanted to go out with him. He was also quarterback of the football team and such a superb athlete that colleges were already courting him with promises of a full athletic scholarship, which he didn't even need because his family was wealthy and could afford to send him to any college he wanted to attend. Jonah's seventeenth birthday present was a red Corvette.

Gary got good grades, a mixture of "A's" and "B+'s" for which he worked quite hard. If he did well on his SATs, he'd get into a good college. He wasn't bad-looking, but not nearly what girls would call handsome. He was a first-string running back on the football team, but no college scouts seemed interested. Gary's parents both worked and brought home a considerable income. Gary drove a seven-year-old Chevy Malibu Z24.

Gary's life would have been fine if he hadn't known Jonah or guys like Jonah.

Things to Consider

Jealousy is as natural a human emotion as love. The problem is that it's a negative emotion, whereas love is positive. Jealousy hurts your self-esteem. If you envy someone else, it means you think he has it better than you. This is where a good communication relationship with your teens is really important. You must help your teens be comfortable in their own skin and happy with their abilities and talents, their looks, their material possessions, their wins and losses. Being comfortable doesn't mean being complacent or self-satisfied or lacking ambition. It means accepting yourself for who you are and not measuring your own worth against others.

Good communication means telling your teens that you value them. The Communication Ethic in Part One suggests some ways to do this. Involve yourself in your teens' lives so you know what they think of themselves. Listen carefully and without judging so they'll never be afraid to talk to you about their lives. Be there for them and always try to communicate.

More specifically, don't preach the old line that who they are as an individual is more important than how they look, what they accomplish, or material success. It's true, of course, but most teens won't understand its real meaning. If you try to convince them of it, you might only make things worse because they'll hear you saying that what they believe is true—that they're not good-looking, talented, or one of life's chosen.

Talk to them about how they can be as good as the people they're jealous of by making the most of their own looks and talent through dedication and hard work. Tell them that they have unfulfilled potential and talk about what that is. Discuss their talents, looks, hopes and desires, anxieties and jealousies. Develop a realistic plan for them to make the most of who they are. Show them all the time that you value them for who they are.

A good defense against jealousy is teaching your teens how to accept the inevitability of life's differences. Talk to your teens about the fact that life normally won't fit their version of what it should be. Tell them that this doesn't mean to accept passively whatever life hands us. It means to work hard, do your best, and take pride in having done as much as you could to achieve your goals.

Rarely a day goes by that I don't find myself feeling a few pangs of jealousy at someone else's good fortune. I feel jealous in spite of knowing that it is a wasteful emotion, that life isn't fair (according to my version of it), and that my own achievements are substantial. So unless your teens are superhuman, don't expect your talking to work miracles. Jealousy is something even saints feel. Your job is to help your teens put their feelings into their proper perspective so they understand that jealousy works in your favor only when it spurs you to work harder to achieve your goals and accept the fact that no one can do more than that.

Three Things You Must Do

1. *Accept* jealousy as a natural emotion.

2. *Build* your teen's self-esteem to combat jealousy.

3. *Help* your teen put feelings of jealousy in perspective.

What to Say and Do

Talk about jealousy as a natural but negative human emotion. Explain how it hurts your self-esteem, and comes from self-esteem that is not all it should be. Say such things as:

- ♦ I know what it's like to be jealous, but I don't like myself when I am.
- ♦ Do you ever feel jealous of someone?
- ♦ I think my feelings of jealousy come from thinking that someone else has it better than me.

Talk to your teens about how important it is to be comfortable in your own skin, happy with your abilities, talents, looks, material possessions, wins, and losses. Explain what that means and what it doesn't mean. Say such things as:

- ♦ If you like yourself, you won't always be comparing yourself with everyone else.
- ♦ It means knowing who you are and not measuring your own worth against others.

Tell your teen that you value him, that you understand his jealousy, but that he needs to rise above it. Say such things as:

- ♦ You're every bit as good as the people you're jealous of. Make the most of your own talents.
- ♦ You need to realize how much you have to offer. Let's go through your assets—you have lots.
- ♦ What is it in others that makes you jealous? Let's talk about what you can change and what you can't. You need to make the best of what you have.

Try talking to your teen about accepting what life gives him, especially when it doesn't fit his version of what it should be. Discuss what this means. Say such things as:

- Lots of things won't fit your dreams, and you may get jealous of others. You know that life is often like that. The question is how do you cope with it.

- You have to accept what life gives you, but having done that, you have to work hard and do your best to achieve your goals.

Help your teen put his jealousies into a proper perspective. Talk about his feelings, hopes, goals, and disappointments. Say such things as:

- Being jealous is normal. What is important is how you deal with it.

- Think about what makes you jealous and see why you feel that way.

- As always, the most important thing is how you make a positive out of a negative.

WORDS AND PHRASES TO USE

- acknowledge your emotions
- be honest with yourself
- be realistic
- caring is good
- change what you can change, forget about what you can't
- don't be ashamed of being jealous
- life will hardly ever fit your dreams
- make a positive out of a negative

What Not to Say and Do

Don't criticize your teen for being jealous. It's a natural emotion. Don't say such things as:

- Jealousy is the same as envy. It's one of the seven deadly sins.

- You're so stupid to be jealous of her/him.

Don't encourage your teen's jealousies. Don't say such things as:

- Some people are just born lucky.

- S/he has everything, don't you think so?

- Life's just not fair.

Don't ignore your teen's jealousies. Don't say such things as:

- Don't be silly.
- I don't want to hear about it.
- You say the dumbest things.

Don't say things that might damage your teen's self-esteem. Don't say such things as:

- There's no point in being jealous. They are just better than you.
- You haven't got a chance.
- Some kids just have a lot more talent than you.
- You're not handsome, and you never will be.
- No matter what you do, you'll never be as good/successful/popular.

WORDS AND PHRASES TO AVOID

don't bother me with that	forget it	just face the facts	you haven't a hope
dumb	get a life	there's nothing to be jealous about	you're a loser
	jealousy is a sin		you're so silly

49 Language

> *When ideas fail, words come in very handy.*
>
> —Johann von Goethe

Marty's mom and dad knew that there were lots of times when they didn't understand a word he said. He said things like "Duh" and "Yeah, right, Mom!" "Duh" seemed to mean "How could you say such a thing?" and "Yeah, right!" meant "No, wrong!" Sometimes he would say things like "I'm going to the movies, not!" Clearly, Marty and his parents spoke different languages.

But that wasn't what bothered them. It was the offensive language they overheard him using with his friends—those four-letter Anglo-Saxon words that most teenagers and parents know but that teenage boys and, increasingly, girls seem to use in every sentence. Mom and Dad could use foul language with the best of them, but they normally saved it for special occasions.

That's what they told Marty. "If you use those words all the time, what do you have left to use when you're really angry?" They also thought but didn't say that using bad language was a teenage boy's macho thing. They were reaching the point where they would have to talk with their son about his language.

Things to Consider

Language is not about who you are. It *is* who you are, at least as far as others are concerned. Crude and coarse or refined and gentle, uncaring and insensitive or nurturing and empathetic, unintelligible or clear as a bell, teens present themselves to others in what they say and do. That's why you're right to be concerned about the language they use.

When you hear teens talking in shopping centers, on buses and trains, outside of schools or at the movies, you make an instant judgment: He's rough.

She's a slut. He's well spoken. She's sweet. You want your teens' language to make a good impression because you know how important superficial impressions can be for giving them the best chance to succeed in life.

It is likely that your teens don't talk the same way to everyone. They will use one kind of language for friends and peers, another for adults, and another for you. You do the same thing when you suit your language to the occasion. You talk differently, using different words and expressions, to your spouse, child, boss, police officer, mechanic, and teacher.

Help your teens understand how important it is to use the right language for the right occasion. This means not swearing in public, not using expressions that the listener won't understand, and not talking to your teacher as you would to a teenage pal. Teens use language to show they're cool, disinterested, unimpressed, unflappable, and in control. Impressing their friends means using the "with it" expressions. Some teens don't want any adults to think they can control them, and they try to make that clear using disrespectful language. This never works to the teens' advantage. It just makes their life more difficult.

There are three guiding principles in language use. The first is: Suit the language to the person and the occasion. The second is: People will identify you with what you say and how you say it. The third is: Use bad language sparingly. If you use curse words all the time, you'll have nothing left for special occasions.

Three Things You Must Do

1. *Recognize* that people believe you are the language you use.

2. *Understand* that your teen will talk the way his friends talk.

3. *Help* your teen learn how to use language that suits the occasion.

What to Say and Do

Talk to your teen about the impression he makes with the language he uses. He may not realize that people label him by what he says and how he says it.

Tape-record breakfast or dinner conversation and get your teen to listen. Talk about his reaction. Say such things as:

- You decide whether you like or don't like people by what they say and the way they say it, right? How do you think you come across?
- Listen to yourself and the rest of us. What's your impression?
- How do you want people to hear you?

Help your teen understand the kind of impression he makes when he talks. Say such things as:

- Whenever I hear kids talking, I get an impression of who they are and what they're like, whether they seem nice or not, intelligent or not.
- Do you care about the impression you make?
- You may think it's wrong for people to judge you when they don't even know you, but that's life. We all form opinions from what someone says and does even if we don't know them.

Explain to your teen that he probably doesn't talk the same way to everyone, and if he does, he is probably making a mistake. He ought to talk differently to friends and peers, to you, and to other adults. And he should suit his language to the occasion. Say such things as:

- You don't use the same language when you talk to me that you use when you talk to your friends. Do you know why?
- You have to be sensitive to those you're talking to. Use words you think they'll understand.
- You need to talk politely in public. That means not swearing.

Show your teen that using the wrong language with you has negative results. Say such things as:

- I know you need to show your friends that you're cool, but that doesn't work with me.
- I don't know if you want to impress me, but you can by speaking to me appropriately.
- Using disrespectful language doesn't help you. It just makes your life more difficult.

Your teen can speak your language. Try working with your teen to learn his language. Don't use it because you will sound either stupid or patronizing if you're not a teenager. But you do need to understand it. Say such things as:

- I've heard some expressions you use with your friends. Can you tell me what they mean?
- How about teaching me your language?
- That hip-hop or rap language doesn't make sense to me. What does it mean?

Talk to your teen about using bad language. Explain that adults hear it as being juvenile, uneducated, and crude. Say such things as:

- I know you use some pretty bad language sometimes. I can't stop you from using it with your friends, but you mustn't talk that way here.
- I realized when I was your age that if I used curse words all the time, I'd have nothing left for special occasions.

WORDS AND PHRASES TO USE

- articulate clearly
- be careful in what you say
- consider whom you're talking to
- don't swear in public
- fit your language to the occasion
- people will label you because of your language
- think about whether you want to communicate something important or just make an impression
- think before you talk
- you are what you say

What Not to Say and Do

Don't set a bad example for your teen. Don't use language you wouldn't want him to use. Don't say such things as:

- You dumb little _____!

Show that you care about what others think about your teen. Don't say such things as:

- You can talk any way you like. I don't care.
- Your language is so bad that there's no hope for you, so say whatever you like.

Don't disrespect your teen. Don't say such things as:

- You're one bad kid.
- There's no way I like having you as my kid.
- Don't you go around shooting off your mouth.

Don't approve of your teen's bad language. Don't say such things as:

- You're right to curse him out.
- If he talks that way, you say it right back.
- I don't care what you say as long as I can't hear it.

Don't belittle your teen's use of teen jargon. Don't say such things as:

- You talk like a moron.
- Talk English, will you?
- Why don't you say what you mean?
- How can I understand you if you talk that way?
- Only uneducated slobs talk that way.

WORDS AND PHRASES TO AVOID

• awful	• dumb	• idiot	• shut up, stupid
• bonehead	• foul	• nonsense	• who cares what you say
• curse	• get out of here with that language	• say whatever you like	

50 Listening

The opposite of talking isn't listening. The opposite of talking is waiting.
—FRAN LEBOWITZ

"Mom, wait till you hear what happened at school today!" Kristen said breathlessly.

"Not now, dear," her mom answered, not bothering to look up from her newspaper.

"Dad?"

"I don't have time. Maybe later."

Kristen walked away, wondering why her parents never seemed to have time to listen to her stories.

She had lots to tell them. New experiences didn't always make sense to her, and she needed to talk about them. She was thirteen and would be a high school freshman in September. She had anxieties about that. Her menstrual cycle had just started, much later than many of her friends, and she wondered if she was abnormal. There was this really cute guy in her class. She really liked him, and he seemed to notice her. What should she do?

Rarely did she and her mom or dad sit down for a nice quiet talk with the television set turned off. They never seemed to go on walks as they used to when she could tell them all the things that were bothering her. Kristen wasn't sure why she needed to talk to them, but she knew that she did. Yet they weren't there for her these days. Too busy. Maybe later. Not now. Another time. Tomorrow. This weekend. Tell your mother. Tell your father.

She'd have to find someone else to talk to. There was this nice older guy who hung around school. He smiled at her and seemed quite friendly. Maybe he'd listen to her.

Things to Consider

Teens love to talk and need to talk. You need to make sure that you're there to listen without interrupting from beginning to end. Listening carefully and honestly without judging encourages teens to tell you the things that are most important to them. Talking enables your teenagers to learn about who they are, to clarify their goals, and to see whom they can rely on. If you're always there for them, they'll learn to trust and rely on you. This kind of relationship will assist you to do a better parenting job.

When was the last time you listened to your teens share their life with you? Do you remember asking your teens how things were going and listening to their answers all the way through without interrupting or judging them? Just occasionally asking your teens how things are going at school isn't good enough. You and your teens have to set apart a time and place in your busy lives when you can give each other your undivided attention.

Let your teen suggest a good time and place for you to meet on a regular basis to share your lives and thoughts. Make sure it is free of distractions. Don't bring your pager or cell phone. Let your teen set the agenda for the conversation. If you have things you want to discuss, keep them until your teen has had her say. Make it a time for listening. Don't argue or interrupt. If you listen carefully and with an open mind, you'll know what to say when it's your turn to talk.

If you have to miss a time, make sure you don't miss it again. Make these times as important to you as a meeting at work. Taking the time to listen shows your teen that you respect her. The response that comes out of careful listening shows that you love and understand her.

You can give teens advice when it's called for. After all, you have the advantage of your life experiences. And it's your responsibility as a parent to guide your children's social and physical growth, but make sure you hear what they are saying. Don't start to lecture them about things. If you've been listening carefully, you'll know the right approach to use. It may be telling a story or giving examples to illustrate what they've been saying. It may be suggesting things to read or people to talk to. Your response needs to be appropriate to your teen and to the occasion.

Three Things You Must Do

1. *Recognize* that your teen loves to talk and needs to talk.

2. *Know* that you have a responsibility to be there to listen to her.

3. *Realize* that you must listen carefully and completely in order to respond appropriately.

What to Say and Do

Teens love and need to talk. Listen without interrupting. Say such things as:

- I want to hear all about it.
- You talk. I'll listen.
- I promise not to stop you or interrupt.

Encourage your teen to share her life with you. Listen without judging.

- I had no idea you thought about things like that. I'm glad you told me.
- How did you like that movie you saw last weekend?
- I heard some hip-hop on the radio the other day. I liked it. Do you?

Set a time and place to meet on a regular basis. Say such things as:

- Why don't we get together Saturday at lunch just to talk?
- Going for a walk will get us away from distractions. No pager or phone.
- A nice drive would be good. Great suggestion.

Let your teen set the agenda. Say such things as:

- What's the agenda for today?
- What's new in your life?
- We can talk about anything you want.

Careful listening will tell you what to say to your teen. Say such things as:

- I'm just going to listen. Unless you ask me something, I'm going to try to keep quiet.
- Yes, I can respond to that. I think something like that happened to me.

♦ Let's talk this through. Suppose you were a parent and your child needed your advice on this. What would you tell him or her?

Make your responses appropriate to your teen and to the occasion. Say such things as:

♦ I know you, I love you, and I think this will make sense to you.

♦ Tell me what you think you should do, and I'll tell you what I think the consequences will be.

♦ You have your own personality, talents, and problems. Let's talk about a solution for you.

WORDS AND PHRASES TO USE

♦ go ahead and talk	♦ thanks for telling me	♦ you can talk about anything you like	♦ you set the time and place
♦ I won't interrupt	♦ that's very interesting		♦ you talk, I'll listen
♦ just you and me			

What Not to Say and Do

Listen to what your teen is saying. Don't put her off. Don't say such things as:

♦ I can't listen right now.

♦ Maybe later.

♦ I'd like to listen, but I have got too much work to do.

Don't push your teen away. Don't say such things as:

♦ Why don't you talk to your mother/father? I'm too busy.

♦ Can't you talk to your brother/sister about that?

♦ Go talk to your friends. They'll understand better than I can.

Don't lecture. Don't say such things as:

♦ Okay, now let me tell you what you ought to do.

♦ This is the best way to solve this problem.

♦ Here's what I would do.

Don't judge. Don't say such things as:

- That's a stupid thing to say.
- That was a dumb thing to do.
- That's terrible. I don't want to hear any more.

Don't argue. Don't say such things as:

- How could you be so stupid?
- You've forgotten everything I taught you.
- You're just another dumb teenager.

Don't miss your regular meetings. Don't say such things as:

- Sorry, I can't make it this week. But I'll try for next week.
- I just got tied up. I knew you'd understand.
- If I miss our meetings, it's not because I want to. I just have more important things to do.

WORDS AND PHRASES TO AVOID

another time, perhaps	I don't have time just now	I'm too tired	tell it to someone else
don't tell me	I'm really not interested	let me tell you what to do	you're overreacting
I can't just listen			

51 Love

To love oneself is the beginning of a life-long romance.

—OSCAR WILDE

Jaimie's parents were kind, sincere, caring people. They wanted the best for their teenage daughter. To this end they encouraged her in every way, helping with her schoolwork, supporting the soccer team she played on, and assisting her volunteer hospital work organized by their church. They were proud of their daughter.

But they left Jaimie wondering if their caring and support was for her benefit or theirs. Was their active interest in her life one more way of keeping control, or did they really love her and want her to be happy and successful on her own terms? Ever since she was a little girl Jaimie had looked for a clear sign that her parents loved her not for what she did but for who she was.

Jaimie knew she was probably being unfair, but she desperately wanted her mom or dad, especially her dad, to say, "I love you"—not because she got "A's" in school or because she scored a goal for her team but out of the blue, for no obvious reason, just say it to her.

She knew what it was like to love someone. That's what she felt for Todd who was in her senior class at school. She didn't love him for marks or sports or anything else but for what he was as a person. Why couldn't she be sure her parents loved her like that?

Things to Consider

There are two aspects to love. The first is loving your child. The second is loving your lover. Parental love differs from romantic love, most obviously in having no sexual content. But both kinds of love have at least one thing in common: In their ideal form they are selfless, wanting only the best for the loved one with no thought of self-interest.

I think it's fair to say that children who haven't experienced parental love may have a tough time feeling love for anyone else principally because they find it difficult to love themselves. You can't love someone else if you don't love yourself.

Love nourishes people of all ages. You need to show your teens that you love them as explicitly as you did when they were infants. Teens are in such a transitional state that everything you can do to give them a sense of self-worth and security through explicit demonstrations of love for them will ease their journey.

It's not enough to do things for your teenagers and assume that they will realize they are done out of love. Helping them, encouraging them, supporting them, and cheering for them are great, but you can do more. You can say, "I love you." You can tell them how proud you are. You can tell them that you admire them as people. You can say that you trust them because of the kind of people they are. You can list the qualities in them that you love and admire.

Love is an action verb. You not only have to say you love your teen, you have to show it by kissing them, hugging them, and putting your arm around their shoulder.

It's easy to love a teen who is lovable. It's much harder to love one who isn't or who rejects your love. But you have to hang in there. Tell your teens you love them in spite of the problems. Say that you will never give up on them even if they reject you. Stay involved.

Sometimes loving your teens means saying no. Teens are not yet adults but are no longer children. Sometimes you need to use your experience and knowledge to protect and guide even though your teens reject your authority. You must do it out of love for your children.

You have an obligation to provide food, shelter, and protection until your children leave home. But these things are not enough. Your biggest obligation is to love your children forever.

Three Things You Must Do

1. *Love* your teen.

2. *Show* your love.

3. *State* your love.

What to Say and Do

Loving your teen means accepting him for who he is. You have helped shape his life, but he is an individual with good and bad points. Accept him for that. Say such things as:

- I love you.
- I can understand your making that mistake. I've done the same thing.
- Nobody's perfect.
- You've done your best. No one can ask for more.

The best parental love is selfless, wanting only the best for your teen, for his sake and not for yours. Encourage your teen in what he wants to achieve. Say such things as:

- That's a great thing to want. I'll help you if I can.
- What matters is what you want, not what I want for you.
- Of course I'd love to see you become a _____, but you need to make your own decision.

Your teen needs to love himself. He will find it hard to love someone else if he doesn't. Say such things as:

- Someday you will love someone because you have lots of love to give.
- You can't love someone else unless you love yourself.

Help your teen develop a good sense of self-worth and security. You can do this by making your love for them explicit in what you say and do. Say such things as:

- I think you're great.
- I'm so proud of you.
- It's great having you as my son.

Do such things as:

- Hug him.
- Kiss him.
- Put your arm around his shoulder.

Love your teen in spite of any problems that exist between you. Never give up on him. Say such things as:

- Whatever happens between us, I'll never stop loving you.
- You are my child, and I love you.
- You can say or do whatever you like, but you're stuck with my love.

Sometimes you must say no to your teen. Your experience and knowledge will come in handy. Say such things as:

- This will make you angry, but I must say no, you can't do that.
- I have got to step in here. I give you as much freedom as I can, but this time I have to stop you.
- I know it's a cliché, but I'm doing this for you.

WORDS AND PHRASES TO USE

• accept	• I'll always love you	• no, I can't let you do that	• trustworthy
• give me a hug	• love doesn't conquer all, but it helps	• proud	• you're great
• I love you			

What Not to Say and Do

Don't expect your teen to be perfect. Don't say such things as:

- Why do you do things like that?
- I'll never understand you.
- You really disappoint me.
- You're a rotten child.

Don't try to live your life through your teen. It's his life, not yours. Don't say such things as:

- This is what you ought to do.
- Don't you want to please me?
- This would be the best thing for you.

- I'll be disappointed if you don't do this.
- It's for your own good.

Don't expect obvious gratitude from your teen. Don't say such things as:

- You could at least show that you appreciate all I've done for you.
- You're an ungrateful kid.
- You selfish brat.
- You don't know all the sacrifices I've made for you.

Don't give up. Don't say such things as:

- Get out!
- I'm finished with you!
- How can I love you when you do things like this?
- You're not my son anymore!

WORDS AND PHRASES TO AVOID

- awful	- disgusting	- hate	- that's not what I'd do
- bad	- empty	- I give up	- unacceptable
- disgrace	- get out	- loser	- you're out of here

52 Lying

Truth is the safest lie.

—Anonymous

"How was school today?" Andrew's mother asked one fall afternoon.

"It was okay," Andrew answered with no great enthusiasm.

"What classes did you have today?" his mother continued, unwilling to let the subject drop in spite of Andrew's less than eager tone of voice.

"The usual," he answered, unwilling to say anything more than he absolutely had to.

"I got a call from your high school this morning," she said. Andrew knew what was coming but said nothing, afraid anything he said would make things worse. She continued, "They asked if you were ill. I asked myself why would they do that since they could see for themselves that you were perfectly fit? So I said, no, he's not sick. Why? They said they were asking because you weren't in school today. I asked if they were sure and said you left for school at the normal time this morning. They said they were sure. I was worried. I wondered if something had happened to you. I thanked them for calling. I've spent the rest of the day worrying about what might have happened to you."

"Sorry, Mom," Andrew said.

"Where were you today? Why didn't you go to school? I want the truth," said his mother.

Andrew didn't know what to say. He certainly didn't want to tell his mom that he and two friends spent the day at a skateboard park and hanging out at a nearby mall. He'd done it a few times before and hadn't been caught because he skipped out of school after home room attendance was taken, and none of his teachers had bothered to call his home.

"I got to school, but one of my friends was feeling real sick and his parents both work, so I helped get him home and took care of him until his mom got home at three-thirty. Then I came home. I was going to tell you but didn't get a chance."

"You wouldn't mind if I called your friend's mom just to make sure he's okay, would you?"

"What's wrong, Mom? Don't you believe me?"

"I believe you. I'm just concerned about your friend. What is his number?"

"I don't know his number."

"Tell me his last name and where he lives, and I'll look it up in the book."

"His name is Jim Smith and he lives on Twenty-eighth Avenue near One Hundred Fifty-ninth Street, but I think he has an unlisted number," he lied.

"I'll just check the book to be sure," said his mom, not believing anything her son had told her.

Things to Consider

You and your teens tell innocent lies to each other, "white" lies that you tell to avoid embarrassment, to avoid hurting someone, to make someone feel good, to preserve good relationships, to conceal private, intimate details. These are the kinds of lies we tell, for example, when someone greets us and asks how we are. Even if we are dying of cancer, we might say, "Fine, thanks. How are you?"

These lies are not the problem. But teens may lie to you about missing school, about using the car without permission, about taking money from your handbag, or about where they are going on Friday night. These are serious lies and need to be stopped if they can. The problem is that teens may lie because of a basic problem in your relationship. You won't stop the lying until you fix the relationship.

Unless a teen is a pathological liar, the problem is usually one of trust. Teens lie because they don't trust you enough to tell you the truth. They are afraid of your reaction. They're willing to lie to you and risk being caught (of course they believe that is unlikely) more than they're willing to face the consequences of telling the truth.

If your teen lies about important things, examine your rules and the consequences of breaking them. If the punishment for lying is no worse than for breaking the rules, then your teen will risk lying. Don't try to solve this dilemma by making the punishment for lying worse than it already is. Try making it easier for your son or daughter to tell the truth.

In most cases breaking the rules and lying about it eventually brings its own punishment. You want to know about this sooner rather than later so you can help your teenager avoid that punishment by getting his act together.

Three Things You Must Do

1. *Distinguish* between social lies and serious lies.

2. *Recognize* that your teen lies mainly from fear.

3. *Build* a relationship of trust in which truth is more important than punishment.

What to Say and Do

Talk to your teen about the difference between social lies and serious lies. Say such things as:

- ♦ You know that lying isn't a good thing to do. But we all have to tell innocent lies sometimes. I just don't want you to get into the habit of telling bad lies.

- ♦ Lies about school, about the car, about money, and about where you go with your friends are serious lies and unacceptable.

Lying is caused by fear and lack of trust. Say such things as:

- ♦ I'm concerned that you think I'm too tough on you when you do something wrong. Do you think I am?

- ♦ Are you afraid of me?

- ♦ Do you trust me to do the right thing?

Of course their answers to these questions may be lies if your teen is truly afraid of you.

Your teen makes mistakes. You need to know about those mistakes to keep your teen from being hurt by them. Say such things as:

- ♦ It's important to tell me the truth about things so I can always be there for you if you need help.

> ◆ Are you afraid to tell me the truth?

> ◆ I don't expect you to tell me everything you do, but if you had a problem, would you tell me?

Try making it easier for your teen to tell the truth than to lie. Say such things as:

> ◆ Whatever you do, it will always be better for you to tell me the truth than to lie.

> ◆ Even if you've made a mistake, almost everything can be put right.

You don't want your teen to be afraid of you. Say such things as:

> ◆ I don't want you to be afraid of me, so whatever it takes to make you trust me, I'm willing to do. Where do you think we should begin?

> ◆ I want to be open and honest with you, and I want you to be open and honest with me. But I'm not sure how to begin. Will you help me?

Don't throw rules away just because you're trying to build a new relationship. Redefine the rules and the consequences of violating them. Say such things as:

> ◆ I'm glad you've come to me. Let's see what we can do to fix this thing.

> ◆ You know what you did wrong. What do you think should happen next?

> ◆ You decide what to do about this mistake.

WORDS AND PHRASES TO USE

◆ afraid	◆ cooperate	◆ honesty	◆ sincere
◆ be honest	◆ fear	◆ lies	◆ truth
◆ consequences	◆ help	◆ nonjudgmental	◆ understanding

What Not to Say and Do

Don't make your teen afraid of you. Don't say such things as:

> ◆ If I ever find out you've done something like that, I'll have your head.

> ◆ Don't let me find you doing anything like that.

> ◆ I know you'd never do that because you know what I'd do to you.

Don't make the lying easier than telling the truth. Don't say such things as:

- If you've done something wrong and tell me, you're in big trouble.
- You know the rules and the punishment for breaking them. So behave.
- Don't ever let me catch you lying to me, or you'll get it.

Don't betray a trust. It will destroy your relationship with your teen. Don't say such things as:

- I don't care what I said, you're grounded.
- Trust has nothing to do with it. You broke the rules, and you're going to be punished.

Don't assume you can get your teen to trust you if you have not had that kind of relationship. Don't say such things as:

- I'm your mom/dad, and I expect you to tell me the truth.
- What do you mean you can't trust me? I said you could. Don't you believe me?
- You'd better talk to me, or you'll be in big trouble.

WORDS AND PHRASES TO AVOID

+ authority	+ dishonest	+ punishment	+ you'd better trust me
+ cheat	+ liar	+ rotten kid	+ you'll be sorry
+ deceitful	+ no excuses	+ strict	+ you'll get what you deserve

53 Maturity

I am not young enough to know everything.

—Oscar Wilde

Paula is fifteen going on twenty-five, as her parents say with fear and trepidation. She started menstruating when she was thirteen, much later than some of her friends, but nevertheless seems to have matured physically very quickly. She has a well-developed body, and if she puts on makeup, she might easily pass for a woman in her twenties rather than a fifteen-year-old child.

Her favorite books are young-adult novels that tell of rape, murder, incest, and addictions. She dates a boy who is also fifteen, and they have been going together for three months. Both her parents work. Paula is on the school swimming team. When she doesn't have a swim meet after school, she has the responsibility of her younger brother until her parents get home. On Saturdays she works at the local Burger King.

Paula's parents are impressed with her mature attitude toward school, sports, and all her family responsibilities. She seems quite adult in her manners and speech, and interacts quite well with adults. But there are times when she seems to be a little girl.

She readily talks to her mother, discussing problems and asking questions, something teenagers often have a problem doing. She still sleeps with the teddy bear her dad gave her when she was four. Sometimes she and her brother fight over the most infantile things, such as who has to clean up after dinner. She is still a virgin, which, given her physical appearance and the experience of so many girls her age, surprises her mother, who lost her own virginity at fifteen in the backseat of a car.

Is this teenager a woman, a child, or something else? How mature can she be at age fifteen? Her parents don't think she has the experience to be considered an adult, but they nevertheless have given Paula increasing control over her own life, over such things as clothes, curfew, study times, and money. They realize this is the way to help her become a responsible autonomous adult.

Things to Consider

Are children maturing faster and earlier? The evidence seems to say yes, both biologically and socially. In a study of 17,077 girls ages three to twelve, 50 percent of African-American girls and 15 percent of Caucasian girls had evidence of pubic hair and breast development at age eight. Another study showed that the average age of menstruation had dropped from fourteen to twelve and a half over the past century. When you add earlier physical maturity to earlier exposure to sex and violence through movies, television, and the Internet, there seems every chance that children lose their innocence at a younger age than ever before in history.

Teens live in both the world of adults and the world of adolescent hopes and dreams. They must make choices in a world of conflicting values and sensibilities based on limited experience and what might be considered only a partial understanding of these choices and their consequences. They must decide to work hard at school or not; to be identified with the jocks, rockers, preppies, or nerds; to wear black, leather, grunge, or J. Crew; to pierce or not to pierce their bodies or be tattooed; to smoke or not; to do drugs or not; to have sex or abstain.

Some of these may not seem like real choices, but there are still matters to be decided and you need to decide how much you will intervene. Do you think your teen is mature enough?

Psychologists say one sign of maturity is how clearly a person understands risk. In a study of how teens perceive risk, adults said the phrase "will definitely happen" meant a 97 percent chance that an event would occur. Teenagers put the chance between 81 percent and 86 percent. This means, for example, that the same risk message given by a doctor to an adult and a teen about the chance of getting a sexually transmitted disease during unprotected sex wouldn't be understood the same way at all.

Regardless of your teens' maturity you still have rules of conduct, but these rules change in scale and interpretation as your teens take on more responsibility for their own lives. Teens who have no rules will feel insecure and even uncared for but will rebel against childish prohibitions and schedules. You need to encourage your teens to get out on their own. The rate at which you do this comes from your knowledge of them and your relationship.

Three Things You Must Do

1. *Understand* adolescence as a transition from childhood to adulthood.

2. *Know* your teen's ability to make responsible choices.

3. *Change* from being your teen's controller to being her advisor, counselor, and friend.

What to Say and Do

Talk about world events, books, articles, movies, plays, radio and television programs, and websites that raise important issues. Say such things as:

- What do you think about this?
- Do you think they are right in doing that?
- What would you do in that situation?

Your teen must decide how hard to work at school, who her public self is, what kind of statement she wants to make with her appearance, and what kinds of risks she wants to take. She has to decide if she will compete, withdraw, or drop out. Talk about these choices with her. Say such things as:

- What do you think about your friends?
- How do you decide how hard you work at school?
- Do you care what people think about you?

How clearly does your teen understand risk? Say such things as:

- If experts say something "will definitely happen," what percent of the time do you think it will happen?
- If doctors say that the chance of getting a sexually transmitted disease is pretty high if you engage in unprotected sex, what percent of the time do you think it will happen?
- If all the evidence shows that smoking is definitely addictive, what percent of the time do you think people who smoke become addicted?

Talk with your teen about what she wants to control in her life. Say such things as:

- I think you need to take more control of your life. What do you think?
- Do you want to make your own study times?
- I want you to decide when you go to bed. Is that okay with you?

Rules have to change as your teen grows up. Get rid of childish prohibitions and schedules. Talk about rules with your teen. Say such things as:

- We have certain rules about what you can and can't do. I think it's time to change them because you're older now. What do you think?
- Let's look at rules for dating, curfews, using the car, choosing clothes, bedtime, watching TV, using the computer, and any others you can think of.

Keep lines of communication open and stay involved in your teen's life. Say such things as:

- What do you think will happen if you do that?
- After high school what do you want to do? What kind of options do you think you'll have?
- How far ahead do you have to plan for things?

WORDS AND PHRASES TO USE

ambition	control	plans	risks
autonomy	danger	preparation	rules
choices	decisions	ready	trust
consequences	maturity	responsibility	what do you think

What Not to Say and Do

Don't get involved in a battle for control over your teen's life. Don't say such things as:

- You'll do as I say.

- As long as you live here, I make the rules.
- I don't care how old you are, you're still my child and my responsibility.

Don't stick to the old rules just for their sake. Don't say such things as:

- I don't care how late your friends can stay out, I want you home by ten.
- You have to be in bed on school nights by ten-thirty.
- You can't date until you're _____.

Don't throw the baby out with the bathwater. Don't abandon all rules. Don't say such things as:

- You're sixteen. I think you're old enough to take care of yourself.
- You have full responsibility for yourself now.
- It's your decision. I'm not going to interfere.

Don't wait until you think your teen is ready for making her own choices before giving her more autonomy. Give her the right to make her own mistakes. Don't say such things as:

- You're too young.
- You haven't proved to me that you're ready.
- That's too important for you to decide.

WORDS AND PHRASES TO AVOID

- awful	- I'm still in charge	- prove it to me	- unapproachable
- closed	- inconsiderate	- secretive	- you're on your own
- I won't help you	- irresponsible	- stupid	- you're too immature

54 Money

I have enough money to last me the rest of my life, unless I buy something.

—Jackie Mason

Hunter found a five-dollar bill lying on the sidewalk. He looked around to see who might have dropped it, but there was no one in sight. He put it in his pocket and figured it was his lucky day. He would put it into his savings account. Each time he wanted something special, he would begin saving a portion of his allowance and the money he made from doing chores around his house and in the neighborhood. Right now he was saving for a new computer game.

Hunter was proud of himself. Most of his friends had to ask their parents for money whenever they wanted something that cost more than their weekly allowance. Often they had to wait for Christmas or for their birthday, and still they had no guarantees.

He always had money for the things he wanted because he never bought anything that cost more than 80 percent of the balance he had in his account. If the item was expensive, he would patiently save until he had 20 percent more than he actually needed.

Not only did Hunter know the value of money, but he had an incentive to find the best price. After all, it was his money he was spending, and the less he had to pay, the more he had for the next item he wanted. His parents were good models for him and had trained him well. Hunter was grateful.

Things to Consider

Money is about choice and control. It gives you power. If you teach your teens to save, to evaluate choices, to search for the best value, and not to spend more than they have, you have put them on the road to personal and financial responsibility and stability.

Teens learn these things through experience and example. You can't begin too early giving your child some control over his own spending. You control income; they control spending. Give them an allowance on a weekly, biweekly, or monthly basis and see how they spend it. Does it last a day, a week, or more? Do they ask for an advance because they've spent everything and now see something they really want? They usually say it's something they need. Resist bailing them out. It's hard, but you'll be doing them a favor in the long run.

Decide on a realistic allowance. Review the amount regularly and adjust it to reflect your teenagers' needs, age, and maturity, as well as family circumstances.

Set a good example for your teens. Examine your own spending habits. Are you a good model of spending and saving? Include your teens in discussions about money, such as family budgeting and household income and spending. Let your teens have some say in issues that affect them—for example, clothes, school supplies, holidays, groceries, computer software, and appliances. Discuss the difference between needs and wants.

Include your teens in planning for the future. Going to school after high school will cost money. Discuss what share of the expenses your teens will be expected to contribute from scholarships, student loans, summer jobs, and part-time work during the year. Give your teens the responsibility for doing the legwork in finding out about financial aid.

Reward your teens for being financially responsible. If they have a part-time job, don't use it as an excuse to cut back their allowance. Make sure they have a bank account. If you can afford it, offer to match their savings dollar for dollar. Buy stocks and bonds for your teens and teach them how to invest money wisely and with a clear purpose and understanding of the cost/benefit—high yield, capital gain, long-term growth, short-term speculation, low risk, high risk. Let your teens research and invest in something that they choose.

Work out a budget with your teens. Review income and expenses. Compare cost and value of items bought. If your teens earn $6 an hour before taxes, they will have to work at least sixteen hours to pay for an $80 pair of Nikes. Is it worth it?

Money is often the greatest source of family friction and breakup. You will be doing your teens a huge favor by preparing them to handle money sensibly and responsibly.

Three Things You Must Do

1. *Give* your teen a regular allowance.

2. *Make* him responsible for his own spending.

3. *Model* good financial habits for him.

What to Say and Do

Teaching your teen about money is teaching him about choice and control. Say such things as:

- Money is a means to an end.

- If you know how to manage your money, your life will be a hundred times easier.

- Some people know the cost of everything and the value of nothing. Don't be like that.

A teen learns through experience and example. Say such things as:

- How much money do you spend each week? Any idea?

- Do you have any money left at the end of the week/month?

- Do you put any money into your savings account on a regular basis?

Discuss a realistic allowance. Review it regularly with your teen. Say such things as:

- Do you think your allowance is enough? What do you think would be the right amount?

- How much do your friends get? (Don't always expect the truth! It's a starting point.)

- If you want your allowance changed, I need to see some figures on your expenses. Can you write out something for me? I need to know fixed expenses, the kinds of things you need to replace on a regular basis, how much you are saving, and a wish list.

Set a good example in your own spending habits. Be a model of sensible spending and saving.

Include your teens in family budgeting. Say such things as:

- I'd like to show you how we do the family budget.
- We have a list of wants, things that we'd like when we can afford them, and needs, things that we can't do without for very long or it will seriously change our standard of living.

If you want to give your teen a credit card, make sure that he understands the rules for using it. Say such things as:

- I want you to have a credit card. It's just for emergencies—if you're stuck someplace and need to take a cab or a plane or a train or make a phone call and don't have the cash.

Reward your teen for making and saving money. Don't cut back his allowance.

Have him open a bank account if he doesn't already have one.

If you can afford it, invest in stocks and bonds for your teen. Help your teen research and invest in something of his choice.

WORDS AND PHRASES TO USE

budget	freedom	need	value for money
choice	income	patience	want
control	investments	savings	waste
expenses	live within your means	thrift	work

What Not to Say and Do

Don't set a bad example. Don't say such things as:

- I don't care what it costs. I want it, and I'm going to have it.
- Nothing's too good for me.
- I can always borrow against next month's salary.

Don't say one thing and do another. Don't say such things as:

- You can't afford that [and then go and buy something you can't afford].

+ You must pay off your credit card in full every month [while you don't].

+ Buying designer clothes is a waste of money [said while you are wearing your Ralph Lauren sweater].

Don't always control your teen's spending. Don't say such things as:

+ You're not allowed to buy that.

+ I gave you the money, so I can tell you how to spend it.

+ You're not good enough with money yet for me to let you buy whatever you like.

Don't bail your teen out too easily. Don't say such things as:

+ Short of money? That's okay. I'll lend you some until next allowance/ paycheck.

Don't discourage your teen from saving. Don't say such things as:

+ I'm not bothering to save for my retirement. I'm going to win the lottery.

+ Saving money is a waste of time. Savings accounts pay too little interest. (They do, but some cash should always be in savings.)

+ Saving money for a rainy day is hogwash. You'll probably be dead before it rains.

Don't penalize your teen for being industrious or growing older. Don't say such things as:

+ Now that you're earning some money, you won't need your allowance anymore.

+ I'm not raising your allowance just because you're seventeen.

+ You're too old for an allowance. If you want any money from me, you'll have to work for it.

WORDS AND PHRASES TO AVOID

+ a no-brainer for making money	+ get rich quick	+ speculate	+ you need to take risks to make money
+ avoid banks	+ money is for spending	+ spendthrift	+ you're too greedy

55 Morals

Morality, like art, consists of drawing the line somewhere.

—ANONYMOUS

"Mom, what if I break school rules to help a friend who really needs me? Is that wrong?" Tatiana, a sixteen-year-old, asked one evening.

"I suppose it depends on what kind of help your friend needs, what rules you have to break to help them, and what your other options are," replied her mom. "Do you want to tell me about it?" she asked Tatiana.

"There's this guy, Brad, in grade twelve. He's almost eighteen. He's a big guy, wrestles and plays on the football team. Well, he keeps hassling my friend Tricia. He purposely bumps into her in the hall and kind of feels her up, if you know what I mean. Or he pats her butt as she passes by. She's asked him to stop, but he won't."

"Has Tricia reported him to the principal?"

"Yeah, but the principal says there's no physical evidence of harassment, so it's her word against his. She said there is little she can do. Her only advice was to stay away from him."

"That's good advice."

"Yeah, but it's not possible. They have classes together, and he's always around where she is."

"What do you want to do that's against the rules?"

"We want to get him into trouble."

"How?"

"We want to plant a stolen copy of a math exam in his locker. I could make an extra copy of a test for Brad's class, and I could put it in his locker while Tricia is playing up to him. Then I could tell Ms. Matthews that I was missing one copy of an exam that I

duplicated and that Brad's boasting about how well he's going to do on her next test. Great plan, don't you think?"

"No, I don't. It's lying and stealing and making false accusations against someone. As bad a thing as Brad is doing to Tricia, you wouldn't make it any better by what you plan. It would make you as immoral as Brad."

"But, Mom, how about an eye for an eye and a tooth for a tooth, as it says in the Bible? That's all we want."

"I understand. My advice is, don't even think about doing it. A better plan would be to video Brad while he's hassling Tricia. I could rent you a small video camera. Then you'd have good evidence."

"Great plan, Mom."

Things to Consider

Morals are principles of right behavior. In my story Tatiana and Tricia think Brad is acting immorally, and Tatiana's mom agrees. Brad is infringing on Tricia's rights by touching her and taunting her when she wants neither to be touched nor taunted.

Our moral code says that each person in our society has the right to do whatever he wants as long as it doesn't infringe on others' rights. This valuable right is the foundation of our liberal democratic society.

Morality combines both rights and responsibilities. In this view, morality becomes sensitive behavior toward others. It tells us to listen to others, to hear what they say, to understand their life situation, and to respond appropriately.

Talk about this version of morality with your teens. Not only do they have the right to choose to act in certain ways, but they also have the responsibility to act in certain ways. Moral behavior demands careful, caring attention to others. It is the opposite of indifference.

Tatiana's proposed revenge on Brad shows her careful, caring attention to Tricia, but it shows indifference to Brad. So it is moral in one sense and immoral in the other. You can't solve one moral problem by creating another.

You might want to impress upon your teens that high moral principles, while needed in any civilized society, can't prevent immorality, or solve moral problems or guarantee justice for victims of immoral acts. Morality can't prevent human experience from being uncertain and ambiguous. You can only ask your teens to be sensitive to each new situation and to listen with care and consideration to what people have to say. The Golden Rule, "Do unto others as you would have them do unto you," is the best guide I know of to morally good behavior.

Three Things You Must Do

1. *Understand* morality as careful, caring attention toward others.

2. *Realize* that moral decisions are neither simple nor easy.

3. *Ask* your teen to do her best but don't expect perfection.

What to Say and Do

Morals are principles of right behavior that you can teach your teenager. Say such things as:

- You don't cheat on exams at school. Why not?
- How do you decide on how to behave toward others?
- Do you know what the Golden Rule is? To treat others as you'd like them to treat you.

Put morality into a practical perspective for your teen by grounding it in practical examples from your life at home. Say such things as:

- If you asked to borrow the car and I said no, I need it tonight, would you take it anyway?
- If your friend asked to borrow a quarter for a phone call, would you lend it to him or her?
- If you were walking home one night and heard a girl call for help, would you help her?

Morality combines both rights and responsibilities. Say such things as:

- If your friend is in trouble, would you ask how you can help, or would you ignore him?

- When you hear people talk about their problems, does it make you want to help them?
- You have a pretty good life. Do you think it would be right to give something back in return?

Talk to your teens about giving careful, caring attention to others. Say such things as:

- Do you or your friends ever do nasty things to other kids at school? How do you think that makes them feel?
- Do you think it's important to think about other people's feelings before you do or say something that might hurt them?

My mother said, "Two wrongs don't make a right." See what your teen thinks. Say such things as:

- Suppose some kid at school beat you up. Would you beat her up if you had the chance?
- If you thought your teacher was being unfair to you, would you try to get back at her?
- Which statement do you agree with: "Two wrongs don't make a right" or "Don't get angry, get even!"

There are no easy solutions to moral problems. Say such things as:

- What do you do when someone makes you angry?
- Suppose you're driving the car and someone cuts you off. Will you go after her?
- Do you think controlling your feelings makes you a better person if what you feel makes you want to do something bad to someone?

Your teen needs to empathize with people. Find out if she is able to put herself in others' shoes. Say such things as:

- When you read about someone's tragedy can you imagine being in that situation?
- Empathy for others is a really important thing to have. Do your friends ever put themselves in someone else's place when they talk about doing something mean?

WORDS AND PHRASES TO USE

▶ caring	▶ empathy	▶ goodness	▶ responsibilities
▶ choice	▶ ethics	▶ honesty	▶ right and wrong
▶ code of behavior	▶ feelings	▶ justice	▶ rights
▶ emotions	▶ friendship	▶ morality	▶ sensitivity

What Not to Say and Do

Set a good example for your teen. Don't say one thing and do another. Don't say such things as:

- ▶ Everybody should be treated equally [and then make racist remarks].
- ▶ You must never cheat in school [while you cheat on your income tax].
- ▶ Nothing is more important than personal relationships [and then criticize your spouse or best friend].

Don't encourage your teenager to be immoral. Don't say such things as:

- ▶ You have to do whatever it takes to win.
- ▶ You can cheat. Just don't get caught.
- ▶ Lying is all right as long as it gets you what you want.

Don't tell your teen that other people are there to be used. Don't say such things as:

- ▶ Most people can't be trusted.
- ▶ Never trust anyone, not even your best friend.
- ▶ People look out for themselves first. You have to do the same.

WORDS AND PHRASES TO AVOID

▶ always look out for number one	▶ it's the law of the jungle— eat or be eaten	▶ me first
▶ cheat	▶ lie	▶ nobody expects anyone else to act morally
▶ do whatever you want	▶ love is just another four-letter word	▶ you're foolish if you trust anyone but yourself

56 Movies

The length of a film should be directly related to the endurance of the human bladder.

—ALFRED HITCHCOCK

"Mom, I'm going to the movies," Catherine said. She was sixteen and a junior in high school.

"Again?" said her mother. "You went to the movies last weekend. Do you have to go every Friday? Why don't you do something else?"

"No, Mom. I've got to see this film."

"I don't think it's such a good idea. All the movies you see are about sex, horror, or violence. I don't think it's good for kids to see these kinds of films, and I wish they'd stop making them."

"I'm sixteen, Ma. These films are fun. I don't take them seriously. Besides, all my friends are going. Anyway, this one's a love story, so you don't have to worry."

"I still don't think you should see so many movies, and I don't approve of what they make in Hollywood these days. I don't see why they couldn't make movies the way they used to."

"Don't worry, Ma, I'll be all right," Catherine said as she went out the door.

Many parents feel the same way as Catherine's mom, that movies have too much murder, sex, and foul language, and producers seem to aim all the junk at teens.

Things to Consider

You might be like Catherine's mom, worried about the kinds of films she sees but not knowing whether you're right to worry or are just being old-fashioned. You might worry that movies are responsible for putting the wrong ideas into

660

teenagers' impressionable heads that cause them to kill other teens at school or join gangs or start cults that do strange and dangerous things.

How do movies affect you? Do they make you do the things you see actors do on the screen? You know that movies can make you feel happy, sad, frightened, angry, or in love. The only movies I ever acted out were the Westerns and war movies I saw as a really young kid. My friends and I would play cowboys and Indians or soldiers. We would shoot each other with toy guns. But we never thought about doing anything like that in real life. We knew the difference between movies and reality.

Today's kids are no different from you and me. They know the difference between fantasy and reality. That doesn't mean your child should see every movie made for today's teenage moviegoers. Many are not worth the price of admission. They're tasteless. Many assume that the moviegoer has the I.Q. of a retarded squirrel. But even these terrible films have some redeeming features as long as you don't take them seriously. I'm sure you can remember seeing such films as *Amazon Women from Outer Space,* which now appears regularly on sci-fi cable channels across the country.

Teenagers can learn from movies that explore relationships, and they need movies that make them laugh at others and themselves—movies that take them out of themselves for a couple of hours and help them forget their problems.

Teens need to see the good and the bad to develop a critical sense. You can help them do this by discussing what they see with them. They will certainly talk about the films with friends. This is an important part of teen culture. Your teens need to be able to participate in that culture.

Remember that your teen is not just any teen. You know your child and what might not be good for her. She is not a stereotypical teen. Do what is right for her.

Three Things You Must Do

1. *Realize* that your teen needs to see the movies her friends see.

2. *Trust* your teen to separate reality from fantasy.

3. *Understand* that seeing good films and bad films helps a teen develop a critical sense.

What to Say and Do

You might think that movies make teens kill other teens at school and join gangs or cults that do strange and dangerous things. If you do, talk about your fears with your teen. Say such things as:

- Don't you think these violent movies make kids do bad things?
- I think all this sex in movies gives kids the wrong idea. Don't you think so?
- Does all the murder in films make kids want to murder people?

Talk about how movies affect people. Ask them about what they see. Say such things as:

- What's your favorite kind of movie? Why do you like it?
- Have you seen any movies that you don't like? Why?
- How does a movie like _____ make you feel?

Many movies made for today's teenagers are not worth the price of admission. Talk about these with your teen. Ask her what she thinks about them. Say such things as:

- Why would you spend your hard-earned money on something like that? Can you tell me?
- Are there any films you wouldn't go to see because they are too awful?
- How do you decide what to see?

Encourage your teens to see films that you think will teach them something important while entertaining them at the same time. You can go to see them together. You can talk about them. But let your teen initiate any serious discussion; otherwise, she'll think you're just using the movie as an excuse for preaching. Keep your questions light. Say such things as:

- There's a film I'd like to see. Want to go with me?
- I hear _____ is a really good film. Have any of your friends seen it?
- I really enjoyed that movie. Did you?
- What did you think of the movie?

Help your teens develop a critical sense by talking about films they've seen. Say such things as:

- Tell me about the movie.
- Who was in it?
- Was it good?
- How was the acting?
- What did you think of the plot?

Your teen needs to be able to talk to her friends about the latest movie. Don't stop her from seeing a movie simply because you don't like it. Let her do what her friends do.

Your teen is an individual. Most teens can keep reality and fantasy separate. If you think your teen would be dangerously affected, however, she probably needs professional help.

WORDS AND PHRASES TO USE

comedy	emotions	I trust you	sense of humor
critical sense	fictionalized account	important	trash
don't take it seriously	fun	okay	worthless
	go ahead	outrageous	

What Not to Say and Do

Don't assume that movies make all teens violent. Don't say such things as:

- Movies are bad.
- Movies are responsible for much of the teenage crime these days.
- Films put crazy ideas into kids' heads

Don't encourage your child to see any and every movie. Ask her to consider the merits of the film before she decides to go. Don't say such things as:

- Go see it. Any film is better than none.
- I use movies as a pure escape. I don't care what I see. You shouldn't, either.

If you push your teen to see "good" films, you may get a strong negative reaction from her. Be subtle. Don't say such things as:

- You always see such crap. Why don't you go to a good film for a change?
- I'll tell you what you can and can't see. You have no taste.
- You can see _____. At least it will do you some good.

Your teen needs to see films her friends see. Don't keep her from seeing films simply as a matter of principle. Don't say such things as:

- I don't care if all your friends have seen it. You're not allowed to see this film.
- Your friends have seen it? Their parents should be doing a better job. You can't go.
- Just because your friends have seen a film doesn't make it right. We have standards.

Your teen isn't some stereotypical teen. Don't treat her that way. Don't say such things as:

- You're just like every other teen. You want to see trash.
- You teenagers are all the same.
- Why can't you be adult about this? Movies like this are for jerks.

WORDS AND PHRASES TO AVOID

crazy	I don't care what your friends do	junk	typical
dumb	idiotic	mindless	you have no taste
how can you stand a movie like that	jerk	stupid	you're all the same

57 Music

I don't know anything about music. In my line you don't have to.
—ELVIS PRESLEY

"Turn down the music!" Billy's mother called up from the kitchen. It was the same thing day after day. Billy's music would come pounding through the ceiling either from his computer or from his boom box, and drive everyone else mad.

His parents realized that their taste in songs wasn't the same as their fourteen-year-old son's. They didn't expect him to like music from the seventies and eighties, nor did they think he had much appreciation for jazz, classical, or opera at his age, although some kids did. They had no intention of trying to force their tastes on him, but they didn't see why they should have to listen to rap and hip-hop twenty-four hours a day, either.

In a perfect world everyone would consider other people's tastes and not play their music too loud. Billy's parents were determined to do a couple of things that they figured would make life better in their household, themselves and Billy included.

First, Billy couldn't play his music so loud that it would impose itself on others. At home, in the car, or at the beach, music was a personal thing not to be shared with others unless requested.

Second, they were going to make sure that Billy was aware of other kinds of music besides what he and his friends played all the time. He didn't have to like it, but he should know it exists. They felt this was especially important now that the schools weren't teaching music appreciation anymore.

Third, they would take the time to listen to Billy's music on the radio and sometimes ask him to play his CDs for them. They wanted to understand the attraction this music had for teenagers and others. In spite of all this, though, Billy remained a fourteen-year-old who tended to play his music too loud!

Things to Consider

Music is a wonderful thing. It expresses emotions in ways that words cannot. Music excites, it soothes, it makes you happy, it makes you sad. Musical tastes vary considerably, and when there are various tastes within a family, it's not just a case of generational differences. Music is a personal thing, and you must allow for that. Avoiding conflict over music requires tolerance and understanding. It also requires consideration of others.

One of the most important things you can teach your teens about music is that others probably don't want to listen to their music. Playing music too loud seems to be a macho thing among teenage boys. Boom boxes invade public spaces and impose their owner's tastes on nearby people whether they like it or not. This is unacceptable, and you should let your teens know that their music must not invade others' space.

A second important thing is to know your teens' music. Listen to what they listen to (on your own terms, of course) and talk about its merits with them. Find out why they like it, how it makes them feel, and what they think of the lyrics. Knowing your teens' taste in music can tell you a lot about their personality that you might not be able to learn in any other way. It would be important to know that your teens like music with racist or sexist lyrics or other antisocial ideas.

Try to give your teens the opportunity to hear and appreciate all kinds of music—country, rock, blues, jazz, musical theater, opera, classical, all the musical genres that they may not choose to listen to at this stage in their lives. Even if they don't like it now, they will thank you for it later on.

Encourage your teen to participate in music at school. They will value that kind of experience for their entire life. If they don't already study a musical instrument, encourage them to begin.

Three Things You Must Do

1. *Encourage* your teen to play and listen to all kinds of music.

2. *Emphasize* consideration for others.

3. *Know* what music your teen likes and listens to, and why.

What to Say and Do

Help your teen understand that musical tastes are a personal thing. Show them that the way to avoid conflict over music is through tolerance, understanding, and consideration. Say such things as:

- Make sure you don't play your music so loud that it bothers others.
- I know you like your music, but not everyone does.
- What would happen if everyone carried a boom box around and played their music loud? It would be chaos. So keep yours quiet.
- The best way for you to listen to your music is through headphones.

Popular music today is often played much too loud by musicians and by listeners. It seems likely that today's teens will suffer severe hearing loss because of it. Encourage your teen to keep the volume down and wear earplugs at concerts. If they are musicians, encourage them to keep the amplifiers turned down to a reasonable level. The problem is that as teen audiences become more and more deaf, volumes will be turned higher and higher.

Know your teen's music. Listen to it and talk about it. Ask him why he likes it, how it makes him feel, and what he thinks of the lyrics. Talk about music with racist or sexist lyrics, or other antisocial meaning. Say such things as:

- Play some music for me that you like, will you?
- That sounds pretty good. What's it about?
- You don't listen to that hate music, do you? I think it's pretty sick. What about you?

Expose your teen to music he might not otherwise listen to, such as country, rock, blues, jazz, musical theater, and opera. Ask him what he thinks of it. Say such things as:

- Would you listen to something I like? I'd like to know what you think of it.
- Tell me what you think about this jazz piece.
- Would you come to the opera with me?
- I'm going to play a range of different kinds of music for you. Tell me which you like best.

If your teen doesn't already study music, encourage him to start now. Say such things as:

- Have you ever thought about learning an instrument? You can choose an instrument you like.
- If you'd like to learn how to play the guitar, I'll buy you one.
- I'm thrilled you want to learn how to play the _____. I'll pay for lessons.

WORDS AND PHRASES TO USE

• beat	• exciting	• noise	• share your music with me
• beautiful	• love	• personal taste	
• consider others	• melody	• practice	• study
• creative/inventive	• musical	• rhythm	• your taste

What Not to Say and Do

Don't set a bad example for your teen. Don't expect everyone to like your music and don't play it too loud. Don't say such things as:

- This is good music. I don't know why you don't like it.
- This is a lot better than the garbage you listen to.
- I'll play this as loud as I like. It's my house.
- If you don't want to listen you can leave.

Don't be inconsiderate of your teen's tastes or dismiss your teen's music out of hand. Don't say such things as:

- How can you pay to listen to that?
- Is that what you and your friends like? No wonder you're always in trouble.
- That's not music. That's noise.

Don't allow music with racist, sexist, or other antisocial meanings. Don't say such things as:

- That tells it like it is.
- At least there is some free speech left.

Don't belittle your teen's taste in music if he happens to like jazz, musical theater, opera, or classical and you don't. Don't say such things as:

- Aren't you the musical snob!
- That stuff doesn't make any sense to me.
- I only like tunes you can whistle.
- I don't like anything that isn't written in English.

Don't discourage your teen from taking music lessons. Don't say such things as:

- I'm not paying for you to study music.
- Only sissies play the piano.
- Why on earth would you want to learn to sing? You can sing well enough already.

WORDS AND PHRASES TO AVOID

• bad	• listen or leave	• that's not music	• waste of money
• crap	• music stinks	• those words tell it like it is	• you have terrible taste in music
• it's my house	• noise		

58 Needs and Wants

Whoever said money can't buy happiness didn't know where to shop.

—ANONYMOUS

"Mom, I need a new Tommy shirt."

"Don't be silly. You have lots of good shirts already. You don't need another one."

"Sure I do. I don't have one of these, and all the guys are wearing them."

"You want one, but you don't need one. You need to understand the difference."

"I know the difference, and believe me, I need a Tommy shirt."

"Forget it unless you want to buy it with your own money."

"I can't afford it."

"Then save your money until you have enough."

"Aw, Ma, that'll take too long."

"Too bad, sweet cakes. That's the deal."

Tyrone's mother was going through what mothers everywhere go through with their teens, boys and girls, about clothing. Tyrone was fifteen and wanted to look like his friends. He would say he needed to look like his friends. His sister, who was thirteen, was the same way about clothes. She needed to dress like her friends, or better than her friends if possible.

For these teens, wearing the latest style of clothing was a badge of membership. It showed that they were "with it." Tyrone and his friends would check one another out at school to see who was wearing the right stuff and who wasn't. Being dressed wrong could threaten one's membership.

It may sound fickle and foolish, but it has been this way for a long, long time. Tyrone and his sister and their friends are simply repeating the ritual of membership, identifying who belongs and who doesn't. This membership extends beyond clothes. It includes taste in cars, music, movies, video games, Hollywood heroes, and, later, colleges and professions.

Things to Consider

The differences between "wants" and "needs" is easy to see at the extremes, but not in the middle ranges. You yourself don't always know whether the new car you choose is more a want or a need. It doesn't need a sun roof, leather upholstery, electronic doors or windows, or a tape deck and CD player with multiple speakers. Yet you might decide that you need these things.

Your teens have the same problem of separating wants from needs. They need what normal teens need, which you may see as simply wants. The last thing you want your teens to be is isolated from their group.

This need leads to other needs: certain kinds of clothing, vacations, sports equipment, music, and cars. Whatever group your teens belong to has membership requirements, and your teens will say they need them. You are likely to say these are not needs but simply wants. In fact, it's difficult to draw the line. If your teens need skis or a snowboard, you don't understand why they need to be top of the line. But your teens will argue that they have to be a certain brand name because that's what cool and in fashion. Otherwise, there is no point in buying anything.

To settle the argument between wants and needs requires diplomacy and understanding. You can be authoritarian and simply say no. Your teens may submit to this or may think you have just doomed them to everlasting isolation because they can't be like their friends.

You can also look for compromise. Talk to your teens about the cost of running a house and raising children. Show them in black and white the cost of things that are needed, and tell them that what is left over is for wants. Work with your teens on estimating how much disposable income can go their way in the form of allowances and payment for work done around the house. Teens can make sensible decisions if they have the right information.

Doing volunteer work is a good way for them to learn the difference between wants and needs. Volunteering at the local food bank puts their circumstances into perspective. Helping people whose lives are reduced to the basic necessities of food, shelter, and clothing will help them realize that what they thought were their needs were, in fact, their wants. Learning to distinguish between wants and needs helps clarify their values. It is part of growing up.

Three Things You Must Do

1. *Realize* that you and your teen will differ on what are needs and what are wants.

2. *Help* your teen understand wants and needs in the context of your family circumstances.

3. *Give* your teen experiences that will help clarify the difference between wants and needs.

What to Say and Do

Distinguish between wants and needs using real-life examples. Say such things as:

- Sometimes I want something so badly that I think I need it.

- I find that when I'm buying a car, there are lots of things I think I need, but I don't. I just want all the "bells and whistles." I don't really need them.

- It's nice to be able to afford everything you want, but most of us can't.

Get your teen to talk about the problem of wants and needs. Say such things as:

- What's the difference between a want and a need? Do you know?

- What do your friends have that you think you need to be their friend?

What kinds of things do your kids think they need? Say such things as:

- I want you to think about what you need and what you want. Tell me what your real needs are and then what your wants are. I want to see if I would agree.

- Help me understand where you're coming from when you say you need this kind of shirt.

- Can you separate your wants from your needs?

Find out what's cool and in fashion. Are these needs or wants? Say such things as:

- Do you think that dressing fashionably is a want or a need?

- What kind of flexibility do you have when it comes to brand names and having the "right" shirt, blouse, shoes, and tennis racket?

- Do you think the cost of being a member of your group is sometimes too high?

If your teen can't distinguish between needs and wants, you may have to say such things as:

- No, you can't have that.
- You're going to have to learn what a need is and what a want is because you don't seem to be able to do that now.

Talk about compromise based on family circumstances. Say such things as:

- Needs for some people are wants for others.
- This is the family income each month. Here is our disposable income after all our needs have been taken care of. Disposable income is for wants. You can see that it isn't much.

Talk about your teen's income, savings, contribution to the family, and disposable income. Say such things as:

- Your allowance is yours to spend as you like.
- The money you earn from your job is all yours/three-quarters yours/half yours to spend on your needs or wants. The rest goes in savings for college.

WORDS AND PHRASES TO USE

- a real need	- decisions	- family circumstances	- the basics
- clarifying	- desire		- values
- cost of friendship	- differentiating needs and wants	- fantasy	
		- fashion	

What Not to Say and Do

You and your teen will have different ideas about needs and wants. Don't say such things as:

- You're wrong. That's not a need, it's a want.
- Just because your friends have it doesn't make it a need for you.
- You don't know what you're talking about.

Don't do or say things that suggest you want your teen to be isolated from his group. Don't say such things as:

- You can't have what your friends have even if it means you lose your friends.
- They're the wrong friends for you.
- You can only do what I allow you to do.

Your teen may think the label is more important than the item itself. Don't say such things as:

- The label doesn't matter.
- It's either these or nothing.

Try to be diplomatic and understanding with your teen. Don't say such things as:

- You can't have that. I don't care why you say you need it.
- I was never like you when I was your age. I knew the difference between needs and wants.

Don't expect your teen to understand family finances without being told. Don't say such things as:

- You should have known we couldn't afford anything like that.
- How can you be so inconsiderate?
- You live in your own little world, don't you?
- You'd better come down to earth.

WORDS AND PHRASES TO AVOID

▶ blind	▶ greedy	▶ you live in your own little world	▶ you're so insensitive
▶ don't you have any values	▶ irresponsible	▶ your friends don't matter	▶ you're wrong
▶ get a life	▶ wake up to reality		

59 Partying

Never give a party if you will be the most interesting person there.

—Mickey Friedman

"Mom, may I have a party?" The dreaded question shot swiftly through the air from daughter to mother one morning at breakfast. Stephanie's mom had been thinking about parties recently because she had read in yesterday's paper about two teens killed in a car crash while driving home from a party at a friend's house. Alcohol had been a factor, according to the police report.

"When do you want to have it?" asked Mom.

"This Saturday night," Stephanie replied.

"Let me talk to Dad about it, and I'll give you an answer tonight," said Mom.

"Okay," Stephanie said.

Mom spent most of that day at work thinking about the party. If they allowed beer, they would have to control driving. Nobody would be allowed to drink and drive. That meant having kids sleep over or having designated drivers.

She didn't want an open-invitation party. And chaperons were also important. They couldn't abandon their house to a bunch of unsupervised teens whose hormones were raging and their judgment clouded by drink.

What about noise? It was late spring, so windows would be open. They wouldn't allow loud music that would bother the neighbors. What should the curfew be? Midnight?

After considering all these issues, Stephanie's parents said yes, she could have a party if she would agree to their rules:

1. Written invitations to no more than thirty kids.
2. Soft drinks would be the norm. No alcohol allowed.
3. Stephanie's parents would be there as chaperons but would stay out of sight.

4. *The party could go on until one o'clock as long as there were no problems.*

5. *Music had to be played at a reasonable level so as not to disturb the neighbors or invite a visit from the police.*

Things to Consider

You might take the view that if the party is at your house, you're in control. My wife and I always believed that we should make our teens and their friends welcome at our place. Then we knew where they were, who they were with, and what they were doing. There were lots of teen parties at our house, and if things got a bit out of hand, we were in the background to get things back under control.

If you're going to let your teen have a party, you need rules. You and your teen should come up with these rules together. Talk them through. Ask your teen her ideas. Find out what works and what doesn't work from her point of view and from her experience at parties.

Party rules are for everyone's good. Here are some general principles to keep in mind:

1. If the party is at your house, you have control.

2. No open-invitation parties. Written invitations should specify the beginning and ending times of the party, dress code, and what people should bring.

3. Put a reasonable limit on numbers for the size of your house and party budget.

4. Decide with your teen what food and drink you will provide and what the kids will bring.

5. No alcohol if your kids are under the legal drinking age. For kids of legal drinking age you might want to allow some beer or wine.

6. There will always be responsible adults somewhere in the house but not spying on the kids. Make your kids feel that they are responsible for their own behavior.

7. Keep the music volume under control. Have a specific place for music and dancing.

8. Keep the kids within the bounds of your property. Tell your neighbors in advance about the party.

9. Have a reasonable curfew for the age of the kids.

10. Nobody will be allowed to drink and drive. Arrangements will be made for a designated driver or for kids to sleep over if necessary.

Three Things You Must Do

1. *Accept* teen parties as an important part of your teen's life.

2. *Decide* if you will allow parties at your house.

3. *Work* with your teen on rules for parties at home or away.

What to Say and Do

Teenage parties are a fact of life. Say such things as:

- Whose party are you going to? Where do they live? What time does it finish? Who're you going with? Is there going to be alcohol? Will the parents be home?

If you always make your teens' friends welcome at your place, say such things as:

- We love having your friends here. (Of course you must show this in the way you treat them. Just saying it won't do the job.)

- Tell your friends you can have the party here.

- Our house is always open to your friends.

You need to have rules for your teens when they go out to parties. Say such things as:

- We need to know where you're going and when you'll be home.

- You must call and tell us when you're on your way home no matter what time it is.

- You must never drink and drive or ride with anyone who has been drinking. You can call us anytime, and we'll come and get you.

Teen parties at your house need rules. Say such things as:

- You've been to lots of parties. Did they have rules?
- What makes for a good party?
- What do you think we need to make your party a good one?
- Can we sit down and come up with some guidelines for your party?

Talk about the things you need for the party. Sit down and make a list. Say such things as:

- Let's make a list of the things we have to do for the party.
- What would you put on the list?

List numbers, invitations, food, drink, music, chaperons, and start and finish times. Praise your teen for their mature attitude and cooperation. Say such things as:

- You have a great attitude.
- That was well done.
- With this kind of approach it should be a great party.

WORDS AND PHRASES TO USE

chaperons	keep the music down	no drinking and driving	responsibility
control	no alcohol	planning	warn the neighbors
invitation only	no crashers	reasonable rules	

What Not to Say and Do

Don't be strict about parties unless your teen is untrustworthy. Don't say such things as:

- You're not allowed to go to parties.
- No, you can't have a party here.
- I don't trust teens in groups of two or more.

Don't make your teen's friends feel unwelcome. Don't say such things as:

- I don't want your friends coming over here and getting my house dirty.

- Why can't you go to your friends' houses? Why must you always come here?

- I don't trust any of your friends. They'll probably steal from us if they get the chance.

Don't make your teen afraid to tell you the truth. Don't say such things as:

- If I ever find out that you've been drinking, you'll be in big trouble.

- Don't ever tell me you've gone to a party without my permission.

Don't just impose rules about parties on your teen. Don't say such things as:

- If you're going to have a party, these are the rules. Take them or leave them.

- You're too young. You don't know anything about throwing a party.

Don't allow an unchaperoned party. Don't say such things as:

- This is your responsibility. We're going out.

- You're on your own. You'd better not leave a mess.

Don't encourage drinking among underage teens. Don't say such things as:

- I know you and your friends are only fifteen, but you have to learn how to handle your liquor someday. You might as well start now.

- I don't care if you drink or not. Just don't let anybody get sick.

WORDS AND PHRASES TO AVOID

- a loud party is a good party
- I used to gate-crash parties all the time
- invite whomever you want
- juvenile delinquents
- parties are for fun, not rules
- rules are for sissies
- untrustworthy

60 Peer Pressure

Every generation laughs at the old fashions but religiously follows the new.
—HENRY DAVID THOREAU

"Did I smell alcohol on your breath last night when you came in?" Craig's dad asked him one Sunday morning.

Craig knew he would get caught one day, and now he had. He was sixteen and had been to a small party at the home of a friend whose parents were away for the weekend. All the kids were hanging out, talking, having soft drinks, and a few guys had brought some beer. Craig wasn't crazy about the taste of beer, but he was offered one and took it.

Now he'd been caught. Craig never got into serious trouble, and even when he did things he wasn't supposed to do, his parents preferred to talk it through rather than fly off the handle as some of his friends' parents seemed to do. They pretty much trusted him to do the right thing, and he generally did. But what was a guy to do if all his friends were drinking beer but he said he didn't like it? They'd just think he was afraid of his parents.

"Yeah, Dad," Craig said. "I drank a couple of beers last night. But I wasn't driving, and it was only two beers. All the guys were drinking, and I couldn't say no."

"Craig," said his dad, "I think we need to talk."

Things to Consider

Sex, drugs, alcohol, schoolwork, sports, clothing, music, movies, video games, cars—these are all part of teenager life, and teens are influenced by peer pressure. Teens "must have" the latest CD, a designer sweater, or a particular kind of car, or see a certain movie. The pressure on teens to know what other teens know and dress the way they dress is just the tip of the iceberg. Beneath the surface you can find pressure to be an "A" student or an "F" student, a preppy or a goth, a rocker or a jock, a straight arrow or a druggie.

Nothing seems more important to teens than being a member of their particular group. The pressures to conform are enormous. Your teen conforms or loses membership.

Know and understand your teen's group. Use this knowledge to help your teen be a member or to change membership. Help them do the right thing and prevent them from doing the wrong thing. By being involved in your teens' life and having open lines of communication, you can understand their wants and needs in the context of their need to be like their friends.

Understand the pressure on teens in the same light as the pressure on you to conform to your group's standards of dress and behavior. As an adult you feel you have more control of your own life, but you still wear certain kinds of clothes, drive a particular kind of car, live in a particular kind of house in a particular neighborhood, and go to particular restaurants and social events.

Talk to your teens about their friends and their activities. Keep up with your teens' schoolwork, leisure activities, the sports they play, the clubs they belong to, and the kinds of parties they attend. Talk about their tastes in music, clothes, movies, cars, food, and drink. Take your teens out to a restaurant, to a movie, to a sporting event, to a show or ballet or opera.

Although some experts think that peer values are everything for teens and parents don't matter, common sense tells you that you have a role to play in your teens' development. Teens learn your values when you practice what you preach. If they have pressure on them to do things that you have forbidden, their regard for you will influence their decisions. The quality of your relationship with your teens can make a difference.

Three Things You Must Do

1. *Recognize* that peer pressure is the most important direct influence in your teen's life.

2. *Know* your teen's peer group.

3. *Make* your relationship with your teen the best it can be.

What to Say and Do

Talk to your teen about the pressures on him. Say such things as:

- Do all your friends feel the same way you do about the clothes you wear?
- What if you don't do what your friends do or what they like or wear what they wear?
- Is it tough being a member of your group?

Your teen's group has values and codes of behavior. Talk about them in specific contexts. Say such things as:

- I was reading about some kids being caught with drugs. Do any of your friends do drugs?
- What do you think about hate on the Internet? Do you ever look at those sites?
- What kinds of groups do you have at school? Do they ever fight?
- I've heard teenagers being given labels such as jocks, nerds, geeks, rockers, goths, and things like that. What would your group of friends be called?

Talk to your teen about tastes in people, music, clothes, movies, cars, food, and drink. Say such things as:

- Tell me what you like these days—in music, movies, clothes, and so on.
- What do your friends like?
- What do you really dislike?

Take your teen to a restaurant, movie, sporting event, show, ballet, or opera. Say such things as:

- Would you like to go out together this weekend? What would you like to do?
- I'll take you to see a movie you really want to see, [teasing] if you don't mind being seen with me.
- You know I love ballet/opera/musical theater. Would you let me take you to one?

Be there for your teen under all circumstances. Say such things as:

- You know you can always talk to me about anything.
- Whatever happens, I'm here for you.

WORDS AND PHRASES TO USE

- be honest with me
- clothes
- disappointed
- drinking
- don't ever think you're alone
- friends
- isolation
- love
- membership
- pressures
- sex
- the right thing to do
- values

What Not to Say and Do

Don't ignore the pressures on your teen. Don't assume that you're the most important person in his life. Don't say such things as:

- I don't care what your friends think.
- I don't think your friends know what's best for you.
- You'll do as I say.

Don't nag your teen about what he wears, what he says, or what he likes. It doesn't achieve your goals. If it did, the repetition wouldn't be necessary. Don't keep saying such things as:

- I hate your hair.
- How can you wear clothes like that?
- Haven't I told you a million times not to use that kind of language?

- I've told you time and time again that you'll end up in trouble if you do that.

Don't ignore the practical activities in your teen's everyday life. Don't say such things as:

- I'm not interested in what you think.
- I'm not interested in what you have to say.
- I'm not interested in what you do.
- I'm not interested in your friends.

Don't abandon your teen, whatever happens. Don't say such things as:

- You're not my child anymore.
- I don't know who you are.
- If you do things like that, I don't want to know you.
- Get out!

WORDS AND PHRASES TO AVOID

- abandon
- disgrace
- forget about your friends
- get out
- hate
- I don't want to know you
- ignorant
- my values are the only important ones
- you'll do it my way
- you have no sense of right or wrong
- your friends don't matter

61 Personality

A bore is someone who, when he enters a room, makes you feel as if some-one has just left.

—Anonymous

Serena, a fourteen-year-old high school freshman, wanted to be a cheerleader, but she knew she didn't stand a chance. She had many of the requirements. She was tall and pretty and got good marks in school. She was athletic and trained in both dance and gymnastics. But she knew she was missing that one thing that cheerleaders had to have above all else: the rah-rah personality.

Serena was cool and laid-back. Nothing seemed to get her really excited. Being a cheer-leader was different. If you weren't ready to jump out of your socks each time your team did something right or the other team did something wrong, there was no place for you on the squad. Serena asked herself why she wanted to be a cheerleader in the first place?

If she was honest, she would answer that it was the costume and the prestige and the attention she'd get. She knew that with her long legs she'd look great in that short skirt and white sweater with the school name across the chest. And all the cheerleaders seemed to have an attitude because not everyone could be one. Most people didn't seem to mind that attitude because they knew being a cheerleader was something special. Best of all, cheerleaders traveled with the teams and always talked about how much fun it was on the bus with all the players flirting with them.

Being an honest person, she realized it never would be. It made her sad but also wiser when, after the tryouts, she was told that she didn't make the squad. She realized that her personality was wrong for the job. In talking to her parents about it, they said that in their experience personality was sometimes more important than talent in deter-mining the direction one's life took. Personality was what made her who she was—as much or more than what she did. They said that the important thing was to accept her-self and to fit her goals to her personality and talents.

Things to Consider

Teens go through many identity crises. Teens live in that transition stage between child and adult where everything seems uncertain, undecided, and impermanent. Most teens think that being an adult will solve all their problems. How wrong they are! Being adult simply means having the freedom to make your own mistakes.

Talk to your teens about who they are. To do this you need to know who they are based on your years of interaction with them as they were growing up. Your relationship needs to be built on a mutual respect of each other's identity. You can draw on your shared experiences, conversations, and observations of them in many different life situations. You know what they like to do in their free time, what clothes they like to wear, the music they like to listen to, the movies they enjoy watching, the kind of boy or girl who attracts them, the subjects they like in school and the subjects they do best in (these can be different), the books they like to read, and the food they like to eat. The list is endless, but to understand your teens' personality you need to know many of these things, if not all.

Tell them stories about themselves growing up. You can explain how others think of them as persons because of what they have said, what they have done, and what they have accomplished in their short lives. Emphasize the good but don't avoid the bad. Put the bad in a positive light by talking about how it can be changed into good. Teens can learn from every experience.

Don't try to make your teens a clone of yourself. Accept them for themselves. If you see yourself in your children, that's fine and natural, but don't push it too far. You can't live your life through your teens. Never pressure them into doing something just because you always wanted to do it but never had the chance, the time, the resources, or the drive.

People aren't perfect. Your children will have their share of problems, faults, shortcomings, failures, and self-doubt. Help them recognize that this goes along with living one's life. It doesn't stop when one is an adult. Show them how you have accepted your own personality, how you have worked with it, and what you have made of your life.

Three Things You Must Do

1. *Help* your teen become happy with who she is.

2. *Show* her how to accept her strengths and weaknesses.

3. *Talk* to your teenager about how others see her.

What to Say and Do

Help your teen see and accept herself for herself. Say such things as:

- You're an interesting person. I know what I like about you. What do you like about yourself? Is there anything you don't like?
- What do you think are your greatest strengths?
- What do you think are your biggest weaknesses?

Talk about the things you have shared and what they have meant to you. Say such things as:

- Remember the time you and I _____. I think you really enjoyed that. Did you?
- Of all the things we've done together, what did you like the most?
- We've done a lot together. I hope we can do more. Is there anything you'd like to do together that we haven't done yet?

Make it your business to know what your teen likes in clothes, music, movies, relationships, school, books, and food. If you don't know, ask. Say such things as:

- What do you like to listen to?
- What good movies have you seen recently?
- Who is your latest heartthrob?

Describe your teen to her. Tell her how you see her. Say such things as:

- You're a very honest person.
- If I ever wanted a good friend, I'd want someone like you.

- You are smart and pretty.
- I can always trust you to do what you say you're going to do.

Explain what others think of her. Say such things as:

- My friends think you're a great kid.
- Other parents wish their kids were as polite as you.
- I think sometimes you need to be more considerate of others' feelings.

WORDS AND PHRASES TO USE

- active	- dreamer	- likable	- realistic
- athletic	- good	- lovable	- smart
- bright	- honest	- musical	- trustworthy
- considerate	- intelligent	- nice	- you need to love yourself

---

What Not to Say and Do

Don't ignore your teen's need to find out who she is. Don't say such things as:

- Grow up.
- You're so immature.
- What do you mean, you don't know who you are? Don't be a stupid teenager.

Don't criticize her likes, dislikes, moods, talents, and shortcomings. Don't say such things as:

- You're so moody.
- I never know who I am talking to.
- You have absolutely no talent at all.

Don't criticize her taste in clothes, music, movies, friends, books, or food. Don't say such things as:

- How can you like such trash?
- It's just a lot of noise.

➤ You look terrible in that.

➤ You have terrible taste in friends.

Don't imagine your teen as a clone of yourself. Don't say such things as:

➤ If I were you, I'd do this.

➤ Don't do that. It's not what I'd do.

Don't pressure her into doing something she doesn't want to do simply because it's what you want to do. Don't say such things as:

➤ Do it for me.

➤ You can do it. I would do it myself if I were your age.

➤ It's what I want you to do.

Accept your teen's problems. Don't expect her to be perfect. Don't say such things as:

➤ No daughter of mine would ever do that.

➤ You know the right thing to do, so do it.

➤ I won't accept any excuses.

WORDS AND PHRASES TO AVOID

➤ bad	➤ idiotic	➤ no excuses	➤ worthless
➤ cheat	➤ inexcusable	➤ stupid	➤ you have a lousy personality
➤ disgusting	➤ lazy	➤ untrustworthy	
➤ dumb	➤ liar	➤ wasted	➤ you're not good enough

62 Popularity

The popularity of a man is as treacherous as he is himself.
—Pliny the Younger

*Martin was very popular with his classmates. George was not. What was the differ-
ence between the two sixteen-year-olds? The difference appeared to be a combination
of social skills, personality, and intelligence, though not success in school.*

*Martin had an uncanny ability to zero in on the needs of others. He knew just what to
say and do that others found interesting, exciting, amusing, and sometimes even useful. The other kids would seek him out to hear what he had to say about the latest movie
or issue at school, or to plan for the football game on the weekend. Martin sincerely
liked people, and the kids could sense that.*

*He was always a source of funny stories and had a great sense of humor. The smile
almost never left his face. He was kind to everyone, even the kids who weren't in his
particular group of close friends. He was rarely intentionally mean to anyone, and he
didn't embarrass or mock other kids. Martin was generous with his time and would try
to help other kids with advice or even money. Although most of the time kids wanted
to listen to him, he was a good listener as well. Martin just seemed to have a knack for
making friends.*

*George was different. If he was honest with himself, he would admit that there were
very few people he really liked, kids or adults. He wasn't a great talker, he didn't have
a good sense of humor, and he would try to make himself look better by putting down
others. Most kids stayed away from George. They didn't enjoy being around him. He
did nothing to meet their needs.*

*George didn't seem to mind being unpopular. He was friendly with two boys who
were very much like himself, and they seemed to understand one another. They went
their own way and weren't members of any of the popular cliques at school. Sometimes*

George felt a little jealous when he looked at all the kids surrounding Martin as he walked through the halls at school. He thought he had just as much to say as Martin, and he was a much better student. But he just didn't seem to fit in the way Martin did. He figured it was just the way things were, and he wasn't going to worry too much about it.

Things to Consider

You want your teens to be popular. You want them to have good friends, to be admired by other kids, to do well socially and academically at school, and to be outstanding in sports. You have memories from your own childhood of what it's like for those kids who are on the outside. You don't want your teens to be those children.

There are a few things for you to consider. First, know what your teens are like not only at home but at school and in the community. How do others see them and react to them? Do they have the social skills that make others want to be around them? Do your teens genuinely like people, and do they convey that to others in what they say and do?

Second, are your teens involved in teams, clubs, musical groups, or church or community groups? These will give your teen the opportunity to take an active role, or even a leadership role if they choose to. Social and leadership skills can be learned in these activities.

Third, are your teens obviously popular, or do they complain about their lack of popularity or seem jealous of others? Envy, jealousy, or resentment at not being as popular as others can lead to social and behavioral problems. Monitor your teens' attitudes carefully.

Fourth, if your teens are shy, encourage them to join activities that bring them into close contact with their peers. Have them reflect on what really interests them about other kids. Suggest that they start conversations with these kids by asking them about these things. Help them realize that people tend to like people who genuinely like them.

Fifth, recognize that some teens will never be very popular with their peers no matter what they do. Yet these children often turn out to be extremely successful and popular adults. Those traits and interests that were problems for them as teenagers can be assets in the adult world.

Finally, be careful that your teens don't seek popularity "at any cost." You don't want them to be popular for the wrong reasons or with the wrong group of kids.

Three Things You Must Do

1. *Recognize* that popularity is important to most teens.

2. *Know* your teen's feelings about popularity.

3. *Help* your teen understand himself in relation to others.

What to Say and Do

You know your teen at home. You need to know him at school and in the community as well. What kind of personality does he have? Watch him interact with others and see what kinds of social skills he has. See if your teen genuinely likes people and shows it in what he says and does.

If your teen wants to be more popular with other kids, say such things as:

- If you want to have more friends, try out for a team at school or join a school club.

- How about joining our church youth group? There are lots of new kids there.

- Think about trying to become one of the leaders of your club.

Talk about what popularity means for your teen. Find out what he thinks about it and what kind he wants. Say such things as:

- Is popularity very important to you?

- What kind of popularity would make you happy?

- What kids are popular at school? Would you want to be like them if you could?

If you have a shy teenager who wants to be less shy, you must encourage him to do things with his peers. Say such things as:

- Try forgetting about yourself and focus on the other person.

- Think about what you like about other kids. Talk to them about it.
- If you show that you like other kids, they'll often like you.

Help your teen accept the fact that he may never be very popular. Say such things as:

- You'd like to be more popular, but maybe you're not that kind of person. Maybe you're meant to have one or two good friends and that's it. Is that okay with you?
- Do you think there are things more important than popularity?
- What would you want to change about yourself if you could? Would it be worth it?

You don't want your teen to be popular for the wrong reasons or with the wrong kids. Say such things as:

- You want people to like you for yourself, not for what you can give them.
- If you give sex in return for popularity, it probably won't last.
- Drugs may make you feel better temporarily, but they can kill you.
- A gang may give you the feeling of being wanted and liked, but it's really just an escape.

WORDS AND PHRASES TO USE

- a few close friends	- get involved	- jealous	- nice
- do you genuinely like people	- good	- likable	- real friends
	- image	- love yourself	- you're fine the way you are
- false popularity			

What Not to Say and Do

Don't show your teen that you are anxious about his popularity. Don't say such things as:

- Why don't you have any friends?
- Why aren't you more popular?

➤ Popularity is an important thing when you are a teen.

Don't try to force your teen to get involved in things he doesn't like to do, just for the sake of being more popular. Don't say such things as:

➤ Go out and join something. Then you'll be popular.

➤ You'll never be popular unless you get off your butt and join some clubs or something.

Don't promote feelings of envy, jealousy, or resentment of kids who are more popular.

➤ I hate those kids who are popular, don't you?

➤ Kids are only really popular if they're conceited little wusses.

➤ Jocks, preppies, and brains—I hate them all. Don't you?

Don't make him feel uncomfortable or inadequate for his personality. Don't say such things as:

➤ Your personality turns people off.

➤ Why are you so shy? Go out and be with the other kids.

➤ You don't like people, so they don't like you.

Don't criticize your teen for not fitting in. Don't say such things as:

➤ Why can't you be like the other kids?

➤ I'm ashamed of you.

➤ Why do you have to be so different?

WORDS AND PHRASES TO AVOID

➤ antisocial	➤ envy	➤ shy	➤ unlikable
➤ bizarre	➤ jealous	➤ strange	➤ unpopular
➤ different	➤ loner	➤ suck up	➤ you don't fit in
➤ dumb	➤ resent		

63 Pregnancy

You can't be just a little bit pregnant.

—ANONYMOUS

"Mom," Jackie said one evening, "Carol is pregnant."

"Carol? But she's only fifteen. How could she be pregnant?"

"You know, Mom. The way anyone gets pregnant."

"I mean, how could she be so dumb as to have unprotected sex?"

"It happens. I know you've told me that I shouldn't have sex because I'm too young, and I appreciate that. But sometimes guys pressure you, and maybe Carol's boyfriend didn't have a condom or didn't think of using it, or whatever. Anyway, I know a lot of girls and guys who have sex without protection. It's just something that gets forgotten."

"That's exactly why teens shouldn't be having sex. You're too immature to realize the consequences of a few minutes of physical pleasure. What's Carol going to do? Have you spoken to her? And what do her parents say?"

"They're very upset. They want her to have an abortion. She doesn't want one. She wants to have the baby."

"If she does, a baby will make her life really difficult. What can she do at age fifteen with a newborn baby to look after? Especially if her parents aren't sympathetic. You need family help to survive in a situation like that. Our society isn't set up to provide that kind of help. If she insists on having the baby, she should think seriously about giving it up for adoption so she can get on with her life."

"I don't think she will. I think she's going to have the baby and keep it. She thinks her parents will come around once the baby arrives."

"Well, I hope things turn out well for her, but I feel very sorry for her and her baby and for her mom and dad."

Things to Consider

The rate at which teenage girls give birth in the United States is among the highest in the industrial world. The National Center for Health Statistics reported that in 1998 there were more than forty births per one thousand girls age fifteen to nineteen. That's considerably lower than the 1960 figure of eighty, but still unnecessarily high.

The drop in the rate seems to result from a number of things: a decrease in the number of girls that age having sex, increased use of birth control, and more sex education in the schools. Nevertheless, the rate is still too high. More needs to be done to lower it still further.

Talk to your sons and daughters about sexual intercourse. First, make sure they know the biological facts of intercourse, a woman's cycle, and the risk of pregnancy and disease. Impress upon them that intercourse has implications far beyond that.

Second, openly discuss the morality of teenage sex. Teenage sex in our society has many dangers, the most obvious being unwanted pregnancy. Being a mother or father requires sacrifice and unselfish devotion. Most teens, even with the best of intentions, would find that difficult—and they should. Teenagers should be free to devote their time to school, sports, music, dancing, parties, maybe a part-time job, and preparing for the future. If they have a baby to look after, that future is now!

Nobody really teaches us how to be good parents. We know that love is not enough. It takes maturity and experience of life, a good education, a secure income, and a nice place to live to raise children. Teens have none of these qualifications.

Keep in touch with your teens to make sure they know as much as you can teach them about avoiding unwanted pregnancies. You are the best judge of your teens' needs.

Three Things You Must Do

1. *Talk* openly about sex and the danger of unwanted pregnancy.

2. *Advise* your teen on all the necessary precautions to prevent pregnancy or disease.

3. *Know* your teen and how much you think she may be at risk.

What to Say and Do

Talk to your teenager about sex, procreation, and love. If you have any doubts about her knowledge, say such things as:

- I tried, as you were growing up, to teach you all about sex, but I'm sure I didn't always succeed. Is there anything I can tell you now that you don't already know?

- Do you know how a man and a woman make love?

- Do you know what a woman's menstrual cycle is and how it relates to childbearing?

- If you were having sex with someone and wanted to prevent pregnancy or disease, what would you do?

Make sure your teen doesn't think of sex as simply another form of physical recreation. Talk about the implications of intercourse. Say such things as:

- I know there is a lot of sex on TV, in the movies, and on the Internet. What do you think about it?

- Sex is an important thing for us to talk about since it's on every teen's mind a lot.

- With whom do you think it is okay to have sex, and when?

Discuss the moral issues of sex. Say such things as:

- Our church forbids sex out of wedlock. What do you think of that?

- Premarital and extramarital sex are considered immoral in our society. What do you think the reasons are? Do you agree with them?

- Do you think you have to love someone to have sex with him?
- Is it okay to have sex with someone you don't love?

Talk about the responsibility of having a baby. Say such things as:

- Can you imagine how different your life would be if you had a baby to look after?
- How do you think a baby would change your life?
- If you had to be responsible for a child, would you still be able to have a normal life?

Talk about what it takes to be a good parent. Say such things as:

- If you had a baby, how would you manage?
- How much money do you need to raise a child? How much would you have to earn each month to pay for food, clothing, and shelter?

Have an open relationship with your teen so she knows she can come to you if she gets into trouble. Simply provide all the love and support and advice you can. Say such things as:

- If you ever get pregnant [get some girl pregnant], don't hesitate to talk to me. I'll do everything I can to help.
- You know you can tell me anything, and I'll understand.

Know your teen. Say what has to be said according to your teen's personality, intelligence, maturity, and sense of responsibility. If necessary, get a prescription for birth control pills for your daughter or make sure your daughter or son has condoms and knows how to use them.

WORDS AND PHRASES TO USE

• abstinence	• condoms	• morality	• responsibility
• babies are not dolls	• fatherhood	• motherhood	• safe sex
• birth control	• love	• parenting	
• casual sex	• maturity	• precautions	

What Not to Say and Do

Don't assume that your teen is not having sex. Don't say such things as:

- You don't ever have to worry about teen pregnancy because you're a good girl.
- I know you would never make a girl pregnant.

Don't assume your teen knows all about sex. Don't say such things as:

- You know all about sex, so I don't have to explain it.
- I bet I can't tell you anything about sex that you don't already know.
- I'd like to talk to you about sex, but I'm too embarrassed. Go ask your friends.

Don't think that if your teen goes to church and understands the rules about sex that she will automatically abide by them. Don't say such things as:

- I know you'd never do anything wrong.

- Sex outside of marriage is a sin, and you'd never be a sinner.
- You know that sex at your age is wrong. I expect you to behave yourself.

If your daughter has an unwanted pregnancy, don't disown her. Don't say such things as:

- You silly little tramp.
- This pregnancy is your problem, not mine.
- You're going to have an abortion whether you want it or not.

Don't lose touch with your teen and their relationships. Don't say such things as:

- You're old enough to do what you like.
- I don't care who it is that you go out with, just don't come to me if you get pregnant.
- Don't talk to me about your relationship. I have got enough trouble with my own.

WORDS AND PHRASES TO AVOID

• birth control is a sin	• don't expect me to help you	• how could you have been so stupid	• tramp
• bitch	• free love	• it's your problem	• whore
			• you're on your own

64 Prejudice

I never believed in Santa Claus because I knew no white dude would come into my neighborhood after dark.

—DICK GREGORY

"Damn those people. Why don't they go back to where they came from?" Dylan's dad said this one Saturday morning after breakfast as he was sitting in the living room reading the paper.

"Who are you talking about, Dad?" Dylan asked.

"Those Vietnamese. They're nothing but trouble. Look at the gangs they belong to and the crime they're involved in. They're no better now than when they were in Vietnam. I ought to know, I almost got killed there," his dad answered.

"Do you think we should ship everyone who gets into trouble back to where they came from?" Dylan asked, not willing to let his dad get away with his prejudices.

"Sure," he answered. "If people don't want to obey our laws, they ought to be shipped out."

"All Vietnamese or just the gang members?" Dylan asked.

"All of them. It would make this a better place to live," replied his dad.

"Dad, that's stupid. There wouldn't be anybody left here. We'd have to send everyone back because there are criminals in every race and national background. Is that what you want?"

"I think this country was founded and built by people from Europe, and there was no trouble until people from other places started messing things up."

"Dad, don't you know your history? People from Europe were fighting each other, stealing, cheating, and killing from the beginning. Maybe we should all go back to our

ancestor's home country and leave everything to the Indians who lived here first," Dylan argued.

"Don't be silly, Dylan. You know what I mean," said Dad.

"Yeah, Dad, I think I know exactly what you mean, and I can't believe what you're saying. They are the kind of prejudiced remarks you can find on those hate sites on the web. Can you really believe such things?"

Things to Consider

If you think prejudice is acceptable in any form or circumstance, you probably won't agree with my advice on what to say to your teen. I believe that prejudice against groups of people because of their race, gender, ethnic or national origin, or sexual orientation is unacceptable because this kind of prejudice contradicts the principles of equality, freedom, and democracy. You need to make sure your teen thinks like Dylan, not his dad. If you think like his dad, then you need to ask yourself why you think that way.

Even if you live in a family in which prejudice is not a problem, you need to talk about it because it is certainly an issue in the community and the nation. Talk about the everyday news reports of people fighting one another because of racial, religious, or ethnic differences. Discuss what is behind "gay bashing" and other hate crimes. Consider our devilish capacity for focusing on the differences among us rather than on the things we have in common.

You and your teen have to face up to your own prejudices each day in one form or another. You might hear an ethnic joke at work. Your teen might hear a racial slur at school. How should you react?

Discuss the reasons and consequences of prejudice with your teen. Examine the sources of hate and discrimination, and the people who profess these things.

In the brief conversation at the beginning of this chapter, Dylan's dad brought up the topic of affirmative action laws, currently a hot topic because they have been repealed in many states. This is a good issue to raise with your teen because prejudice can be discussed from many different angles while asking the question whether legal discrimination is justified as a remedy for historical discrimination.

Finally, you must set a good example for your teen. Prejudice appears to be learned in the home. If you live a life of fair-mindedness and tolerance of others, your teen will likely follow your example.

Three Things You Must Do

1. *Know* your teen's views and attitudes toward prejudice.

2. *Talk* about your own views and attitudes.

3. *Reject* prejudice in yourself and your teen.

What to Say and Do

Don't accept prejudice in any form or circumstance from your teen. Say such things as:

- I can't understand why people are prejudiced against groups. I can see how a person can hate an individual but not a group. What do you think?
- What do you think about prejudice?
- Why do you think some people are so prejudiced?

Discuss the principles of equality, freedom, and democracy. Say such things as:

- Do you think people should be treated equally?
- Do you think you're a tolerant person?
- What kinds of things make you angry with people?

Talk about prejudice as an issue in the community and the nation. Say such things as:

- I feel so sorry for that young man who was beaten and killed just because he was homosexual, and for his family.
- I wonder what was going through the minds of those men who dragged the black man to death behind their truck. Can you imagine someone doing something like that?

Talk about your own experiences with prejudice. Say such things as:

- I know people who say some pretty intolerant things. Sometimes I don't know what to say.
- Are there any kids at school who are prejudiced against others? Do you ever say anything to them? Do your teachers ever say anything in class about prejudice?
- Do any of your teachers seem prejudiced? What makes you think so?

Discuss ways to fight prejudice and the things you and your teen might do. Say such things as:

- I think we need to make sure that we have the courage to speak out if we see or hear something that makes us feel uncomfortable.

Discuss the issue of affirmative action. Say such things as:

- Do you think we have an obligation to actively fight prejudice?
- Are there any racist groups at your school? Would you ever think of joining?
- What do you think we can do as individuals to combat prejudice?

Set a good example. Be fair-minded and tolerant of others yourself.

WORDS AND PHRASES TO USE

accept differences	equity	obligation	tolerant
democracy	equal	racist	unacceptable
differences and similarities	fair-minded	speak up against prejudice	
	freedom		

What Not to Say and Do

Don't condone prejudice in any form or circumstance. Don't say such things as:

- I know that sounds prejudiced, but it's true.
- Sometimes there's a good reason why some people are prejudiced.
- I'm not prejudiced. Those people are really subhuman.

Don't condemn people because of their race, gender, ethnic or national origin, or sexual orientation. Don't say such things as:

- I hate Arabs/Asians/blacks/Hispanics/whites . . .
- I hate bisexuals/gays/straights.
- I hate Buddhists/Catholics/Hindus/Jews/Muslims/Protestants/Sikhs/ Zoroastrians . . .
- I hate men/women.

Don't support "gay bashing" and other hate crimes. Don't say such things as:

- Some people don't deserve to be treated like normal human beings.
- Homosexuals are perverts and deserve whatever they get.
- AIDS was sent by God to punish the sin of homosexuality.

Don't make a habit of telling ethnic jokes. Don't say such things as:

- I like a good ethnic joke.
- If "they" can't take a joke, to hell with them.
- I don't go along with all this politically correct stuff. You have got to call a spade a spade.

Don't give credit or support to organizations that advocate prejudice. Don't say such things as:

- I think the Ku Klux Klan has some good ideas.
- The Aryan Nations are going to save our country.
- Those people aren't crackpots. They know the facts.

WORDS AND PHRASES TO AVOID

- hate	- the wrong people won the war	- they deserve to be discriminated against
- people are not equal		
- some people don't deserve to live	- there are certain kinds of people who just aren't like the rest of us	- those people are always whining and complaining

65 Privacy

The trouble with today's teenagers is that they no longer rebel and leave home.

—ANONYMOUS

Janet's parents called her room her "hole," while she called it her "heaven." It was her own place, her refuge from the world that always seemed to want her to do things she didn't want to do or be someone she didn't want to be. In the privacy of her room she could do what she wanted and be who she wanted.

Janet was fifteen and had just finished her freshman year in high school. She had shared a room with her younger sister until she was thirteen. It was then that her parents decided that she needed her own room, so they changed the study into a kind of bed-sitting room for her.

The once neat and tidy study was now a cluttered combination of "cool" stuff: photos and posters of rock and rap and hip-hop favorites, incense candles, magazine pictures and articles. Some of her friends had gone "retro," covering their walls with Woodstock posters, and photos of Jimi Hendrix, the Mamas and the Poppas, and Elvis. But Janet was modern except for all the candles that gave off a soft, comforting light that made her feel safe and secure.

Every so often her parents tried to clean it. She said there was no way she would change it. The clutter gave her comfort. Her parents were grateful that they had made the room virtually soundproof because the music Janet played at all hours of the night belonged only to her. They treasured her privacy almost as much as she did.

Unlike Janet, her friends Rod, fourteen, and Peter, fifteen, shared a room. They had done so all their lives. They fought about each other's mess, about disturbing each other in the night, about everything.

Their house was small, and their parents did not have the money to build an extra bedroom. But Peter had recently created a private space in the basement to which he could retreat when sharing a room became too much for him. That was the biggest issue, the lack of privacy. Both boys promised themselves that they would never make their own kids share a room.

Things to Consider

There are two different kinds of privacy that teens need: private physical space and private mental space. Whatever the physical setup for your teens, you must respect their right to have private thoughts, private possessions, and private times. You don't always want to know everything your teens say, do, think, or own. Your teens need the opportunity to experiment with things and make mistakes in order to discover who they are.

Don't think that being involved in your teens' lives, loving them, and caring for them and about them means that you have to know everything. There is a fine line between being involved and being nosy. If you have good communication with your teens, you know that they will talk to you about everything that needs talking about.

Because even the best and most well adjusted teens are unpredictable, tell them explicitly that you're not trying to pry into their private lives. If you want to ask them about where they're going or what they're thinking or their latest relationship, frame your question by asking them to tell you if they think you're invading their privacy. Making your concern for their privacy explicit is a good communication practice.

Understanding the need for privacy is part of the mutual respect you need from each other. Never open their mail, read their personal diary, or eavesdrop on their phone calls. If they say something in confidence, keep that confidence. Don't go through their room or their belongings without their permission.

The need for more private physical and mental space is a natural part of growing up. As teens become more autonomous, they show less interest in family activities, less dependence on your approval and advice, and greater need for privacy.

There is one important exception to the teen privacy issue. If you believe your teens might be in danger from what they are keeping private—for example, drugs, illegal activities, stolen objects, illicit sex, or health issues such as bulimic or anorexic practices—you have the right and the responsibility to interfere.

Three Things You Must Do

1. *Accept* your teen's need for privacy.

2. *Give* your teen private physical and/or mental space.

3. *Respect* your teen's privacy as you would expect her to respect yours.

What to Say and Do

Talk about physical and mental space. Say such things as:

- We'll give you your own room as soon as we can.

- This is your space, and we won't come into it without asking your permission.

- Everything you have here is yours, and we won't go snooping around.

When you want to ask your teen about where she is going or what she is thinking or her latest relationship, frame your question. Say such things as:

- We respect your privacy, but we still need to know where you are and who you're with.

- If you think we're being too nosy, please say so.

- We have got to find a balance between your need for privacy and our need to stay involved in your life.

Tell your teen she can talk to you about anything. Say such things as:

- You don't have to tell us anything, but you know we'll listen when you want to talk.

- We don't want to lose touch. We're always here for you.

Show respect for your teen's privacy. Say such things as:

- We know you need your own space. This is all yours—even down to the cleaning!

Talk to your teen about her need for autonomy. Say such things as:

- Finding out who you are isn't an easy job. You have to do that for yourself, but we'll give you all the help and support we can.

- Don't worry about seeming too secretive. We know what it's like to be a teenager.
- Just now your friends seem more important than us. That's okay. You need to do the things your friends do and think what they think.

Talk to your teen about things that go beyond the right to privacy. Say such things as:

- There are some things we must know about even if you think they're your own concern.
- We need to know if you are in any kind of trouble.
- We won't tolerate anything that's immoral, illegal, or threatens your health or safety.

WORDS AND PHRASES TO USE

autonomy	mutual respect	physical privacy	safety
health	off limits	private	tolerance
identity	peers	respect	understanding
mental privacy	personal space	responsibility	

What Not to Say and Do

Don't insist on knowing everything. Don't say such things as:

- What were you up to in your room last night?
- What do you keep in your room that you're afraid to show us?
- I want to know everything.

Don't be nosy or ask questions about things you don't need to know. Don't say such things as:

- I want to know what you're thinking.
- I demand to see what you have in your drawer.
- This is our house, and I have the right to go into any room at any time.

Don't treat your teen as if she doesn't really matter. Don't say such things as:

- ✦ I know you told me that in confidence, but I had to tell your father.
- ✦ We're going on vacation together this summer. Like it or not, you're coming, too.
- ✦ I couldn't keep a thing like that secret even though you asked me to.

Don't worry if your teen shows less interest in family or in your approval and advice. Don't say such things as:

- ✦ I think it's terrible that you don't come to me for advice anymore.
- ✦ Now you only seem interested in your friends.
- ✦ Doesn't your family mean anything to you anymore?
- ✦ Why have you become so secretive?

Don't go to the extreme and give your child so much privacy that it seems you don't care. Don't say such things as:

- ✦ I don't care what you do.
- ✦ I'm not interested in what you do anymore.
- ✦ You want privacy, you've got it. I'll treat you as a boarder, not as a daughter.

WORDS AND PHRASES TO AVOID

✦ anonymous	✦ I have a right	✦ neat and clean	✦ what are you hiding
✦ do whatever you like	✦ I'm not interested in you	✦ no respect	✦ why have you shut us out of your life
✦ go your own way	✦ ingratitude	✦ pigsty	✦ you've hurt me
		✦ secretive	

66 Punctuality

Punctuality is a waste of time.

—A<small>NONYMOUS</small>

"Johnny, there you are. Finally! Do you know what time it is?" said John's mother angrily.

"Yes, I know," John answered sheepishly.

"How can you be so inconsiderate? We told you we had to leave at six and needed you here to look after your sister. It's quarter to seven. We were worried that something had happened to you. Where were you? Why weren't you here at six as you promised?"

"I'm sorry, Dad. Jim and I just lost track of time. We were playing his new video game, and before I knew it, it was twenty after six. I ran all the way home."

Johnny wasn't a bad boy. He was a good student. He was friendly, nice, and well liked by his classmates. He just had a knack for getting involved in things and losing track of time. Often, nothing seemed as important as what he was doing at the moment. Other commitments, appointments, dates, meetings, and classes were forgotten. He didn't intend to be inconsiderate of others, but that's the way people began to see him.

His problem with punctuality wasn't an isolated one. Johnny also had trouble keeping track of things such as his homework assignments, his keys, his wallet, and sometimes even his bicycle. He felt mortified by his lateness and by his losing things. He began to think that something was seriously wrong with him.

Johnny's parents realized that he wasn't an inconsiderate boy, and they felt sorry for his embarrassment when he was late or when he lost things. Rather than yell and scream and punish him they decided to work out a system to help his punctuality, and help him

709

keep track of his things. This involved teaching him how to keep a time planner, giving him a watch that chimed the hours, and presenting him with a tiny voice recorder on which he could record reminder messages to himself.

Things to Consider

Punctuality is an important issue. It affects schooling, extracurricular activities, work, and personal relationships. Most of us interpret habitual lateness as a lack of respect, as being inconsiderate of others, as not caring, or as indicating that someone thinks his own time is more important than others'. Not being punctual can cost you your friends and your job; you can miss planes, trains, and buses; you can miss exams and opportunities. Whatever its cause, people see it as a character fault and something that needs to be fixed.

If your teen has trouble being on time for things, you need to know why. Is it because he is inconsiderate? Does he lose track of time because he gets so totally involved in what he is doing? Is it his way of being in control?

Whatever the cause, people may find your teen inconsiderate, undependable, and perhaps untrustworthy. Teachers, students, friends, bosses, and other adults will be more interested in the consequences of lateness than its cause.

You have friends who are never on time for things. They seem to live in their own little world. If you invite them to dinner at seven-thirty, you know they won't arrive until eight or even later. You forgive them because they're close friends. But you might not be so understanding if they were not.

Your teen's problem is the same. Friends will forgive him, but others won't. The manager at Burger King won't overlook many latenesses, nor will his math teacher.

If you have a teen who is regularly late, the first step is to determine the cause. The second is to talk to him about the importance of punctuality in specific areas of his life and the effect lateness can have on his relationships. The third is to work out a system that will help him be on time, including a system of reminders that he can use. Give him practice so that referring to a time planner or setting an alarm on his watch becomes a habit. Finally, set a good example yourself. If you have had the same problem with punctuality, tell your teen how you overcame it. Be living proof of the importance of punctuality.

Three Things You Must Do

1. *Know* whether or not your teen is punctual or habitually late.
2. *Understand* the causes of his lateness.
3. *Work* with your teen to help him be punctual.

What to Say and Do

If your teen is habitually late, you need to talk to him about it. Say such things as:

- Have you ever thought seriously about why you're late for appointments and classes?

- Do you think it's important to be on time for things?

- Let's look at a few recent times you've been late. Can you explain why it happened?

Discuss the consequences of lateness. Say such things as:

- Do you have any friends who are always late? What do you think about them? Does it matter to you? Do you think it matters to others?

- When people are always late for meetings at my job, most of us think of them as inconsiderate and undependable. Would you?

- What do your teachers and friends say to you about being late? How do you feel about it?

Tell your teen stories from your experience. Say such things as:

- Your dad and I have friends who are always late. We love them dearly, so we allow for their lateness. But other people have made harsh remarks to us about them.

- I had a university professor who was always late for class. Everyone really disliked her because we got the impression that her time was more important than ours.

- I know how angry I get when I have a doctor's appointment and I get there on time only to have to wait for ages before I can be seen. And that's a situation where I know the reasons are generally beyond anyone's control.

Work with your teen if he is regularly late for things. Say such things as:

- I know you feel bad about being late. What do you think we can do about it?
- Here's a watch with an alarm system. It might help.
- This is a little digital recorder that you can use to leave reminders to yourself. It might help.

Be a good example. Be on time for appointments with your teen and appointments that your teen will attend. Explain any problems you've had with punctuality and how you've overcome them. Also explain that being punctual means different things in different contexts. Being on time for a business meeting at 8 A.M. means being there no later than eight, whereas being punctual for a dinner invitation at 7:30 P.M. can mean arriving around seven forty-five.

WORDS AND PHRASES TO USE

◆ appointment reminders	◆ consequences	◆ embarrassment	◆ reasons
◆ awareness	◆ consideration	◆ help	◆ respect
	◆ dependability	◆ planning	◆ trust

What Not to Say and Do

Don't ignore your teen's problem with punctuality. Don't say such things as:

- Being on time for things is highly overrated.
- Don't worry. People can wait for you.
- Just be yourself. Make others adjust to you.

Don't assume that every problem with lateness has the same cause. Don't say such things as:

- I don't want any excuses. Late is late.
- You just don't give a damn, do you?
- It's just that you're inconsiderate of others' feelings.

Don't dismiss the consequences of habitual lateness. Don't say such things as:

- I normally don't care what others think.
- People who get upset are just small minded.
- Some people think being on time is more important than anything else. I feel sorry for them.

Don't refuse to help your teen become punctual. Don't say such things as:

- It's your problem. You work it out.
- I don't know how to help you. Figure it out yourself.
- You don't need help. If you want to be punctual, just be punctual.

If your teen feels bad about his problem, don't make him feel worse. Don't say such things as:

- Your problem is that you don't care about others.
- It's just that you're stupid.
- You could do something about it if you really wanted to.
- How many times do I have to tell you to write appointments down and keep checking your watch?

WORDS AND PHRASES TO AVOID

▸ antisocial	▸ inconsequential	▸ irresponsible	▸ stupid
▸ character flaw	▸ inconsiderate	▸ let them wait	▸ untrustworthy
▸ disrespectful	▸ insignificant	▸ no hope	▸ who cares
▸ failure			

67 Punishment

Getting caught is the mother of invention.

—ROBERT BYRNE

Marissa was supposed to do the dishes and her homework before going out. After dinner she quickly left the table, put some of the dishes in the dishwasher, but left the remainder sitting in a sinkful of soapy water with the pots and pans. She went upstairs briefly, then, before anyone could stop her, she was out the door and gone.

Her mom was sitting in the living room at ten o'clock, Marrisa's school night curfew, waiting for her to come home. Finally, at ten thirty-five, she walked in the door.

"Where have you been?" her mom asked angrily.

"Over at Janine's house," Marissa answered.

"Well, you're in big trouble," said her mom.

"Why?" Marissa asked apparently ignorant of any wrongdoing.

"Are you kidding?" said her mom. "You're sixteen years old and still don't know that you have certain responsibilities to your family and yourself. You're grounded for two weeks."

"Mom, that's not fair," she said. "I didn't do anything."

"What do you mean, you didn't do anything? You didn't clean up after dinner, and you didn't do your homework before going out. And you missed your curfew by over half an hour without calling and letting me know where you were. You call that not doing anything?"

"I thought it was Rob's turn to clean up, and I took my homework to Janine's because we have a test tomorrow. I'm late because Janine's dad was going to drive me home, but he got an important phone call just before we were going to leave and asked me to

714

wait. He didn't want me to walk home alone in the dark. I couldn't call you because he was on the phone."

Things to Consider

We raised three children. I don't remember ever having to punish two of them. The third was punished so often, it became almost meaningless to him and to us. The moral of my story is that punishment is probably not the best way to communicate with your teens about what they should and shouldn't do. Nevertheless, punishment remains an often-used and seemingly necessary evil.

Knowing your teens really well will help you decide what kind of punishment works best with them. Sometimes the best punishment is their own feeling of guilt at having done something wrong.

On the other hand, our teen who was constantly in trouble seemed not to care about the punishment, and if he had a guilty conscience, I never found evidence of it until he was an adult. We never had the feeling that the punishment made any impact on him. He never seemed to share our sense of right and wrong or acknowledge that we and other adults, such as teachers, had the right to tell him what to do.

If your teen does something that needs a punishment, make it fit the teenager rather than the crime. Know your teen well enough to choose a punishment that will have the best effect. After all, punishment isn't supposed to be vengeful, cruel, or unusual. It's supposed to be a deterrent.

The range of punishments is large. You can suspend driving privileges, change their curfew, ground them for a day, week, month, or even a year. You can reduce their allowance or stop it completely. You can make them apologize for their deed privately, or publicly, verbally or in writing. You can administer punishments that grow more severe as the infractions grow more severe. If your teen is a particularly hard, unrepentant rule breaker, you can seek professional help to try to get to the root of the problem.

Examine the rules to see whether or not they need to be changed. Problems disappear when what a teen does is no longer considered a "crime." It may be worth your while to discuss your rules with your teen to see how she perceives their fairness and justice. If your teen is a good person out in the community but breaks your rules at home, it may be your rules that are at fault.

Three Things You Must Do

1. *Use* punishments that effectively teach your teen to change her behavior.

2. *Make* your punishment fit your teen, not the "crime."

3. *Review* your "laws" regularly with your teen.

What to Say and Do

Know your teen. Say such things as:

- ❥ Why do you keep doing that when you know we don't approve?

- ❥ You know that you made a mistake, and I know you won't do it again.

- ❥ How did you end up doing such a silly thing?

Know your teen well enough to know if punishment is necessary. Say such things as:

- ❥ I think you've punished yourself enough. We won't give you any special punishment.

- ❥ You know what you've done wrong. Just don't do it again.

- ❥ You're a good kid. We'll overlook what you've done this time.

Even if your teen doesn't seem to care about punishment, my advice is that you never give up on her. Say such things as:

- ❥ We're never going to give up on you no matter how much you reject our authority.

Don't worry about different punishments given to different teens for the same crime. You want it to fit the teen, not the crime. Tailor them to the child. Say such things as:

- ❥ No more computer games for you until your school grades improve.

- ❥ We've changed your weekend curfew from 11 P.M. to 9 P.M. for the time being.

- ❥ I'm cutting your allowance in half for the next six months. You'll have to work for the rest.

You may need to get help for a teen who is constantly in trouble. Say such things as:

- ✦ I'm concerned about your behavior. I think we need to talk to a counselor about it.
- ✦ If you can't explain why you keep breaking the rules, we need to talk to somebody else.

Review your rules and punishments with your teen and adjust them to take account of your teen's age and level of maturity.

WORDS AND PHRASES TO USE

✦ a onetime thing	✦ apology	✦ learn	✦ responsibility
✦ accountability	✦ don't do it again	✦ maturity	✦ rules
✦ actions have consequences	✦ habitual	✦ punishment	✦ trouble

---

What Not to Say and Do

Don't punish just for the sake of punishing. Don't use it for revenge. Don't say such things as:

- ✦ You're a rotten kid. I'm going to get you for that.
- ✦ You won't get away with it.
- ✦ Wait until you see what I'm going to do to you.
- ✦ You'll be sorry you did that.

Don't punish a teen who doesn't need it. Don't say such things as:

- ✦ Just because you don't usually do this kind of thing doesn't mean you won't be punished.
- ✦ If you break the rules, you get punished, no exceptions.
- ✦ I don't care if you're sorry or not, you're going to be punished.

Even if your child is constantly in trouble, don't give up on her. Don't say such things as:

- I give up.
- You're a hopeless case.
- I've run out of patience. I want you out of here.

Don't give vengeful, cruel, or unusual punishments. Don't say such things as:

- Get me the strap.
- I'm going to beat the living daylights out of you.
- If you disobey me one more time, I'm going to shoot your dog.

Don't use psychological violence. Don't say such things as:

- You're worthless.
- You're a retard.
- You're the dumbest person I've ever known.

Don't keep rules that are unsuitable for your teen's age or that are out of step with their friends. Don't say such things as:

- I don't care if you think it's a dumb rule. You broke it, and you're going to be punished.
- Your friends' parents can make whatever rules they like. You are my son/daughter, and you'll live by my rules or you'll be punished.

WORDS AND PHRASES TO AVOID

- damn you	- I don't care why you did it	- juvenile delinquent
- don't make excuses to me	- I'm going to lock you in your room and throw away the key	- my rules
- habitual criminal		- you'll do what I say or suffer the consequences

68 Relationships

The easiest kind of relationship for me is with ten thousand people. The hardest is with one.

—Joan Baez

"Hey, Phoebe, how would you like to go the ball game with me this afternoon?" Phoebe's dad asked one Sunday morning.

"Sorry, Dad, I can't. I have plans."

"What about next weekend?" he asked.

"Busy then, too," she replied.

"Okay, I'll keep asking," he said, resigning himself to the fact that things had changed between him and his thirteen-year-old daughter. It seemed she had suddenly become a young woman who was more interested in her friends, boys, and talking on the phone than in going places with her dad.

They used to go out together almost every weekend. In the winter they'd go skiing, skating, or to the movies. In the summer they'd play tennis, go to the beach, or watch the local baseball team. It was fun, and Phoebe and her dad enjoyed each other's company. They would talk about almost everything, from her schoolwork to his job. They had a great relationship.

Now Phoebe seemed to have other things to do almost every time he asked. There was still the occasional day at the beach, although even there he saw little of her once they arrived. She was immediately off seeking her friends.

He wondered if he had done something wrong or if it was just a case of her growing up. What worried him most was the possibility of losing touch with her. He had always been involved in her life, and he wanted to stay involved. Their relationship was the most important thing in the world to him. How, he wondered, could he keep that relationship going now that she was a teenager?

Things to Consider

Communication with your teen isn't *about* relationships. Communication with your teen *is* the relationship. You've worked hard at building it over the years, but now you find that you and your child are drifting apart because your son or daughter has become a teenager. Instead of looking to you for companionship and for answers to her questions, now, she seeks out her friends.

Experts say that in the early teen years when they are in junior high, teens break away from the family to form deeper bonds with peers. They need to explore their body and their mind, independently. They will look to their peers for support and form intense friendships in same-sex peer groups.

In the mid-teenage years, arguments and conflicts between parents and teenagers may escalate when they want to make more of their own decisions. They will have close friends whom they will confide in more than their parents. These will be friends with similar interests and talents, and they will spend much time with them, more than they want to spend with you.

In late adolescence when teens are in college or their first job, they will have formed many of their adult values, be quite independent, and want to renew their relationship with you on a more equal basis. They will have one or two very close friends and very likely will have experienced intimate relationships.

Keep your relationship with your teens by understanding that they need their friends as much as or more than they need you, and you will relate to them accordingly. Understand that they seek companionship among kids their own age who have the same needs as they do. Remain involved in their life by talking to them about their friends, experiences, problems, fears, and failures.

You remain the foundation, the "still point," in your teens' lives. Be pleased that they can take you for granted. When they need you, be there for them. When they seek you out, welcome them back with open arms, no matter how brief their stay may be. When they have achieved their independence, you can have a new and even more rewarding relationship.

Three Things You Must Do

1. *Realize* that the quality of your communication and the quality of your relationship are the same.

2. *Expect* tough times in the relationship while your kids are teens.

3. *Be there* for them.

What to Say and Do

Communication *is* the relationship you have with your teens. Say such things as:

- I love seeing you with all your friends.
- Who do you like best of all your friends from school?
- Your friends seem like a good bunch of kids.

Encourage your teen to form strong bonds with her friends and to spend time with them. Say such things as:

- Friends are wonderful, but really good friends are even better.
- I think you'd rather be with your friends than with us today. We can get together tomorrow.
- If you pick your friends wisely, they'll last your whole life.

When your teen is in high school, expect arguments as she seeks more control over her own life. Say such things as:

- I know you disagree with me on this. Let's talk about it.
- I love a good argument, and now you're old enough to give me one.
- Tell me what you think you should have control over now that you're older.

Once your teen is in college or working, you can begin to renew your close relationship. Say such things as:

- It's wonderful to be able to talk to each other the way we talk to friends.
- I think you need to control your own affairs. I'll give you advice if you want it.
- It's your life now. We'll continue to help you when you need it, but you're in charge.

During the years of adolescence stay involved in her life. Say such things as:

- Remember that I'm always here for you.
- I know you're becoming an adult, but if there's anything you need or want to talk about, let me know. I'll help if I can and if you want me to.

Be there to welcome her back at the right time. Make sure you have kept the lines of communication open. Say such things as:

- I've missed our time together. I hope we can start doing things together again.
- Let's go to that new restaurant for dinner on Saturday. You can bring your date along.
- You have your own life now, but I'm glad I can be part of it again.

WORDS AND PHRASES TO USE

adolescence	conversation	I'm here for you	maturity
advice	dependence	independence	relationships
communication	discover	involved	welcome
control	friends	listening	

What Not to Say and Do

Don't be bothered by your teen's growing need for independence. Don't say such things as:

- We used to do so many things together. Now we don't. What's happened?
- I'm hurt that you prefer your friends to your parents.
- You're still daddy's/mommy's little girl/boy.

Don't discourage same-sex peer group friendships. Don't say such things as:

- Why do you need so many friends when you have your family?
- I don't like all these new friends you have.
- With all these new friends, there won't be any room in your life for me.

Accept that there will be arguments and conflicts. Don't say such things as:

- I'm not going to argue with you. You do it my way or not at all.
- You're still my child, and you'll do what I say. I don't care if you are a teenager.
- You're not old enough to control your own life.

When your teen is ready to renew your relationship, don't expect it to be the same as it was before. Don't say such things as:

+ Finally we can get things back to normal.

+ I've missed having my baby talk to me.

+ You're older, but things haven't changed. Now everything can be the way it used to be.

Don't be concerned if your teen takes you for granted. Welcome her whenever she comes back to you. Don't say such things as:

+ You just take us for granted.

+ How can you treat us this way after all we've done for you?

+ You can't push us aside and then expect us to be there for you when you're ready to take us back.

WORDS AND PHRASES TO AVOID

+ bad	+ I'm not talking to you	+ ungrateful
+ hurt	+ immature	+ we won't be here for you
+ I won't tolerate your taking us for granted	+ insensitive to our needs	+ you're ignoring us

69 Religion

There is only one religion, though there are a hundred versions of it.

—G. B. Shaw

George and Mary's families brought them up to believe in God. They went to church with their parents every Sunday when they were small. By the time they were teenagers, they went only on Christmas and Easter. Their parents were not strict about religion and believed their children should have the right to decide for themselves whether to practice their faith or not.

George and Mary met at a church youth group, started dating, fell in love, and after college married and had a son, Brad, and a daughter, Laura. Like their parents before them, they made their kids go to church. When their children became teenagers, they didn't want to go to church. They said they didn't believe in organized religion, that most religious people were hypocrites, and that religion did more harm than good by emphasizing people's differences rather than similarities.

George and Mary had no good answers to their teens' questions about how a loving God could allow such things as the Crusades and the Holocaust to happen. They found themselves falling back on the old argument about God creating human beings with free will, so these evils were our own fault. Brad and Laura came right back and said that God is supposed to know all and see all. Therefore, God would have known when he created people that all this would happen.

It was at this point in the conversation that George and Mary usually tried to change the subject. They remembered asking the same questions when they were teens, but they returned to the religion of their parents. They figured they had nothing to worry about. As long as they didn't try to force Brad and Laura to go to church or to believe the church "line," they'd eventually return to it when they married and had their own kids to raise.

Things to Consider

Parents ask how best to teach their children to be good human beings. Many decide that organized religion is the best way. After all, it worked for them and the generations before them, so it should work for their own kids.

There is a flaw in this argument, and teens pick up on it right away. You can look at the world and say it is good, or you can look and say it is bad. The world has good people who are religious and good people who are not. The world has many evil people who are religious and evil people who are not. Teens ask what the value of religion is when it doesn't seem to make the world a better place to live. It doesn't stop the senseless killing, the starvation, the poverty, the hatred of white for black, Serb for Albanian, Irish Catholic for Irish Protestant, Indian Hindu for Pakistani Muslim, Syrian Muslim for Israeli Jew, Tutsi for Hutu, and so on.

Your best defense is a good offense. Ask your children what they believe in and why. Discuss their values with them and why they think the way they do. Point out that everyone believes in something. Talk with them about what they think is good and what is bad, why the world is the way it is, and how the world might be made better. Talk about why the world exists and where it and all the people in it came from. Point out the wonderful mystery and complexity of life. Could that really have been the result of chance?

If you are not too conservative, encourage your teens to examine many religions. Suggest that a common thread of love and forgiveness runs through all the major ones. You can point out how the failure of organized religion to make the world a better place comes from people losing sight of this love and allowing interpretations of holy Scripture to obscure the basic message that we should love one another as ourselves.

If you don't believe in God and/or organized religion, explain what you do believe in to your teens. They deserve to know what makes you think and act the way you do and why you don't believe. Show them how your own beliefs make sense to you.

Three Things You Must Do

1. *Share* your beliefs with your teen.

2. *Recognize* your teen's need to rebel against your values and beliefs.

3. *Understand* that teens will often return to their religious roots in adulthood.

What to Say and Do

Teach your child your religious values and beliefs. Say such things as:

- Let's talk about what you think of our religion.
- I'm glad you've had a chance to learn about our beliefs even if you reject them right now.
- Like everything else, religion has both good and bad things about it.

Your teen will have lots of practical and philosophical arguments against religion. Say such things as:

- Life has many mysteries. Religion doesn't explain everything.
- If we get rid of religion, what will justify our moral and ethical rules?
- I don't think we need a God to justify why we need to be nice to one another, but how do you explain creation without a creator?

If you're happy with your teen's beliefs, tell him. Say such things as:

- You're everything a parent could hope for.
- I admire your convictions.
- You have good values.

If your child has rebelled against your religion, try discussing it with him. Say such things as:

- What do you believe in? Why do you believe that?
- What do you think is good and what's bad?
- Even if you don't believe in religion, do you believe in God?

Encourage your teen to study other religious beliefs. Say such things as:

- Why don't you look at as many different religions as you can. I think they all have something to offer, and I think that's a good argument in favor of religious truth.

- Think of religion as a way of making sense of the world. That's something we all have to do.
- I think every religion has some version of the Golden Rule at its core. Do you think so?

Don't be afraid to state your own criticisms of religion. Say such things as:

- I think that many people mistake religious concepts for truth.
- Religion isn't perfect. It certainly makes some people intolerant of others.
- I think some people want religion to give them simple answers to complex questions.

Warn your teen about cults. Say such things as:

- I know you reject our religion. But watch out for people who promise you things in order to get you to join their cult.
- Please tell me if anyone tries to get you involved in one of these groups.

WORDS AND PHRASES TO USE

- belief	- explanations	- liberal	- religion
- conservative	- God	- life force	- similarities
- creation	- good and evil	- mystery	- tradition
- differences	- hypocrite		

What Not to Say and Do

Respect a teen's need to explore these issues for himself. Don't say such things as:

- If it was good enough for my dad, it's good enough for me and it's good enough for you.
- Don't turn your back on our traditions.
- What makes you think you know so much?

Don't dismiss the problem of evil if your teen raises it. Don't say such things as:

- People who do evil are really in league with Satan.

- Everything happens for good reason.
- People bring suffering on themselves.

Don't resist defending your religious beliefs against teen rebellion. Don't say such things as:

- I don't have to justify what I believe to you.
- Just because you don't believe in anything doesn't mean that what I believe is wrong.
- I refuse to talk about religion with you.

Don't discourage your child from studying other religions. Don't say such things as:

- Why do you want to waste your time doing that for?
- Ours is the only true religion.
- Do you think our religion isn't good enough for you?

Don't ignore any warning signs that your teen may be associating with a cult. Don't say such things as:

- I know you'd never get involved with any kind of cult.
- I'm not interested in your strange religious beliefs.
- Go join that group if you think they know better than our religion does.

WORDS AND PHRASES TO AVOID

• believe whatever you like, I'm not interested	• hell and damnation	• you'll be damned to hell
• do what you like	• we're the only ones who'll be saved	• you're a sinner
• get out of here		

70 Reputation

If I had done everything I'm credited with, I'd be speaking to you from a laboratory jar at Harvard.

—FRANK SINATRA

Kelly's parents were concerned about his reputation at school. He was sixteen and big for his age. He played on the football team and was a weight lifter. At six feet two inches and two hundred pounds, he was quite intimidating. Their concern came from rumors they had heard that Kelly was confronting other kids at school and threatening them with violence.

"Kelly," they said one morning, "you seem to be getting something of a reputation."

"For what?" he said.

"We hear you've been threatening to beat up some kids at school. Is that true?"

Kelly thought for a moment, wondering how best to present this to his parents who obviously had no idea what had been happening. "Yes, it's true, but you have to understand the situation. It's not what you think. I'm not out there bullying kids."

"We didn't think you'd do that kind of thing. Tell us what's going on so we can relax."

"You know I have a reputation for being a pretty tough guy, and it's true that I won't take any garbage from anyone. But I'm not a bully—never have been and never will be.

"There are guys at school who like to take advantage of kids who are smaller or younger or just don't have the courage or smarts to fight back if someone pushes them around. These kids are tired of getting pushed around, so they came to me to see if I could protect them—like a godfather for kids who get bullied. If a kid needs my help, he asks me, and then I talk to the bully. Usually all I have to do is say a few words and the bullying stops. That's the story."

"Your mom and I are relieved to hear it. But don't you think these kids should just go to the principal about the bullying?"

"They think if they do that it will only get worse. That's why they come to me. I don't mind."

Things to Consider

Your teenagers will have a reputation among their peers. These reputations may be deserved or undeserved. Know what your teens' reputations are. It's also important for you to know what kind of people your teens are so that you know whether their reputations, whatever they are, are deserved or undeserved. Talk to your teens about the kinds of reputations they would like to have.

You can advise them to avoid teens who have a reputation for spreading rumors. Associating with these kids can only get them in trouble, and they may end up being the victims of such rumors. Talk to your teens about how the reputations of people they have as friends can rub off on them. It is called guilt by association. Sometimes this is a good thing if the friends have reputations of being good students, good athletes, nice people, and so forth. It can also be damaging if the reputations are for drugs, violence, poor marks, prejudice, or other negative behavior.

Teens can develop many different kinds of reputations, rightly or wrongly. One of the most loathsome for girls is to be known as sexually promiscuous. There was recently a case in a Wisconsin high school where some kids started a false rumor about a girl, and she suffered terribly from it. Her mother had to take the school administration and the school board to court since they refused to do anything about it after being informed of the problem.

Teens have reputations among their teachers. In the staff room teachers discuss their students at length, and these reputations often precede students to their classes. Teachers may acquire preconceptions of teens that affect their evaluation of the students' work.

Student reputations among teachers include such things as hard worker, bright, intelligent, trustworthy, troublemaker, unreliable, belligerent, bully, slow learner, and irresponsible. This is an area in which you can help your teens develop the right kind of reputation by supervising their schoolwork, keeping in close contact with their teachers, and encouraging them to do their best.

Make sure your teens don't spread false rumors about classmates or teachers. This kind of malicious activity can have terrible consequences for a person. If you think your teens are involved in spreading false rumors, be sure to discuss it with them and help them see the danger in it.

Three Things You Must Do

1. *Know* your child's reputation at school and among his friends.

2. *Know* whether it is deserved or undeserved.

3. *Help* protect your child from a bad reputation.

What to Say and Do

Talk to your teenager about his reputation among other kids. Say such things as:

- ◆ What do kids say about you?

- ◆ What's your reputation with other kids?

- ◆ Do you have the kind of reputation you'd like to have?

Talk to your teen about undeserved bad reputations. Say such things as:

- ◆ Do you think you have a good or a bad reputation among other kids?

- ◆ Do you deserve the reputation you have?

Tell your child to avoid kids who spread false rumors about other kids. Say such things as:

- ◆ Do you know any kids who spread false rumors about other kids?

- ◆ Do any kids spread false rumors about you?

- ◆ I think it's a good idea to stay away from kids who are involved in spreading false rumors.

Help your teen understand guilt by association. Say such things as:

- ◆ You know that you can get a reputation from the kinds of friends you have. Their reputations can become yours.

- ◆ Do your friends have good or bad reputations?

- ◆ People judge you by the kind of company you keep. It's not always fair, but people do it.

Warn your daughters about getting a reputation as promiscuous. Say such things as:

- One of the worst reputations for a girl is that she is promiscuous. I know it's not fair since boys don't have the same problem, but that's the way life is, so you need to be careful.
- You have to pay attention to what you wear, how you use makeup, and what you say and do in public because you can develop a reputation based on those things.

Talk about having a reputation for bullying or being bullied. Say such things as:

- You would never bully anyone, would you?
- Do kids bully you?
- You don't want a reputation as a bully or as someone who is easily bullied.

Talk about the kind of reputation your teen has with his teachers. Say such things as:

- What do you think your teachers say about you?
- Do you have a good reputation with teachers or a bad one?
- What's the best way to have a good reputation with teachers?

Help your teen realize the danger of spreading false rumors. Say such things as:

- I know you realize that you must never spread false rumors about anyone.
- You wouldn't say anything about other kids or teachers that wasn't the truth, would you?
- Saying untrue things about others can make their lives miserable.

WORDS AND PHRASES TO USE

a bad reputation	be careful	guilt by association	rumors
a good reputation	bright	honest	truth
accurate	deserved	lies	undeserved

What Not to Say and Do

Don't ignore your teen's reputation. Don't say such things as:

➤ I don't care what your reputation is among other kids. I know the real you.

Don't condone your teen's spreading rumors. Don't say such things as:

➤ They deserve whatever they get.

➤ You only repeated what you thought was the truth. It's not your obligation to find out the facts.

➤ You can say whatever you like about them; it's your life.

Don't let your teen do things that will give him a bad reputation. Don't say such things as:

➤ It doesn't matter what you wear.

➤ Those wimps need to be taught a lesson.

➤ What you say and how you look are your business.

Don't ignore your teen's reputation among his teachers. Don't say such things as:

➤ If your teachers don't realize what a great kid you are, that's their problem.

➤ I have no respect for your teachers.

➤ I can't believe that all the bad things your teachers say about you are true.

WORDS AND PHRASES TO AVOID

➤ do whatever you want	➤ you can lie about others if you have to
➤ don't pay any attention to your reputation	➤ you don't owe anybody anything
➤ I don't believe it	➤ your teachers don't know anything

71 Respect

> When I was young, there was no respect for the young, and now that I
> am old, there is no respect for the old. I missed out coming and going.
>
> —J. B. Priestley

Tessa's mom received a phone call at work that her daughter had been sent to the principal's office again for inappropriate behavior in class. The previous week Tessa had been removed from class for calling her teacher names and telling her that she didn't know how to teach properly. This morning's story was the same. If it happened again, Tessa would be suspended. She was seventeen, so suspension was a legal remedy for the school in dealing with this kind of disrespectful and disruptive behavior. Suspension could ultimately lead to expulsion. Then Tessa would have to find a new school or get a job.

That evening Tessa's mom confronted her.

"Why do I have to have this trouble from you? Aren't things hard enough for us? Why can't you just show this teacher some respect?" yelled her mother as she walked in the door to the apartment.

"She doesn't deserve any respect," Tessa answered. "All the kids feel the same way I do. It's just that I'm the only one who has the guts to say something to her."

"And look what it's got you. If you do this one more time, they're going to suspend you. Then what will you do? What have you gained?"

"Ma, this teacher is bad. She's always late. She doesn't know what she's talking about. And most of the time we just sit there and read the textbook or copy down notes off the overhead projector. She doesn't mark fairly and yells at us for nothing. She doesn't deserve any respect."

"Yes, she does. Even if what you say is true, she still deserves your respect because she's the teacher and you're just a kid. Besides, there's no way the school is going to let you get away with this kind of behavior."

Things to Consider

One of the biggest complaints about children today is that they don't respect their elders the way children used to. This is, of course, each generation's myth—that their generation was respectful to all grown-ups, especially those in authority, while today's youth show no respect for anyone. Consider the following quotation: "Children today are tyrants. They contradict their parents, gobble their food, and tyrannize their teachers." Sound familiar? The writer is Socrates, a Greek philosopher who was talking about kids in the fifth century B.C.

Kids don't respect grown-ups just because they're grown-ups. That's probably a good thing. Respect must be earned. That's one version of the idea of respect. But there is another.

You often have to respect people because of their position or age even if they haven't earned that respect. You do this all the time with parents, grandparents, teachers, police officers, judges, and others who have some authority over us. The fifth of the Ten Commandments says, "Honor thy father and thy mother." It doesn't say, "Honor thy father and thy mother only if they've earned your respect."

You can help your teens understand this by showing them that respect doesn't mean blind acceptance. Teens can show respect and yet stand up for themselves and take action. If their teacher is not doing a good job, they can talk to the principal. It will take more than just their complaints to get some action, but given sufficient evidence something can be done.

Talk to your teens about the positive aspects of respecting others: It shows that you value them as people, that you understand they're doing their best, and that you don't set yourself up as judge and jury over them. The world won't always fit your ideal version of it. Things don't always go the way you've planned. Realizing this means accepting people for what they are and being grateful you can help them along by showing them the same respect you'd show others simply because they are human beings.

Three Things You Must Do

1. *Encourage* your teen to show respect to everyone.

2. *Explain* that people can forfeit their right to respect.

3. *Extend* the notion of respect to include our whole world.

What to Say and Do

Talk about the myth of respect. Say such things as:

- People like to think that teens today are more disrespectful than teens used to be.

- People like to idealize a past when supposedly everyone respected everyone else.

- I think your generation is great.

Talk about the practical truth of respect. Say such things as:

- I think we should give everyone respect until they lose it. What do you think?

- Respect goes along with some roles in life even if the people in those roles don't deserve it.

Respect doesn't mean blind obedience or passive acceptance. Say such things as:

- You can respect people because of their position even if you consider them incompetent.

- You can respect the title of teacher and still try to do something about a poor teacher.

- If your teacher doesn't deserve your respect, tell the principal.

None of us is perfect. Say such things as:

- I know you find it difficult to respect people you think do things wrong. I suggest you try to understand that they're probably doing their best and what they think is right.

- Does someone have to be perfect before you can respect them?

Make sure to teach your teen that he has a responsibility to take action against people in authority who hurt, harass, abuse, or demean others. Say such things as:

- People who use their position of authority to harm others don't deserve our respect.
- If you know that a teacher or parent harasses or abuses kids, it's your obligation to tell someone about it. Those people don't deserve our respect.

Show respect for your teens and teach them to respect themselves. Say such things as:

- I respect and admire you for the kind of person you are.
- You have all my respect for the way you live your life.
- You should feel really good about yourself. You're a wonderful person.

WORDS AND PHRASES TO USE

abuse	defer	honor	position
accept	deserve	legitimate	reasonable
age	earn	lose	responsibility
authority	forfeit	no one is perfect	role

What Not to Say and Do

Don't believe the myth that kids are less respectful today. Don't say such things as:

- You kids today have no respect for your elders and those in authority.
- Today's kids are so disrespectful compared to when I was a kid.
- We need to teach these kids respect.

Don't teach your teen to disrespect people. Don't say such things as:

- I think your teacher is an idiot.
- The bloody police are like the gestapo.
- Your grandparents are so stupid. I have no respect for them.

Don't teach uncritical respect or passive acceptance of authority. Don't say such things as:

- You show respect to your teacher. I don't care what you say she's done.
- The police deserve our respect. You do whatever they say.
- Your teacher would never do a thing like that. Show some respect.

Don't teach your teen disrespect for people who may be in an inferior position to them socially or economically or from a different background. Don't say such things as:

- You don't have to worry about insulting those kinds of people.
- Don't bother being polite. They won't appreciate it anyway.
- They aren't worthy of polishing your shoes.
- Those people wouldn't understand respect or politeness.

Don't teach your teen disrespect for the environment and the living creatures in it. Don't say such things as:

- I think we should wipe out the grizzly bears. They're nothing but a danger and nuisance to people.
- The earth can take care of itself. It doesn't need us.
- Creating jobs is more important than worrying about the environment.

Don't show disrespect for your teen. Don't say such things as:

- You're a loser.
- I have no respect for you.
- How can you stand yourself?

WORDS AND PHRASES TO AVOID

• disobedient	• don't think about it too much	• obey
• do what they tell you and don't question it	• don't worry about people like them	• stupid
		• worthless

72 Rights and Responsibilities

You can't have one, you can't have none, you can't have one without the other.

—"Love and Marriage," Sammy Cahn and James Van Heusen

"May I borrow the car tonight?" Paul asked his dad.

"Do you have a date with Molly?" his dad asked.

"Yes. We're going to a movie and then on to a party."

"You can have it, but I need you to do a few things around the house for me today. Okay?"

"Aw, Dad, I was supposed to play some baseball with the guys this morning and then go swimming this afternoon."

"Sorry about that, but I'd really like you to help me cut the grass and trim the hedge today."

"Dad, I made these plans ages ago. I can't just not show up."

"Okay. You're off the hook this time. But I think you need to put family first."

"Dad, you're not being fair. You said it was a family car and I could use it as long as I was a good, safe driver."

"Yes, I did say that, and you do have that right because you're a member of our family and you drive very well. But as I've told you before, as a member of the family you also have responsibilities. One of them is to help me keep the house in good shape, and that's what I'm asking you to keep in mind for next time."

Paul's dad had been preaching this theme for a number of years. He was concerned that in today's society nobody recognized that you can't have rights without responsibilities. Having responsibilities gave one rights. He was determined that Paul would realize this, and he felt this was a good opportunity to remind him.

Things to Consider

Teens want adult rights and autonomy, but they rarely want the responsibilities that go along with them. It's hard to get through to them that you can't have rights without responsibilities.

Your kids want the right to dress the way they like, look the way they like, see whatever movies they like, watch whatever TV programs they like, have their own room and privacy, go to bed when they like, study when they like, and work as much or as little as they like. But they don't want the responsibilities that go with these rights: not spending too much of their parents' hard-earned money on clothes, looking like reasonably normal and presentable human beings, keeping their room reasonably tidy and clean, getting enough sleep to stay healthy and alert in school, studying enough to learn the material, and working hard enough to get good grades.

Teach your teens that there are times when their rights can conflict with the rights of others, particularly within the family, at school, or at work. Their responsibility is to respect the rights of others. For example, your family's right to a neat, undamaged, livable house may supersede your teens' right to have a party, provided you recognize your responsibility to let your teens have fair use of the house. Or your teens' right to have a party may rank higher than your right to a quiet evening at home, provided your teens recognize the responsibility not to allow drunkenness or excessive noise, and to clean up afterward.

Your teens might ask why rights and responsibilities go together. There are a few good answers. The first is that you have to work for what you want. Everything costs something, and you have to pay one way or another. You pay for rights by accepting responsibilities.

The second, perhaps less obvious, reason is that if you want to exercise your right to "life, liberty, and the pursuit of happiness," you have to acknowledge your responsibility to parents, siblings, teachers, friends, employers, your community, and society in general because all of these people have helped create a world in which you are lucky enough to have any rights at all.

It may take your teens some time to realize the truth of this relationship between rights and responsibilities, but they ignore it at their peril. Until they understand it and act on it, people will see them as immature, disrespectful, selfish, and as takers rather than givers. But they need your help. You must make sure that your teens learn their responsibilities and live up to them.

Three Things You Must Do

1. *Teach* your teen why rights and responsibilities go together.

2. *Talk* about your teen's rights and responsibilities and your rights and responsibilities.

3. *Talk* about the problem of people who want rights but refuse to accept responsibilities.

What to Say and Do

Explain to your teen that no one can have rights without responsibilities. Say such things as:

- You want to do whatever you want to do, but you can't. Do you know why?

- What would your life be like if we did whatever we wanted and didn't look after you?

- Do you realize that you can't have any rights without responsibilities?

Talk about their rights and responsibilities. Say such things as:

- You have the right to live in this house. That also means you have responsibilities for helping to keep it in good shape.

- You have a right to go to high school. Not every kid in the world has that right. You have the responsibility that goes along with that right of behaving properly, doing your work, and respecting the rights of other students and teachers.

Talk about your rights and responsibilities. Say such things as:

- I have the right to have children. I have the responsibility to care for them properly.

- At work I have the right to be paid. I have the responsibility to do my best work.

- As a citizen I have rights. I also have responsibilities such as obeying the laws and paying my taxes.

Illustrate what you say with as many stories and examples as you can to help your teen understand. Ask him to give examples. You can judge his understanding from these examples.

Talk about the need to pay for everything good in life, including rights. Say such things as:

- If you have a right, it is generally because you earned it or others earned it for you. You have the responsibility to be worthy of that right.

- Some people like to say "the world doesn't owe you a living." They mean that you are expected to work for whatever you want. That's your responsibility.

- "There's no such thing as a free lunch" is another favorite expression. It means you have to pay for everything you get. This is true of rights. You pay by accepting responsibility.

Put the relationship between rights and responsibilities into a larger perspective. The Declaration of Independence says that everyone has the right to "life, liberty, and the pursuit of happiness." Explain how these rights depend on all of us fulfilling our responsibilities to each other and to society in order to protect these and other rights.

WORDS AND PHRASES TO USE

accept	connection	give	protect
acknowledge	earn	mature	respect
appropriate	ensure	obligations	society
community	freedoms		

What Not to Say and Do

Don't let your teen think he can have rights without responsibilities. Don't say such things as:

- It's your right to do whatever you want.
- I don't care what you do.

◆ We have certain freedoms in this country that no one can ever take away from you.

Don't ignore your kids. Don't say such things as:

◆ I don't have time to look after you.

◆ Just stay out of trouble, that's all I ask. Otherwise, you can do what you want.

◆ I don't want anything from you. Just behave yourself.

Don't let your teen ignore the rights of others. Don't say such things as:

◆ That's their problem.

◆ Just tell them to stay out of the way.

◆ You don't owe them anything.

Don't set a bad example for your teens. Don't say such things as:

◆ I don't know why I have to pay taxes. The government just wastes the money.

◆ I don't owe anybody anything.

Don't let your child have rights without responsibilities. Don't say such things as:

◆ You are such a precious child. You don't have to do anything to help me.

◆ What can I give you? Name it and it's yours.

◆ You deserve to have everything you want.

WORDS AND PHRASES TO AVOID

◆ do whatever you like	◆ it's not your problem	◆ no responsibility
◆ don't worry about what people think	◆ it's your right	◆ people are so small-minded
	◆ no obligation	◆ ungrateful

73 Rules

<hr>

Any fool can make a rule.

—Henry David Thoreau

"You know the rules. You're grounded for three weeks. That should give you time to think about what you did. I hope it teaches you a lesson," said Doug's father.

"But, Dad, it was just a speeding ticket. I was only going five miles over the limit, and the cops were waiting at the bottom of the hill. It's not fair," said Doug, a seventeen-year-old high school student.

"The rule is you have to obey the traffic laws. We talked about that when you completed your driver's ed course and passed your test. I helped you buy a car, and you agreed to follow the rules. Speeding is breaking the rules."

"Dad, you break the rules all the time. You speed."

"That's not the issue. I speed occasionally, but I didn't get a speeding ticket. You did."

"It's not fair. I wasn't driving dangerously. The speed limit there is stupid. There haven't ever been any accidents there. They use it to make money. Why should I obey a stupid rule?"

"I'm upset that you broke our rules even more than the fact that you got a ticket. I don't care if the speed limit is stupid. Our rule is that you have to obey the traffic laws whatever they are. If I'm going to trust you to drive a car, I've got to know that you take the rules seriously."

"I do, Dad. This is the first ticket I've gotten, and I've been driving more than a year and a half. I think the rules are fine. I like it that you have rules for me. But you ought to be reasonable."

"I think I am being reasonable. You've got to obey the rules."

"I don't think it's reasonable. It's too much. You know what it's going to teach me?"

"I hope it's going to teach you to remember our rules and to drive more responsibly."

"It's going to teach me not to tell you when I get a ticket."

Things to Consider

Even if they break them, teens like rules. They need rules. It's not surprising. They're going through so many physical and psychological changes that rules are like a security blanket.

Rules do two things. First, they give a sense of what the limits are. Second, they give teens something to rebel against. Rules tell teens what you expect from them. Be sure your rules fit your teens and your family situation. Your teens may say that some rules seem silly because their friends don't have them. Talk about how some rules are "made to measure" and specific to your family. Some are commonsense principles of good behavior in all situations. Family rules can apply to clothes, curfews, dating, schoolwork, tattoos and body piercing, work around the house, and looking after younger brothers and sisters. Universal rules can apply to drinking and driving, drugs, social behavior, obeying the law, and honesty.

Involve your teens in making rules. If they are part of the process, they'll think twice before they complain that a rule is unfair or arbitrary. They may still think some rules are silly or unnecessary, but that's normal, especially as your teen gets older and more mature. Nevertheless, you must have the final say about what the rules are. Regularly review the rules and be open to input from your teens.

Rules should be fair and be seen as fair. Arbitrary or silly rules can have the opposite effect from the one you want.

As a rule of thumb, the fewer the rules, the better. Too many rules make life needlessly complicated. A few good general rules about what is and is not acceptable behavior are enough. Respect for others and taking responsibility for one's own behavior are good general rules that have numerous applications within the family and outside.

Finally, in discussing rules with your teens, illustrate the meaning of rules with specific examples and stories. This gives teens a better idea of how to make sense of them in everyday life. And get your teens to give examples, too. That will tell you if they understand the rules the way you do.

Three Things You Must Do

1. *Have* rules.

2. *Create* the rules jointly with your teen.

3. *Make* the punishment fit your teen.

What to Say and Do

Teens like rules and need rules. Say such things as:

- We have rules so that you know what we think is acceptable behavior and what isn't.

- Rules set the limits on what to do. They don't tell you how to behave within those limits.

Make your rules fit your teen and your family situation. Say such things as:

- Your friends may have some different rules because they're in a different family.

- You know we have two kinds of rules. We have family rules that make sense to us in our family, and general rules that talk about the way to behave in any situation.

- I have talked to your friends' parents. They have the same kinds of rules for their teens as we have for you, though the words are different.

Involve your teen in making the rules. Say such things as:

- Now that you're a teenager, I think we have to make some new rules to help you know what you can and can't do. I thought it would be a good idea to make them together. I wanted to know what you thought we needed rules about. Any ideas?

- I know what kinds of rules I'd like to have for you. Tell me what you think about these.

- I'd like you to jot down some rules that you think are good rules for teens to have.

Review rules as you, your family situation, and your teen change. Say such things as:

- ♦ You're a year older now. I think we need to look at some of these rules again.
- ♦ Are there any rules that you think need changing?
- ♦ How do your rules compare with your friends' rules?

Talk about rules that seem arbitrary or silly. Say such things as:

- ♦ Do you think we have any silly or bad rules?
- ♦ What do you think should be the consequences of breaking the rule about _____?

Give your teen examples and stories to illustrate the meaning of your rules. Say such things as:

- ♦ You have a rule that says you have to be home at ten o'clock on a school night. What do you think that means?
- ♦ Here's what I mean by the rule about studying before you can use the computer for games.

WORDS AND PHRASES TO USE

♦ acceptable behavior	♦ family rules	♦ maturity	♦ safety
♦ arbitrary	♦ general rules	♦ meaningful	♦ sensible
♦ autocratic	♦ good behavior	♦ mindless	♦ silly
♦ fair	♦ limits	♦ necessary	♦ stupid

What Not to Say and Do

Don't let your teen live without some rules. Don't say such things as:

- ♦ I trust you to always do the right thing. You don't need any rules.
- ♦ You know the right thing to do. Forget about rules.
- ♦ If you want rules, you're going to have to make them up yourself.

Don't fail to tell teens what you expect from them. Don't say such things as:

> ❧ You know what I expect. I don't have to tell you.
> ❧ Just be a good person. That's all I ask.
> ❧ I can't spell out what I want, but I'll let you know quick enough if you do something wrong.

Distinguish between different kinds of rules. Don't say such things as:

> ❧ The rules I have for you are rules that every teen should have.
> ❧ Nobody should be allowed to do that.
> ❧ If your friends don't have this rule, their parents are not doing a good job.

Change arbitrary or silly rules. Don't say such things as:

> ❧ Those are my rules, and I'm not changing them.
> ❧ I don't want to discuss it. Nothing will change my mind on these rules.
> ❧ These are the best rules you could have. They'll make you into a good citizen.

Don't think you should have rules for everything. Don't say such things as:

> ❧ What's the rule for talking to us?
> ❧ What's the rule for using the bathroom?
> ❧ What's the rule for hanging up your blouse?

Don't assume that your rules are all crystal clear. Don't say such things as:

> ❧ The rule speaks for itself.
> ❧ Don't tell me you don't understand the rule. It's perfectly clear.
> ❧ You're just trying to find excuses. I don't want to hear about it.

WORDS AND PHRASES TO AVOID

❧ do what you're told	❧ I make the rules	❧ rules are rules
❧ don't you dare question my rules	❧ I'm the parent	❧ that's the punishment
❧ I don't want to hear any excuses	❧ it's perfectly clear	❧ those are the rules
	❧ no exceptions	❧ you can never have enough rules

74 School

School is the opposite of sex. Even when it's good, it's lousy.

—ANONYMOUS

"School sucks," Christine said to her mom. "Teachers are always hassling me, and I don't deserve it. I never learn anything. They don't teach me. I just copy notes. It's a waste of time."

"I'm sure you're exaggerating," said her mom. "You always get good grades, so why are you complaining? Besides, you have to stay in school. What else would you do? I want you to go to college. You're not stupid. It would be a waste for you not to go."

"I don't want to go to college. I'm going to get a job. School is no fun."

"It's not meant to be fun. You're not quitting school. Without a high school diploma you have nothing. You'll spend your life working for minimum wage. What kind of life would that be?"

"Better than sitting in school bored out of my mind."

"No, it isn't because you'd be bored out of your mind doing some kind of brainless job. And it wouldn't end in three or four years. You'd be doing it for the rest of your life. Is that what you want? I don't think so. You're too smart for that."

"I'd get a job selling clothes in that neat shop where I buy my stuff. I wouldn't mind doing that until I get married and have kids."

"You can say that now, but you'd think differently after a few months. What about becoming a businesswoman or an accountant. Or you could go to college and study advertising or journalism. You write well and have a great imagination."

"I wouldn't mind those things if I didn't have to stay in school to get them. I want out."

"Well, quitting school would be a big mistake. I think we need to talk to your teachers. Is that okay with you?"

"Okay. But I don't think it will help."

Things to Consider

Very few successful adults become so without the benefit of formal education. Teens don't have to be at the top of their class, but they need to do well enough to get a diploma and go on to college.

One of my teens was an exception to this rule. He never finished high school but has become an immensely successful businessman—but that was because he had the drive and talent to create his own opportunities. Most teens do not have the entrepreneurial personality or talent necessary to succeed on their own, and those things can't be taught, only developed.

You want your teens to have options. A high school diploma gives them job options they would never have without it. A college degree increases career choices tremendously.

Sometimes school is boring. Teachers can be senseless and cruel. Poor teaching methods can put teens to sleep. The curriculum can seem irrelevant to teenagers' concerns about who they are, how they can maintain or repair relationships, or what their future will be like.

Teens need to learn to cope with both the good and the bad at school. Help them make the best of a bad thing when school is particularly objectionable. Teach your teens how to do their best under all circumstances. Things don't always turn out the way you want them to. The good things in life are seldom easy to get. The secret is to persevere and do your best.

Be involved in your teens' school career. Volunteer your time at the school, go to every parent-teacher interview, be a parent chaperon on school trips, and go to school plays, concerts, and games. Get to know the high school principal and the school guidance counselor so you can talk to them about any problems your teens may have.

Set a good example with your attitude toward education. Understand and support the work that teachers do in and out of class. Lobby for adequate funding for education. Join your school's parent council. Help your teens with projects and homework, and be aware of what's expected of them. Familiarize yourself with their course of study. Encourage them to work hard so that college is an option and not put out of reach by poor grades and work habits.

Three Things You Must Do

1. *Talk* about the high value you place on school for your teen.

2. *Involve* yourself in your teen's school and schooling.

3. *Help* your teen do her best.

What to Say and Do

Talk to your teen about what her life will be like if she succeeds in school. Say such things as:

- ❥ Do you know why school is so important for you?
- ❥ You don't have to be a brain, but you do have to do well enough to graduate.
- ❥ At your age school has to be one of your highest priorities.

Talk about the options a high school diploma and a degree will give her. Say such things as:

- ❥ What do you think you can do with your life if you don't get a high school diploma? Let's talk about the kinds of jobs you could apply for.
- ❥ A good diploma will get you into a decent college, and it will also give you more job opportunities than not having a diploma. Let's talk about what you could do.
- ❥ If you go to college, you will have lots of options.

Discuss any problems she may be having with school. Say such things as:

- ❥ Are you having any problems at school? May I see the kind of work you've been doing?
- ❥ I'd like you to keep a portfolio of your schoolwork so I can see what you're doing and what kinds of things your teachers say about it.
- ❥ What are you supposed to cover in math/social studies/science/English this semester? Do you have a copy of the course syllabus and your texts?

Encourage your teen to get involved in all aspects of school life. Say such things as:

- ❥ Why don't you join a club? What would interest you?

> ❧ Have you ever thought of running for the school council?

> ❧ You need to join a team. It doesn't matter which one as long as you enjoy it.

> ❧ Is there any reason why you don't get involved in school activities?

Let your teen talk about the things she doesn't like about school. Say such things as:

> ❧ When I was your age, I didn't like school all the time. But I hung in there, and I'm really glad I did. What are the things about school that bug you? How are you going to cope?

> ❧ Do your teachers bother you?

> ❧ Is the work too hard or boring, or what?

WORDS AND PHRASES TO USE

❧ academics	❧ diploma	❧ good student	❧ options
❧ career	❧ do your best	❧ hard work	❧ persevere
❧ college	❧ education	❧ I'll help you	❧ priorities
❧ degree	❧ get involved	❧ minimum wage	❧ success

What Not to Say and Do

Don't dismiss the need for a good education. Don't say such things as:

> ❧ You don't have to go to school if you don't want to. You'd be better off working.

> ❧ Education doesn't matter. Most things just need good common sense.

Don't diminish your teen's options. Don't say such things as:

> ❧ You don't have the brains to do well in school. You ought to go out and get a job.

Don't scoff at education for education's sake. Don't say such things as:

> ❧ Schooling is only good if it gets you a good job.

> ❧ Most of schooling is all that philosophy nonsense.

 ♦ You don't need to know all that academic stuff.

Don't discourage your teen from getting involved in school activities. Don't say such things as:

 ♦ You don't want your friends to think you are sucking up to the teachers, do you?

 ♦ Only goody-goodies join clubs.

 ♦ You're not good enough to make a team.

Don't condemn school because of a few bad teachers. Don't say such things as:

 ♦ Teachers get more money than they're worth.

Don't encourage your teen to be a quitter. Don't say such things as:

 ♦ If it's too tough, just quit.

 ♦ You can't do it, so just give up.

 ♦ Don't break your neck over it.

Don't ignore your teen's education. Don't say such things as:

 ♦ Education is your school's responsibility, not mine. That's why I pay taxes.

 ♦ I'm not interested in hearing about your schoolwork.

 ♦ I don't have time to do my work and help you with yours as well.

 ♦ I can't make parent-teacher interviews. I don't have time.

WORDS AND PHRASES TO AVOID

♦ get a job	♦ I'm too busy	♦ not now	♦ waste of time
♦ give up	♦ it's your responsibility, not mine	♦ quit	♦ you're brainless
♦ I can't help		♦ school is pretty useless	♦ you've only yourself to blame
♦ I'm not interested			

75 Self-control

If your conscience won't stop you, pray for cold feet.

—ELMER G. LETERMAN

It was when Todd's mother drove into the garage that evening that she first noticed the holes in the drywall. It looked as if someone or something had punched it in. The indentations went as far as they could into the insulation behind the board. They were flat in the middle, and the board around them was broken and crumbling.

She went into the house and found Todd in the kitchen. He was wearing his Mcburger's uniform and was visibly upset, talking on the phone in a loud voice and pacing back and forth.

"I hate that woman," he said to whoever was on the other end of the phone. "She said I wasn't doing a good enough job, that I was more interested in talking to my friends than serving customers. So I told her she was too stupid to know what I was doing. That's when she told me to change my clothes and get out of there, that I was fired. I told her that she was so full of _____ that her eyeballs were brown. Then I went to the back, grabbed my clothes, and left. If she wants the uniform back, she'll have to crawl on her hands and knees and beg me."

After another twenty minutes of venting his anger, Todd was finished and hung up. His mom had already realized what had destroyed their garage wall. It was Todd. This was not the first time he had demonstrated a serious lack of self-control. She had been called by his school and told that he was being sent home for fighting and destroying school property.

She and Todd talked as she tried to calm him. After about an hour he went to his room. Todd's dad was out of town on business. She called him, and they talked about the latest problem and how they had already let things go too long. They resolved to seek professional help for Todd. They had heard good reports about an anger management program from a guidance counselor at Todd's high school. It seemed to be the right thing to do to enroll Todd. They knew that if he didn't learn some self-control soon, he could be heading for very serious trouble later on.

Things to Consider

Lack of self-control causes some teens a great amount of trouble. Boys are more physically aggressive than girls, and their lack of self-control is more evident. But girls, too, find themselves torn between what they feel like doing and what they think they ought to do. And that's what self-control is—managing the tension between feelings, emotions, and instincts, and thoughts, training, and judgment. It's the filter you apply to experience that tells you what the best course of action is.

Your teens need good self-control in such situations as confrontations with other teens or adults or where sexual intercourse becomes a real possibility; when there are temptations to cheat on exams or opportunities to steal; or when jealousy arises because others have what your teen desperately wants. Teens who are overweight need self-control not to buy that Milky Way. Teen athletes need self-control to stick to their training schedule rather than go to a party and stay out late the night before a competition. Self-control comes in handy when teens are offered a cigarette, a drink, or drugs, and everyone else seems to be joining in. Drinking but not driving needs a strong element of self-control since drinking impairs judgment.

A good set of values can be used to guide teens' reactions to situations. These values come from you since you taught them the difference between right and wrong behavior; from religion, which has given them strong moral and ethical teachings to guide their behavior; from school, which has taught them that the world is a place in which actions have consequences; from everyday interaction with their friends, which has given them experience in making choices; and from their own personality and conscience, which tells them what the right action is.

If your teen loses his temper easily or gets into trouble on a regular basis, you may need to seek professional help for him. It may be a problem of low self-esteem or something much more complicated. If your teen seems to have good self-control, you still mustn't assume that he can do without your support and guidance.

Model good self-control. Don't lose your temper. Don't binge on food or drink. Don't abuse others physically or verbally. Follow the golden mean of moderation in all things.

Three Things You Must Do

1. *Model* good self-control.

2. *Know* your teen's ability for self-control.

3. *Talk* about the consequences of uncontrolled actions.

What to Say and Do

Talk about the problems a lack of self-control can cause. Say such things as:

- ⟩ I know that sometimes people rub you the wrong way. Is it tough keeping your temper when that happens?
- ⟩ Do you have friends who have trouble controlling themselves?
- ⟩ What kinds of things get to you? What do you do about it?

Talk about the tension between what they feel like doing and what they think they ought to do. Say such things as:

- ⟩ How do you decide what to do if you have a choice?
- ⟩ When do you do what you feel like? When do you do what you think is the right thing to do?
- ⟩ Do you think you have good self-control?

Talk to your teen about good self-control. Say such things as:

- ⟩ How do you control yourself if someone teases you?
- ⟩ How do you keep to your training schedule?
- ⟩ When was the last time you had a fight with someone? What do you think about it now?

Discuss the values that your teen has learned. Say such things as:

- ⟩ Does your conscience guide your actions?

♦ What keeps you from hitting someone who has made you angry?

♦ Why don't you cheat on exams if you have the chance?

Talk about the support and guidance you're ready to offer. Say such things as:

♦ If you ever need advice on how to control your impulses, I can help.

♦ You know you're never alone in these things. I'm always available if you need to talk things through.

♦ If you have trouble controlling your temper or any impulses, I can assist you, or if I can't, we can find someone else who can.

WORDS AND PHRASES TO USE

♦ action	♦ considerate	♦ moderation	♦ thought before action
♦ belief	♦ even-tempered	♦ self-discipline	
♦ care	♦ impulse	♦ temptation	♦ thoughtfulness
♦ conscience			♦ values

What Not to Say and Do

Don't refuse to give your teen some control over his life. Don't say such things as:

♦ You'll just have to do as I say.

♦ I don't care what you think or what you want.

♦ You're still a child. You have to do whatever adults tell you, with no back talk.

Don't expect your teen to have good self-control just because you tell him to. Don't say such things as:

♦ Behave or I'll hit you.

♦ You know how to behave, so do it.

♦ Only babies can't control themselves.

Don't encourage your teen to give in to his passions, temptations, or other kinds of potentially self-destructive impulses. Don't say such things as:

- You have to live in the moment and go with the flow.
- Whatever you feel like doing is the right thing to do.
- Don't think too much. Be spontaneous in all things.

Don't disparage the values or institutions on which moral and ethical foundations of self-control depend. Don't say such things as:

- Those things they teach you in church about turning the other cheek are a lot of nonsense.
- If someone insults you, beat the hell out of him.
- Don't believe that religion nonsense. Do whatever you feel is right.

Don't ignore your teen's need for help in controlling behavior. Don't say such things as:

- It's your life.
- I can't help you.
- You're a big boy now. Don't come to me for help.

Don't show your teen that you have no self-control. Don't lose your temper. Don't binge on food or drink. Don't abuse others physically or verbally.

WORDS AND PHRASES TO AVOID

- act on impulse
- be aggressive
- beat him up
- do the first thing that comes into your mind
- don't think too much
- follow your instincts
- forget about self-control
- give in to your passions
- it's not a question of morality
- just react to your gut feeling
- only sissies think before they act

76 Self-esteem

Don't belittle yourself. Your friends will do it for you.

—ANONYMOUS

Jeanne had a sister and brother who were both brilliant high school students. They consistently got "A's" in all their courses. Jeanne was mediocre in most of her academic subjects. Her strength was in the arts. She loved drama and painting, and was hoping to go to drama school or art college after high school. Her talent was obvious to anyone who saw her on stage or looked at her drawings and paintings.

But that wasn't good enough for her parents. Both were successful businesspeople who had little use for such frivolities as the arts. And they were not shy about letting Jeanne know how they felt. They constantly praised her siblings for their fine work but said little about Jeanne's outstanding reports from her drama and art teachers, preferring to point out how poorly she was doing in her other subjects compared to her brother and sister.

Jeanne tried harder and harder to do well so that she, too, would be congratulated by her mom and dad. But it didn't work. Her work didn't get any better, and the criticism got worse. Finally, Jeanne decided to stop trying. She found a group of kids who, like her, were not good students in the "important" school subjects, and she hung out with them after school and on weekends. She began to avoid spending any more time at home than she had to. She started identifying more and more with these counterculture kids; she got tattooed, increased the number of rings in her ears, dyed her hair black, and wore all black clothes with white makeup.

Jeanne didn't really feel comfortable with the drugs and sex that were an important part of her new life, but if she didn't go along with it, her new friends would reject her. She began to put on weight and dislike herself even more than she did before. It was as though she didn't fit in anywhere. She felt that she was not good for anything.

Things to Consider

How do you ensure that your teenagers have good self-esteem? Accept them for who they are. Recognize their strengths and weaknesses. Encourage them to pursue their talents and enjoy success on their own terms rather than yours.

Teens build their identity in the midst of competing demands from parents, friends, teachers, and themselves. Their relationship with you is critical. They must like themselves if they are to enjoy healthy relationships with others and success in their lives. Help your teens develop this self-esteem by being proud of them for whoever they are. I don't mean giving them false praise. Show that you understand them and appreciate them. Help them enjoy their own accomplishments. Praise them for their abilities, their efforts, and their accomplishments. Praising them for hard work and effort has a more positive effect on their self-esteem than praising them for their academic ability or so-called intelligence.

Your teens may have one or more of at least seven different kinds of "intelligence": (1) bodily—the ability to use the body in differentiated and skilled ways, (2) interpersonal—the ability to understand others' moods, intentions, and motivations, (3) intrapersonal—the ability to understand one's own feelings and use them to guide one's behavior, (4) linguistic—skill with words and their meaning, order, function, sound, and rhythm, (5) logical-mathematical—skill with numbers and scientific and formal reasoning, (6) musical—the ability to see meaning in rhythmically arranged sets of pitches and to reproduce them, (7) spatial—the capacity to perceive the world accurately and manipulate these perceptions mentally.

We all have different talents, likes and dislikes, strengths and weaknesses. Helping your teens accept their own particular mix of abilities will help them accept themselves for themselves.

A word of warning: Adolescent girls seem to have a greater problem with self-esteem than boys. Help your daughter develop a positive self-image during those critical years. Show that value by her word and deed: Give her hugs and kisses, and have conversations about her and her relationships. Encourage her with positive yet realistic words of encouragement.

Three Things You Must Do

1. *Help* build your teen's self-esteem through talk and action.

2. *Discuss* self-destructive ideas, actions, and stereotypes.

3. *Love* your teen for who she is.

What to Say and Do

Discuss good self-esteem with your teen. Say such things as:

- ❥ Do you feel good about yourself?
- ❥ Is there anything you'd like to change about yourself? Why?
- ❥ If you don't love yourself, it's impossible to love others.

Talk about your pride in your teen's abilities, efforts, and accomplishments. Say such things as:

- ❥ You always impress me with your hard work and commitment.
- ❥ You are such a good friend to your friends. That's a great way to be.
- ❥ I am so proud of the way you _____.

Show that you recognize your teen's own special talents and abilities. Say such things as:

- ❥ I love the way you have your own special talents and abilities.
- ❥ You're very good at _____.
- ❥ You always do your best. That's very important.

Communicate your love. Do such things as:

- ❥ Give your teen hugs and kisses.
- ❥ Give your teen written messages of love and praise.
- ❥ Give your teen a special present just for being herself.

Encourage your teen in whatever she wants to do. Say such things as:

- ❥ Try it. You have nothing to lose and everything to gain.

- You should try to do anything you want to do. It's the trying that's important.
- People who never fail at anything are people who never take risks.

WORDS AND PHRASES TO USE

abilities	effort	love	self-image
appearance	forgiving	personality	self-love
attitude	happy with yourself	realistic	self-worth
competencies	hard work	self-confidence	stereotypes

What Not to Say and Do

Don't point out your teen's faults. Don't say such things as:

- You don't do well enough in school.
- You're not good enough to make any of the school teams.
- You're not good at any of the arts.

Don't try to turn your teen into someone they're not. Don't say such things as:

- Why can't you be more like your sister/brother/friends?
- Why aren't you a better student?
- Why can't you have more friends?

Don't discourage your teen from pursuing her talents. Don't say such things as:

- That's a waste of time.
- You're not good enough.
- You'll fail if you try that.

Don't call your teen names. Don't say such things as:

- You're stupid.
- You're lazy.
- You're a loser.
- You're a failure.

Don't discourage your teen from trying new things. Don't suggest that she is not good enough to succeed. Don't say such things as:

- What's the point of trying if you're not going to succeed?
- You can't do that.
- Why would you want to try something new? You're no good at that.

Don't avoid physical contact with your teen. Don't say such things as:

- Don't touch me.
- I don't like kissing and hugging. You know that.
- Stay away.

WORDS AND PHRASES TO AVOID

dumb	give up	ugly	worthless
failure	lazy	unintelligent	you don't compare
fat	loser	untalented	you don't have a chance
faults	stupid	waste of time	

77 Sense of Humor

One doesn't have a sense of humor. It has you.

—LARRY GELBART

Greta came home crying. She was fourteen and in her first year of high school. She was crying because she was different from most of the other girls and boys, and today they made her the target of jokes and teasing. She was very tall for her age, already five feet eight, thin, pale-skinned, and very blond. Most of the kids at her school were from Latin American backgrounds, were much smaller than she was, and had dark skin and brown or black hair.

Some of these kids couldn't resist having some fun at her expense. They started calling her the amazon; Sheena, queen of the jungle; La Femme, Nikita; Brunhilde; and beanstalk. Boys and girls both teased her about her height, asking her if she had "manure" in her shoes. Some of the shorter boys purposely bumped into her, their faces coming up only to her breasts. The girls teased her about the number of bottles of dye that it took to make her hair that white.

Greta's reaction was to cry. Her friends told her that she was making a mistake. They told her that she should take all these remarks as a compliment. Laugh at yourself, they said. If you cry, you're giving them the reaction they want. If you laugh, you're laughing with them, and that's a victory for you because they can't get at you.

Greta knew deep down that her friends were right, but she found it too hard to laugh when she was the object of that laughter. Her parents were serious people. Her mom was a doctor, and her dad was a pilot. Neither of them did a lot of laughing about anything. They always discouraged Greta from laughing at things, urging her to be very serious about her studies, to take life seriously because it was a serious thing, and to be quiet, well-mannered, and respectful of others. She had learned over the years that the best way to please them was to do her best in everything, not to make jokes about failures, and to solemnly promise to do better next time. This was not good training for what she was now experiencing in school.

Things to Consider

"Laugh and the world laughs with you; cry and you cry alone." This cliché has more than a grain of truth in it. You can help your teens weather many a rough and stormy time in their lives if you can help them laugh at their problems, whether these problems are at school, with friends, with relationships, with self-image, with teasing, or with you.

Show your teens by your own example that there is virtually no problem in life that isn't made easier if you can laugh at it. What you're really doing is laughing at yourself, telling yourself that nothing in life is so bad that you can't make it better with a sense of humor. If you can help your teens learn this small fact of life and if you can help them develop a sense of humor, you will be giving them one of life's greatest gifts. Here are some basic points to make:

While it's wonderful to make jokes and to laugh at yourself, don't make jokes of others if they're likely to be hurt by it.

Not everyone will share their sense of humor.

Jokes that are racist or sexist are unacceptable.

A good sense of humor is the highest sign of intelligence.

Laughter is the best defense against teasing and inappropriate remarks.

People like you better if you have a good sense of humor. No one wants to be around someone who is always gloomy, who takes everything too seriously, and who never seems to laugh or even smile.

Being a teenager isn't easy. There are lots of moments when crying seems to be the only possible reaction. That's why having a good sense of humor is so important for teens. If they have a natural sense of humor and if you've helped them learn to laugh at life, or have simply taught them to "lighten up," they will always be in your debt.

Three Things You Must Do

1. *Cherish* a good sense of humor in your teen.

2. *Talk* about laughter as the best defense.

3. *Sensitize* your teen to appropriate and inappropriate laughter.

What to Say and Do

Show by example that a good sense of humor can make handling life's problems much easier. Say such things as:

- There is nothing like a good laugh to make you feel better.
- Did you know that smiling is physically better for you than frowning?
- Being able to laugh about your problems helps you solve them.

Talk about the ethics of laughter. Say such things as:

- Jokes are great as long as they're not going to hurt anyone.
- You have to be careful about whom you choose to tease. They may think you mean it.
- Think about how the other person is going to feel before you make a joke about them.

Talk about what makes your teen laugh. Explore her sense of humor. Say such things as:

- You have a weird sense of humor, just like me.
- Is there anything you don't find funny?
- What's your favorite funny movie?

Talk about different tastes in humor. Say such things as:

- Do all your friends share your sense of humor?
- Did you ever tell a joke and nobody thought it was funny?
- Why do you think everybody doesn't think the same things are funny?

Tell your teen that a good sense of humor is a sign of intelligence. Praise her for having a good one or tease her for not having enough of one. Say such things as:

- Last time I looked, animals couldn't laugh or tell jokes, although I may be wrong about that.
- The best people I know have the best sense of humor.

Discuss how to use humor against teasing and insults. Say such things as:

- If people tease, you just laugh with them. The joke is on you, and that's okay.
- People can't insult you if you laugh at them. It literally disarms them.

Talk about the fact that nothing makes your teen more beautiful than a great smile and a good sense of humor. Say such things as:

- Whom do you like being with—someone who is gloomy or someone who smiles?
- After a while you need to have more than a pretty face.
- Isn't it great when you and your friend can laugh together?

WORDS AND PHRASES TO USE

- a great defense against teasing and insults
- attractive smile
- comedy
- defuse the situation
- funny
- jokes
- laughter
- never try to hurt anyone by making fun of him
- politically correct
- sense of humor
- some jokes are in bad taste

What Not to Say and Do

Don't stop your teen from laughing at her problems. Don't say such things as:

- You need to take life much more seriously.
- That's not a laughing matter.
- You should be crying, not laughing.

Don't encourage your teen to pick on people who are different. Don't say such things as:

- Those people deserve to be made fun of.
- They are different from us, so you don't have to worry about hurting their feelings.

Don't set a bad example by taking yourself too seriously. Don't say such things as:

- Don't you ever laugh at me again.
- I would never laugh at a thing like that.
- I can't stand it when people laugh at me.

Don't expect your teen to share your sense of humor. Don't say such things as:

- How can you not think that's funny?
- You have a warped sense of humor.
- You're one sick puppy.

Don't tolerate jokes that are truly racist or sexist, or in any way hateful. Don't say such things as:

- I don't care what kind of jokes you tell as long as they're funny.
- If those people weren't really that way, we wouldn't have these jokes about them.
- There's always some truth in the stereotype.

WORDS AND PHRASES TO AVOID

- a good joke is more important than people's feelings
- being politically correct sucks
- don't laugh
- I don't care what others feel
- if people tease or insult you, insult them back
- life is no joke
- that's the way they really are
- they'll just have to learn to take it
- to hell with them
- want to hear the latest _____ joke

78 Sex

I kissed my first girl and smoked my first cigarette on the same day. I haven't had time for tobacco since.

—Arturo Toscanini

Joan was fifteen. She was bright, pretty, and a member of the soccer team. She had a terrific crush on seventeen-year-old Kevin. He was a brain, really cute, and on the football team. He liked her a lot. They had dated a few times. They had kissed and fondled each other. Then he said he wanted to go further. She was afraid and confused. Her church said it was wrong to have sex before marriage, and she was sure her parents thought the same thing, although they had never talked about intercourse. Her mother talked to her about getting her period and gave her a book on becoming a woman, but that was it. Now she felt these urges. She was also afraid that if she didn't go all the way, Kevin would drop her and find another girl who was willing. He had hinted at it. To whom should she confide? She had tried her friends, who wanted to help but were as confused as she was. Her minister was too old and a man. She finally decided she had to talk to her mom about it.

Things to Consider

Sex! Is there anything left to say to teenagers about sex, or do they already know it all? Before your children were teens, did you talk to them about vaginas and penises, breasts, the first feelings of attraction to the opposite sex (or the same sex), where babies come from, intercourse, menstruation, masturbation, virginity, the rights and wrongs of sexual behavior, love and marriage? Some may answer yes. For many parents, perhaps most, the answer is "No! I was too embarrassed" or "I wanted to, but I didn't know where to start."

You can be sure that most teenagers know the basic mechanics of sex even if you haven't told them. They've learned about it from friends, TV, the Internet, books, magazines, or other sources. But they still need help to make sense of why the sex drive makes them feel and do things they can't explain. Above all they need lots of sympathetic listening and advice when asked for.

You can't start talking about sex out of the blue. For example, when having breakfast one morning, you can't all of a sudden say to your teen, "You and I have to talk about the dangers of unprotected sex," and then quickly stick another piece of toast in your mouth. A good time to talk about sex is when you happen to be talking to your teen about her boyfriend. (This is about heterosexual, not homosexual, relationships.)

Should a fifteen-year-old girl have sexual intercourse with a seventeen-year-old boy or any boy or man? Most of us would answer with a resounding *no!* How do we say that loud and clear while giving our teen's dilemma a sympathetic hearing? Here are some things to consider.

Empathize, putting yourself in your teen's place before you say anything. Make sure you listen. Let her do the talking until you hear her asking for your input. Stay calm. It may be a very upsetting situation, but getting upset or angry will solve nothing and will probably only make things worse. Be grateful that your teen trusts you enough to confide in you. Don't betray that trust by overreacting.

Remember that your teen's life experience is more limited than yours but no less real or important. So take it slow and talk things through thoroughly. Don't be in a hurry. Let the conversation unfold as it will.

Finally, whatever your teen and you conclude will have important consequences for her. You have to trust your teen because what happens next will depend on her. You may both agree that intercourse is a bad idea or even a sin, but what happens next is probably out of your hands unless you lock up your child. The worst-case scenario is that your teen has sex. That's not the end of the world. Pregnancy or disease would be a very bad ending, but life still goes on and everyone has to make the best of it.

Learning how to prevent sexually transmitted diseases and pregnancy using a contraceptive may be the best course of action for your teen. Never give up, no matter what happens. This is your child, and your relationship with her is one of the most important things in your life.

Three Things You Must Do

1. *Tell* your teen everything about the physical aspects of sex.

2. *Talk* to your teen about the moral and emotional aspects of sex.

3. *Caution* your teen about the dangers of unprotected sex.

What to Say and Do

Learn about your teen's feelings about the prospect of having sex. Say such things as:

- Tell me what is really bothering you.
- How do you really feel about this boy/girl?
- How does he/she feel about you?
- Is this boy/girl worth it?

Once you have some understanding about how your teen feels, ask some probing questions to make her think more about what this boy is asking for. Say such things as:

- Do you think if he really cared about you that he would put you in this kind of situation?
- Do you really want to have sex, or is he forcing you to do something you'd rather not do?
- What do you think will happen if you say no?
- Would you put someone you loved in this kind of situation?
- What's more important to you—this person or your feeling good about yourself because you know you've done the right thing?

Now that you're both talking and thinking about the situation, you need to come to a decision on what happens next. Say such things as:

- Let's look at what happens if you do and what happens if you don't.
- You asked for my help, so I'm going to tell you what I'd do in your place.

> ✦ I know how much you care about him and what you're feeling, but I think you're too young.

> ✦ Whatever you decide, I'll always be here for you.

If your teen is truly religious, you can try using arguments from Scripture or other sources of faith and belief. Say such things as:

> ✦ What do you think God would want you to do?

> ✦ What you're considering doing is a sin. Does that bother you?

> ✦ Ask your conscience what you should do. What does it answer?

> ✦ God will love you whatever you do. But there is a right thing to do, and you know what that is.

WORDS AND PHRASES TO USE

✦ be careful	✦ dangers	✦ honesty	✦ safe sex
✦ conscience	✦ differences between sex and love	✦ pregnancy	✦ too young
✦ consequences		✦ right and wrong	✦ trust
✦ contraception	✦ disease		

What Not to Say and Do

Remember that you're talking about sexual feelings and that they are some of the strongest feelings people have. Don't say things that belittle your teen's feelings. Don't say such things as:

> ✦ You're a wicked girl to even think such a thing.

> ✦ If you have sex with him, don't bother coming home.

Don't ignore the fact that it's your teen, whom you know and love. Don't say such things as:

> ✦ What will my friends think?

> ✦ No daughter of mine would ever do such a thing.

> ✦ You're too young to know what love or caring is.

> ✦ You're a stupid, silly girl.

Don't say things that sound too preachy. Don't say such things as:

- God will punish you.
- That's a terrible sin.

Don't say things that are unrealistic. Don't say such things as:

- I'm going to lock you away until you get over these silly feelings.
- I'm going to call his parents right now and forbid him from ever seeing you again.

Don't sever the lines of communication between you. Don't say such things as:

- I don't want to talk about it.
- Never mention that to me again.
- That's something I can't discuss with you.
- Do what you like, but don't come to me with your problems.

WORDS AND PHRASES TO AVOID

bitch	don't talk to me	never	slut/whore
degenerate	get out	not my problem	you're no longer my child
don't bother coming home	it's your problem	sinful	

79 Smoking

A custom loathsome to the eye, hateful to the nose, harmful to the brain, dangerous to the lungs, and in the black stinking fumes thereof, nearest resembling the horrible Stygian smoke of the pit that is bottomless.

—JAMES KING I

Amanda's dad was driving her to her dance class. She was fourteen years old and had been studying ballet, jazz, and tap since she was six. A freshman in high school, Amanda thought she might want to become a ballerina. As they drove up to the studio, they saw a group of girls, obviously dancers, standing outside, smoking.

"Who are those girls?" Amanda's dad asked.

"They're dancers from the senior troupe, Dad. Next year when I'm fifteen, I move up full-time to their group. This year I just dance with them for certain routines."

"Do a lot of the girls smoke?" he asked.

"Some do," she replied.

"They're too young. I'll bet they aren't even sixteen. You wouldn't smoke, would you?"

"What do you mean, Dad? You mean never, like even when I'm grown up?"

"Yeah, I mean that, but I also mean now."

"You can relax. I don't smoke. I don't even want to. It's dumb, and it costs too much."

"Why do those kids do it?"

"Some do it because it helps them stay thin, which is important for a dancer."

"Do you think they have to smoke to stay thin?"

"Some do."

"But you don't."

"No, I don't. Not now anyway."

"I hope you never smoke. Your mom and I used to smoke a lot. Your mom gave it up when she was pregnant with you, and I stopped when you were born."

Things to Consider

A 1994 survey reported that 18.6 percent of eighth-grade kids said they had smoked within the last thirty days; 31.2 percent of high school seniors said the same thing. Teens with friends or family members who smoke are more likely to smoke themselves. White students smoke at twice the rate of black students. Students with no plans for college smoke at twice the rate as those who hope to go on to higher education. Surveys report that boys start smoking because they think it demonstrates maturity and masculinity, or to be accepted by their peers. Girls start in order to keep from getting fat. (Medical reports indicate that smoking has a negligible effect on weight control.)

Know if your teens are smokers. Ask them. They may tell you. If they say no, you may be all right. Most teens try a cigarette at one time or another. Some get hooked. If you think your teens are smoking, you can check out your suspicion in a number of ways. Smoke stinks. Smell their breath and clothes. Smoke stains. Examine their teeth and fingers. See if their friends smoke. Cigarettes are expensive. Do your teens have the money for smoking?

The best cure for smoking is prevention. Talk to your teens about why kids start smoking. Talk about peer pressure and see if your teens feel any pressure. If you are or have been a smoker, you can speak with some authority on the subject. You know why you started—because everybody was doing it. You know why you gave it up—it was making you sick. Or why you haven't given it up—you are too addicted. See what your teens have to say on the subject.

If your teens are at risk, sit down with them and draw up a list of good reasons to smoke and good reasons not to smoke. Talk about the list. Or ask your teens to do some research on the effects of smoking. Have them check antismoking and lung cancer sites on the Internet.

Threats and warnings about the dangers of smoking are negative approaches to the problem. A better approach may be to do something positive. I read of a person who offered to pay his grandchildren the cost of a pack of cigarettes a day, from their sixteenth birthday until they were twenty-one, if they agreed not to smoke. The money would be deposited in an education fund in the bank in their name. It worked!

Three Things You Must Do

1. *Set* a good example by not smoking.

2. *Know* if your teen is or is not a smoker.

3. *Prevent* or stop your teen from smoking through education, financial incentives, and a healthy lifestyle.

What to Say and Do

Know your teen's habits, friends, lifestyle, values, and personality. Say such things as:

- What do you think about smoking?
- Do you have friends who smoke?
- Why don't we try to go jogging together on the weekend?

You must know if your teen is a smoker. Say such things as:

- I'm concerned that you might become a smoker. Do you smoke?
- You'd tell me if you were a smoker, wouldn't you?

Talk about smoking before it is a problem. Say such things as:

- Why do you think some kids start smoking and others don't?
- I started smoking as a teen. It was the worst thing I ever did in my life. Do you want to know why?
- Is there much pressure on you to smoke? Do your friends smoke?

List the pros and cons of smoking. Check the Internet sites on cancer and smoking. Say such things as:

- I know you'd never smoke, but let's try something anyway. Let's see if we can list the good and bad things about smoking.

> ✦ I don't know if you're thinking about smoking or not. In any case, would you mind helping me do some research on the effects of smoking on one-self and others? I thought we could search the Internet.

Talk about mortality. Say such things as:
> ✦ You know all about the dangers of smoking, don't you?
> ✦ Do you know that smoking causes lung cancer and many other life-threatening diseases?
> ✦ Do the dangers of smoking turn you off to smoking?

Offer your teen incentives not to smoke. Say such things as:
> ✦ What would I have to do to guarantee that you would never smoke?
> ✦ What if I were to pay you the price of a pack of cigarettes a day not to smoke?
> ✦ Can I bribe you never to smoke? What would it take?

Express your opposition to anyone smoking, not just teens. Say such things as:
> ✦ I just want to make it clear that I'm against smoking for adults as well as teens.
> ✦ I don't think anybody should smoke, not even adults.
> ✦ I have to be honest with you. When I see anyone smoking, adult or kid, I think he must be a lot dumber than other people.

WORDS AND PHRASES TO USE

✦ abstain	✦ death	✦ intelligence	✦ secondhand smoke
✦ addiction	✦ filthy habit	✦ lung cancer	✦ terrible for your health
✦ at risk			
✦ danger	✦ incentives	✦ peer pressure	✦ weight loss myth

What Not to Say and Do

Don't put them off when it comes to talking about smoking. Don't say such things as:
> ✦ I don't care what you want to talk about. I'm too busy.

+ What you do about smoking is your own affair.

+ There's nothing to discuss. You can't smoke.

Don't threaten your teen with punishment because it will stop her from talking. Don't say such things as:

+ Do you smoke? You'd better tell me the truth, or you're in big trouble.

+ If I ever find out you smoke, I'll throw you out of the house.

+ No child of mine will ever smoke. If you smoke, you're not my child anymore.

Don't ignore the peer pressure on your teen to smoke. Don't say such things as:

+ I know you're strong enough to ignore other kids who want you to smoke.

+ I know you'd never do a silly thing like smoking just to please your friends.

+ I know you'd never smoke just to keep your weight down.

Don't smoke yourself. Don't say such things as:

+ There are few enough pleasures in life. I'm not giving up my cigarettes.

+ I've been smoking for twenty-five years, and I'm in great shape.

+ I don't believe smoking is so bad for you.

WORDS AND PHRASES TO AVOID

+ a cigarette gives me something to do with my hands	+ I don't care what you do	+ smoke if you want to
	+ I like smoking	+ smoking is cool
+ anything you want to do is okay with me	+ if I catch you smoking, I'll kill you	+ there's nothing better than that first cigarette of the day

80 Sports

Running is an unnatural act, except from enemies and to the bathroom.

—Anonymous

Ramon was not a star Little League baseball player. Although his playing never made him a first choice for the league all-star team, his attitude made him a favorite of the coaches and all the other players. No matter what happened on or off the field Ramon's enthusiasm and love for the game and his good sportsmanship were contagious and set an example for all the other players.

Even when the competition was daunting, the training arduous, and the attitude of the coaches and players serious and committed, Ramon focused on having fun playing baseball. He was there to enjoy the friendship and pleasure of teamwork, the feeling of commitment, and the discipline and hard work that helped him become the best player he could be while at the same time helping his teammates to do their best also.

Ramon's parents were thrilled because they had taught him that the most important thing about sports was to love the game, to love playing, and to try to do his best. The outcome, they said, was secondary. Watching him play now they remembered when he got first hit in a game of T-ball at the age of six. They cheered him then as they cheered him now. They didn't mind that he was not destined for great things or professional sports. As they watched him they could see that he loved playing. His feelings were evident in the way he cheered for his teammates and encouraged them even when things went wrong.

His mom and dad went to every game. Whatever Ramon and his teammates did, they shouted encouragement. When he made a good catch, hit the ball out of the infield, or, as was more often the case, missed a catch, or struck out, they were always positive. And when someone on the opposing team did something well they cheered for him also. They never forgot that all these kids had moms and dads who wanted them to do well, and they were happy for them when they did.

Things to Consider

You may have dreams of your teenagers becoming professional athletes and instantly wealthy. Or at least getting athletic scholarships to a good university. You may wish that your teens had the talent to be world-class athletes and perhaps make the Olympic team. Or you may simply want your children to win on a local level. Whatever sporting success you want for your teens, you need to consider a few things.

The most important thing for most teens when they become involved in athletics is the participation. It is not winning, it is not being a star, it is not having a professional career. It is simply having the chance to play. You should want your teens to play a sport so they can enjoy all the wonderful things that sports involve—the chance to work and play with others, to build friendships, to train one's mind and body, to learn good sportsmanship, perhaps to represent one's school.

Pushing your teens to succeed in a sport at ever higher levels of competition and performance is good only if they have the personality, drive, and talent that makes them want this success for themselves as well. For most teens this is unrealistic. Make sure you and your teens talk about their athletics on a regular basis so that you know what they are thinking and feeling. Encourage your teens to play for the sake of playing, not for some dream you may have of their stardom.

Go to your teens' games and watch them play. Even if they lose, make mistakes, and don't do as well as you had hoped, enjoy watching them participate. Make sure their coaches have the best interests of your children in mind, ahead of the glory of winning or building their own reputation. You know that in your own life you have learned more from losing than from winning, from being wrong than from being right. Playing sports should be a positive thing no matter what your teens' ability or level of play. Teach them to play sports for their own sake, to enjoy the moment, to have fun.

Sports are good physically and psychologically, as long as you and your teens approach them with the right attitude. That attitude means loving the game, loving to do your best, and preparing yourself mentally and physcially for the competiton. It also means enjoying yourself, having fun, whether or not you win. Sports are a way for your teens to gain important insights into their personality and to become socially and emotionally mature.

Three Things You Must Do

1. *Encourage* your teen to participate in sports.

2. *Talk* to your teen about how much he enjoys the sports he participates in.

3. *Be realistic* about his talents and ambitions.

What to Say and Do

What are your attitudes and involvement in your teen's sporting life? Ask yourself such questions as:

- Do I actively encourage my teen's sports activity?
- What do I do to help with his training?
- Do I volunteer my time to help in his sport?
- How good do I think my teen is at his sport?
- Do I know what others think of his ability?
- Do I know how hard he is willing to work and train?

If you don't know the answers to these questions, then you ought to find out what they are by talking to your teenager. Say such things as:

- Do you really like _____?
- You've been doing it for years. Do you plan to continue after high school?
- Do you want to be the best?

No matter how good your teen is at his sport, you need to respect his wishes concerning how hard he wants to work at it. You need to know what he is thinking and feeling. Say such things as:

- How far do you want to go in _____?
- I don't want to push you to do something you don't want to do.
- The most important thing is to enjoy playing the game.

Watch your teen compete and see the kind of coaching he gets. If you think your teen's coach is too serious about the sport, say such things as:

- My daughter/son enjoys this sport but just wants to play it for fun.
- I don't think my child needs to be trained as if she was going to be a professional athlete.
- I hope you are teaching my child the importance of fair play and sportsmanship.

WORDS AND PHRASES TO USE

ability/talent	disinterest	hard work	realistic
ambition	drive	health	single-mindedness
attitude	fair play	participation	sportsmanship
conditioning	fun/enjoyment	pleasure	teamwork

What Not to Say and Do

Don't try to fulfill your own sports or financial dreams and ambitions. Don't say such things as:

- I want you to be a champion. Nothing less will do.
- I'm going to make you a star.
- If I'd had your talent, there'd have been no stopping me.

Don't ignore your teen's talents or goals and dreams. Don't say such things as:

- I can't understand why you spend all those hours training.
- Sorry, I can't get to your game. Maybe next time.
- Stop dreaming. You're not that good.

Don't push your teen to do something he doesn't want to. Don't say such things as:

- What do you mean, you want to give it up? Don't be silly.
- I won't let you quit.

- You can't give up after all I've invested in you.
- You're not really hurt. It's just an excuse.

Don't stress winning at all costs. Don't say such things as:

- There are only two kinds of people in sports—winners and losers.
- If you're not doing this to win, you should give it up.
- Don't give me that nonsense about the most important thing being "how you play the game."

Even if you don't like sports, don't discourage your teen. Don't say such things as:

- You're too intelligent to be a jock.
- Don't waste your time playing sports when you could be reading, studying for school, or listening to music.
- Playing that game is too dangerous. I don't want you to do it.

WORDS AND PHRASES TO AVOID

• do it for me	• no pain, no gain	• play through the pain	• winning is everything
• I don't want a child who is a loser	• no sacrifice is too great to be the best	• these days sports are about money	• wuss
• I want you to be the best in the world	• nobody remembers a loser		

81 Stress

The hardest years in life are those between ten and seventy.

—HELEN HAYES

Josh was stressed. The seventeen-year-old loved Liza, but every time they were together, they were constantly fighting. Liza's mother was concerned that Josh might hurt her daughter when she heard him shouting at her, even pushing and shoving. Josh knew he would never intentionally hurt Liza, but sometimes he just got so angry with her that he lost control.

Their relationship had been going on for over a year. Liza loved Josh but was getting to the point where she couldn't take it anymore. It was just too stressful dealing with his moods and jealousy. Finally, she told him that it was over.

Josh said he could never accept this. Liza called his mom to ask her to please keep Josh away from her. Liza's mom also called. Josh's mom said she'd do her best to talk to him, but he was very hard to control. Liza's mom said if Josh didn't leave Liza alone, she'd go to court and get a restraining order. Josh's mom said she understood and would try to keep him away.

Talking to Josh didn't work, and he continued to pursue Liza. Her mother went to court and got a restraining order. Josh's mother tried desperately to persuade him to stay away from Liza but got nothing but more stress and grief for her efforts.

One evening Josh broke into Liza's house when no one was home. Neighbors called the police, and they arrested him. He spent the night in jail because his mom refused to bail him out, hoping it would teach him a lesson. He had caused her so much stress and anguish that she was willing to try anything to get him under control.

Things to Consider

Your teens have their daily quota of stress from school, parents, friends, and relationships. Just getting out of the house in the morning creates stress. Can they get in and out of the bathroom? Do they look good? Did they have breakfast? Have they done their homework? Are they on time? Do they have money for lunch? Do they remember the dentist appointment they have this afternoon?

You can do a number of things to help them. First, talk about things that create this stress. This helps move stress from the inside to the outside where its causes and effects can be seen, analyzed, and dealt with. Be a good listener, offer advice or an opinion, but help your teens find their own solutions.

Second, talk about your experiences with stress. Introduce your teens to methods of stress relief, such as yoga or meditation. Other options include music, dance, reading, and sports, or physical activity such as jogging and hiking. Sometimes starting a hobby can help your teens reduce stress. You might be able to start them doing carpentry, sewing, cooking, or model building. Another coping method is to let them have a pet—a dog, cat, horse, or tarantula. Make sure that your teens' methods for coping don't include drugs, smoking, or alcohol.

Third, in some cases you might need to remove your teen from the situation that's causing stress. For example, if there is a problem at school, such as bullying, harassment, or serious problems with teachers or the administration, your teen might have to change schools.

Fourth, help put the cause of stress into perspective. You can show teens how to keep the "big picture" in mind. Their problem may seem much less significant when viewed in this way.

Fifth, some teens are able to use stress as a motivational device. Talking to them may help them see how to relieve stress by working hard to get rid of the cause. For example, changing study habits can help them cope with examination stress and anxiety. Making a phone call can help them relieve the stress of a problem with a boyfriend or girlfriend.

Sixth, show that you empathize. You've been there. You can help them cope by making them feel good about themselves and by modeling good stress management yourself.

Finally, conversations with your teens may tell you that they need professional help or counseling of some kind because their stress is causing them to say or do things that are out of character.

Three Things You Must Do

1. *Realize* that stress is unavoidable.

2. *Know* the problems that are causing your teen's stress.

3. *Listen*, give advice, and model good coping strategies.

What to Say and Do

Begin by finding out what stresses them. Say such things as:

+ How are things going? I know you were worried about _____. Is that still bugging you?

+ How is school going? Are you worried about the exams coming up?

+ Are you coping with things all right? Are you getting enough sleep? exercise?

Be a model for your teen in coping with stress. Say such things as:

+ Whatever is bothering you, don't look for an easy way out.

+ When I'm stressed try not to look for relief in drugs or other things that will do me more harm than good.

+ There are lots of ways to cope with stress, but doing drugs, smoking, and getting drunk are not options. They can provide short-term relief, but they cause more problems than they solve.

Listen to your teen's problems. Get him talking. Say such things as:

+ I know you're having problems at school. Should we look for a new school for you?

+ Is anyone bullying or harassing you at school? Maybe there is something we can do to stop it.

♦ Maybe you should think about dropping that subject since it is stressing you out so much, and it's not required.

Talk to your teen about methods of stress relief. Say such things as:

♦ You're really stressed. It might be a good time to start a hobby to take your mind off things.

♦ Let's go for a run this Saturday. You might like it. I know it helps me cope with things.

♦ Have you ever thought about starting to dance again? You used to love it so much.

Help your teen put his stress into perspective and think of the big picture. Say such things as:

♦ Do you think this will seem very important six months from now?

♦ Write down your ten biggest problems. Let's see where this fits.

Suggest actions your teen might take to get rid of the causes of stress. Say such things as:

♦ Let's look at the cause and see what you can do to get rid of it.

♦ This is really stressing you. What action can we take to change the situation?

♦ The problem won't go away unless you do something. What can you do?

Talk about the possibility of professional help. Say such things as:

♦ I don't think you and I can handle this ourselves. I know someone who counsels teens on their problems, and I think we should talk to her.

WORDS AND PHRASES TO USE

♦ action	♦ cope	♦ explain	♦ sports
♦ adjust	♦ counseling	♦ hobbies	♦ sympathize
♦ advice	♦ empathize	♦ listen	♦ talk
♦ concern	♦ exercise	♦ solve	♦ understand

What Not to Say and Do

Don't ignore your teen's stress. Don't be unsympathetic. Don't say such things as:

- You're making something out of nothing.
- It's all in your imagination.
- I don't have time for you. Just deal with it. I have my own problems.

Don't encourage destructive solutions to stress problems. Don't say such things as:

- Feeling stressed? Have a drink.
- When I'm stressed, I just pop a few of these pills. They do wonders.
- If I don't smoke, I feel stressed.

Don't ignore the causes of your teen's stress or give him bad advice. Don't say such things as:

- If some kid is bullying you, take him out. That's what I'd do.
- You can't change schools no matter how bad it is.
- You have to face your problems. You can't run away from them.

Don't belittle your teen's stress. Don't say such things as:

- You think you're stressed? You don't know what stress is.
- Stress is good for you.
- This is good practice for life. Stress shows you what kind of person you are.

WORDS AND PHRASES TO AVOID

♦ avoid	♦ it's good for you	♦ run away
♦ be a man/woman	♦ it's your problem	♦ your imagination
♦ coward	♦ loser	♦ you're making a big deal out of nothing
♦ I don't care	♦ nonsense	

82 Studying

Smartness runs in my family. When I went to school, I was so smart my teacher was in my class for five years.

—GEORGE BURNS

Sheila was fourteen. Each day she would come home from high school and get on the phone to her friends. She'd stay on the phone until dinner. After dinner she'd be on the phone again until almost bedtime. Finally her parents got fed up with all of this and told her that if she spent as much time studying as she did on the phone, she'd be an "A" student, which she was not. Sheila answered that she was talking about school with her friends and that this was like studying.

"Nonsense," her mom said. "You spend all your time talking about your other friends. And that's going to change starting today. Here are the new rules." Sheila's mom proceeded to tell her how she could earn phone privileges by doing her homework and studying.

The rules said that Sheila had to be in her room studying, with the door open, at least two hours each day before she'd be allowed to use the phone. That would include one hour before dinner and one hour after. She'd have to do this until the next report card. If her grades didn't show improvement, the schedule would change to one hour before dinner and two hours after dinner. Phone time would be limited to half an hour before dinner and one hour after dinner, both after study time.

She said that if Sheila got into the habit of studying every night, some of the things she learned would undoubtedly stick. Her usual system of cramming for an exam the night before wasn't smart because she remembered almost nothing a few days later. That was the main reason her mom decided on this new approach. She added that she was ready to give Sheila as much help as she wanted for homework and studying. She thought that studying together would be fun. It would take her back to her own high school days, which she remembered fondly. And just maybe she would learn some of those things from high school better the second time around.

Things to Consider

Most teens have poor study skills. Part of the problem is that there are so many more interesting things than school going on in their lives. Friends, clothes, sports, and relationships are far more exciting things to think and talk about than quadratic equations, the conjugation of French verbs, or the economy of Venezuela.

Good study habits require three things: discipline, structure, and quiet surroundings. In order to do the best job in assisting your teens, you need to know their personality, their natural academic ability, and the extent of their commitment to schoolwork.

Personality: Are your teens the studious type? Are they serious? Do they live up to their promises and commitments? Do they make plans? Are they self-motivated?

Ability: Do your teens do well in school? What do their teachers say about their work? Do you think they have high ability but it's not reflected in their schoolwork?

Commitment: Do your teens like school? Do their teachers like them? Are they involved in school activities such as sports and clubs? Are they planning to go on to higher education after high school? Do they already know what they want to be in life? Do they have fairly specific career goals?

Once you have worked through these, you can design a plan for your teens' studying. Remember the three elements needed for good studying are discipline, structure, and quiet surroundings.

Discipline: There should be regular and consistent study every day with no distractions. They should be neither tired nor hungry. Help them develop a study discipline until they have their own. Know whether or not your teens need specific rewards and incentives.

Structure: Studying must be a planned regular activity. Consider your teens' study time sacred; they should not be interrupted or called upon to do chores around the house. Help your teens set up schedules for study based on their high school timetable and the exam schedules. Set up a general schedule for the semester plus specific weekly schedules. Build in days that are study free. Include your participation in their study routine as part of the schedule.

Quiet surroundings: Ideally, your teens have a space in the house or apartment where they won't be interrupted or disturbed by the phone, computer, TV, loud music, or others' conversations. This is especially important in the beginning when your teens are looking for distractions in order to avoid studying. As they develop self-discipline and as studying becomes a habit, they will be less easily distracted.

Unless your teens are geniuses, good study habits, developed early, will help them succeed in school. Success in school will give them options in life that poor school performance won't.

Three Things You Must Do

1. *Give* your teen's study habits high priority.

2. *Know* his personality, ability, and commitment to school.

3. *Develop* a study routine based on discipline, structure, and quiet.

What to Say and Do

You need to know your teen's study habits. Say such things as:

- ♦ May I ask what you've been studying?
- ♦ How do you study each day?
- ♦ What's your study plan for this week?

Ask yourself some questions about your teen, such as:

- ♦ Does my teen like to study?
- ♦ If I tell my teen to study, does he do it without argument?
- ♦ Does my teen plan things ahead or do things at the last minute?

Does your teen need help with schoolwork? Is he good at his studies? Say such things as:

- ♦ What kinds of grades are you getting in _____?
- ♦ Do you have a portfolio of your work that I can look at?

Help your teen set up a good study plan. Build the plan around discipline, structure, and quiet surroundings. Say such things as:

- Let's sit down and plan your studying.
- How many hours each day do you think you need to study?
- When is the best time for you to study?
- Let's see your timetable. You should probably plan to study each subject according to that.
- Do you have some subjects that need more studying than others?
- Where would be a good place for you to study? Somewhere quiet and away from the action.

If your teen needs added incentives to study, talk about what they might be. Say such things as:

- I know that studying isn't much fun for you. What would make it worthwhile?
- Since doing well in school is your way of contributing to the family, I'll pay you for studying.
- If you study two hours every day, I'll increase your allowance by $__ per week.

WORDS AND PHRASES TO USE

ability	discipline	options	rewards
achievement	every day	plan	self-discipline
commitment	learning	priorities	skills
consistency	motivation	quiet	structure

What Not to Say and Do

Show your teen that you value school. Don't say such things as:

- School is not important. I was never a good student.
- School is a waste of time. What matters is your common sense and street smarts.

Don't consider studying unimportant. Don't say such things as:

- I never studied in high school.
- You don't have to study in high school if you have half a brain.

Don't assume your teen will automatically have good study habits. Don't say such things as:

- I think you're much brighter than your schoolwork would indicate. Why aren't you doing better in school?
- I'm sure you know how to study.

Don't give studying a low priority. Don't say such things as:

- You can study later.
- I need you to help me. That's more important than studying.
- You can study anytime, anyplace. I need you now.

Don't expect your teen to teach himself good study habits. Don't say such things as:

- You work out your own study schedule.
- You decide how much you have to study.
- Just cram the night before. That's what I always did, and it worked for me.

WORDS AND PHRASES TO AVOID

- avoid
- do it yourself
- do whatever you want
- I can't help you
- if you fail, that's your problem
- only dummies have to study
- school is really a waste of time

83 Success

Success didn't spoil me; I've always been insufferable.

—FRAN LEBOWITZ

Anita's mom and dad would do everything in their power to help her succeed in high school. She was thirteen and had just reached puberty. Her parents were afraid her academic performance would suffer now that school had to compete with so many other conflicting emotions, urges, and interests. They wanted Anita to succeed as much as her brother, Max, was succeeding. He was two years older and doing very well.

They talked about what they had done with Max and whether or not the same techniques would work equally well with their daughter. They decided that the same principles of success should be good for both children even though some books they consulted said that girls needed praise for effort and boys for abilities. They rejected this argument, knowing that they wanted both their kids to think of success as a process, not just a product. Success, they believed, is a feeling of self-satisfaction that comes from doing your best in whatever you're doing, and that's what they would praise their children for.

They realized that this ran counter to the usual notion of success. For example, most parents and kids thought that high grades meant success in school. In life the common measure of success seemed to be money and power. They could not accept this notion of success for themselves or their children, so they had taught Max that success meant working hard and doing your best at whatever you were doing. If that resulted in high marks, money, or power, that was fine. If it didn't, you were still a success because you gave it your best. Now they were going to teach Anita the same thing.

In sum, they wanted to teach their children that real happiness was in the doing rather than in the having. Success was recognizing and valuing your own efforts. Being realists, they didn't teach their kids to scoff at material success. That was important, too, but they knew that real success and happiness weren't in what you had but in what you did to get it.

Things to Consider

You have great influence over your children's notion of what counts as success. First, your teens know what impresses you about their accomplishments. You've praised or not praised them for what they've done ever since they were born.

Second, your teens know what you say about the things others have done. They hear your favorable or unfavorable comments on the killing someone has made in the stock market, the success someone has made of her business, or the cost of a movie star's lavish new home.

Third, you have shown your teens what you think about your own accomplishments. Your teens know what you think are your own successes and failures.

Here are ways to help your teens become people who are self-motivated, self-assured, self-reliant, willing to try new things, realistic about their own strengths and weaknesses, and who have a strong ethical framework and value hard work and best effort for its own sake.

1. Set a good example. Show your teens that you value your own best efforts.
2. Value education for its own sake as much as for what material advantages it gives.
3. Encourage critical thinking, the value of asking questions and not taking the truth for granted.
4. Be involved with your teens. Listen to what is happening in their lives.
5. Praise their hard work and effort more than the outcome. Tie your praise to specific actions, not just general remarks about how great they are.
6. Encourage them to try new things and not be afraid of failing. Show them that failing is a useful and important part of living.
7. Recognize your teens' own personality and way of doing things. Don't think that they have to do it your way.
8. Help them develop a strong ethical framework for themselves. Discuss everyday issues and problems, and the right and wrong actions. Discuss religious principles and other ethical systems.

Doing these things will help your teens find value in themselves and their relationship to others. That's the real meaning of success.

Three Things You Must Do

1. *Know* what you think is success.

2. *Realize* that success must be your own judgment about yourself.

3. *Teach* your teen that success is not what you have but how you get it.

What to Say and Do

Make your idea of success one that will do the greatest good for your teen. Say such things as:

- ♦ You impress me when you work at something passionately.

- ♦ I think you are most successful when you do something for its own sake, not for what it will get you.

- ♦ I've watched you do things, and I think you are happiest when you're totally involved in what you're doing and you are doing your best at it.

Think about the values you communicate when you label other people as successful. Say such things as:

- ♦ I think the best kind of success is the kind you feel inside you, whether others think you've succeeded or not. What do you think?

- ♦ I used to think that money was the best indicator of success in life. Now I know that it isn't. Do you want to know why I think that?

- ♦ The general view of success is having money and power. Do you think that's a good thing?

Talk about what you think are your own successes and failures. It would be helpful to know your teen's point of view on that, too. Say such things as:

- ♦ I know I see material possessions as a measure of success, but maybe I'm wrong. What do you think?

- ♦ Sometimes I think I will consider this book a success if it sells one hundred thousand copies. But the fact is, just writing it has been a great challenge. I feel that I've already succeeded just by researching and writing it.

- ♦ What do think has been your greatest success in life so far?

Help your teen like and respect herself and try to do her best at everything she attempts. Say such things as:

- Don't look to others for approval.
- Trust your own judgment.
- Never be ashamed to seek help from others who know more than you do.

You can help your teen succeed. Say such things as:

- Don't be afraid to ask questions or admit that you don't know the answer.
- The only stupid question is the one you've been afraid to ask.
- Don't be afraid of failing. Failure can teach you a lot about yourself and what you're trying to do.
- You need to succeed in your own mind first.

WORDS AND PHRASES TO USE

always do your best	confidence	involved	passion
be your own judge	great	know what's important	praise
commitment	hard work/effort	motivated	self-critical

What Not to Say and Do

Don't give your teen the idea that success depends on others' opinions. Don't say such things as:

- What does your teacher think?
- Will you get the highest grade for that?
- What you think is important, but it's what others think that really counts.

Don't teach your teen that the only kind of success is material success. Don't say such things as:

- There's nothing more important than money and power.
- Real success is having a six- or seven-figure income.
- The person with the most toys at the end wins.

Don't set a bad example for your teen. Don't say such things as:

- My book is a failure compared to hers. She sold so many more copies.
- I won't consider myself a success until I can buy whatever I want.
- My idea of success is to drive a Ferrari or a Bentley; to own homes in Palm Beach, New York, and London; and to have my own string of polo ponies.

Don't make your teen feel that her success depends on your opinion of her. Don't say such things as:

- I want you to be the best so I can be proud of you.
- I want you to make me proud by being the first in your class.
- If you're successful in high school, then you can go to the best college.

Don't teach your teen that what matters is what you have, not how you get it. Don't say such things as:

- Nobody really cares how you succeed as long as you do succeed.
- The best measure of success is what you have at the end.
- Real success is something you show off to others.

WORDS AND PHRASES TO AVOID

competition	power	toys	what do others think
fight for what you want	prize	what you have is more important than how you got it	winner
money	reward		
	show off		

84 Suicide

> *Anyone who has listened to certain kinds of music or read certain kinds of poetry or heard certain kinds of performances on the concertina will admit that even suicide has its brighter aspects.*
>
> —STEPHEN LEACOCK

Cortez was a talented and gifted child. He seemed to live in a world different from his parents, siblings, and friends. In elementary school he excelled in most of his academic subjects but was easily humiliated and couldn't take correction. Some of his teachers were able to connect with him and nurtured him. They recognized his academic strengths and helped him with his personal and social weaknesses. His range of awareness, oversensitivity, perfectionism, and idealism made him a favorite target for bullying and teasing.

Cortez knew things intuitively. He was analytical. One could say he really didn't have to "learn" things because they were just "there." But because of this he had little patience with things that he could not intuitively know. He never developed learning skills, so he didn't know how to work hard at learning things step by step as most of us must do. He rejected the idea that there might be areas in which he had to work at learning in the normal way. He expected to be outstanding in everything. He found it difficult to ask anyone for help.

As a result, his peers ridiculed him when he wasn't successful. When he did ask for help, his pleas were dismissed because he was "smart enough to do things on his own." He didn't take drugs or drink alcohol, never missed school, and wasn't a discipline problem. But there were social and emotional issues throughout his early and teen years that Cortez wasn't able to deal with. None of the experts picked up on them, and they eventually led to disaster.

When he was twenty-one, Cortez killed himself with an overdose of sleeping pills. All those traits that made him gifted served to increase his problem of coping with reality.

Looking back on it, the warning signs were there for people to see, but only if they were looking for them.

Things to Consider

Suicide is a leading cause of death among teenagers, particularly teenage boys, who appear to be much more successful at taking their own life than girls. Homosexual boys and girls are two to three times more likely to attempt suicide than heterosexuals.

Know the suicidal danger signs: prolonged feelings of sadness, apathy, inertia, extreme mood swings, lethargy, loss of appetite, loss of interest in personal appearance or hygiene, threats of suicide, preoccupation with death, unexplained decline in school performance, withdrawal from family and friends, giving away possessions, and sudden high-risk behavior.

Only professionals can speak authoritatively on the causes of suicide, but you need to be sensitive to some of the situations that can put a vulnerable or "at risk" teen even more at risk. These situations include the loss of a friend, pet, or family member through death or breakup; family disruption through loss of job, moving, or divorce; genetic predisposition to clinical depression, alcoholism, or schizophrenia; personal failure in school, sports, or relationships; membership in a "doomsday" religious cult; and gifted intellectual ability without commensurate social skills. Don't expect your teen to easily adjust and cope with these situations.

You have a different kind of suicide problem if a family member or your teen's friend or acquaintance has killed himself. Teens may feel guilt because of someone's suicide. They might feel some responsibility for the death if they had a relationship with the person. This can happen especially if there was a recent quarrel or other trouble in the relationship. Some teens have left notes saying they have been driven to suicide because of constant teasing by their peers. If your teen was one of the teasers, counseling is probably in order.

Suicide is an ever-present possibility for teens. Whether your teens or their friends give any indication of such action in either talk or behavior, take it seriously and seek professional advice. Be on guard. In spite of your best efforts, the worst can happen. The better you know your teens, the better you know the chance of suicide being a way out for them.

Three Things You Must Do

1. *Know* that suicide among teens is not unusual.

2. *Recognize* the danger signals.

3. *Seek* help if you suspect any problem.

What to Say and Do

Know your teen well enough to recognize any changes in behavior. Say such things as:

- ✦ Are you having trouble sleeping? You look tired.

- ✦ You haven't been your usual energetic self recently. Is anything bothering you?

- ✦ Has anything bad happened to you? You seem different.

Know if anything bad has happened in his life recently. Say such things as:

- ✦ I know you just broke up with your girlfriend. Do you want to talk about it?

- ✦ Are the kids still teasing you at school?

- ✦ You mentioned something about this new friend and his religious beliefs. What do you know about him and his group? What do they believe?

If you know that members of your family have a genetic predisposition to suicide, you should talk to your teen about it. It's better that he knows to look out for the danger signs than for him to find out when it's too late. (You should seek medical advice if there is a history of mental illness in your family. Only a doctor can give you reliable information on the danger to your teen.)

Be sensitive to cries for help. Say such things as:

- ✦ You mentioned death as a solution for your problems. What did you mean?

- ✦ I know you joke about suicide, but I don't think it's a very funny subject. Would you tell me if you really think about suicide very much?

- ✦ I'd like you to go to the doctor with me. Your talk about death has scared me. If it's really nothing, then you'll just have spent some time to satisfy your old mom/dad.

If your teen has to cope with the suicide of a family member or a friend, say such things as:

- I think _____'s death has really affected you. Why don't you talk to the counselor about it?
- Tell me how you feel about _____'s death.
- I know _____'s death was a shock, but when these terrible things happen, the best thing we can do is talk about it, cry, grieve, and try to move on.

WORDS AND PHRASES TO USE

- death
- feelings
- how do you feel about yourself

- it's not a good solution
- please be honest with me
- suicide

- talk to me
- what are you thinking and feeling
- what's bothering you

What Not to Say and Do

Don't think it can't happen to your teen. Don't ignore the warning signs. Don't say such things as:

- Don't say silly things like that.
- If you keep talking that way, I'm just going to ignore you.
- You're a teenager. Most teenagers feel that way.
- I know you talk about committing suicide, but that will pass and you'll be fine.

If your teen is homosexual, be alert to possible problems with identity, relationships, guilt, and feelings of worthlessness. Don't say such things as:

- AIDS is God's revenge on homosexuals.
- Homos don't deserve to live.
- I can't believe you are homosexual. You'd better get over it.

Don't refuse to talk about suicide. Don't say such things as:

- I don't want to talk about it.

- If we talk about suicide, it may give you ideas.
- It's not a nice thing to talk about. Let's forget it, okay?

Don't be blind to your teen's reaction to stressful situations. Don't ignore his feelings and the need to express them. Don't say such things as:

- You overdramatize everything. Lighten up.
- You'd think you were the first person ever to break up with a boyfriend.
- I don't want to hear your moans and groans. Just cope with it.

Never suggest that your teen was in any way responsible for someone's suicide. Don't say such things as:

- It's your fault.
- You drove him to it.
- You're the guilty party. His blood is on your hands.

WORDS AND PHRASES TO AVOID

- absurd	- grow up	- it's just one of your moods
- crazy	- guilt	- no one can help you
- don't talk to me about suicide	- I'm tired of your moaning and groaning	- silly
		- stupid

85 Tattoos and Body Piercing

Fashions are induced epidemics.

—G. B. Shaw

The thought of your child coming home with a tattoo or with her ears, nose, eyebrows, lips, tongue, or navel pierced and sporting a ring or a stud is enough to strike fear into the heart of even the most liberal parents. Such was the feeling that Brenda's parents had as they looked at their fourteen-year-old daughter who was anxious to show her mom and dad the small tattoo of a rose on her left shoulder and the stud peeking from a hole in the side of her nose.

It wasn't that tattoos and piercing were shocking in themselves to Brenda's parents. There were enough teens and young adults around wearing these fashions that their shock value had largely disappeared. The problem was that it was their daughter who was now tattooed and pierced, who had a ring in each ear, a stud in her nose, and a brightly colored flower needled into her skin. What would be next, they wondered. A ring through her navel and a stud through her tongue? Was this the same girl who last year was studying ballet and jazz at the same studio where she began at age five?

Brenda had come to them when she first decided this was going to be her way of saying good-bye to childhood. The thought of joining the growing number of teens with rings, studs, and tattoos gave her an exhilarating feeling of independence and self-assertion. And she thought she'd look really cool.

"Cool" was one way to describe her parents' initial reaction to the idea. Brenda had had her ears pierced when she was very young and had worn studs since then. But that was a normal, acceptable fashion for women and girls. Now boys and men also wore earrings and fell within the bounds of respectability. Tattoos and rings and studs in other parts of the body went beyond those bounds for Brenda's mom and dad. They were ugly

and repulsive, and could be dangerous to Brenda's health. Yet, when it came to the crunch, they gave Brenda their consent. Now she had done the deed, and they wondered whether they had done the right thing.

Things to Consider

You are legally responsible for your children until they are eighteen. You can say no to body piercing and tattooing. Do you normally discuss fashion and teenage fads with your teens? Do your teens respect your opinion? Do they rarely go against your wishes? Are your teens rebellious and determined to control their own lives?

Tattoos and body piercing are important because they have social and health implications. Make sure that you and your teens understand what is involved. These are not things to be undertaken lightly or in ignorance of the possible short- and long-term consequences and side effects. These things permanently alter your teen's body and require regular care.

Here are some things to discuss with your teen before making a decision.

Short-term considerations: Healing may affect sleeping position, eating, and speaking; no swimming; no direct exposure to the sun for two to four weeks during the healing process; infection; pain; risk of HIV and hepatitis.

Long-term considerations: Changing fashions, tastes, and life circumstances; social rejection; difficulties finding a job; scarring for life; scarred genitalia; fading tattoos; old tattoos on old, flabby skin; painful, expensive removal procedures; wrong name in your tattoo for your current relationship.

Some options: A removable tattoo that can last up to four weeks; clip-on or magnetic rings for the lip, nose, or navel; glue on studs for the nose.

After discussing these issues and options, you and your teens can decide what is best for them. You may choose to say no whatever your teens' desires may be. That's the toughest way to go. Make your views clear. Explain your position and why you hold it.

If you are more flexible and willing to let your teens make their own decisions, be sure to talk through all the issues. If your teen decides to go ahead, check out the place where it will be done and make sure that it is licensed (where required), hygienic, and uses only the best materials.

Three Things You Must Do

1. *Understand* tattoos and piercing as part of a teen's search for identity.

2. *Make* your own position clear.

3. *Discuss* the alternatives.

What to Say and Do

Talk about her feelings and yours about tattooing and piercing. Say such things as:

> ● Look at the rings and studs on that girl. Do you like that?

> ● I must admit I don't find all those things attractive. I've always disliked tattoos.

> ● Are you tempted to get something pierced or tattooed?

Find out how much your teen knows about the risks and procedures. Say such things as:

> ● How much do you know about getting tattooed? Do you know that it hurts?

> ● If you were getting a tattoo, where would you get it done?

> ● Do you know that getting your ears pierced is relatively painless compared to getting other parts pierced such as the lips and tongue?

Talk about the short-term considerations. Say such things as:

> ● Do you ever think about how getting a tattoo or piercing will affect your life?

> ● What do your tattooed and pierced friends tell you about the experience during and after?

> ● Let's look at everything you need to think about before you decide to go ahead with this.

> ● You know there is a chance your body may reject this thing?

Talk about the long-term considerations. Say such things as:

> ● Once you get pierced, you're pierced forever. You'll always be scarred even if you remove the ring or stud.

- Do you think you'll always want to have or wear these things when you get older?
- It's really painful and expensive to remove a tattoo.
- Can you imagine what your tattoo will look like when you're sixty, seventy, or eighty?

Talk about options that your teen can try. Say such things as:

- Instead of getting a real tattoo, why don't you try a temporary one? They have some really good ones that can last a month or more.
- Do you know about clip-on and magnetic rings?

Be sure to make your own views clear. Say such things as:

- I'm against your doing any tattooing or piercing that will change your body permanently. I think you ought to know that.
- If you want a tattoo or piercing, I'm not going to stand in your way, but I want you to know I don't like the idea.
- I'll be happy to help you research a good place to have it done, and we can look at all the precautions you need to take afterward. But you'll have to pay for it yourself.
- If you're going to have it done, make sure it's done right. I'd like to check out the place.

WORDS AND PHRASES TO USE

➧ check it out	➧ fad	➧ I don't like them	➧ scars
➧ do you like them	➧ fashion	➧ long-term considerations	➧ short-term considerations
➧ expensive	➧ health risks	➧ permanent	➧ temporary options

What Not to Say and Do

This is not an issue on which to jeopardize your relationship. Don't say such things as:

- You've disobeyed me. You're going to be seriously punished.

- If you do this, you're no longer my child.
- I forbid you to get a tattoo or to have your body pierced. If you disobey me, don't bother to come home.

Tattoos and piercing are a fashion statement. Don't say such things as:

- You're just the kind of stupid kid who does this.
- Why are you so antisocial?
- What do you think you're rebelling against?

Don't fail to discuss the pros and cons with your teen. Don't say such things as:

- I don't care what you do.
- If you want a tattoo or a piercing, you'll do it without any help from me. I want no part of it.
- Go ahead and do it if you want. It's no big deal. If you think about it too much, you may chicken out.
- I don't think it matters who does it.

If your teen decides to do it, don't ignore the precautions and care they must take. Don't say such things as:

- You're on your own.
- I'm not going to tell you what to do.
- You'll have to take care of yourself. I'm not going to help.

WORDS AND PHRASES TO AVOID

• awful	• I'm going to lock you up	• you must do as I say
• disobey	• I'm in control	• you're out of here
• I forbid	• it's not your choice	

86 Trust

Jesse was troubled. His girlfriend, Terri, was always laughing, teasing, touching other guys at school, and letting them put their arms around her. She was just too friendly, he thought. After all, they had been going out together for almost a year. It made him look like a fool, he said. He wondered what she did when he wasn't around to see. Did she kiss any of these guys, he asked.

Terri just laughed when he said this. "You're just jealous," she said.

Of course he was jealous, he answered. "You're my girl, and I don't want these guys to think you're not."

"You know how I feel about you," Terri said. "You're my main man. We do great things together. I don't want that to change. And don't worry about what I do when you're not around. I'm cool, man. I don't do anything wrong."

"How do I know that?" Jesse asked. "When I see you with these guys, I get really hot inside."

"Well, you'd better cool it," Terri said. "I don't worry about what you do with all the girls around. I've seen you laughing with them. You even gave Victoria a big hug the other day. I saw that, but I didn't say anything. It doesn't bother me. You know why?"

"No, why?"

"Because I trust you! I know you love me, and I trust you to do the right thing. If you love someone, you don't betray that trust. You'd better understand that. If you don't trust me, then nothing I do is going to look right to you."

"But I do trust you. I just don't trust those guys."

"If you trust me, then believe that they're not going to do anything that I don't want them to do. That's what trust is. You've got to trust that I won't do anything to hurt our relationship. If you can't do that, then we have a serious problem."

Things to Consider

There are many different sides to the issue of trust. It's your trust in them, their trust in you, their trust of others, such as family, friends, boyfriends, girlfriends, teachers, police, and other adults.

Their trust in you began when they were born. They depended on you to provide them with the necessities of life and more. They showed their trust in you when they took that first leap into your arms and you were there to catch them.

Now that your children are teens, you must continue to show that they can trust you. A typical comment in any parent-teen argument is "What's wrong? Don't you trust me?" This usually comes when you've refused your teen permission to do something such as borrow the car, go on an overnight stay with friends, go to a concert, stay out late, go to a party, or go to a friend's house when the parents aren't home. The list could go on.

You're no longer dealing with the blind trust of children. Your teens' need to separate themselves from you raises difficult questions of what to say and what to do. How far are you willing to trust them? How far are they willing to trust you? Do they trust your honesty, your understanding, your judgment, your reasoning, your rules, your ambitions, your commitment?

There's a nice expression to describe the constant work you and your teens need to do to keep trust alive in your relationship. It says, "Once again, for the first time." You have the chance to build or diminish each other's trust each time you say or do something. All your values and rules are put to the test in sustaining the relationship.

You and your teens have the chance to show you're worthy of trust by believing that whatever the other says or does, it is with the best of intentions. That doesn't mean you can't talk about things and disagree. It doesn't mean you can't argue or say no. It simply means that you don't mistrust each other's basic goodness or fundamental values.

Without basic trust between you and your teens, all your rules and restrictions will never be enough to make you feel secure in your relationship. Your teens need your trust now more than ever. It is to be hoped that they have earned it over the years, as you have earned theirs.

Three Things You Must Do

1. *Earn* your child's trust from day one.

2. *Trust* them as you would have them trust you.

3. *Understand* that trust is the best foundation for your relationship.

What to Say and Do

Trust is an important issue to discuss with your teen. Say such things as:

- ❧ Whom do you trust? Whom don't you trust?
- ❧ What makes you trust or distrust someone?
- ❧ Do you talk to someone you trust differently from someone you don't trust?

Examine the trust you had in your relationship with him as a child. Say such things as:

- ❧ Remember when you jumped into my arms in the pool? You couldn't swim, but you trusted me to be there for you.
- ❧ Kids trust their parents unless they betray that trust.
- ❧ I've tried to show you over the years that you can trust me. Do you?

Discuss strains in your relationship with them. Say such things as:

- ❧ We can disagree with each other while basically trusting each other. That means we don't doubt our good intentions.
- ❧ Even when we argue, we still don't doubt each other's basic motives.

Talk about how you can refuse him permission and still trust him. Say such things as:

- ❧ I can trust you and yet think that you're mistaken.
- ❧ Even though I trust you, I may not trust the situation you're going to be in.
- ❧ There are situations over which you have no control. I may not trust those situations even though I trust you to do your best in them.

Talk about the areas in which you might not trust your teen. Say such things as:

- I have a basic trust in your goodness as a person.
- I don't always trust your judgment because you don't yet have the experience or maturity to consider all the angles to a situation.
- I can disagree with you, argue, or say no, and still have that basic trust in you.

Talk about trust as the bedrock of any good relationship. Say such things as:

- The bottom line is that you and I have to trust each other. If we don't, then our relationship can't be good.
- If we don't trust each other, then there aren't enough rules, laws, or regulations to make things work. It's trust that makes relationships possible.

WORDS AND PHRASES TO USE

• belief	• credibility	• hope	• responsibility
• certain	• credit	• positiveness	• security
• confidence	• dependability	• relationship	• sureness
• count on	• duty	• reliance	• unquestioning

What Not to Say and Do

Don't encourage distrust of others. Don't say such things as:

- One thing I've learned in life is never to trust anybody but yourself.
- Most people I've ever trusted have betrayed that trust.
- Don't trust anyone, not even me.

Don't betray your child's trust in you. Don't say such things as:

- I had to tell your teacher. It was my duty.
- I know you trusted me, but I couldn't keep it a secret.
- You should never have trusted me.

Don't tell your child that you have no basic trust in him. Don't say such things as:

- Why should I trust you? You're just a child.

> ✸ I don't trust any teenagers, including you.
> ✸ You're not worthy of my trust.

Don't constantly say you mistrust your teen's maturity, judgment, intentions, reasoning, desires, loyalty, or commitment. Don't say such things as:

> ✸ I don't trust anyone who isn't out there earning his own living.
> ✸ You're just an immature teenager. How can I trust you?
> ✸ I wouldn't trust you to make any reasonable decisions about important things. You don't have the judgment or experience.

Don't make your teen feel insecure in his relationship with you or others. Don't say such things as:

> ✸ You must do exactly as I say, or I'll never trust you.
> ✸ Don't trust a teacher or a cop.
> ✸ Don't trust the government.

WORDS AND PHRASES TO AVOID

✸ betray	✸ dishonest	✸ insincere	✸ treacherous
✸ cheat	✸ distrust	✸ liar	✸ unethical
✸ corrupt	✸ doubting	✸ suspect	✸ unprincipled
✸ dangerous	✸ immoral	✸ traitor	✸ unreliable

87 Values

"Julian," his dad said one day. "I think you and I need to talk."

"About what, Dad?" asked Julian, a high school senior.

"About values," his dad answered. "You know that note your English teacher sent us the other day about catching you cheating on that poetry quiz?"

"I told you, Dad, that I was in a panic that morning because I did the wrong assignment, and we were going to get a quiz on poems I hadn't even read, worth 10 percent of our term grade. I need at least an 'A-minus' in the class to keep my English grades up for my college application."

"Do you think that justifies cheating on a quiz?"

"Yes. I mean no. Cheating is wrong. But I had no choice. I would have failed the quiz."

"But you failed it anyway, and now you have a note about cheating on your record."

"It was just bad luck that I got caught."

"You think it would have been all right if you hadn't been caught?"

"Well, yes."

"That's why we have to talk. I need to see where we went wrong in teaching you values. I thought we taught you that honesty was an important value."

"You did. I know that what I did was wrong, but I couldn't help myself. I just had to get a good grade on that quiz. Don't you understand?"

"I think I understand. I think that you don't really value honesty the way you should. I wonder what other values you give lip service to. It seems that when they get in the way of your plans or ambitions, you conveniently forget about them and do whatever

you have to to get what you want. I think your values are wrong. Your real value system revolves around you. Your values say, 'Me first.' Those aren't the values we wanted you to have. We have to talk."

Things to Consider

Values give your life meaning and direction. They tell you what's worth doing and what isn't, and why. They are the foundation on which you build your world. You want to give your teens this foundation so that they can use it for their world as well.

Preaching values won't do the job for your teens. You can say you believe in loving all of humankind and in truth, honesty, tolerance, trust, fidelity, hard work, God, and country, but what you say isn't nearly as important as who you are. Teens learn best from your example. They will be looking for consistency in what you preach and the way you live your life.

Be a role model. In fact, you are a role model whether you want to be or not. Your teens have been watching you for all of their young lives. They know you pretty well from your interaction with them and from what they have seen you say and do in your relationships with others.

Teens are searching for their identity. Accept your teens' search and help them along. Don't take it as a permanent rejection of you and your values. Use it as an opportunity for conversations about those values grounded in everyday life and experience. Talk about things in the news, about movies, books, fashions, war, racism, crime, religion, and about choices and problems they face in their lives. These are all areas of life in which values get clarified.

Talk about personal responsibility. Help your teens understand that they are responsible for whatever they say and do. Ultimately, they make the choice. And that choice reflects their values in the truest sense of the term.

Remember also that your teens' values are best seen in their interactions outside the home. You need to pay attention to how they behave at home, but that may not tell you how they interact with others. The real test of their values is in their behavior in the community, at school, at work, at play, and with friends, strangers, kids, and adults.

Your teens' values are in the process of being created. Don't despair if they're not what you had hoped for at this stage. They're still growing and changing.

Three Things You Must Do

1. *Teach* your teen good core values.

2. *Expect* rejection and rebellion against these values.

3. *Give* your teen increasing responsibility for his own choices.

What to Say and Do

Use real events as a way of talking to your teen about the meaning and direction of his life. Say such things as:

- ➤ What do you think about that case of cheating in your school? Would you ever cheat?

- ➤ Do kids in your school tolerate kids who are different? How do you feel about intolerance?

- ➤ Do you think the Ten Commandments should be on the wall of your classrooms at school?

Talk about the gap between your values and your behavior. Say such things as:

- ➤ I know that sometimes I say one thing and then do another. I know that's hypocritical of me. I guess that's part of being an ordinary human being.

- ➤ Nobody's perfect. What's important is to know the right thing to do and try to do it.

- ➤ Have you ever wanted to do one thing but ended up doing another even when you knew it was wrong? That sometimes happens to me, too, but I try not to let it.

Make explicit the kinds of values you've tried to live by. Say such things as:

- ➤ Even though I lie sometimes, honesty is pretty high on my list of values. Is it on yours?

- ➤ I value tolerance. I don't understand hatred and racism, and my values will never accept them. Why do you think some people hate others because of their color or religion?

- ➤ I think that I value love, gratitude, and a good sense of humor as high as almost anything else. What about you?

Talk about the values your teen seems to be rejecting. Say such things as (and then *listen*):

- You reject going to our church. Why?
- Why do you think how you look isn't important? (Of course your teen does care.)
- Do you think all the values of business and growth are bad? Why?

Be interested in his search for values. Talk about his reaction to events and people in his life. Ask him about movies, music, fashion, and all those things that he likes and dislikes. Say such things as:

- What do you think about movie violence?
- Does the bad language in films and on TV bother you?
- What would you say about the values in films you've seen such as _____?

WORDS AND PHRASES TO USE

choices	honesty	rejection	tolerance
example	humility	responsibility	truth
goodness	love	search	understanding
gratitude	rebellion	sense of humor	virtue

What Not to Say and Do

Don't think that preaching your values will teach your teen good values. Don't say such things as:

- I've taught you the difference between good and bad, so you know what to do.
- Just follow the Ten Commandments.
- I've always told you the right thing to do.

Don't be hypocritical. Don't consistently preach one value but do the opposite. Don't say such things as:

+ Do what I say, not what I do.
+ I always do the right thing even though you may think I don't.
+ I have the right to change my values.

Don't be a bad role model. Don't say and do such things as:
+ I've always done what I said I would do.
+ Don't bad-mouth me. I've always done my best for you.
+ I may not always do the right thing, but at least I try, which is more than I can say for you.

Don't punish your teen for rejecting your values. Don't say such things as:
+ You do what I say or else.
+ If you don't want to accept my values, then you're not my child.
+ You live by our rules, or you leave.

Don't ask your teen questions and then not listen to their answers. Don't say such things as:
+ That's enough. Now let me tell you something about your values.
+ I won't listen to any more of this nonsense. You listen to me.
+ You talk such juvenile rubbish. You just don't know. I'll tell you what you should think.

Don't give your teen the idea that he is not responsible for his own choices. Don't say such things as:
+ It wasn't your fault. They made you do it.
+ You're not responsible for your actions.
+ Don't blame yourself. You couldn't help it.

WORDS AND PHRASES TO AVOID

+ bad	+ hateful	+ loser	+ stupid
+ delinquent	+ immature	+ rubbish	+ ungrateful
+ disgraceful	+ irresponsible	+ simpleminded	+ you don't know
+ evil	+ juvenile	+ sinful	

88 Violence

Never fight someone bigger and stronger than you because he may be Goliath but you're not David.

—ANONYMOUS

Andrew was fourteen, a freshman in high school, and he was scared. He was afraid of some of the violence he had seen and heard about in his school. He wasn't a gang member but had been approached by a number of boys in his class who had told him he'd better join or he'd be all alone. They told him that they were going to join. He had no interest in gangs or violence, and he didn't know what he should do.

He wasn't sure how many of the kids in his school belonged to gangs. He knew that some kids who don't belong seemed to be in clubs and sports and got good grades as well. He wasn't a great athlete, and his grades were good but not outstanding. He wasn't a brain. He had a couple of good friends who had also been approached to join the same gang. None of them wanted to, but what choice did they have? He knew about gangs from what he had seen at school and about other kinds of violence from TV, the Internet, and movies. But except for news reports, he didn't mistake TV, computer, or movie violence for real life any more than he thought that cartoons were real when he was a little kid. He knew the difference between real life and fiction.

Nevertheless, he knew that some of the kids in his school tried to be cool by talking and dressing like macho gang members from the movies. He knew that most of them were just acting and didn't have guns or knives, but he was afraid that some of them might. And he wasn't sure where to turn for advice. Fortunately, he and his parents had always had a good relationship with open and easy communication. His parents made sure there was always lots of good conversation between them and Andrew. Now was the chance for their hard work to really pay dividends.

Things to Consider

Teenagers need to belong. They all wear the same clothes because it's like a membership card in the teenagers' club. They've got to have friends to hang out with, to do things with, to talk with, and occasionally to protect them from other kids. Isolation is the worst thing that can happen to teens. It makes them an easy target for teasing, pranks, and violence. It harms their self-esteem.

But is gang membership the solution? Gangs can serve a purpose. Teenage boys and girls can find a home in them when they can't find a home anywhere else. Yet gangs are violent and get into trouble with school authorities, the police, and other gangs. Violence seems to be a daily occurrence in American society. Research shows that youth gangs and isolated teenage boys do most of the killing, hurting, and damage to other children and to themselves.

You want your children to be safe, happy, and successful in school and in their circle of friends. What can you say to them about their fears of violence and your concerns about them? Here are some important things to consider:

- Your teens need to belong.
- Fear is a strong motivator.
- Is gang membership the only option?
- Who are your teens' friends?
- What gang problems exist in your school and community?
- Do your teens have hobbies?
- Do your teens enjoy sports?
- What opportunities are there to get your teens involved in youth groups, teams, clubs, and so forth?
- Do your teens have older siblings who could advise them?

What to Say and Do

Your teen may have lots of conflicting feelings on violence, some real and some fantasy. Take your time on this one. You need to talk it through thoroughly. Don't rush things. Let the talk find its own rhythm and tempo.

Don't be afraid to bring up the subject of violence in school. Say such things as:

- Is violence a real problem at school?
- Are there gangs at school?
- Do kids ever bring guns or knives to school?

Discuss the possibility of violence involving your teen. Say such things as:

- What do you think about the shootings at the high school in Littleton?
- What do you think about gangs?
- Have you ever been threatened?
- Do kids ever have any fights at your school? Are they serious? Who gets involved?
- Do you have any friends who belong to gangs?

After all these preliminary questions, here are some others that go more deeply into your teen's concerns. Say such things as:

- Do you want to join a gang?
- Are there any other groups or clubs or teams you'd like to join?
- Gangs are not a good option. They will draw you into violence, not keep you from it.
- What do you think will happen if you say no to the boys who suggested you join?
- Would you mind if I talked to your school principal about violence in your school? I won't mention what you've said at all.
- If you were a dad, would you want your son in a gang?

Now go even deeper. Say such things as:

- Why would you consider joining a gang?
- What do you know about the violence in school that you've seen with your own eyes?
- What frightens you most about violence at school? That it will happen to you?

After you've talked this through and made inquiries, you need to suggest to your teen how to come to a decision. Say such things as:

- What do you think you should do?
- Maybe you should try joining the _____ club or the _____ team. You've always been interested in _____. If you don't like it, then we can try to think of other groups for you to belong to.
- We're as concerned about violence as you are, and we'll stand by you in any circumstance.
- What about you and your friends starting a group dedicated to preventing violence at school? You can use movies, music videos, and TV programs to educate kids and grown-ups about ways to help kids settle disagreements peacefully.
- Why don't we have some of your friends over some Saturday morning to talk about your concerns?

Just like your talk about anger, you want to understand what your teen is telling you, to help him manage his concerns, and to help him channel his concerns in a positive direction.

WORDS AND PHRASES TO USE

- action	- death	- gangs	- police
- anger	- defiance	- guns	- pressure
- be careful	- disagreement	- isolation	- territory
- concerns	- fear	- knives	- threats
- control	- fights	- options	- understand

What Not to Say and Do

The important thing to remember here is that your teen needs to feel safe and secure. You don't want to say anything that makes light of this concern. Don't say such things as:

- We're sure you're worrying about nothing.
- We think you're wrong about violence at your school. We've never heard about any.

You must also avoid doing anything that will make him seem like a baby in front of his schoolmates. Don't say such things as:

- We'll take you to school in the morning and pick you up in the afternoon.
- Don't be a sissy.
- You're such a baby.
- Coward!

Finally, you should avoid offering violent solutions to the problem of violence. Don't say such things as:

- When I was a kid, I loved a good fight.
- Kids have to fight to learn how to be adults. We have to fight for everything we have.
- We have a gun in the house, so if any kid comes after you, we'll shoot him.

WORDS AND PHRASES TO AVOID

baby	fight violence with violence	life's a battle	violence
coward		shoot	weapons
don't worry	join a gang	sissy	wuss
fight	kill	stand up for yourself	

INDEX